Brigham Young

BRIGHAM YOUNG

Pioneer Prophet

JOHN G. TURNER

THE BELKNAP PRESS OF
HARVARD UNIVERSITY PRESS
Cambridge, Massachusetts, and London, England
2012

Library of Congress Cataloging-in-Publication Data

Turner, John G., author.
Brigham Young, pioneer prophet / John G. Turner.
pages   cm
Includes bibliographical references and index.
ISBN 978-0-674-04967-3 (alk. paper)
1. Young, Brigham, 1801–1877.   2. Church of Jesus Christ of Latter-day Saints—
Presidents—Biography.   3. Mormon Church—Presidents—Biography.   I. Title.
BX8695.Y7T87   2012
289.3092—dc23
[B]   2012015555

Contents

Preface

A HALF-CENTURY AGO, the historian Philip Taylor predicted that
Brigham Young's life was a "biography which will not be written."
When Taylor wrote those words, several useful biographies of Mormonism's second president already existed, ranging from the hagiographic to
the salacious. No biographer, however, had enjoyed anything close to unfettered access to archival material because the Church of Jesus Christ of
Latter-day Saints would not give scholars access to documents that peered
behind ecclesiastically sanctioned narratives of Mormon history. Because
of such restrictions, Taylor lamented, "[v]ery little of his inner personality
can be seen."[1]

Taylor's warning did not deter all scholars. Stanley Hirshson circum-
vented Taylor's issue of access by relying primarily on non-Mormon newspapers from Young's time. Not surprisingly, his *Lion of the Lord* (1969)
depicts Young as the amorous scoundrel his nineteenth-century detractors
made him out to be. Leonard Arrington, by contrast, having formerly
served in the capacity of Church Historian, enjoyed access to research materials Hirshson could only dream of having received. In *American Moses*
(1985), Arrington provided a rich portrait of Brigham Young as faithful
Latter-day Saints saw him. Arrington captures the playful, astute, and humorous sides of Young's personality, as well as his faith and persistence.
While not blind to Young's human weaknesses, *American Moses* spends
very little time on controversial but central topics such as polygamy and

the Mountain Meadows Massacre. He also does not give full vent to the less attractive aspects of Young's leadership, such as his vindictiveness toward certain church members and his unwillingness to shoulder responsibility when his decisions led to hardships for his people. In *Brigham Young and the Expanding American Frontier* (1986), Newell Bringhurst provided a brief but more balanced treatment, especially on topics such as plural marriage. The American frontier, though, only explains some aspects of Brigham Young's life, and Bringhurst spends less time delving into Young's theological beliefs, spiritual leadership, and development of ritual.

There are several good reasons for a fresh biography of Brigham Young. In the quarter-century since Arrington and Bringhurst published their studies, a vast amount of scholarship on the early Utah period of Mormonism has become available. In particular, these studies permit a much more precise examination of the pivotal events of 1856–1858: the Mormon reformation, the handcart tragedy, the Utah War, and the Mountain Meadows Massacre. In writing *Pioneer Prophet,* I have sought to avoid the parochialism and polemicism that has been endemic to Mormon history by placing Young more fully within the context of mid-nineteenth-century American religion and politics. Finally, greater access to church-controlled primary sources differentiates this study from all previous biographies save Arrington's.

Those sources—journals, minutes, correspondence, and sermon transcripts—provide an often-intimate window into Young's personality and leadership. Such documents exist in relative abundance for Young's life in the church through the early 1860s and become sparser after 1863, when his office clerks no longer kept a journal for him. Many documents, of course, obscure as much as they inform. Young's clerks, for instance, wrote much of his voluminous correspondence, often rendering it impersonal, especially because he presumed federal officials read mail not carried by private courier. Sermons published in the *Journal of Discourses* eliminated much of Young's color, coarseness, and profanity while presenting his ideas in more polished form. Even more problematic is the fact that multiple sources often offer entirely contradictory accounts of the same thing. The field of Mormon history is a hall of mirrors, full of distorted and incomplete reflections of nearly any event. I have relied upon the most contemporary, firsthand, and unedited sources in an attempt to untangle what actually took place. When it was impossible to transcend the limitations of the historical record, I have preserved a sense of ambiguity.

Brigham Young

Prologue

O N NEW Year's Day 1877, Brigham Young and nearly thirteen hundred Latter-day Saints gathered in the southern Utah settlement of St. George. They came to dedicate a temple, the first the church had completed since fleeing Illinois thirty-one years earlier. For three hours, Mormon leaders offered lengthy prayers consecrating the new building.

At the end of the services, Young finally rose. He was ailing from rheumatism and unable to walk. Several men had helped him into and around the temple in a sedan chair on rollers. Despite his infirmities, a man who had delivered thousands of discourses over the past forty-five years would not allow this occasion to pass without comment.

He began by reminding the congregation of the occasion's historic significance. The Mormons had dedicated two temples before the one in St. George, but now they would have the time to introduce what he considered the full range of sacred rituals for the first time. "We that are here," Young said, "are enjoying a privilege that we have no knowledge of any other people Enjoying since the days of Adam." Church members could perform all the rituals necessary to ensure their own eternal exaltation, and they could perform the same ordinances as proxies for their ancestors. "Can the Fathers be saved without us?" Young asked. "No. Can we be saved without them? No." Combined with other ordinances that would bind children to parents and adopt men to spiritual fathers, Young envisioned these rituals as binding together a great chain of redeemed humanity stretching back to Adam. Given the sacred importance of this task, he suggested, the House of the Lord should be crowded after its dedication.

Then, Young's tone gradually changed. Despite the sacrifices of the Mormons who had built the temple, he feared that church members were more worried about money than the eternal fates of their ancestors. They would choose a single dollar over eternal life, and they would give away the people's wealth to their enemies. "[S]ome of this people," he complained, "if they had the power would build a railroad to the bottom less Pit, and would send all they had and the Earth besides to the devil." Too many of the Mormon people, he said, "were damned fools."

Young demanded that his people mirror his own commitment to the Kingdom of God. "[L]et those infernal holes in the ground alone," he instructed the audience, "and let the Gentiles [non-Mormons] alone who would destroy us if they had the power." If they did not heed his words, there would be consequences. "You will go to Hell lots of you unless you repent," he warned.

Building to a crescendo, Young upbraided those who were satisfied with the temple's dedication, a symbol of the Mormons' spiritual commitment and material progress. "I am not half satisfied," Young thundered as much as his aging lungs would permit, "and I never Expect to be satisfied untill the devil is whiped and driven from off the face of the Earth."

To drive home his final sentence, Young took a hickory cane "filled with knots" and struck the pulpit "with such power that he buried three of the knots into the solid wood." The noise reverberated around the hall, and visitors to the temple a century later could still see the marks.

Young's spirit and determination were as strong as his body was weak. He was blunt spoken, pugnacious, and sometimes profane. Through his dedication, energy, and tenacity he had built an earthly kingdom for the Mormon people, and he would fight to defend it until his final breath.[1]

For a religious group amounting to only two percent of the U.S. population, the Church of Jesus Christ of Latter-day Saints has achieved an outsized cultural relevance. Mormons, mainstream and fundamentalist, appear in reality television shows, Broadway musicals, courtrooms, and presidential debates. Some evangelical Protestants accuse Mormons of not being Christians or of belonging to a cult, whereas secular liberals use the origins of Mormonism to cast doubt upon church members' intellect and fitness for high office.

Even though the attitudes of other Americans rankle Mormons at times, most church members have a thick skin. Even the most successful Mormon missionaries, for instance, find their message accepted but rarely. Moreover, one suspects that the church often does not mind the attention it receives, even if much of that publicity comes with misunderstanding and criticism.

There are limits, however, to this forbearance. For the Latter-day Saints, their history is sacred. Mormons venerate their ancestors who first responded to the gospel or who pioneered their way across the American continent, and their church devotes considerable resources to maintaining its historical sites, preserving its documents, and defending the reputation of its former leaders.

Mormons believe that in 1830, God restored his true church on the earth through his chosen prophet, Joseph Smith Jr., to whom he had revealed a set of ancient scriptures translated and published by Smith as the *Book of Mormon*. From the start, non-Mormons attacked both the credibility of the prophet and the historicity of his "Gold Bible." Non-Mormon criticisms of Smith intensified, especially as Smith sought to deflect rumors of polygamy and concerns about Mormon political behavior in Illinois. In 1844, members of an anti-Mormon mob shot and killed Joseph Smith. Debates about Smith's character and historical claims—ranging from his translation of the *Book of Mormon* to his involvement in folk magic to his taking of additional wives—will probably never be settled. For Latter-day Saints, however, such debates and claims have a relevance and immediacy foreign to most other religious groups. Most Presbyterians, for instance, would pay little attention if a scholar published a book slandering John Calvin's reputation. Some Catholics might object to sharp criticism of the current pope, but few would be offended by a similar discussion of an early-nineteenth-century pope.

After the founding prophet's murder, Brigham Young gathered the largest portion of Smith's followers under his leadership, held them together amid persecution and exile, and planted the Mormon kingdom in what became Utah. Young was no less controversial than his predecessor, and non-Mormons routinely accused him of ecclesiastical tyranny, licentiousness, and even murder.

A second prophet to the Mormon people, Young also became a figure of broader significance within U.S. history. After their expulsion from Illinois, the Mormons staked their claim to approximately one-sixth of the western United States, making Brigham Young the greatest colonizer in American history. Young, though, led a church whose claims about marriage and politics extended far beyond the bounds of American religious toleration, and the U.S. government was not content to allow the Mormons to govern themselves in Utah. In the face of federal sovereignty, Young waged a decades-long—and ultimately unsuccessful—struggle for Mormon autonomy. In the process, he brought many of the key political issues of mid-nineteenth-century America into sharp relief: westward expansion, popular sovereignty, religious freedom, vigilantism, and Reconstruction.

Within a Protestant America dedicated to monogamy, monotheism, and Jacksonian democracy, Young advocated the plurality of wives, a plurality of gods, and a unity of power. Given the scope of his vision and the novelty of his beliefs, it is not surprising that he generated intense controversy and opposition. Young's siege mentality, forged in the crucible of anti-Mormon persecution, led him to demonize his enemies, employ violent rhetoric, and condone murders. A leader who understood himself as following in the footsteps of the ancient biblical patriarchs could not readily function within the U.S. territorial system. Convinced that Young—Utah's governor as of 1857—was leading a rebellion against the U.S. government, President James Buchanan sent an army to Utah with Young's gubernatorial replacement. Young eventually learned to live with the presence of U.S. soldiers and officials, but in other ways he defended his kingdom with ever-greater desperation until the end of his life. In the end, Young's ambitions for his church and himself were so great that he could at best bring them only partly to fruition.

LIKE Smith, Brigham Young was an uneducated, rural man born in Vermont who had grown up in western New York. "When I undertook to sound the doctrine of Mormonism," Young recounted twenty years after his conversion, "I supposed a [I] could handle it as I could the Methodist, Presbyterian, and other creeds of Christendom." All of these other denominations, Young argued, if distilled to their essence, amounted to nothing more than petty, fragile human constructs. Mormonism, though, he found to be different. "I found it impossible to take hold of either end of it; I found it was from eternity, passed through time, and into eternity again." His new faith, he often said, became his "all in all."[2]

Just as it was difficult for Young to "take hold" of Mormonism, it remains difficult to get hold of Brigham Young. The diversity and breadth of his experience is astounding. Young spoke in tongues, presided over temple rituals, and led his people in singing hymns and in fervent prayers. More than strictly a religious leader, Young was a pioneer, a federal appointee, and a business magnate. His beliefs and interests, religious and otherwise, were eclectic. Although he condemned them at times, other religions intrigued him, as did theological debates and questions. Young's religion looked for inspiration both in the ancient past and in the American future. He accepted the presence and power of seer stones, healing amulets, and witches, but he also eagerly embraced telegraphs, factories, and railroads.[3] He was a man of great warmth who might sing and dance with his people into the early morning, but he was also moody and prone to outbursts of wrath. Smith's murder and Young's own experiences in Nauvoo, Illinois, altered Young's personality and approach to leadership. His response, which included extreme vigilance against dissent, increased the church's cohesion but also exacted a heavy toll on his followers. Intensely loyal to those he trusted, he was often vindictive for years toward those who crossed him.

How might we make sense of Young's ambiguities and complexities, his strengths and his weaknesses? We should begin by remembering that he was a nineteenth-century man and avoid any tortured attempt to make him palatable for a twenty-first-century audience, Mormon or otherwise. Young believed that God had cursed black people with inferiority and servitude, viewed American Indians as savages inclined toward idleness, and—especially until his later years—made misogynistic comments about women. While distinctively Mormon ideas colored his thinking, in many respects Young approached such matters as did other white American men of his time.

In order to understand Brigham Young we must also reckon with his self-understanding and his religious outlook. Even though some contemporaries and early biographers portrayed him as an opportunist who used the church to gain money and power for himself, it seems obvious that Young was sincere in his faith. Even though he eventually grew wealthy and exercised great power, it is difficult to understand how a prospective Mormon convert in the early 1830s could have viewed the church as a vehicle for self-aggrandizement. Young's highest loyalty was to his church and its kingdom, not to the United States, and certainly not to a shared Protestant moral order that vehemently excluded the Latter-day Saints. He fully accepted that Joseph Smith was God's prophet, his appointed leader of his one true, restored church, and he gradually came to see himself as occupying a similar, divinely appointed position, governing his people in the fashion of a biblical prophet, patriarch, and judge. Thus, Young did not typically distinguish between his own self-interest and that of his church. In his mind, those two things were inseparable.

Young's claims were bold and broad. "Our work, our every-day labor, our whole lives are within the scope of our religion," he stated in 1869, articulating a standard preaching theme.[4] Many American Protestants would have heartily assented to that statement, but Young urged his followers to live it out with a scope and relentlessness that set him and them apart from most American Christians. "[T]he religion that you and I have embraced," Young once told his people, "incorporates the life and doing of man, the life of the angels and all the doings of the angels. It incorporates the life of the Gods and doing of the Gods."[5] Their religion encompassed, he explained, everything from building temples to raising corn and melons to building fortifications against Indian attacks. Forging iron was as much part of the gospel as serving a foreign mission. For Young himself, building temples and building mills and factories were all sacred tasks.

This book is not an appraisal of contemporary Mormonism or an assessment of Mormonism's religious tenets. Instead, it is the story of Brigham Young and the survival, growth, and development of his church, a biography of how a rough-hewn former craftsman brought tens of thousands of Latter-day Saints to the American Mountain West, drove them for thirty years to create his vision of the Kingdom of God, and left a deep imprint—as enduring as the dents in the St. George Temple pulpit—on the landscape of Utah, its people, and their church. Brigham Young was Joseph Smith's successor, but he was in his own right an American religious pioneer.

CHAPTER ONE

A New Creature

He [Joseph Smith] believed that among all the Churches in the
world the Methodist was the nearest right.

—PETER CARTWRIGHT

I WAS baptized under the hand of Ebezer [Eleazar] Miller," scrawled
Brigham Young in his diary when he joined Joseph Smith Jr.'s Church of
Christ on April 9, 1832. Miller baptized Young on a cold, snowy day in
Mendon, New York, about twenty miles south of Rochester. After the
two-mile trip from the stream back to his Mendon home, Young wrote
many years later, "he [Miller] laid his hands on me and ordained me an
elder, at which I marvelled."[1]

For Brigham Young, his conversion, baptism, and ordination heralded a
new beginning, a rupture from his previous life as a rural New York craftsman struggling to reverse his parents' downward mobility.[2] Young's paternal grandfather, Joseph Young, was a Hopkinton, Massachusetts, physician and surgeon who served in the French and Indian War and was killed
when a fence pole fell on him in 1769. Joseph Young had already fashioned misery for his family through heavy drinking and gambling, which
spoiled a promising opportunity to climb into prosperity and left his wife,
Elizabeth, and his children in poverty and distress. "As soon as the sleeping dust of her husband was [de]cently committed to the grave," Brigham's
sister Fanny later wrote, "evry man to whom he ow'd a Dollar was on the
wing." Elizabeth Young sold her Hopkinton farm and bound out two of
her sons, Joseph Jr. and Brigham's father, John, then ages four and six.
They served Colonel John Jones, who owned an estate and gristmill in
nearby Ashland. It was hard work, as the region was "a country broken

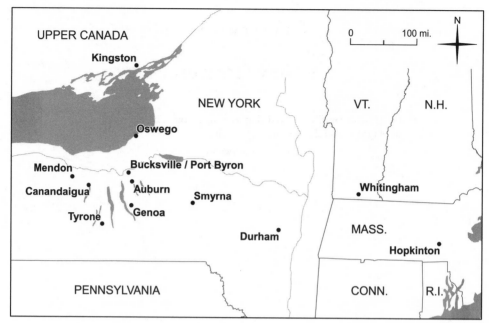

Early life

and rocky, one with rich enough soil, well watered, but one to tax the capabilities of every farmer." Brigham's father, whom Jones's wife often threatened with severe floggings, escaped further torment by joining the Continental Army at age seventeen. After several short enlistments, John Young returned and, without better prospects, resumed work with Colonel Jones, this time for wages.[3]

Given his low economic station, John Young formed an advantageous union by marrying Abigail (Nabby) Howe in October 1785. According to Fanny Young, Nabby married John "sorely against the will of her parents, particularly her Father, for he though[t] it rather beneath him, that his daughter should choose a servant boy, brought up in the kitchen with black, as well as [white ser]vants." Sometime after the birth of their second daughter in 1787, John Young moved his family to the frontier, settling on land southwest of Albany in present-day Durham. Several Hopkinton families had recently moved to the area. John Young undertook the move in a bid for independence and prosperity, as it was unlikely he would ever acquire property in Hopkinton. By 1790, however, the Youngs were back in Massachusetts. Phineas Howe resolved to reclaim his daughter and grandchildren from the wilderness and ordered two sleighs west to return them to Massachusetts. John knew that Nabby's father "had always disliked him," Fanny Young wrote, "and he [John] could not feel willing to place himself under his immediate inspection." Given Nabby's desire for home, however, John relented, suppressed his pride, moved his family into a house on Phineas Howe's land, "and raised corn on shares."[4]

After ten years and the birth of five additional children, John Young pursued a second attempt at independence. From a wealthy brother-in-law he purchased fifty acres of land in Whitingham, Vermont, nestled among the Green Mountains and close to the Massachusetts border. As he struggled to clear the rocky land on his new farm, Nabby bore their fourth son, Brigham, on June 1, 1801. Although she continued to bear children, Brigham's mother at this point was suffering from consumption. Brigham's sister Fanny bottle-fed him in his infancy.[5]

John Young never turned his Whitingham land into a profitable or even self-sustaining enterprise. Instead, he hired out his labor helping other freeholders clear their properties of trees, stumps, and rocks. He also turned to other meager sources of income: one Whitingham publication later identified him as a "poor basket maker." In 1804, the Youngs joined a Yankee exodus known as "York Fever," in which thousands of New Englanders left unprofitable farms in Vermont and western Massachusetts for cheap land and a renewed hope of prosperity. At the peak of this migration, hundreds of sleighs glided through wintry Albany each day on their way to points west. Brigham's father relocated his family to Sherburne (Smyrna, after a division of the township), in Chenango County, New York, about one hundred miles west of Albany.[6]

Now forty years of age, John Young once again plunged into the rigors of building a home, clearing land, and planting crops. Despite his exertions, he never became a successful frontier farmer. The Youngs occasionally went hungry and could rarely provide their children with adequate clothing, let alone anything resembling a formal education. "In my youthful days," Brigham later reminisced, "instead of going to school, I had to chop logs, to sow and plant, to plow in the midst of roots barefooted, and if I had on a pair of pants that would cover me I did pretty well." Brigham and his siblings learned to provide for themselves. "My sisters would make me what was called a Jo. Johnson cap for winter," he recalled, "and in summer I wore a straw hat which I frequently braided for myself." Brigham had ten siblings. His sister Nabby died shortly after their move to Smyrna, but his four brothers and five other sisters lived into adulthood. Even as the elder daughters married and left the household, John and Nabby Young never earned or grew enough to provide more than a hardscrabble life.[7]

Most of Brigham's ancestors were Congregationalists, the spiritual descendants of the New England Puritans. Among his ancestors were both evangelical New Lights, who had supported the revivals that became known as the Great Awakening, and antirevivalist Old Lights. Nabby's maternal grandfather, Ebenezer Goddard, heard "that dear servant of God, Mr. [George] Whitefield," preach in Framingham and signed a New Light petition against the town's established minister. Family lore included a "marvelous" series of events involving Ebenezer Goddard, who became involved in a conflict with Nat Smith, a wealthy and reclusive neighbor. A widow had asked Goddard to administer her estate, which lay on the outskirts of Smith's property. When Goddard refused to cede control of the estate to Smith, "Old Nat" "told him he should rue the day." Shortly thereafter, a servant mysteriously found in the well a set of Goddard's papers that had been locked in his desk. Even more mysteriously, "not a paper was wet." Then the family discovered that "something ailed the milk." The Goddards blamed and flogged a young black servant boy and tied him in a corner. Inexplicable incidents, however, continued. Ebenezer's wife Sybil saw her fine cap suddenly appear, "and before she could possibly get hold of it, she saw one half of it go up [the] chimney, while she caught the other half in her hand." While heating the oven, the family also found a set of books and, later, infant clothing among the flames. At that point, the Goddards dedicated themselves to fasting and prayer and recruited a coterie of local ministers to augment their supplications. Finally, after three days, "there seemed to be a shock through the whole house, not a distress or sorrow, but of joy and assurance that there was a God in the heavens," and from that moment forward the curse was lifted. The family thereafter believed both in the devil's "power on the earth" and in the presence of angels. Their daughter Susannah—Nabby's mother—"believed that Jacob's ladder was not yet broken and that angels still continued to ascend and descend [between heaven and earth]." Brigham's Goddard and Howe relatives bequeathed to their descendants a robust belief in supernatural phenomena.[8]

When the Youngs moved to Vermont in 1801, they entered a region in which a welter of Christian sects had taken root, including Baptists, Universalists, Methodists, and Shakers. According to one local history, the residents of Whitingham circulated tales of witchcraft and housed a smattering of treasure seekers led by Silas Hamilton, a prominent citizen who used a divining rod to direct digging efforts. Rather than joining in treasure-seeking quests, however, the Young family inclined toward backcountry evangelicalism. John Young had married Nabby in Hopkinton's Congregationalist church, but at some point during the first few years of the new century they became Methodists. The Youngs joined the Methodist Episcopal Church, an American denomination that had emerged from the

Anglican reform movement begun in the late 1730s by John Wesley. Despite resistance from Congregationalists and Presbyterians as well as competition from a host of other Protestant sectaries, Methodism spread rapidly in the new settlements of western New York, including Chenango County. "Not infrequently," chronicled William Warren Sweet in his history of American frontier religion, "a Methodist circuit-rider called at the cabin of a settler before the mud in his stick chimney was dry or before the weight poles were on the roof." There was no Methodist church building in Smyrna, but Methodist itinerants regularly passed through on their circuits. "There is nothing out today but crows and Methodist preachers," went a nineteenth-century proverb about inclement weather.[9]

In October 1807, Nabby Young gave birth to her last child, a son the couple named after Lorenzo Dow, the Methodist itinerant whom the family had probably seen and heard at a nearby camp meeting. "Crazy Dow," whose "words . . . cut like a sword," according to an early Methodist circuit rider, operated on the margins of Episcopal Methodism in the early 1800s. "He was as odd-looking as his acts," Brigham later recalled. Unshaven and often unwashed with unkempt hair hanging over his shoulders, the purposefully eccentric Dow ruined horses barnstorming around the frontier in a furious effort to save souls, oppose Congregational establishments, and mock his theological opponents. "You can and you can't," he derided Calvinists in an oft-quoted saying. "You shall and you shan't; you will and you won't—And you'll be damned if you do, and you'll be damned if you don't." Ordained in 1799 as a Methodist itinerant, Dow left his circuit to undertake a preaching tour in Ireland and thereafter operated outside the official confines of the denomination. A relentless opponent of Calvinism, Dow insisted that grace and salvation were freely available to all people through the sacrificial death of Jesus Christ, and he referred to his multitudes of converts as his "spiritual children." Nabby and John Young's choice of names for their last child was not unusual; parents often bestowed the name of a famous preacher on their son, and Dow's fame was without parallel in the first few decades of the nineteenth century.[10]

Methodists were a tiny minority of Americans at the start of the nineteenth century, but by 1850 they claimed one-third of all American church members. Both Enlightenment-era skeptics and more rationally inclined members of the clergy hoped that "enthusiastic" forms of popular religion would wither away, but the American age of revolution instead galvanized a tidal wave of popular, enthusiastic evangelicalism. Part of this torrent, Methodism grew explosively for a number of reasons: its dedicated cadre of self-sacrificial itinerants, its organizational structure (including class meetings, quarterly meetings, and annual conferences), and its egalitarian embrace of vernacular culture. Methodist camp meetings became famous —infamous, to their critics—for singing, shouting, collapsing, and other wild manifestations of spiritual power. In Hop Bottom, Pennsylvania, Methodists full of "holy zeal" turned their meetings into "scenes of confusion" when they exhibited the "jumping spirit." "When much excited," wrote George Peck, "they would commence moving up and down, apparently without effort or a knowledge of what they were doing." Having heard reports of "a singularity called the *jerks* or *jerking exercise*," Lorenzo Dow saw the soil plowed up at one camp meeting ground, where people "had jerked so powerfully that they had kicked up the earth as a horse stamping flies." Especially in newly settled regions of the country, Methodists and other early nineteenth-century evangelicals also reported prophetic dreams, visions, miracles of all sorts, remarkable healings, and other phenomena. Dow claimed the God-given ability to tell fortunes and predict future calamities. Thus, the Young family embraced a rugged faith that emphasized direct encounters with God and ecstatic manifestations of the divine.[11]

Although critics of the revivals described them as hotbeds of spiritual and moral disorder, devout Methodists emphasized a strict moral code. "When I was young," Brigham described his childhood, "I was kept within very strict bounds, and was not allowed to walk more than half-an-hour on Sunday for exercise." Methodists imposed a stringent moral code on their adherents, who typically were "middling people" eager for both eternal salvation and the earthly success they believed would come through discipline and morality. Methodist preachers denounced swearing, licentiousness, and idleness, and they promoted cleanliness and frugality. "The Methodists in that early day dressed plain," wrote early itinerant Peter Cartwright, "wore no jewelry, no ruffles . . . They religiously kept the Sabbath day; many of them abstained from drinking." Though such discipline never brought them any worldly prosperity, Brigham's parents firmly embraced this evangelical moral code. John and Nabby Young forbade swearing, dancing, and music, and they insisted on a strict observance of the Sabbath. Brigham later suggested that his parents had deprived him even of wholesome pleasure. "I had not a chance to dance when I was young," he noted regretfully, "and never heard the enchanting tones of the violin, until I was eleven years of age; and then I thought I was on the high way to hell, if I suffered myself to linger and listen to it." His father did not hesitate to punish lapses in morality and upright behavior. "[I]t used to be a word and a blow, with him," Brigham remarked of his father, "but the blow came first." Alongside her husband's evangelical discipline, Nabby

Young nurtured her children in the "Bible-drenched" culture and prayerful piety of early 1800s America. His mother, Brigham recollected, "taught her children all the time to honour the name of the Father [and the] Son, and to reverence the holy book." While restrained in discussions of his father, Brigham retained a fond memory of his mother's saintliness.[12]

In 1813, the Youngs moved west, to the township of Genoa (possibly Lansingville), near the shores of Cayuga Lake, New York. Shortly after this move, in June 1815, Nabby Howe Young succumbed to her tuberculosis. The family dispersed, with several of the younger children going to live with older married siblings. John Young took several of his sons farther west, around the southern tips of Cayuga and Seneca Lakes to a farm in Tyrone, not far from Brigham's sister Rhoda and her husband John P. Greene. These years after his mother's death marked the trough of destitution and misery in Brigham's childhood. Once again John Young and his sons cleared land—Brigham's brother Joseph remembered "a wilderness country densely covered with heavy timbers"—and tapped sugar maples in the early spring, and they now lived without any female care or companionship. In early 1816, John Young took a large load of maple sugar to the nearby settlement of Painted Post, leaving Brigham and nine-year-old Lorenzo to gather and boil additional sap for several days. Nearly out of flour, the boys subsisted on a robin that Brigham shot until their father returned. Never able to earn enough by farming, John Young and his sons scoured the area for other opportunities to earn money: clearing land, harvesting crops, and bottoming chairs. Now without his mother, Brigham later recalled, "I learned to make bread, wash the dishes, milk the cows, and make butter." After his mother's death and amid his father's absences, Brigham had no choice but to become a self-sufficient young man and at times a surrogate father to Lorenzo.[13]

This training for adulthood served him well, as Brigham soon found himself evicted from his father's home. John Young remarried, to a widow named Hannah Brown. "When I was sixteen years old," Brigham remembered, "my father said, 'You can now have your time—go.'" Although Brigham apparently resented the abrupt nature of his departure, it was not unusual for young men to leave home at this age to learn skills and provide for themselves. Brigham moved back east near Auburn, New York, where he temporarily settled with relatives and looked for work. No longer the frontier, Auburn was a small boomtown in 1817, with a rapidly growing population and an assortment of mills, shops, and taverns. Brigham quickly began to evidence the industry and drive that characterized his adult life. "A year had not passed," he later explained, "until I stopped running, jumping, wresting, [and] laying out my strength for anything useless." He apprenticed himself to a furniture maker, who taught him to make bedsteads, washboards, benches, and chairs. Over the next few years, he helped build the Auburn Theological Seminary for the Presbyterian Church and worked on several of Auburn's finest homes, including the future residence of William H. Seward, who later served as governor of New York and Abraham Lincoln's Secretary of State. Developing a diverse array of skills during these years, Brigham later described himself as a "carpenter, joiner, painter, and glazier." He also worked on a printing press, for he once mentioned boarding with "a journeyman printer" and "working off Ball's Arithmetic." Decades later, he remained proud of his craft skills and industry.[14]

In his later recollections, he described himself as a fiercely independent and somewhat headstrong young man. "I am naturally opposed to being crowded," he later commented, "and am opposed to any person who undertakes to force me to do this, or not do that." As a young man, he both refused to drink and refused to sign a temperance pledge, even when his father urged him to do the latter. "No, sir," he replied, "if I sign the temperance pledge I feel that I am bound, and I wish to do just right, without being bound to do it; I want my liberty." After the founding of the American Temperance Society in 1826, perhaps a million Americans joined it and signed a pledge of complete abstinence from alcohol, a thought unimaginable to earlier generations. Brigham made no such promise. Again showing an independence of thought, he temporarily adopted vegetarianism despite ridicule and scorn. "Young never eats any meat," one of Brigham's roommates told a group of workmen. "I can just throw any man that don't eat meat," he bragged. "Mr. Pratt," responded Brigham, "if you will step here into the middle of the floor I will show you how to dirty coats." Pratt backed down. Having withstood considerable hardship, Brigham had become a young man who could fend for himself and would stand up for himself. He insisted on following his own path. He would not be pressured, and he responded sharply when crossed.[15]

DURING these years, Brigham also began an intermittent struggle to find spiritual satisfaction and assurance. His parents had grown up in a New England that still maintained a sense of religious order, but Brigham experienced a much more diverse and competitive religious pluralism. In particular, he encountered a welter of evangelical movements in what revivalist Charles Finney would later label the "burnt district" of western New York. Brigham described himself as "well acquainted with the Episcopalians, Presbyterians, New Lights, Baptists, Freewill Baptists, Wesleyan and Reformed Methodists . . . more or less acquainted with almost every other religious ism." Given this setting, Young could hardly ignore revivalism. One of his earliest memories included hearing Lorenzo Dow preach, and an "astonishing revival" began in Auburn the autumn after Brigham's arrival and spread throughout the surrounding region.

Brigham later articulated a deep uneasiness and dissatisfaction with Protestant revivalism. He remembered wild manifestations of the Spirit at camp meetings. "Men were rolling and bawling and thumping," he explained in 1845, "but it had no effect on me." Protestant denominationalism also bred confusion. "From my youth up," he complained, "their cry was, 'Lo here is Christ, lo there is Christ;' no, 'Yonder is Christ;' 'Christ is not there, he is here,' and so on, each claiming that it had the savior, and that others were wrong." For a time, Brigham resisted all. He described his demurral as stemming from a rationalistic "inward inquiry" to assess which of the groups most reflected primitive or apostolic Christianity. "I read the Bible," he explained, "and especially the New Testament, which was given as a pattern for the life of Christians, whether as a church or individuals." Brigham shared the belief of many nineteenth-century Americans that they could and should access the teachings of the Bible for themselves—the plain meaning of Scripture was available through common sense without any formal theological education.[16]

Despite his retrospective critiques of revivalism, as a young man Brigham took evangelical claims seriously. When he reached twenty-three years of age, he joined a Methodist church after a one-year period of religious reflection. Brigham later dismissed this decision as a strategic concession to local revivalism. "I joined the Methodists," he joked in 1849, "to get rid of them and all the sects—same as the girl married the man to get rid of him." Yet, at the time of his conversion to Methodism, Brigham insisted on baptism by immersion and threatened to join a Baptist sect should the Methodists refuse to baptize him in that manner. "There are some things," he intimated, "required in the doctrine of the Close Communion Baptists which I cannot subscribe to as well as to most of the principles that you hold in your catechisms, and in the tenets of your church, but . . . they believe in baptism by immersion, and I want to be baptized by immersion." The local Methodists acceded to his wishes and baptized him accordingly. Given other examples of independent thought and action, it seems unlikely that he would have been easily bullied into joining the Methodists. Rather, Brigham had carefully thought through his conversion.[17]

Most of the Young siblings made professions of Christian faith and became Methodists. They eventually affiliated not with their parents' Methodist Episcopal Church, however, but with the Reformed Methodist Church, a small, more radical offshoot. In 1814, a handful of dissident

Episcopal Methodists had formed the Reformed Methodist Church in Readsborough, Vermont, only five miles from Brigham's birthplace in Whitingham. Although the Methodist Episcopal Church always dwarfed such movements, dissenting Methodists formed a number of splinter denominations in the early nineteenth century. Not surprisingly in an era imbued with the "contagion of liberty," some Methodists reacted against the church's episcopal form of government and discipline. As the denomination grew, dissenters also chafed at a perceived drift from the "primitive" [i.e., New Testament] gospel. The Reformed Methodists articulated such grievances. Initially formed by "plain, unassuming mechanics and farmers," none of whom had advanced beyond the status of "local preachers and exhorters," they "renounc[ed] the episcopal mode of church government" and denounced "the methodist travelling connection [itinerant preachers]" as "fallen from the true spirit of religion." They established a denomination with a more congregational form of church government under which churches chose their own ministers and selected their delegates to annual conferences. The Reformed Methodists upheld the Bible as "the sufficient rule of faith and practice," worshiped with fervent ecstasy, demanded the strict observance of the Sabbath, forbade "spirituous liquors," and warned against the "putting on of gold and costly apparel." The small denomination established a handful of conferences in the northeastern United States, including the region of New York inhabited by the various branches of John Young's family.[18]

Most significant in light of the Young family's future religious path, the Reformed Methodists exhibited several of the impulses later central to early Mormonism. Most notably, like a growing number of American Protestants, they looked to restore Christianity to its ancient roots. "They have held and taught," chronicled Wesley Bailey, a Reformed Methodist minister, "that the same faith now, would produce the same effects it did in primitive times." Arguing that "the lapse of ages cannot render void the promises of God," they believed that "faith is the restoring principle" for a church that "has apostatized." In particular, the Reformed Methodists emphasized that "we may now, in this age, pray for the removal of temporal as well as spiritual diseases." Several of the denomination's founders and early members sold their property to follow the example of the early Christian apostles and established a communitarian farm at Shaftsbury, on the New York–Vermont border. The experiment failed, perhaps because of the bitterly cold spring and summer of 1816.

Undeterred by charges of fanaticism, the Reformed Methodists organized revivals at which "hardened sinners" were converted by the "slaying power" of the Holy Ghost. "This was a time . . . something like Pentecost," one Reformed Methodist preacher described an August 1817 meeting in western New York, "for there was shouting, screaming, jumping and falling, which imitates men drunken with new wine." The denomination's founding *Discipline* cautioned against "limit[ing] the spirit of God." "[W]here the fruits of the spirit appear," argued the denomination's founders, "either in male or female, it ought not . . . to be restrained."[19] Previously skeptical of evangelical revivalism, Brigham now embraced one of its more radical manifestations.

For the Youngs, religion was very much a family affair. If anyone had successfully prodded Brigham toward conversion, it was probably his brother Phineas, who joined the Reformed Methodists in early 1824. "[F]rom that hour," he recalled in an 1845 letter to Brigham, "I began to look after my fathers family, and pray for their salvation and redemption from sin." Perhaps fitting given his namesake's alienation from organized Methodism, only Lorenzo Dow Young remained "averse to joining any church, not believing that any of the sects walked up to the precepts contained in the Bible." Akin to Brigham before his baptism, Lorenzo remained "reverential" but hesitated to commit to any denomination. In late 1822, he traveled sixty miles to a Methodist revival in Hector, a town on Seneca Lake, where he "was somewhat affected by the prevailing intense religious feeling" and consented to spend a night on "the anxious seat" for penitential prospective converts. After praying "until two o'clock in the morning," Lorenzo told the assembled ministers that "he had not realized any change," whereupon they rebuked him for "sin[ning] away the day of grace." After a heavenly vision in 1826—in this dream he met his deceased mother and sister—he, "although belonging to no church," "exhorted the people in public and in private to exercise faith in the Lord Jesus Christ." Three of the Young brothers (Phineas, John Jr., and Joseph) were Methodist preachers, as was Brigham's brother-in-law John P. Greene, and Lorenzo preached a similar message without institutional backing. John Young Sr. also transferred his allegiance from the Episcopal to the Reformed Methodists.[20]

For a time, Brigham's brother Phineas found a deep spiritual satisfaction in Reformed Methodism. Shortly after his 1824 conversion, he attended a prayer meeting in Hector, at which he "pray[ed] for nothing but to become holy." Suddenly, "a body of light, above the brightness of the sun," filled him "with joy unutterable."[21] Flush with Wesleyan sanctification, he—along with John Young Jr.—was summoned to the home of Mary Webley, a young woman dying of tuberculosis. They arrived to find the young woman, "to all appearance, breathing her last." Phineas began praying for her peaceful death and transition to heaven, then heard a voice whisper,

"Pray for her recovery." After laying his hands on her and praying, Mary Webley "arose as one from the dead, and sat up in bed and praised God with a loud voice." Phineas established a Methodist church in Cheshire, on the outskirts of Canandaigua and about thirty miles southeast of Rochester. The Cheshire fellowship reflected the impulses of many radical evangelical gatherings: emotional worship, divine healings, and sometimes violent manifestations of the Spirit. "They frequently fell in their meetings with what they called the power," wrote a Canandaigua resident several decades later, "but such things were common among Methodists at the time."[22]

Many Americans, like Phineas Young, found spiritual assurance and purpose following evangelical conversion. By contrast, those who were convinced of their sinfulness and acceded to the revivalist's demands, but then found themselves without any sense of grace often plunged into a state of abject spiritual despair. Brigham experienced such anguish. Even after his "profession of religion," he "often used to get a little puzzled," because the "Evil One . . . would whisper to me that I had done this, that, or some other thing wrong, and inquire whether that looked like a Christian act." Although he rejected Satan's judgment, he struggled with depression. "I was troubled with that which I hear others complain of," he recalled in an 1856 discourse, "that is, with, at times, feeling cast down, gloomy, and desponding; with everything wearing to me, at times, a dreary aspect." His brother Joseph became similarly despondent. "My brother Joseph once said to me (and we were both Methodists at the time)," Brigham recalled, "Brother Brigham, there is not a Bible Christian in the world; what will become of the people?" "For many years no person saw a smile on his countenance," Brigham said of Joseph. "[F]or there being Bible Christians," Brigham concurred with Joseph's assessment, "I knew there were none; and their religion was the religion they liked." Even Phineas eventually succumbed to this spiritual malaise. "I well remember once saying to you," he wrote Brigham in 1845, "that I could not pray as I had formerly done, and your answer to me was that you felt just as I did, you sayed you could hardly pray in your family."[23] By the late 1820s, several of the Young brothers had descended from their evangelical conversions into a slough of spiritual despond.

As Brigham wrestled with this sense of insufficiency and discontent, he drifted between Auburn and the nearby village of Bucksville (later Port Byron) on the newly opened Erie Canal, finding jobs repairing furniture, painting, and possibly working in a factory that produced wooden pails. In October 1824, he married Miriam Angeline Works, five years his junior. Little reliable information exists about Miriam, the couple's courtship, or their early marriage. Like Brigham, she was the daughter of a Revolutionary War veteran, Asa Works, who like John Young had been born in Massachusetts and then relocated to New York State. In 1825, Miriam gave birth to her first child, a daughter named Elizabeth.

In 1828, Brigham and Miriam moved from the Auburn region to Oswego, about thirty miles north on the shore of Lake Ontario. Brigham once referred to having "built a large tannery" in Oswego. He also continued his spiritual searching. In 1860, he exchanged letters with Hiram McKee, an old friend from his time in Oswego who later became a Methodist minister. "How sweet was our communion in old Oswego," McKee wrote Young, "how encourageing our prayrs, and enlivening our Songs." McKee remembered Brigham as a humble, contrite, and pious young man. "I also vividly remember," Brigham replied, "the scenes, feelings and experience of the times to which you kindly allude, when we were fellow seekers after the truths revealed from Heaven for the salvation of the human family." Young may have lost confidence in Reformed Methodism, but he remained a pious Christian seeker.[24]

Brigham and Miriam Young did not tarry long in Oswego. By then, the larger Young family was converging on Mendon, New York, to the southeast of Rochester, a town just entering its boom period and becoming an economic magnet for the region. The Youngs were not unusual in their geographic restlessness. One newspaper editor estimated that more than a hundred individuals streamed both into and out of Rochester each day. In February 1827, John Young Sr. purchased eight acres of land in Mendon and moved there with his wife Hannah and four-year-old son Edward. Brigham's sister Rhoda and her husband John P. Greene were already living in the Mendon vicinity as of 1826. Phineas and Lorenzo Dow Young moved to Mendon at roughly the same time as their father and, with no established Reformed Methodist congregation, "immediately opened a house for preaching and commenced teaching the people." According to Phineas, the local Baptist church and its ministers "seemed to feel a great interest" in their efforts at evangelism. Leaving Oswego in late 1828, Brigham built a house and mill on his father's Mendon land, taking advantage of a small but swift stream running through the property. A dam ran a turning lathe in his shop, which he put to use building furniture and mantelpieces. He continued to build houses, craft furniture, make baskets, and undertake other jobs. During this time, Brigham became good friends with Heber C. Kimball, a Mendon potter and blacksmith who would play a central role in his future.[25]

While the Erie Canal brought the much deeper penetration of commercial market forces and values to western New York, Young mostly stood apart from such developments. Shortly after his move to Mendon, he and his brother Phineas signed a lease for one and a half acres of land for $160 annually. Phineas abandoned his half of the lease within months, and by the following winter Brigham had borrowed $60 from Milton Sheldon to meet his obligations. Brigham later repaid a separate debt to Sheldon by making a picket fence and framing a barn. As evidenced by the fact that he continued to repay debts from Mendon and elsewhere into the 1860s, Brigham probably could not maintain the steep payment schedule for the lease. In 1830, he temporarily left Mendon for employment in Canandaigua, eking out a meager living and trying to avoid sliding into impossible debt.[26]

While repeating John Young Sr.'s life of peripatetic poverty, Brigham also relived some of his father's personal struggles. Miriam bore a second daughter in 1830—named Vilate, probably after Heber Kimball's wife—but then grew ill with the same disease that had claimed Brigham's mother. Brigham recalled that his wife's consumption forced him to prepare breakfast for the family and dress the two girls, leave Miriam in a rocking chair by the fireplace when he departed for work, return home to cook dinner, and put her to bed before finishing up other domestic chores. It was a demanding regimen.

Thus far, there was nothing in Brigham Young's life that foreshadowed any sort of success, let alone greatness. Among the five Young brothers, he was the only one who was not at least an irregular preacher. At best, he would earn enough money from his handiwork to pay off his debts and acquire a small amount of property. Nearly thirty years old with no prospect of obtaining capital, Young would probably never have organized any sort of larger, more profitable economic enterprise. Uneducated and transient, he appeared even less likely to achieve any prominence in civic or political life. There is no record of his engagement with any of the political issues of the 1820s in western New York, such as Anti-Masonry and Sabbatarianism (in particular, an attempt to outlaw Sunday postal operations).[27] As he approached his thirtieth birthday, Brigham Young lived on the economic margins of his society and occupied an unsettled position on the landscape of American religion.

"I was near by and knew something of the doings of the Saints," Brigham Young later stated.[28] In September 1827, as the Young family gathered in Mendon, a farmhand, treasure-seeker, and visionary named Joseph Smith Jr. told his family and a few friends that he had miraculously retrieved a set of gold plates from a hillside as instructed by an angel named Moroni.

Like the Youngs, the Smiths had emigrated to western New York from

Joseph Smith Jr., 1844 *(courtesy of L. Tom Perry Special Collections, Harold B. Lee Library, Brigham Young University, Provo, Utah)*

Vermont, settling on the outskirts of Palmyra, a village ten miles north of Canandaigua and twenty miles to the east of Rochester. Again like the Youngs, the Smiths had failed in their quest for worldly success. In 1825, hopelessly behind on their payments, the Smiths sold their farm, fortunately to a man who allowed them to remain on it as tenants. Occupying roughly the same economic terrain as Brigham Young though lacking his skills as a craftsman, Joseph Smith Jr. hired himself out for an array of odd jobs, ranging from farm chores to digging for treasure. For the latter task,

Smith sought and utilized seer stones. According to Smith's mother, Lucy, the small rocks gave Joseph the ability to "discern things invisible to the natural eye." On one treasure-seeking expedition to the New York–Pennsylvania border in 1825, Joseph met Emma Hale, whom he married two years later. Joseph, although he did not affiliate with any denomination, inclined toward Methodism. Like Brigham, he had attended revivals since his childhood, and he also criticized the enthusiasm, divisiveness, and hypocrisy of evangelical sectarians. Yet one resident of Palmyra recalled that Joseph had caught "a spark of Methodism in the camp meeting." Joseph himself later wrote that he had been "somewhat partial to the Methodist sect, and . . . felt some desire to be united with them." Emma Hale's father and relatives were dedicated Methodists, and Joseph attended a Methodist class meeting in 1828 with the Hales. However, he eschewed a firm commitment to any Protestant church and was instead rapidly moving in a very different direction.[29]

In 1829, after translating what he identified as Reformed Egyptian writing on the golden plates, Joseph delivered the manuscript for what became the *Book of Mormon* to a printer in Palmyra.[30] Among its epic narratives, the new scripture chronicled the journey of an Israelite named Lehi to the New World in the sixth century before Christ, the division of Lehi's descendants into the more righteous Nephites and the unrighteous Lamanites, the appearance of Jesus Christ to these peoples following his resurrection, and the eventual annihilation of the Nephites several centuries later. Living amid people fascinated by Indian burial mounds and various explanations for the origins of North America's native peoples, Smith proposed that the Indians were the descendants of these Israelites-turned-Lamanites. Early Mormons referred to the Indians as "Lamanites"; they also called them "the seed of Joseph" and "the remnant of Jacob" after two of Lehi's Israelite ancestors. Per the *Book of Mormon,* God had cursed the Lamanites for their unbelief "with a skin of blackness." One day, however, they would accept the gospel, become a "white and a delightsome people," and taste millennial glory.[31]

Besides answering the riddle of Native American origins, the *Book of Mormon* announced the restoration of an age of miracles thought to have been lost since the early years of the New Testament church. "[I]f there were miracles wrought then," asked the prophet Moroni after the Nephites' defeat, "why has God ceased to be a God of miracles and yet be an unchangeable Being?" In the years ahead, Smith's followers would attract both converts and derision for their practices of divine healing, speaking in tongues, and ongoing revelation. The *Book of Mormon* denounced those "who deny the revelations of God, and say that they are done away, that there are no revelations, nor prophecies, nor gifts, nor healing, nor speaking with tongues, and the interpretation of tongues." Although early Mormons reported diverse manifestations of divine power, the foremost miracle was the appearance of the *Book of Mormon* itself, which served as a sign that God was speaking to His people as He had spoken both to the ancient Hebrews and the early Christians. Once more narrowing the distance between heaven and earth, God still spoke, at least to those who chose to hear.[32]

Brigham Young, his parents, and his siblings proved receptive listeners. Brigham and his friend Heber Kimball later connected the coming forth of the new scripture with a vision they had seen in the heavens. "The night the plates were found," Young said at an 1845 meeting, "there was a great light in the East and it went to the West and it was very bright although there was no moon at the time. I gazed at it in company with my wife. The light was perfectly clear and remained several hours. It formed into men as if there were great armies in the West; and I then saw in the North West armies of men come up. They would march to the South West and, then go out of sight." Heber Kimball, soon to be Brigham's neighbor in Mendon, reported the same visionary experience. "I distinctly heard the guns crack and the swords clash," he later stated. Kimball claimed to have seen "distinctly the muskets, bayonets, and knapsacks of the men, who wore caps and feathers like those used by the American soldiers in the last war with Britain." Kimball's wife Vilate, John and Rhoda Green, John Young Sr., and Fanny Young beheld the celestial scene with him. Joseph Smith became the burned-over district's most famous recipient of heavenly visions, but the Youngs also belonged to this visionary culture.[33]

Even in a portion of the early American republic thickly populated with visionaries, prophets, and religious reformers, Joseph Smith stood out. The Mormon prophet was a man who tried to burst through nearly all the limitations he encountered. For instance, while many American Christians affirmed that God still communicated with them in the present, the vast majority accepted a closed scriptural canon. There were exceptions. Some Americans published accounts of their revelations and visions, and a few even produced new scriptures or their own revisions of the Bible. Joseph Smith's challenge to the traditional canon, however, was without parallel. In addition to publishing the hefty *Book of Mormon*, he wrote or dictated scores of revelations, which his followers accepted as God's contemporary words and later compiled into additional books of scripture. "Joseph the Seer" was bound by no book, no creed, and—unlike many Protestant reformers filled with a longing for the New Testament church—no particular historical golden age. Instead, Smith and his followers spoke of the "restitution of all things." He eventually promised his followers that through his church they might conquer death, remain with their loved ones for eternity, and create God's kingdom on the earth. Smith also displayed a kinetic energy for forming friendships, creating ecclesiastical councils, and building cities. When he bumped up against the conventions and limits of nineteenth-century politics, marriage, and theology, Smith proposed his own audacious paths. Smith's controversial ideas and practices gained him an outsized measure of notoriety, but a surprising number of men and women accepted his prophetic claims.[34]

When Brigham Young encountered the *Book of Mormon*, though, Smith led only a small band of believers, who soon became known as "Mormons" or "Mormonites." In April 1830, with perhaps forty or fifty followers in attendance, Smith founded what he at first simply termed the Church of Christ. That month, Brigham's brother Phineas stopped at a Mendon inn on his return from a preaching mission in Lima, New York. Samuel H. Smith, the prophet's brother, accosted him with news of "the Golden Bible." Phineas agreed to read the *Book of Mormon* with "a prayerful heart," though he planned to expose the book's errors. He "read every word in the book the same week" and repeated his perusal the following week, but instead of finding the book's errors, he "felt a conviction that the book was true." Brigham's father borrowed Phineas's copy, "read it through," and "said it was the greatest work and the clearest of error of anything he had ever seen, the Bible not excepted." Fanny Young "read it and declared it a revelation." Brigham also saw and read the *Book of Mormon* Phineas obtained from Samuel Smith. Despite these positive responses, no members of the Young family rushed to join the new church, and Brigham did not immediately accept the book's divine claims.[35]

In late August, Phineas and Joseph Young left on a Reformed Methodist preaching tour that took them into southeastern Ontario. On their easterly journey around Lake Ontario, they stopped in Lyons to visit a Reformed Methodist acquaintance, the visionary Solomon Chamberlain. Around 1807, at age nineteen, Chamberlain had a "vision of the night" in which he saw the damned in hell "blowing up the flames and preparing red hot iron to lay their faces on to all eternity." Shaken, he found no comfort in Calvinist Presbyterianism but experienced salvation at a Methodist camp meeting. After an 1816 vision of a meeting house, he attended a Reformed Methodist quarterly meeting and "saw the same house of worship." Further visions of both Satan and Jesus followed, and Chamberlain achieved sanctification and "went home rejoicing." When the Episcopal Methodists rejected his testimony and teaching, he realized "the fallen state that the church was now in" and "the power of the Antichrist." They further soured on him when he—claiming to have communed with a deceased member of the "society"—publicly commanded specific members of the church to repent of their sins. Chamberlain eventually affiliated with the Reformed Methodists and settled in Lyons, just fifteen miles east of Palmyra. While there, he heard about the "gold bible" and visited the Smiths, to whom he gave a pamphlet describing his visions. Recognizing a kindred spirit, Joseph Smith told Chamberlain of his visions and shared an advance copy of the first sixty-four pages of the *Book of Mormon,* which Chamberlain took with him, becoming the book's first missionary. Baptized in April 1830 shortly after the founding of the Church of Christ, Chamberlain determined to proselytize his Reformed Methodist brethren.[36]

Phineas and Joseph Young were taken aback by Chamberlain's message that "every body must believe the *Book of Mormon* or be lost." "Father Chamberlain," Brigham later noted, "preached to Joseph and Phineas in such a manner that they asked him to desist." Reaching Canada, Phineas tried to preach but "could think of but little except the *Book of Mormon* and what I had heard of Mormonism." Partly convinced of Mormonism's claims, Phineas stopped at an Episcopal Methodist quarterly conference in Kingston, Ontario, where he testified about the *Book of Mormon.* He then proceeded to a Reformed Methodist annual conference, which his brother-in-law John P. Greene and Solomon Chamberlain also attended. Chamberlain, who never hesitated to offend an audience, told the attendees that "if they rejected it [the *Book of Mormon*] they would all go to destruction," whereupon they expelled him from the meeting. Phineas Young returned home and "continued to preach, trying to tie Mormonism to Methodism."[37]

Sometime in 1831, Brigham visited Phineas and told his brother "that he was convinced that there was something in Mormonism."[38] Then in the fall of 1831, a group of Mormon preachers from Pennsylvania arrived in Mendon. According to Heber Kimball, the visiting Mormon elders explained Joseph Smith's encounter with the angel in greater detail and emphasized that those who repented and were baptized would "receive the laying on of hands for the gift of the Holy Ghost," whereupon believers would "cast out devils in the name of Jesus" and "should speak with new tongues." The traveling elders, Brigham later recounted, "preach[ed] the everlasting gospel . . . which I heard and believed." That initial response, however, only prompted a combination of belief and further investigation. "I was not baptized on hearing the first sermon," Brigham continued, "nor the second, nor during the first year of my acquaintance with this work." He waited to see if the adherents of this new gospel displayed common sense and morality, and he tested their doctrines by the light of the Bible and prayer. "I reasoned on revelation," he explained, emphasizing the role of rational reflection in his conversion.[39]

Eventually, however, spiritual ecstasy and power overwhelmed that hesitation. Heber Kimball, who a few weeks previously had joined a Baptist church, recalled "pondering upon these things" with Brigham, Joseph, and John Young Sr. Suddenly, "the glory of God shone upon us" and "caused such great joy to spring up in our bosoms, that we were hardly able to contain ourselves; and we did shout aloud, Hosannah to God and the Lamb." Accompanied by Phineas and Heber, Brigham and Miriam—evidently well enough to make the trip—traveled in January 1832 to visit a branch of the church in Columbia, Pennsylvania (Bradford County). The trip gave the visitors an opportunity to observe Mormon fellowship and worship. The Mormons in Pennsylvania spoke in tongues, interpreted tongues, and prophesied. Long accustomed to outbreaks of the supernatural at camp meetings and familiar with Lorenzo Dow Young's visions and Phineas's divine healing, Brigham himself finally sensed the direct connection with the divine that had eluded him during his youth and early adulthood. With the exception of divine healing, radical evangelicals like the Reformed Methodists had largely eschewed the more spectacular gifts of the Spirit, such as speaking in tongues and prophecy. Now, Brigham met Mormon elders who embraced such gifts and practiced them with regularity.[40]

At this point, Brigham hovered on the threshold of baptism. Immediately after returning to Mendon, in February he departed for Canada to report his experiences to his brother Joseph. He rode with John P. Greene as far as Sackett's Harbor, where Brigham had once prayed and worshiped with Hiram McKee. Brigham then continued to Kingston alone. Before making a formal commitment to the new church, he needed to consult with Joseph, always the family's most earnest religious thinker. "I had more confidence in his judgment and discretion," Brigham recounted, "and in the manifestations of God to him, than I had in myself." When he met Joseph, he told him that he had experienced "the power of God." According to Joseph Young's later account, "he reported many things of interest concerning the signs and wonderfull miricles being wrought through the believers in his new faith." "He [Joseph] caught its influence," Brigham reminisced, "came home with me, and was baptized." Now Brigham himself was nearly ready.[41]

In his childhood and early adulthood, Brigham Young had encountered varieties of radical evangelicalism that foreshadowed Mormonism's expectation of restored apostolic gifts and its passion for evangelism and expansion through a largely uneducated itinerant ministry. The Reformed Methodists (along with many other American evangelicals, especially on the frontier and in the backcountry) and early Mormons thirsted for and expected a latter-day Pentecost with powerful and immediate demonstrations of spiritual power. The former prayed for the "slaying power" of the Holy Ghost; Joseph Smith repeatedly promised his followers that they would be "endowed with power from on high." In many other ways—in its appeal to Bible proofs, its expectation of an imminent apocalypse and millennium, and its stark warnings of damnation for those who refused its message—early Mormonism resembled the radical evangelical culture from which it diverged.[42]

North Americans of diverse religious backgrounds converted to Mormonism, from skeptics to pious seekers, from universalists to practitioners of hermetic folk magic. The more religiously esoteric backgrounds of some Mormon converts, though, have sometimes obscured the deep influence of radical evangelicalism on early Mormonism. The Youngs were only one family among many restless and radical Methodists who joined Joseph Smith's Church of Christ. "Most of us are from that body," wrote Mormon editor Edward Tullidge in 1866 with some exaggeration, "from Wesleyan parents, Sunday schools churches." "Brigham and his brothers were Methodists," he continued, "and, spite of our few outward differences, there are no people so much like John Wesley and his early followers in spirit, faith and missionary energy . . . as the Mormons."[43]

Still, there were stark differences between even radical evangelicalism and Mormonism. Joseph Smith's prophetic claims, his embrace of ongoing revelation, and the church's gathering (by the time Brigham converted, a revelation had already specified the location of Independence, Missouri, as "the place for the city Zion," and another revelation encouraged migration to Ohio's Western Reserve) sharply differentiated Mormonism from Reformed Methodism and other varieties of American evangelicalism. Thus, it took considerable reflection and illustrations of supernatural power to convince Brigham to bridge such a wide ecclesiastical chasm. He converted because Mormonism satisfied a skepticism rooted in both rationality and deeply ingrained biblicism and because the elders who witnessed to him displayed spiritual gifts that surpassed anything he had known in Reformed Methodism.

IN APRIL, the Young family began its en masse baptism into Mormonism. Joseph and Phineas, accompanied by their father, made a second trip to Bradford County, Pennsylvania. Phineas and John Young Sr. were baptized on April 5, and Joseph followed the next day. By the time they reached their Mendon homes, several families from Mendon's Baptist church, in which Phineas and the Young family had sparked a "reformation" several years earlier, had converted to Mormonism. The Rochester *Liberal Advocate* reported on April 14 that "*Mormonism* is said to have taken deep root in the Baptist church, in the town of Mendon . . . A number were *re-dipped* on Sunday last." Brigham joined their ranks on Monday, April 9, and was baptized in his own mill stream. "I felt a humble, childlike spirit, witnessing unto me that my sins were forgiven," he later recalled. Brigham had finally found the assurance of salvation he had sought for many years. Miriam was baptized several weeks later, and by the end of 1833 all of Brigham's siblings had joined the new church.[44]

Brigham later claimed to have been the driving force in his family's conversion. "[W]hile I was getting into it," Brigham maintained in 1845, "brother Phineas laid it by." "I preached to him first," Brigham added, recalling his trip to visit his brother Joseph in early 1832. "I claim all of you as the fruit of my labors," he asserted in his role as family patriarch. "I am the first one of the family that embraced it understandingly." Even though Brigham was instrumental in Joseph's conversion, he overstated his role in his family's embrace of Mormonism. Phineas appears to have been the family member who most quickly and eagerly embraced the new faith, and Brigham hesitated to proceed with baptism without Joseph's assent. As in the family's conversion to Reformed Methodism, Brigham initially held back, following the lead of his brothers.[45]

After his Mormon baptism, Young immediately assumed active service and leadership in the church and rarely wavered in his commitment to his new faith. "I was ordained to the office of an Elder before my clothes were dry upon me," he later recalled. Leaving behind family and work, he became an itinerant Mormon preacher, fully dedicated to his new faith. Having found no lasting peace in the evangelical rebirth, Brigham had turned to Joseph Smith Jr.'s Church of Christ and became what the King James Bible termed a "new creature."[46]

CHAPTER TWO

The Tongues of Angels

I am determined that neither heights nor depths principalities nor
powers things present or to come nor any other creature shall
separate me from you.

—JOSEPH SMITH, JANUARY 1836

THE Age of Jackson, in which Americans debated Indian removal, nul-
lification, and the Bank of the United States, was also an era of millenarian visionaries and spiritual wonders. Although mainstream Methodists and Baptists began to shed their rough edges and the intense
supernaturalism of the early-nineteenth-century awakenings, within other
religious movements the veil between heaven and earth continued to part.
Prophets appeared, men and women filled with the Holy Ghost spoke in
tongues, and believers told of angelic visitors. Devotees of Swedish mys-
tic Emmanuel Swedenborg—whose *Heaven and Hell* became an American bestseller in the 1820s—marveled at his reports of the pure heavenly
speech of angels, sought to experience similar visions and wonders, and
sometimes claimed to have communicated with Swedenborg himself.[1] In
the late 1830s, the celibate Shakers witnessed the onset of an "Era of
Manifestations" that included visions, spirit possession, and spiritual
tongues.[2] The Reformed Methodists had emphasized the restoration of
apostolic spiritual gifts, but with the exception of healing they practiced
them only sporadically. When he joined the Mormons, Young converted to
a church that more fully embraced such manifestations of the divine.

Earthly tempests, however, repeatedly shuttered the heavens. During the
first five years of his membership in the church, Young stood by Joseph
Smith's side through many setbacks, including an abortive military expedition, a failed bank, and an inability to stem dissension within the church.

Young's steadiness through those tempests proved central to his rise in Smith's estimation. As others questioned or abandoned Smith, Brigham Young never faltered.

For Young himself, these were years of growing self-confidence and purpose, qualities that ironically came through increased submission to the church and perseverance through its challenges. His intense commitment to his new church temporarily superseded his customarily fierce independence, and Young subordinated himself—albeit sometimes grudgingly—to his prophet and to other ecclesiastical superiors. He still endured poverty but now understood his economic deprivation as a sacrifice for his faith. His peregrinations continued, but his endless movement was no longer rudderless. Through his missionary work and devotion to Joseph Smith, Young became a leader within the church and within his family. At first making little impression on the prophet because of his inexperience and lack of eloquence, Young won Smith's respect through his practical contributions to the church, his ecstatic and musical spirituality, and his indefatigable loyalty. Before his baptism, Young deferred to his brothers' spiritual leadership, and he rarely spoke or prayed aloud at religious gatherings. Now he became an effective and sometimes combative public speaker, surpassed his older brothers within the church hierarchy, and took the place of his father as the patriarchal leader of his family.

AFTER his baptism, Young devoted himself to spreading his new faith. "[I] preacht as opertunity prezented," Brigham recorded in his journal. His early efforts bore fruit when he baptized Rachel Flummerfelt, who along with her husband numbered among the thirty or so Mormon converts in Mendon. The spiritual fervor that had drawn Young into the church lingered over the coming months. Shortly after his baptism, Young and Alpheus Gifford—one of the Pennsylvania elders—gathered at Heber Kimball's home. While they were praying, "Gifford commenced speaking in tongues." Young caught the contagious fire: "the spirit came on me like an electric shock to speak in an unknown tongue, and though I was kneeling looking in an opposite direction, the same moment I turned round on my knees towards him and spoke in tongues also." Other Americans used similar language to describe their experience of God's spirit. Protestant revivalist Charles Finney later recalled the embrace of the Holy Spirit as a "wave of electricity, going through and through me." Except for members of a few small movements, though, Christians in North America and Europe did not speak in tongues. Brigham Young's practice of this New Testament spiritual gift marked him as having moved to a place very much on the fringes of American religion.[3]

Emboldened by this latter-day Pentecost but limited by his wife Miriam's illness, Young continued local attempts at preaching while his brothers Joseph and Phineas joined a mission to Canada. While Vilate Kimball cared for his children and for Miriam, Brigham and Heber traveled to nearby towns to preach, baptize, speak in tongues, and help converts receive the Holy Ghost. Young felt hampered by his inarticulateness and lack of education. "How I have had the headache," he later shared, "when I had ideas to lay before the people, and not words to express them; but I was so gritty that I always tried my best." A full measure of zeal compensated for such deficiencies.[4]

In September 1832, Miriam succumbed to her consumption. "In her expiring moments," Heber Kimball wrote in an early autobiography, "she clapped her hands and praised the Lord, and called to me to help her to praise the Lord."[5] The language resembles common evangelical accounts of believers rejoicing during "beautiful," "triumphant," or "happy" deaths, clapping their hands and shouting praise to God.[6] Young was absent when Miriam died, unusual during an era in which death was sentimentalized and family members kept lengthy vigils at their loved ones' deathbeds. It is uncertain how long he grieved over Miriam's death, which surely reminded him of his mother's from the same illness. Young sought refuge in devotion to his new church, which became and remained his extended family.

Within weeks of Miriam's death, Young left his children with Vilate Kimball and—along with his brother Joseph and friend Heber—began a journey to Ohio to meet the prophet of his new faith. The previous year, Joseph Smith had relocated to Kirtland, a town in northeastern Ohio in a region known as the Western Reserve. Reaching Kirtland in early November, Kimball and the two Young brothers found a man who did not match their preconceptions of a prophet. "I expected," wrote Joseph Young many decades later, "at least I should find him in his sanctum dispensing spiritual blessings and directions [about] how to build the Zion of God on the earth." Instead, and probably decisively for their positive reaction to Smith, they met a prophet much like themselves: young, uneducated, and physically robust. Brigham Young was thirty-one years old, barrel-chested and of medium height, with sandy-red hair, a clean-shaven face, and blue-gray eyes. Smith was four years his junior and a few inches taller, with blue eyes and brown hair. Smith enjoyed wrestling, and he was quick to laugh, even at his own appearance. "I suppose you think I am a great, green, lubberly fellow," he said to one convert arriving in Kirtland. The Young brothers and Kimball found Smith chopping wood in the forest. The prophet stopped, put down his ax, and shook hands with the new arrivals. Brigham offered his assistance, and they all chopped and loaded

wood before going to Smith's house. None of the four men adopted any
pretense to mask their humble origins.[7]

That night, the three guests renewed a debate among Smith's followers
by speaking in tongues during a prayer meeting. Among most evangelical Protestants, including those inclined toward other displays of enthusiasm, speaking in tongues belonged to an age that had long since passed,
and its contemporary practice was a sign of delusion, a badge of lunacy
reserved for fringe movements such as the Shakers. In Kirtland, many of
Smith's followers had formerly embraced the teachings of Presbyterian-
turned-Baptist Alexander Campbell. Along with an assortment of other
Protestant reformers, Campbell was known as a "Restorationist," a man
opposed to creeds and intent on returning to the worship practices and
ecclesiastical organization of the early Christian church as illustrated in
the New Testament. Unlike Smith, however, Campbell believed that most
gifts of the spirit had ceased with the apostolic era of Christianity. A number of Kirtland-area Campbellites converted to Mormonism in 1830, including a preacher named Sidney Rigdon, who soon became one of Joseph
Smith's closest associates.[8]

The Kirtland converts to Mormonism wanted a far more sweeping restoration of New Testament Christianity than did Campbell. Many had visions, and they embraced healing the sick, speaking in tongues, and prophesying. Reports even circulated of Mormon attempts at raising the dead.
Among those who claimed the gift of prophecy for themselves were an
African American convert known as "Black Pete" and a "prophetess"
named Laura Hubbell. Some converts engaged in wild physical manifestations akin to the evangelical camp meeting phenomena Brigham Young
had witnessed as a child and young man. Thus, Smith and other church
leaders confronted the task of consolidating prophetic authority and—like
the evangelical revivalists the Mormons had rejected—separating desired
spiritual ecstasy from unrestrained "enthusiasm."[9]

By the time of Brigham Young's arrival, Smith had discouraged the private receipt of revelations and some forms of religious ecstasy. When the
Young brothers and Kimball spoke in tongues, therefore, some Kirtland
Mormons expected Smith to condemn the practice. Young later recalled
that the controversy revolved entirely around "the gift of tongues that was
upon me" and whether Smith would "condemn the gift brother Brigham
had." Smith, though, pronounced that "it was the pure Adamic language"
and of God. Young also sang in spiritual tongues at the gathering. Several
months after Young's Kirtland trip, Smith presided over an outburst of
tongues at a church council. "[T]he gift was poured out in a miraculous
manner," recorded a clerk, "until all the Elders obtained the gift together

with several members of the Church both male & female." The worshipers prayed and sang praises "to God & the Lamb . . . all in tongues." Brigham Young had converted to Mormonism partly because of the missionaries' practice of spiritual gifts. Now, he participated in the reintroduction of such gifts in Kirtland, and speaking in tongues continued as a distinctive feature of early Mormon spirituality.[10]

Young, his brother, and Kimball spent several nights in Kirtland, listening to the prophet discuss his deepening understanding of God, the afterlife, and the priesthood. Young struggled to assimilate some teachings, such as Smith's explication of three separate "kingdoms" or degrees of heavenly glory. In February 1832, Smith and Sidney Rigdon jointly dictated what became known to Mormons as "The Vision." Elaborating on the imagery and language of Paul's First Letter to the Corinthians, the Vision rejected Calvinist arbitrariness (in which God chose whether to save or damn individuals without regard to their merit) and suggested that the vast majority of humankind would receive some level of eternal blessing. In its three tiers of glory, Smith's Vision also bore some resemblance to Emanuel Swedenborg's division of heaven into three realms. As Smith envisioned, baptized members of "the church of the Firstborn" would become "gods, even the sons of God" and thus exalted dwell with God in a "celestial kingdom." Other people would find their eternal homes in lesser "terrestrial" and "telestial" kingdoms. Only a few "sons of perdition" would suffer eternal punishment. As was true of many early converts to Mormonism, Young's Protestant background did not permit the quick acceptance of such un-Protestant ideas about the afterlife. "[M]y traditions were such," he later reflected, "that when the Vision came first to me, it was so directly contrary and opposed to my former education, I said, wait a little; I did not reject it, but I could not understand it." Rather than causing any spiritual uncertainty, however, such teachings drew Young closer to the prophet. "The time when I first saw Joseph I had but just one prayer," he recalled, ". . . that was all the time I could hear Joseph and hear his doctrine and see his mind." Several decades later, the "contraction of hell" in Smith's vision became a cherished belief for Brigham Young.[11]

The trip to Kirtland began Young's lifelong and loyal attachment to Joseph Smith, which developed quickly and became the most significant and formative relationship in his life. For Young, this was an uncharacteristic development. Proud of his ability to rely on his own reason in religious matters, he had never formed any close attachment to Protestant religious figures. Although Young had converted to Mormonism without meeting its founding prophet, Smith had translated a book Young accepted as sacred scripture. Now, Young became a devoted disciple of a man he viewed as God's chosen leader of his restored church and his earthly oracle. For the remainder of his life, his faith was inseparable from the person of Joseph Smith.

Flush from the events in Kirtland and free to leave his children with Vilate Kimball, Young joined his brother Joseph on a missionary circuit of eastern Ontario during the winter of 1832–33. The brothers trudged on foot through deep mud and snow and then crossed the eastern tip of Lake Ontario on dangerously thin ice. Joseph and Phineas Young, along with several of the Pennsylvania elders instrumental in the conversion of the Young family, had made inroads into Joseph Young's old Reformed Methodist preaching circuit in Canada. Brigham and Joseph now built on those earlier successes, holding forty meetings and baptizing fourteen converts before coming home to Mendon. More confident in his abilities, Brigham then returned to Canada on his own. Evangelizing an audience still imbued with Protestant biblicism, he used the Bible as a means of communicating his new faith. Young never wrote down his extemporaneous sermons, but one diary entry records that he preached from Genesis 48 and 49 and from Ezekiel 37. The latter predicts that God will unite the people of Israel by joining "the stick of Joseph . . . in the hand of Ephraim" to "the stick of Judah." Mormons identified the "stick of Ephraim" as the *Book of Mormon,* and they interpreted Genesis 49 as describing a "branch of the tribe of Joseph which was separated from his brethren," thus supporting the *Book of Mormon*'s narrative of an Israelite family's journey to the New World. Young's approach was typical of early Mormon missionaries, who used the Bible to contend that the *Book of Mormon* provided proof that God had restored the ancient practices of prophecy, revelation, and healing. Equipped with such messages, he reached Kingston, Ontario, where he attended a Reformed Methodist quarterly meeting and preached in the surrounding area, sometimes baptizing as many as ten converts a day. Young had adopted the life of an itinerant preacher, traveling as relentlessly as any Methodist circuit rider, winning men and women to a new faith.[12]

In July 1833, Young accompanied several Canadian converts to Kirtland, where he again met Joseph Smith. For two years Smith had been emphasizing the necessity for his followers to gather in Independence, Missouri (Jackson County), which he identified in a revelation as "the place for the city Zion." At the same time, he also encouraged converts to relocate to Ohio. With large numbers gathering in Kirtland, a May 1833 revelation affirmed the town as "a stake of Zion" and ordered the construction of a temple. While tarrying in Kirtland, Smith told Young to "[n]ever do another day's work to build up a Gentile [non-Mormon] city."

Both Mormonism and Methodism sent young men out to harvest evangelistic fruit in the remote vineyards of the New World. Whereas the Methodists' rural orientation moved "resources from center to circumference" and sought to plant churches on the frontier, the Mormons aimed to draw their scattered converts from the circumference into a new center, gathering them together in preparation for the earth's final days. While sheltering themselves from foretold judgments, they would build up a sacred city. Probably because of their millennial emphasis, Joseph Smith's elders began referring to their movement as the "Church of the Latter Day Saints" and its members simply as "Saints."[13]

After returning to western New York to gather his daughters and few possessions, Young—along with Kimball's family—moved to Kirtland. In the early 1830s, Smith was encouraging his followers to consecrate any property they owned to the church. Young could not answer that call. If "any man that ever did gather with the Saints was any poorer than I was," he later joked, "it was because he had nothing." The move to Kirtland, though, also revealed to Young other, very practical ways that he could help build up his fledgling church. He built houses and furniture for fellow Mormons. Testifying to his skill, Joseph Smith's nephew George A. Smith later recalled Young having "hollowed out a trough from a white wood log to hold soap for his family." Early Mormonism promised its rather down-to-earth converts an "endowment of power from on high" and gave them divine revelations, but the church also sacralized earthly tasks. "When I saw Joseph Smith," said Young, describing an early encounter with the prophet, "he took heaven . . . and brought it down to earth; and he took the earth, [and] brought it up." Young treasured the opportunity to live among the Saints. Given their small numbers and unstable congregations, the Reformed Methodists had never provided the Youngs with the sort of fellowship and lasting community promised by the Mormon doctrine of gathering.[14]

In addition to resuming his trade, Young sought a second wife. Vilate Kimball's generosity had made an immediate remarriage unnecessary, but as a widower with two daughters Young surely felt pressure to find another helpmeet. Both he and Jonathan Hampton, one of Young's converts, courted a woman named Julia Foster, whom Young had also converted to Mormonism. Young told Hampton that "he could have the first chance of popping the question and if Sister Foster did not accept him then he (Young) would try his luck." Julia Foster accepted Hampton's proposal, and Young married the couple, who named their first child after the man who had brought them into the church.[15]

Young quickly identified another prospective wife. She was Mary Ann

Angell, a Free Will Baptist whom Young's brother-in-law John P. Greene had baptized into the church. Sharing Young's penchant for impetuous mobility, Angell had preceded the rest of her family to Kirtland. Emmeline B. Wells, an editor and suffragist in late-1800s Utah, chronicled that Mary Ann "heard him [Young] preach and instinctively felt drawn towards him." The couple secured a marriage license in February 1834, and their marriage certificate dates their union to March 31. A church marriage may have preceded the license date, as a son named Joseph—perhaps after the prophet, perhaps after Brigham's brother Joseph—arrived in October. Young later commented that his new wife "took charge of my children, kept my house, and labored faithfully for the interest of my family and the kingdom."[16]

When she married Brigham, Mary Ann knew she would spend much of her time apart from him. Brigham anticipated a summer preaching trip, departing from the church's custom by requesting permission to travel without a partner. Events in Missouri, however, altered his plans. In July 1833, Missouri vigilantes forced the Jackson County Mormons to agree to depart their Zion within six months, threatening to destroy their property should they refuse. There were several reasons for the conflict, including rumors of Mormon abolitionism and complaints about Mormon spiritual excess. Most basically, however, non-Mormons became alarmed at the sheer numbers of Mormons flooding into the county, purchasing land, and talking of their divine appointment to build Zion in Jackson County. "[I]t requires no gift of prophecy," it was proclaimed at an anti-Mormon meeting, "to tell that the day is not far distant when the civil government of the county will be in their hands." Mormons in Zion considered themselves a persecuted minority, exactly what the non-Mormons feared becoming. After an early November skirmish, the Saints grudgingly left for neighboring Clay County and resentfully endured an impoverished winter.[17]

When church members from Missouri arrived in Kirtland in February, they demanded of Joseph Smith "when, how and by what means Zion was to be redeemed from our enemies." In response, Smith asked for volunteers to accompany him on an expedition for Zion's redemption. In a revelation, Smith likened himself to Moses leading "the children of Israel" out of Egypt to a latter-day Zion. The high council of the church in Kirtland elected Smith the "Commander in Chief of the Armies of Israel." Missouri governor Daniel Dunklin had suggested that he would provide militia protection if the refugee Saints sought to reclaim their lands. With unhesitating submission to his prophet, Brigham Young immediately volunteered as a soldier in Israel's army, soon known as Zion's Camp, and followed Joseph Smith one thousand miles to the Missouri River.[18]

Mary Ann Angell, ca. 1850 *(courtesy of the Utah State Historical Society)*

In practical terms, Zion's Camp was a predictable failure. Given the animosity toward the Saints in Jackson County and the suspicion with which Missouri "Gentiles" (i.e., non-Mormons) regarded them, a battalion of two hundred armed Mormons headed by a prophetic commander-in-chief only made a volatile situation more perilous. The soldiers of Israel—with only a few women accompanying them—presented themselves as settlers bound for the frontier. During Sunday services on the march, elders posed as members of Protestant denominations, with Young preaching the doctrines of the "close communion Baptist[s]." Such amateurish precautions did not prevent word of the march from reaching Missouri, and venomous mobs prepared a hostile welcome. Moreover, just as grumbling plagued Moses during the Exodus, Joseph Smith struggled against malcontents in his own ranks. Sylvester Smith, no relation to the prophet, threatened to kill a bulldog that one of the troops had given to Joseph. Joseph promised Sylvester Smith a whipping in response. According to one marcher, the assembled Saints—many of whom also disliked the prophet's dog—were "dissatisfied with brother Joseph's remarks." Joseph then criticized his perplexed followers for "condescending to . . . the spirit of a dog" and explained that "he had descended to that spirit" only as an object lesson for them. While tempers cooled, the petty disputes disrupted the group's discipline and unity.[19]

Shortly before Zion's Camp reached western Missouri, Governor Dunklin—worried about possible bloodshed—reneged on his offer of assistance, and negotiations between the Missouri Saints and Jackson County representatives over church members' property stalled. As the army camped between the two branches of the Fishing River, two hundred anti-Mormon marauders prepared to attack. A hailstorm frustrated the approaching mob and averted disaster, but it also halted the Saints' approach to Jackson County. Word of Dunklin's decision fully deflated Smith's hope that the Mormon settlers could regain their properties. Although some marchers spoiled for a holy war, the prophet averred that the Saints never intended to "commit hostilities against any man . . . [or] to injure any man's person or property." The Mormon army then suffered further adversity, as a cholera epidemic swept through the camp. In keeping with Protestant convention, Smith and his followers interpreted the disease as the work of the "destroyer," the biblical personification of death. The epidemic claimed fourteen lives, and Smith pronounced it God's judgment on his followers' iniquities. Having marched his army from Ohio to Missouri, Smith now disbanded it without any realistic prospect of Zion's future redemption. The weary marchers straggled back to Ohio. Moreover, irrespective of his cause's justice, by mustering an armed force to "avenge" the Lord of his "enemies," Smith had associated his church in the minds of many Americans with violence and vigilantism.[20]

Many Camp veterans, though, found that despite the debacle their faith in their church and in Joseph Smith was strengthened. Zion's Camp, indeed, exemplifies the parallel worlds inhabited by faithful Mormons and outside critics. For those who remained faithful, including Brigham Young, the trek became not a failed military expedition but a fulfilled spiritual quest. When Brigham's brother Joseph had hesitated to join the army, Smith assured the Young brothers that "if you will go with me in the camp to Missouri and keep my counsel, I promise you . . . not a hair of your heads shall be harmed." Brigham brought with him "a good gun and bayonet, plenty of ammunition, a dirk, an ax, a saw, a chisel, spade, hoe, and other necessary tools," and he gave fellow marcher Wilford Woodruff a butcher knife. En route to Missouri, the marchers encountered a large Indian burial mound on the banks of the Illinois River, in which they found a skeleton of a man with an arrow embedded between two ribs. Smith reported a vision in which he learned that the bones were of a warrior named Zelph, a "white Lamanite" who fought in a great battle described in the *Book of Mormon*. Until at least 1845, Young kept the arrow in his possession, and the party rejoiced at this apparent proof of the new scripture's authenticity. Although Smith interpreted dissension in Zion's Camp as provoking God's wrath, there were also signs of the Lord's pleasure and protection. Smith, in what became known as the Fishing River revelation, told his beleaguered followers that God had "heard their prayers, and will accept their offering." God had brought them "thus far for a trial of their faith."[21]

Young later recalled that Zion's Camp "gave us an experience that Kirtland could not buy. I watched everything that Joseph did and the spirit he did it in." In later accounts, Young did not mention the Saints' failure to redeem Zion and instead credited Smith with staving off additional deaths from the cholera by prodding the Saints to repentance. Veterans at later Zion's Camp reunions remembered the setbacks and murmurings, but they primarily celebrated the faith the march had nurtured. At one such gathering, the veterans recalled Brigham and Joseph Young comforting the camp with "Hark listen to my trumpeters." Originally a Protestant hymn and then a Mormon favorite, the lyrics described a band of volunteers marching "for Canaan's land," its redemption "drawing nigh." While the failure to redeem Zion left some marchers discouraged, the march had filled Young with spiritual exhilaration and dedication.[22]

Back in Ohio, Young unstintingly defended Smith's reputation. He spoke at an August 1834 church trial of Sylvester Smith, who stood accused of making false charges against Joseph. Young testified that he "had not seen anything in his [Joseph Smith's] conduct during his journey to the West unbecoming his profession as a man of God" and specifically affirmed the prophet's handling of Sylvester Smith, adding that it met with "general satisfaction." The next month, Joseph Smith named Young to a seat on the Kirtland High Council for the first time. Joseph may not have redeemed Zion, but he had kept his promise to the Young brothers. Earthly success ultimately was secondary to disciples like Brigham Young who, while others faltered, had demonstrated steadfast loyalty to his Moses. He had passed a trial. During similar trials, more church members would lose their faith in Smith, but regardless of future setbacks Young's loyalty would grow only fiercer.[23]

IN FEBRUARY 1835, Smith called the Kirtland church to a meeting at which he insisted that "God had not designed" the march to Missouri "for nothing." Asking the Zion's Camp veterans to sit together in one part of the meetinghouse, he informed them that "it was the will of God that they should be ordained to the ministry and go forth to prune the vineyard for the last times." Oliver Cowdery, David Whitmer, and Martin Harris, the "three witnesses" who testified to having seen the golden plates, appointed and blessed twelve men, including Brigham Young and Heber C. Kimball, into a Quorum of the Twelve Apostles. "They are to hold the keys of this ministry," Smith stated, describing the quorum several days later, "to unlock the door of the kingdom of heaven unto all nations, and to preach the Gospel to every creature." Young's blessing predicted that he would "go forth from land to land, from sea to sea and shall behold Heavenly Messengers [angels] going forth . . . and that heathen nations shall even call him God himself, if he did not rebuke them." One week later, when all of the twelve had received their blessings, Cowdery spoke to them at length. Noting that they relied on the testimony of others for their faith, he urged them to "receive a testimony from Heaven for yourselves . . . [that] you have seen God, face to face." Reflecting Jesus's instructions to his disciples in Luke 24 ("tarry ye in the city of Jerusalem, until ye be endued with power from on high"), the Mormon apostles would be "endowed with power from on High" before embarking on their foreign missions.[24]

Although Young had earned Joseph Smith's trust through his stalwart defense of the prophet, his rise to prominence in the church also depended on continued displays of spiritual fire. With the twelve apostles chosen, ordained, and blessed, the church announced the ordination of men—including Joseph Young—to another ecclesiastical body, known as the "Seventy." Smith had begun to develop presidencies, councils, priesthood hierarchies, and quorums with the same energy and variety that characterized his revelations and personal relationships. Brigham Young interrupted the blessing of the seventies when he arose and "in the Spirit of God sung a song of Zion in a foreign tongue." He then "delivered a very animated address to his brother ministers."[25] There was more to Brigham Young than loyalty and gritty perseverance; he also exuded spiritual power. When Joseph Smith had first met Brigham and Joseph Young, he likely perceived Brigham's older brother as the greater talent for the church. Several years later, after several preaching missions, Zion's Camp, and continuing displays of spiritual fervor, Brigham had gained the attention and admiration of his prophet and a higher position in the church.

A May 2, 1835 church conference assigned Young a special role on the apostles' first mission, appointing him to "go and preach the gospel to the remnants of Joseph," as the church sometimes called the Indians. Two days later, Brigham Young and his fellow members of the Twelve left Kirtland. Mostly ill-clad and impoverished, with esoteric yet biblical titles, the apostles visited church branches in Pennsylvania and New York and preached to prospective converts. They relied on the hospitality of church members when possible and the uncertain charity of others when necessary. At one stop, Young read "a portion of the Saviour's teaching in the book of Mormon"—probably 3 Nephi, in which Jesus appears to the Nephites, commissions twelve apostles, and delivers a message similar to the Sermon on the Mount—and "spoke about 1½ hours contrasting the religions of the day with the truth." At the end of the month, Young and his brother-in-law John P. Greene traveled to the Seneca Indian reservation on the banks of the Allegheny River in southwestern New York. "[W]ee their saw meney of the Seed of Joseph," scratched Young in his diary, "among them ware two Chefts one a prsbeterin the other a Pagon." The pair preached "among the natives" at a Presbyterian church and gave them the *Book of Mormon*. Joseph Smith had proclaimed that the mission would "open a door to all the house of Joseph," but Young recorded no positive response to his brief efforts among the Seneca.[26]

While traveling, Brigham exchanged tender letters with Mary Ann, his first extant correspondence, offering a glimpse into his interior life that his early missionary diaries rarely provide. Their marriage, probably at first motivated by economic necessity, developed into a relationship characterized by mutual concern and love. The letters reveal a gentle and even romantic side of Brigham Young. "I recived," he responded, "with Joy and gladness this is the first time that I ever saw a letter of yours, but when I came to rede it it was so short that I did not half sattisfy my self a reading about you." Most of their correspondence addressed practical concerns, as Brigham's travels left Mary Ann in precarious poverty. They worried about their baby, Joseph, who was sick for an extended period that summer, and she worried about making clothing to last the three children through the winter. Brigham offered to get any items Mary Ann desired, and she requested an ounce of nutmeg and "any Silk that you would like for a winter Bonnet for me." "I need not tell you that your society would make home much more pleasant to me," Mary Ann reminded him. "I will come as quick as I can," he wrote, ". . . I remaine husban and frend."[27]

When he came home that August, Young found a very different environment in Kirtland. While the apostles were finishing their tour of the Northeast, a church council in Kirtland headed by Smith condemned them *in absentia* for "set[ting] yourselves up as an independent counsel subject to no authority of the church a kind of out law" and threatened them with divine "wrath and indignation." Apparently the apostles' failure to solicit funds for the Kirtland temple sparked the criticism. While Smith and the apostles quickly reconciled, in November the prophet received "the word of the Lord concerning the Twelve . . . they are under condemnation" for a multitude of sins, including insufficient humility and a failure to deal "equally with each other in the division of moneys which came into their hands." Presumably, the apostles had not equitably shared the offerings church members gave them to support their travels. Throughout the fall and early winter, the apostles repeatedly fell out of and returned to the prophet's favor.[28]

Even when on good terms with Smith, the apostles could not get along with each other. Thomas Marsh, age thirty-five, was the oldest of the Twelve and generally presided over the others on that basis. Young ranked third. "The Twelve were in the habit of meeting very often in those days," he later commented, ". . . and if no one of them needed 'cleaning,' they had to 'clean' some one any how." A man who had always cherished his independence and had not backed down from confrontations, Young nevertheless kept his emotions in check. Internally, Young seethed at this discord, for which he blamed Marsh, deeming him both useless and cantankerous. "He was," Young sneered during an 1849 meeting, "like a toad's hair comb[,] up [and] down." Marsh's subsequent excommunication from the church probably colored Young's commentary, but Young clearly resented the criticisms of Marsh, Smith, and Sidney Rigdon. "How much fault have I found with T[homas] B. Marsh, Joseph Smith or S[idney] Rigdon?" Young asked, emphasizing his forbearance. "I never opened my mouth when they lammed it on to me." As a group, the apostles felt insulted by Smith. "We are Apostles it's an insult for us to be treated so," Young remembered Marsh objecting. It seems that Smith's penchant for creating quorums and offices created uncertainty and conflict within the church, especially because he did not always make the lines of ecclesiastical authority clear. Young eventually interpreted Smith's treatment of the apostles the same way he viewed the failure of Zion's Camp. Smith "snobbed us," explained Young in 1847, "and when we proved ourselves willing to be everybody's servant for Christ's sake then we were worthy of power." Young's loyalty usually enabled him to chafe in silence.[29]

Fortunately, Kirtland provided many distractions from both dissension and poverty. In early October, Smith invited the apostles to his house and showed them a set of papyri that, along with four Egyptian mummies, he had recently purchased for $2400. It was a remarkable sum of money, but Smith—and his followers—remained fascinated with documents that he identified as ancient scriptures. The prophet also directed the apostles to attend Kirtland's school, which had in previous years included a series of theological lectures by Sidney Rigdon and remedial lessons in English grammar. Smith's interest in Hebrew reflected the strong Old Testament imprint that characterized his movement. Rather than ordain ministers and build churches, Smith ordained priests and built temples. He emphasized the learning of Hebrew, rather than biblical Greek or Latin. Despite his lack of proficiency in written English, Young gamely endured the school's 1835–36 Hebrew curriculum. He remained bashful about his script, unimproved by this intermittent instruction. "Plese read this," he wrote Mary Ann in 1837, "and keep it to yourself not expose my poore righting and speling."[30]

Such diversions—and reminders of the Mormons' connection to their ancient predecessors—were badly needed because the community's infighting intensified as 1835 approached its end. The prophet grew increasingly testy as other church members criticized his temper and lack of restraint. The dynamic became a vicious cycle, as Smith found fault with nearly everyone who crossed his path. Smith's family, his scribes, and his counselor Sidney Rigdon received withering rebukes from the prophet. When his wife Emma left a meeting early, Smith chastised her so severely that she wept. He even objected openly to his mother's testimony during one church trial. Young testified in support of the prophet at a series of disciplinary cases before the church council; he never supported Smith's detractors, many of whom were tried for manifesting a critical spirit toward Smith. The conflicts were not all Smith's fault—many of his brethren were also young, hot-headed, and sensitive—but he was a prime contributor to the dissension and, for a season, powerless to end it. In December, after weeks of squabbles, Joseph and his brother William came to blows after the prophet called him "ugly as the Devil." William whipped Joseph in the fight. Joseph finally reconciled with his estranged family members after William begged his forgiveness, but the physical attack illustrated the danger dissent posed to Joseph's authority.[31]

In January, the apostles, including Brigham Young, finally confronted Smith and his two counselors in the church's presidency (Rigdon and Frederick Williams) about their lingering grievances. The Twelve remained upset about Smith's letter of chastisement from the previous August. Marsh spoke first, followed by the other apostles, including Young. It was one of the very few times that Young spoke openly against the prophet. Perhaps surprised by the apostles' unity, Smith responded tenderly, asked their forgiveness, and promised not to believe any future complaints against them until having met with them in person. Clarifying the quorum's place in the ecclesiastical hierarchy, Smith also affirmed that the Twelve "are not subject to any other than the first Presidency." In response, the apostles declared themselves fully satisfied. "[T]heir was a perfect unison of feeling on this occasion," Smith's clerk recorded, "and our hearts over flowed with blessing." At the next day's Sunday worship, "the Lord poured out his spirit upon us, and the brethren began to confess their faults one to the other and the congregation were soon overwhelmed in tears and some of our hearts were too big for utterance, the gift of toungs, come upon us also like the rushing of a mighty wind." By mid-January, the church's storm clouds had temporarily parted.[32]

THE first half of 1836 witnessed the church's Kirtland apogee. Mormon spirituality, simmering with tongues, prophecies, and visions since the foundation of the church, now burned white hot. For several years, Joseph Smith had promised his elders that they would "be endowed with power from on High," a prerequisite for the successful fulfillment of their evangelistic missions. While he had shown them repeated glimpses of heaven— spiritual tongues, healings, and revelations—Smith always suggested there was more to come. With the temple nearly completed and harmony in Kirtland precariously restored, Joseph now led the Saints in a series of rituals designed to prepare them for what many had long anticipated.[33]

On January 16, after Smith had received the apostles' complaints, Smith, Oliver Cowdery, John Corrill, and Martin Harris met in the printing office—a loft in the temple—and "wash[ed] each other's bodies, and bathe[d] the same with whiskey, perfumed with cinnamon." A larger group of church leaders, not including the apostles, met five days later. According to Cowdery, Smith and his top counselors "were annointed with the same kind of oil and in the man[ner] that were Moses and Aaron." "The heavens were opened upon us," Smith dictated to his scribe, "and I beheld the celestial kingdom of God," including the "Father and the Son" seated on "the blasing throne of God." Smith also received a vision of the twelve apostles "in foreign lands," including Brigham Young "standing in a strange land, in the far southwest, in a desert place, upon a rock in the midst of about a dozen men of colour, who, appeared hostile." "He [Young] was preaching to them," Smith continued, "in their own toung, and the angel of God standing above his head with a drawn sword in his

Kirtland Temple, 1907 *(courtesy of Church History Library, The Church of Jesus Christ of Latter-day Saints)*

hand protec[t]ing him, but he did not see it." The next morning Young learned of the vision at Hebrew school. The Saints cancelled instruction to discuss "the glorious scenes that transpired on the preceding evening." That night, Smith anointed Thomas Marsh's head with consecrated oil; Marsh then anointed the remaining apostles. Smith blessed the Twelve, and, he recorded in his journal, "the heavens were opened and angels ministered unto us." "Near the close of the meeting," Cowdery wrote, "2 o'clock in the morning, almost all present broke out in tongues and songs of Zion." The heavens remained open in Kirtland for the next two months, with further anointings leading to more visions, tongues, and shouts of hosanna as the temple neared completion.[34]

On February 22, Smith asked Young to cease Hebrew instruction—probably no great disappointment—and oversee the "painting and finishing of the temple." On Sunday, 27 March, hundreds of Saints filled the temple, with many more being turned away when the building reached its capacity. Sidney Rigdon, the church's most forceful preacher, took Matthew 8:20 for his text and suggested that Christ finally had somewhere "to lay his head." The church then sustained Smith as "a Prophet and Seer" and also acknowledged Young and his fellow apostles as "Prophets and Seers and special witnesses to all the nations of the earth, holding the keys of the kingdom." Smith prayed for a great spiritual manifestation upon the Saints, "as upon those on the day of Pentacost." "The latter day glory begins to come forth," sang the choir after Smith finished. "The visions and blessings of old are returning; The angels are coming to visit the earth." The lyrics were more than rhetoric. Several leading members of the church, including Smith, arose and testified that they had seen "angels in the house." Young and his fellow apostle David Patten both sang a song in tongues and then spoke in tongues, with Patten interpreting Young's message as he spoke. That evening, Young and other church officers met with Smith for instruction in the "ordinance of washing," part of the solemn assembly soon to take place.[35]

Three days after the dedication, three hundred Saints gathered in the temple. Smith sent messengers for bread and wine, and tubs of water and towels were prepared for the foot-washing ordinance, the last step—after the earlier washing, perfuming, and anointing—in making the Saints "clean from the blood of this generation."[36] Smith and his counselors in the church presidency began by washing the feet of Young and his fellow apostles. "[T]he brethren," recorded the prophet's clerk, "began to prophesy upon each others heads, and cursings upon the enimies of Christ who inhabit Jackson county Missouri." After asking the Twelve to distribute the bread and wine, Smith retired for the night, leaving the apostles in charge of the meeting. The gathering continued until dawn, "exhorting, prophesying, and speaking in tongues." Some who subsequently left the church later attributed the spiritual excitement to drunkenness from the liberal amounts of wine consumed at the meeting. "Orson," wrote William McLellin, who abandoned the church in 1838, to his former fellow apostle Orson Pratt, "you cannot have forgotten the scenes of drunkenness during the pretended enduement [endowment] in Kirtland in 1836." John Corrill, a leading Missouri Saint present at the assembly, observed after he left the church that a similar report "went out concerning the disciples, at Jerusalem, on the day of Pentecost." Smith's own Kirtland temple experiences culminated several days later when, after a time of prayer, he and Oliver Cowdery "saw the Lord standing upon the breastwork of the pulpit before them." "I have accepted this house and my name shall be here," Jesus told the two men. For Smith and many of his followers, the days in the temple were, in the prophet's words, "a penticost and enduement indeed."[37]

Was it an endowment of power for Brigham Young? Did he see the Savior? Young was reticent when he reminisced about the temple dedication and assemblies, usually emphasizing the temple's arduous construction rather than his own experience of the supernatural. He once affirmed that the Kirtland temple ordinances were "accompanied by the ministration of angels, and the presence of the Lord Jesus."[38] Twenty years after the fact, Young told Wilford Woodruff that he witnessed "a circle of about 40" angels "dressed in white robes & caps" in the temple's upper story: "many personages did appear clothed in white & frequently went to the windows & looked out so that the Brethren in the street could see them plainly."[39] At the very least, Young claimed glimpses of heaven.

THE temple dedication and rituals temporarily liberated the church from the setbacks in Zion and the infighting of the previous fall and winter. It also freed the apostles to resume their missionary travels. In late May 1836, Young left Kirtland for New England, accompanied by his brother Joseph. Although he later commented that he never objected to the missions that took him away from his family, his letters reveal a longing and concern for home and family. "[W]hat shal I say to you to comfort your hart," he wrote Mary Ann from Vermont in early June. "Kiss that lettle son of ours [Joseph] and tell him to make hast and groe so he can goe with me." Young knew that Mary Ann and their children endured sometimes crushing poverty in Kirtland. In January, a church member named Jonathan Crosby had loaned Young a desperately needed twenty-five dollars. "Brother Young said he had nothing in his house to eat," wrote Crosby many years later. "He said he had been standing in the door of the printing office thinking of his condition and felt so bad that the sweat rolled off of him." Young was no richer than when he had arrived in Ohio two years earlier, but he laid plans to improve his family's situation. "I shal be able to return and pay for my house," he wrote her in July, "and I want to repare it this fall so that I can feele contented about my famely when I leve them." Brigham and Mary Ann sacrificed their comfort for their faith.[40]

In Massachusetts, Young visited and witnessed to Mary Ann's relatives and his own, winning their sympathy and interest with his stubbornly biblical defense of Mormonism. Buffeted by stinging rejections from hostile audiences but elated at the baptism of several relatives, Young returned home in September, relieved to again provide for Mary Ann and his children. The couple's family expanded further in December with the birth of namesake twins, Brigham Jr. and Mary Ann.

As a gathering place for the Saints, Kirtland at this time was also renewing and transforming Young's relationships with his extended family. Caroline Crosby, whose husband had loaned Brigham Young money during the impoverished winter of 1835–36, chronicled a Young family meeting at the home of Rhoda Greene, Brigham's sister and the eldest sibling in the family. The purpose was for "Father Young to bless his family":

> The house was crow[d]ed full, we had nice wheat bread and sweet wine all we wanted to drink, it was also called a feast, and so it was a feast of fat things. The brethren and sisters blest one another, but father [John] Young I believe concluded to defer blessing his family untill he could have them by themselves. He seemed rather diffident in regard to speaking, or his mind so much affected by the subject, that he could not express his feelings. Brigham therefore arose and spoke in his behalf. The old gentleman wept freely, as well as many of his family, so that we had weeping, and rejoicing, nearly at the same time.[41]

The occasion at the Greene household reflected the growing importance of extended family connections and patriarchal leadership within the church. The church emphasized gathering, of the Saints to Jackson County and Kirtland, but also of families within the church. In 1834, Joseph Smith ordained John Young as patriarch of his family, authorizing him to give his family blessings with the authority of revelation. Smith subsequently ordained his own father as patriarch for the entire church. Modeled after the biblical Jacob's blessings to his twelve sons, patriarchal blessings held great significance for early Mormons, who treasured them as sacred words of instruction and promise. The blessings identified the recipient's Israelite tribal lineage and promised a variety of benefits, such as prolonged life or the power of healing. They provided a means to bind together generations of believers, bind individual Saints to their spiritual leaders, and connect the church to the sacred events of ancient times.[42]

Brigham devoted time on most of his missionary journeys to proselytizing relatives in New England and visiting with Mary Ann's extended family, and by now siblings, cousins, and in-laws had gathered to Kirtland. Even the parents of Brigham's first wife Miriam, as well as some of her siblings, gathered with the Saints. Not everyone converted and not all the converted remained within the church, but Kirtland restored some of the fractures within the Young family. When John Young remarried in 1815 after the death of Brigham's mother, Brigham and his siblings scattered across western New York. The family partly reunited in Mendon, but then gathered to Kirtland on a much larger scale. Brigham, moreover, now supplanted both his father and elder brothers as the spiritual and practical leader of his family. John Young may have been ordained a patriarch, but it was Brigham who "arose and spoke in his behalf."[43]

By the winter of 1836–1837, the spiritual unity and ecstasy of the temple dedication became a distant memory for Kirtland's Mormon community. Dissension returned, now centered on the misguided creation of a bank. Because of rapidly rising land values and limited specie, Mormon Kirtland—like many western communities—was land rich and cash poor, and a bank resting primarily on land holdings could have alleviated the community's need for liquidity. According to Joseph Young, Smith observed the financial distress of his elders—frequently away from their families on missions—and "conceived a plan of instituting a Bank, with a view of relieving their financial embarrassments." The circulation of notes would facilitate the ability of Smith and others to satisfy their creditors.[44]

In the fall of 1836, Smith sent Oliver Cowdery to Philadelphia to purchase plates for printing banknotes and Orson Hyde to Columbus to secure the bank's charter. The "Kirtland Safety Society" adopted articles of agreement and began selling shares to members of the church; Brigham Young invested seven dollars for two thousand shares. As Hyde took a futile application for a bank charter to a legislature controlled by hard-money Democrats, church leaders began issuing notes without a charter. Although in contravention of an obscure 1816 Ohio law against unchartered societies engaging in banking, the actions were not all that unusual, as other unchartered banks and railroad corporations engaged in similar behavior. Instead of issuing notes of the "The Kirtland Safety Society Bank," bank officers stamped out the word "Bank" or altered them to read "anti-Bank-ing Co." Even if not unprecedented, the clumsy alterations seemed to invite the misfortune that followed.

In the mid-1830s, the American banking system produced a high degree of local chaos, reflected in a mixture of shaky chartered banks, unchartered banks, fraudulent banks, and counterfeiting operations. Many such institutions issued banknotes backed by very little hard money or property. A few Ohio banking frauds printed notes with no intention of redeeming them for specie. The entire system rested upon the confidence of banks and individuals in the myriad forms of paper money. Notes from disreputable institutions might be rejected entirely, while other notes regarded with some suspicion might be accepted at a discount.[45]

For a short while, the establishment of the Kirtland Safety Society notes generated a burst of economic activity and confidence in the town. Buoyed by a steady influx of converts, the town now participated in a national

Kirtland Safety Society "anti-Bank-ing Co." note, 1837, signed by Sidney Rigdon and Joseph Smith Jr., countersigned and reissued in 1849 by Brigham Young, Heber C. Kimball, and Newel K. Whitney *(courtesy of Church History Library, The Church of Jesus Christ of Latter-day Saints)*

boom fueled by a growing population and rising land prices. Men long accustomed to dashed hopes and destitution, like Brigham Young and Joseph Smith, could envision the achievement of their elusive economic goals. Willard Richards, a cousin whom Young had baptized in the fall of 1835, commented favorably on Kirtland's "small, framed houses . . . Some going up almost every day." "Carpenters and joiners," Richards wrote, "command any price." Young plied his trade profitably that winter, overseeing the painting of the Safety Society building, Sidney Rigdon's home, and several other buildings. Young was one of many newly wealthy men, his cousin explained, noting that some "who were not worth a dollar one year ago are now worth their thousands and tens of thousands." Richards attributed the economic effervescence to the bank. "Kirtland bills are as safe as gold," he wrote in January. The Safety Society helped Young prosper for a season. In March 1837, he signed a contract to build a new home, and he also purchased a piece of property—three-eighths of an acre—from Jacob Bump for $500.[46]

Regional newspapers, though, immediately questioned the safety of "Morman Money." "As far as we can learn," editorialized the *Cleveland Gazette,* "there is no property bound for their redemption, no coin in hand to redeem them with, and no responsible individuals whose honor or whose honesty is pledged for their payment." "They seem to rest upon a spiritual basis," the paper concluded. Once circulated, outsiders promptly sought to redeem the notes for specie and quickly drained the bank of its limited reserves. When one non-Mormon organized a run on the bank, rumors quickly circulated that the bank had stopped redemptions, which caused the value of the notes to drop precipitously. Smith tried desperate measures to save the bank, seeking loans and futilely pleading with the Saints to bolster the bank by acquiring additional stock with specie. In February, the Ohio legislature rejected the bank's application for a charter.[47]

The bank's travails widened divides in Kirtland over Joseph Smith's leadership, particularly his accretion of temporal power. Smith had never confined himself to purely spiritual affairs—several of his revelations, for instance, discussed his merchandizing operation, and he had encouraged his Kirtland followers since the early 1830s to consecrate their property to the church. His vision of Zion sought to establish not just a church, but the Kingdom of God on earth. For the moment, that vision crumbled. Almost immediately after the bank issued its notes, grumbling began. "[W]e had a spiritual meeting," wrote Wilford Woodruff in his journal. "Elder Brigham Young one of the twelve gave us an interesting exhortation & warned us not to murmer against Moses (or) Joseph or the heads of the Church." Not surprisingly, the bank's struggles cost Smith the confidence of many followers. "They believed he [Smith] understood spiritual things . . . but they did not believe he knew how to manage temporal affairs," commented Young in a later sermon. The debate, Young recalled in another sermon, "became so public that it was in the mouth of almost every one." Young himself briefly doubted the prophet's leadership. "It was not concerning religious matters," explained Young, "it was not about his revelations—but it was in relation to his financiering." Quickly repenting of this doubt, Young realized that "if I was to harbor a thought in my heart that Joseph could be wrong in anything, I would begin to lose confidence in him . . . until at last I would have the same lack of confidence in his being the mouthpiece of the Almighty." Joseph Smith's prophetic calling—like American banks—ultimately rested upon the confidence of the people, a confidence that many of his followers now lost.[48]

In addition to denouncing criticism of the prophet, Young did all in his power to help Smith save the bank. According to Joseph Young, who in an 1880 letter praised Smith's motives as "unquestionably pure," the prophet "proposed to Br[other] Brigham and Br[other] Hyrum [Smith], that they should commence buying farms." They began to make purchases using notes from the bank of "property round about Kirtland and the adjoining towns." In mid-March, Brigham and his cousin Willard Richards departed for the Northeast on business for Joseph Smith, to raise funds desperately needed to keep the bank afloat, meet with creditors, and make purchases with Kirtland scrip. For instance, Young purchased—probably again with Kirtland money—"a fine tavern establishment" in Troy, New York. Such purchases would disperse the banknotes into the hands of distant individuals unlikely to quickly redeem them, and real estate purchases could provide the bank with additional collateral. Of course, given the bank's troubled state, it was quite likely that anyone who accepted the notes would soon find them worthless. Since he later displayed a shrewd grasp of business arrangements, Young could not have been oblivious to the financial risk anyone accepting Kirtland scrip assumed. He and Smith, however, knew that without such desperate measures the bank was doomed.[49]

While away, Young missed another momentary spiritual peak in Kirtland when the church celebrated its seventh anniversary and performed washings and anointings for those who had not participated at the previous year's temple dedication. Once more, the Saints prophesied, spoke in tongues, and saw angels. The specter of the bank, however, quickly doused this renewed pentecostal fire. Several days later, Smith sharply criticized members of his flock who had "turned tritors & opposed the Currency . . . which has given power into the hands of the enemy." The murmurings of the winter and spring grew into open rebellion in late May, about the time that Young returned to Kirtland. "[M]any & some in high places had risen up against Joseph," wrote Woodruff. Smith attempted to quell dissent from the pulpit, but Warren Parrish, one of the prophet's clerks and an officer in the bank, publicly denounced him. The next day, the church's high council heard charges against Parrish and four other dissenters, including two apostles and one of Smith's counselors in the church's presidency. Because of the high status of the accused and uncertainty about how to proceed, the council "dispersed in confusion." In Kirtland, the bank notes soon gained acceptance only at a severe discount. The Safety Society staggered through the summer of 1837, continuing to issue notes until June, and then dissolved in November.[50]

The Kirtland bank was not alone in its failure to stay afloat. The political war between Andrew Jackson and Nicholas Biddle's Second Bank of the United States preceded a nationwide run on specie that became known as the Panic of 1837. In the spring and summer of that year, scores of banks—including some of the nation's largest in New York City—collapsed. "It was indeed said across the water," wrote a U.S. circuit judge of the panic's international ramifications, "that the 'Yankee nation, from General Jackson to a shoe black, was a fraudulent bankrupt.'" The struggles of the Kirtland bank prefigured the panic, but the panic's effects deepened the anxiety among the Saints, as land values dropped and creditors pressed church leaders to repay loans. Smith faced prosecution for violating the law, and creditors swarmed Kirtland, suing Smith, Rigdon, and other church leaders, including Brigham Young.[51]

Smith never effectively restored financial or ecclesiastical peace in Kirtland. Several members of the Quorum of the Twelve Apostles publicly censured Smith, and others privately doubted his prophetic calling. As Smith left for a trip to Canada, the situation in Kirtland deteriorated further. An open battle between Smith loyalists and dissenters took place in the temple, complete with pistols and bowie-knives. Young missed the altercation; he was in New York on church business and returned to Kirtland only on August 19. Smith arrived home eight days later and finally resolved to take action against the dissidents. At a September 3 meeting, Smith, publicly supported by Young, led a council in disciplining a number of his ecclesiastical enemies, but by then it was too late—nothing could still the opposition. Young later recalled a church meeting at which leading members discussed deposing Smith and installing David Whitmer (one of the *Book of Mormon* witnesses) in his place. When Young vociferously defended the prophet, "Jacob Bump (an old pugilist) was so exasperated that he could not be still." "How can I keep my hands off that man?" Bump said of Young. "I told him if he thought it would give him any relief he might lay them on," Young retorted. According to Wilford Woodruff, Bump had been "the first to Circulate" the bank's notes in January. Young had purchased $500 in property from Bump in March, presumably with soon-to-be-worthless Kirtland notes. For many Mormons like Bump, keen financial distress and a sense of betrayal fueled animosity against the church and its leaders.[52]

In October, Smith and Rigdon were convicted of issuing banknotes without a charter and fined $1,000 each. When they temporarily left Kirtland for Missouri, it gave the Kirtland dissidents a chance to act. Parrish and others who rejected Smith's leadership organized themselves as "the old standard" and pledged to return the church to its original principles. Calling themselves the Church of Christ, the church's original name, they wrested control of the temple and pledged to hold it, "if it is by the shedding of blood." Excommunications held no sway. "Far from flourishing as their prophet had foretold," concludes Smith's biographer Richard Bushman, "the Saints were caught in a downward spiral of personal losses and narrowing opportunities." Smith now prophesied that "peace shall soon be taken from the earth . . . very fierce and very terrible war is near at hand." Hepzibah Richards, a sister of Young's cousin Willard Richards, wryly commented, "It hardly requires a prophet's eye to see that perilous times are at hand."[53]

On December 22, Brigham Young permanently fled Kirtland, taking temporary shelter in eastern Indiana with his brother Lorenzo and leaving Mary Ann and his children behind. He attributed his flight to "the fury of the mob, and the spirit that prevailed in the apostates, who had threatened to destroy me because I would proclaim, publicly and privately, that I knew by the power of the Holy Ghost, that Joseph Smith was a Prophet." Creditors had also added to Young's worries. Mary Ann wrote on January 12, 1838 to tell her husband that one claimant demanded $2500 "of Kirtland monney" and that another creditor "intends to get judgment against you and go on and sell this propperty." "[M]y hart has been much pained to realize the danger your life has been in this place," she wrote. The same day Mary Ann Young penned her letter, Joseph Smith and Sidney Rigdon departed Kirtland, fleeing their ecclesiastical enemies and creditors. Soon after their flight, the printing office burned down in flames and scorched the temple, already in the control of Warren Parrish's "old standard" church.[54]

THE events in Kirtland further convinced many Americans, including some Mormons, that Joseph Smith was simply another fraud in a long line of prophetic con artists. Smith's bank had been an unmitigated disaster, predictions of Kirtland's future grandeur went unfulfilled, and he failed to take decisive action against his ecclesiastical opponents. Smith and those loyal to him lost Kirtland and its temple, roughly one-third of the church's high-ranking officers, and a sizeable portion of the church's entire membership. Brigham Young's confidence in Smith, though, did not depend on the vicissitudes of the church's fortunes or whether or not Smith made accurate predictions of future events. He had accepted Smith as God's prophet in 1832, and the recent missteps did not change that reality. "He was called of God," Young later insisted, "God dictated him, and if He had a mind to leave him to himself and let him commit an error, that was no business of mine." Moreover, through Smith's leadership Young spoke in heavenly tongues, sang songs of Zion, and saw angels.[55]

Young's stubborn loyalty to his prophet earned him Smith's confidence and brought him closer to the prophet's inner fold. Despite his fealty, Young was hardly blind to Smith's weaknesses and mistakes. "Much of Joseph's policy in temporal things," he preached in 1860, "was different from my ideas of the way to manage them." Young concluded that Smith practiced far too much forbearance toward his wayward Saints. When Young assumed leadership of the church in the mid-1840s, he did not repeat that perceived error. Leadership could depend on confidence, but confidence often proved ephemeral. Young concluded that stronger leadership required a firmer foundation.[56]

CHAPTER THREE

Acts of the Apostles

[W]hen a country, or body of people have individuals among them
with whom they do not wish to associate . . . it is the principle of
republicanism itself that gives that community a right to expel
them forcibly and no law will prevent it.

— SIDNEY RIGDON, 1839

LEAVING his wife and children behind in Kirtland, Brigham Young
headed for Missouri. After stopping at his brother Lorenzo's temporary residence in Dublin, Indiana, and rendezvousing with Joseph Smith
and Sidney Rigdon, Young arrived with the prophet in the city of Far West
in mid-March 1838. In 1836, Clay County citizens had met and insisted
that the expelled Jackson County Mormons leave Clay County, Missouri,
where they had taken refuge. Residents of neighboring Ray County did
not want Mormon refugees within their borders either, but state legislation
had carved two counties—Caldwell and Daviess—out of northern Ray
County. Caldwell County would be a new home for the Missouri Mormons, who quickly bought out the few non-Mormon settlers, laid out a
city (Far West), designated a site for a temple, and held elections for the
county's political offices.

When Smith and Young approached Far West, wrote Smith, "an escort
of the brethren . . . came to make us welcome to their little Zion." Young
purchased land on Mill Creek, a short distance northeast of Far West. Suffering from "whooping-cough" and "diseased lungs," Mary Ann shepherded Brigham's five children from Kirtland to Missouri that spring.
Smith instructed Young by revelation "not to leave his family untill they
are amply provided for." Brigham may have expected Mary Ann to repeat
Miriam's path to an early grave, but she regained her health. In keeping
with Smith's promise, Young spent more time attending to his own affairs

over the next several months. The problem of dissent that Smith and Young faced in Ohio, however, followed them west and grew in tandem with renewed conflict with non-Mormon Missourians.[1]

JOSEPH Smith and his supporters determined to take a firmer stand against disloyalty after the collapse of the prophet's authority in Kirtland. Most notably, in April the church's high council excommunicated Oliver Cowdery, Smith's *Book of Mormon* scribe, one of the three witnesses to the golden plates, and assistant counselor in the church presidency, for—among other charges—"insinuating" that Smith had committed adultery with a female servant in Kirtland and for "selling his lands in Jackson County." During Cowdery's church trial, several witnesses affirmed that Smith had never confessed to adultery, and the prophet evidently explained "the girl business" to the council's satisfaction. During the winter and spring of 1838, the church also excommunicated a rash of top leaders in Missouri: David and John Whitmer, also witnesses to the golden plates; W. W. Phelps, a talented editor and hymnist; and two of Young's fellow apostles, William McLellin and Lyman Johnson. The latter had beaten Young's brother Phineas, leaving him with "blood running out of his ears" and an injured stomach. Looking to install leaders loyal to Smith, the church's annual April conference appointed apostles Thomas Marsh, David Patten, and Brigham Young as the "Presidents Pro Tem" of the Missouri church.[2]

The excommunications created a group of prominent and bitter ex-members in Caldwell County. "The dissenters," wrote John Corrill after he himself had left the church, "kept up a kind of secret opposition to the church." The church's leadership soon decided the apostates needed to go. In mid-June, Sidney Rigdon, Smith's fiery counselor, preached what became known as the "Salt Sermon": "If the salt have lost its savour, it is thenceforth good for nothing but to be cast out and trodden under the feet of men." "[I]t was plainly understood," wrote Corrill, "that he meant the dissenters or those who had denied the faith." Leaving no doubt, eighty-three Mormons, including, most prominently, Hyrum Smith (Joseph's brother), signed a letter explicitly warning Cowdery, Phelps, Lyman Johnson, and the Whitmers to "depart with your families peaceably" within three days "or a more fatal calamity will befall you." Many of the dissenters prudently complied. As part of the action against the apostates, a militant faction of the church organized a secret, oath-bound, vigilante society dedicated to quashing further dissent and disloyalty. Known variously as the "Big Fan," "Brother of Gideon," "Daughters of Zion," and the "Danites" (the latter name gaining permanent currency), this movement, led by Sampson Avard, a physician and former Campbellite minister, threatened

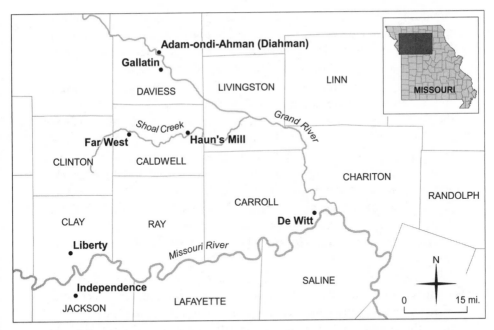

Missouri, 1838

dissenters with violence. "[W]e have a company of Danites in these times," wrote Smith's clerk George Robinson, "to put to rights physically that which is not righ[t], and to clense the Church of verry great evils which hath hitherto existed among us." These attempts to impress conformity and submission backfired, and, alongside renewed efforts to persuade church members to consecrate their property to the church, caused previously loyal members to question the political and economic pretensions of the church's presidency.[3]

While Smith and his loyal followers struggled to contain the problem of dissent, the anti-Mormon threat to the church emerged with renewed strength as the Mormon population in northwestern Missouri grew. Non-Mormon Missourians expected the Saints to limit themselves to newly created Caldwell County, but a few Mormons had settled beyond its borders. Such activity increased when church leaders from Kirtland arrived in 1838. In late May, the prophet and other Mormon leaders had explored a portion of neighboring Daviess County, recognized "an old Nephitish Alter," and then identified nearby Spring Hill as "the place where Adam shall come to visit his people, or the Ancient of days shall sit as spoken of by Daniel the Prophet." By revelation, Smith renamed the area "Adam-ondi-Ahman," and the Mormons considered it to be the land where Adam lived after his expulsion from Eden and blessed his posterity before his death.

Amid the church's ecclesiastical strife, Smith reoriented his followers toward the continent's earlier inhabitants and the origins of the human family. Like Adam and Eve, the Mormons were exiles, from Jackson County and from Kirtland. Church leaders ordered the settlement of all land between Adam-ondi-Ahman (often shortened to Diahman) and Far West. In June, Mormons also began settling in De Witt, a town at the confluence of the Grand and Missouri rivers in eastern Carroll County. Smith envisioned a series of gathered communities, in which the Saints consecrated their land and property to the church, leading to the creation of cooperative manufacturing firms that would provide employment for the Mormons and economic autonomy from their potential enemies. Non-Mormons, whom church members called the "old settlers," "Gentiles," or simply "Missourians," resolved to expel the Mormons in Daviess and Carroll counties before the Saints overwhelmed them politically and economically.[4]

The Mormon settlers and their leaders in turn were determined to avoid a reprise of their expulsions from Jackson and Clay counties. As evidence of an increasingly militant spirit, the Danite militia paraded in Far West on July 4th. The Mormons gathered to lay the cornerstones of the new temple and to declare their independence from their enemies. Sidney Rigdon preached an incendiary oration. After averring that "[o]ur country and its institutions, are written on the tablet of our hearts," he complained about the failure of governments to protect the church from mobs and warned that the Saints would meekly submit to persecution no longer. "And that mob that comes on us to disturb us it shall be between us and them a war of extermination, for we will follow them, till the last drop of their blood is spilled." Young later complained that Rigdon's "oration on the 4th of July . . . was the cause of our troubles in Missouri" and that "Joseph tried to restrain him." At the time, however, Smith endorsed Rigdon's speech and insisted that the Saints would not "be mob[b]ed any more without taking vengeance." The Mormons had professed their readiness to fight.[5]

On election day, August 6, Mormons and Missourians brawled in Gallatin, the Daviess County seat. Rumors swirled, and vigilantism accelerated. Anti-Mormon mobs formed in Carroll and Daviess County, and the state militiamen who mustered, ostensibly to preserve peace, made plain their animosity toward the Mormons. Samuel Lucas, one militia general, suggested that any outbreak of violence "will create excitement in the whole upper Missouri, and those base and degraded beings will be exterminated from the face of the earth." After a mob forced the Mormons to abandon their small community at De Witt, the church leadership made a stand at Diahman. Albert Rockwood, Brigham Young's cousin and a recent convert, wrote in his journal on October 15 that "Oaur lives Honours & Fortunes are pledged to defend the constitution of the U.S.A. and our individual rights and our Holy Religion." As mobs forced outlying Mormon settlers from their homes, Mormon operations moved beyond the defensive. Mormon militias attacked suspected mobbers and confiscated their property. Meanwhile, more church members both despaired of overcoming the growing anti-Mormon forces and grew disenchanted with their own leaders' militant rhetoric. In mid-October, Thomas Marsh and Orson Hyde fled Far West under the cover of darkness. A few days later, Marsh swore an affidavit accusing Smith of threatening that "if he was not let alone, he would be a second Mahomet to this generation, and that he would make it one gore of blood from the Rocky Mountains to the Atlantic ocean." Despite the continued defections, the Saints for a time landed blows against their enemies. Mormon bands attacked Gallatin and other towns and burned roughly fifty buildings, leading John Smith, the prophet's uncle, to exult that "we have driven most of the enemy out of the Co[unty]."[6]

Brigham Young played an exceedingly minor role in these developments, so pivotal in shaping early Mormon identity as a persecuted people. During the early summer, he mostly tended to his own affairs at Mill Creek, rebuilding his finances and Mary Ann's health, though he attended several Far West council meetings and the fiery Independence Day celebration. With numerous fellow apostles recently having become apostates, Young probably wondered about the future of his Quorum of the Twelve. Smith answered such concerns with a July revelation, which a scribe copied into Young's personal journal. It appointed replacements to the quorum, including Young's cousin Willard Richards and future church presidents John Taylor and Wilford Woodruff, and it reaffirmed that the Twelve would undertake a promised mission to Europe. "Let them," it specified, "take leave of my saints in the city Far West on the 26th day of April next on the building spot of my house."[7]

Soon, however, the brewing war interrupted such planning. Along with other Mormons in outlying settlements, Young moved with his family to Far West. Young later claimed that because of his relative anonymity, he could observe the Missourians "unsuspected" and unmolested. "I knew men in the course of the fall," he asserted, "to gather up their flocks and herds, and take their families into their wagons, and then burn up their houses and leave for other parts . . . [and then claim] that Mormons had driven them from their homes and burned their houses."[8] Although other Mormons made similar charges, the allegation strains credibility, as Missouri settlers anticipating mob and militia action against the Mormons would not likely have sacrificed their own property in an attempt to frame the Saints. In late October, David Patten received a mortal wound during the Battle of Crooked River, in which a body of Mormons led by Patten attacked a Missouri militia unit. Between Patten's death and Marsh's defection, Young suddenly became the most senior member of the Quorum of the Twelve Apostles.

Up until the Mormon depredations in Daviess County and the Crooked River attack, Governor Lilburn Boggs had avoided intervention, and several of the state militia generals had sought to mediate a peace. Now, affidavits about Mormon outrages, including statements from recent defectors like Marsh, prompted Boggs—who undertook no independent investigation of the charges—to choose sides. "The Mormons," he declared to the state militia's General John B. Clark, "must be treated as enemies, and must be exterminated or driven from the State if necessary for the public peace." Probably unaware of the governor's order, on October 30 a mob attacked a small Mormon settlement at Haun's Mill, in eastern Caldwell County. Brigham's brother Joseph Young, recently arrived from Kirtland with his wife and children, witnessed the ensuing massacre, in which at least seventeen Mormons were killed. Joseph Young later recounted the story of Sardius Smith, a boy—perhaps ten years old—who hid during the attack but was discovered by an anti-Mormon vigilante after it ended. Sardius Smith's captor "presented his rifle near the boy's head, and literally blowed off the upper part of it." The vigilantes also shot a nine-year-old boy after the fighting had ended. "Nits will make lice," the murderer of Sardius Smith stated, justifying his brutality, "and if he had lived he would have become a Mormon."[9]

Meanwhile, hundreds of state militia troops converged on Far West, apparently prepared to repeat Haun's Mill on a larger scale with state sanction. Smith vacillated between defiance and surrender. Many of his followers expected to fight. "[T]he prophet goes out to the battle as in the days of old," wrote Albert Rockwood on October 28. The Mormons hastily reinforced their defenses. According to Heber Kimball, he and Young were "appointed captains of fifty in a hurry and commanded to take position right in the thoroughfare on which the mob were seen advancing to the city." Smith's defiance evaporated in the face of certain defeat, as militia troops continued to gather outside the city. On October 31, he sent several peace emissaries—curiously, they were mostly men disenchanted with his leadership—to meet with General Samuel Lucas. According to John Corrill, one of the negotiators, Smith "told me to beg like a dog for peace . . . [he] had rather die himself than have the people exterminated." Lucas demanded that the Mormons give up Smith and other top leaders for trial, deed the property of "all who had taken up arms" as restitution for depredations against Missouri settlers, and leave the state forthwith. George Hinkle, lead Mormon negotiator and a colonel in the Caldwell County militia, expedited the surrender of the prophet, Sidney Rigdon, Lyman Wight, Parley Pratt, and George Robinson. Smith believed he was going to negotiate with Lucas; instead, betrayed by either his negotiators or a misunderstanding, he found himself under arrest. "[We] expected," testified Young several years later, "that they would have returned to the city that evening or the next morning . . . but they did not return at all." At first sentenced to execution, Smith—along with his brother Hyrum, Rigdon, and Parley Pratt—was hauled off to a jail in Independence, then transferred to Liberty Jail in Clay County to stand trial on charges of treason.[10]

The Mormons at Far West and Diahman quickly surrendered, bitter at what they understood to be treachery on the part of Lucas and the negotiators. According to Young, when Lucas disarmed the Mormon militia, his soldiers "commenced their ravages by plundering the citizens of their bedding, clothing, money, wearing apparel, and everything of value they could lay their hands upon, and also attempting to violate the chastity of the women in sight of their husbands and friends." General Clark, Lucas's superior, soon arrived in Far West and ordered the Mormon men to assemble. He then read the names of fifty-six additional persons subject to arrest and ordered the rest to leave the state before planting the next year's crops. Rigdon had insisted that republicanism gave a community, even without the sanction of the law, the right to "expel" "individuals among them with whom they do not wish to associate." Though not uncontested, Rigdon's opinion was hardly unusual for its time. In the most lethal example, the 1838 forced march of the Cherokees on their trail of tears to the West killed thousands. Now Missouri insisted that thousands of Latter-day Saints abandon most of their property and leave the state or face extermination. While less deadly, the Mormon expulsion from Missouri was another chilling reminder of the fragility of minority rights in Jacksonian America. The church's principle of gathering—along with its accompanying concentration of political and economic power—inevitably created friction with more powerful and numerous non-Mormons. "I would advise you to scatter abroad," Young remembered General Clark's words, "and . . . become as other citizens." "I [will] see you in hell before I quit my religion," thought Young in response. He escaped arrest by disguising himself in "an old soldier coat and old hat." Regardless of their militant rhetoric and their own vigilante responses, the Mormons met with unmerited cruelty: Boggs's extermination order, the murders at Haun's Mill, the loss of their property, and their forced expulsion from Missouri. Outside of the state of Missouri, Americans tended to be sympathetic with the Mormons' plight, for they were, as one Eastern newspaper concluded, *"more sinned against than sinning."*[11]

With the church's presidency in jail, it fell to remaining leaders, including apostles Young and Heber Kimball, to organize the welfare and removal of the beleaguered Mormons still in and around Far West. Joseph Smith, Hyrum Smith, and Sidney Rigdon guided church policy from Liberty Jail, but in a January 16 letter to Young and Kimball the prisoners explained that "if need be the management of the affairs of the church devolves on you that is the twelve." In a postscript, they commanded the two apostles to "appoint the oldest of those of the twelve who were firs [sic] appointed, to be the President of your Quorum."[12] Fierce loyalty and spiritual fervor had brought Young into Smith's cadre of trusted assistants, but sheer luck—Young was thirteen days older than Kimball—made him leader of his quorum.

Although the Missouri legislature agreed to appoint a committee to study the Mormon grievances, it would not challenge Boggs's extermination order or Clark's directive. With much of their wealth tied up in Missouri property and many of their crops and belongings destroyed by the mobs, the church's leaders faced the daunting task of executing an orderly and safe withdrawal as the mobs continued their depredations. According to Young, after the legislature approved $2,000 in relief funds for the Saints, several crooked anti-Mormon Missourians drove the Saints' hogs into the streets, shot them, and then forced the Mormons to use the relief money to pay for the butchered carcasses. Marauders, meanwhile, periodically rode through the county and threatened to shoot any Mormon man they saw "in houses and woods." Young claimed to have observed the mobs from his house while concealed with his "wife's mantle and bonnet." "Nobody knew but I was a woman," he later joked. At the time, the situation allowed for little such humor, as many church members lacked the resources to feed themselves or transport their belongings and sick relatives out of the state.[13]

Young and other church leaders drew up a covenant to which hundreds of church members pledged to "never desert the poor, who are worthy till they shall be out of the reach of the exterminating order." With great reluctance, the church sold or bartered properties in Jackson County and Far West, often for a pittance. Over the course of the winter, the Mormons trudged out of Missouri, heading for the Illinois border, as that state's governor had offered them refuge. Sleeping exposed to the elements and subsisting on meager rations, the vast majority remained faithful to the church and interpreted their sufferings as further evidence of the judg-ments that would precede the millennium. The Missouri persecutions, wrote Eliza R. Snow, a Mormon schoolteacher and poetess, "might well allay doubts . . . that these are indeed the *last* days." Young's growing prominence in the church having attracted the notice of the mobs, he de-parted Far West with his family in mid-February, as he later wrote, "leav-ing my landed property and nearly all my household goods." For the sec-ond time in a little more than two years, enemies had forced the Youngs to abandon their home.[14]

Along with most of the other religious refugees, the Youngs camped on the open prairie, heading east until their overburdened team stalled near Huntsville, Missouri. After they crossed the Mississippi and reached Atlas, Illinois, Young left Mary Ann and the children in a storehouse and back-tracked to retrieve some of the possessions they had abandoned on the trail. "[D]uring the short interval of three months," Mary Ann later re-called, "I kept house in eleven different places." After crossing into Illinois, the Youngs stopped for several weeks in Atlas and then proceeded north to Quincy, where many of the Saints had taken refuge under the leadership of Sidney Rigdon, who had escaped from jail in early February.[15]

With Rigdon concentrating on seeking political redress and then moving out of Quincy, Young took charge and organized further relief efforts. He also weighed in on perhaps the key question facing the church as it reorga-nized itself. From jail, Smith had conceded in his January letter to Young and Kimball that "the gathering of necessity [is] stopt." In a March revela-tion, Smith recommended tracts of land offered by Isaac Galland, a specu-lator, in Montrose, Iowa, and Commerce, Illinois, on the banks of the Mississippi. However, he refused to identify a single place of gathering and instead counseled the Saints to "fall into the places of refuge of safty that God shall open unto them betwean Kirtland and Far West." Furthermore, Smith backed away from economic communitarianism, suggesting "that there be no organizations of large bodies upon common stock principals in property or of large companies of firms" for the immediate future. Before receiving this letter, however, Young had recommended that the church settle "in companies . . . that they might be nourished and fed by the shep-herds; for without, the sheep would be scattered." In the end, Smith changed his mind and reaffirmed the principle of gathering. The church purchased the tracts from Galland, whose deeds to the Iowa land proved fraudulent. The Commerce claims were bona fide and provided a swampy gathering place for the church on the Illinois bank of the river. The Saints knew their principle of gathering led to almost inevitable conflict with non-Mormon neighbors alarmed at their potential for economic and political power. Alongside the principle of ongoing revelation, however, gathering was the foremost distinguishing characteristic of the Latter-day Saints in the 1830s, and the church refused to abandon it.[16]

Before moving north to Commerce, Brigham Young and his fellow apostles made a final trip to Missouri to fulfill Joseph Smith's July 1838 revelation, which had instructed them to leave for their foreign mission from Far West on April 26. After a week of sleeping on the prairie, they snuck into Far West at dawn and held a conference. The apostles excommunicated a number of apostates, took turns praying, and sang "Adam-ondi-Ahman," surely thinking of a millennial Zion lost for the present.[17] They returned to Quincy and reunited with Joseph and Hyrum Smith, who had escaped during their transfer to a different jail. For Young and the other apostles, the next several months were a time of preparation and instruction as they prepared to embark on their missions to England. After reaching Commerce, Young crossed the Mississippi with his family and settled temporarily in the old military barracks in Montrose, Iowa, purchased by the church.

Beset by dissension, persecution, and imprisonment, the Mormon prophet had enjoyed little time to instruct his flock in matters of doctrine over the previous several years. "I have never have had opportunity to give them," he wrote while in Liberty Jail, "the plan that God has revealed to me." Now free again, he counseled the apostles before their voyage, teaching them a set of "keys," mysteries about the order of heaven. Smith steadily moved his church further away from Protestant, Trinitarian Christianity, and he also increasingly emphasized the order of priesthood hierarchies while distancing the church from the often chaotic spirituality of its early years. Smith taught that "it is not necessary for tongues to be taught to the church particularly, for any man that has the Holy Ghost, can speak of the things of God in his own tongue." By no means, however, did the prophet discount supernatural phenomena. He expected the apostles to encounter both angels and devils. Since the devil could transform "himself nigh unto an angel of light," Smith taught them to verify angelic encounters by shaking hands with purported angels. If "the man takes hold of his hand," Smith warned, "and feels no substance he may know it is Satan." In Smith's heaven, an angel was a "Saint with a resurrected body," and thus today's Saints on earth were tomorrow's angels in heaven and already could greet their angelic brethren as equals. Mormons who thoroughly proved themselves through obedience—made their "calling and election sure" despite all tribulations—could expect even more exalted visitors. The faithful Saint "will have," Smith promised, "the personage of Jesus Christ to attend him or appear unto him from time to time, & even he will manifest the Father unto him." God, Smith taught, was "pure intelligence," intelligence that would flow to faithful Saints through the spirit of revelation. Brigham Young, who had once prayed that "all the time I could hear Joseph and hear his doctrine and see his mind," found his wish granted temporarily.[18]

Young and his fellow Latter-day Saints surely longed for their places in those heavenly councils that summer. Commerce and Montrose were low-lying and malarial, and a relentless wave of feverish sickness swept through the resettled Mormons in July, afflicting Young among many others. By mid-July, the situation had become desperate. At that point, Smith arose from his own sickbed and visited Elijah Fordham and Joseph Bates Noble, two church members on the verge of death. "Brother Joseph went forward," reported Heber Kimball in a letter a few days later, "and took them [the sick] by the hand and commanded the fever to depart from them, and they leaped from their beds and were made whole." Smith crossed to Montrose, Young later wrote, "and commanded me in the name of Jesus Christ to arise and be made whole." "[I]t was truly a time of rejoicing," recorded Wilford Woodruff in his journal. The rejoicing proved transient, as malaria and other illnesses afflicted Young, many of the Twelve, and their families, and the spiritual excitement of July's teaching and healing faded.[19]

For Young and his fellow apostles, tension grew as their departure approached. Smith promised that the church would provide for their families, but a church with few resources after its expulsion from Missouri was in no position to make good that pledge. "[I]f I had known that every one of them would have been in the grave when I returned," Brigham later asserted, "it would not have diverted me from my mission one hour." At the time, however, he wrestled with guilt and unusually chaotic emotions. After John Taylor and Wilford Woodruff became the first apostles to depart for England in August, Taylor's wife Leonora and her three children moved into the Youngs' cabin. "Brother Young Family are all sick, him and all," Leonora wrote her husband. "The[y] could not get a drop of watter." Mary Ann Young was expecting her fourth child. Eventually, Brigham Young summarily told Leonora Taylor to leave and collected four and a half dollars in rent. "Brother Young," she asserted, "said it was a Greivous imposition that the[y] could not have the Room I was in." "He said," she continued, "he would lie in the street if he was me before a Family should be situated as theres was, that Mrs. Young was sick." Offended but powerless to resist, Taylor left to share a house with Sarah Pratt, wife of Orson Pratt. "I tell evry one I left the Room on account of Sister Youngs confinement," Taylor explained, adding that she left Young "to settle that business" with God and asked her husband not to confront his senior apostle about the matter. If the particulars of the conflict remain unknown, the episode hints at an uncharitable belligerence Young rarely displayed during this period of his life, probably brought about by having to leave his family in such an unhealthy and impoverished state. Young apparently regretted his treatment of Leonora, as shortly after he left Commerce, he instructed Mary Ann to pay to "sister Tailor" $4.50, the exact amount he had collected from her in rent.[20]

Young and Heber Kimball, who had served an earlier mission to England, left together in mid-September. Mary Ann Young had given birth ten days earlier to a daughter named Alice, whom the family often called Emma during her childhood. Just one day after Young departed, he wrote the first of a series of letters to Mary Ann, discussing the settlement of various debts that would leave her in even tighter straits."[T]his is all most robing you," he allowed, "but I doe not now what else to doe." Money worries aside, as he traveled Young cultivated his close ties to Mary Ann. In February, while in New York, Brigham expressed deep concern for his wife. "[Y]ou wrote in your letter that your helth was very poor & you a wasting away," he lamented. "[T]his hirts my feelings." Brigham frequently dreamed of his family while away from them; now he had nightmares. "I dremp the other nights you was ded," he wrote Mary Ann. "I waked my self up a weeping and lay awak[e] a while metetaing [meditating] upon our life sast [past] & present." In early March, Young displayed his romantic wit in another epistle home. "Brother Kimball has jest recived a letter from his wife," he jokingly complained, "but Brother Brigham has received but one sence he left home." "I am perswaded," Young continued in the third person, "that he loves his wife & children as well as enny other man if he dos not make quite so much fus about it." "Mary," he continued in the same vein, "I am all most a mind to wright you a love letter & see if that will not bring a nancer [answer] as Brother orson [Pratt] has received 6 or 8 from his wife." Brigham showed himself to be a devoted husband, lamenting the absence of his Mary Ann.[21]

Wrenched temporarily from his wife, Brigham suffered a more permanent familial loss when his father, John Young Sr., died after an extended illness on October 12, 1839 at the age of seventy-seven in Quincy, Illinois. His final years resembled much of his life, full of uncertain poverty and peregrinations. Hannah Brown, his second wife, had remained with relatives in New York State after the collapse of Joseph Smith's Kirtland. John Young Sr. traveled to Missouri just in time to join the Mormon exodus to Illinois, where he lived in a log cabin with his son Lorenzo. After leaving Mary Ann and his children, Brigham had tarried for several days in Quincy in late September. His sparse missionary journal records visits with brothers Lorenzo and John, but it does not include a meeting with his father. Likewise, his published history ignores his father's death. Much as he had been absent on a nearby mission when his first wife died, Young also missed his father's passage from this world. He probably felt that he could not delay his mission indefinitely because of his father's long illness. Such behavior contrasts markedly with Joseph Smith Jr.'s more standard preoccupation with his father's oft-predicted demise, which also finally came in the fall of 1839. Despite Joseph Smith Sr.'s repeated financial setbacks and struggle with alcoholism, his son sought ways to honor him, most prominently by ordaining him as the church's patriarch. While Young venerated his mother, the near-complete absence of commentary about his father in his journals, letters, or later history suggests a relationship that remained less than intimate.[22]

Even if separated from family and in a foreign land, Young used the mission to plunge into familiar activities he enjoyed after three years of turmoil in Kirtland and Missouri. En route to New York City, Young and his companions (apostles Kimball, John Taylor, and George A. Smith along with Theodore Turley and Reuben Hedlock) stopped in Kirtland. Young anointed and blessed John Taylor in the temple—the two apparently on good terms despite Young's conflict with Leonora Taylor. Leaving Kirtland, Young wrote in his journal about a rocky passage on a steamboat from Fairport, Ohio, to Buffalo: "the wind arose about one o clock in the morning I went upon deck and I felt impres in spirit to pray to the Father in [the] name of Jesus for a forgiveness of all my sins and then I fe[l]t to command the winds to sees [cease] and let ous goe safe on our Jorney the winds abated and glory & ouner [honor] & prase be to that God that rules all things." None of Young's companions mentioned the occurrence in their journals or later writings. Perhaps he did not tell them, just as he remained reticent about his vision of angels during the 1836 temple dedication. That Young arose in the middle of the night to beseech God to forgive his sins offers a rare glimpse into his private faith. In addition to embracing the familial and communal aspects of Mormonism, Young remained a man who communed with God in solitude. Moreover, he believed that God heard and responded to his fervent prayer.[23]

At the end of January, Young reached New York, where he lodged with Parley Pratt. In mid-February, while returning to New York from Brooklyn, he leapt to catch a departing ferry boat, crashed onto the vessel, separated his shoulder, and hurt his left arm on an iron ring on the boat's deck. "I hirt my self verry much," he wrote in his journal, "so I was not able to

Willard Richards, ca. 1850 *(courtesy of Church History Library, The Church of Jesus Christ of Latter-day Saints)*

dress my self for 4 or 5 days." In March, Young, in company with Kimball, Smith, Hedlock, and Parley and Orson Pratt, paid $18 for a "steerage passage" aboard the *Patrick Henry,* bound from New York to Liverpool. Young and Kimball shared a lower berth, with the Pratt brothers above them, all of them sick most of the way. Upon stepping foot on English soil, Young exulted with a threefold shout of "Hosanna." He later wrote that he "was so emaciated" that his cousin Willard Richards, who had lived in England since 1837, did not recognize him. Upon arrival in London, Young and his companions met Wilford Woodruff and John Taylor, who had preceded them by several months. After ordaining Richards as a new

Heber C. Kimball, ca. 1853 *(courtesy of Church History Library, The Church of Jesus Christ of Latter-day Saints)*

apostle, the Twelve formally and unanimously affirmed the ragged, gaunt, and still-wounded Young as their "Standing President."[24]

Young's background made him well suited for his mission field. At the depth of a depression deeper and more stubborn than its American counterpart, the British working classes compared to the previous generation were eating less, contracting more diseases, and dying younger. Streets, tenements, and even graveyards suffered from overcrowding as rural areas emptied into rapidly growing cities like Liverpool and Manchester. The British Isles had recently been rocked by Chartism, a working-class movement that erupted in strikes and riots in 1839 when Parliament rejected demands for universal male suffrage and other democratic reforms. Beyond the franchise, Chartism encompassed diffuse working-class frustrations, ranging from anger over a stamp tax that made newspapers more expensive, to high food prices blamed on the Corn Law tariffs, to resentment over an 1834 Poor Law reform designed to confine welfare recipients to draconian workhouses. A government crackdown restored a fragile peace to British cities, but a working-class political party (the National Charter Association) was founded in Manchester shortly after Young moved there in May 1840. Young had known grinding poverty and periodic hunger throughout much of his life, but the squalor of English cities still gave him pause. "I for get how menny bagers [beggars] I saw," he told Mary Ann, "but enuph to take all the pennes [pennies] and copers I can get." The United States had not yet recovered from the banking panic of 1837, but the English situation was far bleaker. "[W]hen I look at the difrents betwene poore People here and in America," he concluded to Mary Ann, "I rejoice that you and the children are there."[25]

The religious landscape was also markedly different from what Young had known. Anglicans, "old dissenters" (Baptists, Independents, and Presbyterians), and "new dissenters" (Wesleyan Methodists) alike all struggled to attract the urban working classes to their churches and chapels. Those living in rural areas, from weavers threatened by the advent of power looms to small farmers squeezed out of livelihood by enclosures and population growth, also suffered economically but were more apt to retain their religious affiliations. Mormon missionaries focused on evangelism rather than on politics or socioeconomic analysis, but with no ties to British elites or the established order they unflinchingly lamented the poverty of the laboring classes, denounced the monarchy's conspicuous consumption, and promised their converts land and employment in Illinois.[26]

Building upon the work begun by Kimball and Richards, the missionaries preached, baptized, nurtured converts, and organized the emigration of British Mormons to the United States. In the mission field, Young first assisted Wilford Woodruff with the explosive growth of the church in Herefordshire, a rural county one hundred miles south of Liverpool. In March, Woodruff had presided over the en masse conversion of a society of fringe Methodists in Herefordshire known as the United Brethren. After John Wesley's 1791 death, his Methodist followers had gradually coalesced into their own denomination. Suspected of political disloyalty by the Anglican-dominated establishment, the denomination's leadership emphasized respectability, and formerly underpaid, unmarried itinerants gradually acquired salaries, status, and spouses. Despite these changes, both Anglicans and other Nonconformists (another term for non-Anglican Protestants) looked down their noses at their Methodist counterparts. In George Eliot's novel *Adam Bede,* a stranger who encounters a female Methodist exhorter comments that Wesleyans are either "bilious" or "ecstatic."[27]

Moreover, as Methodism sought respectability, its unity foundered. One splinter group, the Primitive Methodists—partly inspired by "Crazy" Lorenzo Dow, the same long-haired, animated evangelist whom Brigham Young's parents so admired—clearly fell into the "ecstatic" camp. Resembling the Reformed Methodists of Young's early adulthood, Primitive Methodists—sometimes known as "Camp Meeting Methodists" or simply "Ranters"—held day-long evangelistic prayer meetings, healed the sick, cast out demons, took visions and trances seriously, and engaged the occasional witch in spiritual combat. Whereas the mainstream Wesleyans gradually abandoned their "love feasts," the gatherings remained popular among the Primitive Methodists, who came together to eat bread or cake and drink water from a two-handled mug, listen to evangelistic preaching, sing hymns, and hear converts' testimony. The Primitive Methodists also encouraged female preachers—perhaps one-fifth of their exhorters were women. Dressing "like the farm laborers, miners, and stockingers who came to hear them," Primitive Methodist preachers enjoyed their greatest success in "rural areas and among uprooted newcomers who had yet to find a place in the grimy factory towns of industrial England." In particular, Primitive Methodism thrived in Manchester and the Staffordshire Potteries, two places where Mormonism later took root.[28]

The process of refinement and schism repeated itself, however. According to Job Smith, a convert to Mormonism, the Primitive Methodists expelled a Herefordshire circuit rider named Thomas Kington—known for his revivalistic camp meetings and faith healing—who clashed with "the more formal and better paid preachers of that denomination." Cast out, Kington gathered like-minded believers and preachers into a small Methodist sect known as the United Brethren. Whereas the historian W. R. Ward suggests that mainstream British Methodism ran the grave risk of "becoming a bore," the United Brethren faced no such danger. "They [the United Brethren] were frequently wrought upon," wrote Job Smith, "by what they termed 'the power' which caused strange operations in those who became affected therewith." During prayer meetings, converted young people "would spring up and dance around in a noisy fit of ecstasy." In Herefordshire, the United Brethren numbered roughly six hundred, including fifty or so lay preachers, including some women. The society, asserted Smith, "had a great many very poor people as its members, and a few working men in fairly good circumstances, and one man who might be called wealthy."[29]

Wilford Woodruff had the good fortune to meet John Benbow, the single wealthy man. Benbow immediately accepted Woodruff's testimony, and within a month Woodruff baptized forty United Brethren preachers, including Kington, the society's superintendent. "Glory hallaluyah," wrote Woodruff, "the work of God rolls on." "I felt as if all Herefordshire was coming to be baptized," reminisced Woodruff several decades later. The Herefordshire mission brought Woodruff more than the bliss of evangelistic success; mobs pelted him with rotten eggs and stones as he preached and baptized. Seventy years earlier, young itinerants like Francis Asbury had endured harassment while winning souls for Methodism in the region. Now, some of the grandchildren of those Methodist converts turned their fury on new religious upstarts. Undeterred, Woodruff eagerly recruited Young to join him in this fertile mission field.[30]

Once in Herefordshire, Young immediately plunged into the work of preaching, baptizing, and laying hands on believers "that they might receive the Holy Ghost." After years of toiling in New York and New England with only modest success, Young found the unprecedented response gratifying. "The people are very different in this country to what the Americans are," Young wrote Joseph Smith. "[T]hey do not seem to understand argument; simple testimony is enough for them; they beg and plead for the book of mormon." "[T]here is a grate caul for preaching in this regon of contry," he wrote his fellow apostle George A. Smith. Only a small percentage of prospective converts accepted the apostles' message, partly because of the opposition of Protestant ministers with "jest religion enuph to dam[n] them." Even so, the results outweighed what Young had come to expect in the United States.[31]

Young sometimes earned a hearing from prospective converts by exhibiting the boldness and spiritual gifts that characterized his early years in Kirtland. According to Woodruff, when "opposers" tried to disrupt Young's sermon in a United Brethren chapel, "Elder Young rose up in the power of the Priesthood & in the name of the Great God & according to the laws of the land Commanded order." Like the other apostles, Young also laid "on hands for the healing of the sick." On May 18, Young, Woodruff, and Willard Richards attended the Brethren's annual "feast day" (Young labeled it a "tea party" in his diary) and adapted it to Latter-day Saint purposes. "Elder Young addressed the Saints clothed with the power of God," recorded Woodruff. At the conclusion of the meeting, the apostles laid hands on Mary Pitt, a woman who "had not walked except on crutches for 11 years." "Brother Young," Woodruff remembered many years later, "was mouth, and commanded her to be made whole." Woodruff claimed that "the next day she walked three miles" without her crutches. The Latter-day "love feast" brought another twenty members into the waters of baptism. Young noted that "[a]lmost without exception it is the poor that receive the gospel." Benbow and Kington were notable exceptions, however, as they provided the apostles with the £300 needed to begin publication of the planned hymnal and *Book of Mormon*. With that money in hand, in late May Young left Woodruff and went to Manchester.[32]

Young and his fellow apostles felt at ease amid radical evangelicals in England who engaged in practices that mainstream Methodists and Anglicans would have considered at best enthusiastic and at worst occult. While in Manchester overseeing the publishing efforts, Young promoted an eruption of spiritual gifts, intending to not only reap converts but mold them into men and women of spiritual power. In the late 1830s, Joseph Smith had again discouraged speaking in unknown tongues, and, en route to England, the apostle Parley Pratt had corrected the false notion that "the churches have no gifts unless they have tongues which is the least of all the church, or gifts of the church." Thousands of miles away from the prophet, though, Young displayed the spiritual fire that had characterized his first four years in the church. While visiting a local family, Young and Kimball "sung some and afterwards spake with each other in tongues." After two weeks, though, Young was disappointed that the Manchester converts had not received the gift of tongues. "Br P[arley] P. Pratt and myself talked som time," he scrawled in his diary on Thursday, June 11, "about the nesisity of the Elders having the power of God with them." Having celebrated "wisen week" (Whitsuntide or Pentecost), the Manchester Saints "wanted somthing good," Young wrote Willard Richards. After his session with Pratt, Young explained, during a meeting the next day "we told them to aske fore the blesings of the Lord and get the gifts." Young's comments illustrate a belief that spiritual gifts such as tongues should naturally proceed following baptism and confirmation, in which Mormon elders laid their hands on new converts to bestow upon them the gift of the Holy Ghost.[33]

Soon Young witnessed the desired spiritual outpouring. William Clayton, converted during Kimball's 1837 mission, recorded in his journal that a "Brother Green almost got the gift of tongues." As if to illustrate the practice, Young himself then spoke in tongues. By fits and starts over the weekend, the Manchester Saints—men and women—experienced the gift. Early Saturday morning, Elizabeth Crooks began speaking and singing in tongues as she slept, expressing herself in seven languages over two hours. "[B]y sunday," Young informed Richards, "there was aplenty to rise up in the name of the Lord and speak with other tongues and provisy in the name of Jesus." In the United States, evangelist Charles Finney attracted attention and some notoriety for employing what he termed "new measures" to engineer successful revivals with considerable predictability. On a much smaller scale, Brigham Young and Heber Kimball had laid the groundwork for their converts' baptism with the Holy Ghost. "I recolect in England," stated Parley Pratt eleven years later, "when the Key was turned to open the door upon the Gifts of the Spirit by the twelve." Just twelve hours later, Pratt recalled, "speaking in Tongues, etc. was in Exercise in a variety of places." The practice became common in several English branches of the church.[34]

Divine healing also formed an important component of the mission. The apostles healed through the laying on of hands, through prayer, and through ritual anointing. "I anointed Jennetta," wrote Willard Richards of his ailing wife, "with oil & spirits & myrrh & I seald the blesing upon her by the mouth of br. Heber [Kimball]." Jennetta's health soon improved. The apostles frequently administered to the sick during their travels. "[T]he report went out," Young wrote Mary Ann about a brief trip to Wales, "that we had the same power that the old apostles had it is true." Young and the other members of the Twelve took their callings as priests and apostles seriously.[35]

Young also possessed a strong belief in the spiritual meaning and utility of dreams and therefore recorded countless dreams in his journal and letters. "I doe not know as it will harme enny boddy in the world to know what folks dream," he insisted, "fore there is no harme in dreaming." The night before boarding the ship for Liverpool, he wrote Mary Ann, "[I] asked my Hevenly Father in the name of Jesus to give me som manifestation concerning my jorney across the water." He dreamed of successfully crossing a "large body of water covered with ice and snow . . . like honney comb," which he reported "satesfisd my feeling in agrate mashere [measure]." He routinely dreamed about Mary Ann and his children, sometimes envisioning domestic bliss and sometimes fearing sickness and estrangement. "There is carsly [scarcely] a night but what I dreme of being in my own native contry," he explained in another letter. He saw church members, including Sidney Rigdon, and apostates such as Thomas Marsh. In another dream, he saw several groups of people in the "western contry": a northern group of "saints or Israelits," a southern group of "wicked malicias mobers," and a larger group of people in the East. Although the Saints regularly defeated the mobs, the latter replenished their ranks from the East, where the people "did not seeme to notice enny thing about it." In addition to sharing his own visions, Young took pleasure in the dreams and prophecies of others. Peter Melling, ordained a patriarch by the church, prophesied that Young, Kimball, and James Whitehead "should [not] sleep in the grave till they should see the son of man com in his glory or in the cloud of heaven." The blessing "caused my hard heart to rej[oi]ce in the Lord," wrote Young.[36]

Many prospective converts surely found Mormon concepts of adult baptism, priesthood, gathering, and ongoing revelation (especially the *Book of Mormon*) unusual, but the fact that radical evangelicals often shared the Mormon emphasis on spiritual gifts, visions, and apocalyptic millenarianism made the acceptance of new doctrines easier. At times, Young thought some converts made themselves ridiculous through spiritual excess. "[T]hey get the spirit of Provisi [prophecy] upon them," he joked to his brother Joseph, "and they tell many things that is about so and all we can due is to Laugh at them a little and so pass it off." He and his fellow apostles discouraged the practice of magic, and Young concluded that the Methodist "holy kiss" (a biblical greeting) "was best set aside, or it would lead to evil." Still, Young did not discourage such would-be prophets, and the apostles aimed to channel, not condemn, the spiritual ecstasy of their British flock. For all its divergence from and sharp criticism of the Protestant Christianity of its day, early Mormonism shared—and possibly exceeded—the evangelical expectation of immediate and regular contact with the divine.[37]

Young also engaged in more ordinary activities during his year abroad. He griped about the English weather ("most of the time it is rainy") and was shocked by the pollution plaguing industrial cities like Manchester. "[T]he atmosfer," he reported to Mary Ann, "is so darkened with the cole [coal] . . . that the are [air] is so thick with it the eye cannot penetrate but a little ways." Contrary to an 1833 revelation known as the "Word of Wisdom" that discouraged the consumption of "wine or hard drink" and coffee and tea, the American missionaries embraced conviviality while among their English hosts. Shortly after their arrival, the Twelve "drank of wine that was . . . 40 years old," a gift from a convert in Preston. Young also attended several "tea parties" and developed a taste for the drink. Back in Illinois in November 1841, he asked at a meeting of the Twelve and other "high priests," "shall I Break [the] word of wisdom if I go home & drink a cup of tea?" In its early years, the church oscillated between strict enforcement and latitude, and the council left the choice up to Young, concluding that "a forced abstainance was not making us free but we should be under bondage with a yoak upon our necks." Only toward the end of his life did Young encourage strict obedience to the Word of Wisdom.[38]

As was customary, the apostles had left Illinois "without purse or scrip," but contributions from the English Mormons enabled Young to live more comfortably in England than he had at home. Young claimed to have raised "thousands and thousands of dollars" from the British church, "gather[ing] it up by faith." Young later exaggerated his own penny-pinching. "I do not recollect," he insisted, "of spending more than one penny, needlessly, while in England, and that was for a bunch of grapes." In fact, Young enjoyed purchasing items difficult or more expensive to obtain in America, everything from "Cloggs for the children" to a "Black Silk velvet vest." He sent detailed instructions for a watch to a London craftsman, requesting "one hand to keep the day of the month" and the other to mark the hours with the twelve letters of his name. In addition to occasional "tea parties" and purchases, Young toured cathedrals, museums, and botanical gardens. The peak of Young's trip, as far as tourism was concerned, came in early December when he toured London, visiting Buckingham Palace, Westminster Abbey, the Tower of London (including the Crown Jewels), the British Museum, and the National Gallery. Woodruff and Kimball waited as Young explored the Thames Tunnel, returning with an "exact likeness of it" as a souvenir. According to Kimball, Young "spent his time mostly in looking at thing[s] in London." Perhaps the Mormons' lack of evangelistic success in London explains the burst of tourism. "London was the hardest place in England to get the work planted," Young wrote Eli Kelsey, a missionary in London, in 1851.[39]

The diversions provided welcome relief from Young's unprecedented ecclesiastical responsibilities. In England, Young faced the difficult task of maintaining good relations both among the apostles and with Joseph Smith. Of the apostles, Young was not the most active practitioner of divine healing, the most erudite or eloquent editor, or the most successful evangelist, but he possessed several strengths as the mission's leader. Young illustrated a talent for practical organization. Despite his ongoing difficulty with writing—"exuse erours and mestakes you must remember its from me," he reminded Willard Richards in a postscript—Young regularly corresponded with his fellow apostles and church leaders across the British Isles. Young also oversaw the start of church publications in England, including the periodical *Millennial Star,* a hymnal, and a new edition of the *Book of Mormon.* Young and Richards personally worked on the index to the latter, although Richards, who would subsequently serve Joseph Smith as a clerk, probably did the bulk of the clerical work. When interacting with his fellow apostles he trod cautiously, especially with experienced leaders like Parley and Orson Pratt and Wilford Woodruff. He gave the Pratt brothers prominent positions at church conferences and assigned Parley Pratt the editorship of the *Millennial Star.* Pratt, a talented and prolific writer, happily informed his wife that he was "seated in the presidential chair of a general conference." Instead of feeling threatened by Pratt's talents and reputation, Young put them to good use. Young also defused potential discontent through humor and pragmatism. When Willard Richards asked to visit his wife (whom he had met and married in England), knowing that others of the Twelve could not, Young allowed that there "is a difference betwene 3 months jorny and afue [h]ours ride." "Brigham sayes," he concluded, "come and see your wife." Perhaps most critical to his success as the mission's leader, Young's spiritual fervor and dedication won the respect of his fellow apostles. Young preached boldly, laid hands on the sick for healing, and presided over the Manchester Pentecost. Nearly a decade after his conversion to Mormonism, he retained spiritual assurance and ebullience. If Young's recollection that the Twelve under Thomas Marsh were "continually sparring at each other" was accurate, Young's leadership produced a much more harmonious apostolate.[40]

Moreover, after a majority of the apostles rejected Joseph Smith's leadership in 1838, Young strove to restore his quorum's reputation in his prophet's eyes, carefully and continually reassuring Smith of their loyalty. Young regularly wrote Smith for advice, especially about publishing ventures and ordinations, and he promised to painstakingly follow the prophet's direction. "We desire not to council you," Young and Richards wrote the church's presidency in September 1840, "but to be counseled by you." "[W]e rejoice," they praised Joseph and Hyrum Smith, "that the Church has a *Moses* in these last days (and an *Aaron* by his side) of whom the Saints may enquire, as in days of old, & know the mind of the Lord." The rhetoric was more than obligatory obeisance, as Young repeated such language privately. "May the Lord preserve us from provoking him [Smith]," he expressed to Mary Ann, "as the children of Isreal did the Lord and Moses in there day." Even so, Smith chastised the Twelve on one occasion "because we did not wright to him on the subject of printing the hymnbook and the *Book of Mormon*." Smith's reaction seems inexplicable in light of the apostles' deferential communications. The conflict may have stemmed from an October 1839 church council decision that authorized Emma Smith to publish a hymnal and resolved that "a letter be written to Brigham Young at New York informing him of the same and not to publish the Hymns taken from Commerce." Young and the apostles, though, moved ahead with their hymnal before receiving the letter. Smith probably remained suspicious of the Twelve given events in Kirtland and Missouri. "I have don the verry best that I knew how," Young reacted in private frustration. Smith's displeasure was temporary; in other matters the prophet warmly approved of their activities. "It is likewise very satisfactory to my mind," Smith wrote the Twelve in December, "that there has been such a good understanding existing between you, and that the Saints have so cheerfully hearkened to council." Young achieved this unusual and pronounced irenicism through savvy and thoughtful leadership coupled with his genuine devotion to Smith.[41]

THE British Mission was a bold step for a church in its adolescence. Scarcely three decades had passed since American Congregationalists and Baptists, respectively, had formed their first foreign mission boards, sending a few scattered missionaries to places like India and the Sandwich Islands (Hawaii). As Joseph Smith also did initially, American Protestants had previously conceived of missions as attempts to evangelize Indians. Although some American evangelists, such as Lorenzo Dow, replicated their own personal efforts overseas, the Mormons were the first American religious church or denomination to systematically evangelize Great Britain.[42]

That audacity reaped a harvest more spectacular than the church's success in the United States, as the church in England more than tripled to nearly 6,000 members during the year of Young's leadership. Around eight hundred British converts sailed for America that year, and thousands more followed over the next decade. The Mormon promise of a refuge from a coming tribulation made sense to many Protestant dissenters already imbued with the expectation of divine judgment preceding Christ's return. Other converts emigrated to meet Joseph Smith, and still others simply wanted to escape crushing poverty. At a time when the United States served as an economic refuge for many Britons, the church boosted the potential of the region around Commerce. Parley Pratt promised emigrants "soil as rich as Eden." Moved by the poverty of many converts, Young sought to establish means to help poor emigrants. The Twelve approved Young's proposal that "no one go to America that has money without assisting the poor." As reports from the first emigrants filtered back home, the spirit of "gathering" increased. "[T]he people after joining them selves to the saints," Young wrote Mary Ann, "will even pay their own pasedge to america . . . the promised land." By 1846, nearly 5,000 British Mormons had fled "Babylon" for an American Zion. Down the road, Young would be well positioned to lead those British emigrants, as many possessed memories of his spiritual leadership in England. Even in England itself, the Latter-day Saints remembered Brigham Young for many years. "I have had quite a number take me by the hand," the apostle Ezra T. Benson informed Young fifteen years later, "and say that it was Brother Brigham's voice that they first heard proclaiming the glad tidings of the Gospel."[43]

Although Young continued to miss his family, he adjusted to being apart from them. He complained of fatigue and illness but grudgingly admitted that he enjoyed himself abroad. "I am as happy in this contry as I could be in enny place in the world," he allowed, "whare I had got to be deprived of the socity of my famely." Much of his joy, he told Mary Ann, came from spending nights and meetings with the Saints. "The Brotherin and Sisters would pluck out there eyes for me if it ware nessary," he explained. "They due all they can for my comfort. They feed me and give me close and monny. They wash my feet and wate upon me as they would a little child."[44] At first, he hoped to return in the fall of 1840, then thought he should perhaps stay two years. Joseph Smith settled the question by calling all the disciples save Parley Pratt home after one year. After a final conference, they sailed for New York in April 1841. Voyaging in ill health to lead a mission to a foreign land must have seemed like a daunting challenge to Young, but he returned home in triumph. He had acquitted himself very well during what was his first extended exercise of ecclesiastical authority. Unbeknownst to him, he would face far stiffer challenges in Illinois.

CHAPTER FOUR

New and Everlasting Covenant

From the midst of confusion can harmony flow?
Or can peace from distraction come forth?
From out of corruption, integrity grow?
Or can vice unto virtue give birth?

    —ELIZA R. SNOW (SMITH) (YOUNG), 1842

WHILE Brigham Young oversaw the rapid expansion of the British church, Mary Ann struggled with poverty, sickness, and loneliness. In his absence, she had moved with their children across the Mississippi River to Commerce, Illinois. "I found my family," he later wrote, "living in a small unfinished log cabin, situated on a low wet lot, so swampy that when the first attempt was made to plow it the oxen mired." With his customary energy, Young drained and fenced the lot, finished the house (several blocks away from Joseph Smith's riverside residence), and built an above-ground cellar. One week after Young's return, Smith directed a revelation to him, promising that "it is no more required at your hand to leave your family as in times past . . . take special care of your family from this time henceforth and forever." When Young had reached Missouri in 1838, Smith had given him a similar revelatory promise. Knowing the cost of the British mission on Mary Ann and his children, Young perhaps beseeched Smith for this second revelation. For the most part, Young relished the constant movement of missionary service, but he wanted to finally restore some balance between his ecclesiastical responsibilities and private life. He undertook only several shorter missions in the eastern United States over the next three years. "This evening I am with my wife a lone by my fire side for the first time for years," Young wrote in his journal in January 1842. "We injoi it and feele to prase the Lord." Young's domestic tranquility, as usual, proved fleeting.[1]

Brigham Young, ca. 1845 *(courtesy of Church History Library, The Church of Jesus Christ of Latter-day Saints)*

When Young returned from his British Mission, he found the church's new place of gathering much changed. Most obviously, Smith had re-named Commerce "Nauvoo," drawing upon a Hebrew word which, he explained, "signifies a beautiful situation, or place, carrying with it, also, the idea of *rest.*" When Young had left for England in the fall of 1839, the Mormons were refugees scattered on either side of the Mississippi in tents and crude cabins. By the summer of 1841, Nauvoo was a boomtown of several thousand inhabitants, with more church members living on farms in the surrounding countryside. The church's leadership had proclaimed

Nauvoo the new "cornerstone of Zion," secured a favorable city charter from the Illinois legislature, begun construction on a new temple, and formed "a body of independent military men" known as the Nauvoo Legion, whose troops Smith led as their Lieutenant General, an unusually exalted rank granted by Illinois governor Thomas Carlin. The militia's rapid growth alarmed outside observers, as did the domination of political offices by members of the church hierarchy.[2]

The church's practice of bloc voting also stirred controversy, especially because Smith would attempt to trade votes with either party for political protection. As Young explained in late 1844, "let us vote as kissing goes— by favors." Mormons occasionally threw their support to the Whigs but more often sided with the Democrats. Stephen Douglas, briefly a member of the Illinois Supreme Court and then elected to Congress in 1842, later termed "the Mormons the salvation of the Democracy in Illinois" and recalled that he "was never swindled out of the Mormon vote but once." Responding to complaints about Mormon political maneuvering, the prophet's brother William Smith published a simple retort. The church's political enemies should observe the "Mormon Creed" and "mind their own business."[3]

Recent convert and Major General John C. Bennett played a prominent role in the Nauvoo Legion. Bennett's checkered past included a brief stint as a Methodist preacher, the promotion of the tomato as a panacea for a variety of medical ailments, allegations of diploma peddling related to several attempts to found colleges, the leadership of a newly incorporated Illinois militia unit known as the Invincible Dragoons, and the largely ceremonial title of Quartermaster General of Illinois. Thirty-six years of age, with "black hair sprinkled with grey, dark complexion, and rather a thin face" and possessing "much vivacity and animation of spirit," Bennett impressed Smith as a convert who could immediately raise the prestige of the church and help the Mormons achieve political peace in their new home. By the time of Young's return, Bennett had quickly become the most visible and influential Latter-day Saint in Nauvoo next to the prophet and his brother Hyrum. Bennett served as Nauvoo's mayor and became an "Assistant President" to Joseph Smith. While in England, Young received reports of the "Quarter Master jenerall who had ben Baptised." "[T]hey say he is anointed and a grate man has the spirit," Young relayed in a letter to Willard and Levi Richards. Young added, however, that Bennett "has the spirit of ware [war] and som might think by his speach that there will be ware with the Missourians." Of the fact that others "have the same spirit," Young concluded, "what a pitty." Young's implied criticism suggests that he harbored suspicion about the mercurial Bennett, whose quick path to the prophet's side may well have sparked jealousy in a man who had toiled for years to gain Joseph Smith's trust.[4]

Smith's clear approbation of the Twelve upon their return assuaged any possible envy. He declared at an August church conference that "the time had come when the twelve should be called upon to stand in their place next to the first presidency." When he had first organized the Quorum of the Twelve Apostles, Smith clarified that "the Twelve will have no right to go into Zion, or any of its stakes." Instead, it was their responsibility to "preside over all the church of the Saints among the Gentiles . . . where there is no presidency." Now, pleased with their missionary service and desperate for competent leadership in Nauvoo, Smith broadened the scope of the apostles' authority. In particular, Smith asked the apostles to "take the burthen of the business of the Church in Nauvoo, and especially as pertaining to the selling of Church lands." As had been the case during the church's final year in Kirtland, indebtedness disturbed Smith's peace and threatened his prophetic reputation. The church's Iowa land purchases rested on faulty titles, and Smith had incurred a heavy debt to purchase the church's land in Nauvoo. Only a high rate of land sales to British emigrants and other newcomers would keep the church and its prophet solvent. Smith now gave the Twelve the responsibility for selling land and collecting tithes for the construction of the temple. Young felt compelled to reassure the church "that nothing could be fa[r]ther from his wishes and that of his quorum, than to interpose with church affairs at Zion and her stakes." Responding to his new responsibilities, however, Young quickly issued an epistle encouraging the Saints in the East to deed their properties to the church's primary creditor in exchange for Nauvoo lots. The apostles requested all of the Saints to come to the "places of gathering" and "bring of your substance, your silver, and gold, and apparel . . . cast [it] into the treasury of the Lord." As Smith had stated in a recent revelation, the apostles promised that those church members who helped build the Lord's temple would receive abundant blessings through the sacred ceremonies to be performed within its walls. In September, in a further sign of Smith's approval, Young was appointed to a vacant seat on the Nauvoo City Council.[5]

While he respected Young's talent for organization and business, Smith also promoted Young as a priestly, spiritual leader. In the fall of 1841, for instance, Young assumed a prominent role in the church's ritual of proxy baptism for the dead, first taught by Smith the previous year. Whereas Calvinists hoped that their relatives numbered among the elect, and Arminian evangelicals prayed for deathbed conversions of unbelievers, they both resigned themselves to the possibility of spending eternity apart from unredeemed parents, spouses, and siblings. The Mormons shared such concerns, heightened because Smith taught that God would consider invalid any baptisms performed outside the confines of his restored church, as—according to an 1830 revelation—the "new and everlasting covenant" replaced "all old covenants." Carried to its logical conclusion, Mormon insistence on the proper performance of divinely prescribed ordinances placed the salvation of the Saints' ancestors in jeopardy. Prompted by a vision of his long-departed brother Alvin, Smith had received a divine promise in 1836 that those "who have died without a knowledge of this Gospel, who would have received it if they had been permitted to tarry, shall be heirs of the celestial kingdom." Such promises provided some solace, but Mormons still worried about the fate of their kin who died without having heard the gospel.[6]

Young shared this concern. While in England, he reported to Mary Ann a vision experienced by Ann Booth, a Manchester convert to the church. Booth visited "the Place of departed spirits," lodged in twelve prisons. She saw "one of the 12 apostles of the Lamb who had been martyred in America," David Patten, who proceeded to baptize John Wesley, several other Methodist preachers, and her own grandfather, uncle, sister, and mother. For Young, the vision gave hope for the salvation of "my Dear Mother . . . and my sister that died about 1808." In Nauvoo, Smith created a firm basis for those hopes. Drawing upon a reference in I Corinthians to "they . . . which are baptized for the dead," in 1840 Smith announced a new ritual that appeased Brigham's anxieties and those of his coreligionists. "The Saints," the prophet wrote the apostles in England, "have the privilege of being baptized for those of their relatives who are dead, whom they believe would have embraced the Gospel."[7]

At first gradually and then in a great flood of filial piety, several thousand Nauvoo Mormons plunged into the muddy waters of the Mississippi in vicarious baptisms for their relatives who had died outside the church (and sometimes for others—George Washington, Benjamin Franklin, and the explorer Zebulon Pike were also beneficiaries of the new rite). Seeking to regularize the practice—baptisms had occurred at various points on the Mississippi and record-keeping was spotty—Smith announced in October 1841 that there "shall be no more baptisms for the dead, until the ordinance can be attended to in the Lord's house." The next month, the prophet dedicated a baptismal font, resting on the backs of twelve wooden oxen in the basement of the temple, which was still under construction. The font was patterned after the "molten sea" standing "upon twelve oxen" in Solomon's temple. Young officiated at the first proxy baptisms in the Nauvoo Temple, baptizing Reuben McBride six times in succession for six of his relatives. Soon, he regularly baptized believers, who were immersed in the temple's "sacred pool" to cleanse themselves of sin, search for healing, and, most frequently, offer salvation to their departed kin. At the Kirtland temple dedication, Young had played a minor role, extemporaneously singing and speaking in tongues. His central place at the Nauvoo temple font suggested his new standing as a priestly leader.[8]

The next spring, Smith initiated a select number of trusted followers into a new rite, which became known as "the endowment."[9] In Kirtland, Smith had led the church's high-ranking male leaders in a series of ritual washings and anointings in preparation for an "endowment of power," a pentecostal outpouring of spiritual gifts at the Kirtland temple dedication. The Nauvoo ritual built on the Kirtland experiences but also drew on new sources of inspiration.

In particular, the Nauvoo endowment ceremony was influenced by the Spring 1842 induction of Smith and several dozen other Mormons—including Brigham Young—into Nauvoo's newly established Masonic Lodge. By the early 1840s American Freemasonry had recovered from the anti-Masonic furor that engulfed the northeastern United States in the late 1820s. Freemasonry had largely shed its conspiratorial reputation and had reemerged as a popular fraternal organization. In the late 1830s and early 1840s, Smith became attracted to the Masonic emphasis on secrecy, the fraternity's study of hieroglyphics and other Egyptian esoterica, and its pageantry and ritual. According to Heber Kimball, Smith grew convinced that "thare is a similarity of preast Hood in masonary" and concluded that Masonry was a degenerate form of the ancient priesthood. Accordingly, he ushered leading male members of the church into the lodge, and he openly used the Masonic rite as an inspiration for the church's endowment ceremony. In the words of Joseph Fielding, Masonic ritual could serve the Mormons as a "Stepping . . . Stone or Preparation for something else, the true Origin of Masonry." Scores of church members, then hundreds, joined the Nauvoo Lodge. Mormon Masons soon vastly outnumbered all of the other Freemasons in Illinois, raising objections from other lodges. On April 7, 1842, Young was one of the first three Nauvoo Saints without prior Masonic affiliation who joined the lodge, and two days later he achieved the rank of "Master Mason."[10]

In early May, Joseph and Hyrum Smith invited Young and seven other trusted followers to the same upper room in the lodge and instructed "them in the principles and order of the Priesthood." Smith's assistants had subdivided the room and decorated one section with small trees and shrubs to evoke the Garden of Eden. At the conclusion, initiates passed through a veil (symbolizing the division between heaven and earth) and entered celestial glory. Shortly before the end of his life, Young shared his recollection of the ceremony:

> we were washed and anointed, and had our garments placed upon us and re-
> ceived our New Name. And after he [Joseph] had performed these ceremo-
> nies, he gave the Key Words, signs, tokens and penalties. Then after this we
> went into the large room over the store in Nauvoo. Joseph divided upon the
> room the best he could, hung up the veil, marked it, gave us our instructions
> as we passed along from department to another, giving us signs, tokens, pen-
> alties with the key words pertaining to those signs.

Young believed that he and his fellow Nauvoo Mormons were Latter-day participants in an ancient quest for immortal glory, the fulfillment of which required rites once performed by Adam and Eve, subsequently practiced only in corrupted forms in Solomon's Temple and then later by Freemasons, and now restored to their paradisiacal purity.[11]

The Mormons understood the endowment as a means of penetrating the veil between the human and the divine, securing entrance into the "celestial kingdom," and acquiring "holy mysteries," secret "key words" that would thwart the devil and could bind even God. Participants received secret names, typically connecting them to figures in the Bible or *Book of Mormon*. A few years after the May 1842 endowment, Young referred to his "New Name which is Ancient & refered to Ancient things." Those names and key words provided the Saints with knowledge of "ancient things," the ability to distinguish false spirits from angels, and the opportunity to secure eternal glory. "[Y]our endowment is," Young instructed the crowd at the 1853 dedication of the Salt Lake Temple cornerstone, "to receive all those ordinances in the House of the Lord, which are necessary for you, after you have departed this life, to enable you to walk back to the presence of the Father, passing the angels who stand as sentinels, being enabled to give them the key words, the signs and tokens, pertaining to the Holy Priesthood, and gain your eternal exaltation in spite of earth and hell." Rather than satisfying themselves with a Masonic fraternity in Nauvoo, the endowment established a heavenly and eternal fraternity, in which Latter-day Saints like Brigham Young, blessed with ancient names and dressed in sacred robes, might clasp hands with angels and stride into the presence of the divine.[12]

Protestant visitors to Mormon Sunday meetings in Nauvoo would have found much that was familiar to them: impromptu preaching, hymns (some Protestant and some distinctively Mormon), and the Lord's Supper. As it evolved behind closed doors, however, Nauvoo Mormonism had much less in common with Young's Methodist past. Secret, sacred rituals replaced very public camp meetings and revivals. For evangelicals, individual faith was paramount, as spiritual rebirth brought eternal salvation for all who got off the anxious seat and responded to the altar call. By contrast, Mormons sought the mysteries of heaven and secured their salvation and exaltation through the emerging sacred ordinances of their church. The end of radical Methodist spirituality was perfect holiness, a sanctification possibly attained on earth and then finally in heaven. Mormonism had no end, instead promising a continual increase in spiritual knowledge, power, and dominion. The endowment, therefore, was only one more step in Smith's ritual innovation. The prophet would lead his followers still deeper into the holy mysteries.

Young and the other initiates of the endowment—probably no more than a dozen in 1842—comprised a small group of Joseph Smith's trusted disciples. Variously known as the "Anointed Quorum," the "Holy Order," or simply the "Quorum" or "Council," they dressed in their endowment robes, united in prayer circles, and discussed the struggles facing the church. "Brother Joseph feels as well as I Ever see him," Kimball wrote Parley Pratt, "one reason is he has got a small company, that he feels safe in thare ha[n]ds . . . he can open his bosom to [them] and feel him self safe."[13] Young was now firmly in this inner circle, privy to activities Smith was not ready to share with most church members.

JOSEPH Smith's introduction of proxy baptism and the endowment ceremony brought followers like Brigham Young closer to the center of his theological and ecclesiastical vision. In the early 1830s, Smith had already moved sharply away from Protestant doctrines, talking about eternal matter and intelligences (as opposed to creation *ex nihilo,* out of nothing), distancing himself from the Protestant (and Catholic) understanding of the Trinity, and describing three tiers of heavenly glory. In Nauvoo, Smith presented his new teachings much more boldly, teaching church members about a corporeal God with "flesh and bones" who sent embodied spirits to earth and then gave them priesthood ordinances and keys to enable them to secure their celestial glory.[14]

That celestial glory, moreover, could not be achieved by isolated individuals. Rejecting the more individualistic salvation of evangelical Protestantism while discussing baptism for the dead, Smith—reflecting on a passage in the Book of Hebrews—explained that "we without them [ancestors] cannot be made perfect; neither can they without us be made perfect." At the heart of Smith's ritual vision was the belief that what the priesthood sealed on earth would be "bound in heaven" and a corresponding expectation that only this "sealing and binding power"—rather than faith and good works by themselves—cemented an individual's grip on "glory, and honor, and immortality, and eternal life." For Mormons, the creation of a godly community of Saints bound together by priesthood ordinances became as important as the individual's relationship to the divine. Smith envisioned the exaltation of all would-be Saints across time, stretching back to Adam, who would present this unbroken chain of baptized and sealed humanity to Christ. God, along with those human beings exalted in glory, would continue to people worlds without end. Proxy baptism secured the salvation of the Saints' ancestors, and patriarchal blessings reinforced ties between children and their parents (or other church members if their parents had not joined the church). Smith, though, taught that more rituals were required to ensure that families spent the hereafter with each other. The Mormons needed to seal themselves to each other, beginning with "welding link[s]" between husbands and wives.[15]

The husbands and wives Smith welded together for eternity, however, were often not legally married, at least not to each other. The early history of Mormon polygamy remains shrouded by unreliable, retrospective testimony, usually either from bitter enemies of the church or from staunch defenders of plural marriage's divine origins. As was logical for a prophet committed to the "restitution of all things," from the earliest days of his church Smith considered the marriage practices of the Hebrew patriarchs. In Kirtland, Smith engaged in his first well-documented nonmonogamous relationship, with a servant girl named Fanny Alger. Smith's defenders, and some of his detractors, later described the relationship with Alger as the prophet's first plural marriage. The relationship angered Smith's wife Emma; it also produced allegations of adultery from high-ranking associate Oliver Cowdery, who termed it a "dirty, nasty, filthy affair." By 1836, Alger had exited the relationship; she soon married a non-Mormon. Around the time that Brigham Young and his fellow apostles returned from England in the spring of 1841, Smith was "sealed" to Louisa Beaman, daughter of an old family friend. Joseph Bates Noble, Beaman's brother-in-law and the officiator at the ceremony, recalled that Beaman disguised herself in a man's coat and hat to avoid attracting attention.[16]

Whether Smith was motivated by religious obedience or pursued sexual dalliances clothed with divine sanction cannot be fully resolved through historical analysis. In Nauvoo, he gradually and carefully revealed an elaborate theological edifice surrounding plural marriage. In keeping with church teachings on baptism, Smith insisted that only marriages eternally sealed through the church would bind couples in heaven. In a public March 1844 address, Smith did not specifically mention marriage, but he encouraged his listeners to take advantage of the "sealing power" granted to the Latter-day priesthood:

> Again the doctrin or sealing power of Elijah is as follows if you have power to seal on earth & in heaven then we should be Crafty, the first thing you do go & seal on earth your sons & daughters unto yourself, & yourself unto your fathers in eternal glory, & go ahead and not go back, but use a little Craftiness & seal all you can; & when you get to heaven tell your father that what you seal on earth should be sealed in heaven I will walk through the gate of heaven and Claim what I seal & those that follow me & my Council.

Smith envisioned the creation of a great chain of humanity, with kinship ties cemented by rituals of sealing that God was obligated to honor. Celestial marriage then connected these families together, leading to the creation of ecclesiastical and familial kingdoms that would persist into eternity. Smith's logic created a strong incentive for male church leaders to take additional wives. "I understand that a Man's Dominion will be as God's is," Joseph Fielding wrote in his journal, "over his own Creatures and the more numerous the greater his Dominion." Plural marriage, thus, provided the means by which a man could expand his eternal kingdom and achieve the highest level of celestial glory. At the same time, Smith promised both men and women that if they embraced this new order of marriage they would receive access to priesthood power and tremendous spiritual blessings.[17]

Smith soon pursued polygamy with the same dynamic and chaotic energy that characterized his ecclesiastical organization, business pursuits, and political stratagems. After marrying two other women in late 1841, the prophet was sealed to perhaps eleven women in the first eight months of 1842, most of whom were already married. He and other church leaders viewed those prior marriages as mere civil contracts, while the sealings were eternal covenants full of sacramental blessings and priestly power. Smith ultimately married around thirty women.[18]

Although details remain scarce and contested, it is clear that at least some of the marriages were not just for eternity. "I lived with the Prophet Joseph as his wife," testified Almera Johnson several decades later, implying sexual relations in the visits of Joseph Smith to her.[19] Almera's brother Benjamin Johnson emphasized that to his "certain knowledge he occupied the same bed with her."[20] In an 1892 deposition, Emily Dow Partridge reluctantly testified that she spent the night with Smith on the day of their sealing.[21] It was the only night they shared a bed together, though her opaque statements suggested that she and Smith had sexual intercourse on other occasions. There is some, but not as much, evidence that Smith consummated the marriages to plural wives who already possessed husbands.[22]

Although he did not assemble his wives into a household, coats and hats could not long disguise the prophet's expanding family. Smith surely knew that his marriages would vex his wife Emma, alienate some followers, and ultimately threaten his church's very existence. That he proceeded despite the obvious dangers suggests some combination of theological certitude, megalomania, and an impulsiveness that disregarded future consequences. After the expulsion from Missouri, Smith had maintained the church's policy of gathering, had continued Mormon bloc voting, and had introduced secret organizations and rituals at a time when Americans remained intensely suspicious of such practices. More so than anything else, however, polygamy had the potential to destroy the church from within.

Smith began introducing the doctrine to trusted associates, who termed the principle "celestial marriage," "eternal marriage," the "patriarchal order of marriage," "the new and everlasting covenant of marriage," and "spiritual wifery." A few months after their return from England, Smith discussed plural marriage with several of the apostles. "It tried our minds and feelings," recalled John Taylor. "We saw it was something going to be heavy upon us."[23] While most Mormons reacted negatively when Smith first informed them of the doctrine, the idea of polygamy could not have come as a complete shock. Early Victorian domesticity had not entirely swept the field in the United States. Controversial departures from monogamy included George Rapp's advocacy of celibacy in his Harmonist communities, John Humphrey Noyes's insistence that believers striving for heaven's perfection might abandon marital exclusivity on earth, and the acceptance by some American disciples of the French reformer François Fourier's concept of a "sexual millennium." During his 1836 mission to the Northeast, Young attended a meeting of the Shakers, whose approximately 4,000 adherents gathered in communitarian settlements and practiced celibacy while anticipating an imminent Second Coming. On the other side of the sexuality spectrum, the restorationist Jacob Cochran allowed his married followers in his Saco, Maine, community to take additional "spiritual" spouses. Orson Hyde, the future Mormon apostle, visited a Cochranite community in 1832 and observed their "wonderful lustful spirit, because they believe in a 'plurality of wives' which they call spiritual wives . . . but by the *appearance they know one another after the flesh.*" Young certainly would have heard of the infamous Cochranites when he traveled near Saco during a northeastern mission. Given the curiosity Young evidenced about other religious movements during his travels, Americans' widespread fascination with religiously deviant sexuality, the

Mormons' emphasis on restoring "all things," and rumors about Smith's own sexual practices, Young had surely considered whether God sanctioned something other than monogamy.[24]

Within a few months, Young signaled his acceptance of the new doctrine. In early January 1842, Young officiated at Smith's sealing to the latter's widowed sister-in-law Agnes Coolbrith, a wedding that took place in the upper room of a red brick store owned by Smith. Young cryptically recorded the event in his diary using a Masonic cipher: "J. Smith w[edded] a[nd] s[ealed] Agness." The next month, Young officiated at a second marriage ceremony, the prophet's sealing to Mary Elizabeth Rollins, who was already married to non-Mormon Adam Lightner. Many decades later, Mary Rollins related that Smith informed her that God commanded him back in 1834 "to take me for a wife." Since that seemed impossible, "he got afraid, the angel came to him three times the last time with a drawn sword and threatened his life." Not willing to trust the prophet's word, she needed divine confirmation for herself. "The angel told him," she recounted, "I should have a witness, and an Angel came to me, it went through me like lightning." When Young sealed her to Smith "for time & all eternity," it had little visible impact on her life, for she continued to live with Adam Lightner. By performing two of Smith's marriages, Young had made it clear that he accepted the principle of plural marriage. Polygamy, however, was not meant to be only for the prophet, and Young would soon have to take further steps of obedience.[25]

At some point in early 1842, Smith told him to "go & get another wife." Young recalled that the instruction came in the form of a "command," not a choice. Still, he hesitated. "I felt as if the grave was better for me," he later explained. After discussing the matter with Smith, though, the apostle quickly moved from apprehension to exhilaration. "I was filled with the Holy Ghost," he recalled, "that my wife and Brother Kimball's wife would upbraid me for lightness in those days. I could jump up and hollow [holler], my blood clear as India Rum." Young was "ready to go ahead." Like many others, he followed where his prophet led. No one would marry more women in Nauvoo than Brigham Young. The exact dates of several early polygamous sealings are uncertain, but Young was one of the first men besides Smith to attempt to live out the principle of plural marriage.[26]

Young first proposed to seventeen-year-old Martha Brotherton, a winsome young woman from England who had recently arrived in Illinois with her parents and siblings. Young knew Brotherton from his time in Manchester, where he spent the night at her family's home on two occasions. Young baptized Martha's sister Elizabeth in September 1840, and

Heber Kimball guided Elizabeth toward the gift of speaking in tongues. Young, Woodruff, and Parley Pratt dined with the Brothertons shortly before the apostles sailed for New York. Pratt, editor of the church's *Millennial Star,* praised Thomas Brotherton, Martha's father, as a "man of intelligence, sound judgment, and integrity." The Brothertons emigrated in late 1841 and initially settled in Warsaw, twenty miles from Nauvoo, then moved temporarily to the Mormon capital in March 1842.[27]

Nauvoo soon buzzed with tales of adultery, "spiritual wifery," and apostasy. At the church's annual April conference, Hyrum Smith felt obliged to contradict rumors "about Elders Heber C. Kimball, Brigham Young, himself, and others of the Twelve, alleging that a sister had been shut in a room for several days, and that they had endeavored to induce her to believe in having two wives." The sister in question was Martha Brotherton.[28]

While individuals often responded with disbelief and disgust when church leaders taught them the doctrine of celestial marriage or approached them about becoming plural wives, Brotherton was somewhat unusual in making her disillusionment with the church and its leaders a matter of public scandal. She did so because of John C. Bennett. The mercurial Bennett would lose his church membership in June following allegations of his own sexual indiscretions, and he would soon begin assembling evidence he could use—as one unsympathetic newspaper put it—"to glut his revenge upon the Prophet." Bennett later met with Brotherton in St. Louis, where the young woman and her parents had relocated, and persuaded her to detail her travails in a letter, a notarized copy of which was published in one of the city's newspapers and later included in Bennett's exposé of Mormon polygamy, political power, and sacred rituals.[29]

In the affidavit, Brotherton stated that Young and Kimball persuaded her to meet with Joseph Smith in the upper room above Smith's store, the same room in which Young had officiated at two of Smith's plural weddings and in which he would soon receive his endowment. According to Brotherton, Smith and Kimball left her with Young, who then "arose, locked the door, closed the window, and drew the curtain" before asking her if she would marry him "were it lawful and right." Young then explained the prophet's teaching on the matter: "brother Joseph has had a revelation from God that it is lawful and right for a man to have two wives; for, as it was in the days of Abraham, so it shall be in these last days, and whoever is the first that is willing to take up the cross will receive the greatest blessings; and if you will accept of me, I will take you straight to the celestial kingdom; and if you will have me in this world, I will have you in that which is to come." When Brotherton demurred, Young, after asking for a kiss, went to fetch Smith. According to Brotherton's affidavit, the prophet provided her with glib encouragement: "if you do not like it in a month or two, come to me, and I will make you free again; and if he [Young] turns you off, I will take you on." Young proceeded more cautiously and seriously, asking, "Did you ever see me act in any way wrong in England, Martha?" Brotherton begged for time to consider the proposal. She and her parents soon left Nauvoo, convinced that Smith and his apostles were "deceivers."[30]

After Bennett published Brotherton's affidavit, church leaders and even some members of her own family attacked her character in an attempt to discredit Bennett and restore Smith's reputation. William Smith, the prophet's brother and editor of the Nauvoo *Wasp,* labeled Bennett "the pimp and file leader of such mean harlots as Martha H. Brotherton and her predecessors from old Jezebel, whom the dogs eat." Martha's brother-in-law, John McIlwrick, supported by her sisters Elizabeth and Mary, signed an affidavit testifying that Martha had "stooped to many actions which would be degrading to persons of common decency, such as lying on the top of a young man while he was in bed." Parley Pratt, who had praised Thomas Brotherton's character in February 1842, printed two letters in the British church's *Millennial Star* that incongruously presented Martha's father as a chronic malcontent. Dated before the Brotherton scandal became public, these critiques of Thomas Brotherton are almost certainly later creations. The *Star* further alleged that Martha Brotherton had "conceived the plan of gaining friendship and extraordinary notoriety with the world, or rather with the enemies of truth, by striking a blow at the character of some of its worthiest champions . . . [and] accordingly selected president J. Smith, and elder B. Young for her victims." This rather desperate and vicious smear campaign also targeted several women linked to Smith in Bennett's exposé.[31]

Brotherton's original affidavit does not exist, and Bennett may have altered her claims to suit his purposes. Without his intervention, Brotherton most likely would have disappeared from the historical record. The basic contours of her story, however, are probably true. Brotherton's retelling of Young's theological explanation is a roughly accurate summary of Smith's doctrine of marriage, which promised those who embraced it eternal glory in the celestial kingdom. Moreover, in early 1842 Smith had directed Kimball to marry a British emigrant, and it hardly strains credulity to believe he gave Young similar advice shortly thereafter. In an affidavit of his own, Young did not specifically deny that he proposed marriage to her. Instead, he termed her accusation a "base falsehood, with regard to any private intercourse or unlawful conduct or conversation with me." Unlike Bennett, Brotherton made no attempt to profit from her scandalous exit from the church. She remained in the United States with her parents, suffered an unfortunate marriage to an alcoholic with the surname Purnell, and died in 1864 in Quincy, Illinois, just sixty miles from Nauvoo. Her sister Elizabeth remained faithful to the church and became Parley Pratt's first plural wife in an 1843 ceremony at Young's house.[32]

Undeterred by Brotherton's rejection and the unfolding scandal, on June 14 Young married twenty-year-old Lucy Ann Decker. Smith officiated at the ceremony. At the time she became Young's first plural wife, Lucy Ann Decker was already the wife of William Seeley, whom she had married at around the age of fourteen. Young family lore identifies Seeley as an alcoholic who had abandoned his family, but he was at least still in Nauvoo. Young's account book reveals several transactions with William Seeley in July 1842, during which he paid him a total of $19. Several decades later, Lucy recalled that Joseph Smith had performed the ceremony, with Willard Richards present as the only witness. Presumably her father, Isaac Decker, was aware of the ceremony. Smith married into families with which he had close friendships, and the Young family had known Isaac Decker for many years. Brigham's marriage to Lucy thus strengthened a preexisting bond between the two families. William Seeley probably did not know of or agree to the marriage, unless Young's payments to him represent an attempt to mollify a disgruntled husband. Lucy did not cohabit with Young after the sealing; it is unclear whether she lived with Seeley or with her parents.[33]

It is also uncertain when Mary Ann Young learned of her husband's entrance into plural marriage. Early plural marriages—such as many of Joseph Smith's as well as Heber Kimball's first polygamous sealing—often took place without the consent of first wives. While probably not fully aware of the implications of Smith's emerging theology, when she learned about celestial marriage Mary Ann likely reacted with a combination of displeasure and stoic acceptance. "To say she did not suffer," wrote Charlotte Cobb Godbe in a eulogy of Mary Ann, "when the tenderest chords of her woman's heart were touched, is to say that she was not sensitive, and that no one could say who knew her." Regardless of her initial reaction, Mary Ann quickly signaled her acceptance of the doctrine. Since Smith typically only sealed couples if both parties accepted plural marriage, his May 1843 sealing of Mary Ann to Brigham provides evidence of her acceptance or at least toleration of the practice. On the same date, she served as proxy for Brigham's eternal sealing to his deceased first wife Miriam Works. Mary Ann then further indicated her support in the autumn of 1843 by attending two of Brigham's subsequent sealings.[34]

Young frequently discussed his embrace of polygamy as the simple ac-

Brigham Young,
Mary Ann Angell,
and children, ca.
1845 *(courtesy of
Museum of Church
History and Art, The
Church of Jesus Christ
of Latter-day Saints)*

ceptance of revelatory truth and Joseph Smith's authority. Given that the
sexual morals of many church members resembled those of a seventeenth-
century Puritan or frontier Methodist, the vast majority of polygamous
Mormons embraced plurality not out of lust but through faith and obedience.[35] This does not mean, however, that plural courtships did not involve
sexual attraction, and Young himself acknowledged the presence of attraction and lust. Alluding to the King James Bible's condemnation of lust as
"adultery" in a man's heart, in a November 1847 council meeting Young
allowed that if adultery meant "consenting in his heart to do it if he had
the chance I won't say how often I have been guilty of adultery, but I will
say I never did the act." He resisted temptation. "We brought girls home,"
he related, "after two years mission to England and paid their passage but
did not touch them nor put our arms round them. They married others."
Young probably had been attracted to women on the mission field, quite
possibly including Martha Brotherton. Nor did he have any qualms about
sexual attraction and relations within marriage. Unlike health reformer
Sylvester Graham, who believed that ejaculation sapped male vitality and
health, and unlike the celibate Shakers, Young believed that God created
sexuality for both reproduction and pleasure. "If the Lord did put not the
desire into both men and women," he reasoned pragmatically, "the world
would soon be depopulated." Much like the seventeenth-century Puritans,
the Mormons strictly confined sexuality within marriage but affirmed its
vitality within such confines. Mormon polygamists extended such reasoning to plural unions.[36]

Young's early plural marriage proposals apparently did not disrupt his
own domestic life; however, the spreading practice of polygamy contributed to ecclesiastical turmoil within the church. Several days after Young's
sealing to Lucy Decker, Smith stood before the citizens of Nauvoo and denounced "the iniquity & wickedness of Gen John Cook Bennet."[37] Bennett
had likely joined the church for reasons of self-promotion rather than
faith, and he displayed a similar concern after his excommunication. He
launched a self-aggrandizing campaign to publicize sexual and political
wrongdoing in Nauvoo, which included the publication of an exposé (containing Martha Brotherton's affidavit) and a lecture tour. A bitter series of
accusations and recriminations ensued and opened deep fissures within the
church's top leadership over plural marriage, leaving the prophet temporarily estranged from Sidney Rigdon and Young's fellow apostle Orson
Pratt. The latter apparently contemplated suicide after his wife, Sarah, reported a marriage proposal from Smith. "Br. Orson Pratt is in trubble in
consequence of his wife," Young wrote to Orson's brother Parley, ". . . he

is all but crazy about matters." As did Smith, Young suggested that Sarah Pratt had engaged in adultery with Bennett and then falsely accused Joseph of the same.[38]

Young spent much of the summer and fall attempting to repair those ecclesiastical cracks and rebut Smith's critics within and outside the church. Young and scores of other Mormons loyal to Smith fanned out across the region, denouncing Bennett's allegations. The anti-Bennett campaign marked the beginning of a ten-year effort to deny the doctrine and practice of polygamy. While Nauvoo swirled with rumors and the early days of plural marriage shook the faith of some church members, Young proclaimed himself at peace, entirely unruffled by the scandals and controversies. "I never felt better in my life than I have sence I came home last summer," he wrote Parley Pratt in July. Young saw himself as an anointed high priest who had secured a place in God's celestial kingdom, an apostle devoted to spreading the true gospel, an honorable disciple of Joseph Smith, and a husband of two wives according to divine revelation. He had crossed a Latter-day Rubicon, marrying a second wife and defending Joseph Smith from charges he knew to be true in substance.[39]

Young helped persuade others to make a similar choice, including the prophet's older brother Hyrum, who had succeeded his father as the church's Presiding Patriarch (grantor of patriarchal blessings). Hyrum Smith vigorously rebutted John C. Bennett's allegations of "spiritual wifery." "If an angel from heaven should come and preach such doctrine," Hyrum stated, denouncing polygamy at a May 1843 meeting, "[you] would be sure to see his cloven foot and cloud of blackness over his head." Joseph had not yet introduced his brother to the doctrine of plural marriage, probably because he feared Hyrum would oppose and possibly expose it. William Clayton and Heber Kimball met on May 23 and discussed "a plot that is being laid to entrap the brethren of the secret priesthood by Brother H[yrum] and others." According to Young's later recollection, Hyrum then confronted Young about the doctrine. "I do know that you the Twelve know some things I don't know," he interrogated Young, ". . . is it so?" "I don't know anything about what you know," Young artfully evaded the question, "I know what I know." After Hyrum pressed him on whether Joseph had "a revelation that a man should have more than one wife," Young forced the prophet's brother to "swear with an uplifted hand" never to say another word against plural marriage. "I told him the whole story," Young later explained, "and [he] bowed to it and wept and said, 'God be praised.'" The brothers reconciled forthwith. Within days, Joseph sealed Hyrum to his current wife and his deceased first wife, and

Hyrum married four additional women over the summer. Young was an effective apostle, not only for the church as a whole, but also for its secret priesthood.[40]

Despite his ready consent to plural marriage and his efforts proselytizing for it, Young could not fully escape the vicissitudes and tensions inevitably created by the new doctrine. Though his public loyalty to Smith never diminished in its fervor, even Brigham Young sometimes experienced doubts, if only subconsciously. In particular, he wondered if he would have to make the ultimate sacrifice and allow Mary Ann to be sealed to his prophet. Orson Pratt alleged that Smith had proposed to his wife, and Smith had married Marinda Hyde while her husband, the apostle Orson Hyde, served a mission to Palestine. In early December 1843, Young recorded a curious dream in his diary:

> had a dream thaught I was traveling to the East with my wife in a caredge covrd, it stormed I let the curtins down travel safe along though muddy we turned to come back. Br Joseph Smith sat on the back seat with my wife he whispered to hir said it was wright if she was a mind to nothing more past between them as I drove along the caredge drawd out to be so long I could not see my wife Br J. Smith was on the seat with me I looked back to see my wife but could not Br Joseph said we must goe and get the caredge or part of it that had mary ann in it we got the caredge but saw nothing of mary ann for she was in side and the caredge closed in with curtin and they was Black we was puling it over a Bridg the last I remember.

The latter portion of the dream refers to Mary Ann's death, whereas the beginning appears to include Joseph's proposal of marriage to her. Although Smith never requested that Young relinquish Mary Ann to him, the idea troubled him in his sleep, demonstrating that Young wrestled with his strong love and loyalty to both Smith and Mary Ann. The doctrine of plural marriage imperiled the relationship Brigham and Mary Ann had previously enjoyed.[41]

Moreover, while other followers explicitly sought to link their celestial family to the prophet's, Young did not seek dynastic ties to Smith through his daughters. Young's close friend Heber Kimball offered his fourteen-year-old daughter Helen in marriage to Smith out of his "great desire to be connected with the prophet." Young did not express any such desire. Shortly after Young's sealing to Lucy Decker Seeley, Young's oldest daughter Elizabeth married, and Young moved his daughter Vilate to Boston when she was thirteen.[42]

AFTER a year full of ecclesiastical turmoil over polygamy, Young asked Smith if the apostles should undertake a second mission to England. Instead, Smith dispatched Young to raise money for the temple and the Nauvoo House, a guesthouse then under construction. This time, Young left Mary Ann in much improved circumstances, having moved into a new residence several weeks earlier. As always, he wrote letters to Mary Ann and complained about not receiving epistles from her in return. As was also typical, diseases like scarlet fever and dysentery threatened their children that summer. Mary Ann wrote Brigham that she was "worn down" by listening to their "cries with pain and distress oftimes calling for Father to come and lay hands on them." "The children are all geting better," she reported with relief in an August letter. Sadly, six-year-old Mary Ann, who had been sick with "the canker" (a gangrenous ulcer of the mouth), shortly thereafter became the first of Brigham's children to die before reaching adulthood.[43]

As on Young's 1835 mission, the apostles mostly traveled together, occasionally separating for short preaching assignments or family reunions. They took the opportunity to investigate other religious groups, which they greeted with a mixture of curiosity and derision. En route East, they visited George Rapp's communitarian settlement in Economy, Pennsylvania, remarked on its similarity to "Shakerism" (Rapp's "Harmonists" also encouraged celibacy), and sampled its wine. Young also attended a meeting of the Millerites, a movement led by Deist-turned-Baptist William Miller that anticipated the return of Jesus—based on his reading of biblical prophecy—sometime between March 21, 1843, and March 21, 1844. When the Mormon apostles attended the meeting, the Millerites were at the height of their popularity, which waned after their various predictions of Christ's return proved incorrect. Young sometimes issued bitingly sarcastic critiques of the "sectarians" (i.e., Protestant Christians) of his day. In New York in late August, he opined that "the greatest divine of the day is as ignorant as the dumm ass concerning the things of God."[44]

Despite such dismissals, Young possessed a native religious curiosity. He consulted theological guides from mainstream Christian traditions, such as Buck's popular *Theological Dictionary* and Butterworth's *Concordance*. He listed both on a list of "articles wanted from home," which also included a standard English pronouncing dictionary, his "mason aporn [apron]" (possibly used in prayer circles with other Saints who had received their endowment), and his overcoat. While never a man of erudition, Young studied the Bible, theological guides, and Latter-day Saint texts in an effort to improve himself. Although his spelling never improved and he largely stopped writing his own correspondence after the mid-1840s, he grew increasingly comfortable citing both biblical and *Book of Mormon* passages in his preaching. Young actively sought answers to theological questions that occurred to him. He recorded in his diary a list of "Question[s] to ask Br. J. Smith." Probably reflecting his grief over his daughter Mary Ann's death, concern about "children who die in infinci" topped Young's list. Young also stored up the following diverse queries: "was David a man after gods own hart"; "[What is] the order of ordaining a partriach for the church"; "did you see one of the 3 Nephits in 1840"? The final question referred to a *Book of Mormon* passage in which Jesus promises three faithful Nephite disciples that they will "never taste of death" but instead remain on the earth as his missionaries until his Second Coming. Despite his reputation for down-to-earth pragmatism, Young took an interest in other religious movements, pondered over scriptural passages about patriarchs and angels, and sought more spiritual manna from his prophet.[45]

During his 1843 travels, Young also made time for other diversions. Before leaving Nauvoo, Young had attended a lecture on "animal magnatisem" (or mesmerism), then a popular form of hypnosis that served as a precursor to spiritualism's emphasis on clairvoyant contact with the dead. While in Boston, Young visited the prominent phrenologist Orson Fowler, who examined his head and measured everything from his "amativeness" to his "combativeness." Young scored highest on "grate atachment" and "firmness." Although he later dismissed the phrenologist as "just as nigh being an idiot as a man could be," the fact that Young had undergone a previous phrenological exam in Nauvoo and copied Fowler's reading into his journal suggests that he shared the nationwide fascination with the pseudo-science. As was the case in England, the apostles also made time for tourism. In Pittsburgh, Young visited the "glass works water works iron Boats [and] nale factory." In Philadelphia, he and several others climbed the old State House steeple, sat in the chair used by John Hancock to sign the Declaration of Independence, visited the federal mint, and marveled at "the body of the Mermaid . . . & the Mamouth skeleton" housed in Charles Wilson Peale's museum.[46]

For most of his mission, though, Young raised money for the Nauvoo House by offering a stirring defense of Joseph Smith and a clarion call for the Latter-day Saints to gather to Zion. Wilford Woodruff copiously reconstructed Young's sermons in his journal, the first extended record of his preaching. "[T]he first principle of our cause & work," Young reminded the Pittsburgh Saints, "is to understand that their is a prophet in the Church . . . accountable to God & the Angel that committed the Gospel to him & not to any man on earth." Young also defended the "gifts & graces" of the Holy Ghost, including speaking in tongues, prophecy, and healing. Although Smith and his followers rejected Millerite predictions, the Mormons still believed in an imminent tribulation preceding Christ's millennium. In that light, church members needed to gather to Zion posthaste. "We must build a house," Young exhorted, encapsulating his church's teachings, "& get an endowment & preach the gospel, warn the people, gather the Saints, build up Zion & finish our work & be prepared for the coming of Christ." Young warned that those who ignored the call to gather might taste a "Bitter Cup," and he entreated the Saints to give "all your gold silver & precious things." Heber Kimball allowed that Young "has put the flail on rather heavy." Young, however, explained that his harsh words flowed out of his own devotion to the church. "This work is all," he insisted. "It is my all. If this work does not live God knows I dont want to live." Young's commitment remained steadfast.[47]

That resolute devotion prompted Young to marry additional wives. When Young departed Boston in late September 1843, forty-year-old Augusta Adams Cobb joined his party. Married to the prosperous Henry Cobb, Augusta and Henry's sister Elizabeth had both joined the church in 1832, baptized by the prophet's brother Samuel. Henry rejected the missionaries' message and never joined the church. When Augusta departed Boston with Brigham Young eleven years later, she left behind Henry and most of her children, taking with her only her daughter Charlotte and an infant son. In early October, Young recorded that Augusta's "Babe Died of the consumpsion" in Cincinnati. Augusta "had hir babe put in a tin coffin tooke it with us." A few weeks later, the Nauvoo sexton made an official record of the consumptive death of five-month-old "Brigham Y. Cobb." The choice of names suggests that Young had made a strong impression on Augusta during his northeastern missionary trips.[48]

In all likelihood, that summer Young had taught Augusta the doctrine of plural marriage, prompting her to travel to Nauvoo with the intention of marrying her son's namesake. The principle of celestial marriage gave Augusta a strong theological motivation to exchange a union destined to cease with the grave for one that would secure her future glory and persist for eternity. Brigham and Augusta's marriage, moreover, was born of mutual faith and attraction. She wrote of a "love" that had sprung up rapidly. "Sister Cobb," Young asserted in 1847, "was given me by Revelation but I never did anything till long after she was given until I got the ceremonies performed and all made right." Young's comment makes clear that the relationship included sexual relations after their sealing.[49]

Mary Ann gave her visible assent to Brigham's marriage to Augusta. Perhaps because she agreed to do so, she gained a place in the Anointed Quorum. On November 1, recorded Brigham in his diary, Mary Ann was "admitted into the hiest orderer Preasthood." Freemasons formed lodges strictly restricted to men; Joseph Smith allowed the inclusion of a select number of women, typically those who had signaled their acceptance of plural marriage. The day after her endowment, Mary Ann stood alongside Brigham's sister Fanny as Joseph Smith sealed Brigham to Augusta "for time and all eternity." On the same date, Young wed Harriet Cook, a New York convert just shy of her nineteenth birthday. Young had probably considered a marriage to Cook since at least the previous summer, when he told Mary Ann to "give my love to sister harrit if she is there . . . She is a fine woman." The next spring, he married Lucy Decker's sister Clarissa (Clara), who was two months shy of her sixteenth birthday. By the spring of 1844, Young had four plural wives. Little else is known about the nature of these early plural marriages. Like most other Nauvoo polygamists, Young did not cohabit with his plural wives, apparently did not assume any sort of regular financial support, and had no children by them until 1845.[50]

In early Victorian America, plural marriage's deviation from monogamy was risky, legally and practically. Marrying women who already had husbands was riskier still. William Seeley's apparent abandonment of Lucy Decker mitigated such risk in Young's first plural marriage. Young's sealing to Augusta engendered more notoriety, though. Augusta sought to introduce other women to plural marriage, including Catherine Lewis, who spurned the repeated offers of Heber Kimball and later published an exposé of the temple endowment and plural marriage. Even worse, at a time when Mormon leaders denied the existence of polygamy, Augusta's first husband generated unwanted publicity by suing Augusta for divorce, once unsuccessfully in 1844 and then with success three years later. Both Lewis and George J. Adams, another disaffected Mormon, testified against Augusta at the 1847 divorce proceedings. Probably inaccurately, Adams claimed that Augusta lived with Brigham and Mary Ann, the latter "very much troubled about it." Catherine Lewis corroborated the sexual nature of the marriage with Augusta. Augusta herself later complained that Young had indiscreetly invited her to trysts at Lewis's residence.[51]

In his early adulthood, Young had shown himself to be deliberate and reflective, fiercely independent but not impulsive. Despite his conversion to Mormonism, for the cultural context of the time his life had remained rather conventional, marked by a devotion to church, family, and hard work. His entrance into plural marriage cuts against the grain of his prior behavior. Instead of proceeding carefully, Young proposed to a young British convert and then wedded two married women. Fierce loyalty to Smith and fervent belief helped trump Young's prior caution. His years of increasing ecclesiastical responsibility had also brought expanded self-confidence, leading him to claim the privileges and power that Smith set before him.

The last ritual introduced by Joseph Smith in Nauvoo further enhanced Young's spiritual and ecclesiastical self-confidence. Even after the endowment ceremony, Smith had promised his followers still greater blessings to come. Privy to Smith's intimate theological and ritual thought, Young stated during his 1843 mission that no one in the church possessed the "fulness" of what the Mormons termed the Melchizedek or higher priesthood. "For any person to have the fulness of that priesthood," Young continued, "[he] must be a king and a Priest." Shortly after Mary Ann received her endowment and Brigham's sealings to Augusta Cobb and Harriet Cook, Mary Ann and Brigham attended a prayer meeting at which, Smith's clerk sparsely noted, "B Young [was] anointed and wife." What became known as the "Second Anointing," Smith's final ritual innovation, exalted participants to what Smith termed "the highest and holiest order of the priesthood." Nearly always bestowed on couples, it sealed the bond of those married for eternity with "the Holy Spirit of promise" and ordained a select group of followers as kings and priests and queens and priestesses, exalted godly rulers for eternity. They could now feel fully assured of their salvation and exaltation. After his mid-1820s evangelical conversion, Young had wrestled with spiritual doubt, uncertain whether God or Satan would ultimately claim his soul. For ten years, he had not wavered in his new faith, and he hoped to obtain all of the blessings Smith foreshadowed in his revelations and rituals. Now, Smith assured him that he and Mary Ann would enjoy the fullness of God's promises for eternity. It was a certainty, not a hope.[52]

Through the second anointing, moreover, Smith empowered his closest male followers to "perform all the ordinances of the kingdom of God," sealing others to eternal life and in eternal unions. Only around twenty men and their wives received this privilege before Smith's death. As larger numbers of Nauvoo Mormons received their endowment, Smith and a select inner group received even greater mysteries and became prepared to lead the church with "the fullness of the priesthood" if Smith's premonitions of his early demise proved accurate. Young's inclusion in the ritual signaled that he remained near the center of the prophet's inner circle.[53]

In the meantime, Smith's theology reached its full expression at an April 1844 sermon he preached memorializing his friend King Follett, recently killed in an accident. With Young among the thousands in attendance, Smith discussed his understanding of God, creation, and the eternal destinies of human beings. "What kind of being is God?" Smith asked. "God himself," he then answered, "who sits enthroned in yonder Heavens is a man like unto one of yourselves." Smith explained these teachings on the occasion of Follett's death for a reason. If the Mormons properly understood the common nature of God and humanity, they would have no reason to fear the grave but would instead anticipate an eternal future of glory. God once dwelt on an earth, and human beings if faithful would one day be exalted and godlike. "You have got to learn how to be a God yourself," Smith instructed, "and be a King and Priest to God." God is eternal intelligence, Smith taught, as are human beings—embodied spirits with the ability to become gods by progressing in intelligence and power. God, Jesus, and human beings are, in short, members of the same species, at different stages of development. In a mid-June discourse known as the "Sermon in the Grove," drawing on his interpretation of the Hebrew word *Elohim* (god or gods), Smith forthrightly preached on the "plurality of gods," suggesting that "if Jesus had a Father can we not believe that he had a Father also." The prophet described a council of gods on which the Latter-day Saints could one day take their place, serving a "head God" as kings and priests. On earth, human beings should seek the light, intelligence, and power they might one day exercise as exalted, godlike beings.[54]

The ideas expressed in the King Follett Discourse have often struck non-Mormons as not merely heretical but wildly hubristic for diminishing God's uniqueness and granting human beings a full measure of divine potential. Smith's theology, however, arose in the context of rapidly expanding conceptions of human potential. Calvinism still haunted but no longer shaped much of the American religious landscape. Even one of Calvin's ecclesiastical heirs, the Presbyterian revivalist Charles Finney, preached that "entire sanctification . . . to live without known sin, was a doctrine taught in the Bible." It was still an enormous theological leap from complete sanctification to collapsing the chasm that Protestants believed would always separate human beings from God. Though once hesitant to accept Smith's vision of a three-tiered heaven, Young now enthusiastically embraced new theological ideas. In a letter to his cousin Willard Richards, Young mocked the idea of a "sectarian God, without Body parts or pa[s] sion his center everywhere and cacormfrance [circumference] no where." In much of his own subsequent preaching, Young would articulate what he saw as the implications of Smith's religious cosmology.[55]

WHEN Joseph Smith unveiled his ideas about the commonality of God and humanity in the spring of 1844, he did so amid a backdrop of mounting political and ecclesiastical pressure. Several influential followers were openly opposing Smith because of his accretion of political power, the recent theological developments, and—most decisively—the introduction of plural marriage. The dissenters included William Law, whom Smith had recently selected as one of his two counselors in the church's First Presidency. Moreover, as Nauvoo grew into a thriving if still swampy city rivaling Chicago in size, tensions between Mormons and Gentiles grew. Smith's merger of religious, political, and military power repulsed many who felt threatened by Nauvoo's swelling population, and anti-Mormon committees sprung into existence demanding the Mormons' expulsion or at least the end to their control of Hancock County politics. Whigs in the state legislature led an effort to repeal Nauvoo's charter, now with a large measure of Democratic support. Anti-Mormonism became a rare source of bipartisanship in Illinois, and Smith still faced the threat of extradition to Missouri.[56]

In response, church leaders searched for a way out of this political thicket. Smith began seriously considering moving the church to a new refuge, identifying Oregon, California, and Texas as potential destinations. Meanwhile, after failing to obtain a pledge of protection for the Mormons from any of the politicians presumed to be contenders for the 1844 presidential election, Smith with his trademark audacity launched his own campaign for the White House. "I go emphatically, virtuously and humanely," Smith announced in a mid-April publication, "for a THEODE-MOCRACY, where God and the people hold the power to conduct the affairs of men in righteousness." Both the contemplated exodus and the presidential bid signaled Smith's growing desperation.[57]

Amid growing political threats, in March Smith and trusted associates—including Young—"met in councel . . . a bout 20 to orginise our Selves into a compacked Boddy for the futher advenment of the gospel of Christ." By one of Smith's last revelations, the new council, which included several sympathetic non-Mormons, was titled "the Kingdom of God and his Laws." In theory, the Council of Fifty (as the body was informally known) served as a government-in-waiting for the time when other earthly governments would destroy each other through war and tribulation. More immediately, according to member and council clerk William Clayton, the council possessed several responsibilities: overseeing Smith's presidential campaign; devising the removal of the church to a safer location; restoring "the Ancients [Native Americans] to the Knowledge of the Truth"; and creating "Union and peace amongst ourselves."[58]

Although the Council of Fifty remained a secret organization, Smith's millennial and theocratic vision was not. Smith expected "the entire overthrow of this nation in a few years," and he anticipated a kingdom of Saints arising out of that imminent tribulation. "The whole of America is Zion," the prophet proclaimed in early April, instructing his elders to "build churches where ever the people receive the gospel." While Smith's comment hinted at an end to the doctrine of gathering, Young understood it as a prediction of a glorious and expansive future for the church. Thrilled, he termed Smith's proclamation "a sweepstakes," a further spur to missionary zeal.[59]

Like Smith, Young readily blended temporal and spiritual matters. "We want the Elders," he instructed, "to electioneer for President Smith and we want to build the temple this season." Young also joined in rising Mormon anger against the Illinois and federal governments for their failure to guarantee the Saints' safety from mobs. "[L]et us alone and we will evangelize the world and not make much fuss about it," he said defiantly. "Mob us & we will do it sooner." Non-Mormons in Illinois and dissidents within the church criticized what appeared to be outlandish theocratic aspirations, but in 1844 they were the dreams and succor of an embryonic and threatened kingdom.[60]

Smith pushed ahead with his campaign, in which Young proved a willing political lieutenant. Along with 350 elders, Young left Nauvoo in May for the Northeast, combining his usual duties of preaching and organizing with politicking. Adamantly opposed to both Whig nominee Henry Clay (a "black-leg in politics," according to Smith) and expected Democratic standard bearer Martin Van Buren ("a fop or a fool," Smith had once called him), Smith published a political tract *(General Smith's Views of the Powers and Policy of the Government of the United States)* balancing Whig and Democratic concerns. Young and other elders frequently read the tract aloud and then urged their listeners, primarily members of the church, to cast their ballots for Smith. "[T]he people were well satisfyde," Young wrote Mary Ann about a "political Lector" he delivered in Kirtland, "said they would goe for the Prophet . . . where ever I have spoken on the subject it has taken beyond all my expectation."[61]

Along with several other apostles, Young arrived in Boston for the state convention of what the church called the Jeffersonian Democratic Party. On July 1, Young delivered an evening speech in the Melodeon Theatre promoting his prophet as the best candidate for the presidency. It is jarring to think of Young delivering a political discourse in rarefied Boston, despite his several visits to the city. Young spoke several blocks away from Amory Hall, in which intellectual and abolitionist luminaries (including Emerson, Thoreau, and William Lloyd Garrison) had given a series of lectures that winter and spring on various reform causes. The next winter, ex-Unitarian Theodore Parker drew huge crowds to the Melodeon for Sunday morning sermons. In a city accustomed to intellectual and political agitation, Young's speech nevertheless precipitated a violent response. First, the radical abolitionist Abby Folsom interrupted his remarks, then "young desperadoes" caused a disturbance and brawled with a group of policemen. The meeting came to an early end. "The meeting was broken up," reported the *Boston Evening Transcript*, "with much disorder, and no little confusion, by the interference of interlopers, not of the faithful." Despite the setback, Young planned further political meetings in New England throughout July.[62]

At the time of Young's May departure from Nauvoo, the city was seething with tension and anxiety. Some of the dissidents formed their own church, holding to the *Book of Mormon* and Smith's early revelations but rejecting more recent developments. On June 7, William Law and other now-excommunicated dissenters published the inaugural issue of the *Nauvoo Expositor*, which sought "to explore the vicious principles of Joseph Smith, and those who practice the same abominations and whoredoms." Declaring the *Expositor* a "libellous publication," the prophet ordered the city marshal to destroy the renegade newspaper's printing press, arguing that the dissidents intended to use their paper to stoke anti-Mormon mobs and to further the repeal of Nauvoo's charter. "I was glad when I herd the Nauvoo exspositer was got along with," Young approvingly wrote his cousin Willard Richards from Boston.[63]

Most non-Mormons in Hancock County did not share Young's opinion, and a county constable arrested Smith on charges of rioting. Released by a Nauvoo court, the prophet initially crossed the Mississippi, distressing his abandoned followers. "Some were tryed almost to death," wrote Vilate Kimball, "to think Joseph should abandon them in the hour of danger." Faced with pressure from his followers and Illinois governor Thomas Ford, Smith chose to submit to trial in Carthage, the county seat, while the Nauvoo Legion prepared for battle against mobs which daily grew in number.[64]

In the East, Young heard diverse rumors—"the howlings of Devels," he termed them—about the events in Nauvoo. "Some time the blood is shoe deep in Nauvoo," he joked in a letter to his cousin Willard Richards. "Some times," he continued, "old Jo as they col [call] him is taken by the mob and come to Mo. [Missouri]." "If you are to have a little sport up there," he wrote, expressing his desire to return home soon, "we wish to have a hand in it with you." Young's light-hearted response to Richards attempted to provide some relief from months of rumors and tension, but this time the devils did more than howl. On June 27, vigilantes broke into the Carthage jail and fatally shot Joseph and Hyrum Smith. His body pierced by bullets, the prophet fell from the jail's second-story window. Attempting the Masonic cry of distress, his final words were, "O Lord my God."[65]

WHEN Joseph Smith died, Brigham Young was outside Boston. He first heard rumors of the twin murders on July 9, confirmed in a letter received a week later from Wilford Woodruff. Young sparsely recorded in his journal that he "started for Boston having heard of Bro[ther] J & H Smiths deth." Young and Woodruff spent the morning together. "I here veiled my face and for the first time gave vent to my grief and mourning for the Prophet and Patriarch of the Church," wrote Woodruff, who recorded that he was "bathed by a flood of tears." Young later recalled that although his "head felt so distressed [he] thought it would crack," he did not cry. In front of others, Young avoided emotional displays of mourning.[66]

As had his 1832 conversion to Mormonism, the murder of Joseph Smith decisively altered the future course of Young's life. On the tenth anniversary of Smith's martyrdom, Young said that he could "testify that Joseph is prophet by revelation . . . for I felt him I slept with him I embraced him and kissed him and . . . I ate with him drank with him walked with him handled him." Young loved Joseph as a friend and knew without a doubt that he was God's prophet. He had heard Joseph receive revelations from God and had been there as Joseph unlocked the keys to heaven. "I am [an] apostle of Joseph Smith, Jr., the prophet of God," he emphasized.[67] In twelve years of church membership, Brigham Young had followed Joseph with a stalwart faith that brought him into one of the highest positions in the church. He supported Smith's ill-fated Zion's Camp march and Kirtland Safety Society, embraced the rituals introduced in Nauvoo, and both obediently and fervently imitated Smith's practice of celestial marriage. Under Smith's leadership, Young had gradually developed confidence in his ability to lead others. He could speak with authority, he could preside over sacred rituals, and he could provide financial stewardship for the church. Now, he had to act quickly as a leader in the prophet's absence.

On July 18, Young spoke at a meeting of Mormons in Boston, alongside his fellow apostles Woodruff, Kimball, Orson Pratt, and Orson Hyde. Young did not linger on the events of June 27 or eulogize the fallen prophet. Instead, he looked forward. "Be of good cheer," he told them. "When God sends a man to do a work all the devils in hell cannot kill him untill he gets through with his work," Young said, describing Joseph's mission. "He prepared all things," he concluded, "gave keys to men on the earth and said I may be soon taken from you." For Joseph Smith and Brigham Young, this sealing power formed the heart of their church's mission, a mission that could continue without the church's founding prophet. "Bringing my hand down on my knee," he later recorded, "I said the keys of the kingdom are right here with the Church."[68]

CHAPTER FIVE

Prophets and Pretenders

And many false prophets shall rise, and shall deceive many.
—MATTHEW 24:10–11

QUESTIONS of authenticity were central to antebellum American culture. In a market economy dependent on merchants and banks, Americans struggled to separate genuine currency from "bogus" money, legal title from fraudulent land claims, and creditworthy individuals from confidence men and failures. Antebellum Americans vexed by counterfeit currency also encountered mesmeric healers, skull-studying phrenologists, and spiritualist mediums who claimed a scientific basis for their innovative practices. Thus, it is not surprising that many Americans also debated the genuineness or fraudulency of the prophets and preachers that dotted the religious landscape. Even the adherents of movements with theological affinities sometimes denounced each other as deceitful promoters of nonsense. The Mormons, who claimed to live in the last days, and the Millerites, who predicted Christ's return in 1843 and 1844, regarded each other as preachers of "humbug." Most Protestants lumped Joseph Smith in with other alleged "imposters" ranging from Muhammad to the Shaker founder Ann Lee. Thousands of Americans had accepted Smith's prophetic claims, but even many of these converts later wondered whether he had become a "fallen" prophet.[1]

The Latter-day Saints struggled keenly with such questions, especially after Smith's death, when they needed to choose their next leader. Who was their prophet's true successor, and who were the counterfeits, those the Bible termed "ravening wolves"? Brigham Young convinced most of

Nauvoo's Mormons to accept the Twelve Apostles as the collective leaders of the church. As the Twelve's head, Young quickly became the church's de facto president. He assumed leadership of a church that had been divided before Smith's death, most bitterly over the founding prophet's introduction of polygamy. Young intended to carry out the full extent of Smith's vision, which included completing the Nauvoo Temple, expanding the practice of plural marriage, and establishing a politically autonomous Kingdom of God on earth. Inevitably, that course of action bred opposition within and beyond the church. Disillusioned Mormons and vanquished prophetic competitors saw Young and the apostles as deceivers, men who usurped others' rightful authority. Meanwhile, the apostles, Mormon dissidents, and anti-Mormons in western Illinois all traded accusations about counterfeiting rings in Nauvoo. Young would never convince most Americans to support his religious claims, let alone his political and economic pretensions, but he needed to convince those Latter-day Saints inclined toward the totality of Joseph Smith's prophetic legacy to follow him. To that end, Young needed to complete the temple, usher church members through the promised ceremonies, and then lead them from Nauvoo to a haven safe from their enemies. He had very little time to prove himself a worthy successor.

While Young and his fellow apostles traveled back to Nauvoo from their political mission to the Northeast, others moved to fill the ecclesiastical power vacuum. Young observed the next month that "now Joseph is gon it seamd as though menny wanted to draw off a party and be leders." Samuel Smith, the prophet's younger brother, briefly emerged as a possible successor but died of unknown causes within several weeks. Although William Smith, another brother of the prophet, later accused Young and Willard Richards of poisoning Samuel, the absent Young had been in no position to orchestrate assassinations.[2]

Sidney Rigdon, the only surviving member of the church's presidency, arrived in Nauvoo in early August. Formerly the church's foremost orator, Rigdon had spent most of the past several years outside of Smith's inner circle. He had moved to preside over a branch of the church in Pittsburgh shortly before Smith's murder. Rigdon was opposed to the introduction of plural marriage, and he had not received the second anointing. Nevertheless, Rigdon with great spirit addressed a Sunday congregation, delivering "a message that the church must choose a guardian," and presenting himself for that role. Nauvoo High Council president William Marks, who favored Rigdon's ascension, scheduled an August 8 conference for the church to choose its new leader. Rigdon wanted the matter settled quickly, in the absence of Young and several other leading members of the Twelve.[3]

On the evening of August 6, though, Young and his companions reached Nauvoo and met with Rigdon and Marks the next day. At stake was the totality of Smith's ritual legacy, including the endowment ceremony and plural marriage. Rigdon informed the group that a vision had ordered him to come from Pittsburgh to Nauvoo. "Joseph sustained the same relation to this church as he has always done," Rigdon asserted. "[N]o man can be the successor of Joseph." Rigdon vaguely promised to remain Joseph's "spokesman," the church's guardian. Young was unimpressed. He averred that he did "not care who leads the Church, even though it were [Shaker leader] 'Ann Lee,'" but he needed to know God's choice. Furthermore, he claimed the power of revelation to settle the matter because Joseph had given the apostles "all the keys and powers." The apostles, not Rigdon, had received "the fulness of the Priesthood," the "second anointing" Smith had introduced in 1843. Therefore, only they could ordain others into that "fulness." The apostles promised spiritual blessings, power, and assurance through the long-promised temple rites.[4]

During the morning of the August 8 conference, Rigdon spent two hours making his case. Then Young took the stand in the afternoon and delivered one of the more remarkable speeches in Mormon history, using emotion, derision, and the promise of temple rituals to brush aside Rigdon's claims. Mocking Rigdon's offer to serve as Joseph's spokesman, Young asked the crowd, "Do you want the Church organized or do you want a Spokesman, Cook, and Bottle Washer?" Young ultimately appealed not to any of Smith's revelations or instructions but to the ritual authority the apostles would provide and Rigdon could not. "The keys of the Kingdom are in them," he said of the Twelve, "and you cant pluck it out." "We have a organization that you have not seen," alluding to those select men endowed under Joseph Smith and brought into his intimate inner circle. Under Young's leadership, the Mormons would build the Nauvoo Temple, and if enemies forced them to abandon Nauvoo, he would preside over the endowment in the wilderness. Their salvation and celestial glory hung in the balance, he told the crowd. "We have all the signs and the tokens to give to the Porter [of heaven] and he will let us in," Young assured the church. After he spoke, the Saints with near unanimity voted for the Twelve to lead the church, electing to support the priesthood, the temple, the endowment, the apostles, and—implicitly—Brigham Young.[5]

Retrospectively, many church members claimed that when Young spoke from the stand that day, they saw and heard Joseph Smith. "It was the voice of Joseph himself," George Q. Cannon, a future apostle and counselor to Young, recalled—a miraculous transfiguration. "[A]nd not only was it the voice of Joseph which was heard; but it seemed in the eyes of the people as though it was the very person of Joseph which stood before them." No one would have normally mistaken Brigham Young for Joseph Smith. Josiah Quincy Jr., son of Harvard College's president and future mayor of Boston, described Smith in May 1844 as "a hearty, athletic fellow, with blue eyes standing prominently out upon his light complexion, a long nose, and a retreating forehead . . . *a fine-looking man.*" Young, by contrast, was shorter, barrel-chested, now over forty years of age but still possessing a full head of sandy-red hair. Young lacked Smith's touch for the flamboyant, still clothing himself rather somberly if with more distinction than in his early missionary years. Smith, while sometimes lapsing into frontier vernacular, could also employ soaring rhetoric to match the heavenly mysteries he described. Young's speech was simpler, more forceful, often humorous, and sometimes coarse. In part because of their obvious differences in physique and oratory, the stories of Young seeming like Joseph in appearance and speech gained resonance. Whether or not they experienced something miraculous in the meeting, for some Mormons their sense of Young as Joseph's successor grew quickly. Alluding to the Israelite prophet Elijah having given his mantle (cloak) to his intended successor Elisha, Smith's former scribe William Clayton informed Woodruff in early October that "if you was here you would see the manlte [mantle] of the prophet on brother Brigham very plain."[6]

Forty-eight hours after returning to Nauvoo, Young had engineered the Twelve's ascendance. Technically, Young did not form a new church presidency—in Mormon ecclesiology, a president with typically two counselors. Young, however, unofficially assumed that role, with his old friend Heber Kimball and cousin Willard Richards as his most trusted associates. A few days after the August 8 conference, the apostles chose Young, Kimball, and Richards to superintend the church in North America "and manage the general affairs of the church," and Young sometimes signed letters as "President of the Church of Jesus Christ of Latter Day Saints."[7]

Although Young's preeminence became clear, he trod carefully as a new leader, expressing his love for Joseph Smith and affirming his teachings. Attaching themselves to Smith's legacy, the apostles intended to complete the temple, maintain the city's large measure of political autonomy, and further the institution of plural marriage. Young and his ecclesiastical allies voted in late August "to carrey out all Joseph's vues in all things." Young remained intensely devoted to his prophet. "Elder B Young and myself went and saw Joseph and Hyrum," Kimball wrote in his diary on February 1, 1845, apparently referring to a visit to the Smiths' burial site and an exhumation of their corpses. The coffins had been buried under-neath the under-construction Nauvoo House. Sometime during the winter of 1844–45, Emma Smith arranged for the remains to be moved to a loca-tion she kept secret from nearly everyone. Young may have seen the corpse of his beloved prophet just before it became inaccessible to him. "I saw his body since his death and saw where the bullets pierced him . . . and Brother Hyrum," Young stated on the tenth anniversary of the murders. Young's fealty to Smith was both true to his relationship with Joseph and responsive to the large majority of Mormons who revered their martyred leader. Wisely, though, Young made no attempt to baldly imitate Joseph. "I never pretended to be Joseph Smith," he commented a few years later. "I'm not the man that brought [forth] the *Book of Mormon*." Smith had translated ancient scriptures and dictated revelations; Young never pro-duced a work of scripture and generally eschewed written revelation.[8]

While not presenting himself as a revelator in Smith's image, Young needed to reassure the Saints that Joseph's death had not silenced God's voice and that the Twelve now served as a source of divine authority and knowledge. The August 8 conference had not truly settled the issue of suc-cession. Sidney Rigdon lingered in Nauvoo and began criticizing Smith's later innovations. He threatened to "come out tell all about the secrits of the Church." "He [Rigdon] likewise taught them," William Clayton in-formed Wilford Woodruff, "that Joseph was fallen and that the Twelve were corrupt and wicked, engaged in Bogus making and adultery." In short, Rigdon considered the Twelve a cabal of counterfeit prophets. The apostles responded by convening a public excommunication trial on Sep-tember 8. Young dismissed Rigdon's allegations. "I wonder who is here," he said, "who has seen me make bogus money or any of my brethren the twelve passing Counterfeit money." Getting to the heart of the matter, Young defended his own revelatory authority, even above Joseph Smith's recorded revelations. "[I]f this people have no evidence but the written word," he insisted, "it is quite time to go to the river and be baptised for the remission of their sins." Young possessed a secret, higher authority, "keys that the written word never spoke of, nor never will." Rigdon lost his church membership, returned to Pittsburgh, and formed a church that dwindled into a tiny splinter movement.[9]

Rigdon was vanquished, but Young faced other threats to his leader-ship. After the twin martyrdoms and Samuel Smith's death, Young's rela-tions with members of the Smith family remained prickly. The apostles and Emma Smith approached the settlement of the late prophet's estate with mutual suspicion, exacerbated by the difficulty of separating Joseph Smith's personal property from what he held title to as trustee-in-trust for the church. Even before such conflicts, however, Emma disliked Brigham because of his support for her late husband's practice of polygamy. Back in February 1844, William Clayton, friends with both Joseph and Emma, recorded that "Emma talked a good deal about B[righam] Young and others," almost certainly a reference to supporters of the plural marriage doctrine. After Young's August 1844 return to Nauvoo, he did not meet with Emma. "I cannot say much a bout the famelies of Brs. J. and H. Smith for I have not had time to caul on them yet," Young wrote his daughter Vilate shortly after his return. He finally visited Lucy Mack Smith (Joseph's mother) and Hyrum Smith's widow in mid-September but still apparently made no attempt to mend fences with Emma. Occupied primarily with the task of providing for her family, Emma did not actively oppose the Twelve's ascension. The issue of plural marriage, however, precluded any possibility of ecclesiastical fealty to Young and the apostles.[10]

Despite the rift with Emma, Young expended considerable effort to remain on good terms with other members of the Smith family. He knew that many Mormons venerated both Emma and Lucy Mack Smith. In August 1845, Young learned of the latter's disaffection when he began to use a new carriage that Lucy Smith claimed had been promised her. Departing from his now customary use of clerks for his correspondence, he hand-wrote her an apologetic letter, addressing her as "my mother in the gospel." He sent the carriage that evening.[11]

Young also accepted the unique place of Smith men in the church's hierarchy. "If Hyrum had lived he would have acted for Joseph," said Young at an October 1844 church conference.[12] Previously, he had emphasized that "right of the Patriarchal Blessings belongs to Joseph's family." In this vein, the Twelve ordained Joseph's only remaining brother, William, as the church's Patriarch. They did so despite significant misgivings. One of the church's original apostles, William Smith had refused to join the Twelve's mission to Great Britain in 1839, and more recently he had performed plural marriages without authorization. Since the apostles dearly wanted to keep at least one prominent member of the Smith family in their camp, they overlooked such transgressions. Almost immediately after William's ordination, however, Young heard that he "has been throwing out hints all the time, that the presidency belonged to him." During one conflict with Young, William Smith threatened to destroy the Twelve's legitimacy by moving all members of his family away from Nauvoo. William questioned the legitimacy of the Twelve as anything more than ecclesiastical custodians until a rightful member of the Smith family emerged to preside over the church, and he predicted that "Josephs oldest son will take his place when he arrives to the age of a maturity." At the time of Joseph Smith's death, his son Joseph III was only eleven. Another son, David, was born in November 1844. The potentially divisive issue of lineal succession awaited the boys' maturity.[13]

The breach between William Smith and the Twelve proved irreparable. In August 1845, Young complained in his journal that he found William Smith "preaching a spiritual wife sermon" at a Sunday meeting. The *Warsaw Signal* reported Smith's assertion that "the spiritual wife system was taught in Nauvoo secretly . . . [and that] it was a common thing among the leaders." Such revelations embarrassed the Twelve, who still publicly denied the practice of plural marriage. Despite Smith's indiscretion, the apostles tried to reconcile with him. They visited him to pray for his sick son and commiserate about a wife who had left him because of his recent marriages. In the end, though, the Twelve could not tolerate William Smith's erratic behavior and intermittent chafing against their leadership. Believing that Young threatened his life, Smith left Nauvoo in September and was excommunicated.[14]

An unexpected but more serious challenge to Young's leadership arose from a recent convert to the church. A thirty-one-year-old lawyer and visionary named James Strang claimed to have a letter from Joseph Smith, dated nine days before his murder, appointing him the church's next leader and instructing him to gather the church to southeastern Wisconsin. After founding a community he named Voree, Strang wrote the Nauvoo Mormons to inform them of his claims. The apostles, gathered at Young's house in late August 1844, read the letter and promptly excommunicated the upstart prophet, who proceeded to issue revelations and produced a set of buried ancient plates that served as the basis for his own effort at supernatural translation.

Young dismissed "Strangism" as "not worth the Skin of a Flea," but for a time James Strang was a viable prophetic competitor. As the "Brighamites" struggled with mobs, sickness, and poverty in Nauvoo, some Latter-day Saints saw Voree as a refuge from their troubles. Strang forthrightly claimed to be Joseph's successor; his plates, revelations, and visions provided some Mormons with a different sort of continuity than Young offered. Moreover, Strang at first rejected polygamy and thus attracted Mormons opposed to the practice. As his church grew, Strang drew a number of high-profile converts to his cause, including the *Book of Mormon* witness Martin Harris; the former apostles William Smith (and possibly Lucy Mack Smith), William McLellin, and John E. Page; and the former Nauvoo Stake president William Marks. Isaac Haight, a Mormon who followed Brigham Young to Utah, commented early in 1846 that "many are turning away from the church and from the Twelve apostles to follow a new Prophet." Strang gathered approximately five hundred Mormons to Voree and earned the sympathy of many more on an 1846 preaching mission in the East, a significant movement within a church of perhaps thirty thousand adherents worldwide.[15]

After initially posing a strong threat to Young's leadership, Strangism unraveled from within. Strang chose unreliable and disreputable men like John C. Bennett for some top positions, and he eventually embraced polygamy himself, disappointing many of his followers. Meanwhile, Young's success in leading his followers to their mountain refuge undercut the appeal of Strang, who moved his fledgling and fractious church to Lake Michigan's Beaver Island in 1847. Imitating Smith in death as well as in life, Strang was murdered in 1856 by two disgruntled former members of his church.

Young's refusal to emulate Joseph Smith left a door open for James Strang, but Young provided the church with other forms of sorely needed spiritual leadership. Continuing a practice begun by Smith, he presided over the Anointed Quorum's prayer circles, the sacred and secret gatherings of those who had received their endowment, were loyal to the apostles, and were dedicated to Smith's ritual innovations. At prayer circle gatherings, they dressed in their sacred robes, "offered up the signs & tokens of the Holy Priesthood," prayed together, and discussed the challenges facing the church. Young and his closest allies beseeched God for the sick, pled for divine deliverance from anti-Mormon mobs, plotted strategy, and occasionally added trusted church members to their ranks. More prosaically, the quorum repeatedly prayed for rain and a correspondingly more bountiful harvest in 1845. Young considered these secret convocations essential for the church's welfare. The quorum sometimes met, Young later explained, "every day and in the hottest part of it twice a day to offer up the signs and pray to our heavenly father to deliver his people and this is the cord which has bound this people together." For Young, these sacred prayer meetings provided a private spiritual shelter from the cacophony of dissenters and the responsibilities of leadership.[16]

Publicly, Young continued to provide the sort of priestly leadership he had exercised after his return from England. Such actions took on added significance given his new status in the church. After a brief period of reflection, Young renewed "liberty to Baptize the saints for there dead relitives." As an apostle, Young had prayed with the sick and occasionally anointed them for healing. Now, large numbers looked to him to exercise such apostolic gifts. "[I] laid hands on several sick," he wrote about a visit to the not-yet-completed temple, "which I do daily and thereby keep my self nearly sick." At a December meeting, John Taylor dedicated a newly composed hymn to Brigham Young. Titled "The Seer," the lyrics praised Joseph Smith's restoration of the priesthood and envisioned him pleading the cause of the Saints among the gods in heaven. A few days later, Heber Kimball prayed at another church meeting that God would "Preserve our President & his wife for we must receave our endument through them." The Mormons had expected Joseph and Emma Smith to lead couples through the sacred ordinances of the temple. Now, it would be Brigham Young. While the Saints would never call Smith's successor "Brigham the Seer," he would become his people's chief priest.[17]

IN SOME respects, gaining leadership of the church proved more a burden than a prize for Brigham Young. At times, he relished the exercise of power. For a man who grew up worrying about food and clothing, Young no doubt enjoyed the material benefits of leadership. Still, the Latter-day Saints never adored Brigham Young to the extent they had his predecessor, and Young—alternately social and sullen—did not crave their company and affection to the extent Joseph had. Moreover, Young assumed leadership of a church besieged by political and military enemies and divided internally, a situation fraught with near-constant tension. Guards stood outside Young's house at night and protected him by day from rumored assassins. Losing much of his autonomy and privacy, Young complained of exhaustion, fatigue, and sickness. "I want rest," he said in July 1845 when explaining his refusal to address a meeting. "I am Teaching exhorting Preaching Praying and laying on hands and counseling the whole church all the day long." He rarely shared his most difficult interior struggles, though. "I keep my trials, my troubles and my own feelings to myself," he commented a few years later. "[I] go away, I just go alone, I fight myself and let no one know." Young had several close associates with whom he discussed matters of church business, but many of his own difficulties he unburdened to no one.[18]

Not surprisingly given the events of 1844, many Mormons considered abandoning Nauvoo. Given Young's later reputation as the Mormon Moses, it is noteworthy that he spent much of the next year persuading his flock to stay in their current Zion. Apostle Lyman Wight led a group of Mormon settlers to Texas, once contemplated by Joseph Smith as a potential refuge for the church. Young warned any Mormons considering leaving that "they [Wight and others who led parties away from Nauvoo] Cannot give an endowment in the wilderness." "Dont scatter," he told his flock, ". . . stay here. Sow plant build, put your plow share into the prairies." Young pondered future gathering places, but in the meantime he insisted that "Nauvoo will be the head stake for the Saints to come to and receive their endowment, their anointings, washings, etc., in the house of the Lord." Young himself sometimes needed reassurance from God about completing the all-important task. In January 1845, he, Kimball, and Bishop Newell Whitney spent an afternoon together. They washed and anointed each other before praying. "I inquaired of the Lord whether we should stay here and finish the temple," he wrote in his diary. "[T]he ansure was we should."[19]

Whether the Latter-day Saints could build the temple depended in large part on the activities of anti-Mormon mobs and the church's relationship with several politicians sympathetic to their plight but uncertain in their commitment to protect the church from violence. Young knew that the blood of the Smith brothers had not staunched the flow of anti-Mormon vitriol or calls for the Saints' expulsion. "[E]ither the old citizens or the Mormons must leave," insisted Thomas Sharp, the leading anti-Mormon propagandist, two days after the murders. "The county cannot be quieted until the expulsion of one or the other is effected." Governor Ford, whom Young sometimes blamed for Joseph and Hyrum's deaths, publicly pledged to protect the Mormons from further violence. Privately, however, Ford admitted his impotence to Mormon leaders, reminding them of the recent Philadelphia "Bible Riots" against Catholic immigrants and their churches, during which militia companies often sympathized with the nativist mobs they were ordered to restrain. "I am positively certain," he warned them in late July, "that I cannot raise a militia force in the State who would be willing to fight on your side; or to hazzard their lives to protect you from an attack of your enemies." Nor would Ford employ the Mormons' own "hated legion against old citizens," warning that such a display of ecclesiastical militarism risked the city "being utterly destroyed." Ultimately, the Mormons could expect no protection, because "cases like the present do not seem to be fully provided for by our constitutions." The people, not Governor Ford, ruled western Illinois. Thus, Ford's public promises were merely a governmental bluff, though he was at least kind enough to offer the church fair warning. The Mormons were on their own.[20]

Young vowed to protect the church and himself from mobs and unreliable Gentile governments. "Brigham Young," wrote Sarah Scott of Young's August 8, 1844 speech, "said that if he had been here, he wouldn't have consented to give Joseph up and he would be damned if he would give himself up to the law of the land. He would see them all in hell first." In addition to critiquing Joseph's course, such statements implicitly criticized Emma Smith and others who had encouraged Joseph to return across the river and face arrest. Young had no intention of becoming another sacrifi-

cial lamb. In September, Young noted in his journal that he had nearly
$500 on hand to "send for guns." When Young and several others left
Nauvoo on a short trip in October, one night they "got up loded our firelocks" when an alarm was sounded. Catherine Lewis, before leaving the
church over the issue of polygamy, traveled to Nauvoo in 1845 and observed Young with "a pistol in each side pocket." Joseph Fielding confirmed that "you may see the 12 &c wherever they go with six shooter
Pistols, in their Pockets."[21]

Although Governor Ford criticized "the arming and drilling of your
people, with such exceeding industry," Young had no intention of dis-
banding the Nauvoo Legion or curtailing its preparations. After their expulsion from Missouri and the murder of their prophet, the Mormons regarded the Legion as a necessary response to long-standing anti-Mormon
violence and, quite reasonably given Ford's private communications, their
only source of reliable protection from the mobs. In late August 1844,
Young filled another of Joseph Smith's former offices when the militia
elected him as its next "Lieutenant General." The next month Young
"appeared on the parade ground as Lieutenant General and reviewed the
Nauvoo Legion" with Governor Ford in the audience. Ford had come to
Nauvoo to intimidate anti-Mormons who had circulated news of an impending "wolf hunt" targeting the Saints. Ford's bluff worked this time,
and the anti-Mormons relented.[22]

While a tenuous peace prevailed in Hancock County, the Illinois legislature in late January 1845 repealed Nauvoo's charter. Legally, the charter's
revocation meant the loss of Nauvoo's government, including its militia,
courts, police, and city council. In particular, the Mormons had relied on
Nauvoo's courts to protect them from lawsuits and arrests at the hands
of non-Mormons. Young responded defiantly, sharpening the millennial,
theocratic rhetoric Joseph Smith had employed in the spring of 1844.
"This nation is doomed to destruction," Young declared a few days later,
pointing to Smith's prophecy "that the North & South States will be dissolved." In the meantime, Ford's lukewarm support and the legislature's
hostility meant that the Mormons could rely only on themselves. "The nation has severed us from them in every respect," Young announced, "and
made us a distinct nation just as much as the Lamanites." Like the Indians,
Young suggested, they would get no assistance from American courts and
governments and might be forced to withdraw beyond their jurisdiction.[23]

One portion of Young's response to the charter's revocation involved the
resuscitation of the Council of Fifty, which its members sometimes called
the "living constitution." The latter term suggested the governance of the
church by ongoing revelation rather than by any written set of scriptures

or laws. This body met in early February and elected Young its "standing chairman." Resuming its primary task from the previous spring, the council organized scouting parties to find a place of refuge for the church, still unsure if that new home would be northern Texas or west of the Rocky Mountains in disputed Oregon, Mexican California, or Vancouver Island.[24]

Even before the charter's loss eliminated the legal basis for the city's police force, Nauvoo possessed a reputation for lawlessness and criminality. "[W]e are no longer bound to harbor black legs, Counterfieters, boges makers," Young stated in mid-August 1844. "We know all about them." Church leaders and their opponents both agreed that criminals, including counterfeiters, operated in Nauvoo, but the church rejected anti-Mormon accusations that it sheltered criminals and authorized stealing from non-Mormons. Apostle Orson Hyde warned Young of serious consequences for the church if he did not adopt "some efficient measures to break up a company of bogus makers and route them from this place and also to check stealing and pilfering." Thomas Sharp's *Warsaw Signal,* which had alleged that "Joe Smith" masterminded the circulation of "Nauvoo Bogus," now charged that farmers selling pork in Nauvoo received "spurious coin" as payment. In response, Young blamed anti-Mormon opponents seeking to discredit the Saints. "If they want a method to detect them [the thieves]," he suggested a simple means of settling the question: "give them a ball of lead it would show who were the theives, Mormons or Anti-Mormons."[25]

Partly to fill the civic vacuum created by the charter's revocation, church leaders organized Mormon men into quorums of deacons, charged with the tasks of caring for Nauvoo's poor and maintaining order on the streets. Despite its lack of legal standing, the "old police" force headed by Hosea Stout also remained active, especially in guarding the city against anti-Mormon threats. While Young expressed concerns about criminality, he was most anxious about the threat that both non-Mormons and dissenters posed to the community's unity and security. "[A]n internal inflamation is worse than an external inflamation," he taught, and he proposed solutions to extinguish internal threats. "I intend to get up a whistling school," he announced in March 1845, "and whistle the poor men away." Beginning around this time, groups of young men—known as whittling and whistling companies—conducted surveillance on visitors and other persons considered undesirable, whistled at them, and brandished sticks and knives until they left. Young dared anyone to oppose such tactics. "Every body that hates that go and tattle," he scoffed. "Go it, ye cripples, wooden legs are cheap," he added, meaning that critics would be wasting their effort. Some parties in Nauvoo took the hint. Young noted that "Brother [William] Marks has gone without being whistled out." While Young intended the extralegal harassment as a relatively nonviolent means of removing both crime and unwanted individuals, the *Warsaw Signal* published ominous reports of church-sanctioned violence.[26]

There were more serious instances of vigilantism as well. In early April, according to Hosea Stout, the "Old Police" "beat a man almost to death in the Temple." When Stout discussed the matter with Young, he learned that "he [Young] approved of the proceedings of the Police." The following January Stout nearly killed a suspected spy lingering near the temple by striking him on the head with a stone. Young's approval of violence and vigilantism summoned memories of the Danite vigilantes in Missouri and created an atmosphere in which outsiders and dissenters felt endangered among the Mormons. For his part, Young found allegations of lawlessness in Nauvoo absurdly hypocritical, especially after a non-Mormon jury in Carthage acquitted five men (including Thomas Sharp) of the murders of Joseph and Hyrum Smith. "[I]t would be a new thing under the sun," Young scoffed, anticipating the outcome during the trial, "for Satans Kingdom to bring to justice a man who has murdered a prophet of God." Mormons, fearing for their lives, decided not to testify at the trial; in fact, Young and other top leaders went into hiding to avoid receiving writs summoning them to Carthage. Moreover, throughout much of 1845 Young and others of the Twelve kept "close within doors," fearing attacks from either "Rigdonites" or anti-Mormon vigilantes. Rather than paying obeisance to a legal system that protected anti-Mormon murderers, Young looked forward to the establishment of what he termed "the Celestial law," the imposition of biblical standards of morality by a theocratic church free from entanglement with outside governments.[27]

Amid the challenges of the charter revocation, the ongoing threat of mob violence, and issues of criminality and vigilantism in Nauvoo, Young sought to encourage the beleaguered Saints. If only they would remain united, they would experience unprecedented blessings. "[W]hen we become sufficiently united our enemies would have no more power," Zina Huntington Jacobs recorded a Young sermon in November 1844. ". . . Union will cause the Menlenean [millennium]." Young preached even more hopeful messages the next spring. "Zion is right here," he preached at the church's April 1845 conference. "The millenium has commenced." Statements of millennial hope and promises of future blessings helped the church endure a bleak present. Although the threat of mobbing died down over the winter, the Mormons had reaped a poor harvest the previous fall and now faced mounting poverty and even hunger as spring approached.

Repeatedly, Young sought to bolster their flagging spirits through his words, encouraging them that if they exerted themselves and pooled their money and resources, Nauvoo would "be a fruitful field—like the garden of Eden." The Latter-day Saints, he prophesied, would one day enjoy the peace, rest, and beauty that had thus far eluded them in Nauvoo.[28]

In the meantime, Young maintained his focus on the temple's completion. Through 1845, he regularly visited the temple, offering advice to the many workmen building the walls, roof, tower, and dome. In order to hurry the work, Young called the church's missionaries home to Nauvoo. "We have travelled and preached to them enough," Young said, as he announced an end to missionary work among the Gentiles. "Let the elders stay at home and finish the Temple and get their endowment." Baptisms for the dead and marriage sealings had proceeded intermittently after Smith's death. Young insisted, however, that the Mormons needed to complete the temple to receive their endowments. In May, the Twelve laid the southeast temple capstone. At the ensuing celebration, Mary Ann Young brought a bottle of wine, Brigham raised a toast, and the company cheered. With the temple's structure completed by August, the workers turned their attention to finishing the interior rooms for the promised ordinances.[29]

Despite Young's expressions of millennial hope, the workers were rushing to finish a temple their leaders knew they would probably abandon. Young hesitated to leave what the Saints had rechristened "the city of Joseph." It was hard to stomach the thought of the church's enemies once more forcibly depriving the church of its property and prosperity. "[Y]ou cannot be driven," he insisted, "have your firelocks clean, be ready at a moments warning, to slaughter all that come." "[I]f we leave," he said, holding the door open, "we go of ourselves." While Young and the Twelve considered the church's future, scouts sent west returned in July talking of buffalo herds and mostly friendly Indians, fueling romantic conceptions of a virgin West. "I think those buffalo droves must be a grand sight," waxed Young. By this point, Young believed the church's future home would lie in "Upper California,"—as of 1845 a huge swath of Mexican-claimed territory that included present-day California, Arizona, Nevada, and Utah. At the end of August, the quorum of the anointed voted that three thousand men with their families would go to California the next spring to select the church's future home. Rather audaciously, the quorum "voted that Brigham Young be next Gov[ernor] of Cal[iforni]a and Heber C. Kimball vice Gov[ernor]." In August, Joseph Smith appeared to Young in a dream. "[B]rother Brigham," he told Young, "don't be in a hurry." Young knew the Saints would leave; perhaps the dream strengthened his faith that they could remain until they completed their work in Nauvoo. Young envisioned an orderly, voluntary departure from the City of Joseph sometime after he had presided over the promised rituals.[30]

Despite such hopes, the Saints did not leave on their own timetable. Shortly after church-backed candidates obtained tremendous margins in August 1845 elections, mobs began burning Mormon homes in Morley's Settlement, located in the southwestern part of the county. Newly elected county sheriff Jacob Backenstos, a sympathetic non-Mormon whom the *Warsaw Signal*'s editor Thomas Sharp labeled a "despicable puppy," asked Young to allow the organization of Mormon men into state militia companies. Young angrily demurred. "I should feel myself more degraded in the eyes of the Lord," he jeered, "to be acting under a commission from Gov[ernor] Ford, than I should be to be changed into an affrican." Young often blamed Ford for the deaths of the Smith brothers; he did not see him as a fair mediator between Nauvoo and its enemies. Young believed the Saints had no choice but to solve their problems on their own.[31]

The day the house burnings commenced, Young dreamed of being chased by a mob into a barn. "One [member of the mob] followed me so close that he fell into the same room." Young saw that "it was Tom Ford about 2½ feet high." Fighting back, he continued, "I took his wrists between my fingers & stepped to the door to the mob. & knocked down one after another when I discovered Tom Ford was dead." Young, who dreamed of vengeance, chose instead to evacuate settlements under attack, mobilizing the Saints to provide their brethren with shelter in Nauvoo. "We (the Twelve)," recorded John Taylor, "held a council and thought it advisable as we were going West in the Spring to keep all things as quiet as possible and not resent anything." Righteous anger aside, it was better to give some ground now given the church's contemplated exodus.[32]

Evacuating the burning settlements, however, did not quell the mobs' desire to expel all of Hancock County's Latter-day Saints. Young received word from mob leader Levi Williams "that if we would agree to leave in the spring we might live in peace during the winter." Young vacillated, piqued by the unjust nature of the offer. He did not like the idea of entirely capitulating to the mob. At a council, Young initially "proposed to send a company to . . . surround Williams & company & destroy him, root & branch." When others objected, Young then proposed accepting the deal. However, when the church printed a "Proclamation" in response to the offer, it angered Williams and his followers by referring to them as "the mob party" and by accusing them of burning the Mormon homes. Without clear lines of communication or any sense of mutual trust, serious negotiations between the Mormons and their enemies never commenced.[33]

Meanwhile, skirmishes continued. Young helped organize Nauvoo's defenses and now recruited volunteers to fill Backenstos's posse. Emboldened by Williams's offer of peace but frustrated with the lack of a firm agreement, Young now encouraged Backenstos to apply military pressure against the mobs, leading to a number of anti-Mormon casualties and the temporary occupation of Carthage. "We have been enabled to labor all summer in peace," he lightheartedly motivated Mormon volunteers, "now we can have a respit and take time for a little fun this is fun for us." In an attempt to limit bloodshed he knew would be blamed wholly on the Mormons, though, Young urged Backenstos to confront and arrest mobbers "by surprize or ambuscade" rather than forcing anti-Mormons into a pitched battle.[34]

Publicly, Young "prophesied on the stand . . . that we would have a winter of peace in Nauvoo." Privately, he knew the Saints might have to abandon years of temple building. If a larger war erupted, the Saints would lose the fight and precipitously abandon Nauvoo, increasing the attraction of alternative leaders like Strang and Rigdon. Given his role as the church's founding prophet, Joseph Smith could survive setbacks in Ohio and Missouri. Having only led the church for one year, Brigham Young's leadership might not have survived a chaotic rout at the hands of the mob. "I pray the Lord," Young said, "to hold them off untill we finish the Temple."[35]

Help came from the distrusted state government. Anxious about the potential escalation of fighting in Hancock County, Governor Ford dispatched General John Hardin of the Illinois State Militia to restore peace. Upon hearing of the troop's impending arrival, Young told Sheriff Backenstos "to pray Gen Hardin not to come to this place." Young and his fellow Saints chafed as troops paraded through Nauvoo and Hardin's soldiers searched the temple and other buildings for anti-Mormon prisoners and evidences of Mormon criminality. More helpfully, Hardin brought a political delegation that included Congressman Stephen Douglas, who had been instructed by Ford to pressure the Mormons to leave quickly and peacefully. The delegation provided a conduit for negotiations and helped broker a firm agreement that the mobs would halt their vigilantism if the Saints would agree to depart the following spring. Young initially held out for assurances that non-Mormons would help the Saints sell their property in an orderly and profitable manner, and he hedged on whether the Saints would leave if their properties remained unsold. Eventually, recognizing the weakness of his position, he set those concerns aside and simply agreed to leave in return for a promise of peace. Knowing that the state would not protect the Saints, Young had navigated a military course that had avoided both aggression and passivity. The Mormons had displayed enough mettle to discourage the mobs but had avoided provoking a bloodier conflict. Young knew when to cut his losses. The Latter-day Saints would be driven, but their expulsion felt like deliverance from a far worse fate. Young was ready to lead them out of a Zion that had become their Egypt. "I do not intend to Stay in such an Hell of a Hole," he said of a place he looked forward to leaving. He still had to ensure, however, that the Saints would follow him.[36]

AFTER the Mormons agreed to leave Nauvoo, the mob threat temporarily subsided and Young immediately accelerated preparations for their spring departure. In early October, a church council estimated each family (of five adults) would need three yokes of "oxen between the ages of four and ten," a thousand pounds of flour, five pounds of coffee, fifty pounds of seed, and a "few goods to trade with the Indians." He warned church members to be careful not to sell their property in return for counterfeit money. By November, Young worried about overstuffed wagons, telling an assembly of Saints that "we have come to the conclusion not to build heavy waggons." "We shall have wet prairie," he correctly predicted, "and the heavier the load the deeper you go and the slower you go." Young actively involved himself in the minutiae of the planned exodus.[37]

Over the winter, though, Young switched his attention to the spiritual outfitting of the Saints. In October, the church held its semiannual conference in the almost-completed temple, an edifice three times larger than the building the church had abandoned in Kirtland. Beginning in late November, those brethren endowed under Joseph Smith began meeting in the temple. They dressed in their robes, prayed together, laid hands on sick members of the quorum for healing, and celebrated the Lord's Supper. They also arranged, decorated, and dedicated the rooms in which the Saints would participate in the sacred drama of creation, fall, and celestial glory.

"I truly felt as though I had gotten out of the World," Joseph Fielding described his first visit to the temple.[38] Young surely affirmed Fielding's sentiment. For nearly three months, the temple served as his sanctuary, physically and spiritually. In late November, officers arrived at the temple, ostensibly to either interrogate or arrest Young for undisclosed reasons. Young waited in the temple's attic story until they left. On December 18, a grand jury in Springfield, responding to persistent reports of counterfeiting by Nauvoo Mormons, indicted Brigham Young and eleven other church members, including apostles Parley Pratt, Willard Richards, and Orson Hyde. A circuit clerk's report on the indictments fingered Theodore Turley,

Nauvoo Temple, 1846 *(courtesy of Church History Library, The Church of Jesus Christ of Latter-day Saints)*

whom Young had recently named to the Council of Fifty, as the "chief manufacturer of dies" and suggested that church members had perpetrated the fraud for some years. It remains unclear whether Young or only lower-ranking church leaders like Turley had sanctioned the bogus-making operation in Nauvoo.[39]

Several days after the indictment, officers once more arrived at the entrance to the temple with writs to arrest Young and the other alleged counterfeiters. Alerted to the impending arrest, William Miller appeared outside the temple and deceived the officers through dress and conversation into believing he was Brigham Young. The gullible officers promptly arrested Miller and whisked him away to Carthage before a former member of the church revealed the error. Meanwhile, Young and the other apostles snuck out of the temple "disguised with other mens Hats and Coats." In later years, Young relished telling the tale of "Bogus Brigham." Joking aside, concern about potential arrests stoked a sense of urgency to begin and complete the temple rituals as quickly as possible. The Saints might have to leave Nauvoo, as they had feared, "so early in the spring, that grass might not grow, nor water run."[40]

By early December, the temple rooms were ready. Neither Joseph Smith nor his clerks had recorded the ceremony, and it remained an unwritten rite for several decades. In the Nauvoo Temple, Young expanded and revised what he had learned from Smith. William Clayton sketched the basic contours of the ceremony's sacred drama:

> it is the province of Eloheem, Jehovah and Michael [Adam] to create the world, plant the Garden and create the man and give his help meet [Eve]. Eloheem gives the charge to Adam in the Garden and thrust them into the telestial kingdom or the world. Then Peter assisted by James and john conducts them through the Telestial and Terrestrial kingdom administering the charges and tokens in each and conducts them to the vail where they are received by the Eloheem and after talking with him by words and tokens are admitted by him into the Celestial Kingdom.

Both American Protestants and early Mormons often conflated Elohim and Jehovah, two Anglicized renditions of Hebrew words for God. An 1845 proclamation of the Twelve Apostles, composed by Parley Pratt, referred to the "Great Jehovah Eloheem." By contrast, the temple ceremony suggested a hierarchy of distinct divine beings, including Michael-Adam. After participants were washed and anointed, they passed through the various rooms of the temple's second story, progressing from a premortal existence, into the paradise of Eden, through the fall and the corresponding trials of earthly, embodied life, and ultimately into celestial glory gained through obedience to divinely appointed authorities and ordinances. Participants made covenants with God and their priesthood leaders, and they swore an oath to avenge the deaths of Joseph and Hyrum Smith.[41]

For Young, the Nauvoo Temple was central to his furtherance of Joseph Smith's theology, built around sealing together patriarchal families headed by faithful saints exalted as priests, kings, and—one day—gods. Mormon godhood, as Young explained in several discourses, did not mean divinization in a sense of any fundamental change in a person's nature or essence, since both human beings and gods consisted of intelligence, light, spirit, and matter. Instead, "becoming a God" meant "simply to be in possession of a Kingdom and that makes him an Almighty man to that Kingdom." Exaltation began with patriarchal leadership of families, in which a faith-

Brigham Young, ca. 1845 portrait by S. Van Sickle *(courtesy International Society, Daughters of Utah Pioneers)*. Young is holding the "Law of the Lord," and the Bible and the Book of Mormon rest on the table. The painting was prominently displayed in the celestial room of the Nauvoo Temple.

ful man governed his "innumerable posterity" as "their ruler, savior, dictator, & governor." Temple ordinances enabled the Mormons to create eternal bonds and save their ancestors, creating a great chain of patriarchal kingdoms in eternity stretching back to Adam, "King of all." Then, as Joseph Smith had taught, Jesus would present this restored chain of humanity to God the Father, who would then bestow on them "Power to create worlds ourselves & rule them as Jesus did." Sacred ordinances, including baptism for the dead and plural marriage, were essential to this theological vision. Young envisioned "every one in their order, before God and each other—this is the secret of the whole thing." With Brigham Young as their chief priest, the Saints, their ancestors, their posterity, and their spiritual patriarchs would join together in their advance toward celestial glory.[42]

A great crush of Latter-day Saints came to the temple in December and January. "[S]uch was the anxiety manifested by the saints to receive the ordinances of Endowment," Young journalized, "& no less on our part to have them get the Keys of the Priesthood that I gave myself up entirely to the work of the Lord in the Temple almost night & day." Young frequently spent the night in the temple, often sleeping only a few hours between the end of ceremonies at night and the arrival of the next morning's first group of initiates. Young sometimes played the role of Elohim himself; more often, he oversaw all of the temple's activity, correcting details in the ceremony and maintaining decorum and order among the people. Over the winter, thousands of Mormons passed through the sacred drama, promised to live righteous and moral lives, vowed obedience to the church's leaders, and swore—on the pain of a gruesome death—not to reveal the content of the ceremony and its "signs and tokens." Some Mormons, disillusioned by plural marriage or otherwise disaffected, pronounced the entire affair a spiritual charade. Most, however, felt that the endowment richly rewarded the sacrifices of labor and money they had made for the temple. "[I]t was the most interesting scene of all my life," wrote Norton Jacob, who had toiled for months to build the edifice, "& one that afforded the most Peace and Joy that wee had ever experienced since wee were Married."[43]

As Mormonism's chief priest, Young led the Saints at the temple with a mixture of exactitude, righteous anger, and mirth. By the end of December, Young had grown irritated at the chaos and disorder generated by the unprecedented ritual activity. He announced his intention to stop people (including young children) from passing through the ceremony without invitation, and he complained about lounging, cooking, eating, and cutting and sewing garments in the temple. Two days later, Young had moved from annoyance to wrath, as the ceremony was becoming an open secret on the streets of Nauvoo. "I have been saluted by [people using] the grips & tokens," Young expressed indignant exasperation. "I have felt to slap their faces." "[I] do not like the Dumb Ass that brays in the St[r]eets," he continued, suggesting that the loose-lipped would "go quick to Hell & be damned four fold." Young shut down the ceremonies for a day.[44]

The "lion of the Lord," as the Mormon editor William Phelps nick-named Young, did more than roar in anger. During these weeks in the temple, he also evidenced a tender playfulness that endeared him to the Saints. While he decried untoward levity, Young embraced the presence of music, dancing, and spiritual beauty in the temple. On December 17, after the temple workers completed the evening rituals at half past ten, Hans Christian Hansen "brought in his violin and made Melody unto the Lord, which cheered the hearts of his People." "[W]hile under the power of ani-mation," Young "danced before the Lord," joined by several family mem-bers and friends.[45]

Two weeks later, after another day's ceremonies had concluded, Young led a "French Four," a dance for two couples in which he was joined by Elizabeth Ann Whitney. The temple was full that night, and the floor was soon covered with dancers. After the dancing concluded, Erastus Snow sang "The Upper California," anticipating an exodus to a land where the Mormons could "taste the sweets of liberty" and erect "towers & Temples . . . Along the great Pacific Sea." Responding to Young's invitation, Eliza-beth Ann Whitney then "sung one of the most beautiful songs in tongues, that ever was heard." Whitney's husband Newel and Young interpreted the message, proclaiming that the Lord "looked down upon our devotions & was well pleased." The "Lamanites" (Indians), they continued, would soon convert and "join in the dance before the Lord of Hosts, when our Enemies shall be crumble[d] to dust & fall to rise no more." Young and Kimball then also spoke in tongues. "Altogether," observed William Clay-ton, "it was one of the most touching and beautiful exhibitions of the power of the Spirit in the gift of tongues which was ever seen." Young no longer regularly spoke in tongues. Nevertheless, nearly fifteen years after his conversion to Mormonism and now at the top of the church's hierar-chy, the same spiritual fire burned within him.[46]

Young always remained torn about the Saints' ability and desire to com-bine holy zeal with merriment. His Methodist background left him uneasy with dancing and fiddling, and he believed that such pleasures, if not strictly regulated by the church, would promote sinfulness and inevitably distract the people from more important pursuits. Joseph Smith, by con-trast, had shown Young that a prophet could enjoy everything from wres-tling to dancing. Against his evangelical instincts, Young insisted that "the wicked have no right to dance, that dancing and music belonged to the Saints." They deserved and needed mirth. "We need a little recreation," he stated. "My mind is continually upon the stretch."[47] Young was maddeningly unpredictable, sometimes affirming such activities one week and proscribing them the next. On balance, though, Young and the Nauvoo Mormons preferred to sacralize and control recreational pleasures rather than forbid them. A people uncertain of their future, beset by poverty and mobs, surely enjoyed these aspects of Young's personality and leadership. Young stood above the people as their ecclesiastical hierarch, but he also danced with them late into the night and slept on sofas and pallets amid other church leaders and temple workers.

ON JANUARY 17, 1846, the horses driving Young's new "Omnibus" carriage plunged through a weak bridge while returning its passenger from an evening concert. George A. Smith, the driver, was unharmed, as was the carriage's only passenger, a "Sister Woodard" who was presumably Mary Ellen de la Montague, forty-four-year-old wife of James Woodward. As the distressed horses "remained . . . down between the timbers of the Bridge," Mary Woodward rushed to Young, who got out of bed and hastened to the scene. Young, with the help of several others, "tore the timbers away & let down the horses one at a time on the bottom," rolled them over, and brought them home, where he "washed them all over" with whiskey to prevent stiffness or disease. A few days later, Young returned the team of horses to service. Whether or not Woodward's appearance at Young's house late at night raised any Nauvoo eyebrows, within several weeks she and Young appeared together twice at a new scarlet-covered altar in the temple, fashioning and then refashioning a place in Young's now complex and extended family. Mary first became his ritually adopted daughter, then his wife.[48]

"I have been Amused," Young pronounced in late December, "at the people making [use] of their eyes to see who takes the sisters through the vail." Though unmarried persons also received the endowment, the church structured the ceremony for couples. Men and women, after being washed and anointed in separate chambers, moved through the ritual together. At the conclusion of the drama, the church leader playing the role of Elohim brought the husbands through a veil into the "celestial room," representing the Saints' future passage into eternal glory. Then, the husband joined in shepherding his wife into the celestial room. "Woman will never get back [to celestial glory]," Young explained, "unless she follows the man back." Curious onlookers speculated about plural marriages when church leaders brought ostensibly single women through the veil,

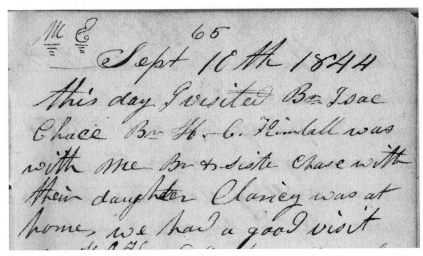

Brigham Young Journal, 10 Sept. 1844, record of marriage to Clarissa Ross Chase
(courtesy of Church History Library, The Church of Jesus Christ of Latter-day Saints)

and some of that speculation probably centered on Young himself. On December 16, for example, Young personally received Augusta Adams, Eliza R. Snow, and Ellen Rockwood "into the upper department" (the celestial room). All three women left Nauvoo as his plural wives.[49]

Shortly after resolving the leadership contest with Rigdon, Young had accelerated his courtship of plural wives, leaving cryptic references to these secret sealings in his diary. He indicated marriages for "time and eternity" with "M.E." and marriages only for "time" with "M.T." In the latter case, echoing the biblical precedent of levirate marriage to the childless widow of one's brother, Young married widows, offering them earthly protection and possible companionship while they (and any subsequent children) remained eternally linked to their deceased husbands. In his first post-martyrdom union, Young married Clarissa Ross, thirty-year-old stepdaughter of Young's friend Isaac Chase. "[T]his day," Young noted, "I visited Br. Isac Chace Br H. C. Kimball was with me Br & Sister Chase with their daughter Claricy was at home, we had a good visit." Nine days later, Young married Louisa Beaman, the first of seven or more of Smith's widows. The sealing took place at Young's house, and he noted in his diary that he "[s]taed at home all day my wife is quite sick." Young recorded in code, "I saw [sealed and wed] Louisa B. Smith." The late 1844 sealings left Young spiritually exhilarated. "[G]rate is the work of the Lord in these Last days," Young wrote after Kimball sealed Louisa Beaman to him "for time." "[T]he Lord is with me continuly," he added the next day.[50]

Young married at least fifteen women between his August 1844 return to Nauvoo and the dedication of the temple, in one busy stretch marrying women on three successive days. Then, during the final month of temple activity, church leaders officiated over marital sealings. First, Young and his existing wives reaffirmed their prior covenants, beginning with Mary Ann Angell standing as a proxy for Young's ritual resealing to Miriam Works. In the case of Joseph Smith's widows, an officiator first sealed the women to Smith "for eternity" with Young acting as Joseph's proxy, then sealed them to Young "for time." The ceremonies confirmed the promises and covenants made in the pretemple sealings; they also illustrated his wives' continued commitment to plural marriage. In the final few weeks of temple activity, Young was sealed to an additional eighteen women, bringing to nearly forty his total number of living wives.

Young was not overly selective about extending the benefits of his eternal kingdom and earthly family to additional wives. "I do not care how many are sealed to me," he only partly joked a few years later, "nor who."51 Indeed, the wives ranged in ages from sixteen to sixty-six and exhibited tremendous diversity of circumstance: Eliza R. Snow, the accomplished, independent poetess and widow of Joseph Smith; Mary Elizabeth Lightner Rollins, another Smith widow who still enjoyed a contented marriage with her non-Mormon husband; Ellen Rockwood, only sixteen years of age. Of the women sealed to Young for the first time at the temple, only one (Margaret Alley) bore him children. A number of the new wives were widows, including Julia Foster, whom Young had converted to Mormonism back in 1833 and then married to Jonathan Hampton. Now, Young stood as a proxy for Julia's eternal sealing to Hampton and became her husband "for time." Young was also sealed for "time and eternity" to his first two mother-in-laws, the widowed Abigail Marks (Works) and Phebe Morton, long estranged from her husband James Angell. He also became a husband to Jemima Angell, Mary Ann's sister, widowed by her first husband and no longer living with her second. The sealings gave women like Phebe Morton and Jemima Angell the opportunity to choose an earthly protector and an eternal husband after prior marriages had brought them bitter disappointment.52

Women kneeled at the altar next to Brigham Young for many different reasons. Clarissa Blake, married to Lyman Homiston at the time of her October 1844 sealing to Young, penned him an acrostic poem and love letter shortly after the ceremony. "[M]y heart," she wrote, "is like a bird let lo[o]se from a long and close confinement and soars aloof on joyful pinions." She anticipated eternal benefits through her new husband. "Onward to guide us, to celestial joys," she described his role. "Upward thou will rise, and we will follow on." Several wives fervently admired Young's spiritual leadership. Zina Huntington Jacobs termed one of his sermons "the greatest that has ever ben Given to the Church, uppon Priesthood, the Godhed, the dut[i]es of Male & Female, there exaltations." While details are scarce, it seems likely that some women actively sought Young as an eternal companion. Indeed, a few women lamented a missed opportunity to join Young's earthly and celestial kingdom. In late 1845, Percis Tippets evidently married another man, then wrote Young regretting the loss of a better match. "[H]ad I known my priviledge at the time of the alliance," she explained, "I should have given you the preference and as my mind seems still to be placed upon you I would ask a place in your kingdom." Women were active participants in the formation of plural marriages.[53]

If motivated by a variety of reasons, most of the women—and perhaps Young himself—probably had only a vague conception of the future shape these marriages would take. Young did not cohabit with his plural wives, who typically remained in their existing living circumstances, but he consummated at least some of these new plural marriages. On October 10, 1844, Young and Kimball visited Ezra Chase, brother of Young's father-in-law Isaac Chase. Further cementing the bonds between their families, Young sealed Ezra Chase to his wife for eternity, then he and Kimball married their daughters Diana and Charlotte respectively. Four days later, Young and Kimball made a clandestine overnight visit to the Chase household, ostensibly to visit their new wives. "No one knew whare we ware gon," scrawled Kimball in his diary. More definitively, Young's plural wives began to "raise up seed" for him. Smith's widow Emily Dow Partridge bore him a son, Edward Partridge Young, in October 1845. Lucy Ann Decker and Harriet Cook also delivered sons, in June 1845 and early 1846, respectively. Many other children followed in the late 1840s. Other marriages, by contrast, were likely not sexual, such as the sealings to his early mother-in-laws. Clarissa Young Spencer characterized her father's sealing with the poetess Eliza Snow as a marriage "in name only," though Snow and Young developed a high level of mutual respect over time.[54]

On one occasion, Young ardently desired a wife also sought by one of his close followers. John D. Lee, an often irascible but sometimes charming man in his early forties, had served Joseph Smith as a bodyguard and quickly earned Young's loyalty and a place on the Council of Fifty. In the spring of 1845, having recently taken his first plural wife, Lee planned to marry sisters Louisa and Emmeline Free. "One day," Lee later wrote, "Brigham Young saw Emeline and fell in love with her." "Bro John D Lee said to me," stated George D. Grant before an 1847 council trying Lee for sexual misconduct, "that Brigham told him if he would give up Emeline to him he would uphold him in time and in eternity & he never should fall, but that he would sit at his right hand in his kingdom." Young married Emmeline, a pretty, dark-haired young woman approaching twenty years of age. Lee married only Louisa. At the 1847 council meeting, Young rebuked Lee for treating his wives cruelly and lasciviously, but he did not take umbrage at his loyal disciple's characterization of their shared romantic interest. Nor did Lee openly manifest any resentment over his loss. In December 1845, Young and Lee visited Emmeline and Louisa, both sick with a fever. Together, the two men "administer[ed] some nourishments & comfort, to them we blesed them & returned." Lee, raised by an aunt after his mother's death and his father's descent into alcoholism, increasingly viewed Brigham Young as a surrogate father. Paternal and ecclesiastical loyalty trumped his interest in Emmeline.[55]

As Joseph Smith had done on many occasions, Young also married women who already had husbands. Out of his approximately fifty-three plural wives, around fifteen women were legally married to other men at the time of their sealings to Young.[56] Some of those prior marriages had failed, others were in the process of failing, but others persisted for many decades. Already married to William Whitmarsh, Emily Haws married Young in mid-January 1846, then completed a property transaction as Whitmarsh's wife in mid-February and presumably remained with him. In one of the more unusual instances, Margaret Pierce had been married to church member Morris Whitesides for six months at the time of her January 1845 sealing to Young, which came one month before her first husband's death of consumption.[57]

Zina Huntington, her parents, and most of her siblings had been devoted members of the church since the mid-1830s. Her father and brothers were priesthood leaders, and Zina—a slender, dark-haired woman with piercing eyes—maintained a firm testimony of Mormonism's truth, spoke in tongues, and joined Nauvoo's Female Relief Society. After marrying Henry Jacobs in 1841, Zina—following a long period of anguished prayer and searching—accepted Joseph Smith's offer of plural marriage. She continued to live with Henry, and two months after her sealing to Smith, she gave birth to a son.

On an unknown date, likely in the spring of 1845, Brigham Young was sealed to Zina. His wife's second plural marriage apparently troubled Henry. Doubts nagged at Zina as well. "The thoughts of my heart or the emotions of my minde causes my very head to acke," she wrote in her diary in early May 1845. A week later, she prayed that God would comfort "Henry in his trouble, for he has not repined a word." Zina provided no details of their sorrows, but she recorded one month later that "Henry

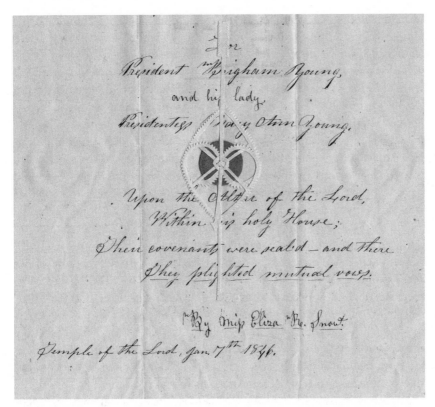

For

President Brigham Young,

and his lady,

Presidentess Mary Ann Young,

Upon the Altar of the Lord,
Within his holy House;
Their covenants were seal'd — and there
They plighted mutual vows.

By Miss Eliza R. Snow.

Temple of the Lord, Jan 7th 1846.

Card created by Eliza R. Snow on the occasion of Young's temple sealing to Mary Ann Angell, 7 Jan. 1846. "Upon the Altar of the Lord / Within his holy House / Their covenants were sealed and there / *They plighted mutual vows.*" Snow artfully created a cut-paper decoration that she attached to the card. The interlocking hearts and the arrow represent romantic love, the knot in the center symbolizes marriage, and the key on the top of the decoration evokes priesthood authority. *(courtesy of Church History Library, The Church of Jesus Christ of Latter-day Saints)*

went to see Pres. B. Young to be counceled upon his and his families situation." If these sparse entries do indeed chronicle the couple's agonized response to Zina's second plural sealing, Henry manifested his peace with the latest development in his marital saga by witnessing Zina's early February 1846 temple sealing, in which a ceremony sealed her to Smith for eternity and as "husband & wife for time" to Young. "Henry B. Jacobs expressed his willingness that it should be so," recorded the temple clerk. He still lived with Zina, who was visibly pregnant with what would be the couple's second son.[58]

Thirty minutes after Henry Jacobs assented to Brigham Young's marriage to his wife, he stood as a witness as Young and Augusta Adams Cobb were resealed to each at the altar. Augusta had delayed coming to the temple, apparently because of doubts about her union with Young. On January 20, she wrote to inform Young that she could not "come up to the Temple this evening with the girls." She had been an active helper in the temple, but her dissatisfaction with her marriage to Young had grown too deep. "I can never be yours in the position you have placed me," she explained. Perhaps the fact that a number of other women had recently joined Young at the altar did not match her initial expectations of plurality. Sixteen years later, Augusta explained that upon her 1843 arrival in Nauvoo, she already had doubts about her choice of husbands. "I should have seen Br Joseph the first thing," she recounted. "But instead of that you exacted a promise of me that I would not see him alone Saying he would certainly over come me." Augusta doubted that any man could do that. "You then Said I had never had to deal with a Prophet of the Lord." Augusta may have projected her later discontents onto her memory of her 1843 sealing to Young, but by early 1846 she had taken the logic of Mormon marriage to an extreme conclusion. "I am resolved to be the Lords wholly for time and Eternity," she wrote, expressing a desire to be sealed to Jesus Christ. If Young would not grant this wish, she added, "I will take the next step and go to Joseph." Augusta wanted both companionship on the earth and the highest level of eternal glory, neither of which she thought she could receive through her marriage to Brigham Young.[59]

Augusta vacillated for two weeks. Then despite her misgivings, she eventually submitted to Young's will. The day after her resealing to Young, she presented several wives "to her husband at the Altar." At least for the moment, her resealing and willingness to participate in the further expansion of Young's family brought her peace. "I felt," she confessed to Young in a letter, "that our love had been like Jonahs gourd, come up in a night, and perished in a night." She expressed relief that God had restored "together with you that love and confidence which I had well nigh lost."[60]

Augusta also played a role in Young's introduction of new ordinances. Through baptism for the dead and patriarchal blessings, Joseph Smith had sought ways to reinforce biological and spiritual ties between children and parents. Now, church leaders sealed children and their spouses to their parents, ensuring the continuation of their relationship in eternity. On January 11, Heber Kimball anointed Brigham and Mary Ann Young as "King and Priest" and "Queen & Priestess unto her husband," respectively. He then sealed Young to his first seven children, along with eldest daughter Elizabeth's husband Edmund Ellsworth. In the Nauvoo temple, most children were sealed to their father's first wife; thus, Mary

Ann Young stood as a proxy for the sealing of her five children to Miriam Works.[61]

Smith, though, had always both reinforced biological ties and sought ways to fashion an ecclesiastical family that transcended biology. In the temple, a new ritual—known as the "law of adoption"—sealed church members to nonbiological fathers and mothers, either because their own parents had not converted or because they desired to link themselves to the kingdoms of prominent leaders. Several books of the New Testament teach that believers in Jesus become his adopted children, grafted into his kingdom; similarly, adopted Latter-day Saints became members of their new father's family and heirs of his kingdom. Church member George Laub wrote in his diary that "this order of Adoption will Link the chain of the Prieshood in such a way that it cannot be seperated."[62] Young later explained that church leaders like himself were "entitled to the Keys of the Priesthood according to linage and blood," carrying in their veins blood inherited from royal ancestors. In light of this claimed ancestry, when Young adopted men and women into his family, he ritually welded them and their sealed children into a priesthood chain that stretched back to Adam. In the process, church members aligned their earthly and eternal futures with those of their ecclesiastical leaders.

On 25 January 1846, Young adopted eight couples, including loyal followers Albert Rockwood, John D. Lee, and George Grant. As with Young's own children, they were sealed to Miriam Works, with Mary Ann again serving as a ritual proxy. "[T]he Spirit of allmighty god attended the administration & filled our hearts to overflowing," Young described the emotions of the day, "& many wept for joy that were adopted into my Family." "Brigham kissed all his children," recorded Thomas Bullock. George Laub, who alongside his wife was sealed to John D. Lee, recorded that Lee promised "to doo unto them as he would unto his own children," and adopted children covenanted "to do all the good for his upbuilding and happyness." Nearly two weeks later, several additional sons and daughters joined Young's family as adopted children. In a departure from the customary practice of having adopted children sealed to a man's first wife, Augusta Adams Young stood next to her husband as the adoptive mother, perhaps as a sign of Young's favor following their resealing.[63]

Amid the feverish pace of ritual activity, many church members probably did not understand the implications of the sealings and adoptions at the temple altar. It was a liminal time for Latter-day Saint family relations, as Smith's plural marriage revelation and the temple rituals disregarded both Protestant convention and civil marriages. The sealings reshaped Mormon families and connected them in new ways. In one case, Young ritually adopted Robert and Hannah Pierce, parents of his plural wives Margaret and Mary Pierce. His parents-in-law became his spiritual children. In some instances, a sense of impermanence and flexibility remained, as parties continued to refashion their family connections. James and Mary Woodward—she was the passenger in Young's omnibus carriage the night it foundered on a Nauvoo bridge—were both sealed to Brigham Young as his adopted children in early February. Two days after Mary became Young's adopted daughter, she married her spiritual father. Sometime after she moved to Nauvoo with her husband, Mary had complained in a letter to Young that James "abused" her and asked Young for her "release from worse than death." Hearing whispers of Nauvoo polygamy, she hoped Young would make her his wife. Perhaps aware of Mary's desire, James may have requested the ritual adoption as a way of avoiding losing his wife. During the press of temple work, Young had little time to reflect on the future consequences of the ceremonies. He and his increasingly unwieldy family would have to wait to work out exactly how the temple sealings would shape their earthly futures.[64]

As THE washings, anointings, and sealings proceeded, Young and top church leaders decided to leave Nauvoo sooner than planned, having received false advice from Governor Ford that the federal government would intervene to arrest church leaders on the counterfeiting charges and prevent the Mormons from crossing the Rocky Mountains. Simultaneously, Young heard rumors that Ford intended to declare martial law under "mob militia" led by General Hardin, who, Young surmised, "will no doubt renew those writs that had been isued for the 12 & others & thereby commence harrassing us again." Ford did not plan to arrest Young or other church leaders, but he did want to hasten the departure of the Mormons and, with them, his biggest political headache. Young, though, feared arrest for understandable reasons. Given ongoing mob activity in Hancock County, he expected anti-Mormons to kill him if he were arrested. By February 2, Young grew desperate in his anxiety to abandon the City of Joseph. "It is my opinion," he told a clerk, "that if we are here 10 days that our way will be Hedged up . . . we want to be 500 miles from here before they are aware of our move." The next day, Young informed church members that they could no longer receive the temple ordinances. A throng gathered at the temple, anxious to participate in the sacred ceremonies before the Twelve left Nauvoo. "[T]his is not the last Temple that we will build," Young declared, attempting to mollify the disappointed crowd. "I am going to load up my waggon & be away from this place immediately," he insisted as he walked away from the House of the Lord. When he later returned to the temple and found the crowd still present, he relented and resumed the rituals. As advance parties crossed the Mississippi into Iowa, Young prepared his own company for the impending departure. On February 8, temple workers performed the final ordinances, took down the veil and altar, and carefully stored the records for the journey west.[65]

After eighteen months in which many Mormons struggled to identify Joseph Smith's true successor amid a host of ravening wolves and counterfeit prophets, the temple rituals marked a turning point. Young had made the completion of the temple for the promised ordinances his highest priority, and he had succeeded. Under his leadership, more than five thousand Latter-day Saints had received their endowment, and hundreds more were sealed in celestial marriage. Young had stood in front of church members in the temple, explaining the endowment ceremony, regulating their behavior, and discussing the church's future. He also exercised the "sealing power" previously held by Joseph Smith, bestowing the prerogative to take plural wives on those men he considered trustworthy and loyal. Even as many Mormons retained their affections for certain members of the Smith family, Young's ritual creation of an extended, ecclesial family created a new and different fulcrum of loyalty within the church.[66] More intimately, Young's own plural marriages and adoptions forged new bonds of loyalty. The two months of temple work greatly augmented Young's position as the church's new leader. Church members practically stampeded the temple to get what Young offered them. For most Mormons, Joseph Smith remained their only Prophet, but for many the temple ordinances solidified Young's standing as Smith's rightful successor and the church's chief priest.

Not everyone was convinced, though, and many Mormons outside Nauvoo remained confused as disciples of Sidney Rigdon and James Strang jousted with representatives of the Twelve. Catherine Lewis, who had hosted Young and Heber Kimball for a night during their 1844 stay in Boston, denounced Sidney Rigdon in a letter to Young as a "wolf in sheapes clothing." Kimball (who desired her for a wife) and Augusta Adams Cobb had introduced Lewis to the doctrine of the "plurality of wives." Although she hesitated to accept the teaching, Lewis remained a fervent supporter of the Twelve and traveled to Nauvoo to receive her endowment. Unwilling to become Kimball's plural wife, she denounced the ceremony as a "ridiculous farce," left Nauvoo and the church, and published a scathing exposé alleging that the Twelve preyed upon the money and innocence of women more gullible than herself.[67]

For Catherine Lewis, Young and Kimball proved to be the wolves, and she was not alone. In fact, perhaps because plural marriage became more visible during the final month of the ordinances, James Strang's threat to Young's leadership reached its peak. For those squeamish about either polygamy or trekking across the plains, Strang's Voree Zion offered an apparently safer, closer, and monogamous alternative. Moreover, neither Emma Smith nor Lucy Mack Smith joined the exodus from Nauvoo. The prophet's mother participated in the endowment ceremony, but Emma avoided the temple and did not consider venturing west under the leadership of a man who practiced and advocated plural marriage. "[T]he Twelve have made bogus of it," she told a servant girl. Sizeable numbers of Saints rejected Young and the Twelve as counterfeit successors to Joseph Smith.[68]

The day after the final ordinances were performed, as some of the companies boated across the Mississippi, the temple's roof erupted in flames, ignited by a stovepipe on the upper floor. A fire brigade extinguished the blaze before it consumed the entire structure, but the fire served as an ominous portent, as did a river accident that killed two oxen. On February 15, Young left Nauvoo, returning only briefly for a meeting at the temple one week later. Young's prophecy of the temple's completion had proven true, but he was driven before grass grew and water ran. Thousands of Mormons straggled out of Nauvoo over the next few months, but the exodus did not satiate mob demands for the total expulsion of the church. Over the summer, vigilantes harassed, threatened, and even whipped Mormons lingering in the city. The departure of most church members and the withdrawal of state forces left Nauvoo nearly defenseless, and a coordinated mob attack in September drove out virtually all the remaining Mormons. Joseph Heywood, one of the church's trustees left behind to sell church properties, described Nauvoo as the "Obomination of Disolation [desolation]" (alluding to an apocalyptic prophecy in the Book of Daniel about the desecration of the temple) and "Hell Town." A second fire gutted the temple in 1848, and a tornado damaged it further two years later. The Icarians, a group of French utopians, salvaged the temple's stone for use in other buildings.[69]

The Mormon departure from Nauvoo also began a new chapter in the church's tumultuous relationship with American political authorities. Wherever the Latter-day Saints had settled, they had clashed politically with non-Mormons, and neither state governments nor the federal government had protected Mormons' property and their liberties. Most other Americans viewed Young and his fellow apostles as the purveyors of a false religion; Young in turn condemned the American government as a counterfeit of true republicanism. "As it regards Whig or Democrat there is no choice," Young had complained before the November 1844 election, "neither of them are republicanism—both are opposite to it." Neither party would defend the right of the Mormons to practice their religion. "They call us *Bogus*," Catherine Lewis quoted Young at a Nauvoo meeting, "but they are all *Bogus*, every one in office, from the President down." Creditors and apostates had driven Brigham Young from Kirtland; mobs had forced him from Missouri and Illinois, and the U.S. government had declined to intervene. "[W]e will go to a land where there are at last no old settlers to quarrel with us," Young prophesied.[70] Mormonism's new leader was determined not to be driven again.

CHAPTER SIX

Word and Will

Let us go, let us go where our rights are secure,
Where the waters are clear and the atmosphere pure,
Where the hand of oppression has never been felt,
Where the blood of the prophets has never been spilt.

—ELIZA R. SNOW (1846)

DURING breaks from presiding over temple rituals, Young and the other apostles examined maps of the American West and read John C. Frémont's narrative of his 1843 journey through the Bear River Valley to California, during which the explorer passed through what he termed the "Great interior Basin," then part of Mexican Upper California. Frémont, known as the "Great Pathfinder," described a vast desert plateau with lakes possessing "no outlet to the ocean," a region "peopled . . . miserably and sparsely." The latter aspect appealed to Mormon leaders, who wanted an isolated sanctuary without any existing white settlements. In August 1845, Young wrote missionary Addison Pratt that they would "probably" settle "in the neighborhood of Lake Tampanagos [Utah Lake] as that is represented as a most delightful district and there is no settlement near there." By January 1846, Young felt assured enough to announce in the temple, "I know where the spot is." Young envisioned the Great Basin, not devoid of humanity but containing very few white people, as the ideal refuge for the Saints.[1]

Along the trail, Young showed himself to be a very different leader than he had been when he sailed to England in 1840. Then, he used patience and humor to build consensus, and he avoided actions that would have left his fellow apostles feeling slighted. In the intervening five years, however, Young had witnessed dissent leading to the murder of his beloved Joseph, and he had spent eighteen months living in fear of arrest or assassination.

Shaken and traumatized by these events, he left the crucible of Nauvoo with a steely determination to make sure that factionalism and disobedience would never lead to a second Carthage Jail. Even though he remained unsure of himself as a prophetic leader, and perhaps in part because of that insecurity, Young brooked no challenges to his authority. Sensitive to criticism, he sometimes lashed out at those who questioned his judgment or complained about their circumstances. At other times, he succored his beleaguered followers with words of comfort, the administration of healing rites, and seasons of recreation. Most decisively, though, Young consolidated his leadership by organizing the successful relocation of thousands of religious refugees to a sanctuary "far away in the West."

AFTER crossing the Mississippi in February 1846, the Mormon refugees stayed at a temporary encampment (Sugar Creek) nine miles west of Nauvoo and then slowly headed across southern Iowa. Fifty-five miles west of Nauvoo, Young stopped at a place called Richardson's Point. Taking his clerk and adopted son John D. Lee with him, Young went into the woods, "cut some crotches," and then "Erected a Table in my Tent which was used as a writing desk." Using his tent for a council room, Young convened a meeting of the church's leadership. Young told them he intended to "put up 300 Pioneers (without a woman) & send them over the Mountains in time to put in Spring crops." The Camp of Israel, as it became known, would race for Zion. Larger groups of Mormons would temporarily remain at various points between Illinois and the Rockies to better provision themselves for subsequent crossings.[2]

Young's hope of reaching the mountain valleys in 1846 collided with the reality of early spring travel on the frontier. "You have herd of a great mud hole which reaches from Nauvoo nearly to this place," Young wrote the apostle Orson Hyde in mid-April from south-central Iowa, a little more than half the three hundred miles to Council Bluffs on the Missouri River. All through the fall, Mormon refugees straggled and staggered out of Nauvoo, their numbers loosely strung between way stations from the Mississippi to the Missouri rivers. They faced not only mud but also severe weather, hunger, and disease. Young's wife Eliza Snow, halfway across Iowa a few months later, wrote of "a growling, grumbling, devilish, sickly time." With the church mired in this slough of despond, many Mormons grumbled about their lack of provisions and sometimes grew envious of church leaders' prerogatives. The church clerk William Clayton, for instance, observed with jealousy the amount of lumber Young and other top leaders received to construct comfortable wagons.[3]

Meanwhile, the Camp of Israel's leader tried every conceivable strategy to build support for his faltering race across the Rockies. Young unrealistically predicted that even an undersupplied vanguard group could make the journey with ease, insisting that the pioneers could travel twenty miles a day on only a half-pound of flour each. He stated that his own generosity to the needy had left him emaciated, and he warned that a failure to cross the mountains would damage the church's credibility and lead the Saints to scatter. In early May, Young lamented that the people "have completely tied our hands by importuning, saying do not leave us behind wherever you go we want to go and be with you." He warned that a lack of unity and obedience "caused Joseph to lose his life" and that the same problem now threatened "to bring me down to my grave." As murmuring increased, Young strove to tighten his control. He threatened those who disrupted Sunday meetings. Most intrusively, he repeatedly discussed having camp captains maintain daily records in order to keep track of the "conduct and behaviour of every person in camp." Church leaders never implemented the plan.[4]

Despite Young's desire for increased control, a quiet protest forced him to abandon his plan to cross the mountains that year. At a church council on May 21, no one voted against a motion "that the brethren outfit the Twelve for the mountains," but only a "part voted in favor, and a part did not vote either way." Conceding defeat, Young won approval for a weak resolution that the church go "over the mountains sooner or later." Frustrated with his recalcitrant followers, Young warned them against continued obstinacy, announcing "that the time had come when I should command them what to do." He threatened those who resisted his authority with "a slap of revelation." Still, no amount of cajoling could move the camp quickly enough, for church members could not follow commands to do the impossible. The camp reached the Council Bluffs at the Missouri River in mid-June 1846, more than two months later than anticipated.[5]

Young publicly took out his frustrations on his downtrodden flock, but he also provided private solace by purchasing food for those running low on supplies, administering to the sick, and organizing relief teams for the most bedraggled Mormons still leaving Nauvoo. Some Mormons, moreover, found deep spiritual comfort in his leadership. "Br Brigham blesed the people," recorded Patty Sessions, a midwife and a widow of Joseph Smith, after one Sunday meeting. "I felt his blessing even to the healing of my body have been better ever since." Anticipating death from another illness in August, Sessions asked Young and others to find her temple clothes for her burial and to record the exact location of her grave. Young and Kimball laid hands on her, but her condition still worsened. "Brigham said," she wrote in her diary, "they must all hold onto me as long as I breathed and 15 minutes after I had done breathing." Sessions again recovered.[6]

The following winter, Young visited John D. Lee while the latter suffered from a fever and stomach ailment. Young placed on Lee's "breast a cane built from one of the branches of the Tree of Life that stood in the garden in the Temple." Cast out into the wilderness, Young had taken with him a piece of the temple's Eden, perhaps as a way to remind himself and the Saints that the temple's divine power and blessings remained available to them. The cane helped Lee focus his mind on "sacred and solemn things," then Wilford Woodruff and Levi Stewart anointed and blessed Lee "with a promise of immediate health." Lee pronounced himself "almost free from pain" the next day. Of course, priestly ministrations, miraculous objects, and other attempted cures sometimes failed, and many Mormons perished on the trail across Iowa. Ultimately, Young recognized that the Saints' best and often only recourse was to strengthen their faith in the midst of suffering. "Some times we lay hands upon the sick & they are healed instantly," he realistically explained. "Other times with all the faith & medicine they are a long time getting well, & others die." Young demanded obedience through authoritarian and sometimes hardhearted instruction, but he also comforted his people through priestly ministrations and genuine displays of concern.[7]

Heartfelt and stubborn faith enabled the Mormons to persevere in the midst of poverty, tragedy, and uncertainty. Many had already drunk deeply from the cup of persecution. Most were intimate with grinding poverty. Although they could have reversed course and headed for Strang's Voree, drifted to St. Louis, or returned to relatives in the East, most chose to keep walking, to keep driving their teams. They interpreted their difficulties through the lens of faith, just as the 1834 Zion's Camp marchers discerned God's providential care and instruction amid defeat and disease. It is not surprising that the Mormons identified themselves with the ancient Israelites leaving Egypt. From the Puritans to African American slaves, many American Christians had viewed their lives through the prism of the ancient Hebrews. No other group of Americans, however, believed themselves to be reliving the sacred history of the Old Testament both in broad strokes and in such minute detail. A frozen Mississippi River that enabled large groups of Mormons to cross quickly into Iowa, a flock of docile quail that alighted on the hungry "Poor Camp" in October, Young's appointment of captains of hundreds, fifties, and tens—all reminded the Mormons that they were recapitulating the sacred wanderings of the ancient Israelites. The Latter-day Saints, though, did more than see mere echoes or repetitions of Israel's past in their present. They believed that the literal blood of Israel flowed in their veins. They were God's chosen and protected people. Rather than an expression of Mormon hubris, their belief, like that of the French Huguenots or the Puritan colonists, sustained their faith despite myriad afflictions. That faith enabled them to share the conviction of William Clayton (expressed in a hymn written during the exodus) that "All Is Well." Correspondingly, these American Israelites viewed Brigham Young as their Moses, a comparison Young encouraged. "I feel all the time like Moses," he told them. Unlike the original Moses, though, Young would reach what Clayton termed "the place which God for us prepared."[8]

If stymied by his people's slow progress across Iowa, Young thoroughly enjoyed himself on the trail. The trek rejuvenated his now middle-aged self. On his way out of Nauvoo, his wagons immediately stalled in the mud trying to ascend a small hill. Young "was there at work in the mud assisting the teamsters," recorded Hosea Stout. Patty Sessions discovered Young in early April "driving his team in the rain and mud to his knes as happy as a king." For Young, the exodus provided now uncommon stretches of personal freedom. In June, he and Kimball "with their wifes went out strawberrying," a pleasant diversion and also essential protection against scurvy. In November, Young and Kimball organized an expedition up the Missouri, cut down trees, built cattle troughs, gathered six pails of honeycomb, and reminisced around the camp fire about their missionary work in England. Young would have maximized his own personal pleasure if he had spent his entire adult life as a Methodist circuit rider, Mormon missionary, or trail guide.[9]

WHILE Young reluctantly discussed plans for the Mormons to winter somewhere east of the mountains, Captain James Allen of the U.S. Army arrived at Council Bluffs in late June. Allen came as a representative of Colonel Stephen Kearny's "Army of the West." By the time of Allen's arrival, the United States had formally been at war with Mexico for six weeks. In 1845, President John Tyler had signed a congressional resolution annexing Texas in the waning days of his administration, and his successor James Polk provoked fighting in a portion of Mexican territory rather baselessly claimed by Texas. Polk simultaneously secured a large portion of Oregon through a treaty with Great Britain, leaving him free to pursue his larger objective of acquiring California. With the United States winning early if costly victories beyond the Rio Grande in northeastern Mexico, Polk wanted American soldiers to advance quickly to the northwestern Mexican provinces of New Mexico and Upper California. Kearny departed for Santa Fe in June, and the army began recruiting volunteers to follow after him. Hundreds of those soldiers would be Mormons.[10]

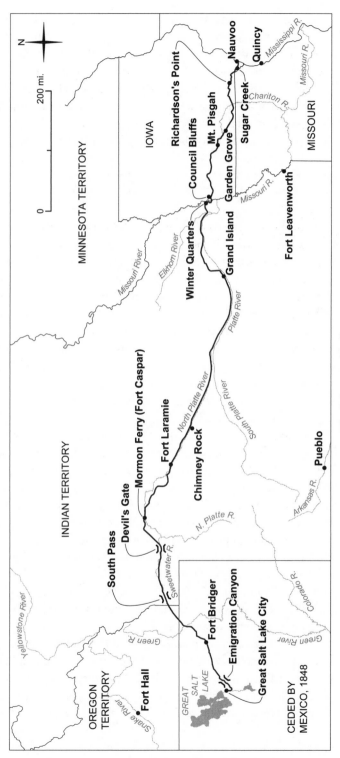

The Mormon Trail

Shortly before leaving Nauvoo, Young had commissioned Jesse Little, a merchant in charge of the eastern branches of the church, to attempt to gain governmental assistance for the exodus. In Philadelphia, Little became acquainted with Thomas Kane, a diminutive young man active in several reform causes whose father possessed solid Democratic connections to Polk. Kane grew sympathetic to the plight of the suffering Saints, viewed them as a potential means of achieving humanitarian and political renown, and announced to Little his intention of accompanying the Mormons to California.

Little and Kane first traveled to the nation's capital. The new president possessed no particular animus against the Latter-day Saints. When Thomas Ford had asked him to send military forces to prod the church out of Nauvoo, Polk had refused to "interfere with them on the ground of their religious faith, however absurd it might be considered to be." While affirming his church's loyalty to the United States, Little somewhat cheekily mentioned to Polk the possibility of assistance from a "foreign power," alluding to British designs on the Pacific Northwest. The threat worked, as Polk, who expected the Mormons to settle on the Pacific Coast, authorized the enlistment to "conciliate them, attach them to our country, & prevent them from taking part against us." While Polk anticipated the enlistment of Mormon men after they had reached California, Kearny's officers interpreted their ambiguous orders as a mandate to immediately recruit Mormon volunteers. Kane raced to Fort Leavenworth to meet Captain Allen, who had already left for Council Bluffs.[11]

Not surprisingly, given their expulsion from Illinois and alienation from the United States, many Mormons greeted Allen with distrust, fearing a plot to harm the church after drawing away hundreds of its strongest men. Young, by contrast, pivoted immediately, temporarily discarding his disdain for the U.S. government. "This is no *hoax*," Young informed his men. He wanted government permission for the Mormons to winter on Indian land, which Allen granted provisionally. Young relished the idea of settling outside the confines of the United States, and he claimed the Saints' right to "straddle the fence" during the war, but he now grasped that American sovereignty would soon extend over the Great Basin and the rest of Upper California. Therefore, he saw potential advantages in forging better ties with the U.S. government. In an August letter, he reminded Polk of Mormon support in the 1844 election and informed the president that "should we locate within the territory of the U.S. as we anticipate we would esteem a territorial government of our own." Most basically, the heavily indebted church needed the hard cash promised the enlistees, much of which the soldiers handed over to the church's leadership. Young promised to care for the enlistees' families in their absence, and after he, Kane, and Allen delivered recruitment speeches at the various Iowa camps, five hundred Mormons marched to Fort Leavenworth to facilitate the imperial destiny of a nation they predicted was manifestly lurching toward damnation.[12]

The result was the creation of the Mormon Battalion, the only military unit in American history recruited on the basis of religion. While other portions of General Kearny's Army of the West suffered casualties at the hands of *californio* forces, the Mormon soldiers endured an arduous but peaceful trek to the Pacific. A footnote to the Mexican-American War, the largest portion of the battalion reached Los Angeles, with a smaller number of sick soldiers and accompanying families wintering at Pueblo (in present-day Colorado) before heading for the Salt Lake Valley. Meanwhile, the Mormons had formed an enduring bond with Kane, who decided to return East after an illness he contracted on the trail. Kane provided the church with a much-needed non-Mormon political ally.

Despite its serendipitous creation and successful march, Young grew bitter in his reflections on the battalion and Polk. In July 1847, he "damned President Polk" in a speech and attributed Polk's enlistment of the battalion as a plot so "that the women & children might perish on the Prairies." He alleged that if "he had refused their enlisting, Missouri was ready with 3000 men, to have swept the Saints out of existence on attempting to cross the Missouri River." Young misjudged Polk, who harbored no ill will toward the church. In hoping the battalion would secure Mormon loyalty to the United States, however, the president misjudged the depth of the Mormons' resentment of their treatment in Missouri and Illinois.[13]

Young's bitterness stemmed in part from dissension caused by the separation of enlisted soldiers from their families and conflicts over the church's appropriation and stewardship of the battalion's clothing allowance. The church used the funds to purchase goods in bulk at St. Louis, sold them at a "heavy per cent," and probably used some of the profits to repay Young for expenses he incurred for the construction of a grist mill that winter.[14] As Young intended, the church as a whole benefited from the battalion's wages, but that necessarily meant that the battalion families reaped a smaller reward from their men's sacrifice. Young blamed shortfalls on unexpectedly high prices in St. Louis, but the soldiers and their wives expressed grief and anger at Young's management of their wages. After seeking provisions while her husband served in the battalion, Fanny Parks Taggert recalled that "the answer I received from President Young made me feel like bursting into tears." Conflicts persisted long after most of the battalion's soldiers had reached the Salt Lake Valley. "I know that

the lowest scrapings of Hell were in that Bot [battalion]," Young maintained, and he rejected the ongoing concerns of the soldiers' wives. "All
their council & wisdom (although there are many good women)," he
joked dismissively, "don't weigh as much with me as the weight of a Fly
Tird." When Allen had appeared at the Missouri, Young made promises
he could not reasonably fulfill to the enlistees and their families. He appointed several dozen bishops to care for the soldiers' families, and he over
and over again urged the emigrating companies to bring the battalion
families over the mountains in 1847. In the end, the church simply lacked
sufficient resources to meet the needs of its many impoverished members.
Young probably could have blunted some of the criticism with a straightforward explanation of the church's circumstances and an apology for his
inability to make good on his pledges. When church members criticized
him, though, Young interpreted it as a challenge to his authority, dug in his
heels, and responded with vitriol.[15]

When facing decisions on the trail, however, he demonstrated much
more supple leadership, as he had done when Allen appeared at Council
Bluffs. After abandoning the rush across the mountains, he pronounced it
"Gospel" that the entire church would winter at Grand Island, two hundred miles west on the Platte. After discussions with Kane and Allen, however, he wisely switched course again and decided that the Camp of Israel
would winter on the west shore of the Missouri, while other Mormons
would remain at the camps and farms constructed across Iowa. Aside from
the virtual impossibility of transporting the far-flung Saints all the way to
Grand Island, the Missouri River provided better grazing and opportunities for trade. Young had demonstrated considerable uncertainty while organizing the exodus; through July he still toyed with vanguard mountain-
crossing expeditions and schemes to settle British converts on Vancouver
Island, off the coast of British Columbia. Ultimately, his decisions to relinquish an 1846 mountain crossing, support the recruitment of the Mormon
Battalion, and concentrate the emigration on the Great Basin all served to
strengthen the church's prospects. Young stubbornly clung to the objectives he articulated for the church, but as circumstances dictated he pursued them with considerable flexibility.[16]

THE 3,500 Mormons on the Missouri ferried themselves across the river,
selected a site about twenty miles above the conjunction of the Platte and
Missouri rivers that became known simply as Winter Quarters, cultivated
peaceful relations with several native tribes, feverishly cut enough hay to
feed their cattle over the winter, and then erected what Young's wife Zina
Huntington termed a small "City of log huts."[17]

In Kirtland, Far West, and Nauvoo, the Saints' Zion always housed a mixed multitude of committed church members, disaffected and former Mormons, and antagonistic Gentiles. Young now wanted to expel sinners, weed out those not fully committed, and arrive in his mountain sanctuary with a purified church. When informed in September that several young men had behaved improperly toward young women, Young ordered them flogged. The whippings sparked objections from the boys' parents and discomfited other members of the camp. Young falsely claimed that "I did not know of it till after it was done." He vigorously defended the punishment, though, surmising that the objections meant that the "Marshall did not whip them hard enough" and warning that if such sexual immorality did not cease "the Law of God should be executed & that would make short work." Young believed biblical law mandated death for extramarital sexual relations. Joseph Smith regularly preached about the need for unity and righteousness; Brigham Young demanded it.[18]

One of the unusual aspects of life at Winter Quarters was the partial emergence of the church's altered and expanded family structures. Though the church still did not publicly announce the doctrine to outsiders, those involved in plural marriages no longer guarded their secrets so tightly. "Here we had now openly," Zina later wrote of the early months of the exodus, "the first examples of noble-minded, virtuous women, bravely commencing to live in the newly-revealed order of celestial marriage."[19]

Such steps required bravery on the part of Mormon women, especially given the sobering conditions of the exodus. Shortly after leaving Nauvoo, Eliza Partridge Lyman found her sister Emily "in a tent surrounded with mud." In her arms, Emily held Young's infant son, born the previous October. Emily stopped at Mt. Pisgah—a Mormon way station one hundred miles short of Council Bluffs—with her mother and stepfather. There, her newborn elicited considerable fascination. She later wrote that "people would stop at our house to see a spiritual child." Visitors debated whether such children possessed the same intelligence as those conceived by monogamous parents. Emily lamented Young's inability to provide companionship and material assistance during the exodus. "Pres. Young had to look after the welfare of the whole people . . ." she recalled. "So you will see he had not much time to devote to his family."[20] With Young occupied by both the practical work of pioneering and the ecclesiastical and political difficulties incumbent to church leadership, many of his wives had to rely on the charity of family, friends, or other church members.

Still, Young expended considerable effort persuading his wives to leave Nauvoo and join him in Winter Quarters, probably concerned that geographic separation would sever marital bonds sometimes only recently formed. Harriet Cook, for example, did not leave Nauvoo with Brigham's company because she delivered the couple's first child on February 10. Beginning in mid-March, Brigham wrote Harriet a series of letters asking her to coordinate departure plans with several other plural wives still in Nauvoo. "Kiss the Babe for me," he wrote tenderly. "The girls talk a gradeal about you and wish you with them." "[T]hey have a tent to themselves," he added of the plural wives then with his camp. Contrary to Brigham's advice, Harriet lingered in Nauvoo. Perhaps because of the trauma of remaining in a half-empty and besieged city with an infant and without a husband, she became deeply unhappy, apparently regretting her marriage. "I have had a variety of feelings since you left," she wrote Young the following summer, mentioning "the powers of darkness that have surrounded me for the past year." She made plans to return to her own family in the East, plans that alarmed and saddened Brigham when he got wind of them. "I cannot have the thaught of you going East," he pleaded with her. ". . . Come here your friends are here we injoy our selves first rate." He offered to send a team or even come himself. Harriet wrestled with conflicting emotions. Eventually, she resolved her doubts, informing Brigham that "the Lord has made known to me the integrity of your heart and that all your intentions were pure before him." She joined him at Winter Quarters in 1847.[21]

Several women sealed to Young but already married to other men now had to make a choice. Mary Elizabeth Rollins remained with her non-Mormon husband, living in Wisconsin, Minnesota, and Missouri over the next fifteen years without forgetting her connection to Mormonism or Brigham Young.[22] Other wives, by contrast, now made a break with their first husbands. Zina Huntington, who had continued living with Henry Jacobs even after her marriage to Brigham, left Nauvoo in an advanced state of pregnancy. With Henry's assistance, Zina gave birth to their second son on the banks of the Chariton River. Just hours later, other Saints helped them cross the river and resume their muddy journey. Shortly thereafter, the marriage effectively ended, as Henry left for a mission to England and Zina began living with members of Young's family at Winter Quarters. From New York, Henry assured her that his "Love is as ever the same and much more abundantly." He looked forward to a future "when familyes are paired together and become one." Although "there will be shiftings in time and revisions in Eternety," he expected that "all [will] be mad[e] right in the End." It is unclear when Henry learned of Zina's new living arrangements—perhaps not until he returned to New York the next year. Though he mourned Zina's loss for many years, he never expressed

Zina Diantha Huntington, ca. 1855 *(courtesy of L. Tom Perry Special Collections, Harold B. Lee Library, Brigham Young University).* To her right are Zebulon William and Henry Chariton, her sons with Henry Jacobs. To her left is Zina Presendia, her daughter with Brigham Young.

any anger against Young. In her diary and letters, Zina revealed very little about her transition to her new husband's family.[23]

Henry Jacobs's decision to keep his anxieties private made Zina's transition into Young's family relatively smooth. Other parties were not as circumspect, and some marital relations remained unresolved for years. In Nauvoo, Young was sealed to Mary Woodward a few days after having ritually adopted Mary and her husband James. At Winter Quarters, Mary Woodward drew Young's ire when she told others about her temple sealing. Terming her mouth *"an open sepulchre,"* Young told Mary to "consider yourself discharged from *me,* and my counsel." Although he encouraged her to "take your cow hide and correct yourself," he also offered to provide food for her and her children in the event of hunger.[24]

Young's letter did not settle the matter, however. According to James Woodward, Mary's longing for Young made her marriage to James untenable. "[I]t is now the common talk," James complained in a letter to

Young, "that you made her covenant not to sleep with me." James professed himself willing to love Mary as his wife or to give her up, "but to live in this way any longer I cannot it will kill me." Seeking clarification, Mary asked Young if "you wish me to raise children by him for you." She remained with James, unhappily, for she still considered herself Young's wife. Mary's letters to Young gradually became more desperate. "I cannot give you up," she wrote, "god dont tell me to." "I took the same privelige *Mary Ann* [Angell] and the *rest* took," she complained to him several years later, "of Choosing for eternity and all earth & hell seeme contrived against me what have I done that there is no place at S[alt] Lak[e] for me & mine." Other women sealed to Brigham Young, including Augusta Adams and Julia Foster, still regarded Mary Woodward as part of their husband's family, but Young himself no longer did.[25]

Young also regretted another of his Nauvoo sealings. Sarah Alley, sister of Young's wife Margaret Alley, informed Clarissa Blake Homiston that Young believed he "had been too hasty in taking you." Clarissa professed herself ignorant of the reason for Young's "disapprobation," which he made evident in a brief and awkward encounter before his departure from Nauvoo. Clarissa remained with her prior husband Lyman Homiston. After they journeyed to Salt Lake City in 1850, Clarissa attempted to renew contact with Young, expressing a desire for reconciliation and requesting the opportunity for her deceased daughter, her only child, to also become Young's wife for eternity. As Young's fellow apostle Amasa Lyman later conceded of early attempts to practice plural marriage, "we obeyed the best we knew how, and, no doubt, made many crooked paths in our ignorance." Young navigated crooked paths in the cases of Clarissa Blake Homiston, Mary de la Montague Woodward, and Zina Huntington Jacobs, but such difficulties never shook his faith in the divinity of plural marriage.[26]

In Winter Quarters, Young began consolidating his polygamous family. Some of his wives still lived with relatives or boarded with other families, but others moved into what Eliza Snow termed "the 2d Mansion of Prest. B. Young." In this "comfortable little log house," Zina Huntington shared a room with Louisa Beaman and Emmeline Free. A core group of sister wives befriended one another, forming an intimate and intensely spiritual *"female family."* At Winter Quarters, several wives laid hands on each other to cure illnesses, mourned with mothers who lost children, pronounced blessings upon each other, and cultivated the gift of speaking in tongues. "This is truly a glorious time," Eliza Snow wrote in her diary, "with the mothers and daughters in Zion."[27]

Not surprisingly given Young's large, unwieldy family, other wives were less content. Namaah Twiss, who had married Young in the temple, complained that she and Mary Eliza Greene had "to sleep in a waggeon" in Winter Quarters. Not immune from the sickness and death that plagued the Mormons at Winter Quarters, plural wife Mary Pierce died of consumption in March 1847. Young preached at her funeral.[28] It was also a difficult environment in which to welcome children into the world. Louisa Beaman delivered a baby boy named Moroni, Young's first child born at Winter Quarters. On January 15, Young held Moroni, and Heber Kimball pronounced a blessing, which Young cherished so much he asked Willard Richards to make several copies of it. Moroni, though, died seven months later from "teething and canker."[29]

Mary Ann Angell Young, the only wife the others referred to as "Sister Young" or "Mrs. Young," befriended "the girls." Augusta Adams informed Brigham that "Mrs. Young appears to have good feelings towards all." Some of Young's wives recognized her position of prominence and apparently held her in high esteem. In a poem, Eliza Snow paid homage to Mary Ann as "Mother of mothers! Queen of queens." Mary Ann involved herself in the pentecostal gatherings of the female family, at least on one occasion singing "a song of Zion," presumably in tongues. For some women, quite possibly including Mary Ann Angell, the shared bonds of a social and spiritual sisterhood compensated for some of the disadvantages of polygamy. Even when Brigham had been her monogamous husband, he had often been away from home or otherwise consumed with church business. Now, a group of women bound to her through sacred rituals alleviated her loneliness.[30]

Young never again rapidly accumulated wives as he had done in Nauvoo, perhaps because the trail revealed the practical difficulties of providing for and managing a large and always evolving family. In July, Young demurred when a man requested him to resolve an unhappy marriage by taking his wife "forever." He still married on occasion, however. In March 1847, Young was sealed to sisters Lucy and Mary Jane Bigelow. According to family tradition, his proposal came while discussing their rebuff of another suitor. The following winter, Young married forty-three-year-old Sarah Malin the same day that he sealed her father to a wife. Several women, including Jane Terry and Melissa Hamblin, made deathbed requests "to be sealed" to Young. Presumably, temple rituals later added them to his eternal family.[31]

Young's attitudes toward women and marriage elude simple interpretation; his many comments on those subjects over the years are full of contradictions. Many nineteenth-century Protestants preached spiritual egalitarianism while resisting earthly forms of equality. In a sense, Mormons followed suit, but in distinctive ways. The endowment and the church's marriage ceremony promised tremendous spiritual blessings and power to both male and female participants. Men and women needed each other to achieve celestial glory. At the same time, they did not participate in such rites as equals. Men and women could become kings and queens, but multiple queens added to the eternal kingdoms of a single patriarch. Shortly after leaving Nauvoo, Young very clearly described the husband as "the head & God of the woman."[32]

Like many Protestant ministers, Young was uncomfortable with the idea of women holding formal positions of leadership. Joseph Smith had established a female Relief Society in 1842 with its own elected officers and hundreds of members, but Young suspended Relief Society meetings. "When I want Sisters . . . to get up Relief Society I will summon them to my aide," Young warned in 1845, "but until that time let them stay at home." He did not explain his reasoning, but Emma Smith's leadership of Relief Society and her blunt talk against polygamy in some of its early meetings probably influenced Young's views. Young later changed his mind, perhaps prompted by some of his plural wives. For now, though, he wanted women to exercise spiritual gifts privately.[33]

Upper-class, Victorian Protestants of Young's day, recognizing the disproportionate number of women in the pews, considered women naturally more religious and righteous than men. Young, perhaps reflecting his hardscrabble, backcountry Protestant upbringing, dissented in derogatory fashion. "A woman is the distirst [dirtiest] creature," he stated, "dirtier than a man." He asserted that "men are honest," but "if a woman wont lie, she is a miracle." With some regularity, he made it clear that he would not take orders from women within his family and that men should act as the leaders of their families and expect obedience from their wives. "The influence of my women over me," he insisted, "is no more than the buzzing of a fly's wing in winter." Men should not kowtow to their wives. "[D]o there Heavy lug[g]ing," he advised, identifying an acceptable form of chivalry, "but don't wash there dishes as some men do."[34]

Young's sense of patriarchy extended to sexuality. Under early-nineteenth-century understandings of coverture, married women became the property of their husbands not only economically but also sexually, a belief that persisted even as new legislation gradually provided married women with more control over their property. Most courts did not accept the concept of rape within marriage, nor did they consider a husband's unwanted sexual advances to be the sort of cruelty that merited a divorce.[35] While some reformers, such as the followers of Sylvester Graham, suggested that women could and should reject their husbands' desire for frequent sexual activity, Young joined most American men in considering sexual access part of a man's patriarchal privilege. His belief in the sexual access of men to their wives partly followed from the church's doctrine of plural marriage, sometimes termed "patriarchal marriage." Men whom God commanded to "raise up seed" by taking plural wives obviously needed such access. "It is perfectly right," Young taught at Winter Quarters, "that you enjoy a woman all you can to overflowing & tell her to keep all about her clean & neat." When a December 1847 council condemned Young's adopted son John D. Lee for his cruel treatment of his wives, including Lee's purported boast that he had "frigged [Young's sister-in-law] Louisa Free 20 times in one night," Young joined in upbraiding Lee but seemed to make light of some allegations. "[T]hats the matter with John," Young laughed, "he has loved his women too much & frigged them too much." Despite the crude humor, Young would not tolerate other forms of domestic violence and granted divorces to those women who chose to leave Lee's family.[36]

For all of his patriarchal rhetoric and his initial opposition to Relief Society, Young at times expressed a much greater appreciation for the talents of women and for their contributions to the church. Perhaps because of his class background and probably in part because of the economic realities of plural marriage, he did not embrace the emerging American notion of separate spheres for men and women. Apart from ecclesiastical affairs, he observed that women in other realms "have a right to meddle because many of them are more sagacious and shrewd and more competent [than men] to attend to things of financial affairs." By necessity, moreover, many of Young's plural wives had to earn money and manage their own finances. He also valued the spiritual contributions of women, within and beyond the household. "I want a wife that can take care of my children when I am away," he said shortly before Joseph Smith's death, "who can pray, lay on hands, anoint with oil, and baffle the enemy." Such a wife, Young explained, would truly be a "spiritual wife." Young's wives administered— engaged in ritual healing practices—not just to their children, but to each other and sometimes to Mormon men.[37]

While Young struggled to work out the earthly implications of celestial marriage for his own family, he claimed the authority to regulate the practice in the church. The Twelve held in 1846 that "no man has a right to attend to the ordinance of sealing except the president of the Church or those who are directed by him to do so." In other words, only Young or those he directed could authorize marriages; in numerous instances, Young disciplined followers for performing sealings without his blessing. He complained that some Mormons used the doctrine to seduce women, sleep with them, and then went "to some clod head of an elder and get him to say their ceremony." Particularly in a church that taught that its members needed the ordinance of celestial marriage for their salvation, the fact that Young successfully claimed this critical priestly prerogative for himself greatly augmented his sacerdotal power.[38]

Like plural marriage, adoption became a more obvious part of Mormon society during the exodus, prompted by Young, who announced in March 1846 that "individuals hereafter [should] be called by ther Name that they received by adoption." Some adopted sons, including John D. Lee, began using Young's surname and addressing him as "Father." While Young and the apostles did not perform any ritual adoptions during the exodus, they kept records of men who sought ritual entrance into their families pending the completion of a new temple. Forging close economic ties with several adopted sons, Young established a family farm near Winter Quarters and asked Lee and fellow adopted son Isaac Morley to manage it, apportioning land to other members of the extended family. At Winter Quarters, Young met repeatedly with his "family organization," a larger conglomeration of three hundred men linked to him by relation, friendship, or ritual. Wilford Woodruff, invited to these meetings along with the other apostles, referred to Young's company as "the tribe of Brigham." Like the biblical twelve sons of Joseph, the twelve Mormon apostles would form their own tribes, their family companies. Big Elk, an aging Omaha chief whom Young met at the Missouri, referred to the Mormon leader as the "Big Red headed chief." Unlike most Americans on whom Indians bestowed such titles, Young acted the part of a tribal chieftain. During the exodus, he settled marital and financial disputes like an ancient Israelite judge, discoursed on theological doctrine, and tried to instill bonds of loyalty among his adopted sons. Young now lived as the patriarchal father of a large clan, but he told his assembled family members, especially those who were his elders, to simply call him "Brother Brigham."[39]

As was the case with plural marriage, adoption became controversial, confusing, and sometimes competitive. Some church members worried that ritual adoption might diminish their own celestial glory. Addressing such concerns, Young spoke at length about the doctrine in mid-February, emphasizing that those men sealed to him would increase rather than diminish their own glory. "[S]ay that I am ruling over 10 sons or subjects," Young explained, "& soon each one of them would have 10 men sealed to them & then would be ruler over them & that would make me ruler over 10 Presidents or Kings." Each faithful man would occupy a position of exalted kingship within this "Chain of the Priesthood." Despite his best efforts to explain the doctrine, the law of adoption still confused Young's followers and kindled dissension.[40]

The morning after his extended discourse on adoption, Young suddenly fell ill and had a vision while he slept. Young reported that he "actually went into Eternity," "came back again," and then fell back asleep. He dreamed of Joseph Smith sitting in a room next to a bright window. When he recovered, Young took the now unusual step of recording his experience in his own handwriting. "I took him [Joseph] by the right hand and kist him meney times," Young began, "he looked perfically natureal, I asked him why it was that we could not be together as we used to live." Joseph assured him they would be together again in the future. Brigham then told Joseph that "the Bretheren have grate anxiety to understand the law of adoption or seeling principals" and asked for a "word of councel." In response, Smith instructed him to "tell the people to be humble and faithful and [be] sure to keep the sperit of the Lord and it will lead them right." He urged the Saints to rely on "the smal[l] still voice" of the Holy Spirit. Finally, Smith showed him how God had organized the human family "in the begining" and reminded Young that "it must be joined to gether so there would be a perfect chane [chain] from Father Adam to his latest posterity." Young placed great stock in dreams as a conduit for divine instruction, but he only rarely recorded them so fully. Although in the dream Smith seemed to affirm the cosmic significance of adoption, following his visionary experience Young no longer emphasized the controversial ritual. Perhaps he felt the "still small voice" prompt him to set the doctrine aside for a time. Adoption faded from immediate importance, though the links between Young and some adopted sons, such as Lee, remained significant.[41]

For Brigham Young, like Joseph Smith, the chief end of humankind was eternal fellowship and familial glory. "[I]f men are not saved together," Young insisted, "they cannot be saved at all." "What is my glory?" he asked. "My family, around me, of one heart & mind." Smith once commented that he would rather go to hell with the Saints than to heaven without them; Young claimed "that he would rather be annihilated than be deprived of his family & of all society in eternity." However much evangelical converts focused their attention on unconverted family members, the nexus of American evangelicalism was individual salvation. By contrast, Young's theology, like that of Joseph Smith, centered around extended families. The Latter-day Saints under Brigham Young created earthly kingdoms, bound for eternity through plural marriages and ritual adoptions, the antithesis of the self-reliant American preached in Massachusetts by Ralph Waldo Emerson. Communitarian in theology as well as in economics, the Mormons rejected the intense individualism associated with religious figures and movements as diverse as Emerson and evangelicalism. What remained unclear, however, was how they could achieve earthly harmony while creating the expanded family structures they expected to persist for eternity.[42]

AT WINTER Quarters, Young busied himself with a host of practical tasks, trying to make his grist mill operational, maintaining peaceful relations with various Indian tribes despite near-constant conflicts over cattle theft, and discussing the logistical challenge of organizing the mountain crossing of the perhaps 12,000 Mormon refugees strung out between Nauvoo and the Missouri. After a year of uncertainty and physical trials, including the death of an estimated 400 Mormons at Winter Quarters during the winter of 1846–47, the future of both the church and Young's leadership remained opaque. James Strang, who criticized Young for "taking out thousands of women and children to perish by famine, flood and Indian war," remained a viable option for Mormons whose miserable experiences during 1846 cast doubt on either Young's decision-making or revelatory authority. Given the physical suffering of the 1846 trail and subsequent winter, it was imperative for Young that the Saints view him as a leader who could provide them with spiritual succor, especially in the absence of physical comfort.[43]

For an early winter's fortnight, however, Young instead gave the church a spiritual browbeating. In mid-December 1846, Young called for a season of repentance and purification, "an entire & thoroug[h] reformation" in which church members would turn from sinful behavior to prepare for the renewed journey west. Young knew that disease and death were breeding doubt. "You must stop," he instructed during the December reformation, "your back biteings speaking evil of the Twelve speaking evil of me . . . or you will be damned." He reminded the Saints that dissent had cost their first prophet his life. "Brother Joseph," he warned them, "being a vary merciful man bore with these things untill it took his life but I will not do it." Young encouraged malcontents to decamp for Missouri, threatening that "if they go with us & continue there wickedness there Heads shall be sevred from their tabernacles [bodies]." The harsh, uncompromising messages probably gave the less committed pause about continuing the journey.[44]

Young pronounced himself pleased with the results of his December preaching. "We have had quite a reformation at this place of late," he wrote Charles C. Rich, a general in the Nauvoo Legion then at Mt. Pisgah, "good feelings prevailing in the breasts of the Saints." Once the fortnight of reformation ended, Young changed his tone and responded to the people's need for recreation and merriment. After an evening meeting, several musicians arrived, and a dance commenced. Around nine o'clock, the assembled Saints sang Charles Wesley's Methodist standard "Come, Let Us Anew Our Journey Pursue." Finally, the group prayed, led by Young, who "thanked the Lord for the privilege of praising God in the Song, dance &c." "After which," recorded Willard Richards, "he gave an address in tong[u]es, then conversed in tong[u]es with Elder Kimball." Such scenes reminded the Saints that seasons of harsh preaching only comprised one aspect of Young's spirituality and leadership.[45]

Two weeks later, Young issued what became his only revelation later canonized by the church. Several days before the revelation, Young shared the contents of a dream, in which Joseph Smith found his mother intently reading a pamphlet. The prophet asked his mother, "Have you got the Word of God there?" When she answered in the affirmative, Joseph replied, "I think you will be sick of that pretty soon." Scriptures and past revelations, the dream implied, were not enough. Three days later, on January 14, Young spent several hours writing—apparently by his own hand—"the Word and Will of the Lord." Heber Kimball properly identified the document as the first revelation "that has been penned since Joseph was killed." It began prosaically by affirming the church's division into companies (with captains of hundreds, fifties, and tens) and explaining in rough terms the responsibilities of those undertaking the 1847 crossing and those remaining behind. Moving beyond the pragmatic, the revelation explicitly identified the Mormons with the ancient Israelites, promising that God's "arm is stretched out in the last days to save my people Israel." Like Young's recent reformation preaching, the text condemned drunkenness and theft, though it also encouraged the Saints to "Praise the Lord with singing, with music, with dancing and with a prayer of praise and thanksgiving." Perhaps most significantly, the revelation insisted that the exodus proceed "under the direction of the Twelve Apostles"; it attributed sacred authority to their decisions and encouraged those complaining about the staggered emigration plan or proposing alternative ideas to submit to the apostles' authority. Police captain Hosea Stout, who recorded the revelation in his diary, rejoiced that it would "put to silence the wild bickering & and suggestions of those who are ever in the way."[46]

The "Word and Will of the Lord" enhanced Young's status as the church's new living oracle and ushered in a season of high spirits at Winter Quarters as the spring journey slowly approached. Mary Haskin Parker

Richards, a niece of Willard Richards by marriage, recorded glimpses of Young's winter merriment in her diary. On January 26, he danced a "mon[e]y musk" with her, followed by a cotillion two weeks later. "Sister Mary," Young told her after the latter, "you have learned me I am very much obliged to you." Evidently, Young's enthusiasm exceeded his ability; along with several other apostles he attended a dancing school organized at the Winter Quarters council house. In early February, Young and the Twelve attended a picnic organized by the "Silver Greys," a club of Latter-day men over fifty years of age. Young declared it a time for mirth. "[I]n a very short time the dancing meetings will all be done away," he advised. Soon they would begin the final organization of the pioneer companies. "[Y]ou may dance all night," he said, encouraging them to enjoy the present, for "there is no harm in it." At the end of the evening, Young, Kimball, Woodruff, and others "with two ladies each danced the Mormon dance, full of life and happiness." The Mormons could poke fun at themselves. Following the dance, William Clayton read the "Word and Will of the Lord" to the crowd. The following winter, Young offered a robust defense of singing, dancing, and merriment. "[W]hoever goes to hell I'll warrant you wont here fiddling or have dancing," he said, "all music is in heaven, all enjoyment is of the Lord." Young's Mormonism remained a faith of physicality, fellowship, and recreation alongside ritual and revelation, a faith that imbued farming, house-raising, and even dancing with sacred significance.[47]

By MID-March 1847, the time for dancing had passed. Young "instructed the brethren to forget dancing, & now commence prayer meetings, & administer the Sacrament."[48] It was time to go. Young had decided against planting crops at the foot of the mountains, hoping an advance party could reach the Salt Lake or Bear River valley in time to plant summer crops. Other, larger companies would follow later in the summer. In mid-April, Young left Winter Quarters. Nearly one hundred and fifty Mormon pioneers traveled with Young, all but five of them adult men. Lorenzo Young had persuaded his older brother to let his ailing and pregnant wife, Harriet Decker Young, accompany the camp. Clara Decker, Brigham Young's eighteen-year-old wife and Harriet Decker's daughter, received permission to come in order to help care for her mother. Lorenzo and Harriet Young brought two sons, and Heber Kimball brought one wife. The pioneer camp included three African American slaves, brought by Mississippi Mormon John Brown, as well as several non-Mormons on friendly terms with the church.[49]

Around four thousand other Americans crossed the Plains to Oregon in

1847, but the Mormon pioneers started earlier and from a more westerly point than most emigrants. Especially since the Mormons used the less-traveled north bank of the Platte instead of the Oregon Trail on the opposite shore, they encountered few white Americans, occasionally meeting the odd trader and more frequently spotting Pawnee and then Sioux Indians. The U.S. Army had no installations between Fort Leavenworth and the Great Basin, and since Stephen Kearny's 1845 march to South Pass there had been no sign of an American military presence on the Oregon Trail.[50]

Elected "General & Commander in Chief," the Mormon Moses fostered spiritual commitment and military discipline. After stopping for a week thirty miles west of Winter Quarters for final preparations, the camp organized itself for the journey on April 16. When the horn sounded shortly after eight o'clock, Young's ritually adopted son Albert Rockwood recorded all 143 men present. Young then "addressed the throne of grace while the [brethren] neeld in a circle around him." After several speeches, the camp's leaders selected captains and organized nighttime guard assignments, and the Camp of Israel finally began the journey Young had wanted to make a year earlier. Young and his captains instituted a strict daily routine. A horn awoke the camp at five o'clock, and after prayers, breakfast, and preparations, the pioneers planned to resume their journey each morning at seven. Other than a one-hour lunch break, Young planned for the camp to travel until early evening, when pioneers would arrange their wagons in a circle for dinner, prayers, and sleep.[51]

Telling his people to march with their guns loaded, Young instilled a sense of watchfulness about Indian attacks that never materialized, though the Pawnee stole several horses and burned the prairie grass ahead of the Mormons to discourage them from hunting buffalo. The encounters with the Pawnee typified emigrant experiences in the mid-1840s, during which very few white-Indian interactions produced open fighting and fatalities.[52]

During the journey's early weeks, Young was largely content with the camp's behavior. He spent little time sermonizing, declaring that "this is not the time for preaching but for doing." On an evening in late May, however, as the camp approached Fort Laramie, Young complained about "the spirit that prevails & has the ascendancy in the camp—levity, loud laughter, whooping, and hallooing." In part, he blamed the frivolity on the few non-Mormons traveling with the camp, alleging that "three or four men who do not belong to the church are enabled to insinuate the Spirit that rules them through the whole camp." He also worried about the influence of the several slaves on the rest of the company. "[T]hose Negros want to dance," he asserted. "[O]thers join in with them & they all become Negros together." Regardless of the source, Young worried that such behavior would cause the Saints to forget their duty to God and to each other. He retreated to his wagon and prayed, called several of the Twelve together later that night, and "wrote some of the word of the Lord Concerning the camp." After writing sixteen lines of revelation, he "did not care to write any more." He was depressed by the camp's spirit, which he believed was endangering their lives. On a recent night, a guard had fallen asleep and lost his gun, placing the camp at risk of an Indian attack. "It is in vain for this camp to go any farther to find a Location for Zion," he told the apostles, "unless we go with pure hearts." The pioneers, he concluded, should either repent or turn back.[53]

When a miserable rain subsided the next morning, Young assembled the pioneers and unleashed a torrent of criticism. "I have let the brethren dance and fiddle," he began, "and act the nigger night after night." Young's strict Methodist upbringing left a greater imprint on his sensibilities than he sometimes allowed. "I would rather see the dirtiest thing you could find on the earth," he stated, "than a pack of cards in your hands." Decisively, though, Young and several other leaders viewed the trek through the lens of the 1834 Zion's Camp failure, which Joseph Smith attributed to dissension, quarreling, and murmuring. Thus, he made clear the consequences for those who sowed dissent. "I swear to you he shall never see home again," he warned. "I will leave them on the prairie." The pioneer camp's leaders feared that the recent frivolity, if unchecked, would eventually place the camp's success in jeopardy. "There are persons here who were there when the destroying Angel visited us in 1834 . . ." Wilford Woodruff emphasized. "I don't want to see such a scene again." In Young's mind, his harsh response to the camp's recent behavior might save it from a similar scourging.[54]

The next day was a Sunday, and the camp did not travel. After morning services, Young and the camp's Council of Fifty members found a secluded spot in the nearby bluffs, clothed themselves in "the priestly garments," and repeated portions of the endowment rites. Young led a prayer for the pioneers, their families, and the battalion soldiers. According to William Clayton, when the group returned, they found the men "still and sober," with no sign of "jesting, nor laughing, nor nonsense." Young's call to repentance had produced the desired effect.[55]

In early June, the pioneers could see Laramie Peak, "crowned with his winter dress," and they soon stood opposite Fort Laramie, an outpost of the American Fur Company about 600 miles from Winter Quarters. Young and several others crossed the river and met not only the traders at the fort but also a contingent of Mormons from Mississippi who had wintered in Pueblo with a segment of the Mormon Battalion. Moving on, the camp ferried its wagons across the North Platte and proceeded along the Oregon Trail, moving more rapidly to stay ahead of the rush of emigrants bound for the Northwest. Many of the Oregon emigrants were Missourians, whom the Saints regarded as at best bitterly anti-Mormon and at worst complicit in the murder of Joseph and Hyrum Smith. Eagerly anticipating every landmark and tributary indicated by Frémont's map, the camp proceeded through hillier terrain and came to an arduous and dangerous recrossing of the swollen North Platte near present-day Casper, Wyoming. After constructing a large ferry boat and finally getting their wagons across, Young instructed a small group of pioneers to remain behind to extract needed money and provisions from the hated Missourians in return for helping them cross the river. The pioneers reached the Sweetwater River, followed its banks past Devil's Gate, and crossed the Continental Divide at the sagebrush-covered South Pass, now enjoying clear views of the peaks that still lay between them and the Great Basin.⁵⁶

Although Young had long since decided on the Great Basin, he now had to choose an exact destination. In late June, the camp encountered two renowned "mountain men" in quick succession, Moses Harris and then Jim Bridger. The thousands of Americans crowding the Oregon Trail behind the Mormon pioneers heralded the end of an era—emigrants in search of farms and then minerals would replace the trappers and traders who had characterized the early American presence in the Mountain West. Men like Harris and Bridger knew the region better than nearly any other white men, but they gave Young conflicting advice. Harris favored the Bear River's Cache Valley to the north, and Bridger recommended the territory between the Utah and Salt lakes. Bridger persuaded Young to go south to his fort, then follow what was known as the Hastings Cutoff, the route into the Great Basin near the Salt Lake that several parties had navigated the past two summers. Partly based on Bridger's advice, Young later directed his people to "the region of the Salt Lake rather than the Utah," so as "not to crowd upon the Utes" who wintered at the streams that flowed into the Utah Lake.⁵⁷

Shortly after the encounters with Harris and Bridger, the company unexpectedly met Sam Brannan, a Mormon entrepreneur who had sailed with a group of Mormons from New York to San Francisco. The intrepid Brannan had journeyed over the snowy Sierra Nevada, encountering survivors of the snowbound Donner Party, some of whom had resorted to cannibalizing their dead companions during an attempt to reach California by snowshoe. After crossing much of the Great Basin, Brannan met Young's party on June 30 while the latter rafted across the Green River. Young and his companions were now nearly 400 miles west of Fort Laramie. Unimpressed with the relative wasteland he had traversed, Brannan encouraged Young to continue to California, but Young remained intent on the Great Basin, "for the present, at least, to examine the country."[58]

From the Green River, the camp traveled to Fort Bridger, which Oregon settler Joel Palmer described as a "shabby concern" occupied by a few white traders and a larger number of Indian wives. At the fort, the Saints met several Mormon Battalion veterans from California, whom they greeted with a Hosanna shout. From Fort Bridger, they crisscrossed streams, climbed steep hills among the mountains, and with locked wheels precariously descended into gullies. Many also endured an incapacitating illness they simply termed "mountain fever" (probably Colorado Tick Fever). On July 12, Young himself became seriously ill—"insensible and raving"—and could not proceed. The Saints "washed & anointed" their president, who survived but recovered slowly. Young largely faded from the camp's decision-making over the next ten days, as Kimball and the other apostles took charge. With Young and a smaller company now trailing behind, the main group of pioneers reached their destination on July 22. By the time Young caught up, Mormons had already dug irrigation trenches, planted potato and corn seeds, and prepared a turnip patch. Young first caught sight of the valley two days later. "We gazed with wonder and admiration," wrote Wilford Woodruff, whose exhilaration Young shared, "upon the vast rich fertile valley . . . Clothed with the Heaviest garb of green vegitation." "President Young," Woodruff recorded, "expressed his full satisfaction in the Appearance of the valley as A resting place for the Saints." The next day, Young expressed his gratification that the pioneers had "reached the *'Promised Land.'*"[59]

Young's leadership of the pioneer camp, along with his role in guiding a larger 1848 party of Mormons to the Salt Lake Valley, became known as the signal accomplishment of his life. The rushed flight from Nauvoo to the Missouri River had come with a sobering cost in terms of death and privation. By contrast, despite its intermittent hardships, the two-and-a-half month journey of 148 men and a few women from Winter Quarters to the Great Basin had proceeded without major mishap. These Mormon pioneers rarely blazed new trails, and they fought no Indians or Gentiles. The Oregon Trail had grown much safer and more populated by 1847, and the camp navigated its more hazardous divergence into the Great Basin both carefully and quickly. The uneventful nature of the trek, though, testifies to Young's leadership capacity and organizational talents. Moving 148 people more than one thousand miles over hazardous terrain without death, hunger, or significant discord could not be taken for granted. When the pioneers received conflicting reports about their destination, some grew uneasy, but the camp held together and pressed on. Young's discipline had inculcated the cohesion, obedience, and vigilance that brought all members of the pioneer camp safely to their destination.[60]

Although some wished to continue explorations, Young said that he recognized the right spot for a settlement when he first saw the valley. "[T]his is the place," he stated at a July 28 meeting.[61] When the pioneers affirmed the decision, Young immediately chose a lot for a new temple. Given his weak physical state, Young did little public preaching, but he shaped policies in private councils. The apostles chose city blocks on which to settle their extended families, including adopted children and those who had journeyed west with the "tribe of Brigham." Under this system of land distribution, only obedient church members (and a few sympathetic fellow travelers) would receive land, the continued use of which depended, in lieu of any legal title, on obedience to Young and other church authorities. Scores of adobe homes, a few log houses, and the beginnings of a fort sprang up in a matter of weeks.[62]

The Great Basin had prior residents, of course. Consumed with the need to quickly establish a settlement, Young had probably given relatively little thought to how the Mormons would relate to the region's native inhabitants. He had purposely avoided more heavily settled Utah Lake, and he discouraged commerce or other interaction with the bands of Shoshone and Utes who utilized the Salt Lake Valley. Young anticipated that the Mormons would eventually convert and civilize the Indians, whom the Saints saw as the cursed descendants of the "Lamanites." Initially, however, Young set aside future hopes of the Indians' redemption in the face of concerns about theft and other potential confrontations. Within days, parties of Utes began coming to the camp to trade, but Young and other church leaders had no sustained contact with Salt Lake Valley Indians that year.

As the Mormon pioneers established the beginnings of what they named "Great Salt Lake City, Great Basin, North America," Young and the other apostles imbued their labors with sacred and prophetic importance. Once he recovered from his illness, Young provided the pioneers with often daily instruction, assigning tasks and organizing work details. He also set the spiritual tone for the new beginning. In early August, Young followed his old New York friend Heber Kimball into a still-cold stream that flowed from the Wasatch Mountains into the Salt Lake Valley. Kimball immersed Young as the latter renewed the baptismal covenant he had first made fifteen years earlier in another icy stream near his Mendon home. Young then baptized the other six apostles with him in the valley. "[W]e had as it were entered a new world," Erastus Snow wrote to explain the impetus for the ceremony, "and wished to renew our covenants & commence in newness of life."[63] The three days of activity culminated with a mass rebaptism of the entire pioneer camp on August 8, the third anniversary of the church's post-martyrdom bestowal of leadership upon the Twelve. For Young, the baptismal waters probably brought a sense not only of renewed commitment, but also of palpable relief. For three years, he had held a fraying church mostly together in the face of dissension, mobs, and uncertainty, and now he had indeed led them into a new world.

The Latter-day Saints were on a divine errand into the wilderness akin to that of their Puritan forebears two centuries earlier. Young and his fellow apostles saw their successful trek over the mountains as the fulfillment of ancient Hebrew scripture. In particular, the Mormons looked to Isaiah's prophecies about the City of Zion being "sought out, A city not forsaken," knew that "the Lord's house shall be established in the top of the mountains," and expected that the "wilderness shall become as a fruitful field." After years of setbacks, dissension, and expulsions, the camp's leadership believed it was witnessing the long-awaited fulfillment of God's promises. Like the seventeenth-century Puritan divines, the apostles characterized their people's relationship to God as a covenant. Should they fulfill their obligations to live uprightly, God would bless the Saints and their new Zion. They would enjoy a future filled with a full measure of glory. The Saints' descendants, Young had predicted upon entering the valley, "may live to the age of a tree & be visited with & hold communion with the Angles [angels]; & bring in the Millenium." If they broke their covenants, they would forfeit their reward and instead could expect divine punishment and rejection. Unlike the way the Puritans had viewed Massachusetts Bay, however, Young did not envision Great Salt Lake City as a "city on a hill," a model community that would inspire Americans to reform their churches and societies in accordance with Mormon principles. Rather, having abandoned hope in the United States, the Mormons intended to raise "a standard and ensign of truth for the nations of the earth," expecting a righteous remnant to seek refuge among them from an anticipated apocalyptic judgment.[64]

Although the Salt Lake Valley technically remained Mexican territory, neither Spain nor Mexico had ever pacified its Indian tribes or colonized the region, and the Mormons expected that the United States would soon claim their new Zion. Young, however, envisioned a mostly autonomous and independent kingdom. "[N]o officer of the United States should ever dictate to him in this valley," he vowed, "or he would hang them on a gibbet as a warning to others." Moreover, notwithstanding the vital role trade with Gentile emigrants played along the Oregon Trail, he called on church members to avoid commerce with outsiders by manufacturing and growing everything they needed.[65]

Young's comments during his first few weeks in the Salt Lake Valley set the tone for the future direction of the society he would lead: a theocratic kingdom resisting encroachments on its autonomy, a society that at best tolerated but could not fully welcome non-Mormons. "[Y]ou don't know," he said of the Gentiles, "how I detest & despise them." Partly because several nonmembers remained with the camp, Young explained that a non-Mormon "may live here with us & worship what God he pleases or none at all." They would tolerate nonbelief but punish any immoral behavior or anti-Mormon animosity. A Gentile, Young warned, "must not blaspheme the God or Israel nor dam old Joe Smith or his religion for we will Salt him down in the Lake!"[66] While expressed crudely, Young's understanding of the rights and responsibilities of religious minorities was mainstream American opinion. In 1821, New York State's chief justice, Ambrose Spencer, stated that non-Christians would be "tolerated" if they did not criticize Christianity, violate standards of morality, or demand equal treatment. Courts in a number of states upheld convictions for blasphemy through mid-century. In rough terms, Young warned non-Mormons that they could not expect better treatment than some religious minorities received in the United States.[67]

LEAVING his plural wife Clara Decker in a hastily built house with several of her relatives, Young left his new Zion in late August, heading back over the mountains to Winter Quarters. Ten days later, on the banks of the Big Sandy River, Young's camp encountered the first company of those Mormons who had left Winter Quarters in mid-June. Under the leadership of Parley Pratt and John Taylor, this emigration camp became much larger than anticipated, and—contrary to Young's January revelation—it contained few poor Saints or battalion families. The pair had also reorganized their camp's leadership as they believed circumstances required. Even before this issue arose, Pratt and Taylor had disappointed Young by choosing to remain with their families in Winter Quarters instead of joining the vanguard group of pioneers. Piqued by what he regarded as insolent disobedience, Young severely chastised Pratt (Taylor's company lagged behind). "I'll spoil your influence," Young threatened Pratt. While Young saw himself as preeminent among the Twelve, Pratt asserted that he and Taylor "hold the keys as well as yourself and I will not be judged by you but by the quorum." Furthermore, Pratt resented what he saw as an arrogation of power that correspondingly diminished the authority of the other apostles. "I've heard you say there is only two of the Twelve that is good for anything," he complained, presumably referring to Heber Kimball and Willard Richards. Young denied making that statement, but he insisted that he, not Pratt, possessed the "oracles" of revelation. In particular, Young sharply defended his right to chastise and correct his top associates. The other apostles present affirmed that Pratt had erred, and after some further resistance Pratt repented and asked forgiveness. "I forgive you," said Young, "but I'll swear to you I shall whip you and make you to stick to me."[68]

Even after the camp victoriously completed its return journey to Winter Quarters, the strained encounter with Parley Pratt—who along with Taylor wintered in the Salt Lake Valley—gnawed at Young. In mid-November meetings of the Twelve, Young made a series of complaints about the pair's behavior: Pratt had committed adultery by marrying plural wives without his permission; Pratt and Taylor had gotten "the Big Head" after their return from England; the pair had misused funds and refused to offer any assistance to Young's wife. "[J]ust as quick as he was in the Quorum," Young complained about Taylor's alleged air of superiority, "he said you are my niggers & you shall black my boots." "I shall never get any rest," he vowed, "until I get in that [Salt Lake] Valley and Parley Pratt and John Taylor bow down & confess that they are not Brigham Young." While Young seethed, the other apostles smarted at Young's public treatment of Pratt and Taylor. Almost to a man they suggested that Young should bring concerns to them in private instead of lambasting them in front of others. Orson Pratt, Parley's brother, asserted that all of the apostles were "equal" and that a majority of the Twelve could overrule Young. "I am the mouth piece," an insulted Young retorted, "and you are the belly." They could either let him treat them as he saw fit, or one of them could take on the burdens of leadership. As the quorum's "King," he would rule "perfectly untrammeled." All save Orson Pratt affirmed Young's right to keep speaking his mind.[69]

The clash with Parley Pratt and Taylor brought to the fore an issue Young had considered for several years, the reconstitution of a "First Presidency" consisting of himself and two counselors. On one level, the point seems entirely technical, as Young had clearly led the church over the past three years. Nevertheless, the subject of the church's leadership structure was of pressing importance to him. If he organized a First Presidency, the church would revert to more familiar forms of leadership, and other members of the Twelve could resume missionary travels. Young could then make decisions without obtaining the assent of the quorum. In large part because of that reduction in authority, many of the apostles resisted what they saw as an unauthorized power grab.[70]

In a series of meetings culminating at an early December 1847 session across the Missouri River in Iowa, a divided quorum tackled the issue of the church presidency. Both Wilford Woodruff and George A. Smith had previously expressed reservations to Young, but only Orson Pratt boldly countered Young's claims, arguing that the apostles had effectively governed the church and that Young possessed no divine authorization to alter the existing arrangement. As the discussion proceeded, Young grew animated and "full of Spirit & Shout," interspersing his arguments with shouting, singing, and hollering. Young scoffed at Pratt's arguments and wore down his objections. "Shit on Congress," he rebuffed Pratt's not overly shrewd comparison of his position to that of the Speaker of the House of Representatives. "When you undertake to dictate and council me it insults me," he rebuked Pratt. Young ended by recounting a dream in which "a personage" came to him, enabled him to contemplate the planets, and "said he could show me in two minutes that the system is correct." "I bel[ieve] the L[or]d God will give me revelations as plain as he ever told Joseph," he concluded before the council voted.[71]

If Parley Pratt and John Taylor had been present, they would have vigorously opposed the formation of a new church presidency, and Young may not have prevailed. Ultimately, however, Young's practical accomplishments and sheer willpower swamped the opposition, and the apostles unanimously appointed Young the church's president and invited him to select his two counselors. As expected, he chose Kimball and Richards. It was now ten o'clock at night. The apostles retired to Orson Hyde's cabin, ate a late supper, sang "the Pioneer song," and drank "Jerusalem Wine & delightful Strawberry Wine." "Our souls," recorded clerk Thomas Bullock, "[were] all rejoicing in the Lord." While the recent council meetings had sometimes devolved into rancor, Young and his fellow apostles now experienced a shared sense of spiritual relief and ecstasy.

Several weeks later, on December 27, church leaders raised the issue of forming a new First Presidency at a spiritually charged church conference. Young's sermon on the occasion reflected his spiritual ebullience. "This is the best day I have seen in my life," he said. "This is a heavenly day, a day of Zion." Orson Pratt then introduced the proposal he had so bitterly resisted. "If I was to go [to] every man and woman [and] ask who is the man," Pratt stated, "they all know the man." The church unanimously affirmed its leader. "I will do right without being trammeled in my feelings," Young vowed. The assembled Latter-day Saints, striking their right hands into their left palms after every word, joined in a threefold shout of "Hosanna! Hosanna! Hosanna! To God and the Lamb! Amen! Amen! and Amen!" As the meeting ended, three violinists played "God save the king."[72]

THOUGH the public unanimity masked the prior tensions, Young must have felt a tremendous sense of both relief and accomplishment. He had endured three years of Strang, Rigdon, and others sniping at his leadership's alleged illegitimacy and predicting the failure of both the temple and the exodus. Undaunted by the Illinois government's unreliable protection, Young had completed the temple and then led the pioneers to plant the Kingdom of God in the Salt Lake Valley. Where dissension had undermined Joseph Smith, Young had taken quick and decisive action to instill loyalty and obedience in those followers who dared question him. "[Y]ou cant tell how this harness feels on you till you feel it," he warned the apostles one year later. "[The apostles] are in the harness and must keep in the line or they will be cuffed."[73] Young and his closest followers shared bonds of affection forged through their years of missionary work, persecutions, and pioneering, but Young did not simply rely on the affection of his associates. He demanded their obedience.

Although Young had settled the question of his own authority, he had out of necessity left many other questions unanswered. He had proclaimed his independence from the United States, but when he repeated the journey across the mountains in 1848 he entered territory now claimed by Washington through a treaty imposed on defeated Mexico. Young predicted the conversion of the Lamanites but discouraged Mormon interactions with them in the valley. Several Mormons from the South had brought slaves with them to the Great Basin—what would their status be in the territory-to-be and the church? With three wives in the Salt Lake Valley, others in Winter Quarters, and still others remaining in Nauvoo and elsewhere, Young's family life also reflected uncertainty. Upon reaching the Missouri, he met two daughters born in his absence (to Clarissa Ross and Emmeline Free, respectively). He now had children by seven different living wives. Young had pressed forward with plural marriage, but while the doctrine exhilarated some Mormons, it confused and disheartened others. In order to answer the many thorny questions facing the church, Young would need adaptability and wisdom as much as stubborn willpower, for he would eventually encounter opponents his personality could not overwhelm.

CHAPTER SEVEN

A New Era of Things

And I saw a new heaven and a new earth: for the first heaven and
the first earth were passed away.

—REVELATION, 21:1

IN JUNE 1848, Brigham Young again set forth from Winter Quarters.
Prodded by the U.S. government's denial of permission for the church to
remain at the Missouri for another season, nearly two thousand Mormons
crossed the mountains that summer. In September, the Saints halted at the
Weber River in honor of "the leader of Israel." When Young overtook
them, he "past [passed] into the valley in his place, at the head of the joyful multitude." The crowd greeting his party sang a hymn composed by
Young's wife Eliza Snow, who praised the arrival of the "great father in
Israel," the "chieftain" of his people. In 1847, Young had left around two
hundred pioneers in Salt Lake City; by the fall of 1848 the valley contained
over four thousand Mormons. "I'm happy to be here," he proclaimed the
next Sabbath morning, "my soul is full of joy." For most Mormons, it had
been, in Young's words, "a dark and dreary time since the death of Joseph
Smith." Now they could begin again.[1]

The political founders of the American Republic saw themselves as entering a "new order of the ages," a Latin phrase *(Novus ordo seclorum)*
included on the reverse of the new nation's official seal. Upon their settlement in the Great Basin, the Mormons similarly entered what they understood to be a new era. They were now free from previous constraints, free
to govern themselves according to their beliefs, and free to openly practice
the doctrine of celestial marriage. The Mormon exodus, however, was far
more than a withdrawal from the antebellum United States. In reliving the

experiences of the biblical Israelites, the Mormons had reentered a more ancient stream of sacred history. In the Great Basin, Young governed the church like an Israelite judge or patriarch, giving his judgment in criminal cases, settling marital disputes, and regularly visiting new settlements to maintain his personal bond with far-flung Saints.

The 1848 Treaty of Guadalupe Hidalgo, however, meant that the United States now claimed sovereignty over the Mormons' refuge. Within several years, Young was the governor of a new American territory, serving at the pleasure of what he considered an irredeemably corrupt government. Inevitably, Young's expansive vision of the Kingdom of God on earth came into conflict with an American nation spreading its political and economic power—slowly but inexorably—toward the Pacific. Through the Bible, their own scriptures, and Joseph Smith's revelations, the Latter-day Saints had long looked forward to the millennial establishment of "a new heaven and a new earth," but even in what seemed to them an untouched wilderness they found that the old earth had not yet passed away.

IN SALT Lake City, Mormons who attended the church's Sunday public meetings—a morning session almost entirely devoted to sermonizing and an afternoon "sacrament meeting" at which the Lord's Supper was served—frequently heard Young preach. The church first held its meetings in a makeshift bowery that used poles and branches to provide shade, then moved them to an adobe tabernacle completed in 1851 (itself replaced by Temple Square's current tabernacle in 1867). When Young occupied the stand, those in the crowd saw a barrel-chested, husky man (one hundred and eighty-two pounds as of 1850) of average height who, while approaching his fiftieth year, still retained his reddish-brown hair and youthful vigor. Young sometimes led the congregation in an opening hymn, and many Mormons commented on his powerful and earnest prayers. From Young's bear-trap-like jaws flowed extemporaneous and often rambling discourses in which he instructed, chastised, and encouraged the Saints in roughly equal measures. Rarely preaching on a scriptural passage as did most Protestant ministers, Young allowed that he typically blended "'a little of this and a little of that'" and made sermonic "suck-a-tash."[2]

Visitors from the eastern United States and Europe who travelled to the American West enjoyed discovering deficiencies of civilization, and Young rarely disappointed those who came to Salt Lake City. Even as growing wealth added the trappings of refinement to his office and homes, the Mormon leader put on few airs of gentility. He was no upper-class Episcopalian or social-climbing midcentury Methodist bent on cultural respectability. In particular, many visitors commented on the public use of profane

Brigham Young, 1850 *(courtesy of Church History Library, The Church of Jesus Christ of Latter-day Saints)*

language by Young and other church leaders. "They curse or condemn with man's curses whenever they pleased," wrote U.S. Army surveyor John Gunnison in 1852, "and such rough language sounds gratingly in refined ears, when it becomes usual in ordinary conversation." At the same time, Young surprised some skeptical outsiders with his wit, intelligence, and fervor.[3]

Young sometimes said that he only swore from the pulpit, but he also employed profanity in private councils. "Shit on the church debts," he pronounced during a heated discussion on the church's liabilities in Winter Quarters. "I say what I please because I know how to say it," he reasoned after one 1849 outburst. "If I did not feel so strenuous I should not use such language." At other points, he knowingly employed crude phrases for effect. "I frequently say 'cut their infernal throats,'" he offered. "I don't mean any such thing." It was better to be passionate than proper. More-

over, Young knew church members excused such minor lapses. "I acknowledged in Nauvoo I was not so good a man as Joseph," he observed
of his language. The crudity and profanity augmented both the earthy humor and fierce anger that characterized many of Young's sermons, but he
and other Mormon leaders made a very strict moral distinction between
ordinary crudity and taking God's name in vain. "[W]hover profanes the
name of God ought to be cut off [from the church]," Young maintained.
"[I]f I hear any swear they shall be caned," he added.[4]

It is impossible to exactly recreate the impact of Young's sermons on the
crowds at the Salt Lake Bowery and Tabernacle. Clerks such as Thomas
Bullock and George D. Watt recorded many of his discourses, using shorthand and abbreviations. Although their notes take us closest to Young's
unvarnished rhetoric, the rushed nature of such work probably makes
Young's sermons appear more broken and less eloquent than they actually
were. At the same time, transcripts edited for publication added erudition
and eliminated the coarseness and colloquialisms that made Young's discourses attractive to many of his listeners. Young's preaching subtly and
persistently shaped Mormon values and religious thought for thirty years,
and he often kept his audience entertained and at attention.[5]

Many theological tropes already standard within Mormonism appeared
in Young's discourses: the sacred design and blessings inherent in the
"fall" and in earthly misery; the corporeal nature of God and his passage
through a similar earthly existence; the celestial reconstitution of earthly
bodies in eternity; and the possibility of eternal progression toward greater
knowledge, wisdom, and capacity. Rather than seek to persuade his followers to believe certain doctrines, though, Young called on them to join
in the practical tasks of building up the Kingdom of God. Without a sufficient measure of prosperity and abundance, the Latter-day Saints in the
valley could not properly serve as an "ensign to the nations," encouraging
and assisting Mormons at the Missouri, in the East, and in Europe to join
them in Zion. Young explained that to accomplish these ends, the people
would have to forgo sermons on "the glories of the eternal worlds." Instead, he would tell them "what is wanting today." The first Sunday after
his return to the valley, the church appointed Young and Heber Kimball to
apportion city lots, and Young soon outlined a plan for the distribution
of outlying farm land. Water and timber, he insisted, would be publicly
owned and controlled. Through tithed labor, the church would construct
public buildings. Through such cooperation, Young believed, his people
would become and remain Saints.[6]

Although similar claims had caused dissension within the church under
Joseph Smith, Young made no distinction between spiritual and "tempo-

ral" matters. The planting of new settlements, raising crops, and searching for iron all were part of the sacred task of building up God's kingdom, and Young drew on his own wealth of practical know-how and experience to direct such activities. He revised building plans for public works projects and offered detailed instruction on the necessary quality and appropriate costs of materials. In a discussion about the construction of a makeshift arsenal, Young pronounced himself "the only man in this valley that understands the duty of an armorer, and he can make any part of a cannon, musket or rifle." At times, Young clearly overstated his knowledge. "I know what would be good for a farmer, blacksmith, wheelwright, or tannery," he asserted. Also, he claimed that "in regard to merchandizing I know better than all other men unless they think as I do." Obviously, Young did not possess the same level of expertise as experienced tradesmen and merchants, but he claimed spiritual knowledge of economic affairs. "I dream about it," he explained, "and understand it by vision and by all the principles." Given this revelatory authority, he argued that the Saints should follow his leadership. For the next three decades, Young's claim over the direction of economic activity provided the greatest source of tension within the church.[7]

The bitter 1848–49 winter, Young's first in the valley, sorely tested the church's morale and cohesion. Late-spring frosts and large, voracious crickets destroyed much of that year's harvest, a portion of which was rescued by the arrival of huge flocks of seagulls that sated themselves on the crickets. Rationing allotted each person a half-pound of flour per day, and some Mormons resorted to sego lily bulbs, wolf meat, and dead cattle to meet their nutritional needs. Young threatened to appropriate cattle from owners who refused to sell them. Given the poor first harvest and harsh winter, some settlers hoped Young would change his mind, abandon the valley, and lead the church farther west. By now, the Salt Lake Valley Mormons had all heard many stories about the riches their counterparts in California were finding.[8]

Sam Brannan, who had led a group of Mormons from New York to California in 1846, was among the first Americans to publicize the discovery of gold at John Sutter's Mill in early 1848. In fact, several discharged members of the Mormon Battalion were on hand when Sutter's partner James Marshall found the first flakes. Hundreds of other Mormons worked in the gold fields, and Brannan obtained substantial wealth through an impressive merchandising operation. Young, who correctly suspected Brannan of less than whole-hearted commitment to the church and its leaders, pointedly asked him to demonstrate his loyalty by sending ten percent of his profits in tithing for the "Lords treasury." He also asked

for a personal gift of "twenty thousand dollars in gold dust" and for another twenty thousand to be divided between Kimball and Richards. Already disillusioned with Young and the church, Brannan demurred, but
the arrival of gold dust bags in Salt Lake City (some of which the church
received as tithing) further stoked Mormon gold fever.[9]

One of Young's foremost objectives was to dissuade would-be "gold
diggers" from decamping for the gold mines. "To talk of going away from
this valley for anything," he maintained, "is like vinegar to my eyes."
Boosting the valley's potential, just as he had predicted an Eden-like future
for Nauvoo, Young again predicted greater prosperity ahead. He maintained that the Great Basin contained rich lodes of gold and silver, but he
warned the Saints to cure themselves of avarice (and develop their land's
agricultural potential) before hunting precious metals. "Gold will sink a
man to hell," Young preached. He pointedly warned those considering an
unauthorized move to California that the church would simply reallocate
any property they abandoned.[10]

Young's pulpit condemnations and curses were only one part of his response to the Gold Rush. He took pride in the role of Latter-day Saints in
the gold discoveries, and he wryly observed that the same unbelievers who
had condemned Joseph Smith as a "money digger" now sought their treasure in California streambeds and mine shafts. "I say you have to follow in
the wake of old Joe Smith," Young joked, "and paddle along to dig for
gold." Of course, Young appreciated the California gold that replenished
the church's tithing coffers and stimulated commerce in the valley, and he
encouraged church members to bring gold dust instead of "foreign coins"
to Salt Lake City. He oversaw the melting of gold dust into fragile coins
during the 1848–49 winter. After the church's minting crucibles broke,
church leaders used the gold deposits to back the issue of handwritten paper currency. In light of the Kirtland bank's failure, the reintroduction of a
church-backed paper currency generated controversy. One skeptic earned
Young's ire for claiming the new scheme was "no better than [the] Kirtland
Bank." Young reassured wary church members that he would "not put a
dollar into circulation without the dust is deposited." Undeterred by criticism, church leaders even reissued some of the old Kirtland Safety Society
notes, countersigned by Young. Once the church obtained better equipment, though, it retired the paper currency and resumed coinage. Young
saw both the coining of gold dust and the issuance of paper currency as a
means to promote Mormon independence from the United States. "I want
to cut off the thread that connects us with the gentiles," he said when explaining the project. The currency fulfilled a practical need for a medium

of exchange (bags of gold dust would obviously not suffice) and served as a visible symbol of a people set apart.[11]

In Ohio, Missouri, and Illinois, the Latter-day Saints had gathered to specific cities, Mormon islands surrounded by an ocean of Gentile settlements. Now, in the Great Basin, they adopted a new model of gathering. Although Young roughly followed Joseph Smith's 1833 "City of Zion" plat when allocating properties in Salt Lake City, the Mormons never created another city with the sacred significance of Jackson County or even Nauvoo. Whereas Smith built cities of Zion, Young more literally established God's kingdom upon the earth. He spoke of the construction of many temples and encouraged the planned dispersal of Mormon emigrants throughout the region.[12]

Beginning with settlements at Ogden to the north and on Utah Lake to the south, Mormon settlers established roughly one hundred colonies over the next ten years. Often at great cost to their personal finances and safety, men and families were called by Young to undertake the hard work of establishing settlements. Church leaders promoted colonization to stake a political claim to a vast territory, to make possible the allocation of land to future emigrants, to promote self-sufficiency in agriculture and other economic enterprises, and to evangelize Native Americans. For example, church leaders voted in March 1849 to send thirty families to Utah Valley "to setle & put in spring crops, open a fishery, introduce schools, [and] teach the Natives." In some instances, settlers simply moved to new areas of their own accord, but it took coordinated effort to quickly establish a string of Mormon colonies that eventually stretched from north to south among the Great Basin's most fertile valleys. Mormons also established footholds beyond the rim of the Basin. In 1851, Young sent colonizers to southern California to establish a settlement near Cajon Pass, resulting in the city of San Bernardino. "Gather the Saints," he instructed the colony's leaders, "and put them in settlements, on the line which now separates us as speedily as possible." Young hoped that Mormon vineyards in California could fully supply the church's need for olive oil, wine, and raisins. In 1855, Young called thirty men to settle at the Las Vegas Springs, which became an Indian mission and an important way station on the route to San Bernardino. That same year, Young dispatched missionaries into the Oregon Territory; they founded Fort Limhi in the Salmon River Valley. By the mid-1850s, the Mormons under Young's leadership had audaciously laid claim to a thousand-mile corridor of colonies and forts within the American West.[13]

A major impetus for ongoing colonization was Young's stubborn pro-

motion of economic self-sufficiency. When the pioneer camp had returned
to Winter Quarters in 1847, Young had praised the Great Basin as "a place
where we can shut out all mercantile communications with the world."
Upon his permanent move to the valley, he insisted that the Saints dedicate
themselves to "home manufactures," thereby keeping the territory's scarce
hard money away from Gentile merchants. He also promoted collective
attempts to produce sugar, paper, wool, and iron within the territory. In
1850, Young recruited nearly two hundred volunteers and sent them south
to establish an Iron Mission. The next year, he reminded the settlers that
their work "is one branch of the Kingdom of God and . . . is as sacred as
any other mission." It was necessary for Young to reiterate the mission's
sacred importance, as many had joined the mission with great reluctance.
John D. Lee, loath to leave behind his family and business interests, accepted his call to the Iron Mission even though it was "revolting to his
feelings." Young did everything in his power to hasten these projects. He
allocated church funds to speed emigrants with skills to the Great Basin,
even expediting the emigration of non-Mormons who could make economic contributions. He begged British missionary Franklin Richards to
find persons—possibly Swedes—who could help the Iron Mission start
furnaces and convert "magnetic ore into wrought, cast, moleable [mallea-
ble], or ductile iron." "[I]f they need converting," he suggested, Erastus
Snow, then leading a mission to Scandinavia, could "convert them."[14]

Despite a seven-year investment of church labor and resources, the Iron
Mission produced only small quantities of useful iron. Attempts to produce sugar from beets also failed in the 1850s, causing Young to more
successfully promote the cultivation of sorghum cane. The church's early
enterprises, hybrids of public investment, whether by the church or legislature, and private capital, largely failed to meet their objectives. Neither
Young nor other Mormon leaders possessed the capital, specified knowledge, or managerial talent necessary to lead large industrial enterprises.
Regardless of such setbacks, Young believed the missions inculcated industry, cooperation, and autonomy. Perhaps most obviously, the Iron Mission
and a later Cotton Mission led to the formation of the southern settlements of Parowan, Cedar City, and St. George.[15]

Although Young promoted economic autarky, he understood that Mormon prosperity rested on its choice location within an expanding United
States. For instance, he ordered several groups of Saints to head for the
gold fields to do precisely what he discouraged church members from doing on their own. The church benefited substantially from an influx of
gold, and it benefited even more from waves of non-Mormon emigrants
that streamed through the territory toward California and Oregon. Great

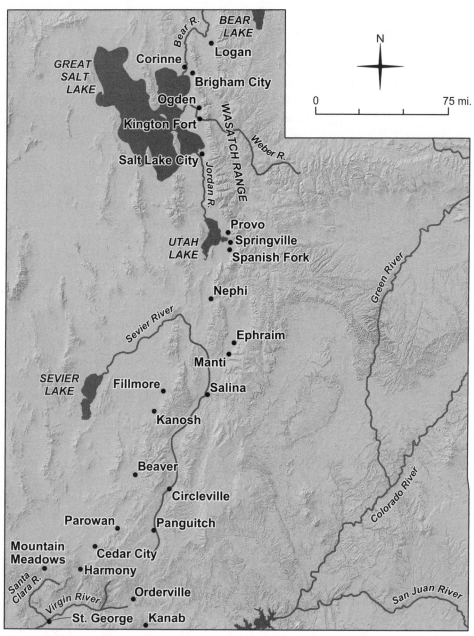

Utah, present-day borders

Salt Lake City quickly became a "mercantile crossroads." Gold-seekers with heavy-laden wagons traded tools, clothing, and currency for desperately needed food and fresh animals. The 1849 harvest and several thereafter quickly ended anxiety about starvation and provided enough of an abundance that the church discontinued its rationing program. No longer eating roots, undesirable meats, and meager quantities of flour, settlers now patronized shops set up by several non-Mormon merchants who swooped into the valley and capitalized on the sudden advent of Great Basin consumerism.[16]

Young's concerns about the Gold Rush and trade, in the end, mirrored his ambivalent attitude toward dancing. There was nothing wrong with seeking riches, but apart from the careful supervision of the church, such activities brought Mormons into spiritually enervating contact with Gentiles, cultivated greed, and threatened a single-minded commitment to the church. More fundamentally, the Gold Rush offered a stark contrast to Young's vision of the Kingdom of God. Instead of the individual pursuit of immediate wealth, Young expected his people to sustain an arduous and cooperative effort to colonize the Great Basin and assist the thousands of impoverished Saints in the East and in Europe to join them. Difficulties and hardships would winnow out the false and halfhearted brethren from among the true Saints. "I am thankful for this hard winter," Young said in January 1849. "It will freeze out some of the hardhearted curses out of the valley." The faithful would remain. California might make men rich, even if it more often dashed such hopes. By contrast, as Young explained a few years later, the Great Basin was "a good place to make Saints."[17]

IN ORDER to "make Saints" and build a kingdom, Young expected the Mormon priesthood, with himself as its head, to govern without interference from the federal government, non-Mormon settlers, or disaffected members of the church. He cared little about political theory or even basic questions of government structure. "[T]here is no difference in reality," Young said in 1849, "between a monarchy, despot, and republicanism." All political systems were grounded in enforcing obedience to "the law," and Young considered the Mormon priesthood "a perfect system of code laws," a system designed to suppress vice and inculcate righteousness. Young suggested that the people, if obedient to the higher, divine law, should not need laws or judges. "If this people will do right as they say they will," he maintained, "they can trample on all laws under their feet." The priesthood, thus, would form the basis of civic life in Mormon settlements.[18]

Only four years removed from Joseph Smith's murder, Young had not forgotten and would not forget that the events that led to Smith's demise originated from within the church. In July 1848 on the trail west, upset about the Saints' failure to heed his instructions about hunting, he had proclaimed himself perfectly insulted. "I don't intend to be shit upon by this company," he warned the trail captains. Once in the valley, Young regularly reminded church members of his preeminence. "I am boss in this valley," he emphasized, describing himself as the church's "master" and "daddy," a leader who could "just walk over all opposition." With varying levels of affection, some Mormons began calling him "the old Boss."[19]

Young had no intention of separating ecclesiastical from political authority, and the church established institutions of civil government intertwined with its priesthood hierarchy. Originally conceived as the "municipal" arm of the Kingdom of God, the shadowy Council of Fifty met regularly for the next eighteen months, functioning as a secret provisional legislature. Presided over by Young, the Council of Fifty included the Twelve Apostles as well as many trusted followers. Initially, church leaders felt no need to draft a written constitution for their settlements; they considered the Council of Fifty the "Living Constitution." Young spoke of the Council of Fifty as the embodiment of God's kingdom, and he explained its "prerogative to dictate [to] all other kingdoms on the earth." Despite such rhetoric, the Council possessed no autonomous power, and political decision-making always emanated from Young and a circle of close advisers. He maintained that he could "dictate this community better than any other man." Brigham Young was the Great Basin's theocratic sovereign.[20]

As such, Young took steps to shield Mormon unity from both criminality and dissent. At Winter Quarters, Young had talked of implementing the "law of God" if ordinary punishments did not stamp out sexual immorality. In the spring of 1849, frustrated with the behavior of young Mormon men, Young believed that time had come. Several Mormon Battalion veterans were frolicking with young ladies, and too many men talked of going to California to seek gold. "The Dandy," joked William Phelps at a church meeting in late February, "thought he should like to be transformed into a right horn of a woman's side saddle." The crowd laughed, but to Young it was not a frivolous matter. There were plenty of "devils" in the valley, he said, that deserved death and should leave before meeting their end. "If a man ought to be killed," he warned, "I just . . . pray that God may enable you to keep your commandments and not lose your cursed heads." It was time for gold-seekers and fornicators to leave the valley. "[Y]ou are in danger of more than you think of," he concluded.[21]

Ira West should have left immediately. For the past two years, the twenty-five-year-old West had known considerable misfortune. Both of his parents died at Winter Quarters, and his infant daughter died while he traveled to the valley in Young's company. The unlucky West also fractured an arm en route. In early March 1849, the Salt Lake City High Council tried him on a string of allegations involving fraud and a failure to pay his debts. Young termed him a "thief and swindler." Both Young and West attended the council meeting. "I want his head cut off right before this people," Young declared, "and they to say Amen, or take some course to stop such infernal doings." Young suggested that, after some prior misbehavior, West had promised to forfeit his head should he repeat his errors. In response, West made a strangely obsequious plea for mercy. "I do not recollect promising my head to Br[other] Young," West said, "but feel to say if I am spared now & am caught in another mean scrape, I am willing my head should go." Young's recommendation gained some support among the council members; another man thought West should at least lose his ears. In the end, the council merely fined West one hundred dollars and excommunicated him.[22]

Young felt that the High Council had shown too much mercy to West and several other transgressors. Thus, the Council of Fifty deliberated over his fate the next day. Erastus Snow repeated the call for decapitation. "I want their cursed heads to be cut off that they may atone for their Sins," he stated, "that mercy may have her claims upon them in the day of redemption." According to John D. Lee's diary, some council members favored a public execution, while others foresaw advantages from a more discreet approach. "The People would know tha[t] he was gone," recorded Lee, "in some strange manner, & that would be all they could sugest, but fear would take hold of them & they wo[uld] tremble for fear it would be thire time next." In the end, Young prolonged West's agony for another week, deciding that the city's marshal would put him in chains and offer him "for Sale to the highest Bidder," apprenticing him until he worked off the fine. Also, following an upcoming election for civil officers and judges, West could be tried and publicly condemned to death. In the meantime, however, should "Ira E. West be miss[ing] on the day of the Election," Young commented wryly, "I motion that we forgive him the debt." Young's final statement encouraged West's extralegal demise.[23]

The church held the auction on March 12. "I told him in W[inter] Q[uarters] he would forfeit his head," Young told the crowd, "there is no sin in killing him—the people may do with him as they please." West, Young explained, had through his sin "incurred a worse curse than the negro." Young did suggest that West "may be made good—the family with the exception are all good." No one rushed to purchase West, so William Major offered a motion "that he die." Major's motion gained no second, and West's brother Chauncey finally took him home.[24]

A few days later, the Council discussed West's case one final time. Young commented that "he did not want any thing said about thiem [West and Thomas Burns, another transgressor] & if any Man could raise Moral courage enough to bring them to him . . . he would show them that he was not offraid to take their Head." Otherwise, he concluded, "[do] as you please with them." Joseph Fielding, a member of the Council of Fifty, reported with dissatisfaction one day later that West was "still at large." "[I]t must not be," Fielding wrote in his journal. The Council, he explained, "is as a Shield round about the Church." Council members had identified other persons "as being worthy of death," and it was "incumbent upon them to cleanse it [the Church] inside of the Platter." Several decades later, the *Salt Lake Tribune,* citing an anonymous informant, asserted that West and another transgressor had been murdered. The *Tribune*'s reporter almost certainly used John D. Lee's journals to write his account. Lee's diary, however, does not reveal West's fate. West and Thomas Burns simply disappear from Mormon history at this point.[25]

When discussing West's transgression, Young articulated the doctrine of blood atonement, which he and other Mormon leaders subsequently advanced publicly. Such ideas had been current among church leaders for some time. In Nauvoo, when a man named Irvine Hodges was murdered by a gang of his fellow thieves, Young explained that his killers "had done even a deed of charity." By preventing him from committing further sins, the murderers had increased Hodges's odds of redemption. At Winter Quarters, Heber Kimball encouraged adulterers to make confessions and be willing to sacrifice their heads. "If I have to make atonement with my head," he stated, "I say do her up." One week after West's auction, Erastus Snow observed that it would have been better for Joseph Smith's faithful followers to have "slain" the apostates in Nauvoo in order to give them "a chance for redemption." Perhaps the only way to save some men for eternity was to kill them on earth. The primary impetus of the doctrine, however, was not theological. Young mentioned beheading West as a means to deter other would-be transgressors.[26]

Crime and sexual immorality were not Young's only worries. He vowed not to let disunity reemerge in the Great Basin. "Whenever a vein [of mutiny] would rise," John D. Lee recorded, "he [Young] would Tap it immediate[ly] then [and] there."[27] Vigorous debate occasionally erupted within church councils, but Young expected his followers to adhere to decisions once made. He also expected members of church councils to keep his confidence. Several weeks after the public auction of Ira West, Young denounced John Pack, a member of the Council of Fifty, for "devulging the secrets of this council" and for warning a man to leave the valley by "intimating that his Life was in danger." Young threatened to drop Pack from the council. "[T]he things that belong to this council," Young exhorted, upbraiding those present, "should be as safe as though it was locked up in the silent vaults of Eternity." Pack pled for Young's forgiveness, suggesting he would have his head cut off if he transgressed again. Pack "wept biterly like a child." The church president accepted Pack's contrition. In the span of a few weeks, two men had promised Brigham Young their heads if they repeated their transgressions.[28]

After West's ordeal, it is not surprising that Pack quivered with fear. Young wanted the threatened execution of God's laws to instill strict obedience and morality in the valley, and at times he appeared satisfied that his "walk and talk" discouraged dissent and criminality. In an 1850 sermon, Young gave thanks that he contended with far fewer "apostate spirits" than had afflicted Joseph Smith.[29] Moreover, although Young regularly complained about lawlessness, Mormon communities in the Great Basin witnessed relatively low levels of crime. By giving an assembled crowd the license to kill petty criminals like Ira West, though, Young gave his blessing to what many outside observers would regard as church-sponsored vigilantism.

ALONGSIDE the pressures of political organization and colonization, among Young's foremost tasks was to fashion a new life for his large family. Most of the wives who would become members of his household traveled to the valley in 1848, along with several women sealed to him for eternity who continued to live with relatives (such as Rhoda Richards, sister of Young's counselor). Young's family grew rapidly. Within five years, he had upward of twenty living children. Also, by the time he reached the valley, Young's oldest daughters Vilate and Elizabeth had both married and made him a grandfather. Vilate named her first child Miriam, after her mother, a choice she expected would please her father.[30]

Similar to the arrangements at Winter Quarters, most of his wives initially lived with each other or with relatives in wagons and tents within the city's adobe fort, southwest of the projected temple lot. On two blocks of property east of the temple site, Young built a long log cabin dubbed the "Log Row," and over the next decade he constructed a number of family residences. A large but fluid group of his wives—around ten or twelve—lived in Log Row. "I know that women can't live many of them together without making fish of one & flesh of the other," Young had observed back at Winter Quarters. Yet a large number of Young's wives did just that. Some members of Young's "female family" found communal living congenial and a welcome antidote to the potential loneliness of plural marriage. Those who could not live peacefully or happily under such cramped and crowded circumstances moved to their own smaller residences. Young spent a great deal of time attending to family matters, frequently socializing at night with one or more of his wives before returning to council sessions or prayer circles.[31]

Mary Ann Angell, sometimes now known as "Mother Young," and her children initially lived in a small storage building near Log Row known as the "corn crib." Responding to an inquiry from the apostle Parley Pratt, Young explained that while polygamous husbands had every right to allocate time with their wives however they saw fit, they should "not forsake the wife of our youths . . . [to] so many of which it would be worse than death for their husbands to withdraw from them." Perhaps with that in mind, Brigham established his official residence with Mary Ann in a home completed in 1854 (called the "Mansion House" or "White House"). Despite the shared residence, however, Mary Ann no longer served as the fulcrum for her husband's domestic life. Nor did she seek a public role within the church. Eliza Snow termed Mary Ann the church's "presidentess," but unlike Emma Smith—and Eliza herself—she never assumed a position of ecclesiastical prominence.[32]

While few records detail Mary Ann's response to her husband's evolving family, the diaries and letters of several other wives shed some light on his construction of a new household. Zina Huntington, her former husband Henry Jacobs (and his new wife), and their two children all traveled in Young's 1848 company. Upon her arrival in the valley, Zina initially relied on her brothers and sister to help provide for her needs. She frequently visited several sister wives, and "the Girls" met together and practiced the spiritual gifts of healing and speaking in tongues. Young was an irregular presence in Zina's life, occasionally visiting her makeshift home or accompanying her to a dinner engagement. In March 1849, she invited Brigham to her home for dinner; two days later he "stayed all night." "A new era of things a wates me," she wrote in her diary the next day. Zina moved to property owned by Young east of the temple site. Temporarily living in her wagon, she resided next to the almost-completed Log Row, where she and sixteen other wives took supper with Young on April 10 after a "family meeting."[33]

By that point, according to Zina's sister wife Eliza Snow, Young had "commenc'd organizing [his family] for living together." One week later, he came to inform Zina that her room was ready. She sat in her wagon "with a hart tender as if believed of a dear friend meditating." Overwhelmed by conflicted emotions, Zina took refuge where the cascading early spring waters of City Creek would muffle her sobs. "I wept," she wrote, "yes wept bitterness of Soul y[e]a sorrow and tears that wore rung from a heavy hart." Even for someone with such fervent belief in Mormonism, beginning to actively live the principle of plural marriage was not an easy step to take. For Zina, it meant ceasing to live with beloved siblings; she may also have mourned a final break from her prior husband. That afternoon, she moved into the Log Row.[34]

The "new era of things" that Zina Huntington entered brought her a mixture of tenderness and sorrow, considerable lonesomeness, and several types of fulfillment. Zina saw Young with some frequency over the next few months. On one occasion, she and Brigham enjoyed "a very agreeable conversation" about Adam and Jesus at an evening gathering. Afterward, Brigham cradled her sleeping three-year-old son (by Henry Jacobs) on their way home. Soon, Zina conceived the only child she would bear Young. Despite a few tender moments with her husband, Zina more often endured feelings of neglect. Eight months pregnant and tending an ill son, Zina lamented "the hours and paneful loneliness that I saw by day & by night." At the same time, she deeply appreciated Brigham's kindness toward her sons by Henry Jacobs. "My two step sons of his," she later wrote, "I do not remember of his ever speaking sharp to them." Within the Young family, she taught at the family's school and, as a midwife, helped deliver children, reflecting her husband's expectation that his wives help support themselves and contribute to his household as their talents and circumstances permitted. Zina was beloved within the family for her devotion to Young's other children. His daughter Susa (by Lucy Bigelow) later described Zina as having "the tenderest, lovingest, most forgiving heart that beat in woman's body."[35]

Through all her struggles, Zina venerated Young as her spiritual leader. She praised the words of one of his sermons as "like aples of gold and pictures of silver." In June 1854, according to Zina's journal, Young preached a sermon in which he "gave his family quite a slant of there weakness if he should call them a round the family alter." Young suspected that instead of praying according to his desires, some of his wives "would be snivelling or praying for something else." Rather than take offense, Zina praised her husband. "[L]ike a God to us he stands," she concluded. Over time, their relationship developed a larger measure of mutual respect. By the mid-1850s, Young's views on female leadership has softened somewhat. When Zina visited with Young about the establishment of a ward-level Female Relief Society in 1854, she wrote that "he greeted me with more kindness than he has for years." Through Relief Society, Zina assumed a measure of ecclesiastical authority, and she occasionally accompanied him on tours of outlying church settlements.[36]

While Zina eventually found a meaningful place in the family, others

Emily Dow Partridge with children Edward and Emily, ca. 1851 *(courtesy of Church History Library, The Church of Jesus Christ of Latter-day Saints)*

never attained such peace. Joseph Smith's widow Emily Dow Partridge steadily continued to bear Young children (seven in all) after her arrival in the valley. Theologically, Young served as a proxy husband for Smith, providing for Emily while raising up children Smith would possess in eternity. In an 1850 letter, Emily worried that Young "may think my affections are entirely placed upon Joseph" but reassured him that "true I love him [Joseph] but no more than yourself." Although she knew that given their proxy arrangement, "the time draws near when we shall be separated forever," she believed that "there is a tie which will ever unite us." Emily, though, never felt secure in the affection she received in return. "I know you cannot love me," she wrote. By 1853, while grieving over the loss of her first child, she found the arrangement intolerable. "[A]s I am not essential to your comfort or your convenience," she requested, "I desire you will give me to some other good man who has less cares." She changed her mind about leaving the family, but she never reconciled herself to the lack of attention Young showed her. Young theorized that plural wives—unlike first wives—could "endure the distant association," but Emily found that distance nearly unbearable.[37]

Augusta Adams, one of Young's first plural wives, was by now thoroughly disillusioned with her lot. Unhappy at having been "constrained" to repeat her sealing to Young in the Nauvoo Temple, she asked Young to grant her a different eternal consort. She still suggested Jesus Christ as her first choice, but she otherwise regularly importuned Young to allow her to be sealed to Joseph Smith for eternity. In April 1848, Young finally gave in and participated in a ceremony in which he promised "to give up Augusta Adams to Joseph Smith in the morning of the first resurrection." Never a discreet individual, Augusta told others about her new family affiliation. Phineas Cook, in whose wagon she traveled to the Salt Lake Valley that summer, described her as "a woman belonging to Joseph Smith." Thereafter, she sometimes signed her letters "Augusta A. Young Smith."[38]

The proxy sealing did not remove Augusta's earthly discontents. She chafed at her relative insignificance compared to Mary Ann Angell, loathed Young's attentions to certain other wives, and—probably accentuated because of the prosperity of her first husband—struggled to adjust to tight quarters, poverty, and hard work. "May God grant me a negro some day," she wrote Young. When Young failed to allay her concerns, she wrote him scores of mournful, plaintive, witty, and acerbic letters, terming the pen her "old faithful weapon." "I am thankfull you are going to have such a delightfull excursion with your Lady [Mary Ann]," she sarcastically observed in 1850. "But expect I should be still more thankfull if you were going to sow holy seed [with younger wives]." She hated Mary Ann's appellations of "Mother Young" and "Queen." Although at Winter Quarters she had expressed fondness for Emmeline Free, she now disliked "dear Emeline['s]" reputation as Young's preferred "consort." According to the later recollections of Young's daughter Susa, Young frequently took Emmeline to social gatherings and "responded to her appeals readily." Her father, Susa explained, "had perhaps the weakness of his strength and he could not pay equal attention to fourteen or fifteen women."[39]

Thus, Augusta felt neglected, financially, emotionally, and sexually. Though approaching her fiftieth birthday, she was upset that Young told her she "should not have any more children," and she suggested that a different proxy husband might expand her family. She once sent a request in writing for Young to spend the night with her, and she insisted that she deserved a husband whom she could "prove . . . in the flesh." Like Emily Partridge, Augusta talked of leaving the family—"I have never in my life felt so much like getting a divorce as I now do"—but stayed.[40]

If Young even read Augusta's letters, he probably reacted with a mixture of irritation and amusement. Augusta addressed him as "Lord Brigham," "his Excellency," "Mr. Proxy," and "Alien." She termed herself "nameless" and, more endearingly given a strong will that could match her husband's, the "Lion of the Lord's . . . Lioness." In any event, Young sometimes refused to see her for months on end. He had no more patience with grumbling wives than whining pioneers. Moreover, his early affection for Augusta dissipated. His "feelings had become seared," she recognized. He did not, however, take her divorce requests seriously, and Augusta apparently made them to prod Young to treat her better. Even when Young placated her with a carriage ride or requested provisions, though, he found Augusta hard to please. When Young sent her a dress, she gave it away and instead asked for "one of the plain linnen ginghams like Zina's if you have any left if not one like Emely's." If Augusta would spend eternity with Joseph Smith, Young probably regarded his loss as a tolerable setback for his celestial kingdom.[41]

Unlike Augusta, a number of discontented wives did sever their ties with Young, including Diana Chase (before an 1849 remarriage), Mary Eliza Nelson (before an 1850 remarriage), Elizabeth Fairchild (before an 1851 remarriage), Mary Jane Bigelow (1851), Mary Ann Turley (1851), Mary Ann Clark (1851), and Eliza Babcock (1853). Most had never become members of Young's household. Mary Jane Bigelow, sister of Young's plural wife Lucy Bigelow, started with Young's company in 1848 but then turned back when she became ill. She crossed the plains with her parents in 1850, moved into a house with Lucy, and then divorced Young the next year. Upset after receiving a "Cool and distant Reseption" from Young at Winter Quarters, Mary Ann Clark Powers remained in Kanesville, Iowa, with her non-Mormon husband. Though she informed Young that she had "not bin a Wife to Mr [William] P[owers]" since her temple sealing, she finally asked Young for a divorce.[42]

Contented wives more rarely recorded their experiences within Young's family. Emmeline Free, who bore Young more children (ten) than any other wife, left behind no diaries or identified letters. Margaret Pierce recalled cheerfully sharing the burden of chores and caring for the children of Young's other wives before the birth of her only son in 1854.[43] Other wives, including Naamah Carter Twiss ("Aunt Twiss" in later years) and Mary Ann's sister Jemima ("Aunt Mima") Angell, also expressed contentment with "the new era of things." "[I]n my marrage relation," wrote Jemima to Young, ". . . I feel so thankful to think I am provided for with a good home & something to do." Even Augusta, whose razor-sharp epistolary sarcasm regularly assaulted her husband's patience, expressed much more positive views of Young and her family life in letters to other family

Brigham Young with unidentified wife, possibly one of several to whom he granted divorces *(courtesy of Church History Library, The Church of Jesus Christ of Latter-day Saints)*

members and friends. There were decided advantages in status and resources through marriage to the most powerful and wealthy man in the territory. Many years later, Zina Huntington explained that polygamy "checks selfishness" in a woman and helps her to "live a bove suspision of her Husbands integrity." Those able and willing to follow Zina's lead found a measure of serenity and contentment within Young's family, but Young satisfied very few who sought companionship, consideration, or romance.[44]

Meanwhile, another of Young's "proxy" wives endured and eventually succumbed to a series of afflictions. A talented seamstress and dressmaker, close friend of several sister wives, and practitioner of spiritual gifts, Louisa Beaman in 1848 traveled with Young to the Salt Lake Valley, pregnant again after the death of their son Moroni. Family tradition and a few scraps of evidence suggest she had also lost a pair of infant twin boys in 1846.[45] In July 1848, Louisa delivered a second pair of twins on the trail near Fort Laramie. After a brief stop, Young, Louisa, and the company proceeded another three miles before stopping for the night. The day after reaching the valley in late September, Louisa wrote her friend Marinda Hyde, "my babes were both taken sik with the bowell complaint." The oldest, named Alvah, died two weeks later. The next month brought false hope, as Alma "seamed well and grew flashy [fleshy]." Louisa's hopes were quickly dashed, however, as the other twin "was taken down again with the same complaint." He soon "breathed his last and I was again left alone." "I am led to think at times," Louisa observed, "that there is not much else but sorrow and affliction in this world for me." Nevertheless, she hoped God would sustain her. "I desire to bear all of my afflictions with patience," Louisa faithfully concluded.[46]

With ten women to share in her grief, Louisa visited her sons' graves in mid-April 1849, then spoke in tongues with Zina Huntington afterward. "O how precious is a sisters kindness," wrote Zina when Louisa likewise comforted her with a cup of tea during an illness. By this time, Louisa herself had been seriously ill with breast cancer for some time; it now entered an advanced stage. Still, with remarkable stoicism she insisted, "I feel as though we had been blesst." Her condition gradually worsened, as her attempts to "docter my breast" failed. The next February she celebrated her thirty-fourth birthday. "It was the last time Louisa was ever out of her room," Zina noted. Three months later, Louisa died at five minutes to noon on May 16, 1850. She had modeled the practicality, faith, and at least outward contentment amid difficult circumstances that Brigham Young wanted all of his wives to exhibit. The next year, the apostle George A. Smith christened the Iron Mission's southern Utah outpost "Fort Louisa," after "one of the first to listen to the Light of Revelation . . . in obedience to the Seal of the Covenant." For reasons unknown, probably to avoid drawing attention to his polygamous family, Young renamed the settlement Parowan.[47]

UNDER Brigham Young's direction, the Mormons had governed themselves since their 1847 arrival in the Great Basin. Since the creation of the Mormon Battalion, however, church leaders had realistically but without any enthusiasm anticipated the extension of American sovereignty over the Great Basin, and they now sought to formalize the nature of their relationship to Washington. In late 1848, the Council of Fifty decided to petition Congress to create a territory named "Deseret," a *Book of Mormon* word for honeybee. The council presumably chose the name for its connotations of industriousness and cooperation. As ambitiously envisioned by Mormon leaders, Deseret incorporated much of the American Southwest, including most of present-day Arizona, Nevada, and Utah as well as portions of Oregon, California, Wyoming, Colorado, and New Mexico.[48]

After sending the petition, however, church leaders gradually grew alarmed at the thought of the federal government's power to appoint territorial officials. Some of Young's close advisers as well as non-Mormon supporter Thomas Kane warned him about hungry hordes of office-seekers and sycophants who would ignore Mormon sensibilities and enrich themselves as rapaciously as the crickets had eaten the valley's crops.[49] Given those fears, the Council of Fifty switched course, holding elections for the "State of Deseret" in March. The settlers unanimously affirmed a slate of candidates, including Young as their governor. Deseret soon developed the trappings of an independent nation, with its own currency, flag, and army. The Deseret General Assembly organized counties, established courts, and incorporated a "Perpetual Emigrating Fund for the Poor," which loaned money to European church members for their journey to the Great Basin. The legislators also granted economic privileges (the control of ferries, toll-roads, waterways, and canyons) to Deseret's leading citizens. In return for $500, for example, Young received "the privilege and control" of City Creek Canyon in Salt Lake City. In one of its final acts, in early 1851 the assembly incorporated the Church of Jesus Christ of Latter-day Saints, empowering the church to "solemnize marriage compatible with the revelations of Jesus Christ," thereby providing polygamy with legal sanction.[50]

In July 1849, when the Mormons gathered to commemorate the second anniversary of the pioneers' entrance into the valley, the church also celebrated its newfound political autonomy. A few days before the gathering, Young's wives Augusta Adams and Eliza Snow scrambled to make an enormous flag for the occasion. "The standard is to be raised on the 24th of this month," Augusta wrote friends, "and we expect to proclaim our Independence." When the day arrived, Salt Lake City's residents awoke to the firing of cannon and the strains of "martial music." Atop a tall liberty pole, Young unfurled the sixty-four-foot-long blue-and-white Flag of Deseret. Serenaded by the ringing of the "Nauvoo Bell" (salvaged from the temple) and loud cheering, Young and the Twelve then entered the Bowery. Dressed in white, the community's young men held a banner welcoming "the Lion of the Lord"; the young women's banner read "Hail to our Chieftain." The crowd included twenty Ute Indians as well as a number of gold-seeking emigrants, some of whom expressed astonishment at such symbols of nationhood. Young led the crowd in vigorously cheering a reading of the Declaration of Independence.[51]

The Mormons, though, were cheering their own independence, not that of the United States. Similar to the way that many African Americans commemorated the anniversary of the transatlantic slave trade's abolition on January 2 but could not wholeheartedly celebrate the Fourth of July, the Mormons privileged their own heritage of liberation and accomplishment. Indeed, while Young venerated the Constitution and Declaration of Independence (the former, he said the following year, "was dictated by the revelation of Jesus Christ"), he minced no words about the politicians and bureaucrats holding sway in Washington, terming them "corrupt as hell." In the summer of 1849, Young was newly embittered toward the U.S. government following its refusal to permit the Mormons to continue using Winter Quarters as a temporary way station. In late August, he predicted that "God Almighty will give the U.S. a pill that will puke them to death and that is worse than a lobelia," a common but unpleasant medicinal treatment. "I am a prophet enough to prophesy the downfall of the Government that has driven us out."[52]

By the July 24 celebration, Young had chosen a different way to formalize relations with the corrupt government whose downfall he predicted. In fact, the establishment of Deseret was partly a gambit to present the United States with a *fait accompli,* much as Americans in California established a state government later in 1849 as an expression of their desire to bypass territorial status. In July, Mormon leaders quickly wrote a state constitution, fabricated the results of a constitutional convention purportedly held the previous March, and drafted a new memorial. In letters to his representatives in Washington, Young explained the new course as a means to avoid the federal government's "appointing power." Following the persecutions in Missouri and Illinois and the failure of the federal government to respond with anything more than token sympathy, Young concluded that the Mormons needed a state in which they could govern themselves. Three days after the July 24 celebration, Almon Babbitt, chosen as Deseret's delegate to Congress, left Salt Lake with the statehood petition. Over the past half-year, Young had presided over a clumsy sequence of political maneuvers, betraying his uncertainty about how to navigate the church's relationship with the United States government.[53]

At the same time, politicians in the nation's capital were bitterly divided about how Congress should incorporate western lands into the union. The 1820 Missouri Compromise and the development of a nationwide two-party system had partly contained sectional divisions over slavery, but the acquisition of a second vast expanse of land through the war against Mexico reopened bitter debates about the place of slavery in the expanding nation. At one end of the political spectrum, Free Soil northerners, committed to the exclusion of slavery from the western territories, demanded the application of the Wilmot Proviso to the Mexican Cession, which would have banned slavery in the entire Southwest. Correspondingly, John C. Calhoun led a faction of southerners committed to the proposition that the national government could not constitutionally deprive slaveholders of their right to bring their property into any federal territory.[54]

Fortuitously for the Mormons, a critical mass of congressmen and senators searched for compromise measures that would preserve both major parties as viable political vehicles in the North and the South. Moreover, with the church still denying its practice of plural marriage, public opinion and political sentiment toward the Mormons were as positive as they would be for the next four decades. The murder of the Smith brothers, the Mormons' expulsion from Nauvoo, and their impoverished journey across the Plains created a narrative of suffering that appealed to non-Mormon sympathies.[55]

Crucially, the proposed Deseret constitution did not include any statement on slavery, an attempt to skirt the issue with the greatest potential to derail the Mormon bid for statehood. While some southerners in Washington wanted an explicit protection for slavery in any Mormon-controlled territory, the omission of anything pertaining to slavery in the constitution or statehood petition satisfied the majority of southern senators and congressmen. Southern Mormons had brought somewhere between fifty and one hundred black slaves into Deseret, and Senator William Henry Seward of New York noted the presence of slaves among the Mormons during an early July 1850 speech. Knowledge of Mormon slaveholding, however, did not rise much above the level of rumor and speculation in Washington, and church leaders quietly assured advocates such as Thomas Kane that slavery would never take root in the Great Basin. Young cautioned the representatives he sent to the nation's capital that they should not insist on free status for Deseret. "In regard to slavery, free soil . . . ," he wrote John Bernhisel, a physician and bearer of the territorial petition, "I can only say that to the latter principle we are favorably disposed, and adverse to the former, nevertheless we do not wish a prohibitory clause [Wilmot Proviso] to attach itself to our Territory in relation to that subject." Instead, church leaders embraced the emerging idea of popular sovereignty, by which Congress would leave the issue of slavery to state and territorial legislatures.[56]

Slavery aside, many politicians were skeptical of Deseret's vast territorial claims, scanty population, and odd name. Even allies like Senator Stephen Douglas of Illinois told Mormon representatives that the statehood effort had no chance of success, and he could not promise that territorial appointments would be favorable. Kane urged Young's representatives to withdraw their petition rather than accept a territorial government and its accompanying federal appointment power. Douglas, though, pointedly informed Bernhisel that it would be meaningless for the Mormons to withdraw their petition. Congress would organize the territory in any event, and it would be called Utah after the prospective territory's most prominent native tribe.[57]

In a fragile compromise, Congress accepted California as a free state, abolished the slave trade in the nation's capital, passed a more coercive fugitive slave law, deprived Texas of some of its western territory, and accepted New Mexico and Utah as territories with no restrictions on slavery. Congress allotted the Utah Territory much less land than Deseret had requested; still, the territory included present-day Utah and Nevada as well as portions of Wyoming and Colorado. To the relief of Mormon leaders, the new president, Millard Fillmore, appointed Brigham Young the territory's governor.

When word reached Utah the following January, a crowd and band greeted Young upon his return to the city from a trip to the northern settlements. The next month, the Deseret Legislature held its final session and dissolved itself. In the fall of 1851, the new territorial legislature adopted Deseret's laws as its own. Young had not intimately involved himself in the petition efforts, and while he would have preferred independence or statehood, he had expressed openness to a variety of political solutions, including a temporary union with California. What he wanted was for the Mormons to run their own affairs. His appointment signaled he had largely accomplished that objective.

Young would not govern without federal interference, however. Fillmore appointed several non-Mormon officials and judges for Utah. Across the West, most territorial appointments hinged more on party patronage than qualifications and experience, and non-residents filled most positions. In many territories, "party hacks" found themselves at odds with local populations. In Utah, however, this dynamic hinged not on individual personalities and particular grievances but instead became a bitter and protracted struggle for political supremacy. Serving at the pleasure of the president, the non-Mormon appointees had little knowledge of and no loyalty to the people they now helped governed. At the same time, although the Mormons regularly and heartily affirmed their loyalty to country and constitution, they ultimately viewed political sovereignty as resting with the Mormon priesthood. "I love my president," Heber Kimball said of Brigham Young at a Sunday meeting shortly before the appointees' arrival. "He is not only the president here but he is the president of the states and kingdoms of this world no matter if they have not elected him." Kimball urged church members to honor their sovereign. "It is for me," he said, "to be obedient to B[righam] Young as to God, as I was to Joseph." The blend of ecclesiastical and political power in Utah, the church's history of persecution, and the fact that many appointees arrived with negative attitudes toward Mormonism all fomented strife between outside appointees and Mormon leaders.[58]

Rather than seeking to camouflage fundamental differences, Young quickly made it clear to the appointees that he would brook no interference with his oversight of the territory's political affairs. On July 19, Broughton Harris, the non-Mormon territorial secretary, arrived in the company of Almon Babbitt and John Bernhisel, two of the men who had been representing the church's interests in Washington. Chief Justice Lemuel Brandebury had already reached the territory, and Associate Justice Zerubbabel Snow, a church member, came with Harris's party. Although Young received the officials and judges cordially, he was privately fuming.[59]

The focus of his wrath was Babbitt, whom Young believed had undermined the church's political prospects. Young disliked lawyers (partly because Joseph Smith regularly found himself the target of lawsuits), and he later mocked Babbitt's fancy tastes and "pettifogging." Fond of politics and non-Mormon society, Babbitt had remained valuable to the church as a legal and political representative despite several clashes with both Smith and Young. "I don't care if he drinks champagne," said Young in 1849, "and knocks over a few lawyers and priests." Now, though, Thomas Kane had informed Young that Babbitt was "gifted . . . with a kind of instinct opposed to truthfulness." According to Kane, Babbitt had antagonized members of both parties in Washington over the issue of slavery, obstructed the nomination of additional Mormons to federal offices, and had spoken in derogatory terms of his own religion. Young used the allegations as an opportunity to both chastise Babbitt and demonstrate to the appointees that he remained in charge of the territory.[60]

On July 23, Young invited Harris and Snow to attend his dressing-down of Babbitt. He began by demanding that Babbitt turn over $20,000 he had brought from the U.S. Treasury to pay for a territorial courthouse. "Politicians are a stink in my nose," Young pronounced. Probably feeling less than comfortable, Harris declared that he had "no interest" in the dispute. "I want you to hear it," Young insisted. Babbitt claimed that Young had illegally used an earlier census to apportion the territory's electoral districts and had scheduled elections for August without Harris's signature. Less diplomatically with Harris temporarily out of the room, Young added that he would rather "stand here and cut throats than suffer law suits and technicalities." Then he threatened Babbitt. "If you interfere with any of my dictation in the elections," he warned, "it will be the last." "You are shitting in my dish and I will lick it out and you too," Young concluded. Babbitt took Young's threats seriously. "I am exceeding fearful this will not work for good to me," he said. Earlier in the conversation, in what may have been an oblique warning of his own to Young, he had maintained that "murder will out one of these days and then all will be known." Eventually, Babbitt affirmed his loyalty to the church and Young, and the conversation proceeded more amicably. Babbitt reported that Fillmore "hoped you would not mingle your religion with your public duties." The president worried that Young would "be as a Prince of this world and a prophet for the next." Young, of course, would not follow that advice, which subsequent presidents would reiterate more forcefully.[61]

Harris, notably, diplomatically distanced himself from Babbitt's positions and never contradicted Young throughout the session. Young apparently intimidated the young secretary. Clerk Thomas Bullock recorded that it was a "new scene for Mr. Harris to behold the Power of the Priesthood." Young reinforced that lesson the next day, when the church held its annual July 24 celebration, with Harris and Chief Justice Brandebury in attendance. Responding to reports (probably false) that the late president Zachary Taylor had opposed even territorial government for the Mormons, Young observed that "as incidental providence would have it, he is in hell and we are here." He warned future presidents that if they opposed the Saints they would soon make Taylor's new home more cramped. Young meant the comment about Taylor to be at least partly humorous, but the non-Mormon appointees in the crowd were surprised that a territorial governor would disparage a recently deceased president.[62]

Still, political concord held for a time. Babbitt turned over the money, and Harris approved Young's oath of office, signed a proclamation establishing judicial districts, and examined the August election returns, in which Mormon voters unanimously chose Bernhisel to serve as their delegate in Washington. In mid-August, Associate Justice Perry Brocchus of Alabama, the last federal appointee, arrived, sick from the long journey and having lost many of his possessions to a group of Pawnee Indians. Brocchus was disappointed to hear of Bernhisel's election as territorial delegate. After his appointment, Brocchus had befriended Mormon representatives in Washington and familiarized himself with the tenets of the church. He then had traveled west with the hope of returning to the nation's capital as Utah's delegate to Congress. Despite his disappointment, Brocchus attempted to initiate good relations with Young. He called at his office and asked for the privilege of speaking at a September church conference.[63]

The ensuing public address, however, backfired. Brocchus began by floridly praising Mormon hospitality. Noting the absence of litigiousness and displaying a surprising knowledge of Latter-day Saint scripture, he alluded to a *Book of Mormon* passage about judges who stirred up lawsuits because they were paid based on the amount of time they spent performing their duties. Since the territorial appointees received their government salaries by the year, he pointed out, they had no such incentive. Next he defended himself against charges of office-seeking. "I repel an imputation that I came in your midst expecting to be returned as your delegate to Congress," he announced, though he added that had the people wanted a non-Mormon representative he "might have been able to do you good." The judge then critiqued what he regarded as the Saints' unjustified lack of patriotism. With astonishment, Brocchus read an extract from a July 24 speech by Utah legislator Daniel H. Wells. He rejected Wells's allegation that the Polk administration had demanded the enlistment of the Mormon Battalion in order to "finish, by utter extermination, the work which had so ruthlessly" begun in Missouri and Illinois. Only those states bore responsibility for the church's persecutions. They were a "private wrong," and the Mormons could not turn to the federal government for redress. While he allowed that Taylor "may have expressed feelings against the L[atter] D[ay] S[aints]," Brocchus absolved the government as a whole from anti-Mormonism.[64]

The Mormons interpreted Brocchus's instruction in patriotism as a gross insult. Wilford Woodruff noted that the judge's suggestion that the Mormons apply to Missouri and Illinois for redress "stirred the Blood of the whole congregation." Woodruff also alleged that the judge had insulted the honor of Mormon women by expressing his hope that they "would become a virtueous people."

In response, Young denounced Brocchus as "either powformally [profoundly] ignorant or corruptly wicked," and he suggested that several members of the congregation could readily prove the judge's office-seeking intentions. Although the church president cautioned that he would not encourage anything that might lead to the "pulling of hair or cutting of throats," he pointedly defended the Saints' patriotism. "We love the government and the Constitution," he clarified, "but we do not love the damned rascals who administer the government." For good measure, he reiterated his belief in Taylor's damnation. "He is dead and damned and I can't help it," Young stated.[65]

Several of the other appointees watched the tongue-lashing, appalled at

Young's implication that Brocchus's life was in danger. Quickly, all but the Mormon judge Zerubbabel Snow stopped cooperating with church leaders. Harris, who had carried $24,000 and the territorial seal to Utah, refused to authorize territorial expenses. Soon, the non-Mormon officials and judges decided to leave the territory with the $24,000. "Mormonism was a little to[o] warm for their relish," Young wrote the apostle Amasa Lyman. "I felt like kicking the poor curse[']s arse out of the territory," Young recounted the next summer. He attributed the Saints' harsh reaction to their fear of persecution. "Many in their imagination," he explained two years later, "saw us all hung, shot, drown, murdered massacred in evry imaginable shape that you could think off [of]."⁶⁶

Both sides, using a blend of truth, exaggeration, and base falsehoods, engaged in a furious campaign to control the response of the national government. At first, it seemed the appointees' accounts of theocracy, polygamy, violence, and sedition would have serious repercussions for the church's political control of Utah. In December, Bernhisel reported that "it is considered a settled matter that Governor Young is to be removed" and that a military force would occupy Utah to "enforce the laws." Young and other leaders discussed a renewed application for statehood, suggesting that if the federal government persisted in sending hostile officers to Utah, the Mormons would revert to their provisional Deseret government. "They may send another governor here," he informed the territorial legislature in February, "but I shall govern the people by the Eternal Priesthood of the Son of God." If an army crossed the mountains, Young conveyed to his representatives in Washington, the soldiers "had better bring their bread and dinner with them for I very much doubt their getting it here." The church, he suggested, would again move to a new location in order to pursue self-government and its ability to obey God's "higher law." In the event of such a federal response, Young probably had not decided whether to accommodate, flee, or resist.⁶⁷

In the nation's capital, Mormon representatives prudently chose not to pass along such threats, instead rebutting the appointees' charges and insisting upon Mormon loyalty to the nation. Portraying themselves as the victims of oppressive office-seekers, the Mormons styled themselves as Latter-day descendants of the American patriots forced to defend their right to self-government. With the help of Thomas Kane, Salt Lake City mayor Jedediah Grant colorfully lampooned Brocchus's drunkenness, Brandebury's personal hygiene (he allegedly wore "the most Disrespectful Shirt, ever was seen at a celebration"), and the indolence of the whole group. Remarkably, the church outmaneuvered its opponents, partly because the appointees lacked powerful political allies in Washington and partly because of the church's adroit and coordinated response. The government sided with the Mormons, depriving the "runaway judges" of their pay and keeping Young in office.[68]

THE conflict with the first territorial appointees both emboldened and alarmed Mormon leaders. Despite the church's political triumph, the officials' allegations about plural marriage gained broad circulation, and in 1852 both John Gunnison and Howard Stansbury published accounts of Mormon polygamy. Sometime in late 1851 or early 1852, Young decided to acknowledge and defend plural marriage. Although an abrupt change in official church policy, Mormon leaders had gradually spoken more openly about "plurality" since leaving Illinois. In early 1851, several months before the arrival of the federal appointees, Young boldly announced his own practice of polygamy during a Sunday discourse. "I have more wives than one," he stated. "I have many I am not ashamed to have it known."[69]

The church revealed the doctrine by publishing the discourses from a special conference in late August 1852 in a special edition of the *Deseret News*. Later termed the church's "philosopher and show-speaker" by a French visitor, Jules Remy, the apostle Orson Pratt robustly defended plural marriage on the grounds of religious freedom, theological necessity, biblical tradition, and revelation. Pratt, an erstwhile opponent of polygamy, argued that God had instituted plurality so that righteous men could share the blessings of Abraham (a large progeny) while creating bodies ("tabernacles") for God's preexistent spirit children.[70] Over the previous four weeks, Young had been laying the groundwork for Pratt's address, obliquely approaching the issue of polygamy. Alluding to rumors of his sixteen wives and fourteen children, Young joked that his critics underestimated his "possession." "I am enlarging on the right and on the left . . . Abraham like," he jokingly corrected the rumor.[71]

More seriously, Young made two basic defenses of Mormon plurality. As the Mormons would contend for the next four decades, he argued that governments had no right to forbid something that was a matter of religious freedom. "There is not a constitution [or] law in any state in the union that forbids a man having two wives if that man lays it down as . . . a principle of faith [or] creed," he insisted. Obviously, according to Young, the federal government had no right to interfere in Utah's domestic institutions. He suggested in a September 1852 letter that "as for Congress they might as well abolish slavery in the South as plurality in Utah." If popular sovereignty made slavery a territorial matter, surely plural marriage also fell outside federal control.[72]

Young also connected plural marriage with exaltation into the celestial kingdom. "The Lord Almighty created you and me," Young taught, "to become a God like himself." Each resurrected and exalted Saint would, like Adam had once done, "organize an Earth, people it, redeem it, and sanctify it." That future glory hinged on the Saints' embrace of plurality. At the special conference, Young emphasized that without Joseph Smith's revelation on celestial marriage, "there is not a man [who] can be a God."[73]

Beginning with the 1852 conference, the Mormons made a host of other public arguments for polygamy, suggesting that the institution prevented the evils of prostitution and adultery, provided a surplus of female church members with righteous husbands, and followed the examples of not only the biblical patriarchs but of Jesus and God the Father themselves.[74] Shortly after the conference, Young dispatched a large group of missionary elders to present the doctrine to church branches in the United States and Europe and defend the institution at public meetings and in print. Though Young predicted that the principle would "sail and ride triumphantly above all the prejudices and priestcraft of [the] day," Mormon missionaries and publications convinced precious few non-Mormons, and the large British church hemorrhaged members as news of the doctrine arrived overseas. Parley Pratt termed the doctrine a "choker," a stumbling block that impeded missionary efforts. In Utah, though, the announcement served the vital purpose of openly providing a clear theological rationale for a principle most Mormons found difficult to embrace and to practice.[75]

Despite his sanguine conference prediction, Young knew the revelation would create a political firestorm in Washington, correctly foreseeing a "formidable opposition." In the nation's capital, Utah's congressional delegate John Bernhisel predicted that the publication would "prevent us most effectually from obtaining a single dollar" and would provide pretense for removing Young from office. Indeed, the public admission changed the dynamics of the church's relationship with the rest of the country. The church had managed to carve out a measure of sympathy from other Americans because of its forced expulsion from Illinois, but the open practice of polygamy made the narrative of the "suffering Saints" viable no longer. Going forward, it would be much more difficult for the church to successfully navigate disputes like the one over the "runaway judges." Bernhisel, however, was wrong when it came to the announcement's immediate political consequences. Fillmore left Young in office. Though both he and his successor Franklin Pierce appointed additional non-Mormon judges and officials, they did not eliminate territorial appropriations, withhold Young's salary and expenses, or seek federal action against Mormon polygamy.[76]

By the end of 1852 Brigham Young had accomplished the utterly improbable. Nearly 20,000 Latter-day Saints occupied Great Salt Lake City and a series of settlements stretching from San Bernardino in California to northern Utah. Each year, companies of Saints—novelist Wallace Stegner famously called them "villages on wheels"—added thousands of Mormons to the territory's population. After the privations of initial settlement, the Mormons had achieved subsistence and a few signs of prosperity. Given the uncertainty of the succession after Joseph Smith's murder and the challenges of exodus and settlement, it is remarkable that more than half of the church's membership followed their Moses over the Rocky Mountains. That shared experience of persecution and exodus welded a perennially fractious church into a "people," who through their relative isolation and efforts at kingdom-building had established a "near nation" in the Great Basin. Even more remarkably, Young achieved this growth, prosperity, and stability while openly espousing theocracy and polygamy and did so without producing any challenge from the U.S. government.[77]

At a September 1850 church conference, Young's followers sustained him for the first time as their "Prophet, Seer, and Revelator." One year later Heber Kimball called him "our Prophet, Priest, and King Revelator and Seer." Young declared that it was "immaterial" to him whether he formally held such titles. Regardless, he joked, "I have been very profitable to the people." The congregation laughed in agreement and appreciation.[78]

For a brief moment, Young stood at the head of the Kingdom of God on earth as it rolled on nearly unimpeded through the Great Basin. It could not so last.

CHAPTER EIGHT

One Family

Eve had no land to sell nor yet to buy
But they might have all they could occupy
—BRIGHAM YOUNG, DECEMBER 1847

THE whole kingdom are one family," Brigham Young told an 1848 meeting of his extended family.[1] Utah's Mormons spoke English with a variety of British accents, and by the mid-1850s Scandinavian Mormons in Utah held Sunday services in their own languages. They came from a variety of socioeconomic backgrounds and from different religious upbringings. In one respect, though, they were strikingly similar. Whether born in the United States or Europe, nearly all were white.

A handful of black Americans—free and slave—had joined the church in the 1830s and 1840s, and a small number of Native Americans ("Lamanites," in Mormon parlance) had converted to Mormonism. In the early 1850s, Mormon missionaries began to win converts in the Pacific, especially in the Sandwich Islands (Hawaii). Still, despite their small numbers, nonwhite peoples had occupied a central place in Mormon thought from the church's beginning. Young himself briefly served an Indian mission in 1835, and Joseph Smith had predicted that he would preach to southwestern Indians in their own tongues. "Joseph committed to me the keys to open the gospel to every Lamanite nation," Young stated at Winter Quarters in December 1847. The exodus to the Great Basin gave Young and the church an opportunity to fulfill that sacred obligation. Like many Latter-day Saints, he expressed delight at the idea of living amid the Indians. "Joseph wanted to go among the Lamanites," Young recounted on the trail in 1848, ". . . and now we are kicked right amongst them. I say

Glory, Hallelujah."[2] Concern for the Indians' redemption, however, took a backseat to the more pressing business of establishing Mormon settlements across the Great Basin. As the Saints flooded into their promised land, they displaced the prior inhabitants of the land in much the same way as the ancient Israelites had conquered the Canaanites. Young displayed very little anguish about this process, which mirrored the broader conquest of the American West by white settlers and the U.S. Army. Still, especially after the Mormons gained clear supremacy in the Great Basin, theological imperatives ameliorated the way that they treated the now-marginalized native peoples.

Young also devoted considerable thought, and even emotion, to persons of African descent. Only a handful of African Americans settled in Utah during Young's lifetime, but numbers had little bearing on the salience of racial questions for white Americans. Race, not just slavery, was of great political and cultural import across the United States, especially as the political conflicts that led to the Civil War intensified. States and territories in the Midwest and Pacific West, many of which had minuscule black populations, rushed to pass legislation depriving blacks of citizenship rights. While most white Christians accepted their shared ancestry with black people, even most white opponents of slavery saw black people as their ecclesiastical, political, and social inferiors. Young's harsh conclusions about both the earthly and eternal places of black people, and the passion with which he expressed them, were not unusual in the mid-nineteenth-century United States. The vehemence with which Young expressed his racial views, however, contributed to the long-term exclusion of black men from the Mormon priesthood and black men and women from the church's most sacred ordinances.

BEFORE the Mormons arrived, the Great Basin's native peoples had already endured and adapted to the presence of Europeans and Americans. The initial areas of Mormon settlement contained both Shoshone (mostly to the north) and Ute (mostly to the south and east) Indians, loose conglomerations of bands present in the region since around the thirteenth century. At a relatively early date, bands of Shoshone became equestrian, and by the early nineteenth century, certain bands of Utes had also acquired horses. Long accustomed to taking captives during wars and through raids, powerful, equestrian Utes increased such practices in response to a reliable market for Indian slaves and servants among Spanish and then Mexican residents of what became the American Southwest. They sold captive Shoshones, Paiutes (who lived farther to the south), and Utes from rival bands. Both the Shoshones and Utes had then further adapted to the arrival of trappers and mountain men, to whom they sold skins and, on occasion, captive children. Thus, the Mormons encroached on native peoples who, rather than being helpless victims of European incursions or settlement, had developed new and sometimes violent strategies for surviving in a repeatedly altered world.[3]

In ways reminiscent of other European-Americans before them, the Mormons saw the Indians simultaneously as religious kindred and as savage enemies. European explorers and settlers had pondered whether the native peoples they met were the lapsed descendants of the Ten Lost Tribes of Israel. A few Puritan ministers in seventeenth-century New England saw themselves as divinely chosen agents of salvation to a people regarded as ripe for conversion. As Puritan-Indian relations quickly deteriorated into brutal warfare, however, the Indians were sometimes recast as the Old Testament Amalekites, the cursed descendants of Esau whose utter destruction God commanded. Even those Indians who converted to Christianity typically disappointed American colonists, who found that the converts did not look or act like white Christians. As Indian populations declined precipitously, eastern Americans regarded native peoples with a mixture of indifference, romanticism, and scorn, though westward expansion regularly renewed both hopes for conversion and calls for extermination.[4]

Into this recurring American story of evangelistic hope, disappointment, and destruction, the Latter-day Saints brought their distinctive scriptural beliefs. The *Book of Mormon* identified the Indians of the Americas as the "Lamanites," the cursed, dark-skinned descendants of the wicked people who had wiped out the righteous Nephites several centuries after the birth of Jesus. God had tasked the Mormons with bringing the modern-day Lamanites back to the true faith. "The Savages are not yet grafted in the Olive Tree," Young explained upon his departure from Winter Quarters in 1847. "They are now as a withered branch before the Lord." Once the Lamanites fulfilled their Israelite lineage by embracing the gospel, God would remove the curse he had placed on them, they would become "a white and a delightsome people," and they would assist in building the millennial kingdom. The *Book of Mormon* suggested and Joseph Smith had taught that the "remnant of the house of Jacob" would "marshal themselves, and shall become exceedingly angry, and shall vex the Gentiles with a sore vexation." Converted Indians, thus, would serve as God's foreordained vehicle of millennial judgment against the United States and its people. The redeemed Lamanites would become, Young explained a few years later, "the Lord's battle axe."[5]

The coming forth of the *Book of Mormon*, Young said, had "taken off" the Lamanites' curse. The exodus meant that the work of Indian redemption could now begin in earnest, as the Mormons would have ready opportunities to teach their faith to the natives they encountered. Other strategies, moreover, would supplement preaching missions and hasten the whitening of the Indians. When Young first entered the Salt Lake Valley in 1847, he had emphasized that the Saints "would be connected with every tribe of Indians through America & that our people would yet take their squaws & dress them up teach them our language & learn them to labour & learn them the gospel of there forefathers & raise up children by them." After several generations, he predicted, "they will become A white & delightsome people & in no other way will it be done." Mormon men could hasten the whitening of the Lamanites by marrying Indian women. "If you take a white apple graft and plant it in a red apple tree," theorized Heber Kimball, "it will bring forth a white apple." Israelite blood would wash away the Lamanites' curse. While Young and Kimball discussed such ideas in the language of Mormon scripture and theology, some federal Indian agents and Protestant ministers encouraged marriage between white men and Indian women as a means of absorbing—and whitening—a shrinking native population and obtaining Indian land. Intermarriage was typically forbidden when the roles were reversed, however, both in Mormon communities and throughout the West. Young observed that it was "against law for a [white] woman to take an Indian husband." "The governing principle is in the husband," he clarified, "and by prayer they will bring forth white children." Preaching missions, efforts at civilization, and intermarriage could all further the Lamanites' redemption.[6]

In 1847, Young had purposefully avoided settlement in the Utah Valley (east of Utah Lake to the south of Salt Lake City) because of its heavy use by various bands of Utes, known as Timpanagos Utes or "Fish-Eaters." Some Utes lived year-round along the streams that flowed into Utah Lake, and others arrived from points farther south during the summertime peak of the fishing season. In addition to attracting Utes who subsisted on its fisheries, the Utah Valley also became a destination for stolen Mormon livestock. When Mormon settlers interfered with the Utes' traditional means of subsistence, some Ute bands responded by stealing Mormon livestock and horses, driving them south and then up into the Utah Valley's canyons.[7]

In return, in late 1848 some Mormon settlers called for violent reprisals against the prior occupants of the land. Young initially rejected such calls. "A many Elders have prayed to be among the Lamanites," he complained, "and now they want to kill them." He reminded his restless followers that "they [the Indians] are the Children of Abraham, the descendants of Israel

. . . the remnants of Israel." Young also told the settlers that they should not hold the Indians to white standards of morality in cases of theft, a sentiment he repeated frequently over the next three decades. After several more months of cattle theft, Young changed his mind. In February 1849, several Mormon scouts met with Little Chief, one of the leading Utah Valley Utes. Little Chief complained about former members of his band who stole Mormon cattle and encouraged "the big white Capatan [Young] to send up some men and kill those . . . mean Ewtes." Little Chief's motivations are unclear. Perhaps he aimed to use the Mormons against his own enemies, or perhaps he simply wanted to curry favor with the leaders of the rapidly growing Mormon population. In any event, he warned the Mormon scouts that inaction would only breed more thieves. Prompted by this suggestion, Young dropped his previous inhibitions about killing Indians. He authorized an early March expedition that tracked the Indians and, after they refused to surrender, killed all of the party's men save one sixteen-year-old boy.[8]

Shortly after the expedition's victory, with thousands of additional emigrants expected in the fall, the Council of Fifty in March 1849 authorized the creation of a Utah Valley colony, initially called Fort Utah and later known as Provo. Of the Ute bands in the valley, the Council intended to "improve their Morals, to make Fishers of them, and then the Saints can buy the Fish of them for a trifle, which will preserve their good feelings." Several dozen Mormon families moved south to establish the settlement. Maintaining good feelings quickly proved impossible. Three settlers killed an Indian who refused to surrender a shirt the whites claimed had been stolen. According to an account written several years later, after shooting him, the settlers cut open his abdomen, filled it with rocks, and sunk the corpse in the Provo River. The Indians responded to the crime by increasing their cattle raids and driving their horses through Mormon crops. Unable to stop the attacks on their own, settlers wrote Young to ask for his counsel, probably hoping that he would authorize military action against the Utes.[9]

Young again initially resisted such calls. "[T]he Indians are wild, uneducated, naked [and] destitute," he explained in January 1850, "and they mostly steal from necessity and think it no harm." The settlers, he noted, would not shoot civilized and more educated white men for similar misdeeds. As he had done the previous year, though, Young changed his mind. Utah Valley leader Isaac Higbee reported at a January 31 council meeting that the settlers unanimously supported a campaign. "They [the Indians] say the Mormons have no captain," Higbee added, seemingly goading Young toward action. "I say go and kill them," Young decided without further hesitation, concluding that his forbearance had made the Indians more hostile. Captain Howard Stansbury and his Lieutenant John Gunnison of the U.S. Topographical Engineers, on a surveying mission in the Great Basin, affirmed Young's decision "to use up the marauders." Stansbury offered Young "the use of every thing I have," including guns. Once Young had decided to fight, he proceeded without any equivocation. "They must either quit the ground or we must," he said ten days later. "We have to maintain that ground, or vacate this." In order to steel the members of the expedition for what lay ahead, Young provided the campaign with the highest possible Mormon religious sanction. "Joseph prophesied," he said, "many of the Lamanites will have to be slain, many of them by us." Presumably because of the strain of the war, Young and the apostles held nightly prayer circles at his home for several consecutive days.[10]

When he declared war on the Utes, Young made clear that the warriors would receive no quarter from his militia. "We shall have no peace until the men are killed off," he said, though he intended to "let the women and children live if they will behave themselves." Young's subsequent comments suggested that men might be spared if they separated themselves from hostile bands. Militia commander Daniel H. Wells ordered his men to "[t]ake *no hostile Indians as prisoners.*" On February 13, Mormon militiamen captured a group of Indians at Table Point on the southern end of Utah Lake. "They were induced to come in," John Gunnison wrote a few weeks later, "on the assurance of the whitemen being friendly to them." The militia disarmed the Indians. "[W]e shall deal with them in the most summary manner as soon as another day favors us with its light," Wells informed Young. In a postscript written the next morning, he asked for Young's advice regarding "the disposal of some 15 or 20 Squaws and children who probably belonged to some 11 warriors who met their fate in a small skirmish this morning." While some of the warriors may have tried to escape, their deaths were mainly the result of a premeditated execution. "[I]n the morning," Gunnison informed, "all disarmed & the male Indians were all shot." Young praised the operation following his receipt of the dispatch from Wells. *Let it be peace with them or extermination,*" Young affirmed. By this point, most of the fighting was over, as surviving Ute warriors escaped the militia by retreating into the mountains. The grisly scenes continued, though. Abner Blackburn, a participant in the expedition, helped the U.S. Army surgeon James Blake decapitate the slain Indians in order to send their heads to Washington for medical research.[11]

The February 1850 campaign served as the Mormon conquest of Utah Valley. Including the executions of Ute warriors, the militia killed at least several dozen Indians, including some former Mormon allies. A few months later, Young explained that when he had joined the church, he had approached the Lamanites with an open mind, "but my natural disposition and taste it loathes the sight of those degraded Indians." White settlers and explorers often traveled to the West with romantic expectations about its native peoples, but contact with actual Indians often replaced those preconceptions with feelings of revulsion. Only a very few white Americans proceeded beyond that revulsion to true understanding and respect, and Young was not one of those few. Even though the Great Basin's Utes "are as bright as any in America," he concluded, they were "fallen in every respect, in habits, custom, flesh, spirit, blood, desire." Young had envisioned successful missions and co-existence with converted Indians. Although he had initially responded to conflicts by calling for restraint, he eventually initiated military reprisals wholly disproportionate to alleged Indian crimes. Perhaps at moments of stress, Young's disgust at the Indians' present condition made it easier for him to authorize their deaths.[12]

In the fall of 1850, Mormon settlers established the beginnings of eight Utah Valley towns. The rapid Mormon colonization of the valley—and then more distant portions of the Great Basin—reshaped and limited the options available to its native peoples. The swelling population of Mormon settlers steadily depleted the Utah Valley fisheries, especially when settlers sent loads of fish to Salt Lake City. Game was already scarce in the neighboring mountains. Disease ravaged Ute encampments. For the Indians, their old earth had indeed passed away, and the new order of things was decidedly to their detriment. Those Indians who remained in the valley gradually found themselves reduced to begging and occasional trading, further establishing themselves in Mormon eyes as an impoverished, primitive, and cursed people.[13]

Recognizing the shift in power, some Ute bands perceived opportunities to gain food, supplies, and enhanced prestige and power. Chief Walker (*Walkara* or *Wakara*), a renowned leader of a powerful, slave-trading band of equestrian Utes with a base of operation in the Sanpete Valley to the south, aggressively courted the Mormons as allies against his Shoshone enemies and other bands of Utes. When Walker heard of the outcome of the February campaign, he informed Mormon leaders of his approval. The following month, he was baptized and became an unreliable Mormon ally for the next few years.[14]

By then, Young had pivoted back to conciliating potentially friendly Utes. In early May 1850, he wrote Walker, Black Hawk, and several other Ute chiefs. "We cannot live with bad Indians," he explained. "We can live with good Indians, and will do them good." Young claimed revelatory authority in the letter, telling the recipients "God talks to Mormon chief," and he signed the letter "Big Chief." Two weeks later, Young met twenty Ute band leaders in Utah Valley. "We want to smoke the pipe of peace and be friends," Young announced. He asked Thomas Bullock to read his recent letter, which included Young's assurance that the Indians "need not leave this land." Probably confusing them, he then asked them if they wanted to sell their land to the Mormons. They demurred at that request but otherwise responded favorably to his peace overtures. As the meeting continued, Young showed one way in which he differed from other white American "Big Chiefs." The Mormons in attendance sang two hymns, and Young then gathered the Utes into a circle for a sermon. At the close of his sermon, Young spoke in tongues, and the Utes responded that they understood his words. Young now rarely spoke in tongues, the practice so fundamental to his first ten years in the church. That he did so in front of the Ute chiefs suggests that the church president felt unusually strong emotions—or an unusually strong sense of the divine—at the meeting. Joseph Smith had a vision in 1835 that Young would speak to hostile Indians in the Southwest in their own tongue. If Young believed that Smith's prophecy was now being fulfilled, he kept such thoughts to himself. The following month, 126 Indians were baptized into the church, probably with little understanding of the religion they publicly embraced.[15]

Even if the baptisms resulted more from the Indians' military setbacks than sincere conversions, they provided some hope that the Mormons might achieve missionary success among Great Basin Indians. By the fall, however, mounting frustration led Young to a more sober conclusion. In a November 1850 letter to John Bernhisel, a Mormon representative in Washington, Young identified "naked Indians and wolves" as his people's chief nuisances. Settlers could eventually dispatch the wolves, "but worse, by far, are wild men than wild beasts." The Mormons meant the Indians no evil, Young insisted. "We would have taught them [the Indians] to plow & sow, & reap & thresh," he maintained, "but they prefer Idleness and theft." Identifying a number of possible reservation lands, such as the eastern slope of the Sierra Nevada, Young contended that removal would hasten the arrival of civilization and also that Indians would more quickly assimilate when separated from their hunting and fishing grounds. Ultimately, Young anticipated his people occupying the Great Basin's arable land, and, in his mind, only the Saints would make proper use of it. "Let the Indians be removed," he argued, "we can then devote more time to agriculture, raise more grain to feed the starving millions desirous of coming hither." Indian removal, he concluded, would benefit the Indians, the

Mormons, and all other Americans who would pass through the Great Basin.[16]

Young's call for a Ute reservation was very much in keeping with developments within U.S. government policy. Many Americans shared Young's view that the Indians could only be civilized (and thus preserved) by being forcibly separated from their traditional but no longer viable means of subsistence. Only then would they become industrious and sedentary farmers. In the same year that Young called for the removal of Deseret's Indians, U.S. Indian Commissioner Luke Lea called for the forcible restriction of each tribe to a "country adapted for agriculture" and for government agents to assist the Indians' transition to civilization. For Young, a Ute reservation remained a distant goal, for only the U.S. government could legally sign treaties extinguishing native title to territorial land.[17]

Meanwhile, the Mormons at first fostered and then eliminated one other Ute vehicle of prosperity. When the Mormons arrived in the Great Basin, "Spanish" traders still traveled up a well-established trail from New Mexico to the Utah Valley, but Indian raiders soon perceived the possibility of a new outlet for their contraband. Shortly after the 1847 pioneer camp arrived in the Salt Lake Valley, an Indian trader approached Mormon settlers with two children for sale. It was inevitable that settlers would purchase children, as traders occasionally killed unsold captives to facilitate sales. In 1847, an Indian named Batiste brought two captives to the Mormons' Salt Lake Valley fort and offered them for sale. When the pioneers refused, he killed one of the prisoners, a boy of about sixteen. Charles Decker, married to Young's daughter Vilate, bought an eighteen-year-old "squaw."[18]

Charles Decker gave the young woman to his sister, Young's wife Clarissa (Clara), presumably as a servant. Kahpeputz, or Sally as Clara named her, quickly became acquainted with Young's extended family and their religion. In 1849, Zina Huntington Young sang in spiritual tongues while at home one evening. She felt God's spirit leading her to "go and bless Clarry Decker." She did so, and also extended a blessing to "Sally (the lamanites that Charles Decker bought)." "I lade my hands upon her hed," wrote Zina in her diary, "and my language changed in a moment and when I had finished she said she understood every word." Sally might have told Zina of the pain she experienced because of her separation from her family, for Zina "told her that her mother and sisters ware coming." For Zina, the blessing meeting was a "positive proof" of spiritual power. It is impossible to know how Sally interpreted the experience.[19]

Sally remained a member of Brigham Young's household for nearly three decades. "She has lived in my family ever since," Young stated in 1852, "has fared as my children and is as free." Despite that statement,

Sally Young Kanosh (Kahpeputz), 1878 *(courtesy of the Utah State Historical Society)*

however, Sally ultimately did not live as Young's other children. Young later informed a visitor that it was difficult to "rear Indian children," mentioning a woman he had obtained as a child. "At first she slept outside," Young told his guest, "and preferred the meat she gathered from the gutters instead of good fried beef." Now, Young concluded, Sally had become an excellent housekeeper and was "ready to vomit now at the recollection of her former habits." The 1860 census groups her with the other female help in the household.[20]

Mormon ally Chief Walker had long been one of the most audacious, wide-ranging, and successful Ute slave raiders. "[W]hen he cannot get what he thinks they [captive children] are worth," Young testified in 1852, "he says he will take them to the Navaho Indians or Spaniards, and sell them, or kill them." Such tactics induced Mormon settlers to purchase the children, which in turn increased Walker's incentive to take additional captives. "I have seen Walker's slaves so emaciated," Young said, "they were not able to stand upon their feet." Since Young and other Mormon leaders largely discarded the possibility of mass conversions of adult Indians, such quasi-adoptions also provided a means to encourage a rising Lamanite generation to embrace the gospel. Young "counseled the brethren to buy up the Lamanite children as fast as they could and educate them and teach them the gospel so that [in] not many generations they would be a white and delightsom people." Young thus encouraged the purchases for practical and theological reasons, and the Utah legislature in 1852 passed "An Act for the Relief of Indian Slaves and Prisoners," allowing settlers to indenture Indian children for up to twenty years. Gradually, though, the Mormons eliminated the Ute slave trade by preventing Mexican traders from operating in the Great Basin. The Fish-Eaters could no longer rely on Utah Lake's bounty, and dominant Ute bands could no longer support themselves by selling captives. The Great Basin's native peoples steadily saw their options for sustenance and autonomy vanish.[21]

When President Fillmore appointed him Utah's governor, Young also became the territory's *ex officio* superintendent of Indian affairs. In 1852, Young explained that his "uniform policy . . . [was] 'that it is better and cheaper to feed and clothe the Indians, than to fight them.'" That conclusion was not original to Brigham Young. For example, a group of Indian commissioners that negotiated a series of 1851 treaties with California tribes concluded that "it is *cheaper* to feed the whole flock for a *year* than to *fight* them for a week." Probably no one else employed the maxim as frequently as Young did, though. For the next thirty years, he consistently reminded Utah settlers calling for military reprisals against Indians that it was "cheaper to feed them." Like other American leaders, Young wielded blunter instruments of control when charity and civilizing efforts failed to pacify Utah's native peoples. When conflicts with Indians proved intractable, he would "chastise" the Indians through military action, and once prodded to action, he meted out harsh retribution. In 1853, he attributed the survival and safety of Utah's settlements to his willingness to "kill every soul of them [the Indians] if we had been obliged to do so." Still, after the bloody conflicts of 1849–50, Young's Indian policies for the subsequent decade became more noteworthy for their relative benevolence and patience. Both the church and the federal government devoted some resources to Indian relief and agriculture, though clashes between Young and U.S.-appointed Indian agents inhibited the successful application of any consistent Indian policy in the territory.[22]

For the most part, Indians played only an awkward and largely un-wanted role in the early Mormon settlement of the Great Basin. Young's overriding objective remained bringing as many Saints to Zion as possible, creating a firm foundation that could not be dislodged. All of his policies regarding native peoples, from pacifying them with food, to killing those hostile to settlers, to asking Washington for their removal, furthered this grand objective.[23] As the Saints struggled to achieve prosperity and peace in their new home, Young perceived only an awkward and inferior place for the Indians, both within his own family and in the Kingdom of God expanding its dominion over the Great Basin.

WHILE often frustrated with the present condition and behavior of the Great Basin's Indians, Young at least inconsistently affirmed the Mor-mons' obligation to restore the Indians to their ancient faith and usher them into a glorious millennial future. By contrast, Young concluded that God had cursed another dark-skinned people with much bleaker earthly and eternal prospects.

During his early years in the church, Young made almost no comment on black Americans. Though he probably saw few African Americans in the hinterlands of western New York, Young had grown up in a state in which slavery was declining but remained legal until 1827. An 1821 con-stitutional convention in New York, moreover, granted only a small per-centage of free black men the right to vote. Like almost all white Ameri-cans, Young thought of black people as an inferior and separate class of degraded human beings. Occasionally, however, he had experiences that contradicted such general views. Once during his early missionary travels, he mentioned the generosity of a black man who responded to a call for donations.[24]

After 1844, Young spent more time with the church's small number of black members. Jane Manning, a black woman born in Connecticut who had worked as a servant in the Smith household, briefly lived with Young's family after Smith's murder. Green Flake, who traveled west as Mississippi convert James Flake's slave despite a sojourn in Nauvoo, drove a wagon into the Salt Lake Valley several days in advance of Young's arrival in July 1847. Beginning in 1848, free black Isaac James, who married Jane Man-ning, worked as a coachman for Young.[25]

The Latter-day Saints reflexively understood two key biblical passages as pertaining to African peoples and identifying them as divinely cursed. The fourth chapter of Genesis narrates God's curse of Cain following his murder of his brother Abel; God subsequently places a "mark" on Cain to protect him from retributive justice. Genesis's ninth chapter relates

Jane Elizabeth Manning James, n.d. *(courtesy of Church History Library, The Church of Jesus Christ of Latter-day Saints)*

that after Noah's son Ham "saw the nakedness of his father," Noah pronounced a curse upon Ham's son Canaan that he would serve his uncles Shem and Japheth. Although neither biblical text specifies the skin color of any of the individuals involved, many European Christians—especially after the advent of the African slave trade—came to posit that these curses had been laid upon those with black skin. In particular, Europeans utilized the Curse of Ham as a justification for the enslavement of Africans. In the United States, many antebellum white Christians, and even some black writers, accepted this basic exegesis, and proslavery apologists utilized the passage exhaustively in their biblical defenses of southern slavery. Thus, European and American whites came to view dark skin as a symbol of God's curse and a badge of inferiority. Many white Christians presumed that African Americans labored under a permanent curse, though a few theorized that conversion would not only whiten African souls, but would also lighten the skin of converts' children.[26]

Dark skin as a consequence of God's curse was a significant trope in the *Book of Mormon,* and other Mormon scriptures extended that reasoning to persons of African descent. The *Book of Moses,* Smith's 1830 revision and expansion of the first several chapters of Genesis, specified that "the seed of Cain were black." A later scripture, though it did not specify dark skin, suggested significant ecclesiastical consequences for the ancient curses. The *Book of Abraham,* translated by Joseph Smith in 1835 and published in 1842, identified an Egyptian pharaoh as "a descendant of the loins of Ham" and "a partaker of the blood of the Canaanites" and further described him as "being of that lineage by which he could not have the Right of priesthood." Mormon scriptures also contained more egalitarian teachings. The Lord "inviteth them all to come unto him and partake of his goodness," reads the *Book of Mormon*'s 2 Nephi 26:33, "and he denieth none that come unto him, black and white, bond and free, male and female . . . all are alike unto God." Nevertheless, in keeping with mainstream white American attitudes, Joseph Smith and many other early church leaders described black people as subject to biblical curses.[27]

Despite the Mormons' inheritance and adaptation of white Christian racism, several black men were ordained as elders in the Mormon priesthood during the church's early years. Still, while they welcomed a few black men as minor church leaders, white Mormons by no means sought to create a racially egalitarian Zion. Nauvoo restricted voting, civil offices, and militia service to white men. The city also prohibited marriage between blacks and whites. Smith on one occasion enforced the ban on intermarriage by fining two black men for planning to "marry white women." Such measures and actions would have raised no eyebrows in Illinois, which like much of the American Midwest had enacted similar state laws. Indeed, for all of the North's internal disagreements on the issue of slavery, most white northerners, especially those living outside New England, staunchly affirmed black inferiority and abhorred the specter of large free black populations. Jane Manning recalled being threatened with arrest in Peoria unless she could produce "free papers." When the authorities relented, she and her family continued to Nauvoo. A number of midwestern states, including Illinois, passed laws criminalizing the settlement of free blacks within their borders in the late 1840s and early 1850s.[28]

Having matured as an ecclesiastical and political leader in a "sea of Negrophobia," it is surprising that Brigham Young's first recorded comments on the issue of black church members conveyed a more egalitarian mind-set. In March 1847, a strange musician and prophet named Warner (or William) McCary appeared in Winter Quarters. Born a slave in Mississippi of mixed European and African ancestry, McCary somehow escaped and moved to St. Louis, then was baptized in Nauvoo and married a white woman before relocating to Cincinnati and building a congregation around his own prophetic and messianic authority.[29]

After his popularity in Cincinnati waned, he and his wife traveled to Winter Quarters, where McCary presented himself as an Indian prophet. Despite this pretense, reported Wilford Woodruff, most observers considered McCary "to be a descendant of Ham." The next month, McCary met with a church council and complained to Young about various sorts of verbal abuse at the hands of church members. "[S]ome say there go the old nigger and his White Wife," began McCary, still claiming to be of native descent. Young reassured McCary that race had no bearing on an individual's standing within the church. "Its nothing to do with the blood," he said, rejecting contemporary arguments for the separate creation of different human races, "for of one blood has God made all flesh." Young added that "we have one of the best Elders an African in Lowell [Massachusetts], a barber" named Q. Walker Lewis. With McCary still unsatisfied, Young stressed "we don't care about the color." Acting erratically and bizarrely, McCary spoke of himself as Adam, disrobed and asked to be examined for a missing rib, and eventually agreed to perform in the council house to raise money for a projected move over the mountains with the church. Young probably did not mean for his spontaneous reassurance to McCary to endorse black Mormons' full equality within the church but rather to calm McCary and give himself the opportunity to appraise a bizarre situation. Still, it is noteworthy that he apparently raised no objection to McCary's interracial marriage.[30]

After Young's pioneer camp left Winter Quarters, McCary fell out with remaining Mormon leaders and departed; local Mormon leaders in Iowa later alleged that McCary—known as the "Nigger Prophet"—gained sway over church members and had himself sealed to several white Mormon women. Young would have learned of these alleged sexual escapades upon his return.[31]

In December, Young met with William Appleby, who had recently served as the president of the church's eastern branches. In Lowell, Appleby had encountered Walker Lewis, the black elder in Massachusetts. Appleby discovered that Lewis's son (Enoch Lovejoy Lewis) was "married to a white girl" and fellow church member. "I wish to know," Appleby wrote Young, "if this is the order of God or tolerated in this Church, i.e. to ordain Negroes to the Priesthood, and allow amalgamation."[32] When Appleby met with church leaders, he further informed them that Enoch Lewis's white wife had given birth to a child. Young responded harshly to Appleby's report:

> If they were far away from the Gentiles they would all have to be killed—when they mingle seed it is death to all. If a black man & white woman come to you & demand baptism can you deny them? the law is their seed shall not be amalgamated.

> Mulattoes are like mules they can't have children, but if they will be Eunuchs for the Kingdom of Heaven's sake they may have a place in the Temple.

Young's ideas about mixed-race sterility, including the mule analogy, were standard fare among white Americans into the early twentieth century. Still, despite its condemnation of miscegenation, Young's response to Appleby suggested that persons of African descent might receive some of the church's ritual blessings.[33]

Young's beliefs about the place of black people within the church soon hardened, and he made clear that all black people—not just those who married white women—lived under a divine curse. During a February 1849 council meeting, Lorenzo Snow—brother of Young's wife Eliza Snow —suggested that the church should "unlock the door" to the African race so that its members would have "a chance of redemption." It is unclear what Snow meant, perhaps either an emphasis on missions to African Americans or their access to sacred church rituals. Regardless, Young in response "explained it very lucidly that the curse remains on them because Cain cut off the wives of Abel to hedge up his way and take the lead but the Lord has given them blackness, so as to give the children of Abel an opportunity to keep his place with his descendants in the eternal worlds." By murdering Abel, Young theorized, Cain had deprived both Abel and his wives of increasing their progeny. From that time forward, Young repeated his conclusion that God had punished the "seed of Cain" with blackness, which meant an inferior position within society, the church, and, ultimately, in the "eternal worlds." At some point, after Abel's posterity— nonblack people—had received their blessings in full, God would remove the curse. Until then, Young insisted the church could not alter "the true eternal principles the Lord Almighty has ordained." Under Young's leadership, the church did not ordain black men as elders, did not allow black men or women to receive the endowment, and did not seal the marriages of its few black members.[34]

The Mormon drift from relative egalitarianism to racial exclusion partly resembles the trajectory of other American religious movements. Though

American Protestants were divided over the issue of slavery (the largest Baptist and Methodist denominations split along sectional lines in the mid-1840s), they were largely united through their belief in the inferiority and undesirability of black people. By the mid-nineteenth century, many evangelical churches—including the Methodists—had backed away from tentatively egalitarian beginnings. It is thus not surprising that the Mormons followed suit.

Although fragmentary documentation obscures the reasons for Young's hardening position, his revulsion over the specter of interracial procreation apparently played a major role in his thinking. Perhaps most fundamentally, a church that emphasized forging links between the generations and eternal sealings between its members would not find it easy to incorporate black Americans within this ecclesial family. Though some white Protestants posited the idea of a segregated heaven, most—happily or unhappily—expected they would coexist with black Christians in heaven. Focused primarily on individual salvation, perhaps Protestants did not fret over the racial characteristics of those who would spend eternity glorifying God. Mormons, by contrast, emphasized the eternal continuation of earthly relationships through ritual sealings. The church encouraged its adherents to build eternal family kingdoms through participation in sacred and intimate rituals, the sort of experiences white Americans would be very unlikely to share with black men and women. Excluded from the church's most sacred rituals, black Mormons would thus not share celestial glory with their white counterparts. For a church that sealed people on earth to bind them together in heaven, the exclusion of black Mormons from church offices and most rituals meant the eternal perpetuation of earthly inequities.

Despite the ecclesiastical restrictions, a small number of blacks traveled to the Great Basin. Initially, most came involuntarily. By 1850, approximately eighty enslaved and thirty free black men and women lived in Utah, the slave population augmented by a group of Mississippi Mormons that brought their human property to the valley in 1848. Probably seeking to mask the presence of slaves in Utah from antislavery politicians in Washington, a census taken in 1851 both understated the number of slaves in the territory and falsely suggested all would soon go to California. As was the case in most western states and territories, Utah blacks could not vote, hold territorial offices, serve on juries, or serve in the state militia. In 1852, the state legislature referred to the territory's "white legalized Government." Mormon leaders did not anticipate the growth of a large black population, slave or free. In the final decade before the Civil War, however, issues pertaining to slavery and free black people took on great importance even in western territories unlikely to develop sizeable black populations.[35]

Just as Utah's Mormons brought their marital and financial problems before Brigham Young, they sometimes asked him to help resolve disputes involving slaves. In the spring of 1851, a number of the Mississippi Saints were preparing to leave for California. Although their slaves would become free upon reaching the Golden State's soil, the owners evidently wagered that other forms of material enrichment would amply compensate them. William Crosby, a minor church leader planning to join the California expedition, wrote Young shortly before the group's departure. William Lay wanted to take his slave Hark to California but lacked the money to purchase Hark's wife, owned by John Bankhead. Taking Hark, therefore, would split up the couple. Crosby also informed Young that Green Flake acted "Lying disafected Saucy to Brother Flakes wife." James Flake had died in 1850; his widow Agnes now owned Green. If Green Flake gained his freedom in California, Crosby warned, "he would leave his Black wife and git him a white woman." Green needed a firm hand, Crosby explained.[36]

Young tried to find a joint solution to both problems. "[I]t would not be wisdom to part Man and Wife," he counseled Crosby. Despite noting that "we do not wish to encourage the Sale of Blacks in these vallies," Young tried to broker a transaction. Perhaps Lay or Bankhead would exchange Hark or his wife for Green Flake, thereby preserving the marriage and providing Agnes Flake with a more tractable servant. Although he expressed concern for the married slave couple, Young otherwise did not indicate that the slaves' wishes should influence the arrangements he suggested. In any event, he observed, the slaves would become free when they entered California, which had recently joined the Union as a free state. "I therefore," Young concluded, "would not be very strenous to take many of them to that country."[37] As his advice about Hark Lay and Green Flake illustrates, Young as the church's leader could not avoid some involvement in decisions that impacted the lives of human beings held as chattel in Utah.

Along with around one-third of Utah's enslaved population, Hark Lay ended up in California, with or without his wife. Neither William Lay nor Bankhead acquired Green Flake, who evidently impressed potential owners no more than he had impressed Crosby. Even though Bankhead was upset about a runaway "nigger not coming back," church clerk Thomas Bullock noted that "he will not take Green." Agnes Flake went to California without Green. According to the later recollection of Agnes Flake's son, Young accepted Green Flake's service to the church as a tithing payment from his owner.[38]

During the early 1850s, Young's comments on the issue of slavery were a bundle of contradictions. Young had expressed a preference for the Mormons to occupy "free soil," but both the Deseret Constitution and the 1851 Organic Act establishing the Utah Territory purposefully made no mention of slavery. "Shall we lay a foundation for Negro slavery?" he asked in a June 1851 sermon. "No God forbid!" Like many northerners critical of southern slavery, though, Young sharply opposed abolitionism because he associated it with political radicalism and an undesirable racial equality. He maintained that "to abolish slavery it would be throat cutting to themselves (the whites) and damnation to the blacks." Like many northern Democrats, Young did not want to live amid black slaves, but he loathed abolitionism.[39]

At the start of the 1852 legislature, the clerk Thomas Bullock read a carefully prepared message from Young to the assembly. In the speech, published in the *Deseret News* and probably crafted in part with national politicians in mind, Young addressed the twin issues of Indian and African slavery. "My own feelings are," Young maintained, "that no property can or should be recognized as existing in slaves, either Indian or African." In terms of Utah's small black population, he called for a middle ground between making African Americans "beasts of the field" and elevating them to full equality with their superiors. Young envisioned black people as the servants of benevolent white patriarchs, not slaves to cruel owners.[40]

Strangely, just two weeks later Young contradicted his previously stated opposition to slavery by urging the legislature to codify its existence in the territory. "I am a firm believer in slavery," Young now declared. When the Council (the assembly's upper chamber) first took up an "act in relation to African slavery," he outlined several rationales for the proposed law. He observed the wealth that southern Mormons had invested in slaves, but he also made a strong theological defense of the institution, maintaining that "[i]nasmuch as I believe in the Bible, inasmuch as I believe in the ordinances of God, in the Priesthood and order, and decrees of God, I must believe in slavery." For Young, the heart of the issue was that Africans were cursed by God with dark skin and servitude. Furthermore, arguing that American slaves enjoyed a "much more comfortable" life than European workers, Young suggested that a well-treated slave "is much better off than if he was free." The argument, common in southern critiques of northern as well as European capitalism, reflects Young's familiarity with working-class England and his relative lack of personal experience with southern slavery. Like many proslavery apologists, Young suggested that the institution was a positive good, both for slaves and their owners. Probably with an eye to Washington politicians, though, Young recommended changing the name of the bill to an "Act in Relation to Manual service."[41]

After a committee reworked the legislation, Young returned to the assembly in early February. Probably because some of the legislators—all church members and many holding high-ranking ecclesiastical offices—had scruples about the law, Young spoke more forcefully. "Any man having one drop of the seed of Cane in him Cannot hold the priesthood," he declared, "& if no other Prophet ever spake it Before I will say it now in the name of Jesus Christ." Young also repeated his severe teaching on miscegenation. "[I]f any man mingles his seed with the seed of Cane," he insisted, "the ownly way he Could get rid of it or have salvation would be to Come forward & have his head Cut off & spill his Blood upon the ground." Young had a simple answer for members of the legislature who wondered whether the territory's Organic Act permitted the bill. "If you will allow me the privilege [of] telling right out," he told the legislators, "it is none of their damned business what we do or say here." Cursed as slaves and excluded from the priesthood, Americans of African descent had few political rights in the Kingdom of God. Young allowed that they were citizens, but they could not vote or hold offices. As did many white Americans at this time and long afterward, Young feared that abolition or black suffrage would lead to black rule. "Negroes shall not rule us," he declared. Neither the federal government nor "inferior" races should interfere with the church's right to govern the Utah Territory. At least during this one legislative session, Young approached the issue of slavery with the same racial venom with which he addressed mixed-race marriage.[42]

With Young's support, in early February 1852 the assembly passed "An Act in Relation to Service," codifying the type of servitude Young envisioned. The statute, which never employed the word "slave" or "slavery," nevertheless made Utah the only part of the Mexican Cession open to black slavery. Rather weakly, the law allowed the importation of slaves "if it shall appear that such servant or servants came into the Territory of their own free will and choice." It also required "masters or mistresses" to provide their "servants" with comfortable housing, food, clothing, recreation, and eighteen months of schooling during their youth. Probate courts could free slaves if their masters treated them cruelly, and the statute allowed sales and exchanges of human property only if slaves freely gave their consent.[43]

Young's endorsement of slavery was fraught with political risks, as he well knew. Young and other church leaders were fortunate that Congress apparently failed to notice the codification of slavery in Utah. Reliable news of Utah slavery might have imploded the fragile political consensus that supported the extension of popular sovereignty in the early to mid-1850s. Public knowledge of legal slavery in the territory would at the very least have further complicated the church's political relationship with Washington. By the end of 1852, though, American politicians were outraged by the Mormon announcement of polygamy and thus paid no attention to Utah's legalization of slavery.[44]

The extent to which Mormon masters fulfilled Young's vision of benevolent servitude remains unknown—few sources give voice to the enslaved. Some black slaves in the territory left clear evidence that they did not regard their owners as benevolent patriarchs. On the same day in March 1849, two Mormons wrote Young letters informing him about runaway slaves. One of the slaves, a woman, fled to Young's house, reluctant to return to her owner for fear he would "correct her." Young's counsel in the case remains unknown. At least in other cases, however, Young enforced the 1850 Fugitive Slave Act, passed along with the creation of the Utah Territory in the Compromise of 1850 and bitterly reviled in antislavery portions of the North. In July 1852, Young forwarded an advertisement for a "runaway negro" to territorial marshal and church member Horace Eldredge, pointedly reminding him that if he should encounter the escaped slave, "the Fugitive Slave Law will no doubt be honored."[45]

Not surprisingly given Young's theological horror over the prospect of "amalgamation," Utah's slavery legislation also criminalized interracial sexual relations. The penalties were not as harsh as those Young had previously suggested in private. Instead, they prescribed a $500–$1,000 fine and a prison term of up to three years for any white person engaging in "sexual intercourse with any of the African race." By this time, most states and territories outside New England had banned black-white intermarriage. In particular, western states and territories rushed to do so despite their often minuscule populations of African Americans. Utah's sweeping legislation criminalizing all black-white sexual relations was more unusual, but not without precedent. No evidence suggests any Utah court enforced the law against black-white sexual intercourse during the years the provision remained in effect.[46]

At the end of 1852, Young commented that the "Act in Relation to Service" had discouraged the further growth of the territory's black population, slave and free. He praised the statute as having "nearly freed the Territory of the colored population; also enabling the people to control all who see proper to remain." Most western politicians would have affirmed these twin goals of discouraging both slave and free black populations. Indeed, both Oregon and New Mexico enacted provisions criminalizing the settlement of free blacks within their borders. Utah's slave population never again grew beyond several dozen, and its free black population also remained very small. Young did not want that fact to change and on that basis argued against seeking Utah's admission to Congress as a slave state. "[I]t is a curse to any Community to have them in it," he objected in a discussion of an 1856 bid for statehood. "Keep the blacks out and let the white men do the work and the people will rise." Regardless of constitutions and laws, he argued, persons of African descent would be in "perpetual slavery."[47]

Outside of church councils, Young was more humane than his racial rhetoric would suggest. After moving to California in 1851, Agnes Flake later regretted leaving her slave Green behind. In 1854, through the apostle Amasa Lyman, she asked Young if he would send Green Flake to her in California. If Young agreed, a third party "would purchase the negro and pay for him." Young responded that while "Green Flake worked for me about a year," he had since moved to Cottonwood Canyon and now suffered from ill health. Young did not offer to have him sold. Green Flake married a Mississippi-born slave; he appeared on the 1860 census as a "common laborer," living with his wife, Martha, and their two children.[48]

Isaac James, Young's black coachman, received an unusual share of his generosity. The church president paid James around one dollar a day, but by the mid-1850s Young had granted him more than a thousand dollars of credit. Young knew that James could never have repaid such a debt given his meager wages. Instead, the extension of credit probably represented Young's fondness for his black servant.[49]

"I Have two Blacks," Young commented in 1851. "They are as free as I am." Even if James and Flake were free to leave Young's service, they were not as free as their employer. They could not vote in Utah, did not possess most other basic citizenship rights, and could not marry according to the teachings of the territory's quasi-established church.[50]

In 1862, Congress abolished slavery in American territories, thus ending a geographically unusual incarnation of the peculiar institution. The exclusion of persons of African descent from the Mormon priesthood and from full access to church rituals, however, did not end for more than another century. Despite its broad empowerment of men—and sometimes women—through spiritual gifts and ecclesiastical responsibilities, Brigham Young's Mormonism remained deeply hierarchical, fostering unequal relationships between leaders and followers, men and women, and white people and members of other races. Young talked of creating a chain of humanity back to Adam, but he by no means envisioned all individuals as equal links in that familial chain. Young saw black Americans at best as servants expected to remain quiescent.

Jane Manning James, who along with her husband Isaac had briefly worked for Brigham Young, outwardly fit that mold. She remained a faithful Latter-day Saint, attending Sunday worship for decades. Yet her exclusion from temple rituals gnawed at her. In 1890, she petitioned Apostle Joseph F. Smith for her endowments. Divorced from Isaac around 1870, Jane also asked to be sealed to the deceased Walker Lewis, whom Young had praised in 1847 as "one of our best elders." Jane observed that Lewis had been a Mormon elder, ordained in the years before the priesthood ban. Finally, she stated that Emma and Joseph Smith had invited her to be adopted into their family, and she now requested that privilege as well. "I am Couloured," she reminded Joseph F. Smith in a postscript. Two months later, not having received an answer, she sent a second letter repeating her requests. "[P]lease answer this," she added in another postscript, "that my mind may *be saisfid* [satisfied]." Although church authorities allowed her to enter the temple to be baptized for her deceased relatives, they politely refused all her other requests. Finally, according to Joseph F. Smith, Wilford Woodruff and his counselors "decided that she might be adopted in to the family of Joseph Smith as a servant." James accepted Woodruff's offer. A servant on earth, she would be a servant in eternity. Still unsatisfied, however, Jane Manning James—whom church leaders termed "Aunt Jane" or "Black Jane"—continued to request full temple privileges.[51]

Given the racial context of the mid-nineteenth-century United States and the attitudes of other Mormon leaders, it makes little sense to lay the entire blame for the church's discriminatory policies at the feet of Brigham Young. Only a leader with an ardent commitment to racial egalitarianism, which Young did not possess, would have maintained the church's early relative openness to black Americans. Ecclesiastical discrimination was the norm among white American Protestants, and it is no surprise that the Latter-day Saints followed suit. However, Young's adamant contention that such discrimination rested upon "eternal principles" fostered a policy of exclusion that his successors saw little choice but to perpetuate.

CHAPTER NINE

Go Ahead

Brigham is the article that sells out West with us—between a
Roman cutlass and a beef butcher knife . . . how can I make you
know a good *Blade?*

— JEDEDIAH GRANT AND THOMAS KANE (1852)

WITH predictable victories over Utah's Indians and the more surprising triumph over the "runaway judges," Brigham Young in 1852
stood at the height of his political power while the church enjoyed several
years of relative peace and prosperity. Thousands of Latter-day Saints
crossed the plains each summer and the church steadily built up the line of
settlements that extended from Salt Lake City to nearly the California
coast. The Utah Mormons numbered more than twenty thousand by the
mid-1850s. "[I]t will be *mormondom* all over," Young exulted.[1]

Young knew it would take years of arduous work to achieve that audacious vision. "'Do not hurry me,'" he told his people in 1852, "is one of
the prominent characteristics of my history."[2] Young did not like others to
pressure him, but he himself vacillated between his avowed deliberateness
and a tremendous impatience to build up the Kingdom of God. On certain
matters, he adopted a policy of patient waiting. For example, he was not
concerned about either the rapid conversion or extermination of the Indians. If he could merely preserve peace and good relations with Utah's native peoples, a chosen few would convert, and he expected the remainder
to wither away to irrelevance.

While content to let the passage of time solve certain problems, Young
felt a growing impatience to secure the church's political autonomy. "[T]he
American character is Go a head Davy Crockett like," he once instructed
the territorial legislature, emphasizing its need to take the initiative in the

absence of assistance from Washington.[3] Also, by the 1850s, Young grew intensely frustrated with what he perceived as spiritual declension in Utah, and he responded by calling the Saints to new depths of contrition and new heights of dedication. Young wanted to ensure that committed and obedient Saints populated Zion's valleys, and he warned disaffected Mormons and antagonistic federal officials to leave the territory. Through his impatience to build up a kingdom of righteous Saints, Young adopted rash measures that exacted a high physical and emotional toll on his followers.

AFTER his 1847 return from the valley, Young talked about beginning work on another temple as soon as the pioneers had built homes for their families. He foresaw the "almightiest big Temple that ever was, instead of a nasty little one."[4] The project's successful completion hinged on the people's willingness to tithe their labor and wealth; hence, Young waited until the territory began to enjoy a measure of prosperity. If the Saints died before completing temple rituals for themselves and their ancestors, their descendants could perform the ordinances on their behalf. In 1853, the Saints broke ground for a temple in Salt Lake City, but construction proceeded haltingly over the next several decades.

In the meantime, the church began using the city's new Council House for both government business and ecclesiastical rituals, namely endowments and marital sealings. Young frequently used the "intermission" between the two Sunday services to seal couples in marriage, and he periodically went to the second floor of the Council House to preside over the endowments. A few years later, the church began construction on what would be known as the Endowment House, used for endowments, sealings, and baptisms for the dead. As he had done in Nauvoo, Young involved himself in the Endowment House's minute details, dictating "the pattern for the cushion for the altar in the sealing room." Several of his wives, including Eliza Snow and Naamah Carter ("Aunt Twiss"), also helped prepare the rooms. Young did not resume ritual adoptions, either because of the confusion the ordinance had caused during the exodus or simply because he believed such sealings could only be performed in the temple.[5]

Most Sundays, Young gathered the apostles and other close associates for a prayer circle, after 1851 often meeting in the Council House's "temple room." Dressed in their temple robes and repeating the sacred signs, Young and his followers prayed, then conversed upon diverse subjects. In early 1853, Thomas Bullock, a clerk, listed the evening's topics as including the "*Book of Mormon,* Punctuation, Familiar Spirits, Rappers [spiritualists], Revelation." The prayer circles were a chance for Young to unburden himself, to freely speak his mind on subjects he was not yet prepared to broach in public. "Brigham Young rolled out revelation upon revelation," Thomas Bullock recorded after a March 1852 prayer circle, "in regard to the creation of the world." "Adam," Young explained, "came to the Earth when he assisted to form it and he then partook of the fruits of the Earth and became Earthy [corporeal]." The Saints, Young taught, should seek to emulate Adam. When we "receive our resurrected bodies," he concluded, we will have "the privilege of going as Adams forming an Earth and doing likewise." As resurrected, exalted, and godlike beings, they would one day organize and people celestial kingdoms. As the organizer of this world, Adam served as the archetype for Saints, who would organize their own kingdoms on future worlds.[6]

After broaching these ideas in the privacy of the prayer circle, Young elaborated on them several weeks later at the church's annual April conference. He objected to the New Testament accounts of the birth of Jesus because they allowed infidels to blaspheme that "God is a whoremaster and Jesus Christ a bastard." Young countered with an alternative theory of messianic parentage that included his interpretation of the Fall: "Our Father in Heaven begot the Spirits in the eternal worlds . . . then organized a tabernacle. When our Father in Heaven came in the garden of Eden, Father Adam came with a celestial body, brought one of his Wives named Eve. They then stayed and ate of the fruits of the Earth until they produced seed from native element and were made mortal." Therefore, Young concluded, Adam "is Michael the Archangel, is the Ancient of Days, is our Father, our God, and the only God we have to do [with]." It was this Father, not the Holy Ghost, who then produced a son with Mary, no longer a virgin. "If [you] believe that our beloved Savior was begotten by [the] Holy Ghost," Young joked, "be very careful when you confer the Holy Ghost [on women] . . . you may beget them a child."[7]

Young subsequently identified Joseph Smith as the source of his ideas. "It was Joseph's doctrine that Adam was God," he said in 1860. It is more likely that Young expanded on ideas Smith had introduced toward the end of his life. Smith had taught that God was an exalted man who had once dwelled upon an earth, and he had identified Adam as the Archangel Michael and "the father of all, the prince of all, the ancient of days." While most Christians interpreted the latter title from the Hebrew Book of Daniel as referring to God the Father or Christ, Smith believed it referred to the "oldest man," the "head of the human family." He looked forward to a future date when Adam would present a chain of redeemed and sealed humanity to Christ. By the end of Smith's lifetime, moreover, other

Mormons had creatively elaborated upon his ideas. William Phelps, Smith's clerk and frequent ghostwriter, composed a fictional story revolving around the figure of Adam. In Phelps's "Paracletes," a heavenly being (Milauleph, representing Adam) takes a wife ("one of the 'Queens of heaven'") to earth, receives a physical body, reproduces, sins, accomplishes his mission, and eventually returns to his "father and mother in heaven." Adam does this according to the example of his "elder brother" (Jesus). Adam's path, moreover, is one his own Father had walked "in eternities before." While they may or may not have read Phelps's story, most of the Mormons who traveled west with Brigham Young had passed through the endowment ceremony in the Nauvoo Temple. In that sacred drama, Michael-Adam is one of three divine beings who, along with Elohim and Jehovah, create the world, whereupon Adam passes through an earthly existence before resuming his place within the divine hierarchy of heaven.[8]

Young's identification of Adam as the Saints' God moved beyond these antecedents. In Young's formulation, Adam stood "at the head of it all," including Christ. Young elaborated on Adam's relation to humanity in an October 1854 conference sermon. "He is the God and Father of our Lord Jesus Christ, both body and spirit," Young preached, "and He is the Father of our spirits, and the Father of our flesh in the beginning." Young posited that exalted human beings—Adam and Eve—had given birth to spirit children who later received bodies on earth. Exalted Latter-day Saints would one day return to their parents. "[W]hen you see your Father in the Heavens, you will see Adam," he explained. "When you see your Mother that bear[s] your spirit, you will see Mother Eve." Adam himself might have his own father in heaven (perhaps Jehovah), but for human beings on earth, Adam was God the Father, the pivotal figure in the creation and governance of the world. Although Young often used standard Christian language, encouraging the Saints to imitate Jesus, Adam also served as a human-divine archetype: an exalted man who had built a new world and established a kingdom whose increase would never end. Through the church's ordinances, Mormon men could embrace those same privileges.[9]

Some Mormons greeted Young's teachings enthusiastically. "Father Adam, our God, let all Israel extol," wrote Eliza Snow in early 1855, two months after Young delivered several sermons on the subject. Young's identification of Adam as humanity's God, however, raised jarring questions in a church that primarily consisted of converts reared in Protestant, Bible-drenched societies. Genesis 2 taught that God had formed Adam "from the dust of the ground." In response to that objection, Young taught that Adam was born in the flesh on another planet, made from its dust, and then came to earth as an exalted, resurrected being. Still, the teaching raised many other questions. Should the Saints worship Adam? Pray to Adam? Many church members responded to the new doctrine with a mixture of confusion and quiet unease.[10]

Apostle Orson Pratt, an autodidact in mathematics and astronomy, felt compelled to make his unease known. In the 1850s, Pratt and Young were moving in different theological directions. Central to Young's faith was his belief in eternal progression or increase. Both gods and the Saints as future gods would forever progress in knowledge, intelligence, independence, and progeny. By contrast, Pratt asserted that God the Father and Jesus had arrived at a fullness of knowledge and wisdom and that human beings could eventually become equal in those and other divine traits. "There is a *plurality* of substance," Pratt explained a few years later, "but a *unity* of quality; and it is this unity which constitutes the one God we worship." For Pratt, such logic reconciled Joseph Smith's apparently contradictory beliefs in the oneness of God and a plurality of gods. A few years later, Pratt further explained that the fullness of divine attributes existed in the Holy Spirit's "boundless ocean," omnipresent particles of spirit matter or intelligences.[11]

Pratt left Utah in September 1852 to defend the doctrine of plural marriage in the eastern United States. Bothered by Young's recent teachings about Adam, Pratt informed his traveling companions that "Adam is not the God that he is praying unto." In Washington, Pratt began publishing defenses of polygamy and other theological treatises in *The Seer,* a short-lived periodical that convinced few non-Mormons on the matter of plural marriage. In an 1853 letter to the missionary apostle, Young declared that "many points" in *The Seer* were "not *sound* doctrine." When Pratt returned home and attended a Sunday evening prayer circle, Young pointedly criticized him on several counts, emphatically rejecting Pratt's belief in an equal sharing of divine attributes by exalted beings. Unbowed, Pratt countered that he could not stomach Young's belief "that Adam was our God or the Father of Jesus Christ." Young was upset at Pratt for other reasons as well. Without seeking Young's approval, Pratt had published an autobiography of Lucy Mack Smith, containing what Young considered "thumping lies." The apostle had also published a text of the church's marriage sealing ritual in the *Seer.* Pratt apologized for these actions, but the two men locked horns over Adam.[12]

The ensuing theological dispute revealed several important aspects of Young's leadership. Despite his reputation for pragmatism, he was not content to merely give his followers practical advice and instructions.

Though Young was not a scholar or intellectual, he had a theologically speculative mind. Young enjoyed chatting about such subjects in the confines of the prayer circle, and when he was convinced of a doctrine's truth, he felt compelled to share it with his followers.

At the same time, Young's doctrinal concerns and theological curiosity differed from Pratt's systematic and intellectual approach to theology and science. Young had no interest in an extended theological debate with Pratt, and he could not tolerate expressions of doubt about his doctrinal leadership. Instead, Young insisted that church members, and especially fellow leaders, accept him as the oracle through which divine revelation and truth now flowed to the church. Pratt considered the scriptures and Joseph Smith's revelations authoritative sources that he could use to test the truthfulness of any doctrine, including those articulated by Young. In a heated 1856 discussion on the topic of Adam, Young put forth his beliefs with the full sanction of revelatory authority, informing Pratt that "things were so and so *in the name of the Lord*." The apostle refused to accede to Young's judgment, insisting "that the President's word in the name of the Lord was not the word of the Lord to him." Still unconvinced the next month, Pratt clarified that he "preferred to receive the written revelations of J[oseph] S[mith]." This attitude was unacceptable to Young. Though he cited both scripture and Joseph Smith's revelations as authoritative sources in his sermons, Young claimed that the "living oracles" were more valuable "than all that has ever been written from the days of Adam until now." Smith had left behind an expanded canon, but to Young, God's ongoing instructions took precedence.[13]

The conflict between Young and Pratt simmered for years. Young's understanding of eternal progression maintained a strong sense of hierarchy, preserving distance between God and human beings and between leaders and their followers. Orson Pratt failed to recognize that distance, and despite promises to the contrary he continued to espouse doctrines that Young regarded as speculative and misguided. Several times in the mid- to late 1850s, Young privately chastised Pratt. In 1856, he warned Pratt that he would never become "Adam," suggesting the apostle would not achieve the highest level of celestial glory and godhood. Characteristically, Young did not keep his chastisements private. The next year, while criticizing Pratt's beliefs about the Holy Spirit, Young told a congregation that Pratt "drowns himself in his own philosophy."[14]

At the same time, though, Young recognized that many church members had not embraced his teachings on Adam. He could not tolerate Pratt's open opposition, but he would not impose his beliefs on the church's membership. By 1857, Young conceded that "[w]hether Adam is the personage that we should consider our heavenly Father, or not, is considerable of a mystery to a good many." The Saints could consider Adam, his father (Jehovah), or his grandfather (Elohim) their God. "I do not care for one moment how that is," he groused. God had provided his son, Jesus, with a human body, so that human beings—of the same species as God and Jesus —could follow the same path toward celestial exaltation. Young stopped advancing the Adam-God doctrine in public with frequency, much as he had set aside ritual adoption after leaving Nauvoo. Young sensed he had gone ahead too quickly. He could reintroduce controversial teachings when the Saints were more ready to accept them. There was no need to hurry.[15]

For Brigham Young, as for Joseph Smith, an integral part of godliness— for Adam, for Jehovah, for Elohim, for Latter-day Saints on the path toward exaltation—was eternal increase. *"None but the Gods,"* he said in a description of the celestial world, "will be allowed to multiply *and increase."* Two decades later, Young clarified his belief that Adam and Eve had produced spiritual offspring "in the celestial world." On earth, the Latter-day Saints provided bodies for those spirit children when they produced mortal offspring. While plural marriage enabled the individuals involved to secure a larger share of eternal glory for themselves, marriage and childrearing also granted Mormons a chance to participate in this larger drama of the human family.[16]

For a decade, from Joseph Smith's secret introduction of plural marriage through the public announcement of the doctrine, Brigham Young had both expanded and reshaped his family life. In 1854, he and Mary Ann moved into a new principal residence, known as the Beehive House, and two years later a large number of his wives began occupying an adjacent building, known as the Lion House. Young's household included a sizeable number of servants, including the adopted Indian Sally and African American Mormons Isaac and Jane Manning James.[17] Young took breakfast in his own residence, but he assembled his entire family at the Lion House each evening for supper and prayer. Zina Huntington served as the family's midwife, Clara Decker raised Margaret Alley's children after the latter's death, and Aunt Twiss took charge of the Lion House meals. With the more permanent housing arrangements, Young's family life moved into a period of greater stability.

As always, though, there were subtractions and additions to the family. Margaret Alley died in 1852 shortly after giving birth to the couple's second child. Clarissa Ross Chase died in 1857. She had borne Brigham four children, and he remained close friends with her stepfather Isaac Chase.

Lion House and Beehive House, ca. 1855 *(courtesy of Church History Library, The Church of Jesus Christ of Latter-day Saints)*. In the center of the photograph, the "President's Office" and "Governor's Office" sit adjacent to each other. The church's "Tithing Office" occupies the story above the "President's Office."

Despite the early deaths of two wives, the steady birth of children increased Young's family size significantly during the 1850s. In 1858, the Ute chief Peteetneet visited Young and asked him how many children he had. The chief laughed when Young gave him an accurate count of forty-seven. Peteetneet claimed only two.[18]

Young was no longer especially interested in the further expansion of his household via marriage. With some regularity, women sent letters requesting to be sealed to him, sometimes grounding their requests on visions or revelations from God. Young usually ignored such entreaties but occasionally grew annoyed. "[W]hen I wish to have any woman sealed to me," he upbraided one persistent supplicant, "I shall reveal the fact. I am not guided by revelations coming through any woman."[19] In the 1840s, Young had not been overly selective about his wives, asserting that women had the right to choose their husbands. Given his wealth and status, that policy would have proven impractical over the long run. After the rush of marriages in Nauvoo, Young had consolidated a household in Utah and was not in any hurry to add wives to it.

After not marrying since his 1848 return to the valley, Young married five women between 1852 and 1856. Only one woman, however, represented an addition to his household. Eliza Burgess, a native of England, had already lived within his household as a servant.[20] Harriet Barney, who ended a nine-year marriage to William Henry Harrison Sagers shortly before her 1856 sealing to Brigham Young, joined the household and bore Young a son. Young married divorcées Mary Oldfield and Catherine Reese "for time and eternity," but neither woman joined his household.

In another instance, Young pointedly refused to acknowledge a new wife's standing within his family. Amanda Barnes, whose first husband, Warren Smith, was murdered in the 1838 Haun's Mill Massacre, came to Utah in 1850 as the unhappy wife of a second Warren Smith, who had embraced plurality and alienated Amanda in the process. Just days after their arrival in the Salt Lake Valley, Amanda wrote Young, informing him of Warren's verbal abuse and financial neglect and asking him for assistance. Subsequently, she asked Young to seal her for eternity to Joseph Smith, a ritual for which she needed a proxy. When she went to the Council House in January 1852 for the ceremony, Young suggested a man whom Amanda found unacceptable. With great reluctance, Young agreed to serve as Joseph's proxy, though he warned Amanda that he would not make her part of his household or otherwise provide financial support. "I should have faulterd," Amanda wrote him one month after the sealing, "when I saw your reluctant and gloomy felings the last time I saw you up in your office." Several months later, Warren and Amanda Smith divorced. Incorrectly blaming the church president for the dissolution of his marriage, Warren Smith complained publicly about Young having taken his wife.[21]

Despite their understanding at the time of the sealing, Amanda soon resented her exclusion from Young's acknowledged family. In a letter to Young, she lamented that she remained impoverished while others "enjoy your sosiety and have blesings heaped uppon them." Several years later, she upset her proxy husband by discussing their marriage at a social gathering. Young held firm in his refusal to provide Amanda with either money or a place in his household. When in 1868 she asked Young for coal, he replied that that given its scarcity he could "obtain no more than sufice the wants of those whom duty prompts me to provide for." In other words, he had no obligation to support her. Forced to provide for herself, Amanda developed a sense of pride in her self-sufficiency. "I left him [Warren Smith] and took my children and began to do for myself," she wrote in the mid-1850s. "I have got along first rate since that time." When Amanda Barnes Smith died in 1886, her *Deseret News* obituary did not mention any connection to Brigham Young.[22]

Young also refused to welcome back women who had been separated or estranged from him. Mary Woodward, for instance, futilely entreated the church president to permit her to join his household in Salt Lake City. Similarly, Young rejected the overtures of Clarissa Blake, who along with her prior husband, Lyman Homiston, emigrated to Utah in 1850. Clarissa had done something to upset Young back in 1845, and he had concluded that he "had been too hasty" in taking her as a wife. Once in Utah, Clarissa attempted in vain to effect a reconciliation. In 1858, Lyman married a second wife, an Englishwoman named Amelia Milner. Rejected by her eternal husband and feeling slighted by her earthly husband, Clarissa moved to Manti, Utah. At this point, Young quietly intervened. He wrote a cryptic letter to Bishop Warren Snow, explaining that Amelia had "pretty nigh left" Homiston and noting that Lyman intended to winter in Manti to reunite with Clarissa. "It will be perfectly right," he discreetly informed Snow, ". . . for br. Homiston's first wife to get a bill of divorce and be sealed to br. Homiston." Evidently, Clarissa was to obtain a divorce from Young and then be sealed for eternity to Lyman. Clarissa was surprised at the counsel, but she conveyed her willingness to obey. Two weeks later, though, Lyman Homiston died at the age of 81, probably before the planned divorce and sealing took place. Although Clarissa mentioned a dispute with Amelia in an 1861 letter to Young, she affirmed her belief that "plurality is the foundation of my hopes of salvation and exaltation in the Kingdom of God." She died in 1863, buried as "Clarissa Blake Young," staking her claim to the eternal privileges the church president had attempted to deny her.[23]

Despite keeping several women on the extreme margins of his family, Young went to great lengths to persuade one temple-sealed wife to join his household. Unlike in the cases of Amanda Barnes or Clarissa Blake, Young had a deep attachment to Julia Foster. While a widower, Young had converted Foster to Mormonism in 1833 and had been interested in marrying her at that time. He later became her proxy husband when she was sealed for eternity to Jonathan Hampton at the Nauvoo Temple. After he left Nauvoo, Young had written his brother Joseph and informed him that "sister Hampton must be braught with the Saints." Julia, though, stayed in Nauvoo and married Thomas Cole the following year. Five years later, Julia's second marriage ended in abandonment. She then wrote Young of her desire to rejoin the Saints, without mentioning her marriage to Cole. Young quickly instructed his representatives to procure any "necessary provisions for her transportation to this place." Two years later, missionaries visited Foster and her children, rebaptized them, and brought them west. The day after their arrival in Salt Lake City, Julia and her two eldest sons (including Brigham Young Hampton) called on the church president.

Initially, Julia lived in the Lion House, though she eventually moved to Ogden with her two youngest children.[24]

In addition to managing the complex affairs of his own family, Young also exercised church-wide authority over matters of marriage and divorce. Polygamous unions generally required his consent or that of other delegated leaders. "[I]f you whant a wife," Albert P. Rockwood instructed a group of men in Provo, "you first ask Brigham, then the Perants & next the female." Young encouraged the Saints to embrace plurality, so he responded positively to most requests even if he doubted a marriage's prospects. Solomon Chamberlain, who had been instrumental in the conversion of Young's family in the early 1830s, requested Young's permission to marry in early 1857. "I am willing that brother Chamberlain should take another wife," Young wrote Chamberlain's bishop. "How long will he keep her?"[25] In this case, it seems that the seventy-eight-year-old Chamberlain failed to find a bride. Though he used requests as opportunities to address deficiencies in morality, tithing, and obedience, Young could not set the bar overly high, as many Saints were hesitant to enter plural marriage.

Young received countless reports of marital strife and requests for advice. During his final winter in Nauvoo, Young issued a curious threat to an abusive husband. "[I]f your wife goes back to live with you on or by my councel and you should abuse hir," he warned in a handwritten letter, "I shall look to it take hir . . . and cherish hir, and be a savior to hir and your children." Given the spate of plural marriages Young contracted that winter, the recipient probably took Young's threat seriously. In most cases of spousal abuse, Young recommended that the couple try to live together in peace, promising a divorce to the wife if the abuse continued. Young also displayed little patience with men who neglected their wives. In 1856, he learned of a man who had left his blind wife "destitute of means." "If you do not attend to this matter forthwith," he threatened, "I shall send a *servant* after you."[26]

More unusual dilemmas sometimes required creative solutions. In 1857, Mary Richardson wrote Young about a seemingly intractable marital problem. Mary and her husband, Edmund, had once been members of a Presbyterian church. In 1853, the couple with their two children moved to Utah, converted to Mormonism, and settled in Manti. Edmund, however, was "incapable of having [additional] children," she explained, partly because of an "ailment" and partly "done voluntarily in consequence of Gentile feelings and tradition." Regardless of the exact cause of Edmund's self-inflicted impotency, Mary worried that her husband could not receive the "ordinances of the temple, the endowments, sealings." Perhaps her worry stemmed from Deuteronomy's prohibition on a man "wounded in the stones" entering the temple. Should she remain with Edmund and risk her exaltation, or should she leave him and marry someone without such a handicap? At the very least, given the link between progeny and celestial glory, Edmund could provide only very limited eternal benefits.[27]

Young regarded impotency as valid grounds for the dissolution of a marriage. John Benbow, instrumental to the success of Young's British mission, took Agnes Taylor as a plural wife in the Nauvoo Temple. Agnes, the apostle John Taylor's sister, refused to live with Benbow when the latter proved physically unable to consummate the marriage. "[F]or a woman to be in such a situation of impotency," Young told Benbow, "it is death to her, and I would not live three weeks in such a situation." Mary Richardson, by contrast, wanted to remain with Edmund for eternity, so Young in this case made a different proposal. "[I]f I was imperfect and had a good [fertile] wife," he wrote Mary, "I would call on some good brother to help me that we might have increase." Should Edmund agree to this plan, he would "have a place in the Temple, receive his endowments and in eternity will be as tho' nothing had happened to him in time." Perhaps Young felt Edmund needed to accept this arrangement as a way of proving himself worthy of the temple ordinances, or perhaps he simply felt Mary Richardson deserved a larger share of celestial glory. Edmund and Mary agreed to Young's plan, and he sealed them to each other at the Endowment House in April.[28]

"[I]n the counsel we recieved from you on a former occasion," Edmund wrote six months later, "you have the sincere gratitude of our hearts." While requesting ritual adoption as Young's son, Edmund pledged himself to "faithfully to carry out your counsel, and instructions, as those of a father." According to several sources, Young sanctioned Mary's marriage to Frederick Walter Cox, another Manti resident with whom she bore two sons in short order. Mary then returned to Edmund, who raised the boys as his own.[29]

Young's advice helped preserve some marriages, but others—monogamous and polygamous—were beyond saving. Young and other Mormon leaders decried divorce in their sermons. Indeed, divorce ruptured the links in the eternal chain that the Latter-day Saints reconstructed through their rituals. Children of divorced couples could not be sealed to both of their parents. Yet Mormon theology also required couples contented enough to bear children, and divorce thus could provide a means for women to fulfill that theological imperative in a new family. Young therefore displayed to Mormon women the same pragmatic, liberal attitude regarding divorce that he adopted within his own family.

In 1849, Sarah Phelps asked her husband William Phelps (formerly Joseph Smith's ghostwriter) for a divorce. Phelps denied that he had mistreated her in any way, and Young initially rejected her request. Claiming that her husband treated her as a "menial slave," Sarah professed herself unable to follow Young's counsel. "True I did choose him," she explained, "But I was then incapable of choice. I had been beguiled like Mother Eve." Now she should have a true choice. "Is this not a woman's right?" she asked Young. Young agreed. "All by freedom," he told Phelps, "and nothing by force." "Were Brigham a wife," he asked, displaying an ability to empathize with an unhappy wife, "would he want to be forced to live with a husband he did not love?" Sarah obtained her divorce. "[T]here was No law in Heaven or on Earth," Young later observed, "that would Compel a woman to stay with a man either in time or Eternity." Given Young's attitude and a lenient divorce law, Utah polygamists had an unusually high divorce rate for the remainder of the nineteenth century. It is worth noting, however, that women risked losing custody of their children in the event of divorce.[30]

Young may have responded sympathetically to some unhappy plural wives, but he chastised men seeking divorces. Rejecting one such supplicant, Young "said that when a man married a wife he took her for better or for worse, and had no right to ill use her, and if she shit in bed and laid in it until noon; he must bare it." He further threatened that men who mistreated their wives in order to prod them into asking for a divorce would find themselves "in the worlds to come, alone." Similarly, Young told another man that "if you have drawn a red hot iron between your legs and scorched yourself bear it without grunting." He observed that he offered such advice against his pecuniary interest, as he charged ten dollars for a certificate of divorce.[31]

Young later both qualified and expanded his emphasis on female agency. In an October 1861 sermon he ordered withheld from publication, Young informed women that they could not separate themselves from "righteous" husbands even if he signed a divorce certificate for them. "[Y]ou may just as well tear off a piece of your shirt tail," he explained, "and lay it by and call it a divorce so far as any good that piece of paper . . . will do you." In partial contradiction to what he had told William Phelps in 1849, righteous husbands would retain their unhappy wives in eternity even if they lost them on earth. At the same time, however, Young provided a noteworthy exception to this general rule, claiming a teaching directly "from Joseph the Prophet." Young explained that if "a woman can find a man holding the keys of the priesthood and higher in power and authority than her husband, and he is disposed to take her he can do so." In this case, the woman did not even need to obtain a divorce. Although Young described this option as a matter of female agency, he thereby also provided a rationale for the plural marriages that he—and Joseph Smith—had contracted with previously married women.[32]

Plural marriage had become more regularized in Utah than it had been in Nauvoo, but the rules for Mormon marriage and divorce remained flexible. Within his own family, Young persistently encouraged some women to join his household while making clear his unwillingness to support others. He could decide such matters on a case-by-case basis. Within the church more broadly, Utah's peculiar institution proceeded according to Young's discretion.

IMMEDIATELY adjacent to the Church President's Office on Young's Temple Square property lay the Governor's Office, aptly symbolizing Utah's union of political and ecclesiastical authority. Utah's elections were the nation's least suspenseful, as the Mormon people without party or factionalism, without violence, and with unanimity or minimal dissent affirmed men nominated by the hierarchy. "[Y]ou know this people well enough," Young wrote non-Mormon ally Thomas Kane in 1854 when offering him the position of territorial delegate to Congress, "to be certain that they will vote as they may be counselled." Young gave instruction to local Mormon leaders to be sure that elections produced the desired results. As was common in many states until later in the nineteenth century, voters cast numbered ballots, and election officials recorded their names. This procedure added an element of coercion to Utah elections, though church-supported candidates retained overwhelming margins even after the 1878 adoption of a secret ballot.[33]

Young did not regard the ad hoc political authority of the priesthood as inimical to the sovereignty of Utah's people or to American republicanism, which he defined as the people's right "to choose their own rulers." In his mind, there was no conflict between republicanism and priesthood authority, because the Saints had submitted to the authority of the priesthood when they were baptized into the church, when they made their sacred covenants at the Nauvoo Temple, and when they followed the apostles to the Great Basin. Young occasionally referenced Joseph Smith's concept of "theodemocracy," and he frequently insisted that priesthood rule represented both the will of God and the will of the people in Utah. Democracy as practiced in the rest of the United States produced division and strife, whereas the Mormons' "democracy of Heaven" produced harmony and unity. In the minds of many other Americans, Young and other church hierarchs trampled on fundamental American political values of democracy and republicanism. For Young and his supporters, by contrast, it was the national government that sought to tyrannize the people of Utah. When Young received word in early 1854 that President Franklin Pierce intended to appoint a new set of non-Mormon justices for Utah, his anger boiled over. "We will rid ourselves," he wrote territorial congressional delegate John Bernhisel, "of as many such white livered, blackhearted, sycophantic Demagogues, as the Administration shall send." In Young's mind, the American territorial system denied the Mormon people their basic right to self-determination and self-government.[34]

Pierce's appointees were not the only unwanted 1854 arrivals in Salt Lake City. In August, Lieutenant Colonel Edward Steptoe reached Salt Lake City with 325 U.S. soldiers. While en route to the Pacific, Steptoe's command wintered in Utah to investigate the 1853 massacre of John Gunnison, who along with seven other men had been killed by a group of Pahvant Utes while on another surveying mission. While other Americans speculated that Mormon elders seduced or kidnapped women as polygamous brides, the Saints were certain that Steptoe's men intended to corrupt and take away young Mormon women. Trouble soon arose, as fraternization proceeded despite a steady stream of pulpit warnings to Mormon women and denunciations of lecherous soldiers. The indiscreet Lieutenant Sylvester Mowry found himself infatuated with Mary Ann Ayers Young, whom he termed "as hot a thing as you could wish." Mary was Brigham's daughter-in-law by his eldest son Joseph, then away on a mission. Her father-in-law put a quick end to the budding affair. "Brigham sent me word," Mowry wrote a friend, "that if I took her away he would have me killed before I could get out of the territory." Mowry took the threat seriously. "He is a man of his word in little matters of this sort," the captain noted. Steptoe ordered his philandering underling to stay out of Salt Lake City. Love affairs were not the only problem. On Christmas Day 1854, a riot broke out between the soldiers and the city's Mormon residents, evidently including Brigham Young Jr. Still, Brigham Young Sr. regarded Steptoe himself as a gentleman, and he and the colonel remained on good terms through the winter. Steptoe even signed a petition supporting Young's reappointment as governor.[35]

Meanwhile, Young's relations quickly soured with a Pierce appointee, Chief Justice John F. Kinney. The judge, a rotund, pompous, and politically opportunistic Presbyterian, had struck up friendly relations with the Mormons in Iowa while holding a seat on that state's supreme court. In Utah, Kinney quickly angered Mormon leaders by invalidating a territorial statute that forbade Utah's courts from citing the common law or other nonstatutory legal precedents. The legislature had enacted the measure in part because the Anglo-American concept of common law could have provided a basis for antipolygamy prosecutions. In a Sunday morning sermon, Young publicly denounced the judge's decision, contending for Utah's right to exclude the common law. He also made clear that his highest loyalty was not to the U.S. government. "My Kingship [and] Governorship submit to the Priesthood," Young proclaimed. Kinney considered Young's rhetoric treasonous. "The avowed doctrine of the 'great Apostle,'" he wrote U.S. Attorney General Caleb Cushing two weeks after Young's sermon, "is that the authority of the Priesthood is and shall be the law of the land."[36]

By this time, Young had learned that President Pierce had appointed Steptoe as his gubernatorial replacement. Young regarded Steptoe as a gentleman, but the colonel soon dramatically revised his opinion of the church president. After deciding against mounting a military expedition to capture or kill Gunnison's murderers, he felt hoodwinked when the Pahvant chief and Mormon ally Kanosh produced six rather unimpressive-looking natives to stand trial for the murders. Steptoe blamed Young for his embarrassment when a court convicted three of the defendants on a lesser charge, and he retracted his earlier endorsement of Young. Before he left the territory in April, Steptoe wrote President Pierce a scathing indictment of what he termed "fanaticism in the mass of the people, and a religious oligarchy, or rather Monocrasy." The problem, he informed Pierce, was not just polygamy. The Mormons were also thoroughly alienated from the national government. The church possessed within its people "the germ of a mighty State." When Steptoe declined the governorship, Pierce ignored Judge Kinney's offer of himself and never nominated a second replacement. Although his four-year term expired, a simultaneously defiant and bemused Young retained his office in the absence of a replacement. "I shall be Governor as long as the Lord Almighty wishes me to govern this people," he enjoyed saying.[37]

When the Steptoe Expedition left the territory in the spring, a number of its officers took Mormon women with them. In a fiery discourse, Young expressed regret that the soldiers had escaped punishment for their immorality. "We ought to have slain them in the middle of the day," he asserted, "and hung up their bodies or thrown them to the wolves." Young equated the soldiers' actions to the anti-Mormon mobs that had victimized the Saints in Missouri, and he warned that the Saints possessed every right to "get redress by the same laws of mobocracy." If any "more mobs come [to Utah]," he warned, the Saints would be justified in "cut[ting] their damned throats." Washington should realize that the Saints would not be driven from Utah. They would hide in the mountains, and, if cornered, they would fight. Given the likelihood of future army expeditions and forts, Young's words portended conflict.[38]

Other events further corroded the church's relationship with the federal government. In the midst of an 1853 clash with the Ute chief Walker, Young authorized a militia expedition against Fort Bridger, suspecting that indomitable mountain man Jim Bridger was selling arms and whiskey to hostile Indians. One hundred and fifty men captured the fort but not their chief prey, who sped to Washington and told anyone who would listen that Brigham Young had stolen the outpost and trade he had carefully cultivated for several decades. John Bernhisel rankled Young by informing him that Congress wished him to avoid confrontations with mountain men. "Please say to all who advocate such policy," Young dictated a letter in response, "Kiss my arse, damn you." Diplomacy was not one of Brigham Young's many talents. The revised letter omitted the colorful insult but retained a threat: "we cannot well prevent fools from exhibiting their folly, & keep your pet Bridger there, if you wish to preserve him, for if the legal officers get hold of him . . . he may be strung up between the heavens and the earth." Presumably, the tactful Bernhisel kept this idea to himself.[39]

If Young regarded Kinney with suspicion and Bridger with disdain, he soon loathed William Drummond, who arrived as one of the territory's associate justices in 1855. The roguish Drummond, who had left his wife and family in Illinois, brought a prostitute with him to Utah. Even Kinney regarded him as "in consequence of his immoral conduct . . . entirely unworthy of a place upon the bench." Within a few months, Drummond was not only at odds with Brigham Young but in a Millard County jail, accused of assaulting Levi Abrams, a merchant and rare Jewish convert to Mormonism. Drummond's case hinged on the legality of a probate court's authority to proceed with a case against him, and local leaders withdrew the charges rather than risk Kinney truncating the prized authority of the probate courts. Like Kinney, Drummond left the territory in 1856. "If Judge Drummond does return, he should be removed from office," Young told Bernhisel, terming the departed Drummond "vain as a peacock and ignorant as a jack-ass."[40] Drummond never came back. Instead, he became one of the church's most bitter and effective enemies in Washington. The Saints had survived the allegations of the "runaway judges," but as Steptoe, Bridger, Kinney, Drummond, and other federal officials carried reports of Mormon theocracy and immorality to Washington, anti-Mormon sentiment in the nation's capital steadily waxed.

Church leaders hoped that the Democratic Party's doctrine of popular sovereignty would shield Utah's domestic institutions from federal interference, and Young keenly followed national political developments. In April 1854, his Sunday prayer circle spent an evening engaged in "conversation on the new nebraska bill." The next month, Congress passed the Kansas-Nebraska Act, which overturned the Missouri Compromise and opened the territories of Nebraska and Kansas to slavery should their residents so choose. In shepherding the bill through Congress, however, the Mormons' political ally Stephen Douglas inadvertently opened up unbridgeable sectional divides in both of the two major parties. Southern Whigs abandoned their party to support the expansion of slavery, whereas many antislavery northern Democrats found the Missouri Compromise's repeal a pill too bitter to swallow. Out of that political chaos, an assortment of Know-Nothing nativists, Whigs, and antislavery northern Democrats coalesced into a new Republican Party. In 1856, the Republican platform linked slavery and polygamy together as the "twin relics of barbarism," the unholy fruit of popular sovereignty.[41]

Democrats, however much they disliked polygamy, correctly understood the Republican position on polygamy as a backdoor attempt to regulate territorial slavery. Thus, many southern Democrats opposed antipolygamy efforts. If Congress could declare territorial polygamy a crime, why could it not prohibit slavery's further expansion? According to Utah's congressional delegate John Bernhisel, Douglas expressed his opposition "to any interference with any local or domestic institution, for the reason that if the principle were once recognized it would apply everywhere, to all religious sects, slavery, etc." At the same time, though, the Democrats recognized that any perceived support for the Mormons would imperil the party's doctrine of popular sovereignty. Indeed, in order to discredit Douglas's political creed, in 1857 an abolitionist newspaper mocked the Mormons as "freaks of popular sovereignty." As early as 1854, therefore, Young complained to Douglas that the Democrats were bent on convincing voters "that the mormons are no pets of ours." The Saints thus found themselves without any reliable allies in Congress.[42]

Despite these political storm clouds, Young felt no compulsion to kowtow to either Washington or federal officials in Utah. While he regularly affirmed his attachment to the Constitution and the government, even the Saints' own publications included bitter invective against Washington and federal appointees. "Whenever you feel to indulge in a train of remark designed for the ears of the saints only," Bernhisel pleaded, ". . . ask the reporters and printers not to give publicity to them, for they greatly tend to alienate our friends." Young disregarded Bernhisel's advice. In fact, he found it inexplicable that eastern newspapers interpreted his words as disloyalty, especially when fire-eaters like Senator James

Rhett of South Carolina preached resistance to federal oppression and southern states contemplated secession. "[A]ny person or people can say and do what they please with perfect impunity," he once complained, "except the Mormons." With the South and its northern allies defending the sovereignty of both states and territories, Young concluded that he should contend equally vigorously for Mormon sovereignty. With each clash between federal appointees and the church, Young grew more impatient to unshackle Utah from the territorial system's limits on self-government.[43]

RESOLVING the church's position within the United States was an ongoing concern, but Young devoted most of his energies to building up his kingdom's unity, economy, and size. In the mid-1850s, Young revived the principle of consecration, dormant in the church for two decades. In an 1831 revelation, Joseph Smith had called upon church members to consecrate their properties, from which the church would return an amount to each family sufficient for its subsistence. Persons who accumulated more than they needed for their subsistence would then give the "residue" to support the poor and other church needs. The initial attempts to practice consecration proved short-lived, breaking down amid confusion and resistance. Now, Young called on the Saints to finally embrace the sacrificial commitment Smith had commanded. Consecration would give the church a revenue source in addition to tithing, and it would bind wavering Saints to the church and to their homes. "You may feel it best to stay where your treasure is," Young suggested, offering consecration as an inoculation against apostasy.[44]

In response, church members signed deeds assigning their property to "the Church of Jesus Christ of Latter-day Saints . . . Brigham Young, Trustee in Trust for said Church." Young even consecrated (to himself as Trustee in Trust) $200,000 worth of property, including his homes, his farmland, and his six gold watches. The Ute chief Arapeen deeded all of San Pete County to the church, one slaveholder dedicated an "African servant girl" (valued at $1,000), and one idealistic settler consecrated his young daughter (to whom he did not assign a monetary value).[45]

In the end, the mid-1850s consecrations were purely symbolic. The church never reassigned surplus consecrated property for other ecclesiastical needs. Congress had not extinguished Indian title to any land in the Utah Territory, and for the church to more actively function as a landholding behemoth would only have retarded that process. Moreover, no more than half of the territory's church members embraced consecration, an impressive display of dedication but hardly indicative of future harmony should Young have moved forward. Church members thus retained individual control of their property.[46]

Young also inconsistently advanced another, more quixotic reform, the creation of the Saints' own phonetic alphabet. Young and other early Mormons understood speaking in tongues as a foretaste of the divine language of heaven, which Adam had spoken but which had then become a Babel of confusion. Young disliked the confusion caused by local dialects, and spelling always vexed him. A new alphabet, containing one letter or symbol for each sound in the English language, could correct the latter problem and make it easier for foreign converts to quickly develop the ability to communicate with their new co-religionists. Young was not the first noteworthy American to promote such ideas. For example, Benjamin Franklin had designed a phonetic alphabet during his late-1760s stay in London. Clerk George D. Watt, Young's counselor Willard Richards, and several others created what became known as the Deseret Alphabet, mostly containing symbols with no resemblance to Latin letters. Young and his apostles discussed the project in prayer circles, and he helped revise the proposed symbols.[47]

Young praised the results as "a step and partial return to a pure language which has been promised unto us in the latter days." In the late 1850s, Young authorized the publication of a primer, dictionary, and the *Book of Mormon* in the Deseret Alphabet. Despite his enthusiasm, the new system never gained popular acceptance. Young saw no point in forcing his people to adopt something they greeted with apathy and skepticism. He usually sensed when he had pushed his people beyond where they were willing to follow.[48]

Back in 1846, Young had predicted that a vanguard group of pioneers could speed their way to the Great Basin, relying on limited rations supplemented by stalwart faith. As the Saints straggled across Iowa, he blamed his followers for preventing the pioneer camp's departure. Young was no fool, though. Instead of attempting the impossible, he deferred his trip until the following spring. A decade later, he abandoned such caution.

By then, tens of thousands of Latter-day Saint pilgrims had made what Wallace Stegner termed their "rite of passage, the final, devoted, enduring act that brought one into the Kingdom." For many emigrants with insufficient means, the church's Perpetual Emigrating Fund (PEF) paid their passage with the understanding that they would later repay those debts. In 1855, four thousand English Mormons came, and that fall apostle Erastus Snow reported to Young that he had accrued a debt of nearly $50,000 for the season's emigration. Most emigrants failed to make the repayments, which hampered the church's ability to pay its creditors and the PEF's ability to gather more poor to Zion.[49]

Despite the PEF debts, Young moved ahead with several ambitious and costly plans. Most significantly, in early 1856 he organized a hybrid public-private venture, known as the Brigham Young Express and Carrying Company (or simply the Y.X. Company), to transport mail, freight, and passengers from Missouri to California. Young intended for the company to create way stations along the "Mormon Trail," creating a means for the emigrants to resupply themselves. Also, in 1855 Young ordered Erastus Snow to purchase an enormous steamboat engine in St. Louis and ship it to the Salt Lake Valley. Intended for the territory's iron works, the massive piece of machinery barely made it past the Missouri River. The next year, Young sent two associates to help complete the engine's journey west.[50]

Young distinguished, though, between the PEF and ventures designed to build up Utah's economy. He was leery of charity and handouts that might encourage indolence. "No man or woman in Utah is desserving of food or clothing unless they work for it," he explained, and no one deserved a free ticket to Utah, either. Young badgered PEF recipients about paying their debts. "I calculate to put the screws on to men," he threatened with characteristic hyperbole, "sell their property & if you cant pa[y] the debt I will sell your wives & children at vendue [auction]." Even had fewer other projects drained the church's coffers, Young would not have allowed such PEF deficits.[51]

Young was determined to economize, but without retarding the flow of Mormons to Zion. He told those in charge of planning the subsequent year's emigration that he was "thrown back upon my old plan," for those receiving PEF assistance to "make hand carts and let the emigration foot it." Young had long considered this inexpensive but arduous form of transportation, occasionally used by impoverished American emigrants on the Overland Trail. Even before Joseph Smith's death, he once suggested that "if the Saints only knew the necesity of gathering they would go on a hand cart." Now Young sent his associates in England and the eastern United States detailed plans for the construction of handcarts "without a particle of iron," saving the much higher expense of purchasing wagon teams. Although Young suggested each family should bring ninety days of rations, he predicted "a company of this kind should make the trip in sixty or seventy days." Once the Saints became accustomed to traveling by handcart, they should travel "20, 25 & even 30 [miles] with all ease, and no danger of giving out" until relief teams from Utah met them on the Upper Platte or even in Laramie. Young saw no reason why faithful Saints should object to handcarts. "If they have not faith enough to undertake this job," a church epistle announced, ". . . they have not faith sufficient to endure, with the saints in Zion, the celestial law which leads to exaltation." Crossing the plains and mountains by handcart thus became an article of faith and a requirement for the church's European poor.[52]

Young's confidence fired some of his subordinates with a zeal akin to his own. Apostle Franklin Richards, who oversaw the 1856 emigration as he returned from England to Utah, sanguinely trumpeted the virtues of the plan. Others foresaw problems. Apostle John Taylor confessed reservations in a series of letters to Young. "I wish to use care with the first companies especially," he wrote, suggesting that the church provide them with ox teams to carry extra provisions and any weak or infirm Saints. Taylor worried about "throwing a great many into the wilderness in a helpless condition." Many emigrants were coming from English cities like Manchester and Liverpool; they had no experience with the sort of conditions they would encounter on the American frontier. Young did not share the apostle's sense of prudence. He even wrote Taylor that "it is all right not to provide wagons for infirm persons to accompany the hand carts for it would encourage infirmity. . . . There would soon be but few able to walk." Young's zeal, absorbed by followers like Franklin Richards, trumped Taylor's caution.[53]

Thus, in 1856 nearly two thousand Mormon emigrants became their own beasts of burden. After boarding Liverpool ships and traveling by rail to Iowa City, they waited for contractors to finish their handcarts. The first three companies left for Utah in June. Despite handcart breakdowns and considerable hunger, they made the crossing in good time and reached Salt Lake City in late September and early October. The Y.X. way stations would not materialize for another year, but relief wagons provided the companies with needed supplies before the more arduous portion of the journey. (The church required the emigrants to pay for the supplies upon arrival in Salt Lake City.) The death rate for the companies was congruent with typical overland travel. Young considered the first companies' arrival the fulfillment of prophecy. He rejoiced that "[i]t is now reduced to a moral certainty, that the Saints can cross the plains in this manner."[54]

The exultation was premature. Earlier reports from the East had informed Young of two additional handcart companies. Although Young at the end of September professed himself unsure whether they had ventured forth or decided to winter in the East, prudence would have dictated the dispatch of additional relief trains. On October 4, Franklin Richards arrived in Salt Lake City with the worst possible news. The final two handcart companies—and several other Mormon trains—were en route, far from their destination and in grave peril from starvation and the onset of winter.[55]

Once in possession of this news, Young wasted no time in organizing a heroic relief operation. In a meeting with Richards, Young carefully went through what the remaining companies would need in terms of flour, wagons, and mules, often suggesting amounts greater than those recommended by his assistants. "That is my religion," Young announced at a hastily called meeting, "that is the dictation of the Holy Ghost that I possess, it is to save the people." Within days, the relief trains climbed into the mountains.[56]

Over the next few weeks, the members of the Willie and Martin handcart companies—named for their captains, James Willie and Edward Martin—trudged forward as the snow fell and their rations were cut to a mere pittance. Their extremities froze, and many bodies gave out simply because they lacked food. "[M]any of the deceased," reported a member of the relief expedition to Young, "pulled their hand cart during the day and died the same evening." In mid-October, having already lost fifty-six of its members, the trailing Martin Company crossed the Platte River for the final time. There, short of South Pass, a bitter snowstorm stopped the group in its tracks. Over the next week, the deaths mounted as the company largely gave up hope. The relief wagons finally met the companies and averted a much worse disaster, though the treks remained macabre in their closing stages. "A few of the brethren of the handcart companies," George Stringham informed Young, "was so frozen that the flesh dropped off of the frozen parts." The Willie Company, after nearly seventy deaths, entered Salt Lake City on November 9. By the time the Martin Company reached its destination three weeks later, it had lost roughly 150 of its nearly 600 members, a death rate much higher than that of any other Mormon pioneer company.[57]

Young had reacted impressively to the crisis, inspiring and coercing the Saints to provide as much succor as they could to the beleaguered companies. The handcart companies—and their rescue—rightly came to symbolize the devotion and self-sacrifice of the Latter-day Saints. Mormon leaders, though, could have prevented most of the deaths. Most obviously, the Willie and Martin companies should not have ventured forth in August, and even though the first three companies made the trek relatively unscathed, better provisioning could have spared them considerable hardship. Even before the scope of the tragedy was clear, some church members expressed reservations about Young's leadership. "There is a spirit of murmuring among the people," stated Heber Kimball in reference to the hand-cart companies, "and the fault is laid upon brother Brigham."[58]

Young refused to shoulder any blame for the tragedy. "[M]y skirts are clear of their blood," he responded to Kimball's statement. He also down-played the emigrants' losses and hardships. Even after the Martin Company's fate became known, Young insisted that "few, comparatively, have suffered severely, though some had their feet and hands more or less frosted." Still insisting upon the superiority of the handcart method, he asserted that "the mortality has been much less than attends well fitted animal trains traveling in good season." He also stated that the 1834 Zion's Camp march was "many times more taxing upon the health and life of a person." In his youth, he had without complaint crisscrossed the eastern United States in poverty and hunger. Why should the handcart emigrants complain about their hardships?[59]

At the same time, he publicly denounced his subordinates. In an early November sermon, he chastised Franklin Richards and his assistant Daniel Spencer for "rush[ing] men, women and children on to the prairie in the autumn months." He lambasted the pair again at the church's April 1857 conference, and they then met with Young in the latter's office. "[H]e told us to acknowledge our falts and that his chastizement was Just," wrote a shaken Spencer in his diary. The pair made the desired confessions, but they felt that at the very least all of those involved in organizing the emigration should have shared the blame.[60]

Richards and Spencer escaped rather lightly compared to John Taylor. In the same November sermon, Young asserted that "John Taylor had put his foot on the people coming to this place by hand carts; he did every thing he could against it in secret." Taylor's obstruction, Young claimed, had led to the disaster. "Taylor designed to have them caught in the snow," Young alleged, "that his word might be fulfilled." When the *Deseret News* published Young's sermon, it omitted the sharp words against Taylor. As the tragedy was unfolding, Young had written the apostle to criticize him for promoting measures that would have incurred additional emigration expenses. "[W]e do not hold in very high estimation your financial talent and ability," Young informed Taylor. In this case, Taylor sharply rejected Young's critique. "I did not consider that a few dollars were to be put in competition with the lives of human beings," he fired back. Rarely did Young's apostolic subordinates criticize him so boldly.[61]

Despite his protestations and accusations, Young as the architect of the plan bore a large measure of responsibility for its poor execution. By itself, his economizing did not lead to any deaths. Indeed, his "old plan" met its objectives of providing transportation for healthy people at rock-bottom prices. Not all of the emigrants were young and healthy, though, and Young's austerity certainly made their journey unusually onerous. Moreover, his disregard for prudence turned what should have been a cautious experiment into a poorly organized mass movement with deadly consequences for the members of the Willie and Martin companies. Although Young called for subsequent PEF emigrants to rely exclusively on handcarts, only a few additional companies crossed the plains with handcarts until Young permanently shelved the plan in 1860. That year he finally conceded that it was a "hard task" for emigrants to pull their own provisions.[62]

IN ADDITION to saving scarce money, Young expected the handcart plan to discourage all but the most committed Latter-day Saints from traveling to Zion. By the mid-1850s, moreover, he was also deeply distressed about those Mormons already in their promised land. Young was a shepherd not easily satisfied with his flock, and his discontent led to a season of spiritual tumult that became known as the "Mormon reformation." Unlike the Protestant Reformation, it was not a time of doctrinal innovation or ecclesiastical reform. Instead, Mormon leaders demanded repentance and rebaptism. While the reformation left some church members with a greater sense of spiritual assurance and exhilaration, its chilling and bloody rhetoric also bred fear and disaffection.[63]

It is impossible to pinpoint a catalyst for the Mormon reformation. The mid-1850s brought a series of scourges to Utah, as drought, crickets, and livestock deaths afflicted the Saints. "We lived chiefly on Weeds which we gathered from the Fields or the Woods," wrote Joseph Fielding. Only rigid austerity prevented hunger from progressing to true starvation. While such challenges were real, they were hardly unprecedented. Indeed, given the first two decades of the church's existence, the mid-1850s were an unusually extended hiatus from external persecution. Internal divisions also posed a minimal threat at this time. Still, always vigilant against the danger of dissent, Young felt troubled by a small but growing number of Gentiles and disaffected Saints in the territory. In response to such concerns, Mormon leaders regularly emphasized the need for absolute obedience to church authorities. On the eve of the reformation in Provo, the church clerk George D. Watt reminded a Sunday congregation that "Brigham Young is an absolute Monarch & it is his right to be so . . . if Brother Brigham tells us to do anything we should not question his right in dictating us in every thing." Young worried that the Saints were insufficiently righteous, obedient, and united, slowly drifting away from the ardor with which they had first embraced the church. Young and other church leaders determined that a spiritual crisis existed, and they called the people to new heights of dedication.[64]

In order to combat perceived spiritual sloth, Young sent the Twelve on preaching missions to Mormon settlements, and he organized a "home missionary" program to monitor and improve the morals and spirituality of the people. By March 1856, Young decided that such measures were insufficient. It was time, he announced, for the elders "to put away their velvet lips and smooth things and preach sermons like pitch forks tines downwards that the people might wake up." Six months later, Mormon leaders began hurling those pitchforks. In mid-September 1856, Young delivered a fiery sermon in Salt Lake City, forcefully condemning a multitude of sins, ranging from adultery to dishonesty to a failure to tithe. Mincing no words, he complained that some Saints kept their "brains . . . below their waistbands." He warned that the "whole people will be corrupted if we do not lop off those rotten branches." At the same time, he held out the prospect of forgiveness and spiritual empowerment, calling on the repentant to repeat their baptisms and "receive the Holy Ghost and then live in it continually." Sinners could choose between repentance and flight. Otherwise, they deserved excommunication and possibly death.[65]

Young's sermon might have become merely one of his many jeremiads save for the corresponding efforts of Jedediah Grant, who after the 1854 death of Willard Richards had become Young's second counselor in the church's First Presidency. Grant, a tall, square-jawed, forty-year-old "sledgehammer," demanded the people's repentance, confession, and ritual renewal in return for their continued church membership. After his sermons, several whole communities unanimously renewed their spiritual covenants in the waters of baptism. Young, Grant, and others preached reformation sermons for several months, calling on the Saints to confess their sins and sometimes singling out individuals—especially persons in positions of authority—as being in particular need of repentance. "Misdeeds are not only publicly denounced," wrote Franklin Richards, soon to be singled out for his mistakes relating to the handcart companies, "but the doers and their misdeeds are named before the public congregations." Church leaders stopped celebrating the sacrament of the Lord's Supper in meetings, withholding spiritual succor until the Saints manifested a proper degree of repentance and righteousness.[66]

Public preaching then evolved into private counseling. Over the next few weeks, Grant devised a Mormon catechism, a list of questions local leaders posed to church members in order to gauge their repentance. The list included queries about murder, adultery, drunkenness, and tithing. Re-

Jedediah Grant, late-nineteenth-century engraving of earlier photograph *(courtesy of Church History Library, The Church of Jesus Christ of Latter-day Saints)*

flecting Grant's obsession with personal cleanliness, it also asked the Saints whether they bathed weekly. Young responded to the latter requirement by observing that "he had tried it . . . [and] was well aware that this was not for everybody." While wary of bathing, Young thoroughly approved of Grant's reformation leadership. In early December, Grant died, probably of pneumonia. Many Mormon leaders attributed his death to the intensity of his reformation efforts and willingness to baptize so many penitent sinners in winter waters. The reformation "has Cost him his life," said Young.[67]

In Young's mind, one sign of lukewarm commitment was the hesitancy of many church members to enter into plural marriage. During the reformation, Young pointedly reminded the congregation that "multitudes of pure and holy spirits [were] waiting to take tabernacles." Righteous men, he argued, had an ongoing responsibility to create those bodies. "If my wife had borne me all the children that she would ever bare," he explained, "the celestial law would teach me to take young women that would have children." Mormon men and women signaled their renewed commitment to their religion by responding to such calls. Letters from men and their bishops poured into Young's office, requesting permission to take additional wives. Young's clerk Thomas Brown pronounced himself "astonished at the number of applications for permission to take wives." Pleased with the response, Young told most supplicants to "go ahead." With particular satisfaction, Young noted that the handcart "Sisters . . . are almost all married off; they are much in demand." The Saints took the reformation preaching of their leaders to heart.[68]

The marital stampede led to a decrease in the marriage age. "Nearly all are trying to get wives," Wilford Woodruff wrote the following spring, "until there is hardly a girl 14 years old in Utah but what is married or just going to be." Woodruff himself offered his fourteen-year-old daughter Phebe in marriage to Young, who informed the apostle that he was no longer marrying "young wives."[69] Although marriages of fourteen-year-old girls were not unheard of in the rest of the United States (the legal age of consent was often twelve for wives), such unions were very rare. Mormon leaders, by contrast, blessed an unusual number of early marriages, especially during the reformation. Writing to one supplicant, Young granted him permission to wed a thirteen-year-old girl but instructed him to "preserve her intact until she is fully developed into Womanhood."[70] Similarly, he counseled another applicant to "'Go ahead' but leave children to grow."[71] Even so, Young found some requests distasteful. "Old Father [seventy-three-year-old James] Alread brought three young girls 12 & 13 years old," he once complained. "I would not seal them to him. They would not be equally yoked." The issue arose repeatedly during early 1857, and while Young recognized it as a problem, he granted local leaders and families considerable latitude. For the most part, his deep satisfaction over the matrimonial response of the Saints trumped such concerns. Thus, while refusing to countenance some early marriages, Young usually encouraged men to grab what he termed the "long tail of the 'Reformation.'"[72]

Just as the American South was a slave society even though only a minority of white men owned slaves, Brigham Young's Utah was very much a polygamous society despite the fact that only a minority of Mormon men were ever married to more than one woman at the same time. Polygamy was an obvious feature of Mormon communities, and polygamous men held the top political and ecclesiastical offices in the territory. Although the spate of marriages in 1856–57 led to a subsequent rise in divorces, the reformation enhanced plural marriage's place within the church and within Utah society.[73]

During the reformation, Young also forthrightly preached the doctrine of blood atonement, previously only briefly mentioned in public. Atonement for sin required a blood penalty, one paid with temple sacrifices in ancient Israel and then satisfied in traditional Christian theology by Christ's sacrifice. Young, however, warned that the death of Jesus would not absolve all sins. "[T]here are transgressors," he explained, "who, if they knew themselves, and the only condition upon which they can obtain forgiveness, would beg of their brethren to shed their blood, that the smoke thereof might ascend to God as an offering to appease the wrath that is kindled against them." Young articulated the doctrine repeatedly over the next few months, presenting such bloody logic as a form of spiritual charity. When facing individuals whose sins could not "be atoned for without the shedding of their blood," Young asked, "Will you love that man or woman well enough to shed their blood? That is what Jesus Christ meant." In a chilling perversion of the golden rule, Young suggested that killing people before they had the opportunity to forsake their salvation "is loving our neighbor as ourselves." Young's comments were not spontaneous hyperbole. He had believed in the doctrine for at least ten years, discussed blood atonement on several previous occasions, and now more forcefully and fully explained his ideas.[74]

Young's preaching terrified some of his listeners and made many others uncomfortable. "He made the Harts of many tremble," journalized the apostle Wilford Woodruff. It was never quite clear exactly which persons should suffer blood atonement, but possible victims—or willing participants—included adulterers, murderers, violators of the covenants made in the endowment, and those who had committed the biblically opaque sin of blaspheming the Holy Spirit. At least a few Mormons offered their lives as a sacrifice for their sins. Isaac Haight, president of the church's Cedar City stake, wrote in October 1856 of one adulterer: "I think he has deeply repented of the sin and Says that if the Law of God requires his Blood to be Spilled he will most willingly comply with Any thing required that he may be saved." Young informed Haight that "this time, in the name of the Lord, remission and pardon, even of adultery, are promised to all that truly repent." Young's response no doubt reassured Haight's inquirer.[75]

Even if Young primarily considered the doctrine a prod to repentance, several brutal acts of violence indicated the dangerous nature of his rhetoric. On October 29, 1856, at the height of the reformation in Manti, Thomas Lewis was castrated. Lewis was a Welsh immigrant in his early twenties; a few weeks earlier, he had been excommunicated from the church because he had nearly killed Manti resident John Price with a shovel. More recently, he had threatened to kill his brother-in-law Isaac Vorhees and had been sentenced to five years in prison. While being transported to the penitentiary, according to his mother, Elizabeth Jones, Lewis "was taken out of the wagon a blanket put round his head & . . . like a pig by taking his Testicles clean out & he laid at this place in a dangerous state he was out two nights & part of two days before he was found." Manti bishop Warren Snow had ordered her son's castration. Two later anti-Mormon exposés alleged that Lewis had courted a woman also desired by Bishop Snow, but the incident may also have simply stemmed from Lewis's violent behavior.[76]

Elizabeth Jones wrote to Young for an explanation. Young was aware of Lewis's crimes and punishments, for local leaders had discussed the Price incident with him. According to Jones, Young had authorized her son's transportation in handcuffs to the Salt Lake City penitentiary. Now she asked the church president if her son's punishment was "right and righteous." Young responded with a letter that, while expressing sympathy, offered a theological justification for the castration by alluding to the concept of blood atonement. "I would prefer that any child of mine should lose his life in atonement for his sins than lose eternal salvation," he counseled. The following spring, when other church leaders questioned Snow's judgment, Young defended the bishop. "I will tell you," Young insisted, "that when a man is trying to do right & do[es] some thing that is not exactly in order I feel to sustain him." Snow kept his bishopric. Though he condoned it afterward, it is uncertain whether Young had authorized Thomas Lewis's castration in advance.[77]

Young did explicitly authorize extra-legal violence on at least one occasion during the same winter. In January 1857, a pair of non-Mormon horse thieves (John Ambrose and Thomas Betts) were released from the Salt Lake City penitentiary, whereupon they headed for California. Young instructed church leaders to take action should Betts and Ambrose attempt to steal livestock on their way. "[W]e do not expect there would be any prosecutions for false imprisonment," Young reassured his bishops, "or tale bearers left for witnesses." "Be on the look out now," he added a few days later in a letter to bishops farther to the south, "& have a few trusty men ready in case of need to pursue, retake, & punish." In other words, if local leaders imprisoned or killed the men, they would be acting with impunity. Vigilantism was a common response to horse thievery in the nineteenth-century West. At a time of rising tension with the federal government, moreover, Young had heard reports that the thieves would spread rumors about Mormon injustices after they reached California.[78]

Young's advice apparently contributed to two separate incidents of violence, neither of which involved Betts and Ambrose. On February 17 a group of men attacked a camp on the banks of the Santa Clara River in southwestern Utah. In all likelihood, the shooters intended to kill Ambrose and Betts. They instead wounded four men, including John Tobin, a convert from Gunnison's second surveying mission to Utah who had courted one of Brigham Young's daughters before marrying—apparently with reluctance—the daughter of the apostle Charles Rich. The shooters' poor selection of targets caused future embarrassment for Young when newspapers incorrectly alleged that he authorized the attack to settle a grudge with Tobin.[79]

Meanwhile, Bishop Aaron Johnson of Springville used Young's directive as a justification for ordering an assassination. At the height of the reformation in Springville, William Parrish decided to flee the territory. Johnson interpreted Young's instructions about Ambrose and Betts as a more general authorization to take action against apostates, and he identified Parrish as a potential horse thief. Johnson recruited spies to learn of Parrish's departure plans, apparently to ensure that he settled his debts before leaving. Later that spring, Young would instruct some of his bishops to let "none go who are in debt to the P.E. Fund or otherwise without first paying the same." With the church's highest leaders advocating blood atonement for apostates, moreover, Johnson may have decided that Parrish's decision to leave the faith and the territory warranted death. The operation went awry. Assassins killed William Parrish and his son William, but they also fatally shot Gardiner ("Duff") Potter, one of Johnson's spies, in the process. Another son of William Parrish fled, and when the perpetrators escaped punishment, rumors circulated that Young had ordered Parrish's death.[80]

When Young visited Springville four years later, he felt compelled to address such talk. Making what would have been a reasonable argument for vigilantism at the time, he began by claiming that William Parrish was a horse thief sent by a California gang to establish stations for such activities in Utah. He told the congregation of Springville Saints not to "whine" about Parrish's death and joked about having "God Almighty . . . arrested for drowning the Egyptians in the Red sea." Young described himself as "too big a coward to ever hurt anybody," and he observed—quite correctly—that there was no evidence to suggest that he had ordered the murder. "You need not undertake to accuse me," he cautioned his listeners, "and think that I advised and planned this, that and the other." "I cannot be implicated in any of them," he added. While Young denied culpability, he simultaneously condoned extralegal justice. "[T]here has been a great deal done," he commented, "quite a number killed, and, I believe, many more ought to have been." Presumably, horse thieves were not the only men who deserved death.[81]

Orrin Porter Rockwell *(courtesy of Church History Library, The Church of Jesus Christ of Latter-day Saints)*

During these years, Young maintained friendly relations with reputed killers, including Bill Hickman, a ruffian and sometimes lawyer whom journalist George Alfred Townsend later called "a human hyena." Young was well aware of at least some of Hickman's crimes. Joseph Young informed his brother back in 1849 that "Inocent Blood . . . will Be found Driping from the hands of William Hickman," whom he labeled a "cold Blooded Murderer." In March 1853, a clerk in the Church Historian's Office recorded matter-of-factly that "last night the notorious Ike Hatch was shot in his bowels when riding in the Big Field with Bill Hickman." Young and other church authorities, however, did not take action against Hickman. Young also remained on good terms with Orrin Porter Rockwell, to whom Joseph Smith had promised divine protection if he never cut his long and typically braided or plaited hair. Rockwell, who was suspected, tried, and acquitted in the 1842 attempted assassination of Missouri governor Lilburn Boggs, gained further infamy in connection with a string of murders in the 1850s and 1860s. In 1857, Young recruited Hickman and Rockwell to help operate a U.S. government mail contract secured by the church. The church president's relations with Hickman and Rockwell suggested to both Saints and outsiders that he condoned their actions. In 1860, Salt Lake City mayor Abraham Smoot warned Young that Hickman's frequent visits to his office led people "to suppose he is sanctioned in all he does by the President."[82]

Vigilantism had a long tradition in the United States, serving to enforce standards of morality, punish criminality, and silence political opposition. Extralegal violence took many forms in the middle portion of the nineteenth century. For years, antiabolitionist mobs had harassed and attacked vocal opponents of slavery. Abolitionists also took matters into their own hands when the law failed them. Boston abolitionists, for instance, formed a Vigilance Committee to rescue African Americans from "man-stealers" operating in the North after the passage of the Fugitive Slave Act. In the western United States, proponents defended the actions of posses and vigilance committees as deterrents against crime waves in newly settled areas. In San Francisco, vigilance committees, fueled by political and ethnic divisions and apparently enjoying broad support among the city's Protestants, meted out summary justice to mainly Irish-Catholic criminals. In July 1857, Young called for a "Vigilance Committee" to punish both Mormon and non-Mormon criminals. "And I say to all such characters," he warned, "if you come here and practice your iniquity, we will send you home quick." Young's stance was not all that unusual. Other western communities also took the events in San Francisco as a model.[83]

Utah, of course, differed in important ways from other parts of the mid-century American West. Unlike in San Francisco, there were no widespread political or ethnic divisions fueling vigilantism, and there was no apparent popular demand for extralegal violence. In comparison to other western states and territories, indeed, Utah was remarkable for its lack of organized vigilante activity.[84] In Utah, though, the governor and head of the territory's quasi-established religion lent his approval—at least after the fact—to shadowy acts of retribution that alarmed even some loyal Mormons. Ordering the deaths of horse thieves was unremarkable in the American West, but Young also condoned the castration of Thomas Lewis and the Parrish-Potter murders and suggested that an unspecified number of other individuals deserved to die. Brigham Young, who had feared for his life while on the margins of Illinois society, created a climate in which men and women on the margins of Mormon society lived in a similar state of fear.

Scores of disaffected Mormons left the territory with the 1857 spring thaw. "The fire of the reformation," journalized Hosea Stout, "is burning many out who flee from the Territory, afraid of their lives." Young saw this flight as removing the church's spiritual dross. "The Territory this season," he wrote George Q. Cannon in July, "has taken an emetic," spewing out "Lawyers, Loafers, Special pleaders, Apostates, Officials, and filth." Previously, Young had recognized that as much as he wanted a unified Kingdom of God on the earth, he had no expectation of achieving such unity until the advent of the millennium. "I expected there would be goats mixed among the sheep, until they are separated," Young said in 1853. Growing impatient with his mixed multitude, Young had prodded some of those goats out of the way.[85]

YOUNG was pleased with the spiritual results of the reformation. In addition to the surge in plural marriages, other measures of spiritual commitment also increased, such as tithing and attendance at church meetings. In Mormon communities, wards—the smallest geographic units of the church—began holding worship services on a more regular basis, creating something more akin to Protestant congregations. Young, meanwhile, was busy presiding over endowments and sealings at a rate not equaled since Nauvoo. "President Young," wrote Wilford Woodruff, "has hardly time to eat, drink or sleep, in consequence of marrying the people and attending to the endowments." Most of the Latter-day Saints had responded to his insistent calls for repentance, sacrifice, and obedience.[86]

For some, the intensity of the reformation produced spiritual ecstasy of the sort Young had often experienced in Kirtland. In December, settlers in Manti and the vicinity held a four-day conference. According to the Manti ward's clerk, "the Fire of the *Reformation* glowed with great intensity." While the hard-edged preaching undoubtedly caused some to tremble, it also produced an outpouring of spiritual gifts: "Brethreren generally confessing their Sins and wrong doings and receiving forgivness & testimonies to the Gospels power the presence of the Holy Spirits, Angels, and the Spirit of Joseph Smith. Angels singing; Tongues &c &c." Brigham Young had spent his young adulthood seeking assurance that God had forgiven his sins. At least some church members in that same spiritual predicament found spiritual assurance through their experiences of confession and ritual renewal.[87]

It was not easy being a follower or associate of Brigham Young. He was demanding and pugnacious. He frequently excoriated his followers for their errors while refusing to acknowledge his own. Many of his economic initiatives did not succeed, ideas such as consecration and the Deseret Alphabet failed to take hold, and the handcart emigration ended in macabre tragedy. Certainly, Utah's hard times and Young's mid-1850s leadership created rumbles of discontent and contributed to a minor wave of apostasy. At the same time, Young retained the firm support of most Mormons. As the reformation euphoria of Manti illustrates, Young's religious leadership was far more than bellicosity and blood atonement. Moreover, for many church members, the sheer accomplishment of Young's early church presidency—the thousands of Saints brought to Zion and the ongoing settlement of the Great Basin—covered his missteps and faults and sustained his leadership during times of economic, spiritual, and political tumult.

In the spring of 1857, Young finally shifted the tone of his counsel and preaching. He told bishops to stop making reports of the Saints' confessions. Instead, they should provide repentant sinners with spiritual assurance. In the early spring, mass rebaptisms occurred, and church leaders restored the sacrament. "[N]ever did I hear a more comforting sermon," Young's wife Zina Huntington described one sermon. "[He] told how our Father felt towards us it was most glorious." The calls to repentance came with the promise of blanket forgiveness for all but the blackest sins. For some, that promise brought tremendous spiritual relief. Indeed, while impending judgment was the dominant theme of the reformation, Young had always held out the promise of celestial joy for the faithful. "When you are prepared to see our Father," Young preached during one of his September 1856 reformation sermons, "you will see a being with whom you have long been acquainted, and He will receive you into His arms, and you will be ready to fall into His embrace and kiss Him, as you would your fathers and friends that have been dead for a score of years." By the spring, such hopeful messages became more frequent, and talk of blood atonement and hellfire subsided.[88]

The spiritual crisis created by Young and Jedediah Grant had ended, but Utah's Mormons would enjoy only a short season of peace. Since 1847, the Latter-day Saints had lived without any imminent danger of external persecution. "That is the longest rest," Young said in August 1857, "that the Saints had ever at one time." By the time Young reflected on those ten years of peace, he knew that a large United States army was marching toward Utah.[89]

CHAPTER TEN

The Whirlwind

They say they'll send an army,
To set the Mormons right,
Regenerate all Utah,
And show us Christian light.

—PETER O. HANSEN

ONE OF the more curious scenes of the Mormon reformation came at the territory's legislative assembly, which moved from Fillmore to the new capital of Salt Lake City in 1856. In late December, Brigham Young addressed a joint session of the territory's two legislative chambers. If the legislators got "the Holy Ghost," Young suggested, they could "make laws that no gentile power can break." After the speech, the legislators unanimously voted "to repent and forsake our sins and be rebaptized for their remission." That night, they formed a line and passed buckets of ice-cold water to a baptistry on the city's Temple Block. Woodruff termed their mass rebaptism "a New feature in Legislation." It was a period of intense spirituality, and Woodruff reckoned that "every one received the Holy Ghost." He supposed outsiders would regard the action as an example of theocratic "treason" because of the blatant union of church and state.[1]

Officials in Washington were worried about Mormon loyalty, but not because of legislative baptisms. In early 1857, church leaders made a tactless attempt to resolve their longstanding feud with Washington over political appointments. In January, with Governor Young's approval, the territory's legislative assembly composed a memorial for incoming president James Buchanan. The memorialists warned that if Washington continued to appoint "office seekers and corrupt demagogues," Utah's citizens would "send them away." At the time, Mormon leaders were at odds with Utah's three federal justices (two of whom had left the territory) and an assortment of federal Indian agents and surveyors. A draft of the memorial had been even more incendiary, threatening federal appointees engaged in "swindling operations" with "summary punishment." The draft had also rejected the right of the national government to "distress" Utah by "locating in our midst an ungovernable and reckless soldiery." Still, even with the excision of some especially inflammatory portions, Utah's legislators—and Young—had issued an undiplomatic challenge to Washington. Buchanan would respond to it by sending the U.S. Army to extinguish what he concluded was a Mormon rebellion against national authority.[2]

YOUNG'S 1851–52 clash with the "runaway judges," the 1854–55 conflicts with Steptoe's expedition, and his regular denunciations of federal officials had not produced any serious consequences for the church. Given that apparent political immunity, Young probably saw little risk in frankly conveying his demands to Washington. Moreover, he thought that Buchanan's election to the presidency augured well for the church's political goals. "Prest. Fillmore was our friend," Young wrote to his non-Mormon political ally Thomas Kane before the new president's inauguration, "but Buchanan will not be a whit behind." Both Buchanan and Stephen Douglas, his rival for the 1856 Democratic nomination, supported popular sovereignty, but the Pennsylvanian Buchanan was even more sympathetic to the concerns of southern slaveholders. Northern opponents of slavery's expansion considered Buchanan a "doughface," a northerner with southern sensibilities. While not sympathetic to slavery, Buchanan feared its ability to destroy the Union and worked to mollify the southern half of his party. Young probably expected that Buchanan's commitment to popular sovereignty rendered any action against Mormon polygamy unlikely. As it turned out, Young badly misjudged the "Old Public Functionary."[3]

Two days after Buchanan's March 4 inauguration, the Supreme Court in *Dred Scott v. Sandford* ruled that neither Congress nor territorial legislatures could enact bans on slavery in American territories. The decision eviscerated the notion of political sovereignty, though Douglas weakly claimed that slavery could not flourish without territorial codification. *Dred Scott* reignited sectional tensions still smoldering from the previous year's violence in Kansas, the caning of abolitionist Senator Charles Sumner by a southern congressman, and the presidential election. Embroiled in such controversies, Buchanan had given little thought to the Mormons. His inaugural address, which included a ringing defense of the right of "the people of a Territory . . . to decide their own destiny for themselves," excluded any mention of Utah.[4]

Nevertheless, Utah promptly became one of the new president's fore-

James Buchanan, ca. 1857 *(courtesy of Library of Congress)*

most concerns. A few days after the inauguration, John Bernhisel reported to Young on a "pleasant" interview with the new chief executive, whom he found "free from prejudice." Then in mid-March, Bernhisel delivered the Utah legislature's memorial to Buchanan, who instructed him to pass the document along to Secretary of the Interior Jacob Thompson. The next day, Thompson informed Bernhisel that he regarded the memorial as a "declaration of war."[5]

The diplomatic Bernhisel might have mollified the administration had the memorial been the only problem. In rapid succession, however, a barrage of letters arrived in Washington, written by disaffected federal appointees who had left their posts in Utah over the past year. "[I]t is impossible for us to enforce the laws in this Territory," asserted justice W. W. Drummond in a letter published in the *New York Herald* several days after Bernhisel met with Thompson. "Every man here holds his life at the will of Brigham Young." Drummond alleged that non-Mormons who questioned church authority were "murdered, robbed, castrated, and imprisoned." Taking note both of Drummond's letter and the church's request for an all-Mormon slate of appointees, the *Washington Star* announced that the "Mormons are practically in a state of rebellion." Chief Justice Kinney and Utah Surveyor General David Burr also submitted complaints to Washington about this time, both recommending that a military force accompany a new, non-Mormon governor to the territory. Almost overnight, Buchanan had an unanticipated Mormon crisis on his hands.[6]

Some members of the Democratic Party, including Buchanan's close ally Robert Tyler (son of the former president John Tyler), perceived political benefits from a military campaign against Utah. "I believe that we can supercede the Negro-Mania [over Kansas]," Tyler wrote Buchanan in late April, "with the almost universal excitements of an Anti-Mormon Crusade." Buchanan himself did not appear to embrace this political calculus, as the administration made no attempt to inflame or capitalize on anti-Mormon sentiment. Instead, without fanfare and without any public comment, in May Buchanan ordered 2,500 troops to Utah to install Young's replacement. The president reached this decision without a thorough investigation of the charges against Mormon leaders, and Young received no official word of Buchanan's decision in advance of the army. While Buchanan correctly understood the Mormon challenge to federal sovereignty and acted entirely within his authority, there was no armed rebellion or other crisis in Utah that required the precipitous dispatch of an army.[7]

Although Congress was not in session to discuss or otherwise sanction Buchanan's decision, it appeared to have bipartisan support. At first, Stephen Douglas hesitated to denounce the Mormons, suggesting that "Mormonism in Utah is not so bad as represented." He added that the "idea of Gov. Young taking an airing in a carriage with his twenty-six wives, with their three children each, seems to me to be beyond the bounds of credibility." Douglas, though, concluded that "the popular sovereignty doctrine is not intended for Utah." Former Illinois representative Abraham Lincoln, whom Douglas would best in an 1858 bid for a Senate seat, noted that Douglas's rejection of popular sovereignty for Utah proved that his "doctrine was a mere deceitful pretense for the benefit of slavery." When he revised his remarks for publication, Douglas fully abandoned his former Mormon allies and declared it "the duty of Congress to apply the knife and cut out this loathsome, disgusting ulcer." Young and Mormon leaders did not forget or forgive his betrayal.[8]

Meanwhile in Utah, Young proceeded in ignorance of the political fire-storm. In late April, the governor left the territory on a monthlong trip to Fort Limhi, a Mormon Indian mission on the Salmon River in the Oregon Territory in present-day Idaho. The large company included three of Young's wives (Zina Huntington and sisters Lucy Ann and Clara Decker), Indian chiefs Kanosh and Arapeen, and an array of top church leaders. Along the trail, the travelers sang "O Stop and Tell Me Red Man," a hymn written by William Phelps. "He'll come for your redemption," they sang, the lyrics predicting the Lamanites' providential deliverance, "and break the Gentile yoke." Young bestowed gifts on Bannock and Shoshone Indians, and several chiefs came to the fort to see "the Big Mormon Chief." While other Mormon leaders pressed the Salmon River settlers to marry "squaws," Young told them to demur if they did not feel prompted to do so by the "spirit." Young, who had always found traveling an invigorating break from the constant press of church business, thoroughly enjoyed the trip, and he later contemplated the valleys to the north as potential refuges for his people.[9]

Back home, Young heard rumors of Washington's discontent as Bern-hisel and a batch of eastern newspaper articles reached Utah. Young ordered a clerk to read the newspaper articles at a Sunday meeting in mid-June, then "made a few remarks about the trash that has been read" before proceeding to other topics. While Young did not appear to take the tales of pending military action seriously, he worried that the furor would impede Utah's case for admission into the Union, and he was concerned that rumors of war would discourage merchants from offering the church credit in St. Louis. Young professed bewilderment over the talk of an army coming to Utah, writing to Thomas Kane that the government should get its priorities straight. "When shall we have a rail road," he asked, "or are the people too busy about nigger and mormon affairs to think about such a noble enterprize?" Nevertheless, he had taken steps to prepare for the eventuality of military conflict. In the spring of 1857, the church had begun a reorganization of the territory's Nauvoo Legion, enrolling and mustering the territory's men in local militia companies. In June, Colonel William Dame in southern Utah reported an enthusiastic response, observing that "some few are enroled as young as fourteen," while "[s]ome Aged Fathers wished to be called buoys yet." As the militia's new lieutenant general, Young selected Daniel Wells, a long-time Nauvoo Legion leader whom Young also chose as a replacement for Jedediah Grant in the church's First Presidency. While not a match for the U.S. Army in either numbers or resources, the Nauvoo Legion gave Young a credible military deterrent. Over the summer, Young took additional precautions. He requested militia officers and business agents to covertly bring or ship am-

Parley P. Pratt, n.d. *(courtesy of Church History Library, The Church of Jesus Christ of Latter-day Saints)*

munition to Utah, and he asked representatives in St. Louis to keep "men and animals on hand" in order to send an extra mail to Utah should they perceive any unusual movements of "soldiers or politicians."[10]

In addition to bringing more rumors of the Utah Expedition, another batch of eastern mail that arrived in late June brought reports that the apostle Parley Pratt had been murdered in Arkansas. Pratt was a beloved figure among the Saints, who treasured his writings nearly as much as the *Book of Mormon* itself. In the mid-1850s, Eleanor McLean had converted to Mormonism, left an abusive husband, married Pratt, and attempted to take her children to Utah. In late May, Eleanor's husband, Hector, tracked Pratt from St. Louis to Arkansas, pulled him into a thicket of trees, stabbed him three times, and shot him in the neck. Although Young acknowledged Pratt as a new martyr alongside Joseph and Hyrum Smith, his response was somewhat muted. He and Pratt had clashed repeatedly during the early years of Young's leadership of the church, though Pratt had since proven his loyalty and shown a sacrificial willingness to undertake missions. Young later suggested that Pratt had deserved his fate. Alluding to

Pratt having taken additional plural wives without authorization in the mid-1840s, Young explained that "Bro. Parley's blood was spilt, I was glad of it for it paid the debt he owed, for he whored." Young had forgiven Pratt for that and other offenses, but he had not forgotten.[11]

On July 22, Young and about 2,500 invited guests began traveling to an alpine lake at the headwaters of Big Cottonwood Canyon, gathering to celebrate the tenth anniversary of the pioneer camp's descent into the Salt Lake Valley. As usual, the celebration blended Mormon pride and American patriotism. "[T]he stars and stripes," the *Deseret News* reported, "were unfurled on two of the highest peaks in sight of the camp and on the tops of two of the tallest trees."[12] Partway through the festivities, Abraham Smoot, Porter Rockwell, and several others arrived from the east with the news that a new governor, a set of territorial appointees, and 2,500 soldiers led by General William Harney were en route for Utah. Also, the federal government had cancelled a mail contract obtained by Young's Y.X. Carrying Company; the Mormons could now communicate with the rest of the country only via California or by private messenger across the Plains. The messengers' arrival transformed rumors—not unusual as far as Utah affairs were concerned—into reality. The crowd hardly knew what to make of the news. After passing a Young-sponsored resolution that "if Harney crossed the *South Pass the buzards* Should *pick his bones,*" the Saints returned to their dancing and mirth.[13]

Given the military odds, it seems incomprehensible that Young would talk of fighting the U.S. Army. Young, however, lived with fresh memories of anti-Mormon persecution. The death of Joseph Smith and his own traumatic experiences of evading arrest and escaping Nauvoo left him with scars that healed very slowly. Young worried about a reprise of past horrors. "The mail not coming in regularly is ominous," Young had said during an interruption in service two years earlier: "they always stopd the mails in Kirtland, Missouri, & Nauvoo when there was a fuss on hand." In his mind, if the Saints simply allowed the army to march into the territory, they would be inviting their own destruction, and he considered his own life very much at risk. Though his prior experiences help explain Young's reaction, his choice to resist carried incredible risks for the church he led.[14]

The next Sunday, Young laid out a theological response to the crisis. He read Daniel's prophecy that God would one day establish a kingdom "which shall never be destroyed . . . but it shall break in pieces and consume all these kingdoms, and it shall stand forever." That kingdom, Young interpreted, was the Saints' mountain Zion. Young was not typically inclined toward millennial speculation. Joseph Smith had disagreed with

William Miller's prediction of an imminent Second Coming, and Young usually focused on the more immediate tasks of kingdom-building. Still, like other Latter-day Saints, Young anticipated what Mormons sometimes termed the "winding up scene," the coming judgment on the nations of the world that would be followed by the spread of God's kingdom across the earth. The United States' sectional discord and its approaching army now suggested the more rapid approach of these final days. Young was not one to box himself into a theological corner, though. "I don't profess to be such a Prophet as were Joseph Smith and Daniel," he cautioned, "but I am a Yankee guesser." Young used such prophecies to reassure the Saints of God's providential care for them against military odds they all knew were enormous.[15]

Young's rhetoric became angrier and more vengeful, and he resumed talk of political independence. "I shall take it as a witness that God designs to cut the thread between us and the world," he explained in an early August discourse published in the *Deseret News,* "when an army undertakes to make their appearance in this Territory." Such language may have seemed politically provocative, but Young informed his St. Louis business agent Horace Eldredge that there had been "considerable pepper extracted" from newspaper accounts of his discourses. Young's verbal response to the expedition crested in mid-August with a sermon that apparently contained too much pepper for any sort of publication. Equating the U.S. Army with the vigilante killers of Joseph Smith and Parley Pratt, Young encouraged the congregation to "lift the sword and slay them." Elias Smith, Mormon legislator and judge, commented in his diary that Young had "laid down the law and the Gospel and the course that would be pursued in the event that our enemies should come upon us, so plain that none could misunderstand it." William Staines, the territorial librarian and a frequent officiator at the church's Endowment House, termed the address "the Greatest Decourse [discourse] . . . ever herd by Man." The church president, he added, spoke "in the language [of] a Revelator."[16]

From late July through mid-September, Young formulated his political and military strategy. He immediately ruled out one potential solution to the crisis. Amid rumors that army troops intended to hang him "with or without a trial," Young made clear that unlike Joseph Smith he would not sacrifice himself to save his people. "I will try to take care of number one," he insisted. "[W]ere I thrown into the situation Joseph was," he reiterated the next March, "I would leave the people and go into the wilderness, and let them do the best they could." Young categorically ruled out adding himself to the ranks of Mormon martyrs.[17]

With twelve hundred miles separating Salt Lake City from the Utah Expedition's staging post in Kansas, church leaders did not panic. Their immediate military objective was limited to keeping the army from reaching Mormon settlements that fall. Church leaders planned to slow the troops' advance with militia raids on supply trains and other forms of harassment. If all else failed, the Nauvoo Legion would resist the army's descent into the Salt Lake Valley. When the expedition failed to fully depart from Fort Leavenworth until mid-July, Young's desired outcome became more likely. Perhaps like the handcart companies the year before, the troops would be unable to reach Utah's settlements before snow halted their progress. "[W]e think they will not reach above Laramie this year," Young wrote to Nauvoo Legion quartermaster Lewis Robison at Fort Bridger, "and then something will probably turn up to give them another direction." While some American politicians hoped the distraction of the Utah campaign would temper disputes over slavery, Young hoped "bleeding Kansas" or another crisis would distract other Americans from the Mormons. Given the ongoing political and vigilante battles for control of Kansas, Young's strategy had some merit. Buchanan himself considered Utah a relatively low priority. "Kansas is vastly more important at the present moment than Utah," he reassured Robert J. Walker, the Kansas Territory's beleaguered proslavery governor. Young believed national politics, time, the weather, and the Lord were on his side.[18]

If the Nauvoo Legion failed to stop the expedition's advance, Young planned to evacuate and burn Salt Lake City. "I shall lay this building [the Salt Lake Tabernacle] in ashes," he preached in his fiery mid-August sermon, "I shall lay my dwelling houses in ashes, I shall lay my mills in ashes, I shall cut every shrub and tree in the valley, every pole every inch of board, and put it all into ashes." He would cache livestock, grain, and families and "make a potters field of every Canyon they go into." According to the Gospel of Matthew, the priests used Judas's thirty pieces of silver to purchase "the potter's field, to bury strangers in." In Young's analogy, Utah's canyons would become fields of blood, the final resting places for as many troops as Washington cared to send. The ancient Israelites had survived seven years of famine through careful planning. The Latter-day Israelites, Young reasoned, could survive a seven years' siege. He ordered a Mormon retrenchment, abandoning a number of outlying forts and way stations and entreating settlers in California and Carson Valley to return to the Great Basin.[19]

In August, Young sent emissaries to outlying portions of the territory to disseminate strategy and shore up Mormon resolve. Apostle George A. Smith, who had founded the church's Iron Mission in Parowan, traveled to southern Utah. With the apostle, Young had sent orders for the people to

George A. Smith, n.d. *(courtesy of Church History Library, The Church of Jesus Christ of Latter-day Saints)*

harvest their grain and hoard it as well as their ammunition. "[T]hose who persist in selling grain to the gentiles, or suffer their stock to trample it into the earth," he instructed local bishops, "I wish you to *note* as such." For two weeks, Smith traveled across the arid and hauntingly beautiful region, watched militia companies drill, and instilled local congregations with martial zeal. He informed settlers that the U.S. Army was preparing a "war of extermination" in which it would hang Brigham Young and other "principal leaders" without a trial. Smith made clear that he expected the settlers to strictly obey Young's orders. "Will we sell them grain or forage?" he asked. "I say damn the man who feeds them; I say damn the man who sympathizes with them; I say curse the man who pours oil and water on their heads." In late August, Iron County's militia commander William Dame reported to Daniel Wells that local Mormons had made every effort to secure "all the grain in every settlement," were guarding every inlet in southern Utah, and were "willing to act upon any command." Still displaying the effects of the reformation's emphasis on obedience and commitment, Mormons in southern Utah prepared to defend Zion from its enemies.[20]

In the event the Nauvoo Legion fought the U.S. Army, Young also sought to recruit the territory's native peoples to his side. While depositing a set of Mormon scriptures and other church articles within the Salt Lake temple foundation on August 13, Young beseeched God to "turn the hearts of the Lamanites even the sons of Jacob unto us that they may do thy will and be as a wall of defense around about us." Indian allies had the potential to cause terror on the Overland Trail, delay the expedition's advance, and even help the Mormons inflict an embarrassing defeat on the initial detachment of troops. "Instruct the Indians that our enemies are also their enemies," Wells wrote Dame, ". . . for if our enemies kill us off, they will surely be cut off by the same parties." However, instead of embracing what the Mormons saw as their millennial role, most of Utah's Indians sought to avoid taking sides while turning the crisis to their own advantage.[21]

On September 1, Young met with a group of native leaders from across the territory, including Mormon allies Kanosh and Ammon, as well as Paiute leaders from Santa Clara and Harmony in the south. The previous day, Dimick Huntington, Young's most trusted Indian interpreter, had met with a group of Indians north of Salt Lake. Young, Huntington informed them, had given "them [the Indian chiefs] all the Beef cattle & horses that was on the road to Cal Afornia the North Rout." At the September 1 meeting, Young told the central and southern Utah Indian chiefs that they could take "all the cattle that had gone to Cal the southe route." Young also asked the chiefs to join him in a fight against the U.S. Army. "[T]hey have come to fight us and you," he explained, "for when they kill us then they will kill you." The chiefs demurred, stating that they preferred to "raise grain" instead of fighting. Noting that previously he had told them "not to steal," the chiefs expressed their astonishment at Young's change of course. A man who still claimed to be the governor of an American territory had encouraged them to attack emigrant wagon trains and prepare to fight the U.S. Army.[22]

Young had sown the wind, and American emigrants reaped the whirlwind. After six weeks of mounting tension, war sermons, and threatened violence against Gentiles passing through the territory, members of the southern Utah Nauvoo Legion treacherously massacred a large wagon train on September 11.

The "Arkansas company," most of whose members came from that state, was a loose conglomeration of emigrant parties that arrived in Salt Lake City in late July and early August. Later known as the Fancher-Baker train for two of its leaders, the company took several hundred head of cattle on the southern route to California. The emigrants passed through settlements in which local leaders echoed the wartime messages of the church hierarchy. In mid-August, the group stayed near Nephi in central Utah. "The Bishop sent out to them requesting them to move for they were destroying our winter feed [pastures]," reported Samuel Pitchforth. "They answered that they [w]ere American Citizens and should not move." Pitchforth also recorded that the emigrants sought—presumably unsuccessfully—to purchase flour. Moving to the south of Fillmore, the emigrants camped next to Corn Creek. Coincidentally, stopping for the night across the creek was George A. Smith, in company with the southern Utah Indian chiefs en route to Salt Lake City for their meeting with Young. According to the somewhat later reconstruction of Jacob Hamblin, recently appointed president of the Santa Clara Indian Mission, "a Strang atmosphere Serounded [surrounded]" the emigrants. Hamblin, who was traveling with Smith, remembered that the apostle predicted that "Some evle would befall them before they got through." After the Fancher-Baker train moved on, subsequent groups of emigrants found the local Pahvant Indians agitated when a number of Indians and livestock died from what might have been anthrax. Later on, Young and others repeated false rumors that members of the Arkansas company had brought trouble upon themselves by poisoning the creek and an ox they had given to the Indians.[23]

Tensions crested as the emigrant train reached southern Utah. Colonel William Dame in Parowan strictly enforced Young's ban on sales to the Gentiles. Dame sent men to assault William Leany, a Mormon settler who had the temerity to give food to one of the emigrants, a man Leany had known in Tennessee.[24] Although the emigrants would surely have been wary of inciting opposition given the obvious tensions of 1857, Mormon-Gentile animosity was mutual, and there is no reason to presume that either Mormons or emigrants acted like saints in their interactions. In Cedar City, emigrants frustrated with their inability to purchase supplies became angry and apparently made threats against the settlement's mayor, Isaac Haight (also the church's regional stake president), and its bishop, Philip Klingensmith.[25]

Haight, who was a Nauvoo Legion major, ordered John D. Lee, Young's ritually adopted son and a "farmer" to the Indians at nearby Harmony, to recruit local Paiutes for an ambush on the Arkansas company. From the start, local leaders sought to cover their tracks. According to Lee's later account, he and Haight decided to "make it *an Indian massacre* . . . so that it could be laid to them, if any questions were ever asked about it." Since 1854, the Mormons had sheltered the southern Paiutes from slave-raiding Utes, who terrorized them by abducting their children. Mormon missionaries and Paiutes together built a fort at Santa Clara, and the missionaries both evangelized the Indians and helped them expand the amount of land they had under cultivation. The Paiutes carefully distinguished between the *Mericats* (Americans) and the *Mormonee*. More so than most of the Great Basin's native peoples, the Paiutes had indicated their willingness to fight alongside the Mormons against the U.S. Army. They would never have raided a large, well-armed train of their own accord, but Lee persuaded a group of Paiutes to join in the ambush and spoils.[26]

The attack took place on Monday, September 7, at the Mountain Meadows, a cool, relatively lush expanse above the Santa Clara Canyon, where the emigrants had camped to refresh their animals before the push across the desert to San Bernardino. It was not far from where unknown assailants had attacked John Tobin's party earlier in the year. The flaws in the plan immediately became apparent. The emigrants were far too numerous and capable for a disguised Lee and the Paiutes to overcome. They circled their wagons, dug in, buried their dead, and returned fire. The attackers succeeded in capturing much of the train's stock, but the ambush became a protracted siege, and the Indian participants in the attack became disillusioned.

The previous evening, Haight had convened a council meeting in Cedar City to gain broader approval for the planned ambush. In the face of unexpected opposition to Haight's course, the council finally agreed to send an express letter for Young's advice. Haight did not send a rider north immediately, but when he received word of the attack, he ordered James Haslam—a musician in the militia—to leave for Salt Lake City. When Haslam passed through Nephi, Samuel Pitchforth recorded that the express letter informed Young that the "emigrants who went through a short time since was acting very mean." After a two-hundred-and-fifty-mile ride north, Haslam reached Salt Lake City on Thursday. The church president immediately dictated an answer, and an exhausted Haslam departed again one hour later, carrying the following message back to Cedar City: "In regard to emigration trains passing through our settlements we must not interfere with them untill they are first notified to keep away. You must not meddle with them. The Indians we expect will do as they please but you should try and preserve good feelings with them. There are no other trains going south that I know of if those who are there will leave let them go in peace." Young's response reflects the new policy he had articulated to the Indian chiefs in early September. While Young discouraged settler attacks on the emigrants, he did not wish the settlers to restrain Indian attacks.[27]

By the time Haslam returned to Cedar City on Sunday, September 13, Mormon militiamen and some remaining Paiutes had slaughtered most of the surviving emigrants.[28] Haight and his militia superior, William Dame, may have believed that the emigrants knew of Mormon complicity and would cause trouble for the church if they reached California, or they may have felt the need to finish the deed before trailing emigrant trains reached the area. Regardless, acting on orders from Haight and apparently Dame, on Friday morning Lee approached the emigrant corral with a white flag and offered them passage to Cedar City. Telling them they needed to take precautions to avoid instigating another Indian attack, Lee required the emigrants to surrender their weapons and exit the meadows according to his precise instructions. The wounded and small children would travel first in wagons, the older children and women would then proceed next, and the men would bring up the rear in a single-file line flanked by armed members of the militia. Despite their misgivings, the hungry, thirsty, and nearly hopeless emigrants accepted Lee's terms.

The trek began. After a short distance, John Higbee, a key planner in the operation and a major in the Cedar City militia, shouted "Halt!" On Higbee's signal, the members of the militia shot the emigrant men at point-blank range. Most died instantly. Meanwhile, Mormons and possibly some remaining Paiutes butchered the women, wounded, and most of the children. The attackers mercilessly shot, stabbed, and slashed the throats of emigrants who pled for their lives. They spared seventeen children considered too young to provide credible reports about the crime. Local families took in the surviving children until the U.S. Army returned them to eastern relatives eighteen months later. In all, about one hundred and twenty men, women, and children died. The Mormon men quickly looted the wagons and bodies; the Paiutes, deprived of the most valuable spoils, stripped the bodies of their clothing and took anything of value overlooked by the militiamen.

White mass murders of Indians and African Americans were not unusual in nineteenth-century America. Seven years after the Mountain Meadows Massacre, a unit of Colorado volunteers attacked a Cheyenne encampment at Sand Creek, in the southeastern portion of the Colorado Territory, killing around one hundred and fifty men, women, and children. The Sand Creek Massacre took place at a time of unrest between white settlers and several bands of Cheyenne and Arapaho warriors, though the attacked village had been inclined toward peace and contained few warriors. There were several massacres of African Americans in the mid-1870s American South, though in these instances white southerners primarily targeted black men for political purposes rather than engaging in the wholesale slaughter of women and children. White-on-white massacres, however, are a very rare occurrence in the history of the United States. Even during the Civil War, both sides took pains to avoid killing civilians. The 1838 Haun's Mill Massacre in Missouri forms one exception, as do the events at Mountain Meadows. A heinous crime executed after careful deliberation and subterfuge rather than in the heat of any battle, the Mountain Meadows Massacre testifies to the extreme levels of anxiety, hatred, and avarice present in 1857 Utah.

Local leaders instructed the perpetrators to keep silent about their deeds and then undertook a remarkably ineffective cover-up. Lee talked, and rumors spread quickly among the territory's native peoples. Only two weeks later, U.S. Indian Agent Garland Hurt fled the territory with a reasonably accurate report of Mormon involvement in the massacre.[29] In early October, William Cox, stake president for Mormon San Bernardino, reported that "there is a great Excitement here at this time on acount of the Masacre of atrain of Americans Some Where near the mountain medows." According to Cox, local non-Mormons talked of raising a company to "go to the Batle ground and find out wheather the Saints had any hand in it or not." California newspapers soon reported on Mormon participation in the butchery. "[W]ho can be so blind as not to see that the hands of Mormons are stained with this blood?" asked a letter printed in San Francisco's *Alta California*. George Q. Cannon reported that the state "would boil over with volunteers to go and clean out the 'Mormons,' if the Government would only call on them." The massacre created a nightmarish political problem for Young and the Mormons.[30]

The question of whether or not Brigham Young ordered or was otherwise complicit in the Mountain Meadows Massacre quickly became a subject of heated debate and remains so to this day. In 2002, the historian Will Bagley—proud of his "Mormon heritage" but no longer a church member—documented a long history of denial, obfuscation, and obstruction on the part of church leaders in relation to the massacre, symbolized by "pages ripped from dozens of 1857 journals." Bagley concludes that Young sent George A. Smith to southern Utah in August 1857 to set in motion the destruction of the Fancher-Baker train. More recently, three historians employed by the Church History Department depicted the massacre as the work of local church leaders. Past persecution and wartime fervor overcame moral scruples and led Mormons in southern Utah to dehumanize and destroy their Gentile enemies. They allow that "errors were made" by Young, but they include his mistakes among those of James Buchanan and many others.[31]

There is no satisfactory evidence that Young ordered the massacre; the most straightforward reading of Young's letter to Haight is exculpatory. Many years later, Young instructed his associates to put the copybook containing the letter "into a safe where it will be secure and at hand if called for."[32] Although Young at one point falsely denied that the letter was in his possession, probably because it tacitly encouraged Indian attacks, the church president believed that his instructions to Haight could exonerate him.[33] Given his political objective of keeping the army away from Mormon settlements, moreover, there was no good reason for Young to order a massacre with the potential to focus the full fury of the American government on Utah.

At the same time, Young bears significant responsibility for what took place at Mountain Meadows. Southern Utah leaders had almost certainly received word of Young's decision to no longer discourage Indian attacks on emigrant wagon trains. The new policy may have led local leaders like Haight and Lee to presume that their ecclesiastical superiors would condone the initiation of an ambush. Given the Saints' palpable animosity toward non-Mormons and apostates in Utah, a more prudent and responsible leader would have calmed rather than inflamed anti-Gentile sentiment and restrained rather than encouraged Indian attacks on American civilians. The several acts of violence during the previous winter—the Thomas Lewis castration, the shootings at the Santa Clara River, and the Parrish-Potter murders—all suggested how easily violent rhetoric and incautious decisions could have unexpected and deadly consequences. Despite those lessons, during the early stages of the Utah War Young fomented the hatred and anxiety that made it conceivable for Mormons in southern Utah to slaughter men, women, and children. Young's saber-rattling, militia operations, and Indian policy contributed to the most unusual mass murder in the history of the American West.[34]

The 1857 massacre at Mountain Meadows contributed to a long-term worsening of already tense Mormon-Gentile relations, in part because Young failed to undertake an aggressive ecclesiastical investigation into the mass murder and hold its perpetrators accountable. After a late-September report on the massacre to Young, John D. Lee provided him with a written account of the Indians slaughtering the emigrants in retaliation for the alleged poisoning of the ox carcass and the spring at Corn Creek. Young drew on Lee's report when he repeated the same narrative to Commissioner of Indian Affairs James Denver. Still acting as the territory's superintendent of Indian affairs, Young asked the federal government to

Brigham Young, ca. 1857 *(courtesy of Special Collections, J. Willard Marriott Library, University of Utah)*

reimburse him for $3,527 for gifts purportedly distributed by Levi Stewart to "sundry bands of Indians near Mountain Meadow" on September 30, 1857. The gifts, which ranged from steers to clothing to butcher knives, were plunder from the Fancher-Baker train.[35]

It remains unclear exactly what southern Utah leaders privately told Young about the massacre in the fall and winter of 1857–58. Even if they attempted to shroud their own participation and that of other southern Utah Mormons, their explanations would likely not have satisfied the church's president. Brigham Young was not a gullible man. He knew as well as anyone that the Paiutes would not have made an unprompted attack on the Arkansas company, and he soon heard rumors of what had actually taken place.[36] Young feared that full knowledge of Mormon responsibility for the massacre would foment anti-Mormon sentiment across the country and embolden federal judges, giving him good reason for wanting the truth buried in the shallow red dirt of southern Utah.

In June 1858, Jacob Hamblin, who knew of Mormon leadership of the attack, gave the apostle George A. Smith an "account of the Massacre at Mountain meadows." Hamblin's visit prompted Young to send Smith to southern Utah, accompanied by several others. The group visited the site of the massacre, stayed with John D. Lee in Harmony, and then held hearings in Cedar City and Parowan. "John D. Lee and a few other white men were on the ground during a portion of the combat," Smith wrote Young after the conclusion of his investigation. By this point, Smith—and Young—must have known a great deal about the actions of the massacre's ringleaders. Yet Lee, Haight, and others appeared to remain not just in good standing but in Young's own personal favor. Over time, Young's inaction led many observers, Mormon and Gentile, to reach the conclusion that he condoned the slaughter.[37]

As the grisly events in southern Utah unfolded, Captain Stewart Van Vliet, a U.S. Army quartermaster who had encountered the Mormons at Winter Quarters a decade earlier, arrived in Salt Lake City. General Harney had instructed Van Vliet to ascertain the availability of lumber and other supplies for the army, to scout out a possible location for the planned army outpost in Utah, and to report on Mormon intentions. The captain confirmed news that the army had just reached Laramie, and he expected that the troops would winter at Ham's Fork, a river crossing nearly two hundred miles to the east of Salt Lake City. Van Vliet also confirmed that Buchanan had detained General Harney to deal with ongoing violence in Kansas, replacing him as the Utah Expedition's commander with Colonel Albert Sidney Johnston. The news bolstered Young's hope that "if we Can Ceep the peace for this winter I do think there will be sumthing turn up that may save so much shedding of blood."[38] Thus, Young's meeting with the quartermaster came at a time when he felt confident of his strategy's success.

Young did everything in his power to make Van Vliet feel personally welcome, taking the captain through his garden, orchard, and house and introducing the visitor to his family. The church's president, however, also gave Van Vliet a clear view of the iron fist lurking behind the velvet glove of his hospitality. "[I]f they [the troops] come they could not have an article," Young told the captain, "this was said to him as between gentlemen—

not for his report to [the] government." Van Vliet also spoke more bluntly behind closed doors, warning Young that "if this Territory should resist the orders of the [war] department we should be committ[in]g an overt act [of treason]." Young was not intimidated. On Van Vliet's final day in Salt Lake City, he attended Sunday meetings in which Young gave "Uncle Same Considerable Hell fire." In a final private session before Van Vliet's return, Young made clear his refusal to retreat even to the pre-expedition status quo, insisting that "we will not have neither their soldiers or officers any more here at all." He repeated his threat to close the Overland Trail and stop restraining Indian attacks. He vowed to evacuate and burn Mormon settlements and even suggested that Mormons across the country would retaliate for army depredations in Utah. "I shall Carry the war into their own land," Young vowed. The Mormons' visitor gave no sign of being shocked by such defiance. Upon his departure for Washington, Van Vliet professed his friendship and sympathy, but his report to Buchanan helped the president conclude that the Mormons were now in armed rebellion against the government.[39]

The day after the quartermaster's departure, Young issued a governor's proclamation as a response to an invasion "by a hostile force, who are evidently assailing us to accomplish our overthrow and destruction." Noting past persecutions and claiming constitutional rights of self-government and self-defense, Young resolved to "[f]orbid all armed forces, of every description, from coming into this Territory under any pretence whatever." Citing his authority as governor and superintendent of Indian affairs, Young declared martial law, stating that "no person shall be allowed to pass or repass into, or through, or from this Territory, without a permit from the proper officer."[40] The Overland Trail and Utah's borders were now closed. Young's application of martial law to an entire territory and against U.S. troops was unprecedented. On the heels of his strong language to Van Vliet, Young apparently was taking all possible measures to let the army know it would have a fight on its hands should it attempt to force its way into the Salt Lake Valley. Given Young's hope that something would distract the army from Utah by the following spring, the proclamation was a distinctly unwise and dangerous step. It quite predictably served only to enrage the army and the Buchanan administration while providing a solid pretext for treason indictments against Young and other church leaders.

Meanwhile, Colonel Edmund Alexander's Tenth U.S. Infantry was on the Sweetwater River west of Devil's Gate, roughly two hundred miles to the east of Ham's Fork (and still four hundred miles from Salt Lake City). Several supply trains preceded Alexander, and the remainder of the Utah

Expedition—six companies of dragoons (mountain infantry), followed by Johnston and his civilian charges—lagged far behind. While some of Alexander's subordinates longed for their commander to make a headlong plunge for Salt Lake City via Echo Canyon, Alexander himself hesitated to take any bold steps before his superior's arrival. The Utah Expedition was strung out, vulnerable, and without strong leadership in its vanguard.

In order to hamper the army's progress, Young's militia commanders launched a campaign of obstruction and harassment. Some elements of the plan had been in operation since August. For instance, the Mormon militia burnt grass alongside the trail to make it harder for the army to feed its animals. By late September, Young grew less confident that the army would stop short of its destination. When Alexander reached Ham's Fork (inside Utah's boundaries at the time), Young sent the colonel an assertive letter demanding that he "retire forthwith from the Territory." Alexander, of course, did not retreat, but the cautious colonel was unsure of how to proceed. When Alexander sent infantry volunteers on muleback scouting missions, Young derisively ordered militia leaders at Fort Bridger to lure "that Jack ass cavalry into an ambush and take them without firing a gun or at least without killing anybody." The contemplated ambush never took place, but Mormon raiders struck at the army's other weak spots. Within a span of twenty-four hours, Major Lot Smith and two dozen mounted militiamen captured and torched three army supply trains, including two months' supply of the expedition's food. Young exulted when he learned of Smith's triumph, pronouncing himself in a letter to his commanders "highly pleased with the bloodless success which has so far attended your labors."[41]

Although even during the raids the two sides took care to avoid pitched battles, the Utah War did not proceed without bloodshed. At the end of October, the Nauvoo Legion in northern Utah arrested six mysterious visitors from California. Known as the Aiken Party for its members John and Thomas Aiken, the group had entered the territory without the "permit" required by Young's martial law proclamation. While their intentions remain unknown, it seems that they intended to profit in some manner from the arrival of the U.S. Army in Utah. At some point, Mormon leaders concluded that at least some of the men were army spies. "One of the men," wrote Homer Brown in Nephi, "had a letter of recommendation from a commander of the U.S. Station in Callifornia to Col. Johnson stating that the bearer was a man that could be trusted." Brown added that the "letter fell into Brighams hands, and thus he found out who they were." Young gave two of the men permission to winter in the territory. The four others headed south toward California escorted by Porter Rockwell and several other men, who murdered them one hundred miles south of Salt Lake. Given Brown's comment, it seems probable that Young sanctioned their deaths. After his excommunication from the church, William Hickman later claimed to have shot a fifth member of the party (Horace Bucklin) at Young's behest, though no evidence corroborates that allegation. The sixth member of the party apparently survived and escaped to California.[42]

In addition to his likely complicity in the deaths of four members of the Aiken Party, Young sanctioned the murder of Richard Yates, a trader who had spent the previous few years operating in the mountains between South Pass and the Salt Lake Valley. Mountaineers sold gunpowder to both Mormons and Indians, but they now anticipated an unprecedented windfall with the army's pending arrival. The Mormons tried to buy Yates out, and Young ordered the confiscation of his property if that attempt failed. When Yates refused to sell out and the U.S. Army purchased his gunpowder, the Nauvoo Legion arrested the trader. On October 15, Daniel Wells informed Young that the Mormon militia had arrested Yates, who had "been passing to and from the enemy's camp (and it is believed) as a spy." For years, Mormons and mountaineers had competed for the economic benefits of trade and ferry operation in northeastern Utah. Men like Jim Bridger had also been political thorns in Young's side. Now, in a time of war, church leaders saw them as military enemies. A few days later, on October 18, Wells alerted Young that he had sent "*Yates* on the road to the City, a prisoner in charge of Wm. Hickman."[43]

The trader never made it to Salt Lake. In the 1870s, Hickman, now excommunicated from the church, described encountering Young's son Joseph Angell Young during the trip. "[He] said," Hickman wrote, "that his father wanted that man Yates killed." That night, Daniel Jones, Hosea Stout, and two others came to Hickman's campfire and "asked if Yates was asleep." When that proved to be the case, "his brains were knocked out with an ax." When he made this accusation, Hickman—along with Brigham Young, Wells, and Hosea Stout—was under indictment for Yates's murder, so he had a strong incentive to point the finger at his former superior. Wells, Joseph A. Young, and Jones all stoutly rejected Hickman's narrative.[44]

Contemporary evidence, though, renders Hickman's account plausible. A journal kept by one of Brigham Young's clerks records the October 16 arrival of Joseph A. with Wells's October 15 express containing the news of Yates's arrest. In response, Young instructed Wells "that no mountaineer be let to go at large whose operations are against us, or who are in favor of the enemy." He added that "Bishop Callister has an undoubted right to cut off those whom he cant fellowship." At the time, Thomas Callister was a Nauvoo Legion colonel at Fort Bridger. In this context, "cut off" implies murder. A courier with Young's response reached Wells on the morning of October 17. Hosea Stout's journal places Yates in the company of Hickman the next night, and Joseph A. Young was also there, having left Salt Lake City for Echo Canyon that morning. Young thought that mountaineers trading with the enemy deserved death. In his mind, they were traitors. By mid-October, his wartime policies had moved beyond ordering "bloodless" ambushes to countenancing bloodshed.[45]

Meanwhile, even as Young celebrated Lot Smith's raid, Colonel Alexander tentatively began moving his troops up Ham's Fork to the northwest, hoping to approach the northern Salt Lake Valley via Bear River. Young conditionally ordered a lethal attack. "If they undertake to swing round into Cache Valley or the Malad [Valley]," the well-informed Young wrote Wells, "let sleep depart from their eyes and slumber from the eyelids, both day and night, until they take their final sleep; pick off their guards and sentries & fire into their camps by night, and pick off officers and as many men as possible by day." Young also sent Alexander a more desperate and insistent directive to leave the territory, and the church president made it plain that he had no intention of backing down. "With us it is the kingdom of God, or nothing," he wrote.[46]

An order from Johnston arrived and resolved Alexander's indecision, instructing him to rendezvous with Johnston at Ham's Fork and then proceed west together. The Nauvoo Legion intended to attack the army should it advance past the charred remains of Fort Bridger, which the militia had evacuated and burned in early October. Tensions reached a peak in Salt Lake City on November 11, when a report arrived that the army would reach the city in only twelve days. Four days later, Young asked those attending his Sunday evening prayer circle "to pray that the soldiers might return, and that we might not have to shed their blood." Those supplications were partly granted. Punishing winter weather killed thousands of the army's horses and livestock and dramatically slowed its advance. Johnston spent twelve days advancing the thirty miles from Ham's Fork to Fort Bridger. The army's mounted regiment followed in Johnston's wake; one civilian accompanying the dragoons described the trail as "one vast slaughter yard." Meanwhile, Wells instructed his commanders in the field to strike should the army continue past Bridger. "[F]rom the time they leave Bridger," he ordered, "torment, harrass, and commence killing them." He would regard such an advance, Wells informed Young, "as a sure indication that the Lord wants them used up [killed]." Johnston, though, reluctantly abandoned any hope of pushing forward the remaining sixty miles to Echo Canyon. Instead, the Utah Expedition's 1857 campaign halted and went into winter quarters at hastily constructed Camp Scott. Johnston would wait until the snow melted.[47]

Young had achieved his immediate goal. "Brigham Young has taken the cream of the army of the United States," he crowed, "and stopped them from going any further."[48] While the Nauvoo Legion's harassment campaign had helped retard Alexander's progress, that success mostly hinged on the army's late and staggered start. With his orders, moreover, Young had come dangerously close to instigating a shooting war. With both sides having placed more than a thousand men in the field, the suggested ambush of Alexander's mounted infantry and the planned strike against an army advance both carried the potential for mass bloodshed. That war would almost certainly have led to the church's political annihilation. Fortunately, Young's commanders moved cautiously and understood that he only wanted to initiate armed hostilities should the army definitively move toward Echo Canyon.

Still, as 1857 drew to a close, Young and his church had entangled themselves in a military and political dilemma from which there was no ready escape. In mid-November, intelligence of Young's continued defiance and Mormon military actions startled and infuriated administration officials. By late November, Young's replacement as Utah's governor, Alfred Cumming of Georgia, and several other appointees were with Johnston at Bridger. The new chief justice of the territory, Delana Eckels, assembled a makeshift grand jury that indicted Young and other Mormon leaders on charges of treason. In his first annual address to Congress, Buchanan stated the need for four additional regiments so that an "imposing force" could bring an end to the conflict. "This is the first rebellion that has existed in our territories," he declared, "and humanity itself requires that we should put it down in such a manner that it shall be the last." Johnston and his officers, meanwhile, salivated at the thought of concluding their march in the spring and meting out the strictest possible punishment. Both Johnston and administration officials talked of opening a second front from the Pacific Coast.[49]

Young had threatened to cut the thread between Utah and the rest of the United States. That thread was now effectively cut. Young's formerly expansive Great Basin kingdom had withdrawn into a narrower line of settlements, no longer received mail from the eastern United States, and faced the prospect of overwhelming military opposition from multiple directions. The Mormons had bought out Utah's most prominent Gentile merchants and had lost their political allies in Congress. Young's kingdom was now isolated, shrinking, and embattled. If captured, Young faced a realistic prospect of execution. At best, he possessed half a year to find a way out of this predicament.

THE Utah War's winter hiatus meant that Young's existence resumed some usual patterns. He regularly sealed couples at the Endowment House, granted divorces, visited his properties, and began laying the groundwork for new projects for the territory's elusive economic self-sufficiency, such as a cotton-growing initiative in southern Utah. The army's presence, however, loomed large. As he had throughout the fall, Young spoke frequently from the stand, emphasizing his standard themes of obedience and unity with greater than usual insistence. For the Mormons to have any chance against an enemy with superior numbers, firepower, and resources, they could not afford dissent or a lack of common purpose. Young drilled this lesson into congregants all fall, telling them to trust their leaders. Unity was so crucial, he explained, that the Saints should not let their minds form their own supplications during Sunday meetings or prayer circles. He observed that his request for perfect unity and obedience was inimical to the American exaltation of independent thought. "[O]ur fathers have taught us," Young complained, ". . . that every man and woman and every child old enough to speak, argue, read, reflect, &c., must have minds of their own and not listen to anybody else." In his early adulthood, Young had agreed that ordinary Americans could and should use their common sense to ascertain religious truths for themselves. Now, he insisted that such notions "must be checked in this people." Young may have downplayed his prophetic calling at times, but during this crisis he insisted that the Saints recognize his words as the "voice of God to this people."[50]

In public, Young continued to project an air of confident defiance. He asked Albert Carrington, editor of the *Deseret News,* to draft yet another memorial for the territorial legislature to send to Congress. Complaining that the government had not responded to their prior year's memorial, the Mormons reiterated their demand for the right to choose their own officers and laws, and they requested several hundred thousand dollars in reimbursements for Indian expenses. The Mormons styled themselves as Latter-day Thomas Jeffersons and Patrick Henrys, defending their right to self-government at any cost. Young knew the memorial would cause another "tremendous uproar," but he did not mind. For good measure, the church printed what he termed "some spicy correspondence," his incendiary epistles to the army officers from the past fall. One week later, he threatened that if the army persisted in its attempt to take his life, he would "make Millions of them Bite the Dust." Young gave Washington no sign that he was prepared to back down.[51]

Privately, the conflict exacted a heavy toll on the church's president. Young often bragged about his physical stamina, and he loved it when visitors commented on his youthful appearance and relative lack of gray hairs. Yet at fifty-six years of age, he was old by mid-nineteenth-century standards, suffering intermittently from rheumatism and possibly from chronic urological problems. His ecclesiastical, political, and economic responsibilities remained vast. In February, he complained that he had to "do more business in an hour than Any presidet, king, or Emperor has to perform in a day." Even apart from the constant stream of visitors to his office, he added, "I have to think for the people Constantly." Young's trademark vigor diminished somewhat as the months progressed.[52]

One possible sign of that strain came through Young's frequent recounting to his clerks of unusual and sometimes intimate dreams. In various dreams, Colonel Johnston and his old nemesis Lieutenant Sylvester Mowry tried to kill him, enemies chased him into a ravine, and a California emigrant first attacked him with a bowie knife before deciding to take his own life. In yet another dream, a woman approached him privately and indicated that "she wished to have connection with him." Young noticed that she was naked with a "handsome form," "her belly having no signs that she had ever had a child." Rebuffing her seduction, Young "asked her if she thought he was such a damned fool, as to have connection with any woman that was not his wife." The following January, Young dreamed that one of the new territorial judges ordered him to relieve himself in public. "In following the ruling of the Judge, he [Young] besmeared himself," recorded a clerk, "he wanted to find some place to clean himself, but could not, for every where he went, the women were looking at him." The intimate disclosures and the hints at Young's sexuality were out of character for a man usually circumspect about such topics.[53]

Young spent the winter months searching for a way to resolve the conflict. As early as October, he recognized that if he wanted to score a military blow against Uncle Sam, the Nauvoo Legion would have to attack that fall when the army was weakened from its long march and before it could resupply and reinforce itself. Young never seriously considered mounting an offensive, though. Instead, he ordered the creation of a new "Standing Army of Israel" to counter expected American springtime reinforcements. Young envisioned a brigade of between one and two thousand mounted riflemen to augment the Legion's militia troops, but he had to ask volunteers and their communities to supply the horses and provisions. Young had long sought to create a self-sufficient economy; he now tried to create a self-sufficient army. The U.S. Army may have bungled its fall 1857 march, but given time it possessed military advantages the Mormons could not overcome.[54]

Many outside observers believed the Mormons would again undertake an exodus, speculating on a number of possible destinations, from Central America to Sonora, Mexico, to Russian Alaska. Young apparently gave passing thought to Alaska, but he never seriously considered leaving Utah. He argued that if the Saints occupied any desirable land, the U.S. government would soon be on their heels again.[55]

The Mormons would remain in the Great Basin, but they were hemmed in, with an underequipped and impoverished militia, and without reliable Indian allies. In early March, Young received news of a Bannock Indian attack on Fort Limhi, the Mormon missionary outpost in the Oregon Territory he had visited the previous spring. Two Mormon missionaries died, five were wounded, and the Indians drove off several hundred cattle. Young ordered the fort's evacuation. The raid further exposed the hollow sanguineness of Mormon rhetoric about a military alliance with the Lamanites. Six months earlier, he had spoken of the Kingdom of God spreading across the world in the rapidly oncoming last days. Now, Young was slowly coming to grips with what seemed to be the final months of his earthly kingdom. In early February, Young had sent John D. Lee to explore the Virgin River valleys to identify "a resting place for his famely & that of the 1st Presidency [Heber Kimball and Daniel Wells]." At best, in the eventuality of a shooting war with the U.S. Army, church leaders would survive as fugitives.[56]

Bleak as the military and political situation appeared, Young turned out to be only one of several parties eager for a solution. On February 25, the church's trusted non-Mormon advocate Thomas Kane arrived in Salt Lake City. As news of Lot Smith's raids and Young's proclamation of martial law reached the East, Kane had thrown himself into an attempt to broker an amicable resolution. In December, Kane had traveled to the nation's capital to seek Buchanan's blessing on a peacemaking trip to Utah. The president initially discouraged him but then gave the idea lukewarm support in late December. Buchanan hoped that if Kane conveyed the administration's resolve to subdue the Mormon rebellion, Young would come to his senses and cease resisting the army. The president refused Kane any official standing but supplied him with letters commending him "to the favorable regard of all officers of the United States." With Buchanan's quasi-endorsement in hand, Kane departed for Utah to manufacture his own solution to the standoff.[57]

Kane traveled to California via Panama, then traveled incognito to Salt Lake City on the southern route. Declaring his "joy and surprise," Young

Thomas Leiper Kane, ca. early 1870s *(courtesy of L. Tom Perry Special Collections, Harold B. Lee Library, Brigham Young University)*

sent a carriage to bring the visitor to his Beehive House mansion the evening of his arrival. Kane brought welcome news that private cracks existed in Buchanan's firm public resolve to subdue the Mormons. "I suppose they are united," Young lamented, referring to the administration. "I think not," replied Kane. Buchanan had sparked a revolt among northern Democrats by supporting a proslavery Kansas constitution, and northerners suspected him of continued efforts to annex Cuba as additional slave territory. A run of bank failures, meanwhile, had plunged the country into a financial panic. The president, Kane correctly surmised, wanted to end what had become an embarrassing and costly Utah campaign.[58]

Kane, who approached seemingly intractable problems with a romantic flamboyance, intended to solve the Mormon crisis by turning Young into a peacemaker and driving a wedge between Colonel Johnston and his civilian counterparts. To accomplish the first end, he sent letters to Washington describing a division between Mormon warmongers on the one hand and Young on the other. The Buchanan administration and incoming Utah governor Alfred Cumming, Kane argued, should embrace Brigham Young as a paragon of restraint who had prevented his rabid fanatics from attacking the army. Kane's portrayal was a very creative fiction. It blatantly ignored Young's actual rhetoric and actions from the previous year and invented out of whole cloth the purported division within Mormon ranks.[59]

Before he began the daunting task of persuading skeptical non-Mormon officials to accept his depiction of Young's leadership, Kane had to get the church president himself to play along. He asked Young to demonstrate his goodwill and humanitarianism by sending provisions to the army. Taking substantial license from what the president had told him in December, Kane offered Mormon leaders an apology from Buchanan and dangled the possibility of a presidential pardon. Young's initial response was unenthusiastic. Mormon horror at the thought of thousands of soldiers within striking range of their homes and women was unchanged. After two weeks, Kane began the journey to Camp Scott to apprise himself of the army's intentions. At the last minute, Young sent a messenger after him with a letter, in which Young offered to deliver a herd of cattle and twenty thousand pounds of flour to the army. For all his animosity toward the army, Young relished the thought of an army "very destitute of provisions" relying on his generosity, and he wanted a peaceful resolution of the standoff. From this point forward, Kane and Young worked in tandem, and the Utah War became a grand exercise in diplomatic theater.[60]

Kane knew that Johnston would respond skeptically to his mission and antagonistically to Young's offer. In fact, in a draft of the letter to Kane, Young initially stated his expectation that Johnston would "utterly refuse" the gift. The previous fall, Young had sent a load of salt to the army, with an accompanying letter suggesting Johnston might fear that it was poisoned. Johnston had dismissed the idea of receiving succor from an enemy of the U.S. government, and he did so again in March. Probably because Kane wanted to sow discord between Johnston and Cumming, he clashed with Johnston at every opportunity, pronounced himself insulted, and initiated steps to challenge the expedition's commander to a duel. Johnston made sufficient apologies for the perceived slights to avoid the latter outcome. At the same time, Kane established good relations with Cumming, whom he even attempted to recruit as his "second" for the proposed duel. Nevertheless, after several days, Kane had to report discouraging news to Young. Johnston, with sufficient supplies and expected reinforcements, still intended to move his troops into the Salt Lake Valley irrespective of Mormon resistance.[61]

Young now proved that he could provide some theatrics of his own. Probably in response to Kane's news and advice, Young publicly announced that he would not fight the army after all, declaring military resistance both futile and not worth a single Mormon life. If the Nauvoo Legion killed American soldiers, Young argued, an overwhelming military response would ensue, and their enemies would steal their land and improvements, just as they had done in Missouri and Illinois. Still, he could not simply accede to the army's invasion. Instead, he would do as the Russians had done and evacuate "Sebastopol," the Black Sea port destroyed and vacated by the Russian Army during the recent Crimean War. If Johnston entered the valley, the army would find it deserted and torched. This was the contingency plan Young had discussed the previous August. Even if previously broached, though, the announcement of what became known as the "Move South" was a very public about-face. It was also a signal to the army, incoming Governor Cumming, and the Buchanan administration that there would be nothing to govern should an uninvited army enter the valley.[62]

Young left with the first group of evacuees, traveling the forty miles to Provo on April 1. Within days the narrow road out of the Salt Lake Valley toward Provo was clogged with Mormon families and their teams and wagons. Simply transporting Young's own personal property was a massive undertaking; his workers carefully inventoried and packed up several tons of clothing, furniture, foodstuffs, church publications, and even one harp and two trombones. Given the close proximity to Salt Lake City, he and many other church members shuttled back and forth between their new and former homes over the next two months. Before deciding whether they would move farther south, Young awaited word from Mormon expeditions into the western desert and for a more detailed report of the army's intentions. Meanwhile, he planned the construction of a series of houses in Provo for his family, sending urgent letters to Daniel Wells requesting nails, posts, and other building supplies. "[M]y heth [health] has improved fast scence I left home," he wrote Wells. "[Y]ou would think so if you could see me runing over this town to day." During the 1846 exodus, Young had proven himself a capable leader amid constant challenges, and it was exhilarating for him to oversee a similar operation a decade later. "I had not finished my house [in Salt Lake City] until I wanted to leave it and build better," he stated in June. "I'm a man of enterprize."[63]

As the Mormons began their evacuation, new governor Alfred Cumming accepted an invitation from Young (made via Kane) to visit Salt Lake and claim his office without an army escort. Kane believed that if the Mormons welcomed Cumming it would undercut the rationale for the army's presence. Cumming quickly warmed to the idea of saving lives on both sides by establishing a cordial relationship with the Mormons. Army officers complained that Cumming had been "fooled by this nincompoop [Kane]." Kane and Cumming, each accompanied by one black servant, were escorted down Echo Canyon by Porter Rockwell and a Nauvoo Legion detachment. Having "caught the fish," Kane told Young upon their arrival, "now you can cook it as you have a mind to."[64]

Young proved a skillful chef. Church leaders sized up Cumming as a corpulent alcoholic of limited intelligence, fortitude, and morals. George A. Smith's first impression of Cumming was that "he had more chops than brains," and Young soon heard rumors of Cumming's alleged lechery. While Young extended every official courtesy to the new governor, Young instructed church leaders to give him a reception "cold enough to freeze peaches." Young pointedly informed Cumming that he "would rather burn everything he had than submit to them [the army] five minutes." Afterward, he observed that Cumming "desired the destruction of this people." Young hoped the governor would appraise the situation and quickly decide to return east.[65]

Cumming, who dearly wanted to make his appointment viable, was not easily discouraged. Though he was taken aback by the ongoing evacuation, Cumming persisted in efforts to win over his skeptical new constituents, and he remained in Salt Lake City and the vicinity for the next month. During this time, Kane and Mormon leaders carefully managed his movements and interactions. Young ordered the reopening of the city's *Globe* restaurant for Cumming and any associates, specifying that it was to be staffed "*exclusively* with *male help.*"[66] Kane continued his efforts to widen the divide between Cumming on the one hand and Johnston and more antagonistic appointees on the other. By May, Kane was drafting some of Cumming's letters to Washington.

On April 25, church leaders invited the new governor to address a Sunday congregation. Cumming, it turned out, was no more adroit than Justice Perry Brocchus had been seven years earlier in a similar setting. While Cumming quickly reassured the Mormons that he would not interfere with their "social habits," he offered to assist any persons who had been constrained in their desire to leave the territory. "He also appealed to the *Women*," recorded Hosea Stout, "as he called them to back him up [and] said that he depended on them for support." Like most outsiders, Cumming presumed Mormon women were discontented members of polyga-

mous unions. None other than Young's wife Augusta Adams arose to dis-
abuse the new governor of that notion. Privately, Augusta had repeatedly
demanded freedom from what she considered Young's neglect. She now
declared that she had "known nothing but liberty since I have been
here."[67]

Cumming received other and stronger indications of Mormon unity and
determination. Gilbert Clements, a Mormon merchant, mocked Cumming's comment that the army would protect the people from the Indians,
and while he appreciated Cumming's stated desire to tolerate polygamy, he
pointedly reminded the Georgian that anything else would be akin to the
national government meddling with southern slavery. Apostle John Taylor,
probably by prior arrangement, became so incensed in his comments that
Young intervened to encourage him to "not be so personal in your remarks
[to Cumming]." Thousands of Latter-day Saints shouted their approval
when Taylor insisted that *those troops must be withdrawn before we can
have any officers palmed upon us!*" "The whole of the congregation," recorded one of Young's office clerks, "was enthusiastic in denouncing any
other authority than Brighams and his associates." When Young followed
Taylor with calming words about his "friend Governor Cumming," the
latter surely breathed a sigh of relief. When Young affirmed that had it not
been for his influence over the people, they would have destroyed Johnston's army, Cumming believed him. During the afternoon's tabernacle
meeting, Young mentioned the possibility of moving to a "fine country in
the north of Mexico [Sonora]." According to a clerk, church leaders made
sure Cumming received a report of Young's comment before nightfall.
Cumming had heard rumors of a Mormon exodus out of the country;
coupled with the Move South, they made Cumming fear that he would be
a governor without a people.[68]

The new governor now swallowed Kane and Young's gambit wholeheartedly. "I can do nothing here without your influence," Cumming quite
realistically conceded to Young, and he did everything in his power to gain
that influence.[69] In a letter to Speaker of the House of Representatives
James Orr, drafted by Kane, Cumming now identified Young as the "head
of the peace party" and even surmised that some Mormons "hate him
[Young], in consequence perhaps of his pacific measures." The previous
fall, Cumming had threatened Young with the "penalties awarded to traitors." Now he praised his gubernatorial predecessor as a man of peace.
Assisted by Kane, Young and Cumming established some mutually benefi-
cial common ground. Young would not impede the army's entrance into
the valley, though he refused to abandon the Move South until certain
of the army's intentions. Cumming, for his part, promised to shield the

church from any unwarranted army actions and from Chief Justice Delana Eckels's grand jury. Kane's far-fetched stratagem had succeeded brilliantly.[70]

For all practical purposes, Cumming became Young's deferential junior partner in the church president's attempt to check the power of the army and other administration appointees. In May, Young reported dreaming of an "exceeding friendly" Governor Cumming. "[W]e must be united," Cumming told his predecessor, "we must act in concert." After this brief discussion, Young related, Cumming "commenced undressing himself to go to bed with him."[71] Even in his dreams, Young seemed assured of Cumming's friendship and subordination.

General Johnston (he had received a promotion to brevet brigadier general), meanwhile, seethed over the concord established by these strange political bedfellows and waited impatiently to complete his army's march to Salt Lake City. Thus, Cumming's political alliance with Mormon leaders did not end the standoff. Young remained uneasy about the army's plans and the possibility of treason trials for himself and other church leaders. By mid-May, Young had ruled out a further retreat to the inhospitable landscape of the Great Basin's western desert, but church members continued to vacate the capital and points north, swelling Provo and other Utah County settlements.

Especially after Cumming's April embrace of Mormon leaders, more church members questioned the necessity of the burdensome evacuation, and a number of disaffected Mormons took advantage of the governor's offer to escort them to Camp Scott. Others dragged their feet and remained in Salt Lake or the northern settlements. After three years of unremitting hardship and turmoil, beginning with the failed crops of 1855 and stretching through the reformation into the present crisis, some Mormons lost their confidence in Brigham Young and their faith in the church. "Many was Apostatizing Daily from us," wrote Henry Ballard, a member of the Nauvoo Legion. Young, though, still refused to relent. Presuming that the soldiers intended to plunder the city and rape its women, Young hoped that "burning the city would reduce inducement for the army to come into Utah." Even if Johnston respectfully sheltered his soldiers at a distance from any Mormon settlement, the completion of the Move South would demonstrate the unity and obedience of the Saints and register a visible protest against Buchanan's Utah policy. Young's only stated regret was the potential loss of the Salt Lake City temple's foundation. Despite some defections and considerable grumbling, most Mormons followed orders. Young later claimed that the evacuations "prove the people were willing to move when they were told."[72]

The Mormons never lit their torches. On the heels of the interventions from Kane and Cumming, other surprising developments helped end the standoff. Unbeknownst to all parties in Utah until early June, Buchanan had chosen to seek a peace roughly along the lines Young, Kane, and Cumming had already discussed. In April, the president issued a proclamation that promised a vigorous military campaign against continued Mormon resistance but also offered "a free and full pardon to all who will submit themselves to the authority of the federal government."[73] It was simultaneously an ultimatum and an olive branch. Buchanan would enforce federal sovereignty, but he did not want to prosecute an expensive and potentially unpopular war against the Mormons, nor did he want to make martyrs of Young and other leaders by trying them for treason.

On June 7, two "peace commissioners" arrived in a mostly deserted Salt Lake City to announce the president's terms to Mormon leaders. They were former Kentucky governor Lazarus Powell and former Texas Ranger Ben McCulloch. In the spring of 1857, McCulloch had been Buchanan's first choice as Utah's new governor, a dubious honor he promptly declined.[74] The commissioners refused to discuss either the merits of Buchanan's accusations against the Mormons or their history of persecution. Although they gave assurances of the army's intention to respect the settlements, they informed Young that the president's offer was nonnegotiable. If church leaders accepted the pardon, there would be no trials for Utah War offenses, but otherwise the commissioners could not restrain the judges' future intentions.[75]

It was not easy for Young to embrace the offer. Like many white Americans who lived among actual slaves, Young feared political subordination and equated it with a state of slavery. "I would rather live in those rocks, and eat roots," he told the commissioners, "than be a miserable slave to their [the army's] whims." Young allowed that the Nauvoo Legion had burned army supply trains and plundered the army's cattle, but he otherwise protested his innocence and that of his coreligionists. Nevertheless, he accepted Buchanan's terms. "If a man comes from the moon and says he will pardon me for kicking him in the moon yesterday," he joked, "I don't care about it; I'll accept of his pardon." He made clear that he expected the army to quarter itself at some distance from the city, and he would never put himself at the mercy of a hostile judge's court. "Our necks shall not be given to the halter," he said at a breakfast with the peace commissioners the next day.[76]

It had taken several months to complete the process, but Young had slowly backed away from the precipice. As the church president had made clear on several occasions, he had no interest in a glorious defeat, a last stand like that made at the Alamo or like that which George Custer would make some twenty years later. As Joseph Smith had done in Missouri and Young himself had done in Nauvoo, Young ultimately chose to make a strategic retreat rather than to fight a hopeless battle.

On June 13, Johnston's resupplied and reinforced army resumed its march and prepared to fight its way down Echo Canyon if necessary. Two weeks later, the troops and their camp followers spent an entire day passing through the empty streets of Salt Lake City. The absence of fighting and the lack of either cheering or even sullen crowds lent a hollow air to the army's triumph. The soldiers built Camp Floyd, named for Secretary of War John B. Floyd, forty miles away from Salt Lake City. At the time, it was the nation's largest military garrison.

Young refused to acknowledge the war's conclusion as a defeat. "They gloat over it as having obtained a victory," Young wrote the day of the army's march through the capital, but "we consider them badly whipped." After an overnight carriage ride, Young quietly arrived back at his Beehive House mansion on July 1. According to a church clerk, Young kept "all his gates closed & locked & bolted & has a guard on his door at the East entrance where people are admitted." Young remained largely secluded for weeks, fearful of legal prosecution and lynch law and quite possibly despondent over the war's outcome. "President Young," church clerk Robert Campbell wrote in late July, "still keeps sentinels at his East entrance, and is not seen outside of his walls." Young had failed in his attempt to exclude the army and nonresident federal appointees from the territory. "When a sufficient power was put on foot to put success beyond all doubt," bragged Secretary of War Floyd in his 1858 annual report, "their bluster and bravado sank into whispers of terror and submission." Stripped of his political offices, with events having proved his defiance futile, he returned as a survivor but not as a victor.[77]

NEITHER Brigham Young nor James Buchanan gained very much from the Utah War. Buchanan had sent thousands of troops to Utah to install a governor, but the Mormons would not accept the legitimacy of outside rulers. Utah's Latter-day Saints had not abandoned either polygamy or their theocratic claims, both of which made them continued objects of fascination, suspicion, and outrage to many other Americans. Moreover, while Buchanan had asserted federal sovereignty over Utah, deep divisions over slavery and westward expansion continued to imperil the Union itself. Three years later, a number of individuals who had joined together to subdue the Mormons would fight each other.

Although Buchanan's pardon saved the church and its leaders from more severe consequences, Mormon resistance had been costly. Mormon leaders temporarily ended nearly all emigration from Europe to Utah, the church called home missionaries, and Young directed Latter-day Saints living in California to relocate to Utah. Young's Y.X. Carrying Company, which church members had helped establish through donations of property, collapsed with the administration's cancellation of its mail contract. Militia service, the ban on the sale of foodstuffs and ammunition to 1857 emigrant trains, and the Move South's interruption of the 1858 growing season all contributed to massive economic hardship. Hard money became so scarce in the territory during the military conflict that the church introduced the Deseret Currency Association and printed its own banknotes, which were secured by several large herds of horses and cattle. Young incurred some losses, but Utah's many impoverished citizens bore the economic brunt of his decision to resist the army's approach.[78]

At best, the Mormon actions against the expedition in 1857 bought Young enough time to make Buchanan wary of taking any measures that would precipitate fighting and bloodshed. Young defended his resistance on that ground. The "check which the Army received," he argued in an October 1858 letter to Stewart Van Vliet, "evinced to the people that we were in earnest and would not tamely submit to being used up [killed] at the dictation of anonymous and lying scribblers."[79] Furthermore, he later told a Mormon congregation that without Mormon resistance, the army "would have strung up you and I."[80] While it is hardly evident that Mormon resistance was decisive in the army's failure to reach Salt Lake City in the fall of 1857, the winter's pause in the expedition's advance meant that Kane's intervention, the Mormon courtship of Cumming, and word of Buchanan's proffered pardon all reached the city before the troops. For the remainder of his term, Buchanan supported Cumming's attempts to curb the threat of judicial investigations into a host of matters ranging from polygamy to the Mountain Meadows Massacre. Stiffer than expected Mormon resistance had embarrassed Buchanan politically, perhaps dissuading him from embracing measures that would have produced renewed confrontation with church leaders. For the time being, with the army camped forty miles from Salt Lake City, a sympathetic, sometimes inebriated governor, and a hesitant administration in Washington, Young still wielded *de facto* control over many territorial affairs.

Nevertheless, the Utah War heralded the eventual end of Mormon theocracy in Utah. Cumming and Buchanan would depart from the scene in 1861, and what Young termed the "Black Republican" Party would hold power in Washington. The Republicans had fewer qualms about taking federal action against polygamy and church control of Utah politics. Buchanan had reaffirmed the right of the federal government to appoint the territory's officers and judges and place troops wherever it deemed necessary. Future administrations would eventually wield those powers, especially after the Civil War further scuttled the concept of popular sovereignty. The Mormon quest for political autonomy, while not fully over, had suffered a crippling blow from which it would never recover. In the same way, while Young retained much of his authority within the Utah Territory and still contended against federal sovereignty, he would never again be quite the same man and leader who had called out his troops to block the advance of Johnston's army.

CHAPTER ELEVEN

Let Him Alone

Fight on, 'til all your *men* be dead
And Mormon saints your *widows* wed!
—ANONYMOUS, *MORMONIAD* (1858)

B Y LEADING the Latter-day Saints across the Rocky Mountains, colonizing a large swath of the American West, and bringing Utah into
armed confrontation with the U.S. Army, Brigham Young had become
a figure of national and even international renown. Mormonism was
famous—more accurately, infamous—as America's homegrown religion.
When Philip Schaff, a theologian and church historian, returned to his native Germany, he lamented that "concerning nothing have I been more
frequently asked in Germany, than concerning the primeval forests and the
Mormons—the oldest and newest products of America." Exposés of Mormon domestic life, books that chronicled trips through the Utah Territory,
and attempts to debunk the new religion's founding scripture all sold well.
"Well we are a curiosity ain't we?" Young allowed.[1]

In 1861, Samuel Clemens—soon to become known as Mark Twain—
spent two days in Salt Lake City and later penned a mostly good-humored
account of its most famous citizen. Twain was en route to Nevada, accompanying his brother Orion, that territory's first secretary. The writer later
recalled that Young largely ignored him in favor of his brother and several
more important dignitaries. "When the audience was ended and we were
retiring from the presence," he wrote in *Roughing It* (1872), "he put his
hand on my head, beamed down on me in an admiring way and said to my
brother: 'Ah—your child, I presume? Boy or girl?'" Although the meeting
took place, Twain's reconstruction was probably fanciful. Then, using a

fictional Gentile as his "unreliable" source, Twain targeted Mormon polygamy. He portrayed a husband beset with anxiety over his wives' materialistic demands and confused over the identities of his progeny. Twain's account culminated with Young embarking on a misguided attempt at marital frugality:

> Bless you, sir, at a time when I had seventy-two wives in this house, I groaned under the pressure of keeping thousands of dollars tied up in seventy-two bedsteads when the money ought to have been out at interest; and I just sold out the whole stock, sir, at a sacrifice, and built a bedstead seven feet long and ninety-six feet wide. But it was a failure, sir. I could *not* sleep. It appeared to me that the whole seventy-two women snored at once. The roar was deafening. And then the danger of it! That was what I was looking at. They would all draw in their breath at once, and you could actually see the walls of the house suck in.

The portrait of the polygamous bedstead became a staple of anti-Mormon humor, utilized by the satirical *Puck* to lampoon Young's grieving widows after his death. As he conceded in *Roughing It*, Twain had received only a superficial impression of Young's personality and habits. The church president, according to other sources, slept alone.[2]

Despite its author's wit (the humorist declared the *Book of Mormon* "chloroform in print" and deemed it a miracle that Joseph Smith had remained awake while translating it), *Roughing It* also contained more serious material. Twain included two appendices, the first a rather inaccurate summation of Mormon history which included the claim that Young had impersonated the martyred Smith to win affirmation as the prophet's successor. A religious iconoclast himself, Twain took issue not with Mormon theology but with Brigham Young's political power. He described the church president as a theocratic "absolute monarch" who defied the will of the U.S. government. The second appendix used a dubious source to allege that Young had used a purported revelation to order the massacre at Mountain Meadows. For Twain and for many Americans, Young was simultaneously an object of mockery and a cause for alarm.[3]

Even before the Utah War, popular fascination with Mormonism had fueled sales of the pseudonymous, mostly fictional, and wildly popular *Female Life among the Mormons,* purportedly written by "the wife of a Mormon elder" named Maria Ward. The novel portrayed Young as a cunning impostor, who believed in Mormonism only as a "fable" he could "make profitable to himself." Ward's Young blunders his way across the American continent, steals beautiful girls from younger men, and encourages his fellow patriarchs to confine women in cellars to prevent their escape to the States. Similar in tone to popular anti-Catholic works of fiction, anti-Mormonism became a niche genre in American literature.[4]

A few authors made more serious efforts to explain the church president's personality and leadership. "Few men can persist in believing him a hypocrite," wrote John Hyde after leaving the church in 1856, "after hearing him thus pray, either in his family, or in private meetings, or in public." Hyde, who suggested that Young's sincerity made him more dangerous than Joseph Smith, identified Young's bona fide enthusiasm for Mormonism as "the real reason of Brigham's triumph." Some careful non-Mormon observers reached that same conclusion. Richard Burton, a British explorer who published an account of his 1860 stay in Utah, termed Young "the St. Paul of the New Dispensation: true and sincere." Both Burton and Horace Greeley, the influential editor of the *New York Tribune* who interviewed Young during an 1859 visit to Utah, found him unprepossessing, forthright, and without a trace of fanaticism. "In appearance," wrote Greeley, "he is a portly, frank, good-natured, rather thick-set man of fifty-five, seeming to enjoy life, and be in no particular hurry to get to heaven." Hoping to gain valuable Gentile advocates for himself and the church, Young smoothed his rougher edges for such distinguished guests.[5]

As both Greeley and Burton perceived, Young's character and personality were far more complex than most caricatures suggested. His public discourses were often crude, rambling, and full of bluster, but in private they experienced a different man. "In council," wrote John Hyde, "he is calm, deliberate, and very politic; neither hastily decided, nor easily moved when decided." "His followers deem him an angel of light," Burton observed, "his foes a goblin damned." Most representatives of the U.S. government who held office in Utah sharply inclined toward the latter view, but enough assessed him more positively to muddy the political waters. Moreover, many of Young's close associates experienced both the angel and the goblin. Young excoriated fellow church leaders in public, then salved their wounds with private tenderness. Living with those contradictions, many of his followers craved his approval even as they feared his fury.[6]

In October 1859, Governor Alfred Cumming discussed the difficulties of his office with Latter-day Saint writer and editor William Phelps. Cumming pronounced the Mormons "a damned *hard set*," but he averred that he "got along well enough . . . by 'minding my own business.'"[7] Partly because of Cumming's embrace of that simple creed, Young had escaped the most dire possible outcomes of the Utah Expedition. Political conflicts occurred with some regularity, but Washington simply deferred their resolution, giving Young a renewed opportunity to direct Utah's politics with relative impunity.

Still, it was not a return to the early and mid-1850s. Young complained

Alfred P. Cumming, ca. early 1860s *(courtesy of Church History Library, The Church of Jesus Christ of Latter-day Saints)*

that the infusion of non-Mormon soldiers and camp followers had produced a corresponding increase in crime. Within months of the war's conclusion, Young began complaining about a Gentile "clique" that included U.S. Indian Agent Garland Hurt, U.S. Surveyor David Burr, U.S. Marshal Peter Dotson, the new federal judges, and several merchants. In conversations and letters, Young accused the clique of seeking to foment discord so that its members might continue "sucking government pap." The army and the "clique" on the one hand and church leaders and their few allies on the other hand regarded each other with mutual hostility and suspicion. Symbolic of the new reality was the November 1858 launch of the anti-Mormon newspaper *Valley Tan,* a name applied to the territory's home manufactures, beginning with shoe leather "tanned in the valley" and later applied to the output of local distilleries. Young stated that the paper did not merit the Saints' attention, but the venom of his private comments directed at the "miserable little sheet" suggests otherwise. Although still small, the territory's non-Mormon population had reached a critical mass, enabling non-Mormon merchants and other residents to threaten Mormon economic and cultural hegemony.[8]

The most immediate political threat to Young and other church leaders came from the territory's three federal judges—Chief Justice Delana Eckels and his associates Charles Sinclair and John Cradlebaugh. Having made plans at Fort Bridger to prosecute Mormon leaders for both treason and polygamy, Eckels temporarily left the territory after realizing how difficult it would be to actually secure convictions. Sinclair, a Virginian whom Young derided as the "baby Judge," persevered a bit longer. In November 1858, he convened a grand jury. Partly because church leaders denied they had committed any treasonous acts, Sinclair informed his grand jurors that he would not "take Judicial cognisance" of Buchanan's pardon. Instead, he would investigate acts of treason—a capital crime, he reminded his grand jury—committed before and during the war, and he also planned to prosecute Mormon polygamy. In addition, Sinclair heard a case against James Ferguson, accused of slandering and intimidating George Stiles, a former justice and church member. After church leaders had accused Stiles of adultery and excommunicated him in December 1856, vigilantes had burned his legal books and papers in a privy. Stiles fled the territory early the next spring.[9]

During the grand jury investigation of Ferguson, Sinclair subpoenaed Young, whom the judge suspected of masterminding Stiles's travails. Church leaders feared that Sinclair wished to find a way to get Young to Camp Floyd, where he might be killed, either judicially or by an army mob. The church president grudgingly appeared in Sinclair's Salt Lake City courtroom, one of his first public appearances since the army's march through the city. A number of church hierarchs, armed with "pistols and knives," accompanied Young to the courtroom. "During the greater portion of the time," wrote a correspondent to the *New York Times,* "he rested his head upon his hand, and his countenance wore a careworn, melancholy expression." Young never testified, and a Mormon-dominated jury ultimately acquitted Ferguson. The church president observed that "there had not been a Judge in Utah, that had been so completely taken up and set down on his arse in the mud, and had his ears pissed into as Judge Sinclair had been." The judge left the territory in 1859.[10]

While Sinclair had devoted much of his time and resources to a relatively inconsequential case, no responsible federal judge could ignore crimes like the Mountain Meadows Massacre or unpunished murders like those committed in Springville during the Mormon reformation. At first glance,

Judge Cradlebaugh seemed like an unlikely man to take on such cases. On his way to Utah, he crossed paths with the departing Chief Justice Eckels, whom he found irrationally anti-Mormon. In early November, the bedraggled and mildly frostbitten Cradlebaugh reached Ephraim Hanks's way station to the east of Salt Lake City. "The Judge has the appearance of being an ox driver," reported Hanks. "[H]e was very roughly dressed, has only one eye, but that is a very good one." In contrast to Eckels, Cradlebaugh suspected that the Mormons had been misrepresented by their opponents. His one good eye soon perceived enough unpunished injustice in the Utah Territory to change his mind.[11]

Taking up quarters at Camp Floyd, Cradlebaugh heard testimony about the 1857 Parrish-Potter murders in Springville and several other unsolved crimes in Utah Country. He also intended to investigate the Mountain Meadows Massacre. In January 1859, the territorial legislature redrew Utah's judicial boundaries and relocated Cradlebaugh's district court to Carson Valley in present-day Nevada, meaning that neither the Parrish-Potter murders nor the massacre would remain under his jurisdiction. The redistricting would not take effect until May 1, though, so the undeterred judge proceeded with his planned investigation. Believing that friendly witnesses would need protection and hostile witnesses and suspects would need coercion, he asked the army to provide an escort for his court. General Johnston, fuming over a church he described to his superiors as "at war with the freedom and morals" of the United States, happily obliged. Thus in March 1859, Cradlebaugh and several companies of the U.S. Army's Tenth Infantry took up quarters in Provo. For Young and other church leaders, these developments confirmed their worst fears about the true intent of the Utah Expedition.[12]

Suspicious that crimes had gone unpunished because of the complicity of the church hierarchy, Cradlebaugh aimed his judicial hooks at big fish rather than small fry. In his charge to the grand jury, the judge alleged that both the Mountain Meadows Massacre and the Parrish-Potter murders were sanctioned by "some person high in the estimation of the people." Church leaders privately worked to undermine his proceedings. "We learn of one nerve here in Provo that is shrinking a little," George A. Smith informed Young, in reference to a potential grand juror or witness. "I will try & poultice it." Some Mormons, though, willingly if fearfully testified. Orrin Parrish, despite predicting his "head would sure be cut off" if he traveled half a mile outside of town, identified some of his father and brother's killers to the grand jury.[13]

It was all to no avail. Despite the assistance of fresh arrivals from Camp Floyd, Cradlebaugh could not corral his most prominent suspects. He sent marshals to arrest Bishop Warren Snow of Manti in connection with the Thomas Lewis castration, but Snow evaded arrest. Cradlebaugh later complained of a "general stampede" as alleged criminals and witnesses fled into the mountains. "There seems to be a combined effort on the part of the community," he complained to his grand jury, "to screen the murderers from the punishment due them." Sneering at the uncooperative grand jurors, the judge informed them that he would refuse to prosecute "gentiles" and Indians whom Mormons accused of crimes. Instead, he told them, he would "turn the savages in custody loose upon you." Church leaders, in turn, accused their judicial enemies of bribing and coaching witnesses in order to obtain damaging testimony. Cradlebaugh dismissed his grand jury, and the army escorted his few remaining prisoners to Camp Floyd in early April.[14]

As April proceeded, rumors swirled around Salt Lake City that Johnston would send troops to occupy the capital and arrest Young. The suspicions were mutual, for the Nauvoo Legion's surveillance operation sparked army fears of Mormon raids. Young had been willing to attend Sinclair's court in Salt Lake City, but he feared appearing before what he termed Cradlebaugh's "Star-Chamber" at Camp Floyd, believing that he would fall prey to a military lynch mob. Church clerks began packing up ecclesiastical records, and Young renewed talk of laying waste to the territory's property. Young called on Governor Cumming and implored him to take a firm stand against the army. When Cumming cautioned Young that he could not openly defy the army, Young explained that his faith mandated resistance to military or political oppression. "My religion is true," he stated to Cumming, his eyes tearing up as he spoke, "and I am determined to obey its precepts, while I live. . . . I love my religion above all things else." Composing himself, Young made it clear to Cumming that he would not back down: "I will not be nosed about by the military, and *I will not go into their Camp alive.*" The crisis soon passed. Johnston regarded Young as a traitor, but he did not intend to precipitate a war by attempting to arrest the church president.[15]

Cradlebaugh decided to use the weeks before his reassignment to make arrests in connection with the Mountain Meadows Massacre. Escorted by another military detachment, his party traveled south to investigate the massacre site. According to U.S. Army Captain Reuben Campbell, the party observed "human skulls, bones, and hair, scattered about, and scraps of clothing of men, women, and children."[16] From Cedar City, the judge issued warrants for the arrest of forty alleged perpetrators, most of whom had already fled.

Then, Cradlebaugh's quest for justice came to an abrupt and unexpected halt. In response to complaints from Cumming, President Buchanan had decided that only the territorial governor could request army escorts for judicial investigations. "Our judicial system does not prosper under military protection," he chided justices Cradlebaugh and Sinclair, "and was not made to be backed by bayonets." U.S. Attorney General Jeremiah Black informed the judges that they should merely try "the cases brought before them" and leave prosecutorial discretion to the district attorney.[17] The Buchanan administration's decision was a thorough vindication of Cumming, a humiliation for the justices, and a welcome reprieve for Young. When Cradlebaugh grudgingly relocated to Carson Valley, Young rejoiced at the departure of his *"one eyed enemy."*[18]

Even though they had issued a severe rebuke to Cradlebaugh and Sinclair, members of the Buchanan administration wanted the territory's U.S. district attorney, Alexander Wilson, to identify and prosecute the perpetrators of the Mountain Meadows Massacre. Black instructed Wilson that the massacre merited his "special attention" and expressed his frustration that the ringleaders remained at large. U.S. Indian Agent Jacob Forney and several military officers had provided Washington with roughly accurate accounts claiming that John D. Lee and other local Mormon leaders had orchestrated an attack on the Fancher-Baker train, negotiated the emigrants' surrender, and then slaughtered its members. Forney cited Jacob Hamblin, a Mormon missionary to the Paiutes, and his wife as witnesses who could incriminate Lee, Isaac Haight, and six other men. Meanwhile, accounts of the massacre continued to appear in newspapers across the country. President Buchanan was concerned enough to question Thomas Kane about the matter, leading Kane to press Young to provide him with affidavits and evidence about the massacre.[19]

In the summer of 1859, Chief Justice Delana Eckels, having returned to Utah, planned to seek indictments in the massacre, even without a military escort. According to Eckels, Young had offered his assistance if someone other than the judge would select the jurors and if a church member executed the writs. Eckels refused, in his words, to make terms "with criminals." When the judge held court at Nephi, jurors fled, and Eckels proceeded with a grand jury composed primarily of non-Mormon camp followers. With no ability to make arrests in southern Utah, Eckels gave up, concluding that District Attorney Wilson's cozy relationship with the church neutered his passion for justice. The judge informed his superiors in Washington that "an Attorney who understood his business and would try, could show that Brigham Young directed the Mountain Meadow massacre."[20]

The investigations of judges Cradlebaugh and Eckels probably enhanced

Young's desire for the full extent of Mormon leadership and participation in the massacre to remain shrouded. Young did not impose ecclesiastical sanction on those who had organized, led, and condoned the massacre. Haight, Lee, and the many others involved in planning and carrying out the murders remained church members in good standing. Haight resigned his stake presidency in 1859, while William Dame retained his positions in Parowan. Moreover, Young continued to bestow fatherly attention on Lee, who he knew had been "on the ground" at Mountain Meadows. Lee became the presiding elder of the small southern Utah settlement of Harmony in December 1861, a position he held for the next three years. Despite knowledge to the contrary, Young still placed the full blame for the slaughter on the Paiutes, and he callously complained about the "farcical" expense of a government escort that returned the young children who survived the massacre to relatives in the East. In his desire to protect the church and himself, Young decided that the risks of full disclosure outweighed those of inaction. Severe ecclesiastical punishment of the perpetrator would probably have produced tale-bearers, and grand jury investigations and trials would have inevitably reopened questions about his wartime rhetoric, martial law proclamation, and Overland Trail policy.[21]

In May 1861, Young went to Mountain Meadows and looked at the makeshift monument that members of the U.S. Army under Major James Carleton had constructed in memory of the massacre victims. On top of a twelve-foot mound of rocks, a wooden cross bore an inscription from the New Testament epistle to the Romans: "Vengeance is mine; I will repay, saith the Lord." Young probably took offense at the suggestion that the Latter-day Saints merited divine wrath. According to fellow traveler Wilford Woodruff, Young suggested that it should read, "Vengence is mine and I have taken a little." God had punished the emigrants, either for their own misdeeds or for the misdeeds of other Gentiles.[22]

Several sources assert that members of Young's party destroyed the monument. Dudley Leavitt, then a resident of southern Utah, later told his sons that Young ordered the monument's destruction: "He didn't give an order. He just lifted his right arm to the square, and in five minutes there wasn't one stone left upon another." There is some corroborating evidence for Leavitt's recollection, though not his dramatic details. In the early 1890s, Samuel Knight told Andrew Jenson, an employee of the Church Historian's Office, that the monument had been desecrated, "perhaps by som[e] of Prest Youngs company." These accounts are probably inaccurate. Edwin Purple, a non-Mormon mail agent, led a party of stagecoaches from Los Angeles to Salt Lake City that same spring and detoured to visit the massacre site. Purple recorded seeing the monument, and his visit came after Young's company had returned north. A massive flood the following winter might have been responsible for the monument's destruction.[23]

Even if he did not order the monument's destruction, Young's words on his 1861 trip south denigrated the massacre's victims and defended the Mormon murderers. Young visited Harmony and spoke in John D. Lee's "family hall" and also spoke privately with Lee, who recorded the church president's statements on the massacre: "Pres. Young Said that the company that was used up at the Mountain Meadowes were the Fathers, Mothe[rs], Bros., Sisters & connections of those that Muerders the Prophets; they Merritd their fate, & the only thing that ever troubled him was the lives of the Women & children, but that under the circumstances [this] could not be avoided. Although there had been [some] that wantd to betreyed the Brethrn into the hands of their Enimies, for that thing [they] will be Damned & go down to Hell."[24] Young's callous justification of the deaths of unarmed men, women, and children resembled the way that many white Americans of his time responded to white massacres of Indian villages. It is possible, of course, that Lee's own desire for Young's approbation and protection influenced what he heard and recorded. At the same time, Lee's statement represents an expansion of the sentiment Young had expressed at the monument itself. By 1861, Young knew that Mormons bore responsibility for the crime and wanted to make sure that their fellow church members shielded them from prosecution. For Young, everything else was secondary to the preservation of the church, including the standards of morality the Latter-day Saints usually shared with other mid-nineteenth-century Americans.

THE failure of the judicial investigations marked the true end of the Utah War and left Young feeling considerably more secure. As news of the administration's position reached Utah in May, Young reemerged from a yearlong absence at the church's meetings. "I am yet alive," he joked. "More than that, I ain't half dead."[25]

Still, Young contended with his own physical frailties as he reached his sixtieth birthday. In the early 1860s, dentists gradually pulled a large number of decayed teeth from his mouth, leaving Young to wonder whether the extractions would hinder his ability to speak clearly. Eventually, a dentist removed his few remaining molars and made him a set of false teeth. Young also suffered from rheumatism, complained of "tic doloreaux" (a neuralgia involving severe facial pain), became corpulent (a forty-five-inch waist in 1864) and somewhat stooped, and endured urological problems. Privately, he seemed at peace with his physical decline. Young candidly discussed cures for such ailments as "deranged" (i.e., constipated) bowels and hemorrhoids when he felt his remedies of choice might relieve others' discomfort. To relieve constipation, he swore by enemas of "composition" mixed with consecrated oil.[26]

Other than mentioning his tooth extractions, though, Young made few public concessions to this private reality and gave no sign of scaling back the scope of his ambitions or activities. He suggested that with "good common food," "exercise sufficient," the observance of the Word of Wisdom, and the avoidance of physicians, human beings could stave off the aging process. On occasion, Young even boasted of his continued virility. "I could find more girls who would choose me for a husband," he jested on the eve of the Utah War, "than can any of the young men." In 1862, he observed that he would reach the age of seventy in nine years. "Do you think I shall give up then?" he asked. "No. I expect my head will be as good and my intellect as bright, and my mind will be more vivid than it is to day." Perhaps Young made such boasts to reassure the Saints and himself that he possessed sufficient vigor for continued leadership.[27]

In May 1859, Young finally returned to the Salt Lake City tabernacle's pulpit and offered a theological interpretation of the past two years. While God remained faithful, Young knew that some Latter-day Saints had not. Some had left the territory after years of poor harvests or simply because what they found in Utah did not match their expectations of Zion. Church members, Young suggested, should thank God for the persecutions that had winnowed out the apostates. Proof of God's providence and favor had come through divine preservation of the church and its leaders from the U.S. Army, treason indictments, and Gentile appointees. For the next few months, Young preached regularly, mostly emphasizing central aspects of Mormon theology: the embrace of light, intelligence, and truth found in the church; the necessity for the Saints to honor their leaders and sacred covenants; and the anticipation of a millennium in which exalted Saints would achieve godhood and become "Saviours upon Mount Zion" for the remainder of the human family.

Building upon one of the emphases of Joseph Smith, Young sought to collapse the space between heaven and earth and the distance between eternity and the here-and-now. "Our religion is the foundation of all intelligence," he stated, touching on the core of his faith. "It is to bring heaven to earth and exalt earth to heaven and to prepare all intelligence that God has placed in [the] heart[s] of [the] children of man to mingle that with that intelligence that dwells in eternity." Young pointed the Saints toward their future existence on a "celestialized" earth, when they would come into "the immediate presence of the Father and the Son." The exalted Saints "shall inhabit different mansions," he foretold, "and worlds will continue to be made, formed, and organized, and messengers from this earth will be sent to others." At the same time, however, that glorious future always maintained an intimate connection with the Saints' current work. "We shall make our home here," he continued, "and go on our missions as we do now, but at greater than railroad speed." "Every faithful member of the Church of Christ," he explained several years later, "will always be found in all his earthly occupations and pursuits attending to this business of unifying ourselves."[28]

This correspondence between the Kingdom of God on earth and its future exaltation helped Young imbue the mundane tasks of kingdom-building with sacred significance. "We are not going to wait for angels," he instructed in 1862, "or for Enoch and his company to come and build up Zion, but we are going to build it." The Saints should busy themselves with the tasks at hand. "We will raise our wheat, build our houses, fence our farms, plant our vineyards and orchards, and produce everything that will make our bodies comfortable and happy, and in this manner we intend to build up Zion on the earth." The Saints' millennial glory, Young taught, depended on building their earthly Zion in preparation for Christ's return. "What are we come here for," he scrawled into an account book in 1864, "to be taught the corse we shauld persu here after." Human existence, Young believed, was a school for life eternal. By dedicating themselves to the tasks before them, church members would prepare themselves to inhabit a millennial city they were building with their own hands.[29]

Although American Protestants created a host of voluntary societies in the mid-nineteenth century to promote both evangelism and social reform, Young's efforts at kingdom-building necessitated a much higher level of collective enterprise than was customary within Protestant America. Young once identified a "gathering and social spirit" as "the order of heaven." Despite his emphasis on "absolute independen[ce]" as an integral part of godliness, the Saints' individual exaltation, economic self-sufficiency, and political sovereignty all required interdependence, not individual autonomy. As he had taught in Nauvoo, Young saw priesthood ordinances as creating a great chain of interlocking kingdoms. "[E]ach father, being a son," he explained, "will always, throughout time and eternity, be subject to his father as his king, dictator, father, Lord and God." Correspondingly, each son would become a father and receive the same eternal fealty from his posterity. "We without them cannot be made perfect," Young said. "Neither can they without us be made perfect."[30]

What was true for eternity was true on earth. Besieged by their enemies, the Latter-day Saints needed strict adherence to common goals for their survival and advancement on earth. As the territory emerged from the economic disruptions of the mid- to late 1850s, Young continued to promote home manufacture. The purchase of imported goods, he believed, gave non-Mormons economic leverage over the Saints and also exerted a corrosive cultural influence. If church members produced everything they desired, they would become "an independent people." Young finally gave up on the southern Utah Iron Mission, but he pushed forward with other initiatives. Church leaders directed hundreds of families to the territory's southern valleys—Utah's "Dixie"—to raise cotton and tobacco. Young quit his use of tobacco in 1860 (he also reduced his consumption of coffee and tea), and he calculated that home production of tobacco would keep an annual $60,000 out of the hands of non-Mormon merchants. If the Saints were going to disregard the Word of Wisdom, he argued, "we can save the money, and still break it." Despite Young's advocacy, tobacco cultivation remained limited in the territory. The colonists' efforts to grow cotton achieved some success in the early 1860s, fortuitously coinciding with the Civil War's disruption of the southern cotton market. Over the long run, though, the Cotton Mission never became self-sustaining.[31]

Young's initiatives enjoyed their share of successes as well. Perhaps the most well conceived, in terms of its promotion of both economic self-sufficiency and the church's other goals, was the "down-and-back" system of cross-Plains emigration established in 1860. Bringing converts to Zion remained a primary objective. "[A]ll Elders should understand that after baptism comes the gathering," he wrote apostles Amasa Lyman and Charles Rich, then directing the church's European Mission, ". . . and that *everything* which in the least impedes the gathering tends directly to hinder the great work in which we are engaged." The Perpetual Emigration Fund, the handcart companies, and the short-lived Y.X. Carrying Company had all failed to overcome the financial impediments to the church's gathering. Thus, Young searched for yet another plan. Beginning on a limited basis in 1860, church leaders called upon members to donate wagons, oxen, and men to send church trains east in the spring and return the same season loaded with emigrants, merchandise, and machinery. While traveling east, the "missionaries" deposited flour and other necessities at several church-owned depots along the trail. They also sold surplus Utah flour in the Midwest. On their return, they brought—in addition to emigrants—carding machines, cotton gins, and other supplies.[32]

For most of the 1860s, two or three thousand converts came to Utah each year by means of this new system of mass migration. They did not receive a free ride. The indigent borrowed the fare ($41 in 1861) from the church, though unlike the earlier PEF emigration, the church itself did not accrue much if any cash indebtedness. It was an ingenious way of using what the territory possessed—men, livestock, and a sense of common purpose—to overcome its shortage of hard money. By the time the transcontinental railroad (completed in 1869) greatly eased the financial and logistical burden of gathering, Brigham Young had presided over the organized emigration and settlement of more people than anyone else in American history.[33]

Despite the continued flow of Mormon emigrants into Zion and Young's wishes to the contrary, the Mormons found themselves economically dependent not just on each other but also on the very army they regarded as a menace. At first, Young grudgingly permitted the Saints to sell to the several thousand soldiers stationed at Camp Floyd. He then plunged into his own quite profitable trade with his former enemies. Apostle George A. Smith described the army's presence as a "regular windfall" for the Mormons, and the brisk sales of lumber and foodstuffs to the army meant an unusual influx of specie. When the army evacuated Camp Floyd (renamed Camp Crittenden) in 1861, it resold many of its purchases for a fraction of the original prices. Young, who bought through several representatives to avoid attracting attention, took advantage of the army's sale by acquiring for the church sixty tons of flour, iron, and machinery, as well as an enormous number of wagons and mules. Bringing him particular satisfaction, Young received the army's flagstaff and flag as a gift from the camp's departing colonel, Philip St. George Cooke.[34]

Despite his fear that wealth and Gentile goods and customs would corrode his people's faith, Young had no interest in presiding over an isolated backwater. Utah, as Young put it, was a natural "halfway house" between the Missouri River and California. The Pacific and Overland telegraph companies contracted with Young to construct around five hundred miles of the final line, which was joined in Salt Lake City in October 1861. The Pony Express, telegraph companies, and freighting operations all served as sources of jobs and trade for the territory. Even before the U.S. Army had settled into Camp Floyd, Young resumed his efforts to persuade Congress to route a projected transcontinental railroad through the territory. In addition to the direct economic benefits reaped from such projects, Young gained a number of powerful non-Mormon business allies, relationships that proved helpful when he faced political threats.[35]

While both attempting to stimulate home manufacture and capitalize on national economic developments, Young put the brakes on mining operations. He wanted the church to profit from any valuable mineral deposits but worried that reports of rich strikes would bring an overwhelming influx of non-Mormons to Utah. "If gold was discovered here," Young cautioned in 1861, "the gentiles might overrun us and break us up." Young's fear was well grounded. The late-1850s discovery of the Comstock Lode in Carson Valley accelerated the effort of non-Mormon settlers in Utah's western third to detach themselves from Mormon political control. Congress responded to non-Mormon appeals for political redress from alleged "Mormon Outrages" (such as the "prostitution" of women as polygamous brides and the incitement of Indian attacks) by creating the Nevada Territory in 1861. That same year, the creation of the Colorado Territory cost Utah a large amount of its easternmost land. As mining discoveries pushed east in the 1860s, Congress sliced off further portions of Utah and assigned them to Nevada, to which it granted statehood in 1864. Young warned that a Utah mining boom would "weld upon our necks chains of slavery, groveling dependence and utter overthrow." He encouraged the Saints to claim any known finds for themselves, but he wanted them to be circumspect about new discoveries. "[D]o your best," he cryptically responded to one correspondent, "to keep things dark, for it is far better to be poor than to be distroyed."[36]

Young was in no danger of poverty himself. His personal wealth continued to grow. In 1859, he told the journalist Horace Greeley that he was worth $250,000. Although one non-Mormon businessman claimed that Young possessed an "abundance of Cash means & can pay if inclined to do so," most of his wealth rested in real estate. As Trustee-in-Trust for the church, Young also oversaw a further vast array of enterprises and held much of the church's property in his own name.[37]

Young lived in the commodious Beehive House mansion, with three parlors containing space for family celebrations and social gatherings, decorated tastefully enough to impress the politicians and journalists who visited Young in Utah. Over the span of several years, he fastidiously requested his eastern business agents to purchase a carriage "of the best material and workmanship, of the latest, best most fashionable, and approved style"; carpeting made of "a good sized, well twisted thread, made of long-stapled, coarsish, good wool"; a set of opera glasses "nicely cased in *roan* calf instead of patent leather"; a dozen pairs "of best French kid gents gloves (*goatskin,* not sheepskin)"; and a grand piano. Such acquisitions announced Young's status as a gentleman of means, refinement, and status. When he showed fellow church leaders his pianos, furniture, and other domestic acquisitions, he exhibited a pride quite understandable given his modest roots.[38]

Probably in light of the stark poverty of most Utahans, Young sometimes felt the need to defend his wealth and economic power. "God heaps property upon me," he said, "and I am in duty bound to take care of it."

Questions about financial stewardship had badly damaged Joseph Smith's authority in Kirtland, and Young made it clear that he would not tolerate such criticism. "I am not to be called in question as to what I do with my funds," he instructed an 1860 tabernacle audience. Suggesting that rumblings of discontent reached his ears, though, he on several occasions rejected the notion that church tithing sustained his income or lifestyle. "[M]y private affairs are not amalgamated with the public," he explained. "Brigham Young and the Trustee-in-Trust are two persons in business . . . kept as strictly separate as is the business of any two firms in the world."[39]

Young's explanation was technically true. His clerks carefully kept accounts—often in the same ledger—for both Brigham Young as an individual and the Trustee-in-Trust. There was considerable amalgamation, however. If Young needed funds, he drew on the resources of the church before incurring debts from non-Mormon merchants. By 1865, for instance, Young had contracted a half-million dollars in debts to himself as Trustee-in-Trust. He used such funds to pay the taxes and debts of friends and indigent church members, to buy equipment for the territory's home manufacturing enterprises, and to purchase clothing, food, and tobacco for family members. In a more general sense, his wealth hinged on his ecclesiastical position, by which he had obtained choice real estate holdings and the ability to conduct nationwide business through church representatives in St. Louis and the east. The legislature had granted Young a number of concessions involving timber, herding, and water rights, all on the public domain.[40]

By the early 1860s, Young also managed a vast array of enterprises, including farms, mills, a cotton factory, and a lumberyard. He listed nearly two hundred employees in the early 1860s, and through the wages of his workers and his support of his family he provided for over one thousand individuals. Many of these workers were indebted to Young, and he often paid them in kind rather than in scarce cash. When he hired David Hilton in July 1858, Young's business manager and son-in-law Hiram Clawson noted that he was to be paid "$1.75 per day during the busy time if he works longer and times not so busy his wages to be less, he is to be paid in anything we have except cash or store pay, is promised some better clothing." Young was a fair but economical employer. In 1868, Young's clerk and reporter of church discourses George D. Watt asked him to raise his pay from $3.50 to $5.00 per day. When Young refused, Watt threatened to quit, prompting a public tongue-lashing from the church president that evening. Young would not tolerate other church members attempting to pressure him in such a manner. With Watt already heavily indebted to the church's tithing office, moreover, Young considered the request an insolent sign of ingratitude. Some church members chafed at Young's privilege and power, but many others probably saw him as an indispensable source of what prosperity the territory enjoyed. At the very least, large numbers of Latter-day Saints depended on Young for employment and depended on the church tithing stores for necessities. Later in the 1860s, the growing presence of non-Mormon merchandizing operations in Utah would test those economic bonds.[41]

For the Latter-day Saints, the outbreak of the Civil War was full of ironies. Young found it curious that President "King James" Buchanan, so eager to quell a Mormon rebellion, took no stern measures against the seceding southern states. "[I]f President Buchanan had been a smart man," said Young, "he would have hung up the first men who rebelled in South Carolina." General Johnston, once eager to use the U.S. Army to crush Mormon resistance, now fought against that same army as a rebel and died during the April 1862 Battle of Shiloh. As their former enemies turned their fury on each other, Young anticipated that the conflict would benefit the Saints. At the very least, he predicted, apparently with full seriousness, "the brethren will have many wives to take care of."[42]

Abraham Lincoln, whom Young variously termed "King Abraham," "Old Abel," and "Old Abe," suggested in his second inaugural address that God had afflicted the entire nation with the scourge of war as a just punishment for the sin of slavery. Young agreed on the divine nature of the punishment, though the sin he identified was the country's mistreatment of the Latter-day Saints. "[A]s the Jews did in killing Jesus," Young pronounced, so the U.S. government would "pay" for Joseph Smith's death. Again like Lincoln, Young observed that northerners and southerners prayed to the same God for each other's destruction. Young, though, seemed pleased with the thought that both sides might have their prayers answered. After the fighting began, he told his associates that he "earnestly prayed for the success of both North & South." The war, Young hoped, would distract the Union government from meddling in Utah affairs and finally leave the Saints to govern themselves.[43]

Young had no sympathy for either side in the Civil War. "We are not by any means treasoners, secessionists, or abolitionists," he explained in 1862. "We are neither negro-drivers nor negro-worshippers." Young still contended that there was nothing peculiar about African slavery; it was a divinely ordained institution. When he insisted to Horace Greeley in 1859 that Utah would enter the Union as a free state, though, his stance was more than political posturing. Young accepted the arguments of Hinton Rowan Helper's stridently anti-slavery *The Impending Crisis of the South,* a book that Greeley distributed across the country. While unsympathetic to the human plight of the South's slaves, Helper argued that slavery had retarded the South's economic progress and thus the prosperity of most of its white citizens. "[I]f they would abolish slavery," Young suggested along similar lines, "and institute free labor they would be much richer than they are." Like most white northerners, Young felt his society would be better off without any black people, free or enslaved.[44]

Most states and territories in the West, including California, Oregon, and especially New Mexico, contained enough Confederate sympathizers to cast their loyalty in doubt.[45] The dynamics in Utah were different. When Young and other Mormons made statements that appeared to favor the Confederacy, it was largely because they feared that Lincoln and the Republicans would turn their attention to Utah if they quickly defeated the South. Thus, Young stated that he "would be glad to hear that [Confederate] General [P. G. T.] Beauregard had taken the President & Cabinet and confined them in the South," but he made it clear that he "did not wish Utah mixed up with the secession movement." When the telegraph line reached Salt Lake City in October 1861, Young wired the president of the Pacific Telegraph Company: "Utah has not seceded, but is firm for the Constitution and laws of our once happy country." Young was careful with his language. He was "firm" for the Constitution, not for the Union or its present government. In short, Young and most of his co-religionists were simply pro-Mormon during the crisis. Mormons did not rush to enlist in the Union Army, and there were no displays of wartime fervor in Salt Lake City. Young offered "to furnish a home guard for the protection of the telegraph and mail lines and overland travel within our boundaries," but he was opposed to Mormons providing the Union with either money or manpower. "I will see them in Hell before I will raise an army for them," he declared in late 1861.[46]

With the telegraph line, wartime news came on "lightning's wing," and Young avidly discussed national affairs with other church leaders. As usual, he positioned the church for a variety of possible outcomes, centered around his desire for the Kingdom of God's autonomy. The conflict rekindled the millennial hopes Young had expressed at the outset of the Utah War. As Americans slaughtered each other, they might pave the way for the Saints' long-awaited return to Jackson County, where a New Jerusalem would arise upon the soil of the Garden of Eden. Should the nation collapse, he wrote Utah's congressional delegate William Hooper, "Utah,

Brigham Young, ca. 1864 *(courtesy of Church History Library, The Church of Jesus Christ of Latter-day Saints)*

in her rocky fastnesses . . . [would] step in and rescue the constitution."[47] After God's judgment upon the U.S. government, the Saints would emerge as the nation's unexpected saviors.

The departure of the Utah Expedition's final troops in July 1861 temporarily fulfilled Young's hopes. "They were whipped in coming to Utah," he exulted, "[and] are worse whipped in leaving." One month later, Young asked Daniel Wells to "quietly revive the Military through the Territory" by reorganizing the Nauvoo Legion's companies and by amassing guns and ammunition. As the army's threat waned, Young also resumed a more active social calendar, attending dances and parties with some frequency. In January 1861, George A. Smith reported to his fellow apostle Orson Hyde that at a recent social gathering "President Young danced as wildly as any boy till midnight." In 1862, he once attended five parties over the span of one week. Young's participation in such recreations signaled the palpable reduction of military and political tension.[48]

The Utah Territory never went for long without a fresh political crisis, however. Governor Cumming, a southern Democrat, left the territory after Lincoln's inauguration. Rumors reached Utah that the new president would appoint as his replacement Broughton Harris, one of the original 1851 appointees who had clashed with Young and then fled the territory. Young expressed his hope that "if Harris did come the boys & dogs would piss on him." Harris did not come. As governor, Lincoln chose an obscure Indiana politician, John Dawson, who managed to become the shortest-tenured governor in the territory's politically tumultuous history.[49]

The new governor, as yet unconfirmed by the U.S. Senate, promptly enraged his hosts by vetoing a legislative act calling for a convention to renew Utah's statehood petition. Church leaders intended to revive the state government they had abandoned to become a U.S. territory, hoping that the national government would accept Utah statehood as a *fait accompli*. "I will lead the people on to victory and glory if they elect me their Governor," Young asserted on December 22. "I wish we were a State and in 10 days these Gentiles will hustle out or lie low." The next day, however, church leaders learned of Dawson's veto. The governor claimed that the Utah legislature should have sought congressional approval for the planned convention and that the time frame for holding planned elections was too short. Dawson, though, subsequently admitted that he suspected the Mormons of disloyalty and wanted to block granting "the ulcer *polygamy* . . . sovereign protection." Young surely knew the nature of Dawson's actual objection to the petition. "[Y]ou take a man like him [Dawson] who has been an Editor for 15 years," said Young, "and you will find him to be a Jackass."[50]

Dawson did not long remain an obstacle. The governor, according to a church clerk, "threatened to shoot [*Deseret News* writer Thomas] Stenhouse if he publishes anything about his wishes to sleep with Tom Williams['s] Widow." Albina Williams purportedly drove the governor off with a "fire shovel" and then presented an affidavit about the incident to Young. Dawson left Salt Lake City on New Year's Eve, accompanied by a group of known ruffians. "[H]e has not selected a choice set of men," Young commented to Stenhouse. While stopping for the night at Ephraim Hanks's way station, Dawson was attacked by his traveling companions, who "beat him almost to death and drove off & left him in his gore." Rumors circulated for years that Dawson had been castrated. After recuperating, Dawson continued his journey, writing to Lincoln from Fort Bridger that he had been assaulted by "a band of [church-sanctioned] Danites." That was probably not the case. Young wanted Dawson out of the territory, not dead, and certainly not wounded and making allegations against the church hierarchy. Stenhouse, who published an exposé of Mormonism after his 1871 excommunication, suggested that church leaders had hatched a plot to entrap the disliked governor "into an offence." The attack, however, had "dreadfully annoyed" Young, who "had a greater desire to disgrace the Government in his [Dawson's] person than to see him 'whipped.'" Fortunately for Young, the Senate failed to confirm Dawson's appointment and Lincoln showed no interest in the governor's plight. Two months later, two of Lincoln's judicial appointees also left the territory.[51]

Meanwhile, the Saints moved forward with their plans for self-government. Young employed rhetoric similar to that used in the months preceding the Utah War. "If they undertake to install their officers here at the point of the bayonet as they did in '57," he warned with customary bluster, "they will not fare as well as they did then." Given their potential ability to disrupt the Overland Mail route and telegraph line, Young speculated that the Saints now posed a greater military threat to government, especially in light of the Civil War. A January 1862 statehood convention adopted a slightly modified version of the old State of Deseret constitution and nominated Young for governor in elections scheduled for March. "We will ask Congress to admit us into the family of States," Young announced. "What if they do not? We have got a Government and what are they going to do about it?"[52]

Nearly ten thousand Mormons unanimously cast their ballots for Young as Deseret's governor, and in April he delivered his first governor's message to the new state legislature. The legislators then passed an act "making the laws of the Territory of Utah in force in the State of Deseret," created a court system, and elected senators to Congress. Young emphasized that he "did not want to annul the territorial government," and although the *Deseret News* published the assembly's proceedings, the Saints did not accompany either the elections or the assembly with a public celebration as they had done in 1850. Also, unlike in 1857, Young took steps to avoid giving offense to Washington politicians. After instructing Albert Carrington to draft the memorial to Congress, he asked congressional delegate William Hooper to make sure it did not contain "any objectionable sentiments." Young moved much more cautiously than he had five years earlier.[53]

While the application for statehood was pending, Young took advantage of a welcome opportunity to demonstrate his church's wartime loyalty. In April, U.S. Army Adjutant General Lorenzo Thomas, by order of President Lincoln, sent a telegram to "Mr. Brigham Young," authorizing the church president to raise a cavalry company of approximately one hundred men to protect the Overland Mail route in northern Utah and what is now southwestern Wyoming against Indian depredations. It was an unusually explicit recognition of the true locus of political power in the territory, probably explained by the fact that Dawson's replacement had not yet reached Utah. Just three days later, Lot Smith, who had conducted raids against the U.S. Army in 1857 as a Nauvoo Legion major, led the militia company east to patrol the mail and telegraph route. In August, though, angered that the U.S. Army had decided to station a regiment of California volunteers in Utah, Young pointedly declined the army's request for Smith's men to march to Laramie. "[I]f the Government of the United States should now ask for a battalion of men to fight in the present battlefields of the nation," he explained the following spring, "while there is a camp of soldiers from abroad located within the corporate limits of this city, I would . . . see them in hell first." Thus ended Utah's only military contribution to the Civil War.[54]

By that point, it was clear that Congress had not grown any more receptive to the idea of Utah statehood. John Bernhisel, who returned to serve as territorial delegate to Congress for two years in the early 1860s, informed Young in a late February letter that he did not know of "a single member either of the Senate or of the House who will vote for the admission of our Territory into the Union as a State." Implacable opposition to Mormon polygamy, along with concerns about theocracy and the Mountain Meadows Massacre, rendered Deseret's bid entirely futile. Instead, Congress passed the Morrill Anti-Bigamy Act, which threatened polygamists with fines and imprisonment, annulled Utah's implicit legal sanction of polygamy, and, in a blatant attempt to strip the church of its economic power, ruled that no territorial religious corporation could possess more than

$50,000 in property. In a public address, Young affirmed the divine nature of polygamy and warned Congress against undertaking "to dictate the Almighty in his revelations." The next year, Young instructed his representatives in the nation's capital that he would not abandon polygamy in order to gain statehood.[55]

After Congress's rejection, the Deseret legislature continued on as a "ghost government," meeting every January in an elaborate charade to listen to Young's "governor's message" and symbolically affirm the territory's laws. Young informed the legislators that they should remain ready to assume their lawful responsibilities. "We are Called the State Legislature," Wilford Woodruff summarized Young's January 1863 message, "but when the time comes, we shall be called the Kingdom of God . . . the time will Come when these men will give laws to the Nations of the Earth."[56] The language evoked the dormant Council of Fifty's claim to constitute the political Kingdom of God upon the earth.

That kingdom would not arrive anytime soon. By July 1862, the regiment of U.S. Army soldiers—volunteers recruited in California—was on the march to Salt Lake City. The administration's primary concern was an upsurge of Indian attacks on Overland Mail stages and telegraph lines that passed through Utah, but a number of officers within the army's San Francisco–based Department of the Pacific also worried about the loyalty of Utah's Mormon population. The fact that Young—unlike in 1857—organized no military response to the new intruders revealed the hollowness of his recent rhetoric about political independence and resistance.

Colonel Patrick Edward Connor, a fiery Irish immigrant, nominal Catholic, and veteran of the U.S. war against Mexico, commanded the mixed unit of infantry and cavalry. Amid considerable competition, Connor would distinguish himself as one of the nation's foremost haters of Indians and Mormons, but the Latter-day Saints were the immediate object of his venom. Even before reaching his new post, Connor accused its Mormon population of disloyalty and warned that those who uttered "treasonable sentiments in this district . . . must seek a more genial soil, or receive the punishment they so richly merit." After a brief foray to Salt Lake City on a scouting mission, Connor declared it "a community of traitors, murderers, fanatics, and whores." He informed his superiors that Young ruled the territory with "despotic sway" and ordered the execution of those disobedient to his will. "The Federal officers," he relayed, "are entirely powerless, and talk in whispers for fear of being overheard by Brigham's spies." Rather than quarter his troops at the abandoned Fort Crittenden, Connor detoured his men through the capital and then bivouacked them on a pla-

Patrick Edward Connor, ca. 1866 *(courtesy of Library of Congress)*

teau overlooking Salt Lake City from the east. From that position, he could "say to the Saints of Utah, enough of your treason." The colonel christened his location Camp Douglas, named for the Saints' late political nemesis Stephen Douglas. Deprived of the opportunity for wartime glory on eastern battlefields, Connor grasped an unexpected chance to resolve the "Mormon question" through a display of federal power. Though he and Young apparently never met, Connor became one of Young's most persistent and creative antagonists.[57]

Shortly before Connor's encampment, Stephen Harding, an antislavery advocate from Indiana, had arrived in the territory as its new governor. Harding, whose initial sympathies for his constituents evaporated within weeks, interpreted Mormon predictions of the country's dissolution as disloyalty. The Mormons, he wrote Secretary of State William Henry Seward, anticipated that they would "step in and quietly enjoy the possession of the lands and all that is left of the ruined cities and desolated fields." Like Connor, Harding wanted the U.S. Army to use its presence to "make treason dumb." Young certainly was aware of the governor's growing antipathy. In late October, he offered his private assessment of "that thing that is here that *calls himself* Governor." "If you were to fill a sack with cow dung," Young suggested, "it would be the best thing you could do for an imitation." Harding's December 1862 message to the legislature turned Young's private derision into overt animosity. After endorsing the Emancipation Proclamation, which the *Deseret News* deemed unconstitutional, Harding warned the Mormons to abide by the federal antipolygamy law. He went so far as to express his horror that "a mother and her daughters are allowed to fulfill the duties of *wives* to the same husband." On Young's advice, the legislature refused to print the address.[58]

While Harding seethed over what he considered Mormon disloyalty, Young openly violated the Morrill Act. In January 1863, he was sealed to Amelia Folsom, the "handsome and magnetic" daughter of church-employed architect William Folsom. She was twenty-four years of age, thirty-seven years younger than her husband. The marriage surprised many in Utah, as it had been seven years since Young had taken a wife.[59]

The sealing angered at least one of Young's other wives, who penned him a caustic Valentine's Day greeting. In verse, she mentioned seeing her husband and his new consort at the stately new Salt Lake Theater and, mockingly, observed how "young" he had "grown of late." She also questioned her husband's judgment that she had "no reson to mermur." One possible candidate for the anonymous poet, who described herself as "not old, nor . . . so young," is Emmeline Free, then thirty-six years of age. On February 9, Emmeline bore Young her ninth child, a son either stillborn or who died later the same day. Until Young's marriage to Amelia, Emmeline was regarded by many observers as her husband's favorite, and several later accounts describe her as deeply wounded by Young's marriage to Amelia. At the same time, several of Young's other wives who had resented Emmeline's privileged position were quietly delighted at her displacement.[60]

The marriage to Amelia undermined some of Young's own statements about plural marriage. Probably in response to non-Mormon conceptions of Latter-day Saint polygamy, Young emphasized the spiritual underpinnings of plural marriage and downplayed the role of sexual attraction in such unions. "I never entered into the order of plurality of wives to gratify passion," Young stated in 1861. "I am almost sixty years old," he added,

Brigham Young and Amelia Folsom, ca. 1863 *(courtesy of Church History Library, The Church of Jesus Christ of Latter-day Saints)*

"and if I now live for passion, I pray the Lord Almighty to take my life from the earth." Young embraced polygamy to obey Joseph Smith, not to satisfy lust, but his was not a "Puritan polygamy." The sealing to Amelia Folsom demonstrates that attraction continued to play a role in his marital choices. Simply put, an aging Brigham Young was in love. Although Young defended polygamy as a theological imperative for "rais[ing] up a holy nation" and sometimes spoke as if wives served little purpose beyond childrearing, the fact that Amelia bore him no children did not in any way diminish his affection for her. Young's daughter Susa Young Gates later described her father's marriage to Amelia as "surely a love match."[61]

Young's relationship with Amelia became a matter of considerable gossip. Thomas and Fanny Stenhouse, Ann Eliza Young (who published an exposé of Young's family life after her acrimonious divorce from the church president), and non-Mormon reporters all published unflattering accounts of Young's attentions to Amelia. For example, Fanny Stenhouse asserted that at balls, "after dancing with each of his other wives who might be present—simply for appearance sake—the remainder of the evening was devoted to her [Amelia]." "Polygamist, as he professes to be," sighed Ann Eliza Young, "he is, under the influence of Amelia, rapidly becoming a monogamist, in all except the name." Ann Eliza also portrayed Amelia as a volatile and domineering presence who feuded with her husband's other wives and periodically exploded in rage at Young himself. In a similar vein, a correspondent for the *New York World* reported in 1869 that Amelia greeted Young stonily after the latter had spent the night with another wife, then kicked over the breakfast table and spilled an urn of hot tea on his Sunday best. Young's daughter Susa (by Lucy Bigelow), by contrast, posited that Amelia "refrained from any act or word which would give occasion to natural reactions in the household." Even Mary Ann Angell, who more than any other wife possessed cause for jealousy, expressed fondness for a woman younger than two of her daughters. "[T]ell Amelia I do not forget her kindness," Mary Ann wrote Brigham in 1873. It is difficult to reconcile these contradictory sources.[62]

In earlier discussions of polygamy, Young had sometimes emphasized his equal treatment of his many wives and had suggested that a first wife should retain a preeminent position within a polygamous household. Perhaps because Mary Ann Angell did not retain that position within Young's own household, he now dismissed the idea. "Every old woman thinks she must go to Every party," he complained one year before his marriage to Amelia, "and Many a first wife thinks she should be a Queen and the rest of the wives surfs [serfs]. But this I do not believe in." Amelia later denied the appellation of "favorite wife," but Susa Young conceded that her father "could not pay equal attention to fourteen or fifteen women" and recognized Emmeline and Amelia as his successive favorites. Irrespective of the notoriety she generated, Amelia became Young's most significant female companion for the remainder of his life. He frequently escorted her to the theater and dances, and she accompanied him on several of his tours of Mormon settlements. When Young established a winter residence in St. George in the 1870s, he brought Amelia as his consort during those months.[63]

Shortly after Young's sealing to Amelia, territorial judges Thomas Drake and Charles Waite informed President Lincoln that Young had "taken a young wife, after an assiduous courtship, lasting several months." Governor Harding, with outrage but without accuracy, alleged that Young was "about evry week adding to his Harem, the unprotected and demented victims of his villainy." Harding, convinced that "to find a *traitor at heart* you have, with fewest exceptions, *only to find a Mormon*," reported that Young was stockpiling arms and ammunition and developing deadly new weapons to use against the U.S. Army.[64]

In early March, the insults and accusations evolved into a full-blown political crisis. Utah's congressional delegate, John Bernhisel, informed Young that a Senate subcommittee was considering legislation prepared by Harding, Waite, and Drake that would have limited the jurisdiction of Utah's county probate courts, given the federally appointed U.S. marshal the power to select jurors, and granted the governor complete authority over the territorial militia (previously exercised by the legislature). On March 3, church leaders convened a large meeting in the tabernacle at which Young preached an incendiary discourse. When he forwarded his remarks to the territorial secretary, Frank Fuller, Young allowed that he had employed some "expressions rougher than is usual." In a church transcript of his remarks, Young attributed Harding's actions to a national conspiracy of "Black-heart[ed] Republicans, rabid abolitionists, or negro worshipers" who intended to provoke the Mormons into an armed response and then impose a "military despotism" on Utah. In "such an attempt," Young warned, "they will then learn who is Governor." A mass meeting in Salt Lake City passed resolutions asking for the resignation or removal of the governor and judges. Colonel Connor and judges Drake and Waite provided U.S. officials with versions of Young's remarks rougher still. In these accounts, Young labeled Harding a "nigger worshiper" and called on the people "to attend to" his removal should the governor not go voluntarily. Harding, Waite, and Drake all refused to leave. Justice Waite wrote Lincoln that, among other outrages, Mormons had accosted him on the street and threatened him with death.[65]

Believing that Connor was about to arrest Young, church leaders on two separate occasions raised a signal flag on the Beehive House, summoning hundreds of armed Mormons to defend their president. Connor, whose men would have been badly outnumbered by a fully mobilized Nauvoo Legion, repeatedly warned his superiors of a potential Mormon attack. "[I]f the present preparations of the Mormons should continue," Connor informed, "I will be compelled for the preservation of my command to strike at the heads of the church." Though he encouraged prudence, U.S. Army General-in-Chief Henry Halleck authorized Connor to seize "arms and military munitions intended for use against the authority of the United States." In the end, for all their posturing both Young and Connor preferred to avoid a military collision. The furor eased as both sides awaited direction from Washington.[66]

Young's business relationships now paid dividends. Edward Creighton of the Pacific Telegraph Company informed Young of his willingness to counteract the federal appointees' charges. Hiram Sibley, a founder of the Western Union telegraph company, wired his former associate Anson Stager, now head of the Military Telegraph Department, to inform Lincoln that Harding's removal would "save us millions." In late spring 1863, Lincoln removed Harding and all three of Utah's justices. James Doty, who as Utah's Superintendent of Indian Affairs had remained on cordial terms with the Mormons and the army, became the new governor. Brigham Young had once more achieved a remarkable political victory. Never a Republican firebrand on polygamy, Lincoln had no interest in provoking a fight with the Mormons. Thomas Stenhouse met with Lincoln in Washington and reported the president's attitude: "if the people let him alone, he would let them alone." Young wanted a president who would mind his business and not interfere with Mormon control of Utah. Lincoln played that role.[67]

Connor remained, founded a lively daily newspaper (the *Union Vedette*), and began a campaign to attract non-Mormon prospectors to Utah. He found little encouragement from his superiors, though, in his crusade against Mormonism. When Connor placed a provost guard opposite the Salt Lake City Temple Block, his new commander General Irvin McDowell corrected him. "The question is," wrote McDowell through his adjutant, "are we at this time . . . in a condition to undertake to carry on a war against the Mormons—for any cause whatever—if it can possibly be avoided?" McDowell reminded Connor that his only task was to "protect the overland route." Young, meanwhile, warned that if "Gen[eral] Connor crosses my path I will kill him," and he suggested that the Lord would have been pleased if the Saints had "*cut him* [Connor] and bound him out to a gimlet maker and sent the soldiers back to California." Despite animosity between Young and Connor, tensions between Utah and the national government eased for the remainder of the Civil War.[68]

THE federal government was the gravest, but not the only, challenge to Young's authority. Since leading the Latter-day Saints to the Great Basin, Young had faced no serious internal threats to his leadership. Still, he had not lost his vigilance against the danger of dissent. "Joseph was never afraid of anybody but those who professed to be saints and his friends," Young observed, "and it was those characters that led him to the slaughter." Because of that perennial fear, Young still reacted vindictively toward perceived slights to his authority. In April 1861, Young pronounced himself "mortified" when Orson Hyde, president of the Quorum of the Twelve, opened a conference meeting before his arrival. "[H]ow would you feel," he asked Hyde at the apostles' evening prayer, "if you had a work to do which God & the heavens held you responsible and . . . another man should rise up & take it out of your hands Before the people as if you were not qualified to Do it or was neglecting your duty?" Hyde, a frequent target of Young's chastisement, meekly defended himself and then promised not to repeat the offense.[69]

In order to illustrate the hazards of apostasy, Young publicly humiliated those who strayed. In 1857, Thomas Marsh, Young's former apostolic superior who had been excommunicated after betraying Joseph Smith to his enemies in Missouri, asked the church president to welcome him back. Invited to Salt Lake City, Marsh arrived impoverished, humbled, and handicapped by a paralyzed arm. Publicly sizing up the "infirm old man" at a Sunday meeting and noting Marsh's professed scruples about plural marriage, Young pronounced himself skeptical that Marsh "could get one wife." Contrasting Marsh's decrepitude with his own health and virility, Young held up the apostle-turned-apostate as a visible warning of dissent's cost: "If any want to apostatize, I want them to look at brother Marsh." In Utah, Marsh became a pitiable figure beset by poverty and mental illness. He periodically sent Young requests for clothes, which Young probably granted. In 1860, Marsh called at Young's office, and Young "talked about old times with him, and sung a Hymn they had Sung together in old times." Marsh commented that Young's display of kindness "made him feel good." After Marsh became thoroughly submissive, Young showed charity and mercy to his former superior.[70]

Few Mormon men long withstood the pressure of Young's disapprobation. They either submissively accepted his chastisement or left the church. Apostle Orson Pratt's theological rebellion formed an exception to this rule. In the mid-1850s, Young had repeatedly chastised Pratt for promulgating unsanctioned, speculative doctrines and for opposing Young's identification of Adam as God. That conflict came to a head in 1860. Annoyed for years at Pratt's intellectual independence, Young convened a meeting of top church leaders in January and read a discourse that Pratt had prepared for publication in the *Deseret News*. It repeated Pratt's belief that the attributes of God—rather than God Himself—should form the object of the Saints' worship. Young scoffed at the idea of worshiping divine attributes in which human beings could eventually achieve an equal share. He worshiped God, a God of flesh and bones, a Father in every sense of the word. Young insisted that Pratt accept him as the revelatory arbiter of correct

Orson Pratt, ca. 1863 *(courtesy of Church History Library, The Church of Jesus Christ of Latter-day Saints)*

doctrine and confess his error. Pratt refused to budge. "I am not going to Crawl to Brigham Young and act the Hypocrite and Confess what I do not Believe," he declared. "I will be a free man." Young characterized his wayward apostle as "a mad stoubern Mule." The council adjourned at midnight with Pratt and Young still at loggerheads.[71]

Pratt finally decided to become less stubborn, making a public apology in the tabernacle. That confession, however, failed to satisfy Young. Pratt had apologized for his lack of submission but had not conceded that he had actually been in error. Young convened a second council in April to bring matters to a final resolution. Pratt's tabernacle sermon, Young complained, "makes me appear to be a tyrant and [suggests that] because I am the President of the church every man's will and judgement must bend to mine." Young wanted the Latter-day Saints to embrace him as the church's living oracle, to see him as the font of true doctrine. Ideally, he wanted a submission that flowed from sincere acceptance, not grudging obedience. As he had done in January, Pratt initially refused to budge, maintaining that scripture, Joseph Smith's revelations, and reason supported his positions. Young then made plain the stakes. "Orson," he delivered an ultimatum, "it is for you to call the 12 together & do as I have suggested or do as you please. [Otherwise] It will be brought before [the] conference and you will be voted as a false teacher, & your false doctrine discarded." Young stated that he was merely fulfilling his calling as the church's president. "It is my duty to see that correct doctrine is taught," he said, "& to guard the church from error."[72] Ironically, after complaining that Pratt made him out to be an ecclesiastical tyrant, Young exacted Pratt's submission when he could not extract it voluntarily.

The next day, the apostles, including Pratt, discussed the case, then dressed in their temple robes and prayed. Pratt finally acceded to his brethren's advice. They submitted a revision of Pratt's January sermon to Young, who pronounced himself satisfied. Young told Pratt that "he never wanted the subject, to be mouthed again, and wished those in the room, not to mention it."[73] A chastened Pratt remained within the fold, but Young never fully forgave him. He saw the apostle's intellectual independence as an ongoing threat to the church's unity.

Young was now a much different leader than he had been when he led the Twelve Apostles to England. Then, he had led gingerly, giving his fellow apostles positions of authority and correcting them gently to avoid wounding their pride. Young's later treatment of high-ranking church members like Orson Hyde and Orson Pratt illustrates a much more heavy-handed approach to leadership. Always cognizant of the events that led to Joseph Smith's death, Young took no chances with anything resembling disloyalty. He understood how to wield power and exercised it with vigor and sometimes with bravado. Young's chastisements of his ecclesiastical associates cost him a certain measure of their affection, for the feelings of men like Franklin Richards, John Taylor, Pratt, and Hyde remained bruised.

Fear was only one of Young's leadership tactics. He expressed his admiration for Pratt's dedication and oratory even at the peak of their disagreement. "[I]f Brother Orson were chopped up in inch pieces," Young stated a few months after Pratt's humiliation, "each piece would cry out Mormonism was true." Young sometimes expressed his love for his ecclesiastical subordinates quite tenderly. For example, while ordering Daniel Wells to prepare for possible bloodshed in November 1857, he wrote his militia commander letters of comfort when his infant daughter Luna died after a long illness. Because of his harsh, often public rebukes, Young did not have the unalloyed love of many church leaders. In addition to his ecclesiastical, economic, and political successes, however, his more private displays of concern and friendship helped him retain their respect. Those close to him understood his complex and sometimes unpredictable nature. They admired his strengths and had no choice but to live with his flaws.[74]

On the heels of the renewed conflict with Pratt, Young faced the emergence of the first serious schism within the church since its colonization of the Great Basin. Joseph Morris, an English convert, gradually became convinced that he was a new prophetic successor to Joseph Smith. In several ways a throwback to pre-Nauvoo Mormonism, Morris spoke in spiritual tongues and was uneasy about polygamy. In a series of letters to Young, Morris offered the church president a subordinate position under Morris's prophetic leadership. Young's clerks labeled the rambling epistles "balderdash," "twaddle," and "bosh."[75] Morris then began promulgating revelations, many of which were critical of Young. "He [Young] surpasses in wickedness," God announced through one such revelation, "all that have ever lived before him, or that will ever live after him." Morris's appeal was reminiscent of James Strang's in the late 1840s. "Brigham had been barren," wrote Thomas Stenhouse twelve years later. "Morris was overflowing." By the summer of 1861, Morris had formed his own church, which grew to include some five hundred baptized members. His followers gathered within a jerry-built encampment (Kington Fort) at the mouth of Weber Canyon, consecrated their property, and anticipated Jesus's imminent return. Just as the Saints linked the future spread of their kingdom to God's promised destruction of the United States government, so Morris coupled the deliverance of his followers to divine judgment upon Brigham Young and the Mormons. "Secession must be infectious," reported an amused correspondent for the *New York Times*.[76]

Then, Morris fulfilled Young's hope that his church "would soon fizzle out." The upstart prophet made a series of specific and inaccurate predictions about the Second Coming, and the Morrisites imprisoned three disenchanted members who attempted to leave Kington Fort and reclaim their property. In June 1862, after the Morrisites had ignored legal writs for three weeks, Chief Justice John F. Kinney and Frank Fuller, territorial secretary and acting governor—both non-Mormons friendly to Young—authorized the use of the Nauvoo Legion as a *posse comitatus* to free the prisoners and arrest the Morrisite leaders. It was an opportune time for such an action, falling between the evacuation of Camp Crittenden and Connor's arrival. Hundreds of militia men approached the fort on June 13 and issued an ultimatum demanding surrender within thirty minutes. It is unclear how long the militia waited for a response, but after some passage of time, militia artillery fired a cannon shot that killed two of Morris's followers and wounded a young girl. After the militia stormed the fort, its leaders shot and killed Morris, a top associate, and two women. The troops hauled ninety prisoners back to Salt Lake City and brought Morris's body to the capital, where thousands of eager onlookers waited for a glimpse at the corpse of "the Weber River prophet." The following spring, Governor Harding pardoned those prisoners convicted of crimes, and Connor escorted a group of Morrisites to a settlement at Soda Springs in the newly formed Idaho Territory.[77]

Young's comments on the conflict provided further evidence of the subtle way that the 1857–58 Utah War had changed the church president's approach to the national government. Previously, Young had spoken his mind with little heed to potential reactions in Washington. Now, he worried that the federal government would blame him for the bloodshed at Kington Fort. He wrote John Bernhisel, again Utah's territorial delegate, and told him to rebut such talk with the fact that "the whole affair was . . . conducted and enforced solely by officers of Federal appointment." Young suggested Kinney had acted in haste. "He [Young] would not have disturbed them," Young asserted in a tabernacle discourse, "but Judge Kinney thought the Law must be honored." Despite his disavowal of responsibility, the assault on the fort would never have proceeded over Young's opposition. Informed that Young had blamed him and termed him "weak in the Upper story," Kinney told Wilford Woodruff that he had "not taken any step without Counciling Preside[n]t Young" and that the complainants against the Morrisites had only sworn their affidavits after consulting Young. The church president played no public role in the crisis's handling, but he was keenly interested in the Morrisites' fate. Woodruff recorded that he spent an "Evening in President Youngs Office waiting for a messenger from our armey to bring the News of affairs with the Morrisites."[78]

While Young had never been overly alarmed about Joseph Morris, a different Joseph posed a more fundamental threat. Despite his dislike for

Emma Smith (remarried to non-Mormon Lewis Bidamon), Young maintained tender feelings toward Joseph Smith Jr.'s sons, including Joseph III, whom the Mormons frequently called "young Joseph." Through the 1850s, many Utah Mormons held out hope that Joseph III and his three younger brothers would eventually travel west and join their branch of Mormonism. In 1860, however, Joseph Smith III assumed leadership in Illinois of what became known as the Reorganized Church of Jesus Christ of Latter Day Saints (RLDS). The Reorganization movement rejected polygamy, the move to Utah, and—therefore—Young's leadership. Against abundant evidence, Joseph III denied that his father had practiced plural marriage. He also distanced his church from Smith's introduction of temple ordinances, theocratic claims, and later theological creativity. Even so, after Young heard that "young Joseph" had joined the Reorganization, he promised that when he and his brothers "make their appearance before this people . . . [we] will say—'Amen! we are ready to receive you.'"[79]

As long as the "Josephites" remained in the Midwest, they posed no immediate ecclesiastical threat to the "Brighamites," but RLDS missionaries came to Utah in 1863. Young received them coldly and publicly denounced the "apostates" who followed "Young Joseph Smith." He blamed these unfortunate developments on Emma. "[M]ore hell was never wrapped up in any human being than there is in her," he said publicly, and he now declared that Joseph's sons "will never lead the church." While the RLDS Church never found many converts in Utah itself, it gained a significant number of members in states such as California and Illinois.[80]

Another reminder of the contested nature of Mormonism continued to nettle Young. It stemmed from the history dictated by Lucy Mack Smith (Joseph Jr.'s mother) and published in 1853 by Orson Pratt as *Biographical Sketches of Joseph Smith the Prophet, and His Progenitors*. In 1861, Young ordered George Q. Cannon to send "to the *pulp tub* of the paper makers" any remaining copies of the book. Several years later, Young unleashed a tirade against the book after encountering a copy at the home of the apostle Ezra T. Benson in Cache Valley. Young called on church members to burn or otherwise destroy any copies of the objectionable history. The occasion also apparently prompted him to again convene a council to review Pratt's publications, which the council agreed should be destroyed. Young made it clear that Pratt's church membership hung in the balance and grew more bitter in his denunciations of the apostle as the months proceeded. During a Sunday afternoon sermon in the southern settlement of Beaver, Young bluntly announced that "Orson Pratt would go to hell." Pratt, now a white-haired, long-bearded, aged-looking man serving a mission in England, once again responded with contrition, publishing an apology in the

Millennial Star and writing to Young that his own erroneous writings deserved destruction.[81]

Young was annoyed when Pratt had first published Lucy Smith's memoir, which he termed "a bundle of lies" in 1855. Still, in the mid-1850s the publication of the *Biographical Sketches* was merely one mistake among Pratt's many alleged errors. By the mid-1860s, Young had endured the lingering conflict with Pratt, the conflict with the Morrisites, and Joseph Smith III's emergence as the Reorganization's president. Young felt the danger of dissent with renewed strength. Lucy Smith's book offered an alternative history of the church, one focused on the Smith family and largely confined to the church's roots in New York and Ohio and its persecutions in Missouri. Although the book preceded the Reorganization, it suited the RLDS understanding of the church's past quite well. Other than a brief mention of his conversion, Young scarcely appears in Lucy Smith's account. A reader of her history would not appreciate the significance of the Quorum of the Twelve Apostles, the temple ordinances, or plural marriage. In short, Lucy Smith's book posed a subtle challenge to Young's authority as head of the church.[82]

Young was keenly aware of the church's need to control its history. For many years, the *Deseret News* serialized a "History of Joseph Smith" that, while brief on plural marriage and temple ordinances, nevertheless included such subjects. In Young's mind, a church could not retain its unity and stability with two histories, two theologies, or two presidents. "There is but one man upon the earth, at one time," an 1865 critique of Pratt affirmed, "who holds the keys to receive commandments and revelations for the Church, and who has the authority to write doctrines by way of commandment unto the Church." Young believed that God had appointed him that man, and he was determined to retain his position.[83]

"BRIGHAM's power is evidently on the wane," asserted Patrick Edward Connor in May 1865, "the scepter is leaving his hands, and he is becoming desperate."[84] The general, who claimed to have a "peculiar way of managing" Young, was engaging in decidedly wishful thinking. During the Civil War, Young had rid the territory of two disliked governors while ignoring the Morrill Act with impunity. While the bloodbath in the eastern United States had not helped the Mormons achieve statehood for Utah, the war had provided Young with some political breathing space. Connor's attempts to bolster Utah's non-Mormon population had largely failed, and Young still controlled the territory's politics and militia while exercising a large influence over its economic development. The church resumed baptisms for the dead in its Endowment House, and each year more than a thousand Saints received their endowments and hundreds were sealed in marriage. In the summer of 1865, Young visited forty-nine Mormon settlements, delivering sixty-five discourses en route.

Shifting gears with the Union's imminent victory, church leaders organized a large celebration of Lincoln's second inauguration in March 1865. Though neither Young nor Connor made an appearance, a troop of U.S. soldiers and a group of Nauvoo Legion militiamen both promenaded through the streets of Salt Lake City. One month later, Young lowered the flags over the Beehive House to half staff and draped his gates in crepe following the assassination of Lincoln, whom two years before he had labeled "as wicked a man as ever lived."[85]

Young had successfully parried most federal attempts to encroach on Mormondom since the Utah War's conclusion. If Connor exaggerated his claim of Young's demise, the reconciliatory atmosphere surrounding Lincoln's second inaugural and death obscured the challenges Young would face in the years ahead. Indeed, while it partly shielded the Mormons from federal interference for four years, the Civil War's long-term consequences were disastrous for Young's attempt to secure the Kingdom of God's autonomy. By 1865, the Republican Party had abolished one twin relic of barbarism and passed legislation outlawing territorial polygamy. Although initially a "dead letter," the Morrill Act was a template for future federal action against Mormon polygamists.[86] Before the Civil War, westward expansion had produced bitter sectional divisions over slavery, divisions that impeded the assertion of federal power over those territories. Now, Washington was more free to devote its attention to the West's conquest, settlement, and economic exploitation and integration. While wary of conflict with the Mormons during the war, after its conclusion the army decided to keep troops at Salt Lake City because high-ranking officers accepted Connor's argument that only a strong military presence would discourage Mormon harassment of Salt Lake City's Gentile population and the incitement of Indian attacks on the Overland Trail. After the Civil War's conclusion, therefore, Mormon control of Utah's politics and economy became more imperiled. Young, though, had always hedged his bets, keeping one foot in Deseret and the other in the United States, anticipating the imminent millennium while focusing on building up his earthly kingdom.

CHAPTER TWELVE

The Monster in the Vale

He rides on a rail
With smoke for his trail,
And that's how the monster comes into our vale.
— JABEZ WOODARD, 1869

IN MAY 1867, when Young arrived home after one of his regular tours of the southern Utah settlements, Salt Lake City's Mormon population greeted its president like a returning king. Having turned sixty-five the previous year, a rather portly Brigham Young now sported a neatly trimmed gray beard to complement his still-full head of slowly graying hair. American flags festooned the capital's buildings, the Nauvoo Legion provided an escort, and throngs of the church's youth greeted Young's party. Probably with some hyperbole, John D. Lee estimated that 25,000 persons—five miles in length—filed passed Young's Beehive House mansion. Young's tours and returns were public celebrations, in which church members displayed their loyalty to their president. Communities sang songs composed in Young's honor, lined their streets, and greeted him with banners such as "Hail to the Chieftain of Israel," "Welcome, Brigham, the Friend of Mankind," "Zion's Chieftain Ever Welcome," and "Welcome to President Brigham Young and the Nobles of Israel." Of Young's 1872 trip south, non-Mormon Elizabeth Kane informed, "It is a sort of Royal Progress in a primitive Kingdom."[1]

The sea of acclamation that greeted Young on his tours masked a more complicated relationship between leader and followers. Mormon settlers might abstain from coffee, tea, and tobacco during his visits and then resume such consumption after his departure. They might unanimously affirm communitarian efforts in church meetings but then subsequently undermine them. Underneath the regular displays of unity at church conferences, division and uncertainty were increasing. Whereas in earlier years Mormons had sometimes quietly ignored Young's economic directives, such as his calls for the consecration of property, some church members now openly rebelled. The 1869 arrival of the transcontinental railroad—the "monster" in the "vale," as one Mormon writer termed the iron horse—further reduced Utah's isolation from the rest of the United States and stoked tension over Young's economic policies. Shortly after the railroad's completion, a group of prominent Mormon men began publicly criticizing his leadership, leading to a series of excommunications and the formation of a rival church.

Meanwhile, during the years following the Civil War, Young parried multiple threats to Mormon control of Utah's economy, politics, and legal system. After a decade of relative peace with Utah's native peoples, Young worked for several years to end a string of Ute raids against central and southern Utah settlements. The Nauvoo Legion eventually suppressed the Indian raids, but other threats mounted. Non-Mormons ever more boldly challenged the church's economic and political supremacy in Utah by pushing ahead with mining ventures and by organizing their own political party. By the early 1870s, moreover, Utah's non-Mormon governors and judges grew more combative toward Young and the church, symbolized by Young's 1871 indictments for both "lewd and lascivious cohabitation" and murder.

Young responded to everything with his customary faith in the future of his kingdom against all odds. That others believed he could not maintain the church's grip on Utah's economy in the wake of the railroad simply led him to push his followers to embrace an even higher level of cooperation and self-sacrifice. Young also displayed a resourcefulness that surprised his enemies. In keeping with his role in the completion of the transcontinental telegraph, he did not oppose the railroad. "I shall ride on it myself when I get to be President of the United States," he joked before conceding that he had become too old for that office. Young also mostly eschewed the inflammatory rhetoric of the 1850s and early 1860s. He no longer made public threats against either ecclesiastical dissidents or political opponents. Gone were the pulpit fulminations against earlier governors and vows to fight the U.S. Army. As a local writer, Edward Tullidge, later commented, the "Lion of the Lord" could play the fox when circumstances warranted.[2]

FOR many years, observers of Utah affairs had anticipated that the railroad would undermine Young and his church by bringing a host of Gentile

Brigham Young and party in southern Nevada, 1870 (courtesy of Church History Library, The Church of Jesus Christ of Latter-day Saints). Young is seated on a chair near the center of the photo, with apostles Erastus Snow and George A. Smith to his left and sons Brigham Jr. and John Willard to his right.

settlers and merchandise to the territory. A. G. Browne Jr., a journalist who had accompanied the U.S. Army to Utah in 1857, predicted that "the first shovelful of dirt thrown on its [the railroad's] embankments will be the commencement of the grave of his religion and authority." Also, some non-Mormons in Utah and politicians in Washington hoped that the Civil War's conclusion would bring about a concerted federal effort to extirpate Mormon polygamy and theocracy. At war's end, however, the transcontinentals extended only roughly forty miles west from Omaha and forty miles east from Sacramento. The federal threat lay dormant for several years as well, with Andrew Johnson no more interested in reconstructing Utah than the defeated Confederacy. Young anticipated renewed threats to Mormon polygamy and theocracy following the end of the Civil War but instead found himself facing an entirely unexpected conflict. On the same day that Robert E. Lee surrendered to Ulysses S. Grant, a bloody war began in Central Utah. The resulting violence temporarily arrested Mormon colonization and also highlighted the limits of Young's influence over both settlers and Indians.[3]

Despite retrenchment during the Utah War and the loss of territory to Nevada and Colorado, in the early and mid-1860s Young directed the establishment of new settlements in present-day Idaho and to the southwest on the Virgin and Muddy Rivers in both Utah and Nevada. Also, in previously settled areas of Central Utah, forts grew into larger outposts, and the Mormons expanded into new valleys. Young wanted Mormons to occupy fertile valleys and mineral-rich areas before others claimed them. Mormon expansion continued to impoverish, displace, and often frustrate Utah's native peoples, especially the Shoshone in the northwestern region of Mormon settlement and Utes in central and eastern Utah. As traditional means of subsistence disappeared, native populations steadily fell. Despite Young's "cheaper to feed them than to fight them" axiom, neither the Mormons nor federal Indian agents provided the Indians with food or presents sufficient to compensate them for their steady loss of traditional resources.

The increased presence of the U.S. Army and militias during the Civil War, moreover, augured ill for the American West's native populations. In Utah, Patrick Edward Connor's hatred for Indians matched his hostility toward Mormon leaders. In January 1863, Connor's men marched toward a Shoshone village on Bear River, guided by the Mormon scout Porter Rockwell. In the process of routing the warriors they encountered, Connor's men took no male prisoners and killed many women and children in the process. Two Mormon settlers visited the battlefield, counting 235 dead Indians, "besides Squaws and Papooses that are badly wounded . . .

Brigham Young, ca. 1867 *(courtesy of Church History Library, The Church of Jesus Christ of Latter-day Saints)*

left their to perish by Col Connor." The clash at Bear River—viewed as a battle by the army and a massacre by its critics—earned Connor the brevet rank of brigadier general. Though the *Deseret News* initially praised the expedition, Young later criticized Connor, both for losing men to wounds and frostbite and for his wanton treatment of the Shoshone.[4]

For years, non-Mormons had regularly alleged that the church cultivated the Indians as allies against the U.S. Army and American emigrants passing through the Utah Territory. "Brigham Young has complete control of the Indians," complained Connor to his superior in April 1863.[5] Two years later, Utah's native peoples badly discredited Connor's assertion. The Ute chief Black Hawk *(Antonga)* and his band of warriors drove off a cattle herd near Manti and then ambushed a pursuing Nauvoo Legion detachment, killing two Mormon militiamen. The raid was prompted by an altercation in Manti between a settler and another minor chief, but it stemmed from years of poverty and episodic tension with Mormon settlers. Following the example of his late relative Walker, Black Hawk gained influence over a diverse collection of Ute bands and warriors. Over the ensuing months and years, in what became known as the Black Hawk War, raiders regularly captured valuable herds of Mormon stock. Meanwhile, the Nauvoo Legion fruitlessly tracked Black Hawk's band, desperate to capture its antagonist but wary of stumbling into ambushes. Indians scalped Mormon women, and settlers angrily shot "friendly" Indians. From Salt Lake City, Young groped for ways to both end the raids and restrain his more vengeful co-religionists.[6]

Shortly after the initial raids, Young chastised apostle Orson Hyde for suggesting he request "outside aid." "You would find if this aid [a federal army] were down there with you," Young lectured, "it would be far better to have the Indians to war with and to deal with than to have to war and deal with them." Young wanted Camp Douglas to wane, not wax, so he ruled out asking for military assistance. Young's desire aligned with that of the army, which informed Utah's Superintendent for Indian Affairs Orsemus Irish that the Mormons settlers would have to fend for themselves.[7]

The army's demurral was fortunate for the Utes. If interested in the task, General Connor, whom some citizens cheered as "the exterminator," would have pursued Black Hawk's band more ruthlessly and effectively than the underequipped Nauvoo Legion. In the summer of 1865, preparing for an expedition against the Sioux and Cheyenne, Connor ordered one of his subordinates to "not receive overtures of peace or submission from Indians, but . . . attack and kill every male Indian over twelve years of age." While deplored by many easterners, Connor's mentality was not unusual among whites in the American West. "The Indians must be exterminated," declared the Nevada *Daily Territorial Enterprise* the very month the Black Hawk War began. While some of Young's decisions had tragic consequences, he was not an "exterminator." Indeed, when he received word of the first deaths, Young discouraged hasty and broad retribution. "[W]hile we consider such outrages altogether unbearable and we will not submit to them," Young instructed a local militia commander, "we have no desire to inflict indiscriminate punishment upon both the innocent and the guilty."[8]

Instead of immediately seeking vengeance, Young worked to shore up Mormon relations with other Ute chiefs. In June 1865, at the invitation of Superintendent Irish, Young traveled to Spanish Fork to preside over a council with the territory's leading Ute chiefs. The U.S. government offered the chiefs sixty years of annuities in return for their removal to a reservation in the Uintah Mountains in northeastern Utah. Young and the church had a keen interest in the council's outcome. By extinguishing Indian title to much of central Utah, the treaty would enable the Mormon settlers to become more than mere squatters under American law.

The chiefs in attendance expressed due respect for Young. "Brigham is the great Captain of all," stated the Pahvant chief Kanosh, the Mormons' most reliable Ute ally, "for he does not get mad when he hears of his brothers and friends as the California Captains do." Kanosh praised Young's straight talk and accused past federal Indian agents of employing "two tongues." Still, Kanosh and Sanpitch, chief of San Pete Valley, opposed ceding their lands in return for a gift of any amount. Young reasoned with them bluntly, telling them that the government—and Mormon settlers— would take the land whether they accepted the terms or not. Although Young promised that the Indians could live among the Saints, he also informed them that "we shall occupy this valley and the next, and the next, and so on till we occupy the whole of them."[9] Young hoped that the chiefs who signed the resulting Spanish Fork Treaty would restrain Black Hawk and other younger, more restless warriors. Young staked his honor on his belief that the chiefs would never get better terms than those currently proposed, and all of the Utes except for Sanpitch finally agreed. The church president affixed his signature to the treaty as a witness. Although still disgruntled, Sanpitch added his name one week later.

Young was pleased with the result, partly because his starring role at the deliberations signaled his ongoing authority over territorial affairs. Not only the territory's *de facto* governor, he remained its *de facto* superintendent of Indian affairs. "A few words of explanation and counsel from myself," he recounted, "removed all their feelings of aversion and they consented immediately to sign the treaty." Young did not grasp the full extent of the Utes' unease and resentment over their declining fortunes. Although most of the chiefs probably considered him more trustworthy than the American civil and military officers, that trust was shallower than Young realized.[10]

The Spanish Fork Treaty did not arrest Central Utah's descent into violence. During the early years of Mormon settlement, Young's militia had overwhelmed the Timpanogos Utes in Utah Valley, and his conciliatory posture had quickly ended an 1853 conflict with Walker. Now, he vacillated between chastisement and conciliation. In July 1865, Young was only thirty miles to the northeast when two settlers near Salina were killed, prompting him to order the Nauvoo Legion to pursue Black Hawk's band into the mountains. Furthermore, he declared that those Utes who did not actively align themselves with the Latter-day Saints placed their lives at risk. "[I]f these Indians who profess to be friendly will not help bring them to justice," Young instructed the settlers at Manti, "do not let them stay with you but treat them as Enemies." In what became known as the "Squaw Fight," the militiamen stumbled upon six tepees and proceeded to kill more than a dozen men, women, and children. The slaughter gave Young pause. He now reemphasized his "cheaper to feed than fight" maxim, asked Superintendent Irish to seek a peace treaty with hostile Utes, and instructed San Pete Valley residents to "stop fighting altogether." Black Hawk, though, rejected Young's overture and launched a deadly raid against settlers in Ephraim who were caught unawares partly because of expectations of peace. By early 1866, Navajo Indians partly inspired by Black Hawk's example began raids on southern Utah settlements. Ready markets for stolen Mormon cattle in both Santa Fe to the south and Denver to the east also encouraged the raids.[11]

Young now switched tactics once again. Convinced that Sanpitch and other ostensibly friendly Utes were aiding the Mormons' Indian enemies, Young wanted to force them to betray Black Hawk's location. In March 1866, with Young's authorization, Nauvoo Legion district commander Warren Snow arrested Sanpitch and eight other Indians and incarcerated them in Manti. After Snow threatened that his men would shoot the hostages if hostilities continued, Sanpitch evidenced a desire for cooperation. Acting on Sanpitch's intelligence, Snow's men captured and executed three alleged raiders in Nephi. A few days later, militiamen murdered a Ute woman and boy who had participated in a failed attempt to free the prisoners. Sanpitch and his fellow inmates then succeeded in escaping, but the militia wounded Sanpitch in the jailbreak, tracked him for several days, and killed him. Although the scheme had failed badly, Young defended the hostage plan and Snow's actions. "I do not know that any better course could have been taken in relation to Sanpitch and the others than has been," he wrote Snow. For many years, Young had maintained a stubborn confidence in Snow, unshaken by the latter's role in the Thomas Lewis castration and by early setbacks in the Black Hawk War. Later in the war, Young finally replaced Snow—whose health was failing—with a new local commander.[12]

Sanpitch's death caused previously friendly Utes to become disenchanted and afraid; several bands took shelter in central Utah canyons. According to U.S. Army Colonel Orville Babcock, with whom Young discussed the war that spring, Black Hawk refused to meet with Utah's new superintendent for Indian affairs, Franklin Head, for fear of Mormon "treachery." Militia operations failed to capture Black Hawk or other principal leaders, but they incited new cycles of reprisals. Following several raids and altercations, militia in the isolated settlement of Circleville arrested a group of twenty Indians whom they suspected of collaborating with Black Hawk. After an escape attempt, the settlers held a council meeting in which they decided to execute all of the captives except four young children. Retrospectively, Young condemned the cruel act, but there is no evidence that he or other militia commanders investigated the slaughter or reprimanded those responsible.[13]

After a year of erratic wartime tactics, Young's Indian policy was in tatters. In the 1850s, the relative success of the Paiute mission and the baptisms of several key Ute leaders had suggested the possible redemption of the people the Latter-day Saints regarded as the "Lamanites," Israel's New World remnant. More prosaically, baptism often symbolized a tribal leader's political and economic alliance with or subordination to the church. Earlier Indian missions and baptisms had made smoother the path of Mormon colonization. Now, those vital alliances had frayed. In late April 1866, about the same time as the Circleville Massacre, Young met with Kanosh, who by now found himself suspected of supporting Black Hawk despite his deep ties with the church. In the strongest possible terms, Young threatened that if ostensibly friendly Indians did not begin fully cooperating in the effort to locate Black Hawk's band, the church "would have to cut them all off."[14] Whether by "cut off" Young meant death or excommunication, his chilling warning suggests the extent of his frustration.

The war also revealed limits on Young's ability to control the behavior of Mormon settlers and some of his own ecclesiastical inferiors. Orson Hyde, president of the church's Quorum of the Twelve Apostles and the presiding authority over the Central Utah settlements, consistently articulated a much more vengeful attitude in the wake of Indian raids. Especially during the first eighteen months of the conflict, Mormon settlers hesitated to follow Young's instructions to fortify themselves and abandon small and indefensible settlements. Also, in disobedience to Young's calls for restraint, settlers exacted vengeance upon those Indians who had not participated in raids. For example, in June 1866 James Ivie murdered one of Kanosh's Indians in anger over the death of his father at the hands of Black Hawk's raiders. Young pronounced Ivie "as much guilty of murder as if he had stepped up and killed a white man," but a local jury acquitted Ivie, who claimed that he acted under military orders from Nauvoo Legion commander Daniel Wells. Ivie's bishop, Thomas Callister of Fillmore, called the jury's decision "nonsense."[15]

Shortly after the failed hostage-taking scheme, Young oscillated back to a renewed and ultimately successful emphasis on vigilance and conciliation. He issued a directive to abandon dozens of small and indefensible settlements such as Circleville and called for even more "thorough and energetic measures of protection."[16] After more than a year of depredations, Mormon settlers finally heeded his calls for vigilance. Young sent $5,000 worth of food to a band of starving Utes on the Uintah Reservation led by Tabby, who had been drifting into a hostile posture. He also sent a shipment of flour to Kanosh and encouraged local settlers to feed the Indians generously. Along with similar acts by Superintendent Head, Young's conciliatory moves prevented additional Ute defections.

In July 1866, three months removed from the angry sentiments he had expressed to Kanosh, Young rebuked the residents of Springville for their actions and attitudes toward the Indians. Still angry over Ivie's crime, he threatened that settlers who killed innocent Indians would have to pay with their own blood in order to maintain their eternal salvation. He also warned that those who "feel as though they should wipe out the Lamanites" needed to repent. Young allowed that "evil passions" sometimes led him to feel the same way. "I could take the elders of Israel and slay them all [the Indians]," he stated. If he should order that wholesale murder, however, he would "bring a curse upon this people they would not overcome for many years." Although the settlers should defend themselves with vigilance, it was time to welcome the Indians back to their homes. "They buried their fathers and mothers here, and children," he stated, "and this is their home." Young showed unusual empathy for the Indians' plight. "When we came in," he recalled, "[there were] great hordes [of] fish in this lake in abundance and they came here to catch the fish." It was the Mormons' duty to feed the Indians, he added, because "we are living on their possessions and in their homes." While he insisted that the Saints were not "interlopers" because God had brought them to the Great Basin, both peoples possessed the land, and the Saints had to provide for the Indians, whose sustenance they had imperiled. His Springville audience would almost certainly have preferred to listen to a bellicose war sermon. Indeed, few political leaders in the American West would have called for restraint and co-existence under similar circumstances.[17]

Although the fact was unknown to Young at the time of his speech, in the previous month Black Hawk had received a wound that eventually brought his rebellion and life to premature ends. Raids continued, but the Nauvoo Legion inflicted more significant casualties on its enemies by the summer of 1866. Black Hawk himself ceased hostilities after a meeting with Superintendent Head in August 1867. "The vigilance which our people have maintained this season in San Pete has had a salutary effect upon the Lamanites," Young explained. Even though raids continued sporadically into the early 1870s, large-scale fighting ceased, following the deaths of perhaps seventy whites and probably twice that many Indians.[18]

The later experiences of Kanosh and his Pahvant Ute band reflect the legacy of Mormon settlement and the vagaries of the Indian policies of both Brigham Young and the federal government. Although the U.S. Senate never ratified the Spanish Fork Treaty, Young and federal Indian agents encouraged the Pahvants to abandon their Fillmore County homeland and move to the Uintah Reservation. Mormon settlers quickly encroached on the Indians' old land, leading to the creation of a town named Kanosh City. The Pahvant chief and a contingent of his people established a new farm near the Mormon settlement, apparently with Young's blessing.[19]

Kanosh, meanwhile, became indirectly connected to Young's family. For many years he had wanted to marry Sally *(Kahpeputz)*, the Indian girl adopted by Young's wife Clara Decker in 1847. "Kanosh wants to have a talk with Sally before he goes away," Dimick Huntington reported to Young in 1856. Kanosh would not get his wish for two decades. Several later sources suggest that Sally was very reluctant to leave Young's household and return, at least in part, to a lifestyle she had long ago involuntarily left. In 1877, though, Sally finally married the Pahvant chief. After taking the train with Kanosh and Bishop Thomas Callister to Nephi, Sally refused to ride on top of a wagon filled with her belongings. "[W]hat shall we do?" Kanosh wired Dimick Huntington. Sally and her new husband eventually reached Kanosh City. When she died the next year, she was buried in temple clothes given to her by Brigham Young. Kanosh and Sally had both passed through the endowment ceremony, in a sense becoming members of the church's extended ecclesial family. Even redeemed Lamanites, though, occupied a very uncertain and unequal position within that family. Though adopted by Young's wife, Sally had become a servant, not a daughter. Kanosh was among Young's most trusted Ute allies, but he needed Young's permission to remain on his traditional land.[20]

Even if his policies and rhetoric were humane in comparison to the brutality of contemporaries such as General Connor, Young presided over the military and demographic conquest and diminution of Utah's Indians. Very rarely did he express any scruples over that typically American result. The Black Hawk War only temporarily reversed Mormon colonization, and the territory's native population continued its precipitous fall as the Latter-day Saints fulfilled what they saw as their manifest destiny to occupy Zion. When he first came to the Great Basin, Young had envisioned a much different future for the region's Indians. "Joseph committed to me the keys to open the gospel to every Lamanite nation," Young had stated.[21] That optimistic and expansive vision of Indian redemption had quickly foundered upon conflicts over Zion's scarce resources and the daunting cultural gap between the Mormons and their prospective Indian converts. Thereafter, Young articulated a much more modest prediction that only a tiny "remnant of Israel" would embrace the Gospel. A portion of Utah's surviving native peoples did indeed convert to Mormonism, often amalgamating Latter-day Saint teachings with native practices and beliefs. For most Paiutes, Utes, and Shoshone, however, Mormon colonization of the Great Basin under Young's leadership had unleashed devastating consequences.

As the Black Hawk War crested in 1866, two murders that same year raised fears among Utah's non-Mormons that Young was making a renewed effort to intimidate Gentiles through violence. In March, Newton Brassfield was shot shortly after a marriage to Mary Emma Hill, who was already married to a polygamous Mormon then absent on a church mission. U.S. judge Solomon McCurdy had informed Hill that her plural marriage's illegality rendered a divorce unnecessary. The *Union Vedette* contended that the murder "was a deliberately planned scheme, concocted and advised by men high in authority in the Mormon Church." In a discourse at the church's annual April conference, Young denied any involvement in or knowledge of the crime, but he condoned the murder by adding that were he "absent from home," he "would rejoice to know that I had friends there to protect and guard the virtue of my household." As Young had previously done on a number of occasions, he stressed that husbands— and friends on their behalf—had the right to take vengeance on their wives' seducers.[22]

Judge McCurdy wired Edwin Stanton, asking him to delay the planned removal of troops from Camp Douglas. Convinced of the threat, Lieutenant General Ulysses Grant instructed General William T. Sherman in St. Louis not to muster out the volunteers in Utah "until others are there to take their place," lest "the Gentiles will all have to leave the country." Sherman in turn sent Young a threatening telegram, noting that "our country is now full of tried and experienced soldiers, who would be pleased, at a fair opportunity, to avenge any wrongs you may commit against our citizens." Young, who disclaimed any knowledge of the murder, informed Sherman that men "who have taken more wives than one in this community," just as much as their monogamous counterparts, would take action to keep their marriage beds inviolate. Sherman, it turned out, did not fully trust non-Mormons in Utah and accepted Young's accusations against the political and military "clique" in the territory. Rather remarkably, the general recommended to Grant that "if the Gentiles will stir up strife they must take the consequences, but if they hold their tongues and mind their own business we will keep the present peace, and leave the Great Questions of Polygamy and the sanctity of Religion to the Law making Power." Brigham Young had asked no more of Utah's non-Mormons.[23]

Six months later a second murder created a similar sensation. Dr. John Robinson, a former Camp Douglas surgeon, collided with church leaders when he attempted to file a preemption claim for undeveloped land within the expansive Salt Lake City limits. Territorial lawmakers had set those limits to prevent unwanted homestead claims. When Robinson built a shack on his claimed land, the city police tore it down, prompting him to challenge the city's charter in court. A non-Mormon U.S. judge ruled against Robinson, though the doctor planned to appeal. On October 22, someone knocked on Robinson's door late at night and begged him to provide a brother with medical assistance. Decoyed out of his house, the doctor was shot within minutes. Patrick Edward Connor, mustered out of the army the previous spring, immediately pinned the murder on "Brighams destroying angels." Robinson, he alleged, was "shot down like a dog, for appealing to the Courts, for his rights." The *Union Vedette* reported the testimony of the sister of Robinson's widow that the doctor's murder came shortly after an argument with Young's counselor and Salt Lake City mayor Daniel Wells over the destruction of a bowling alley owned by Robinson. Young naturally denied the insinuations. "I have not the least idea in the world who could perpetrate such a crime," he stated in a tabernacle sermon. At the same time, he warned anyone tempted to homestead on his land: "If they jump my claims here, I shall be very apt to give them a preemption right that will last them to the last resurrection." In the cases of both Brassfield and Robinson, he chose his words carefully to deter other non-Mormons who might consider wooing Mormon wives or jumping church members' claims. Young's blunt talk increased suspicion that the church hierarchy sanctioned anti-Gentile violence.[24]

Expecting that the completion of the transcontinental railroad would cripple Mormon control of the territory, Utah's non-Mormons hoped that allegedly Mormon acts of violence would not go unpunished for much longer. By the end of 1866, the Union Pacific Railroad only extended a little more than halfway across Nebraska, and the Central Pacific Railroad had not yet reached Nevada. Still, construction was accelerating, and Young worried that the railroad's arrival would bring a host of non-

Mormon settlers to Utah and bolster the economic power of non-Mormon merchandizing houses. Young considered most non-Mormon merchants at least tacit supporters of the political and military clique that sought the overthrow of Mormon political and economic supremacy. Economic carpetbaggers, they were "[m]issionaries of evil" and the church's "avowed enemies." On at least one occasion, Young singled out Jewish merchants as the particular target of his contempt. "There are Jews here," he warned in the spring of 1869. "They are not our friends. Do not trade with them. They do not Believe in Jesus Christ."[25]

Young expected non-Mormon merchants to pursue their own self-interest, but he believed that the territory's Mormon merchants also valued mammon more highly than the welfare of the church and its members. Like leeches, they drained an industrious and righteous citizenry of its economic blood, charging the highest possible prices for the goods they imported or otherwise obtained. "They will get sorrow," Young warned in 1864, and "the most of them will be damned." Three years later, Young noted that one of the earliest of Joseph Smith's revelations instructed a merchant to "sell goods without fraud," a commandment Young accused the city's Mormon merchants of breaking by selling merchandise at inflated prices. Young's criticisms were not unusual in post–Civil War America. As railroads extended the sway of city-based wholesalers and bankers across the Great West, many Americans in the western hinterland concluded that merchants and bankers profited at their expense through corrupt and cruel practices.[26]

Knowing an economic battle loomed, Young made plans to hold as much ground as possible. The first prong of his response was a boycott of non-Mormon merchants, announced in 1865. Many Mormons failed to comply with this directive, but enough toed the line to persuade twenty-three Gentile merchants to offer their stock to the church. Even so, non-Mormon trading houses continued to thrive. Walker Brothers, run by former church members, was the territory's largest merchandizing operation. Annually it cleared upward of a half-million dollars by the end of the decade.[27]

Aware of the need for a more coordinated and coercive response, in December 1867 Young revived the School of the Prophets, an institution established by Joseph Smith in Kirtland in which church elders washed each other's feet, shared spiritual experiences, and received instruction in theology and secular branches of knowledge. In its second Mormon incarnation, the School of the Prophets was open to priesthood holders who observed the Word of Wisdom and promised to obey church leaders in all matters. The School of the Prophets drew hundreds of men to biweekly meetings in City Hall, and church leaders established branch schools in more than a dozen Mormon settlements.

Rather than a place for formal instruction, the revived School of the Prophets served as a forum for the coordination of economic policy, political decision-making, and doctrine. At one of its first meetings, Young emphatically returned to a controversial teaching, declaring that "Adam was Michael the Ark angel & he was the Father of Jesus Christ & was our God & that Joseph taught this principle." Back in the 1850s, Young had dismissed controversy over Adam's exact place in the chain of divine beings. At an 1871 school meeting, he now clarified that "Eloheim, Yahova, & Michael, were father, Son, and grandson." This divine family "made this earth & Michael became Adam," humanity's God. The assembled priesthood leaders discussed a wide variety of other topics: remedies for grasshopper invasions (axle grease on fruit tree trunks, whiskey sprinkled on trees, and dense herds of sheep to trample the pests were among the creative suggestions); the hygienic disposal of human excrement; and the purported advantages of plural marriage, ranging from men's greater procreative opportunities to a disincentive for masturbation.[28]

Especially during the school's first two years, though, Young mostly used the institution to further his economic war against Gentile merchants. He regularly inveighed against "trading with our Enemies" and eventually made such commerce grounds for expulsion from the school. In addition to firming up the boycott of non-Mormon trading houses, Young revealed the second and most popular prong of his response to the railroad. Under his direction, Mormons would help build it. The church—and individual church members—needed cash, and by drawing upon local and often indebted laborers Young could easily offer the railroad companies terms no one else could match. "The price he pays is not satisfactory," the Central Pacific executive Leland Stanford informed his partner Mark Hopkins, ". . . [but] his followers will not work for any one else while he wants men without his sanction." Young, as Trustee-in-Trust for the church, secured the contract—worth over two million dollars—to grade one hundred and fifty miles of the Union Pacific line, approaching the Great Salt Lake from the East. With Young's consent, several other church leaders obtained a four-million-dollar contract to grade a portion of the Central Pacific line. In May 1868, Young announced the Union Pacific contract, expressing thanks that it would keep "away from our midst the Swarms of scalliwags that the construction of the railway would bring here." In letters, he termed the contract a "god-send" for the church, and he hoped that it would improve congressional opinion toward the Latter-day Saints. Now that the railroads eliminated the rationale for the early 1860s "down-and-back" emigration and merchandizing teams, the contracts also provided an impetus for the church's effort to gather its converts, who could then work on the projects to pay off their church debts.[29]

Thus, under Young's leadership hundreds of Mormons helped grade the railroads that finally met in May 1869 at Promontory Summit, thirty miles west of Brigham City. Though it did not prevent him from bidding on the work, Young was disappointed that the railroads bypassed the Mormon capital by taking the northern route around the Great Salt Lake. Although the contracts had proven an economic boon, the Union Pacific—in financial straits despite years of lavish government subsidies—failed to meet its obligations to Young. The church president spent the next several years pressing the railroad for a settlement while asking his own creditors and subcontractors for patience. Partly because of Young's atypical tardiness in meeting his financial obligations, some Mormons accused him of acting like a corrupt railroad baron, lining his pockets while railroad laborers received rock-bottom wages and subcontractors and creditors awaited payment. The charges were at least partly unfair, as most of Young's difficulties began with the Union Pacific's failure to meet its obligations in a timely manner. Young rankled workers, though, when he talked of the need to reduce wages in order to make Mormon enterprises more competitive.[30]

Young attempted to overcome his financial difficulties by moving ahead with plans for a railroad to connect Salt Lake City with Ogden (where the transcontinentals intersected). The Union Pacific agreed to contribute iron rails and other materials, and church members contributed their labor to settle tithing or emigration debts or for payment in stock or railroad tickets. Young sold bonds for what became the Utah Central Railroad, intending to use the proceeds to pay off his Union Pacific subcontractors. The further demands on church members produced grumbling. At an August 1870 meeting of the School of the Prophets, the apostle George Q. Cannon referenced "a wide spread feeling of discontent and distrust in relation to moneytary matters in connexion with President Brigham Young and the Railroad." Predicting the railroad's profitability, Young nevertheless insisted that profits were beside the point. "We ought to take hold of it for the sake of building up the Kingdom of God," he instructed, "whether it pays or not." When church members remained slow to purchase the Utah Central bonds, Young threw his whole prophetic weight behind their sale. "It is the mind and will of God," he declared, "that the Elders of Israel should take the Utah Central Rail Road Bonds." Eventually, church leaders found enough buyers and celebrated the railroad's completion in January 1870. Although the Corinne *Reporter* mocked the project as "a train-way over a level plain the unparallel distance of thirty-five miles," it bears noting that other American churches did not build railroads of any length. Following the Utah Central's completion, Young proceeded with a Utah Southern Railroad and Utah Northern Railroad that slowly linked the outlying Mormon settlements with Salt Lake City. The railroads facilitated everything from Utah's internal commerce to the construction of the Salt Lake City Temple. Ironically, despite Young's determination to keep such enterprises in church hands, the Union Pacific later acquired control of the major Mormon-built Utah railroads because they proved unprofitable under church management.[31]

Although Young's initiatives co-opted the railroad's impact to some extent, its construction had indeed increased the presence and influence of non-Mormons in the territory. The railroad town of Corinne became a base for non-Mormon economic activity and threatened Mormon political control of northern Box Elder County. Despite his best efforts, Young had failed to eliminate the presence and power of Gentile merchants or to significantly curb the prices charged by Mormon traders. Thus, Young now moved forward with his economic strategy's crown jewel: church-directed cooperative merchandizing. He instructed Mormon merchants to develop a plan to purchase eastern goods collectively and then retail them at much lower prices. Mormon merchants would earn reduced profits, but they would undercut their non-Mormon counterparts and keep Zion's wealth within its borders. The result was the Zion's Cooperative Mercantile Institution (ZCMI), a joint-stock company established in 1868 that purchased and wholesaled eastern goods. In 1869, ZCMI retail stores appeared, first in Salt Lake City and then in the outlying settlements, swallowing up independent merchants by purchasing their stock. Merchants who invested in the enterprise displayed a ZCMI sign on their storefronts, consisting of an "All-Seeing Eye" and the phrase "Holiness to the Lord." The signs underscored the sacred significance Young lent to the enterprise. An inscription high above the Nauvoo Temple's main entrance included the phrase "Holiness to the Lord," probably taken from its appearance on Aaron's priestly headdress in ancient Israel. The all-seeing eye, meanwhile, was a symbol common to both Christianity and Freemasonry, and it appears in early architectural drawings of the Salt Lake Temple.[32]

ZCMI was a colossal financial risk for the church, for most cooperative merchandizing efforts in the late-nineteenth-century United States ended in failure. Farmers' cooperatives formed by the Grange movement, for example, were quickly undercut by city wholesalers.[33] Although ZCMI's ecclesiastical backing brought it unusual advantages in the marketplace and

William Jennings's "Eagle Emporium," 1869 *(courtesy of Church History Library, The Church of Jesus Christ of Latter-day Saints)*. The Zion's Co-Operative Mercantile Institution sign above the entrance reads "Holiness to the Lord" and contains an image of the all-seeing eye of God.

ensured its short-term success, its creation stoked controversy within the church. A correspondent for the Dun & Company credit bureau observed in 1869 that ZCMI had caused "wide spread dissatisfaction throughout the territory." That dissatisfaction existed most intensely within the economic elite of Mormon society.[34]

Several Mormon merchants, including the prosperous William Godbe (described by another credit agency correspondent as a "smart, active little fellow"), wanted Young to relax his grip on the territory's economic development, embrace mining, and cease his antimerchant fulminations.[35] Godbe shared these and other frustrations with Elias Harrison, the editor of the city's high-brow *Utah Magazine*. As did Brigham Young, Godbe and

Harrison coupled economic and spiritual concerns. Godbe and Harrison believed that Mormonism had lost its early spiritual core, especially church members' ready access to visions, revelations, and spiritual gifts. During the fall of 1868, while Young was laying the foundation for ZCMI, Godbe and Harrison traveled to New York City. While there, the two men patronized Charles Foster, a spiritualist medium who convinced his audiences partly because the spirits he summoned wrote their names in blood on his hand or arm. In their sessions, the recently departed spirit of Heber C. Kimball spoke through Foster, and the pair subsequently received messages from such diverse personages as the German naturalist Alexander Humboldt and Jesus Christ. Godbe and Harrison contrasted Kimball's spiritual piety with Young's temporal ambitions. The spirit visitations confirmed for Godbe and Harrison that they were meant to reform the church, freeing it from Young's oppressive leadership and elevating Mormonism to a higher plane of intelligence and freedom.[36]

Spiritualism had burst onto the American religious landscape in 1848. In Rochester, New York, sisters Maggie and Kate Fox began presiding over séances in which spirits made "rapping" noises to convey messages from beyond the grave. Such phenomena partly grew out of an earlier movement known as mesmerism, in which individuals who believed themselves gifted with a certain "magnetic fluid" or "animal magnetism" used that gift to heal the sick by placing them in trancelike states. Mesmerizers traveled around the United States (especially New England) in the 1830s and 1840s, and some of their subjects began receiving revelations and messages from the dead. During the second half of the nineteenth century, millions of Americans participated in some form of communication with spirits, typically with the assistance of a medium such as Charles Foster. Spiritualism had a particular appeal to individuals beset with intellectual or doctrinal doubts about their faith, which partly explains its attractions to Godbe and Harrison. They wanted to believe, and they wanted license to believe differently than Young taught.[37]

Spiritualism became associated with a rejection of orthodox Protestantism, a diminution of biblical authority, and radical political causes and sexual practices. In different ways, those tendencies also described Mormonism. Both Mormons and spiritualists spoke of replacing dead forms of religion with "science," "rationality," and "progress." Some Mormons experienced angelic visitors, and others saw their departed friends and family members in dreams. Just as for millions of other Americans, the possibility of communication with departed spirits did not seem incredible to many Latter-day Saints. Moreover, as James Strang and Joseph Morris had demonstrated, because Young eschewed Joseph Smith's form of revelation he left an opening for men who presented themselves as more abundant and regular sources of divine communication. "[H]ere comes a man," the *Salt Lake Tribune* wrote when Charles Foster visited Utah in 1873, "who gives people more revelation in ten minutes than they have received through Brigham Young in twenty-five years."[38]

Young often manifested a relatively tolerant attitude toward other religions, claiming that most possessed some truths. Accordingly, he allowed visiting Protestant ministers to speak in the tabernacle, and—despite his anger at Jewish merchants—he gave money for a Jewish cemetery in Salt Lake City. Spiritualism, though, Young denounced from the start as the "work of the Devil," a counterfeit form of revelation. Young believed that mesmerizers could indeed put their subjects into trances through the use of "animal magnetism," but he did not accept that those individuals received either healing or heavenly communications. Whereas Godbe and Harrison believed an infusion of spiritualism might liberate Mormonism from Young's despotic rule, Young saw spiritualism as encouraging religious chaos. Both Latter-day Saints and spiritualists rejected some of the same shibboleths of Protestant Christianity, but Joseph Smith and Brigham Young—unlike their spiritualist counterparts—had replaced them with a new set of scriptures, an ecclesiastical hierarchy, and the practical tasks of building the Kingdom of God on earth.[39]

Upon their November 1869 return from New York, Godbe and Harrison began quietly forming a network of dissenters. After ignoring the cooperative drive and then supporting it half-heartedly, they began quietly opposing Young's economic agenda in the pages of Harrison's *Utah Magazine*. As late as the spring of 1869, Young did not foresee the coming storm. He officiated at Godbe's plural marriage to Charlotte Cobb, Young's stepdaughter by Augusta Adams. "I would have bet my last dollar on him [Godbe] being true to you," Brigham Young Jr. later consoled his father.[40]

In the fall of 1869, the dissenters began to announce their views more openly. In the pages of the *Utah Magazine*, Harrison lamented the "fatal error" held by many Mormons "that God Almighty *intended the priesthood to do our thinking.*" Instead, he encouraged, "[t]hink freely, and think forever." That same publication editorialized in mid-October against Young's attachment to agriculture and "home manufactures," declaring that only the open and vigorous development of mining could provide Utah's citizens with the currency they had long needed and the financial means to develop their own industries. Otherwise, warned Harrison, residents of Utah would remain impoverished within a backward economic system reliant upon barter. The editorial marked an open assault on Brigham Young's leadership. [41]

The church president, now fully aware of the threat, quickly brought the issue to a head. At the School of the Prophets, Young denounced the rebellion and scheduled an ecclesiastical trial for Godbe, Harrison, and several other men. Given Young's past fulminations against apostates, his hyperbolic responses to Orson Pratt's theological independence, and his harsh words toward Joseph Smith's sons, the dissenters probably expected to meet the full fury of Young's wrath.

As it turned out, Godbe, Harrison, and the other dissidents overestimated their potential support while badly underestimating their opponent. Unlike in the 1850s, there was no talk of cutting throats or sending men to "hell across lots." Young orchestrated a hearing remarkably free of rancor and allowed the eloquent and forceful Godbe and Harrison to air their views fully. While affirming his belief in Young's right to have succeeded Joseph Smith and that "polygamy is true & eternal," Harrison took issue with the priesthood's purported claim of "infallibility" and criticized Young's economic policies. While conceding that not all of his decisions had produced financial success, Young countered they might still serve God's purposes, and he also pointedly remarked that Godbe had grown wealthy under the policies he now criticized. "I do not pretend to be infallible," Young clarified, "but the priesthood that I have on me is infallible." Godbe and Harrison were free, free to reject church authority, turn away from the gospel, and eventually "taste the second death and lose their identity." True Saints would persevere in righteousness and obedience, gradually enjoying greater quantities of "intelligence," "truth," and "light." Godbe and Harrison stood firm. The council "handed [them] over to the buffettings of Satan." The church imposed its most severe penalty, excommunication. Young, however, had presided over a calm, restrained trial, and in the process he had compellingly affirmed his own Mormon faith.[42]

The merchant Henry Lawrence, Eli Kelsey (an editor and a son of Young's wife Mary Oldfield), the writer Edward Tullidge, Orson Pratt Jr., and James Cobb (son of Young's wife Augusta Adams) all followed Godbe and Harrison's lead. Thomas and Fanny Stenhouse hesitated for a season before also joining what became known as the "New Movement," as did Young's former clerk George D. Watt. Unlike Joseph Morris in the early 1860s, Godbe and Harrison had attracted several of the territory's leading economic and literary lights. Many of the men had previously enjoyed Young's esteem and trust, making the rupture unusually painful for the church president. The Godbeites, as the group was also known, quickly formed what they named the Church of Zion, initially intending to reform rather than to reject Mormonism.

Although its meetings in late 1869 and early 1870 drew significant crowds, the new church acquired few actual converts. It quickly turned out that the Godbeites intended to replace Brigham Young's Mormonism with something few Latter-day Saints would have recognized as their own religion. Within months of their excommunications, Harrison stated that Mormonism was a "species of spiritualism," and the New Movement quickly rejected or deemphasized its more distinctly Mormon aspects (from polygamy to a corporeal God). Mormons who considered Young's temporal leadership a declension from Joseph Smith's foundation would not find the latter among the Godbeites. By the end of 1870, the New Movement had stopped calling itself a "church," gathered more for intellectual lectures than for worship, and more openly embraced spiritualism.[43]

Despite its tiny membership, the New Movement mounted an ongoing threat to Young's hegemony over Utah. The *Salt Lake Daily Tribune and Utah Mining Gazette,* the successor to the Godbeites' *Mormon Tribune,* became the territory's most significant non-Mormon publication and a constant journalistic thorn in Young's side. It adopted a stridently anti-Mormon tone and promoted Utah's economic development in ways contrary to Young's vision. In 1871, the Godbeites also founded the Liberal Institute, a free-thought counterweight to the Salt Lake City Tabernacle. In a magnificent downtown edifice, the institute hosted worship services for a variety of non-Mormon religious societies (from Jews to "Josephites"), lectures, political meetings, and séances. The institute gave Mormonism's opponents a secure, commodious, and visible platform.[44]

The Godbeites sought a political alliance with the territory's leading non-Mormon businessmen and politicians. Although initially divided over the Godbeites' agonized defense of plural marriage, the two sides stumbled their way toward the creation of the "Liberal Party," the territory's first independent political party. In response, Mormon leaders began referring to the church ticket as the "People's Party." The People's Party initially won overwhelming electoral majorities in Utah, but the presence of a vigorous opposition meant that those elections made up for their lack of suspense with a full measure of rancor.

Young's response throughout had been muted. He was away from Salt Lake City on an extended southern tour during the Church of Zion's first conference in April 1870. Young informed the apostle Albert Carrington that his policy toward the Godbeites was to "let them severely alone."[45]

Church leaders made derisive comments about the Godbeites and warned church members of the dangers of apostasy. Mormons who attended Godbeite meetings sometimes reported that church leaders employed retaliatory measures against them. Still, unlike in 1856–57, there was no talk of blood atonement for apostasy, signaling a transition to a new era. Young would no longer publicly condone violence, as he had done after the murders of Brassfield and Robinson. The confrontational tactics Young had employed in earlier decades were ill suited for Utah in the early 1870s. With the arrival of the railroad, Utah's isolation from the rest of the country had markedly decreased. Young knew it and adapted accordingly.

As THE Black Hawk War waned and the New Movement developed, the federal threat to Young's kingdom reemerged after an extended respite. President Andrew Johnson had continued Lincoln's policy of neglecting Utah affairs while appointing non-Mormon officials and judges. Utah territorial delegate William Hooper, a prosperous merchant and key ZCMI figure, sanguinely and correctly predicted that while "Andy is Yet at the White House" the Mormons had little to fear. Congress transferred an additional degree of longitude containing valuable mining strikes from western Utah to eastern Nevada, but it did not pass more draconian proposals, one of which would have entirely dismantled the Utah Territory. In contrast to his frequent discussion of the Civil War, Young made few comments on the Reconstruction-era policies that produced bitter divisions within the Republican Party. Terming Negro suffrage a "vexed" question, Young doubted "that there is any President who could be obtained who could swallow all the niggers there are without bolting [vomiting]." He probably meant that the Republicans could not incorporate black voters without destroying themselves politically.[46]

While Congressional Reconstruction produced a venomous reaction from white southerners and galvanized a resurgent Democratic Party in the North, measures considered radical elsewhere proved uncontroversial in Utah. The territory's voters, Young informed Thomas Kane in an 1869 letter, had adopted black suffrage by a vote of fourteen thousand to thirty. Especially in light of Young's earlier stated opposition to black political rights, the vote was a rather ironic example of Mormon political obedience. Both California and Oregon refused to ratify the Fifteenth Amendment, but in Utah—previously the first far-western state or territory to legalize black slavery—it generated little opposition.[47]

Young's own political views had changed little since before the Civil War. He shared the national Democratic Party's preference for a limited central government and greater local control. He would have agreed with many Democrats and—as the Grant administration proceeded—reformers within the Republican Party that the national government had become a corrupt and oppressive behemoth to the detriment of ordinary white Americans. Young was not, however, a limited-government Democrat at the territorial level, where the church hierarchy in partnership with the Mormon-controlled legislature happily undertook internal improvements and public-private business ventures. Young's goals were to preserve his ability to direct Utah's government and shield church members (and especially hierarchs) from prosecution in the courtrooms of federal judges. In short, Young wanted to stop the national government from applying the tools of southern Reconstruction to the "Mormon problem."[48]

Heralding the end of Washington's benign neglect of Utah, Vice President Schuyler Colfax visited Salt Lake City in October 1869 and demanded Mormon obedience to the Morrill Anti-Bigamy Act. "[O]ur country is governed by law," Colfax lectured, "and no assumed revelation justifies any one trampling on the law." Colfax's sharp warning foreshadowed the Grant administration's harder line on Utah affairs.[49]

Polygamy aside, the main points of conflict within the territory revolved around courts and land. Under Utah law, marshals appointed by the wholly Mormon legislature impaneled juries. This arrangement made successful polygamy prosecutions impossible. Also, the territory's probate courts, whose judges were appointed by the legislature, still claimed original jurisdiction in both civil and criminal cases. As illustrated in the issues surrounding the John Robinson murder case, non-Mormons also complained that municipalities effectively excluded them from obtaining desirable land in the territory. In 1868, Congress had for the first time established a land office in Utah, but incorporated cities and their officials—church members in nearly all cases—mostly controlled the process of land distribution and sales. Thus, while many church leaders were obvious violators of the Morrill Act, in many other disputes they had the law on their side.[50]

Territorial opponents of Mormon supremacy, therefore, worked hard to get those laws changed, traveling to the nation's capital to lobby politicians to embrace their cause. In early 1870, the writer and editor John Beadle and Robert Baskin (the attorney who had represented John Robinson) eagerly testified before the Republican-dominated Congress about everything from Mormon juries to Young's public profanity. In February, Representative Shelby Cullom of Illinois introduced sweeping antipolygamy legislation. The bill proposed to limit the jurisdiction of the territory's probate courts, strip voting and preemption rights from those who refused to swear under oath that they neither practiced nor believed in polygamy, give federally appointed officials the authority to impanel juries, and convict men on the basis of "cohabitation . . . with more than one woman as husband and wives." As an enforcement mechanism, the bill would have authorized the president to send up to forty thousand troops to Utah, which boasted a population of slightly more than one hundred thousand.[51]

Utah's Mormon population was predictably outraged at the proposed legislation. "The slavery from which the blacks of the South have been emancipated," editorialized the *Deseret News,* "would be delightful compared with the crushing bondage which this Bill would bring." It was an affront to which the newspaper believed white, Anglo-Saxon men should not submit. Referring to Baskin, the *News* threatened that a "Vigilance Committee in search of a criminal might make the mistake of hanging the owner of such a countenance." When it came to Washington politicians, Young still privately displayed the acerbic wit he had publicly deployed in the mid-1850s. "I have a proposition to make to [senators Aaron] Cragan [*sic*], Wade and all such men," he wrote William Hooper, Utah's congressional delegate, in 1868, "when my old niger has been dead one year, if they will wash their faces clean they may kiss his ass." As Congress debated the Cullom Bill, Hooper politely encouraged Young to restrain his rhetoric. "[N]othing my dear friend," Hooper warned, "do they now so much desire as some act or speech of yourself & others which would kick the beam and thus enable them our enemies to carry their point of robbery & plunder." Young had already learned this lesson, however. Just as with the Godbeite trial, Young responded much more cagily than his detractors expected. There were no public denunciations of "King Ulysses" or threats to slay an army should it march on Utah. Instead, Young preached on the need for calm and peace.[52]

In another sign of Young's shrewder political approach, thousands of Mormon women gathered at the tabernacle to affirm their commitment to "Celestial Marriage." The assembled women pledged themselves, in the event the Cullom Bill became law, "to aid in the support of our own State Government." "[L]et us stand by the truth if we die for it," resolved Amanda Smith, who had quietly been sealed to Young as a proxy wife in 1852. Eliza Snow, also Young's wife and Mormonism's most prominent female leader, disputed the notion of Mormon women as enslaved to polygamous men. Knowing that the territorial legislature would soon grant women the ballot, she observed that "to us the right of suffrage is extended in matters of far greater importance." In February 1870, partly as a preemptive rebuttal of the Cullom Bill, Mormon legislators made Utah the second territory in the nation (after Wyoming) in which women could vote. (Women could not vote in any state.) As Apostle Orson Pratt observed, the measure would "increase our votes one Hundred per cent." The territorial legislature's vote was unanimous, meaning that Utah's peculiar politics had granted suffrage to African Americans and women in successive years without any apparent internal controversy.[53]

Shorn of its most draconian provisions, a weakened version of the Cullom Bill passed the House in March 1870, but the measure died in the Senate. Mormon Utah had narrowly escaped the federal government's cudgel once again.

In the absence of new legislation, President Grant expected his Utah appointees to assert federal control over the territory through other means. In the spring of 1870, new territorial governor J. Wilson Shaffer reached Utah. A former aide to General Benjamin Butler during the Union Army's occupation of New Orleans, Shaffer determined to make himself governor in fact as well as in name, and he regarded his new wards much as he and Butler had viewed obstinate Confederates. "I am fully satisfied that this people are worse than their enemies ever charged," the governor wrote Secretary of State Hamilton Fish two weeks after his arrival in Salt Lake City. He alleged that Young's "absolute power" had sanctioned "murders and assassinations," and he insisted that Grant support legislative measures to reform the territory's judicial system. "As the law now stands," he reported in July, "the Mormons have entire control, and a verdict in favor of the Government or a Gentile cannot be had." The governor promptly made his own round of appointments to minor territorial offices, replacing Mormon (or sympathetic non-Mormon) incumbents. "Brigham Young clearly is beginning to feel that we have a President and a Government," he bragged.[54]

That fall, Shaffer struck perhaps the most effective blow against Mormon control of the territory since the arrival of Albert Sidney Johnston's Utah Expedition. For years, the Nauvoo Legion had provided the Latter-day Saints with a military deterrent against federal intervention. During congressional deliberations over the Cullom Bill, some representatives had expressed concern over the possibility of armed resistance, noting that the Mormons drilled thousands of militia men. Young had deployed the Nauvoo Legion during the protracted Black Hawk War, and the militia was a major factor in his ongoing influence over Indian affairs in the territory. In September 1870, Shaffer ordered the cancellation of a planned territory-wide militia muster and appointed Young's old nemesis Patrick Edward Connor the territorial militia's major general. Despite Shaffer's imminent death from tuberculosis, he stood his ground. Four days before his death at the age of forty-three, he informed now former militia commander Daniel Wells—whom the governor pointedly addressed as "Mr. Wells" rather than "Lieutenant General"—that he would not compromise with "an un-lawful military system." Although some Mormon militia units continued to drill without gubernatorial sanction, Shaffer's action significantly weakened the church's military deterrent (against either Indians or the federal government). In keeping with his recent approach, however, the church president avoided public comment on the matter, again deeming it more politic to maintain a lower profile in response to federal threats.[55]

Building on Shaffer's lead, the next year former congressman, Civil War veteran, and new territorial Chief Justice James McKean launched a judicial campaign against Mormon polygamy and theocracy. McKean, a wiry, gray-bearded son of a Methodist preacher, attacked plural marriage with evangelical zeal. Young and many other Mormon leaders had openly violated the 1862 Morrill Act, but no judge in Utah had attempted to prosecute a polygamy case. The lack of a legal basis for plural marriages posed a challenge, as did the presumed hesitancy of Mormon jurors to convict their co-religionists on the basis of a law they regarded as oppressive and unconstitutional. McKean, whom the apostle George Q. Cannon labeled Mormonism's "most unrelenting, persevering and active enemy," was not easily discouraged by such legal niceties. Rather than use the Morrill Act, he made Utah's own territorial law against adultery and lewd and lascivious cohabitation the basis for indictments. He also held, contrary to territorial law, that the federally appointed U.S. marshal would empanel juries in his court, giving himself the means to stack juries with non-Mormons.[56]

While he rejected the constitutionality of both the Morrill Act and McKean's subversion of territorial law, Young could probably see advantages in a series of anti-polygamy trials that would make legal martyrs out of church hierarchs. The specter of a murder indictment, however, soon raised the stakes. William ("Wild Bill") Hickman agreed to implicate Young in the 1857 death of non-Mormon trader Richard Yates. By the mid-1860s, Hickman had become disillusioned with Young's leadership and more interested in mining ventures. Before his excommunication, Hickman threatened to reveal incriminating facts about Young and the church. "I am willing," Young dared, "you should tell the whole world what you know about Mormonism or my private and public character." Three years later, Hickman did just that. Suspected of a long train of church-ordered as well as freelance murders, Hickman met with Deputy U.S. Marshal Sam Gilson and turned state's evidence.[57]

In late September, church leaders got wind of Hickman's arrangement, and Young spent the next several months debating whether he should risk his life in a capital case before a hostile judge. At first, Young seemed inclined to stand trial, telling his associates that he would not "be exposed to assassination here as Joseph was in Carthage jail." He had assurances of protection from General Regis de Trobriand, a French native on friendly terms with Mormon leaders since assuming command at Camp Douglas in 1870. Also, while Young expected to be convicted in McKean's court, he and Mormon leaders predicted the judge's strategy would not prevail upon appeal. Church leaders hired a team of non-Mormon lawyers (including the former Nevada representative Thomas Fitch, who had opposed the Cullom Bill) and prepared to contest McKean in court.[58]

McKean, meanwhile, had assembled a non-Mormon grand jury. On October 2, U.S. Marshal M. T. Patrick served Young with a writ for his arrest on the charge of "lascivious cohabitation." With Young in poor health at the time, Patrick left him in the care of deputies. The marshal then arrested Daniel Wells, George Q. Cannon, several other church leaders, and Henry Lawrence, a Godbeite polygamist. The next week, thousands of Latter-day Saints crowded the streets outside the courtroom as Young appeared before McKean and posted $5,000 bail. In rejecting a motion to quash Young's indictment, Justice McKean made clear what he saw as the pending trial's import: "The government of the United States, founded upon a written constitution, finds within its jurisdiction another government—claiming to come from God—*imperiam in imperio*—whose policy and practice, in grave particulars, are at variance with its own. . . . A system is on trial in the person of Brigham Young." Many members of Utah's non-Mormon community exulted at the rise of a "new judicial era." The *Salt Lake Tribune* crowed that Utah's version of "Boss Tweed" was about to follow the example of his New York counterpart, who had just lost an election. The Corinne *Reporter* rejoiced with each legal setback endured by the man it variously insulted as the "hoary libertine," "the butcher of Zion," and the "high priest of Hell." Not all non-Mormon opponents of the church, however, considered McKean's actions wise, believing that economic development and non-Mormon emigration presented less controversial means of breaking the church's stranglehold on the territory. Young's old nemesis Patrick Edward Connor—now a civilian engaged in mining ventures—reportedly conveyed to Young "a strong hope & belief that you would get clear of all your troubles soon."[59]

The church president initially professed himself unconcerned about his indictment and arrest. "It is as easy as an old shoe," he said to a *New York Tribune* correspondent. Privately, though, he seethed over the proceedings. A former Reformed Methodist himself, Young blamed "the power of the Methodist Church" for the current persecutions.[60] A Methodist minister had recently held a camp meeting in Salt Lake City, Judge McKean was a Methodist, and Methodist U.S. Senate chaplain J. P. Newman regularly preached against Mormon polygamy.

The dynamics of the judicial holy war shifted when Young, accompanied by his wife Amelia Folsom, left Salt Lake City for southern Utah on October 24. Young claimed that his trip had been planned for some time, and he attended the dedication of a temple site in St. George two weeks later. The church president, however, slipped out of the city late at night. "[Y]ou left none too soon," Wells wrote the next day, adding that "it is not generally known that you are away." Young had departed because of his imminent arrest on charges of murder. A few days later, the marshal arrested Wells, Hosea Stout, and William Kimball in the death of Richard Yates. The prisoners were housed at Camp Douglas, and Young would have joined them had he not begun his trip. As rumors swirled that the army would mount an expedition to capture him, Young stayed in the apostle Erastus Snow's St. George mansion. According to George A. Smith, "a sufficient number of the brethren" stayed in the house "to protect him [Young] from assassination." Local church leaders instructed St. George Saints to plead ignorance if questioned by strangers about Young's presence.[61]

Young was unsure whether to return to Salt Lake City to stand trial. He briefly considered fleeing farther south, mentioning to Wells that they could "continue a line of settlements into Mexico" before cryptically informing his counselor that it looked "a little stormy and bad for a trip to Mexico this fall." Young also asked non-Mormon political ally Thomas Kane to investigate the possibility of securing a tract of land in British Columbia and a corresponding guarantee of religious freedom from the British government, a suggestion Kane quickly rejected as impossible. Meanwhile, Mormon leaders furiously sought a means to secure McKean's removal or otherwise obstruct the trials. Young and George A. Smith warned Wells that the Gentile "Ring" had used women to befriend the "hired girls" working in the homes of Mormon leaders. In return, Young recommended that "a few female detectives" might befriend the wives of McKean and Governor George Woods and gather damaging personal information.[62]

After Young failed to appear for an early December court date, McKean leniently rescheduled the trial for early January and did not order the forfeiture of Young's bonds. Young thus had several more weeks to consider his options. He worried less about his eventual judicial fate than about his immediate safety. Most church leaders and the church's non-Mormon attorneys encouraged Young to return, in part because of newly appointed

U.S. Attorney George Bates's sympathy. The church had quickly established good relations with the destitute Bates, offering him five hundred dollars after he lost everything in the October 1871 Great Chicago Fire. Bates declined the gift, but he soon made it clear that he did not affirm McKean's course of action.[63]

Young did not want to return to Salt Lake City without assurances that he could post bail and avoid confinement at Camp Douglas. Bates asked U.S. Attorney General Amos Akerman to endorse granting bail to Young. After obtaining advice from President Grant, Akerman deemed the proposal inappropriate "while Young absconds." McKean also refused to give Young any special treatment. Bates, though, had already told Wells that if Young returned he would either be granted bail or be placed under house arrest. Worried about the security of telegraph lines, Young sent a telegram to Wells using the church's substitution cipher:

> Can I be assured of getting bail if I come home? We understand they have a thousand troops at Camp Douglas. Bates may have it in his mind to spring a trap upon me, get me to camp and let men come in there who would assassinate me If there is the least apprehension with you or the brethren of anything of this kind then I should want you to have two thousand men distributed in the city ready with materials for such an emergency.

Wells, who throughout the fall had leavened hot-headed Mormon calls for a militant response to McKean's court, now told the men at a School of the Prophets meeting to "be ready with your Arms and Ammunition . . . keep them where you can put your hands upon them at a Moments notice—and be sure to have your powder dry." Young warily slipped back into Salt Lake City on December 26 at midnight.[64]

On the second day of the new year, Young was arrested by prearrangement with the U.S. marshal. McKean refused to grant Young's request for bail but asked the marshal to place him under house arrest with every possible convenience. "Brigham seemed perfectly cool and unconcerned," informed the Corinne *Reporter,* which even praised the church president's "virtue" in submitting to the court. Young's trial would have begun a week later, but the proceedings came to an abrupt halt when William Clayton, territorial auditor and church member, refused to pay the court's expenses. This prompted Bates to request the delay of all pending trials. Young remained under a very loose house arrest, nominally guarded by the marshal while several of his "boys" also held watch at all times. He attended the theater on January 11, and the famous phrenologist Orson Fowler examined his head later in the month.[65]

Meanwhile, a test case regarding the legality of McKean's actions reached the U.S. Supreme Court. Salt Lake City Alderman Jeter Clinton, a trusted member of the church, had ordered the destruction of $20,000 worth of liquor owned by non-Mormons who had refused to pay the city's steep liquor license fee. In McKean's court, an entirely non-Mormon jury had convicted Clinton of malicious destruction of property. In April 1872, the Supreme Court's unanimous *Engelbrecht v. Clinton* decision overturned the conviction, ruling that McKean had violated territorial law through his jury-selection process. McKean, Robert Baskin, Joseph Walker, and Henry Lawrence attended the court to listen to its ruling, as did George Q. Cannon. The *Engelbrecht* decision quashed all of the pending indictments, including Young's for both lascivious cohabitation and the Yates murder. Young and church leaders quietly rejoiced over the decision but expected no pause in the ongoing war for judicial and political control of Utah.[66]

Indeed, the very day after the *Engelbrecht* decision, Mormon representatives in Washington presented Young with yet another political dilemma. Fearing an adverse decision, McKean had already drafted legislation to legalize the tactics he had employed in the 1871 prosecutions, and he persuaded Indiana Democratic Representative Daniel Voorhees to introduce a bill that would allow federally appointed officials to control the jury-selection process. The measure would also have permitted cohabitation as sufficient evidence in polygamy cases.[67] George Q. Cannon, a savvy political operative whom the *New York Tribune* described as "stout of flesh, low of stature, rubicund [ruddy] of countenance, and ready of tongue,"[68] warned Young that the church should protect itself against this new legislative threat. When transmitting sensitive information from Washington to church leaders, Cannon wrote in Hawaiian, relying upon his fellow former missionary Joseph F. Smith to translate. In this instance, Cannon suggested that the church should "fee some of the members of Congress":

> If reported by the committee and it comes before the House [it] will cause a great deal of discussion and difficulty to kill said Bill in that position, because the members are afraid to vote against it. We think its defeat is important, and we think we can defeat said Bill by giving a few thousand dollars. What is your mind? Shall we try? If you wish us to do this, it would be well for you (bro. Wells) to arrange through Lew Hills, with Kountze Brothers at New York. . . . Should the proposition meet your mind, and you do anything about it, a despatch by telegraph might be a guide to us as to what to do.[69]

Smith translated the letter on April 26, and several days later Daniel Wells quickly reassured Cannon that "all necessaries will be attended to." In mid-May, Young by telegraph informed Cannon of "Three Thousand dollars placed [to] your credit at Kountze Brothers, New York."[70]

Utah congressional delegate William Hooper had informed Young that the ex-Mormon mercantile house Walker Brothers was prepared to spend $200,000 to ease the Voorhees Bill's passage through the House. While Young disliked the uneconomical nature of bribery and sometimes told his representatives simply to trust in the Lord for help, he authorized such measures on occasion. In the early 1860s, on the recommendation of John Bernhisel, he paid a Washington middleman in return for assistance in getting his Indian expenses approved. The church also expended funds to purchase favorable newspaper coverage, a common practice in nineteenth-century America. The church's political opponents regularly alleged that any Gentile judge or official whose actions appeared sympathetic to church leaders must have taken a bribe from them. George Bates, the U.S. attorney tasked with prosecuting Young for murder, felt obliged to inform Attorney General George Williams that "Brigham Young has not wealth enough to buy me." Still, after Governor George Woods and other non-Mormon officials accused Bates of acting as if he was counsel for the defense, he lost his job. By the spring of 1872, Bates was with Hooper and Cannon in Washington, and he later found work as an attorney for the church. Such developments increased suspicion that he had been bought, if not with an outright bribe then through the promise of business.[71]

The Mormons, of course, were hardly the only Americans with a less than saintly record when it came to political ethics. In September 1872, newspapers reported that the directors of the Union Pacific Railroad Company had enriched themselves, their stockholders, and their political friends through a scheme that involved the awarding of inflated construction contracts to a subsidiary company, the Crédit Mobilier. As Congress had subsidized the completion of the transcontinental railroad, those involved had lined their own pockets with government largesse. The directors of the Union Pacific, moreover, had then sold Crédit Mobilier stock to politicians (including Vice President Colfax) at below-market prices. Given the extent of Gilded Age corruption and the tremendous nationwide antipathy against Mormon polygamy ("public men are as much afraid of being suspected of having sympathy with 'Mormons' or 'Mormonism' as they are of the small-pox," observed Cannon), it would have been politically unwise for church leaders to rely only upon persuasion and personal relationships in the pursuit of their political goals. A well-placed bribe often worked wonders in a national capital rife with corruption.[72]

In the spring of 1872, the Mormon bribe apparently proved decisive.

"The Mormon Problem Solved," 1871 *(courtesy of Library of Congress)*. The caption reads: Brigham—"I must submit to your laws—but what shall I do with all these?" U.S.G.—"Do as I do—give them offices."

During the week after Young's telegram, both Mormons and their Utah opponents, including Judge McKean, feverishly lobbied the members of the House Judiciary Committee. Sagging under the weight of the Crédit Mobilier scandal and continued fissures over its treatment of the ex-Confederacy, the Republican Party was heading toward an election-year schism. Ultimately, a group of self-styled Liberal Republicans nominated Horace Greeley for president, who favored a hands-off policy toward both the South and Utah. Several southern Democrats, meanwhile, had privately told Cannon of their sympathy for Utah. While their constituents might have supported action against Mormon polygamy, most Washington politicians merely wanted to leave town and begin the election campaign in earnest. In May 1872, after several contentious sessions, the House Judiciary Committee could not find a majority to report the Voorhees Bill to the full House. For the second time in three months, church leaders celebrated a political triumph. When the Republican Party dedicated itself in 1856 to eradicating the "twin relics of barbarism," few Americans would have predicted that Mormon polygamy would prove a more stubborn target than slavery or that federal authority over Utah affairs would remain contested for so long. After a decade in which the Republican Party held the White House and typically enjoyed large majorities in Congress, the Latter-day Saints still practiced plural marriage and Brigham Young remained the lynchpin of Utah politics, business, and religion.

DESPITE the recent victories, Young's position was more tenuous than ever. Church leaders could no longer persuade Washington to remove hostile governors and judges, and they had lost authority over Utah's militia. Although certain Mormon scriptures predicted that the Indians would one day execute God's judgment upon the Gentiles, Indian raiders had instead wreaked havoc on outlying Mormon settlements. Young had tried every possible tactic to eliminate the profits of non-Mormon merchants, including a church-ordered boycott and church-backed cooperative merchandizing. Surprising his political and ecclesiastical enemies, Young replaced his ham-handed rhetoric and actions of the mid-1850s with more adroit and less inflammatory tactics. In so doing, Young displayed an impressive ability to adapt to changing circumstances even as he more fully entered old age. He even nominated his son Willard (by Clarissa Ross Chase) for a West Point cadetship in 1871.

Still, while the Zion's Cooperative Mercantile Institution became the most significant wholesale and retail business in the territory, it did not sweep the field. Walker Brothers, for instance, saw profits plunge in 1869 only to sharply rebound thereafter. Young's policies delayed the growth of non-Mormon enterprise in Utah, but they could not stop it. With President Grant now demanding additional legislation to eradicate Utah polygamy and theocracy, moreover, it seemed only a matter of time before Congress enabled the prosecutions that had thus far eluded McKean. By then, the judge would have a new and unexpected ally—one of Brigham Young's own wives.

CHAPTER THIRTEEN

The Soul and Mainspring
of the West

When I leave this frail existence—
When I lay this mortal by,
Father, mother, may I meet you
In your royal court on high?
—ELIZA R. SNOW (1845)

MANY nineteenth-century Americans saw the West as a quick path to great riches. They came to make their fortunes out of white pine forests, prairie soil, bison herds, and placer gold. The descendants of men and women who had sought buried treasures in the burned-over district of western New York now sought gold and silver in western canyons and mountainsides. Prospectors hoped to beat others to those resources and quickly make their fortunes, then return to families and homes back east. Many ultimately decided to stay in the West, but even once mining became industrialized, miners remained peripatetic, readily moving on in search of better wages.

Brigham Young and the Latter-day Saints, by contrast, made the Great Basin their permanent home. Young anticipated the Mormons' eventual return to Jackson County, and he regularly contemplated contingency plans should the U.S. Army force them out of their Rocky Mountain Zion. Still, he intended to build an earthly kingdom that would endure. "The Latter day Saints will stay here," he explained, "and labour and make it their homes—but the balance will go, as soon as the bottom drops out of these Mines, and become as white pine & other once boasted Mines, but are now forsaken." The Mormons, he suggested, were different from other white Americans passing through the Great Basin's canyons and valleys. If others wanted to get in, get rich, and get out, the Latter-day Saints should get in, stay in, and help fellow church members to do the same.[1]

As Congress continued to reduce Utah's size and even contemplated its complete dismemberment, Young doggedly pushed ahead with Mormon colonization. In the late 1860s, under Young's direction settlers haltingly established new colonies in southern Nevada, with the renewed intention of cultivating cotton, sugar, and olive oil. Settlement also continued apace along the Virgin River in southern Utah, in territory Mormon leaders spoke of as Utah's own "Palestine." In the mid-1870s, Mormons established colonies deep into Arizona, and missionaries explored potential settlements in northern Mexico. During these years, Mormon settlers also built new towns in southern Idaho. "In the course of a little time," Young predicted in 1870, "we shall have the controuling power in Ida[h]o." Visiting the southern settlements that same year, Young declared that "Mormons rule Nevada." Such predictions were fanciful; the church would never control political developments in neighboring states and territories. Indeed, during his 1870 trip to southern Nevada, he and other church leaders discussed a potential war with the United States and the need for hideaways within the canyons of the forbidding southern landscape. Not all of the new colonies succeeded, and the constant threat of federal opposition to polygamy and theocracy lent an air of fragility to the entire enterprise of kingdom-building. Nevertheless, Young's stubborn confidence in his church's future paid dividends. Of the roughly three hundred and sixty Mormon settlements established during Young's three decades in Utah, more than one-third were founded during the last ten years of his life. The Latter-day Saints, Young correctly foresaw, would grow in numbers and strength while building their Zion on land others mainly wanted to exploit. "We are the Soul," he said, "and the Mainspring of the West."[2]

Even as Mormon settlers carved out their church's lasting presence within a broad swath of the American West, Young's own presence now seemed much less permanent. His attacks of rheumatism came more frequently and were more painful, prompting him to spend several months of each winter in more temperate St. George. As long as he could, he approached old age and disease as opponents his iron will and stubborn faith could subdue. On his 1870 trip to the southern settlements, a gastrointestinal illness attacked several of Young's traveling companions, including his son Brigham. "The same feeling came upon me," Brigham Jr. wrote in his diary, "but father sat there and shook his fist at me & I managed to choke it down." Young himself "fought off the feeling, produced his medicine and was very active in treating the sick."[3]

By 1874, Young began experiencing other intractable health problems. In the fall of that year, he began retaining urine due to an enlarged prostate. For a fortnight, his nephew and physician Seymour Young emptied his bladder with a catheter until he learned to catheterize himself. The problem recurred the following year, and Seymour Young again provided similar treatment. The church president was so grateful that he gave his nephew a parcel of Salt Lake City real estate.[4] Fifteen years earlier, Young had boasted of his fine health and virility. By the mid-1870s, gray-headed and gray-bearded, and sometimes unable to walk, he frankly discussed the ravages of aging. In January 1876, showing compassion for another old man experiencing similar urological trouble, he sent a catheter to William Stevens. The detailed instructions for its use included a suggestion to lubricate it with "consecrated oil," reflecting Young's tendency to imbue even such an unpleasant task with a reminder of the sacred.[5]

Young's decreased physical capacity forced him to slow the pace of his activities. He dedicated his remaining years to institutions, relationships, and ideas that he hoped would long survive him. Shortly after his seventieth birthday, Young began to get his affairs in order. He updated his will several times and began to clarify the tangled relationship between his own property and that of the church. He reared his eldest sons as ecclesiastical leaders, and he took actions to reorder the leadership succession that would follow his eventual death. Until the final days of his life, though, Young prodded his often weary followers to higher levels of commitment and dedication. Despite substantial opposition, he promoted the formation of cooperative and communitarian orders across the Great Basin. With far greater support from his followers, Young oversaw the completion of a temple in St. George and presided over a renewed emphasis on the church's sacred ordinances. All the while, Young found himself besieged by legal and political threats from non-Mormons in Utah and the U.S. Congress.

ONE of Young's most obvious legacies was his large family, which had quietly expanded in the late 1860s and early 1870s. While the Godbeites agonized over and then discarded their plural wives, Young endured no such self-doubt. Five years after his marriage to Amelia Folsom, he was sealed to Mary Van Cott, the former wife of Augusta Adams's son James T. Cobb. At the age of fifteen, Mary had contracted a civil marriage to Cobb, who was not yet a member of the church. At the time, her father, John Van Cott, was away from Utah as president of the church's Scandinavian Mission. Young later reassured John Van Cott that he had blessed the marriage because he was "reliably informed that Mary's affections were placed upon James." The marriage failed, however, and the couple obtained a civil divorce in 1867. In January of the next year, Mary—now twenty-three—became Young's wife. Young moved Mary and her mother into a home purchased for them in Provo, partly with the intention of spending more time there himself. Though she did not rival Amelia Folsom in his affections, Young bestowed considerable attention on his new wife, who escorted him on a trip to southern Utah in the spring of 1869. In 1870, Mary bore Young his fifty-eighth and final child.[6]

A few months after his sealing to Mary Van Cott, Young married Ann Eliza Webb, also twenty-three years of age and the daughter of a stalwart church member, Chauncey Webb. In December 1865, prompted by Ann Eliza's mother, Young had encouraged Elias Smith, Salt Lake City's probate judge, to grant Ann Eliza a divorce from James Dee on grounds of "abusive treatment." Judge Smith granted the divorce shortly before Christmas, and Ann Eliza returned to her parents' household with two young children. She soon had multiple suitors. In July 1867, her bishop informed Young that "a young man in this ward" wished to marry her but hesitated despite her "Bill of Divorce from her former husband." Because divorces did not necessarily cancel a husband's eternal, ecclesiastical claims, the suitor wished to know whether Ann Eliza was "entirely free and clear from any obligation to him [Dee]—for Time and Eternity." Apparently on the same day as the anonymous suitor's inquiry reached him, Young escorted Ann Eliza on a walk and informed Chauncey Webb of his own matrimonial interest. Ann Eliza knew Young and his family quite well. She had filled some minor acting roles at the Salt Lake Theater, which Young regularly patronized, and she was friends with several of Young's daughters and wives through visits to the Lion House. Ann Eliza was sealed to the church president in April 1868. Young did not feel for her the sort of affection or attraction he felt for Amelia Folsom or Mary Van Cott. When Ann Eliza refused to move into the Lion House, Young built her a cottage nearby, in which she lived with her mother.[7]

After the marriages to Mary Van Cott and Ann Eliza Webb, Young agreed to be sealed for eternity to several women who had long importuned him for the privilege. For two decades, Elizabeth Jones had endured a tumultuous family life. A woman of some means, she left Wales as the wife of David Thomas Lewis, married Captain Dan Jones shortly after her arrival in the Salt Lake Valley, and then divorced Jones in October 1856. One day after her divorce, her son Thomas Lewis was castrated by an extralegal posse, and Young conveyed to her his approval of the punishment. Elizabeth then married a third husband, whom she also divorced. In the late 1850s, she asked Young to marry her. "I belong to you," she wrote the church president, adding that he had previously caused her to marry against her wishes. "Had you Have acted the right part toward me I should have Been another woman," she stated. Young admired the woman many Mormons called the "Welsh Queen"; he publicly praised her generosity toward poor emigrants from Wales. He was unwilling to marry her, however, and she eventually returned to Captain Jones.[8]

Seven years after Dan Jones's 1862 death, Young and Elizabeth finally knelt together at the Endowment House altar. Ann Eliza Webb later alleged that Young married Elizabeth because her property in Provo interfered with his factory-building plans, an obstacle removed after Elizabeth's move to Young's eight-hundred-acre Forest Farm property east of Salt Lake City. Jones owned land north of the woolen factory, and she did leave Provo after her sealing to Young. She did not deed the land to Young until 1876, however. Although Ann Eliza portrays Elizabeth as deeply unhappy with the result of her marriage, given her entreaties in the 1850s it seems unlikely that she was a simple victim of avarice. Nevertheless, she—like several of Young's other wives who spent time there—did not find contentment at Forest Farm. Chores at the farm, including cooking for a large number of workers, were grueling. In 1875, Young instructed one of his workers to "say to Sister Jones unless she takes care of the farm I shall have to place some one in possession who will take care of it." Now sixty-one years of age, Elizabeth Jones probably found her married life more arduous than she had imagined.[9]

Like Elizabeth Jones, Lydia Farnsworth had long wanted to be Brigham Young's wife. In 1855, two decades after her marriage to Elijah Mayhew, she met with Young and expressed her "conviction that I belong to you." Two years later, she repeated her desire "to be sealed to you for Eternity." At the time, Young curtly dismissed her request. For unknown reasons, Young changed his mind in 1870. A few months after the sealing, she announced herself as "Lydia Young" in the 1870 census. Still, if she considered herself Young's wife, she remained a member of Elijah Mayhew's extended household. She lived with several of her grown children in a house near one occupied by Elijah and his other two wives.[10]

Finally, in 1872 Young was sealed to Hannah Tapfield, known in Mormon circles for her poetry. Although Tapfield had also been married for decades, her husband Thomas King did not belong to the church. Thus, according to church teachings, she needed a sealing to a "righteous man" in order to secure her salvation. After her sealing to Young, she continued to live with King. After King's 1874 death, Young sent her a gift of flour, cornmeal, sugar, and sago. "I sincerely appreciate the kind and delicate attention," she wrote, expressing her thanks. Altogether, in ceremonies spanning nearly five decades, Brigham Young had married at least fifty-five women. After his sealing to Hannah Tapfield King, Brigham Young—

probably the most oft-married man in America—was never again sealed to any living woman.[11]

Ever since his move to the Great Basin, Young had attempted to inculcate a sense of unity and interdependence among his household wives and children. Like many devout Protestants, Young assembled his family for prayer each afternoon or evening, often interrupting or delaying church business for that purpose. He once excused himself from George A. Smith when the hour for prayer came, informing the apostle that "he always thought it would be of a great benefit to his family in the after life if he set the example to pray punctually with them." Young also upbraided his wives and children who absented themselves from prayer, once dictating a formal request that they "receive kindly and obey" his counsel "when prayer time comes that they all be at home." Sometimes he followed fervent prayers with impromptu sermons to his family.[12]

That sense of common purpose was difficult to maintain as his family continued to grow, symbolized by the gradual dispersal of wives and children away from the Beehive and Lion houses. Probably because Mary Ann Angell preferred a more secluded existence away from the Beehive House's social and ecclesiastical activity, she moved back to the nearby "White House" shortly after 1860. Lucy Decker, Young's first plural wife, now became the Beehive House's chief female resident. Wives with many children, such as Emily Dow Partridge, Emmeline Free, and Clarissa Decker, moved out of the Lion House, probably finding it ill suited for their large families. Augusta Adams and Zina Huntington, with small households, moved out as well. Young purchased a number of Salt Lake City homes for his wives, typically kept at least one wife at Forest Farm, and eventually bought additional homes in Provo, Logan, and St. George. In 1873, construction began on a new official residence that Young called the Gardo House and the *Salt Lake Tribune* dubbed the "Amelia [Folsom] Palace." In his will, Young left the home to Amelia Folsom and Mary Ann Angell, both of whom had lived in the home for a short time in 1876 before it was damaged in an explosion.[13]

Several of Young's wives achieved a high degree of visibility and prominence during these years, rebutting non-Mormon assertions that polygamy enslaved women. In a patriarchal and hierarchical religion, Young often reminded women that they were subject to their husbands (the "Lords of Creation") and an exclusively male priesthood. In other ways, though, he sanctioned the expansion of women's roles within the church and civil society. "We believe that women are useful," Young said, "not only to sweep houses, wash dishes, make beds, and raise babies but that they should stand behind the counter, study law or physic, or become good bookkeep-

Gardo House *(courtesy of Church History Library, The Church of Jesus Christ of Latter-day Saints)*

ers." He went so far as to endorse the desire of one woman to attend the Woman's Medical College in Philadelphia. The very nature of Mormon ritual, meanwhile, required women to officiate in temple ordinances performed at the Salt Lake City Endowment House. Without the participation of women, Mormon men could not obtain salvation and celestial glory. Young's wife Eliza R. Snow was a fixture in the Endowment House, introducing Mormon women to the church's most sacred teachings while they made their covenants and performed sacred ordinances on behalf of their ancestors. "Aunt Eliza," wrote Young's daughter Susa Young Gates, "was the high priestess in the temporary House of the Lord." Through such ritual work, Snow and several of Young's other wives gained official positions of high ecclesiastical status and influence.[14]

Although hostile to the women's Relief Society after Joseph Smith's death, Young allowed its revival on a local level in the mid-1850s, and several of his wives played leading roles. In 1867, preparing for his economic battle against non-Mormon merchants, Young called for the systematic reestablishment of Relief Society, which focused its efforts on home manufacture and thrift. Eliza Snow became head of the revived society, which promoted everything from grain storage to silk culture. For Young, Relief Society existed largely to promote the virtues of domestic thrift and housekeeping, but in the process it created formal positions of leadership and visibility for Mormon women. Snow helped local bishops establish ward-level Relief Societies, and she later also organized the church's Young Ladies' Mutual Improvement Association. Young's wife Zina Huntington also played a prominent role in Relief Society reorganization.[15]

Over the thirty years of his church presidency, Young said so many different things about women that with selective quotations from his discourses one could turn him into either a misogynist or a proto-feminist. Neither portrait is accurate. Young did not advocate temple work or Relief Societies as steps toward equality for women, either in the world or church.

Eliza R. Snow, Cairo, Egypt, 1873, during a trip to Europe and the Middle East with other church leaders *(courtesy of Utah State Historical Society)*

Instead, he sanctioned wider opportunities for female leadership because he needed the talents of Mormon women for the all-consuming task of building up the Kingdom of God. In the process, though, Young came to appreciate women's talents in new ways. In 1875, he commented that Eliza Snow and Emmeline Wells "have given as good exhortations as any elder can give." Young especially recognized Snow's intellectual and organizational capabilities. He once gave her a gift of newspapers, and he discussed political matters with her, publicly praised her poems, and regularly gave her a seat next to himself at dinner and during family prayers.[16]

Plural marriage continued to try the hearts of many of his wives, however, who could less easily detach themselves from the burden of polygamy. Augusta Adams, sealed to Joseph Smith for eternity but still Young's earthly wife, occasionally resumed her bitter complaints about his neglect. In December 1861, upset at her exclusion from a family party, she informed him that "while ruminating this morning upon all my grievances and the indignities I had endured I inadvertantly said *S__ t upon him.*"[17] While never as open with her complaints as Augusta Adams, Emmeline Free resented the fact that Amelia Folsom became her husband's preferred consort. She lived the last few years of her life as an invalid, a "dope fiend" addicted to morphine, according to Young's daughter Susa. The ledger of Young's family store documents Emmeline's frequent acquisition of morphine, a common relief for many chronic illnesses in the late nineteenth century. Young's correspondence reveals an ongoing concern for Emmeline's welfare. In December 1874, for example, Young telegraphed Emmeline from St. George, encouraging her to "ferment" and then take some medicinal roots. Despite such attempts, she died in 1875.[18]

Financial concerns plagued several wives. In the 1870 U.S. Census, Young reported two million dollars in assets and an annual income of one hundred thousand dollars. Depending on his own financial circumstances and his whims, Young could be either miserly or generous. Zina Huntington praised her husband for his generosity toward children in need. "I do not know how many orphans he has reared to maturity," she wrote in a later autobiography. At the same time, despite his wealth it was expensive for Young to maintain his wives, children, servants, and workers. Various wives earned some money through midwifery, sewing, and teaching, but most relied on their husband to meet their expenses. When they had exhausted their own means, Young's wives typically obtained necessities from their husband's "family store." In 1870, according to a clerk's ledger, Augusta Adams (no young children) drew $245 on the store, Ann Eliza Young (two young children) $322, childless Amelia Folsom $513, Emily Partridge (three children at home) $259, and Emmeline Free (seven children at home) $1,272. Even if she no longer received the lion's share of Young's attention, Emmeline and her large family did not suffer from financial neglect.[19]

By early 1874, his railroad debts and the effects of a nationwide economic panic caused Young to impose a measure of austerity on his family. "I don't want any of my folks to go to the Coop Store [ZCMI]," Young instructed his storekeeper John Haslem, "for they have got enough to eat and drink and wear I know." Young anxiously sought tenants for property he owned, and he instructed his business associates to "borrow no money" on his account because he had "no means of paying it." The restriction in expenditures generated resentment, especially because Young himself and Amelia Folsom (in his company during his months-long stays in St. George) seemed immune from it. That year, Augusta Adams obtained $89 in goods from the family store, Emily Dow Partridge $242, and Emmeline Free $1119. "I feel quite ashamed to be known as a wife of the richest man in the territory," the periodically disenchanted Emily confided to her diary in 1875, "and yet we are so poor." "I do not know why he is so loth to provide for me," she lamented, adding that Young "provide[d] sumptuously for some of his family." According to Emily's journal entries, Young refused to provide means for her to visit her aging mother, neglected to fix up her house and lot, and forced her to pay her own taxes.[20]

For the most part, Young's wives economized and kept their discontents within the family. Nearly all retained their belief in polygamy. Even Augusta Adams expressed spiritual satisfaction despite her often virulent criticism of her husband. "Their Father," she wrote about her children in a letter to Young, "Wether it is Br Joseph or your Lord ship, is a King and Their Mother is or will be a Queen thats sure."[21] Young, for his part, readily conceded that no polygamous husband could always satisfy all of his wives. "Where is the man who has wives," he asked in a sermon, "and all of them think he is doing just right to them? I do not know such a man; I know it is not your humble servant." He was not always as callous as Emily Partridge's complaints would indicate. In July 1877, he cordially discussed Emily's financial distress with her and granted some of her wishes. For the moment at least, she felt reconciled with her husband.[22]

While Young never expressed any doubts about the divinity of plural marriage, he apparently had some regrets about the way he had structured his family life since leaving Nauvoo, which may partly explain the family's dispersal in the 1860s and 1870s. Susa Young Gates later wondered whether her "father was thus settling his wives out into homes of their own to correct what he esteemed to be a mistake of his early judgment."[23] Young had wholeheartedly obeyed what the Mormons often simply termed "the principle." Plural marriage brought him a large earthly kingdom, augmented his status among his people, testified to his faith, and even produced companionship and occasional romance. Polygamy also introduced into his household considerable disharmony and financial strain. Young's creation and maintenance of a large polygamous household was a bold experiment and—not surprisingly—only a mixed success.

Young spent more time with a select group of male church leaders than he did with any of his wives, Amelia Folsom included. "Brigham Young is more frequently in his society than with any of the Madame Youngs," joked the journalist George Alfred Townsend about George A. Smith. The rotund, bellicose, and bewigged Smith had become Young's First Counselor after Heber Kimball's death in 1868. Smith had a rare ability to offer Young gentle suggestions and criticism without arousing any sensitivity on the church president's part. For some time, Young had relied on a fluid circle of trusted advisers instead of the formal layers of the church hierarchy (including the Quorum of the Twelve). By the early 1870s, those in Young's inner circle included his counselors Smith and Daniel Wells, the apostles George Q. Cannon and Albert Carrington, and business associates like John Sharp, Hiram Clawson, and Horace Eldredge. The young, energetic, and diligent Cannon earned Young's trust partly by providing him with frank assessments of other church leaders. Cannon, who related to Young much the way Young had subordinated himself to Joseph Smith, began editing the *Deseret News* in 1867 and later became the church president's most trusted representative in the nation's capital. For his political savvy and ecclesiastical clout, a non-Mormon author later dubbed Cannon the "Mormon Richelieu." "Squire Wells," a tall, gangly, red-haired man, had for many years commanded the Nauvoo Legion and supervised Salt Lake City's public works department. In 1866, he became the city's mayor as well. Sharp, for his part, possessed Young's complete confidence when it came to business transactions. Although Young always set the broad contours of church policies, he relied heavily on these loyal associates to manage political, economic, and ecclesiastical affairs.[24]

Young also cultivated as leaders his three sons by Mary Ann Angell: Joseph Angell, Brigham Jr. ("Briggy"), and John Willard. It was clear as early as 1855 that Young was thinking about their future place in the church hierarchy. That year, he ordained to the apostleship eleven-year-old John Willard, the first son born to Young after his endowments and sealing to Mary Ann. John Willard did not assume any active role as an apostle until the following decade; for the time being, his ordination remained unknown to nearly all church members. In 1864, Young privately ordained his two oldest sons—Joseph and Briggy—as apostles and then "set apart" his three apostolic sons as "assistant counselors" within the church's First Presidency, privately bestowing high ecclesiastical authority on them. Despite their ordinations, none of Young's sons had received a place within the Quorum of the Twelve until Brigham Jr. filled an opening in 1868. It remained unclear to many church members whether seniority among the apostles rested upon ordination as an apostle, ordination into the Quorum of the Twelve, or uninterrupted service within that quorum. In any event, Young's private ordinations of his sons—especially John Willard—seemed designed to make it likely that at least one of them would one day hold his father's office.[25]

Of course, Young's sons had to choose whether to embrace their given roles. By his own account, Brigham Jr. was "wild" as a young man. Despite later stories about the church president interrupting his children's youthful courtships, Young was not a parental killjoy. "I would rather," Young stated, "my children would spend their early life sliding down Hill, skating, riding Horses, & not go to school one day." His own childhood had been devoid of both recreation and schooling. While he wanted his children to obtain both, he valued the former—along with practical experience—more highly. Young did not overly worry when his children engaged in adolescent antics and youthful frivolities, as Briggy had done. By his mid-twenties, Briggy had decided to walk more closely in his father's path, and by the late 1860s all three elder sons became key business associates of their father. In 1873, Young formalized the inner circle of advisers he had come to trust. At the church's semiannual conference in April, John W. and Brigham Jr. were publicly sustained as "assistant counselors" to their father, along with Lorenzo Snow, Albert Carrington, and George Q. Cannon.[26]

In 1874 and 1875, Young was staggered by the deaths of several beloved family members and close advisers. Alice Young Clawson, a daughter by Mary Ann Angell, died of complications following premature childbirth in December 1874. "The sad circumstance is pretty severe on my system but I shall be able to overcome it," a grief-stricken Young telegraphed Mary Ann. The following summer, only a few weeks after Emmeline Free's death, Young received the news that his eldest son Joseph Angell had died unexpectedly of "congestive chills." Unlike brothers Brigham Jr. and John Willard, Joseph Angell had not become a member of the Quorum of the Twelve or the First Presidency. It is possible that Joseph's role in the railroad schemes that had produced so much financial distress caused his father to lose some confidence in him. In 1875, Joseph's wife Clara Stenhouse wrote her father-in-law that Joseph had recently dedicated himself to serving the church in Sevier County "as his only redemption from past follies." Clara added that Joseph's efforts were straining his health but that her husband desperately wanted his father's "approbation." When Brigham tasked him with overseeing the construction of a planned temple in Manti, Joseph felt the satisfaction of receiving his father's approval. His sudden death cut short those efforts.[27]

Young rarely showed outward grief and discouraged public displays of mourning. He had kept his tears to himself after Joseph Smith's death, and he did not participate in deathbed vigils for his first wife Miriam or his father. When his daughter Mary Eliza Croxall (by Clarissa Ross) died in 1871, a "shocked" and sickened Young cancelled all business and simply remained inside for a day. As the summer of 1875 drew to a close, though, Young's emotions were unusually ragged. One month after Joseph Angell's death, George A. Smith died. For four decades, Smith and Young had been at the center of the church's history: the 1834 Zion's Camp march, the 1840–1841 mission to England, the tumultuous events of Nauvoo, and the exodus. At his friend's funeral, Young uncharacteristically wept.[28]

The *Salt Lake Tribune* mercilessly lampooned Young's two remaining eldest sons, Brigham Jr. and John Willard, as unworthy beneficiaries of nepotism. Mocking him as "porcine Prince Briggy" or simply the "Fat Boy," the *Tribune* reported with glee on Briggy's girth and purported violations of the Word of Wisdom, namely an apparent fondness for Havana cigars.[29] Brigham Jr. remained a steadfastly obedient son and frequently traveled with his father, but the more magnetic and eloquent John Willard ("Apostate Johnny," per the *Tribune*)[30] preferred to operate at a distance from Utah and his father. Dapper and mustached, alternately prosperous and penniless, he frustrated his creditors and distressed his father. John Willard's letters are filled with vows to return to Utah after settling his affairs, but the tug of business always pulled him east again. On more than one occasion, Young paid John Willard's debts to induce him to actively assume ecclesiastical leadership and remain in Zion. *"I want you here,"* Young concluded a December 1875 letter to John Willard. Pleading with his son to come home from New York City, Young added a handwritten postscript: "O Jonna I pr[a]y for you and yours continuly. If you nue [knew] how I want to see you, you would come. my dear Jonna, I due hope you will see as we see thing[s]. I send your dear Br Brigham & Br [William] Stanes to prevale on you to come home and stay with us. m[a]y god Bles my d[e]ar Boy." When John Willard returned in February, Brigham Jr. wrote in his diary that "Father & Mother welcomed their son for whom they had longed especially since the death of Jos. A."[31]

Young then took a step designed to keep his prodigal son nearby. Given former assumptions about Joseph Smith's children, Young's earlier creation of familial tribes, and themes of kingship and priesthood royalty within Mormon theology, it was widely assumed that Young wanted either John Willard or Brigham Jr. to succeed him. Further stoking such speculation was Young's choice of John Willard to replace George A. Smith as his First Counselor. With Brigham Jr. assisting, Young privately ordained John Willard to that position in March 1876, a decision affirmed at the church's October conference. Many years later, the apostle Joseph F. Smith told Charles Nibley that he had suggested Brigham Jr. as a wiser choice. Smith's bold statement prompted a predictably sharp response from Young: "I have got Brigham and I have got you and I want John W." Perhaps sensing others might share Joseph F. Smith's objection, on the day after the announcement of John Willard's elevation Young preached a sermon on Jacob receiving his father's blessing instead of his older brother Esau. As was nearly always the case, Young got his way. John Willard seems to have expected to be his father's successor, but he did not have the respect of other church leaders. Perhaps with that in mind, while he clearly hoped that one of them would eventually lead the church, Young did not try to engineer the immediate succession of either son.[32]

A few months after the 1873 elevation of John Willard and Brigham Jr. as Young's assistant counselors, another family member forced Young back into federal court. In July of that year, supported by a Methodist minister and backed by the territory's leading Gentile lawyers and politicians, Ann Eliza Webb Young sued Young for divorce in James McKean's federal district court. Alleging that Young treated her with emotional, physical, and financial neglect, she sought $1,000 in monthly alimony, $20,000 in legal fees, and $200,000 from his future estate. In response, the church president argued that since his marriage to Ann Eliza had no legal basis he owed her nothing.[33]

Americans relished scandals that combined popular interest in both religion and sex. Since late 1872, major newspapers had publicized accusations of adultery against Henry Ward Beecher, the nation's most renowned Protestant preacher and brother of novelist Harriet Beecher Stowe. Beecher engaged in an affair with the wife of his friend Theodore Tilton; the resulting scandal captured the national interest for many years, partly because Elizabeth Tilton several times retracted and then restated her charges while Beecher steadfastly maintained his innocence. At first glance, Brigham Young and Henry Ward Beecher had little in common. Fawned over by parishioners and luminaries, the minister of Brooklyn's Plymouth Church had discarded the already desiccated Calvinism of his ministerial father and unapologetically replaced it with promises of Christian love and earthly happiness. Beecher gained a legion of admirers for his witty and eloquent rhetoric. Meanwhile, Young was reviled by Protestants of all theological stripes as a religious deviant. In the public mind, though, the two sometimes became associated as paramours of young women, objects of fascination and derision. Young even linked himself with Beecher on occasion. "I believe he is as earnest in his belief of free love and that he thinks it just as right for him to cohabit with twenty-eight women as for Brigham Young to have twenty wives," Young jabbed. In other words, Beecher was a hypocrite, while he was simply living out his sincere belief in celestial marriage. Both Beecher and Young, though, provided sensationalistic grist for the mill of American journalism. Newspapers from San Francisco to New York provided generous coverage of Ann Eliza's charges against her husband.[34]

Ann Eliza's divorce suit proceeded slowly. With McKean ill, another federal judge twice quashed the suit on procedural grounds. Meanwhile, Young's brother-in-law Hiram Clawson and Ann Eliza discussed a settlement that included a divorce and $15,000. Ann Eliza hesitated. In September, she wrote Clawson to say that she gave Young twenty-four hours to accept those terms but warned that she had "stronger inducements" to "go before the eastern public and in person acquaint them with my wrongs." It is unclear which party ultimately rejected the settlement, but the "insubordinate rib of the Prophet," as the *Salt Lake Tribune* called her, made good on her threat.[35]

Ann Eliza seized her moment. She had an offer from P. T. Barnum, but her manager James Pond steered her toward James Redpath's Lyceum Bureau, based in Boston. Unconcerned with maintaining an air of neutrality regarding the divorce suit, Judge McKean provided Ann Eliza with a public endorsement to take with her. Beginning with stops in Laramie, Cheyenne, and Denver, she told audiences about the Mormon endowment ceremony, provided a list of Young's wives, and exhaustively denounced her husband's miserliness. "The things which I suffered opened my eyes to the hollowness of Brigham Young's pretentions to sanctity of character," she concluded at the end of her first Denver lecture, "and unveiled the system of which *he* was the head and *I* one of the many victims." Ann Eliza joined the growing but still controversial ranks of itinerant female lecturers, alongside suffragists, spiritualists, and a few evangelical reformers. She packed lecture halls, earned generous fees, and became an overnight celebrity and newspaper darling. Her lectures became the basis for her 1875 autobiography, *Wife No. 19*, a pastiche of firsthand vignettes of Young's polygamous household combined with secondhand accounts of

Ann Eliza Young, ca. 1875 *(courtesy of Library of Congress)*

episodes like the Mountain Meadows Massacre. Ann Eliza alleged that Young had banished her to Forest Farm, rarely visited, and when he occasionally appeared cruelly berated her for wasting food on the hired help. Endearing herself to the bulk of her readers, Ann Eliza described her rejection of Mormon religious teachings and her new anchor "in the sheltered haven of Christian belief." Although she had been born into the church, hers was a classic American captivity narrative, chronicling an escape from lustful and heretical savages.[36]

In April 1874, George Q. Cannon informed Young that Ann Eliza had spent a week in Washington and "lobbied at the Capitol every day." Noting the politicians' interest, Cannon jeered that "[w]hen a drunkard and a whore unite, the product should be filthy." Washington newspapers used Ann Eliza's statements about the ecclesiastical obedience of Mormon jurors to urge passage of the Poland Bill, a measure adopted in June that curtailed the jurisdiction of Utah's probate courts and created a process for the selection of balanced—i.e., Mormon and non-Mormon—juries.[37]

For the church and Brigham Young, the passage of the Poland Act actually averted worse outcomes, such as a measure granting federal officials sole authority to impanel juries. Still, the first significant Utah legislation in a dozen years set the stage for several key court battles. For example, the Poland Act ensured that Ann Eliza's divorce suit would proceed in McKean's federal courtroom. The next February, the judge ordered Young to pay Ann Eliza $500 monthly alimony pending the suit's resolution. Ironically, while Young denied the validity of the marriage in question, McKean's ruling asserted that any marriage contracted in Utah "according to the forms of the 'Church' of which Brigham Young is the head . . . is a lawful and valid marriage." Young refused to pay, and McKean held him in contempt and sentenced him to one night's imprisonment. Accompanied by Daniel Wells, business associate William Rossiter, and his nephew and physician Seymour Young, the church president spent a night in the penitentiary, while several hundred supporters gathered near the jail. According to Seymour Young, his uncle had a good night's rest.[38]

Having made his point, Young paid the portion of McKean's judgment pertaining to attorney's fees but still refused to pay the alimony. Almost immediately after Young's brief imprisonment, President Grant removed McKean from office. Both church leaders and their opponents presumed that the judge lost his position because of his strident anti-Mormonism. "Woe be unto all the carpet-baggers of Babylon who tarry in Zion," commented the *Tribune* with a tone of mocking lamentation, "refusing to bow down to the assassin and tithing thief of Utah." While the details remain uncertain, it seems that McKean's removal more likely resulted from a political spat unconnected to Young's imprisonment.[39]

Following McKean's ouster, the territory endured a spate of short-tenured chief justices over the next two years. In November 1875, Associate Justice Jacob Boreman, presiding in the absence of a chief justice, sentenced Young to house arrest until he paid back alimony. New Chief Justice Alexander White then rescinded Boreman's decision and ordered Young's release. Yet another chief justice, Michael Schaeffer, reduced the alimony but ordered a seizure of some of Young's property for its payment. Young simply dug in his heels. "I will spend the remainder of my days in prison before I will pay them one cent," he informed two of his sons. Finally, the case went to trial in April 1877. Schaeffer accepted Young's argument that his marriage to Ann Eliza was illegal and dismissed her suit. The fact that Young won the case on the basis of the marriage's illegality, however, augured poorly for the future of Mormon polygamy. With the Poland Act having stripped a measure of church influence over the territory's courts, federal prosecutors were eager to proceed with polygamy prosecutions.[40]

After the furor subsided, Ann Eliza found that marital, financial, and spiritual contentment all continued to elude her. In 1883, she remarried again. Moses Denning was a wealthy Manistee, Michigan, lumberman and banker who had fallen in love with Ann Eliza after attending one of her lectures. Denning, a father of five, divorced his wife to marry Mormonism's most famous apostate, who finally had the palatial house she had wanted from Brigham Young. Although Ann Eliza eventually divorced her third husband and faded into obscurity, for a few years in the 1870s she was an effective opponent of Young and his church. Indeed, Ann Eliza Webb was the most formidable female antagonist Brigham Young ever encountered.[41]

WHILE it portended future legal trouble for Mormon polygamists, for Young himself the divorce suit ultimately was only an embarrassing distraction. He had survived the campaigns of countless runaway officials; he could endure one runaway wife. Far more serious was ongoing speculation regarding his role in the Mountain Meadows Massacre.

By the early 1870s, fifteen years had passed since the butchery at Mountain Meadows, and none of those involved had even stood trial. On one level, such a failure of justice was not an aberration, as mass murder in the years surrounding the Civil War frequently went unpunished. John Chivington, the Methodist preacher turned Indian fighter, suffered only ignominy (in some quarters) for his leadership of the 1864 Sand Creek Massacre, and the white southern "redeemers" who slaughtered their black enemies in Colfax, Louisiana, also escaped retribution. Indeed, it was all too common for white Americans to kill Indians and African Americans with little fear of punishment. It is astonishing, though, that members of a reviled religious minority who killed one hundred and twenty white, Protestant emigrants eluded prosecution for nearly two decades.

Young feared that federal judges would make him the target of any inquiry into the Mountain Meadows Massacre. Thus, though Young repeatedly promised to support an impartial investigation, he hardly clamored for justice, nor did he mete out timely ecclesiastical punishment to those local leaders considered most suspect. Indeed, Young's continued signs of friendship toward John D. Lee rankled some church members, especially those in southern Utah familiar with Lee's role in the treacherous butchery. George Hicks, a settler in Harmony, wrote Young in 1868 to ask why Lee had not lost his church membership. Hicks commented that while he had once taken comfort from Young's public, though unspecific, denunciation of the massacre perpetrators, he now wondered whether the church sanctioned the crime. "Can it be posable," Hicks wrote, "that the Church . . . fellowships a Company of men *whose hands have been Stained with the blood of innocent women and children?*" The letter touched a raw nerve in the church president, who dictated a reply blunt even by his standards. Given Hicks's anxiety about the massacre, Young offered the baseless speculation that Hicks had been "a participator in the horrible deed." "In such a case," Young counseled, "if you want a remedy,-rope round the neck taken with a jerk would be very salutary." Otherwise, Hicks had no reason for his angst. The massacre, Young insisted, "does not concern" uninvolved Latter-day Saints. Hicks should mind his own business.[42]

After years of inaction, in October 1870 church leaders quietly excommunicated Lee, Isaac Haight, and George Wood. According to the apostle Franklin Richards, those cut off from the church were "not expected to reenter in this estate," that is, in this life. It is unclear why Young sanctioned the excommunications at this time. The action shocked Lee, who never expected to face any lasting displeasure from the man who had ritually adopted him in the Nauvoo Temple. They had maintained a friendly relationship since the massacre despite Young's knowledge of Lee's involvement. Young saw Lee on his trips to southern Utah, ate and lodged with Lee, sanctioned his taking of additional wives, and entered into business arrangements with him. When he received word of his expulsion, Lee presumed that Young had acted out of necessity, to stop the "mouths" of "apostates & Godbyites" implicating him in the massacre "on the grounds that he houlds Men in the church who are reported to be in it." When he heard that Young had forbidden his future rebaptism, Lee became more pained and sought an audience with the church president. Stunned by Young's change of course, Lee complained that if "it [the massacre] was wrong now, it certainly was wrong then." Young for his part claimed "that they had never learned the particuelars until lately." Lee countered that "the whole Truth was then told to you," and he rightly complained that many others shared the responsibility for what had occurred. If Young had indeed learned new details about the massacre, ecclesiastical sanction certainly should have fallen upon a far broader group of men. Lee correctly noted that non-Mormon pressure for action was increasing again, but such agitation was not unprecedented. Even had the church publicly announced the excommunications, the action would hardly have satisfied Young's critics. Thus, more than a decade removed from the massacre, Lee was bewildered by his surrogate father's newfound displeasure.[43]

Despite the ecclesiastical action, Young was not yet ready to deliver up the guilty to a hostile judge. In November 1871, with the twice-indicted Young in St. George, Daniel Wells sent warning that "writs were out" for Lee, Haight, and others. In April 1874, Lee visited Young in St. George, and the church president received him "with the kindness of a Father" and invited him to share in a splendid repast. George Hicks, not having followed Young's earlier advice, lost his church membership after sending a letter to the *Salt Lake Tribune* noting that Lee rode his horse "by the side of Brigham's carriage." "Birds of a feather," concluded Hicks, implying that Young shared in Lee's well-known guilt. The warm welcome, however, was Young's final meeting with Lee.[44]

The wheels of justice finally began to turn. Three years earlier, Philip Klingensmith had sworn an affidavit that incriminated Lee, Haight, William Dame, and John Higbee as those with local military responsibility for the massacre. Klingensmith, former bishop of Cedar City but only a private in the Nauvoo Legion in 1857, recalled that Haight claimed "orders from headquarters" but did not know whether Haight meant Parowan or Salt Lake City. A few months after the June 1874 enactment of the Poland Act, a grand jury indicted Lee, Haight, Dame, Higbee, Klingensmith, and several others for murder. The territory's deputy U.S. marshal, William Stokes, found John D. Lee hiding in an animal pen near his house in Panguitch. Dame was arrested shortly thereafter. Young was clearly worried about his own legal jeopardy. In preparation for his own potential defense, he asked Daniel Wells to find the copybook containing his September 10, 1857 letter to Isaac Haight "and put it into a safe where it will be secure and at hand if called for." Territorial authorities, however, did not seek his arrest.[45]

In July 1875, Lee and Dame prepared to face trial in Beaver, Utah. Former U.S. Attorney George C. Bates, now in the employ of the church, provided Young with regular updates by telegram. In mid-July, Bates reported that Lee intended to turn state's evidence and provide testimony against "all on the ground," i.e., those Mormons at the site of the massacre. Lee implicated Isaac Haight and John Higbee, but not Dame, let alone George A. Smith or Brigham Young. He stated that he had reported to Young the "exact facts of the transaction" shortly afterward and that Young had "wept like a child." Uninterested in low-hanging fruit, the prosecutors called off the deal.[46]

Young and George A. Smith provided testimony in affidavits sent by telegram. Young testified that he had responded to Haight's inquiry by ordering that the emigrants be allowed to "pass through the country unmolested." Some of Young's statements, though, departed from what is otherwise known about the events following the massacre. He asserted that he had not met with Lee for "two or three months" afterward, even though the Church Historian's Office could readily have confirmed that Lee met with Young less than three weeks after the massacre. The church president also claimed that he had stopped Lee from giving a full account of the massacre because he did not wish his feelings harrowed up. The apostle Wilford Woodruff's journal, by contrast, confirms that Lee had discussed the slaughter in at least some macabre detail in his meeting with Young. In his affidavit, Young denied any knowledge of the disposition of the emigrants' property. It seems incredible that he would not have asked such questions of John D. Lee or others. Even George Bates suggested that Young had been overly circumspect. "Your father's deposition might have gone much farther and still kept within the truth," he wrote John Willard Young. It is unclear what Bates meant, perhaps that Young might have done more to either clear his own name or implicate the perpetrators of the crime. At the very least, Young told precious little of what he knew about the massacre, and Judge Jacob Boreman refused to accept Young's affidavit-by-telegram as evidence.[47]

The prosecution, which included longtime Mormon political nemesis Robert Baskin, sought to convict Lee but seemed more committed to convincing the public of Young's complicity. In his opening statement, Baskin stated that he would "show the jury some of the part taken by Brigham Young in this affair." Star witness Philip Klingensmith provided damning testimony of Lee's guilt in decoying the emigrants out of their corral, but he could not say whether or not Lee had actually killed anyone, nor could he attest that anyone in Salt Lake City had ordered the massacre. Klingensmith also recounted meeting with Young after the massacre and receiving strict instructions to maintain secrecy about the affair. Lee's attorneys concentrated on the emigrants' supposed offenses during their journey through the territory and blamed the Indians for compelling local Mormon settlers to assist in the massacre. According to the *Tribune*, nine jurors (at least eight of whom were church members) voted to acquit Lee, one non-Mormon remained uncertain, and two other non-Mormon jurors voted to convict. George Bates speculated that the prosecutors had not even presented all of their evidence, instead hoping to use Lee's acquittal as political fodder in their attempts to persuade Congress to allow them to exclude church members from jury service in Utah.[48]

With the jury hung, Lee remained in custody awaiting a second trial. Baskin, though, had succeeded in his larger objective of arraigning Brigham Young and the church before the court of public opinion. In his closing argument, Baskin accused Young of obstructing justice by instructing the perpetrators to keep silent about the massacre. "In no other community on God's earth," Baskin charged, "could this heinous crime be allowed to slumber eighteen years." Baskin also accused Young of ordering Klingensmith and Lee to steal the emigrants' property for the church. *Tribune* editor Fred Lockley, in one of his many reports from Beaver, could only explain the participation of so many men in such a brutal deed by the "favorite priestly maxim, 'mind your own business.'" Although few newspapermen considered it a surprise, the trial's result angered both Lockley and a number of national editors. "[I]t does not seem possible," suggested the *New York Times,* "that any one who has paid attention to the evidence can have any doubt that the prosecution have convicted the Mormon hierarchy of being accessory to, if not issuing orders for, the massacre." Awaiting a second trial, Lee sat in the territorial penitentiary in Salt Lake City for nearly a year, refusing innumerable requests to implicate Young.[49]

Bates warned John Willard Young that U.S. Attorney William Carey was seeking evidence to indict his father as an accessory to the massacre after the fact. According to Bates, Carey would allege that Young as Utah's governor failed to have Lee arrested after the latter's report of the massacre, oversaw the church appropriation of the spoils, and allowed Lee and Haight to sit in the legislature despite his knowledge of their guilt. Bates also reported that prosecutors intended to charge George A. Smith as accessory before the fact. Brigham Young was in some legal peril. Both Lee and Klingensmith had clearly stated that they had reported the facts of the massacre to Young shortly after the slaughter. The church president needed to protect himself, Bates urged. In order to demonstrate that the massacre resulted from "a little band of Religious fanatics, Mormons all, at Cedar City," Bates strongly encouraged Brigham Young to leave men like Lee and Haight "to their [own] fate."[50]

Young followed Bates's advice. Utah's new U.S. Attorney and prosecutor Sumner Howard reported to Attorney General Alphonso Taft that church leaders were innocent and had provided "aid in unraveling the mystery of this foul crime." In the courtroom, Howard made it clear that John D. Lee alone was on trial. He dismissed charges against William Dame, and in response to statements made by Lee's attorney "defied the defense and the whole world to produce one particle of evidence connecting any authorities . . . with the atrocities of this case." Young's counselor Daniel Wells even testified at the trial, signaling to the jury his approbation of Howard's course. Several Mormon witnesses came forward and testified that Lee had murdered women, and an all-Mormon jury found Lee guilty of first-degree murder.[51]

Lee alleged that Young and other church leaders had selected him as their "scapegoat." "Wells was sent here to have the thing cut and dried which he did to perfection," Lee informed his wife Rachel. The verdict dissolved the fidelity Lee had long maintained toward his surrogate father. In Lee's mind, Young had decided to offer his blood as an atonement for the sins of all those complicit in the massacre. Blood atonement, Lee explained to another wife, Emma, "is one of his peculiar ways of showing his kindness to some men by killing them to save them." That type of friendship, Lee observed, "is getting too thin, it is too much like the love that a hungry wolf has for an innocent lamb."[52]

While the presiding judge, Jacob Boreman, accepted Lee's obvious guilt, he made clear his belief that others should share in Lee's fate. "[T]he massacre," he alleged as he sentenced Lee to death, "seems to have been the result of a vast conspiracy, extending from Salt Lake City to the bloody field." Boreman further observed among Mormon leaders "a persistent and determined opposition to an investigation of the massacre." Noting the obvious concord between Howard and Mormon leaders, Boreman and other church opponents accused the prosecutor of accepting a bribe.[53]

Lee's lawyer, William Bishop, stopped pursuing his appeal when his client ran out of money. "I am sorry that you were unable to raise the money to carry the case up to the Supreme Court of the United States," Bishop coldly informed Lee, "for I do think we could have reversed the case in that court." Lee chose to die by firing squad. In an unusual procedure, in March 1877 authorities brought him back to Mountain Meadows for his execution. "I have been sacrificed in a cowardly dastardly manner," he stated on the day of his death. While professing himself a true believer in the Gospel of Jesus Christ as taught by Joseph Smith, Lee now asserted that Young was "leading people astray." As the executioners prepared to do their duty, Lee uttered his final words, "Aim at my heart." After the soldiers fired, Lee immediately fell back into his coffin, dying in the firm belief that he had "done nothing wrong designedly." In 1856, some twenty months before the massacre, Lee had written Young that "I never felt to flinch, but on the contrary would have esteemed it a prevelige to have Stepped between you and the cannons Mouth to have Saved you from death." By the time of his death, Lee no longer felt that way about Brigham

John D. Lee, 1877 *(courtesy of Church History Library, The Church of Jesus Christ of Latter-day Saints)*. Lee is sitting outside of the guard house at Fort Cameron, shortly before his execution at Mountain Meadows.

Young. Still, unknowingly echoing the language of that earlier letter, the *Salt Lake Tribune* reported that the "old man never flinched."[54]

At Mountain Meadows, Lee demurred when again asked about the role of church leaders in the massacre. However, in February he had prepared a written "confession," which he gave to U.S. Attorney Sumner Howard and which appeared the day after his death. In it, Lee detailed the involvement of many Mormons in the massacre, placed a heavy measure of blame on Isaac Haight, and portrayed himself as a reluctant participant who had saved the lives of several emigrant children. Lee suggested that George A. Smith had prearranged the company's destruction during his August 1857 trip to southern Utah by carefully verifying that local Mormons would "pitch into" any emigrant company "making threats" as it passed through the region. Also, Lee claimed that he had given Brigham Young a "full history" of the massacre shortly afterward, "except that of my own opposition." He added that after a night of prayer, Young reported that God had affirmed that "it was all right for that deed to be done."[55]

Lee agreed to write an autobiography for his attorney, William Bishop, to help posthumously pay his legal bills. By the time of his execution, Lee had only reached 1847 in his account. Bishop, though, was most interested in the events in Utah and in particular in Lee's account of the actual massacre. He had Lee's 1875 statement about the massacre, access to Lee's 1857 journal (from which at some point twelve pages were removed), and may have obtained an additional statement from his condemned client. From these sources, Bishop constructed a new "confession." A sparse version of this account appeared in newspapers a day before Lee's execution, and an expanded form appeared a few months later as *Mormonism Unveiled*. "The Mountain Meadows massacre," Lee alleged in the brief version, "was the result of the direct teachings of Brigham Young, and it was done by the orders of those high in authority in the Mormon community." Lee recalled that George A. Smith had "taught the people that it was their duty to kill all emigrants." *Mormonism Unveiled* added the assertion that when Smith visited southern Utah "to prepare the people for the work of exterminating Captain Fancher's train of emigrants . . . he was sent for that purpose by the direct command of Brigham Young." Had Lee made such accusations against Smith and Young in 1875, he probably would not have been executed for his crimes. By 1877, Lee was embittered by Young's betrayal. Bishop was worried about competing against other purported Lee confessions for book sales. In the end, Lee's statements are so obviously self-serving and contradictory—and, in the case of *Mormonism Unveiled*, probably embellished by Bishop—that one should hesitate before accepting them as evidence.[56]

Partly because of Lee's confessions and partly because Isaac Haight, John Higbee, William Dame, and others escaped prosecution, the death of a single man did not slake the non-Mormon thirst for justice with respect to Mountain Meadows. Even Sumner Howard informed the U.S. attorney general of his belief that "Young had the benefit of the property of the murdered Emigrants and defrauded the United States" by claiming it as his gift to the Indians.[57] John Willard Young and several associates considered ways to counter Lee's published confessions, such as by hiring a journalist like George Alfred Townsend to publish stories about the massacre more sympathetic to Young and the church. David Calder, Young's former clerk and editor of the *Deseret News,* drafted a petition to newly inaugurated Rutherford B. Hayes asking for a full federal investigation into the massacre and affirming Young's long-standing willingness to cooperate.[58] In May, Young and Daniel Wells gave an interview to a *New York Herald* correspondent in which they asserted that Lee and a few other sinners took advantage of the emigrants' boorish behavior and the unsettled state of the territory to gratify their desire for plunder.[59] The inchoate public relations campaign soon ended, though. No amount of friendly journalism or further statements from church leaders would have removed the dark stain the Mountain Meadows Massacre had left on Young's reputation. Likely realizing the impossibility of convincing their critics, the church president and his associates mostly let the matter rest.

As NATIONAL observers of Mormonism fixated on Ann Eliza Young and John D. Lee, Brigham Young remained focused—at least in public—on his own long-cherished objectives. Shortly before Lee's first trial, Young traveled through the settlements of the San Pete Valley, never commenting on the case or the massacre. In Manti, he presided over a unanimous vote to build a temple, which eventually rose above a stone quarry on a prominent hill overlooking the community. In Ephraim, the trip culminated with an attempt to persuade the settlers to consecrate their property and labor in a cooperative effort known as the United Order. On June 27, Young and seven of the church's apostles baptized each other with the following words: "I baptize you for the remission of sins [and the] renewal of your covenants with a promise on your part to observe the rules of the United Order."[60] Over the next several weeks, hundreds of San Pete Valley Mormons once again entered the baptismal waters in a sign of renewed dedication to their church and its economic unity.

For Brigham Young, the temple and the United Order were two sides of the same sacred task of binding church members together on earth and in heaven. At the church's October 1872 conference, Young articulated his vision of a city "after the Order of Enoch." "I would arrange for a little family," he began, "say about a thousand persons." The various households would assemble at mealtime in a dining hall that would seat five hundred persons. A few community members would do the cooking. Whimsically, Young imagined that a miniature railroad would pass under the table delivering everything from steaks to tea on demand. Freed from domestic drudgery, the community's women could go right to their work every day, making bonnets or clothing or working in factories. Since no one would want to wash five hundred people's dishes, Young suggested that "we could have a few Chinamen to do that." Groups of Latter-day Saints should live like extended families, biological and ecclesial, on earth and in heaven, bound together by both blood and sacred rituals.[61]

Although it evoked the sort of family organizations the Mormons had experimented with during the exodus, Young's 1872 conference talk primarily represented the logical conclusion of his decades-long emphasis on economic cooperation and unity. When he discussed the merchandizing cooperative in 1869, he commented that it was a "stepping stone to what is called the Order of Enoch, but which is in reality the order of Heaven." A minor character in Genesis and the New Testament, Enoch so pleases God that he is immediately "translated" into heaven. Joseph Smith, in his scriptural expansion of Genesis, greatly enhanced Enoch's significance. After Enoch builds a city, "the Lord called his people Zion, because they were of one heart and one mind, and dwelt in righteousness, and there was no poor among them." In anticipation of divine judgments upon humanity, God takes Enoch's city, the city of Zion, into heaven. Young wanted to recreate that heavenly city on earth.[62]

As Young noted, the New Testament (and the *Book of Mormon*) recorded that some early Christians had practiced a form of communitarianism, keeping "all things in common." The sooty misery of working-class England, moreover, had left Young with a lingering belief that capitalism could produce an existence worse than chattel slavery. While Utah was admittedly far removed from such horror, Young retained a skepticism about capitalist development despite his partnerships with railroads and telegraph companies. The Panic of 1873 had proven devastating for the territory's economy, demonstrating to Young the grave danger of relying upon outside or non-Mormon capital. ZCMI, though, had survived, and a series of cooperatives in the northern settlement of Brigham City had continued to prosper amid the economic storm. After forming a cooperative store back in 1864, the Brigham City settlers under the leadership of apostle Lorenzo Snow had added a tannery, a shoe shop, a woolen factory, and a stock herd. The cooperative's employees received pay in scrip, redeemable at the enterprise's various departments. Now, Young wanted other communities to replicate Brigham City's cooperative spirit and profitability. Young was more aware than ever of his mortality. If the Latter-day Saints were going to achieve a higher level of economic unity under his leadership, it was now or never.[63]

The United Order movement was thus born, beginning in early 1874 in St. George under Young's supervision. In March, residents of St. George who joined their community's United Order approved a founding document, consisting of a preamble and articles of agreement. The preamble referenced "the struggle between capitol [*sic*] and labor resulting in Strieks of the workman and also the oppression of monied monopolies." It also blamed speculation and capitalist overreach for the current economic crisis and the fact that for many families the necessities of life had become uncertain. The antidote of unfettered capitalism would be "self-sustaining . . . home-manufactures," including cotton and wool. Utopian elements seeped into the agreement. If they pooled their resources, the Saints would achieve such great economic efficiency that they would have more time to devote to the "cultivation and training of our minds." In St. George, church members consecrated their labor and property, and foremen under the direction of the order's leaders took charge of manufacturing and agricultural activities. Private property was not abolished, however, and individuals received dividends and wages based on their contributions and labor.[64]

Beginning in early 1874 and continuing for about eighteen months, Young dedicated his energy to organizing and sustaining United Orders in Mormon settlements. "Pretty much all the preaching now," stated Young's clerk James Jack, "is on the order of Enoch." Young called on Mormon communities "to live as one family as did the *[Book of Mormon]* Nephites while they were faithful." In this vision, the Latter-day Saints would consecrate their property and resources to common management, divide labor according to specialized ability, and eliminate disparities of wealth. Young sought to impress on the Saints that this was not merely an economic arrangement. "To me all labors are spiritual," he told the settlers in St. George, "our labor is one eternal spiritual work." In addition to pooling their resources, he wanted those entering the order to promise to pray with their families and keep the Word of Wisdom.[65]

Most communities, and individual wards in larger cities, opted for limited forms of cooperation. Several Salt Lake City wards attempted a single cooperative enterprise, such as shoemaking, reflecting Young's current fixation with the home production of wooden-soled shoes. A few remote settlements attempted to fully live out Young's communitarian vision. In 1875, around twenty-five Mormon families who had relocated from the difficult Muddy Mission in Nevada formed a new settlement in southern Utah named Orderville. Probably because they brought few means with them, residents of Orderville embraced life without private property and even ate together in an enormous dining room. Orderville's population nearly quintupled within five years of the settlement's idealistic beginnings. Settlers made their own silk and soap, looms and leather. Families drew from a central storehouse based on individual need. The intense spirit of cooperation boosted the prosperity of all for a few years. In the summation of the novelist Wallace Stegner, Orderville achieved "a communism of goods, labor, religion, and recreation such as the world has seen only in a few places and for very short times."[66]

Orderville's enthusiasm aside, many Mormons greeted the United Order warily, no more eager to consecrate their property now than they had been back in the 1830s or 1850s. Brigham Young Jr. found that in most of the northern Utah communities in which he attempted to start United Orders, barely half of the settlers would give their assent. Wealthy church members, who obviously had much more to lose should the orders prove unsuccessful, were especially hesitant. When Young initiated the San Pete Valley rebaptisms in June 1875, he was attempting to revive an ideal that was already flagging. In the settlement of Moroni, he warned that those who "say the United Order [was] born prematurely" "are full of lies and will not be gathered on his [Christ's] right hand." Even some top ecclesiastical leaders displayed a lack of enthusiasm. Young singled out Orson Hyde, the apostle who presided over the San Pete settlements, for particular chastisement. "Brother Hyde," Young declared, "had not the spirit or he would have seen the United Order."[67]

Perhaps most emblematic of the struggle to bring the United Order to fruition was Young's unwillingness to consecrate all of his own property. In June 1874, he announced that he was "going into the Order with all that I have." Just two months later, though, he conceded that he did not trust anyone else to manage his major enterprises, including a woolen factory in Provo. Back in 1872, he had informed the apostle Wilford Woodruff that he wanted to begin the Order of Enoch by placing one thousand families on his farm, giving them ten acres each. Unfortunately, he told Woodruff, he could think of only "two men that I think would do right & that is you & me." If Young did not trust others with his property, it is hardly surprising that many church members did not trust him with theirs.[68]

Brigham Young won the loyalty of the Mormon people when he trudged across mud and ice to preach its gospel in Canada, when he arrived as an emaciated apostle in England, when he risked his own life to remain in Nauvoo until the temple's completion, and when he led the pioneers to the Great Basin. He was at his most inspiring as a leader when he shared in the sacrifices that he demanded of others. When non-Mormons arrested Young or even insulted him, Latter-day Saints rallied to his defense. Especially as the years progressed, though, Young more often asked the Mormon people to make sacrifices he seemed unwilling to share. Though he had ridden in a wagon, they should push handcarts to Zion. Though he retained his wealth, others should consecrate all of their more meager property. Such contradictions or disparities did not cause most Mormons to reject his leadership, but they made many less willing to comply with his more burdensome requests.

From the start, the *Salt Lake Tribune* had denigrated the entire affair as the "Order of Euchre" and had suggested that Young was simply trying to fleece his impoverished followers. "If the Profit don't make the rich men fork over as well as the poor," chided the *Tribune,* "we shall think him an unjust, discriminating Profit."[69] Young's unwillingness to risk his own property and enterprises lent credibility to such accusations. The United Order, however, was not a money-making scheme for Brigham Young. Seventy-two years old when the St. George United Order was organized, Young probably did not expect to live very many more years, nor would he have stood to gain in any direct sense from the scores of United Orders formed across the territory.

Instead, the United Order was a desperate rearguard action to stave off Utah's dependence upon outside capital and non-Mormon bankers and businessmen. Boycotts of Gentile merchants and ZCMI's cooperative merchandizing had slowed down but not reversed that long-term trend. The United Order was Young's final attempt to accomplish an impossible economic objective. Although Young had promoted economic cooperation for decades, the United Order itself was hastily and poorly conceived. Young advanced the idea relentlessly for eighteen months, but he did not make it a test of fellowship or otherwise force his people to embrace economic unity. In the majority of Mormon communities, the United Order ideal quickly withered, as church members withdrew from the agreements and local orders dissolved. Even Orderville eventually abandoned the experiment. In the early 1880s, a mining boom in southern Utah made Orderville seem desultory and backward, as residents elsewhere gladly snapped up imported goods. Orderville Mormons began to envy their neighbors. The Orderville United Order finally collapsed in 1885. It had proven impossible to translate the City of Enoch back to earth.

If the Latter-day Saints could not create heaven on earth, they pushed ahead with their sacred work of forging ties on earth that would persist in heaven. In early 1877, Young and other church leaders dedicated the St. George Temple, the first completed since the exodus from Nauvoo. Laborers on the temple received no wages for the work. The church required individuals to donate ten percent of their labor to public projects like the temple, and others gave far more. "[T]his Temple in St. George is being built upon the principle of the United Order," Young explained in 1875.

St. George Temple, ca. 1876 *(courtesy of Church History Library, The Church of Jesus Christ of Latter-day Saints)*

While workers occasionally grumbled that the church should provide more food for their families, they made enormous sacrifices to build the temple. Church members who hesitated to embrace the United Order gave their financial support and labor to the temple. As had been the case back in Nauvoo, Young involved himself in the minute details of the temple's construction, aided by his annual winter residence in St. George. When he was back in Salt Lake City, temple foremen telegraphed him constantly with questions about architecture, building supplies, and labor.[70]

In late 1876, Young ordered the closure of the Endowment House, and on New Year's Day 1877 church leaders dedicated the St. George Temple. "We thank thee, God for Inspiration," a choir sang at the January temple dedication, "Poured out upon our Living Head, Who holds the keys of Revelation, and ordinances for the dead." Young had become increasingly feeble, and he was unable to walk due to an attack of rheumatism in his feet. Instead, he was pushed into the temple on a "sedan chair with rollers," then carried up a staircase to one of the sealing rooms. Young's body was breaking down.[71]

Despite his infirmities, Young remained a constant, guiding presence in the temple, once again becoming the church's chief priest. Befitting a church that accepted and expected ongoing revelation, there was always a belief that church leaders could revise sacred rituals in keeping with increased understanding. Accordingly, Young spent the next two months attempting to perfect the endowment ceremony. The ceremony included a "lecture at the veil," in which the officiator explained to participants the broad outlines of what Mormons regarded as the divine plan for human salvation. In Young's St. George temple formulation, Adam came to earth as a resurrected, exalted, and immortal god, accompanied by his wife Eve. They became mortal by eating the "forbidden fruit," a necessary and good step "that man might be." Adam and Eve's transgression enabled the embodiment of spirit children they had already created "in the celestial world." Adam eventually returned to the spirit world, but he returned "in the spirit to Mary and she conceived." By emphasizing Adam's role in the creation and redemption of humanity, Young more subtly introduced his earlier identification of Adam as humanity's god to those Mormons who passed through the ceremony in St. George.[72]

Young used a crutch and walking stick to ascend to the top of the temple font to witness the first St. George baptism for the dead. He also now called on the Saints to pass through the endowment ceremony for their dead relatives, giving participants a means of securing celestial benefits for their ancestors. In March, Young himself passed through the ceremony for John Twiss and Moses Whitesides, the respective deceased first husbands of his plural wives Naamah Carter ("Aunt Twiss") and Margaret Pierce. Young also received the second anointing for his wives' former husbands. According to Susa Young Gates, both Naamah Twiss and Margaret Pierce asked Young for the privilege of being anointed unto him instead. However, he refused to "rob the dead" and insisted on thus honoring their first husbands.[73]

Young had intended to perform the temple ordinances for his father as well, but being too feeble, he deputized those tasks to his son. Brigham Jr. and Elizabeth Young Ellsworth ritually sealed their grandparents, John Young and Nabby Howe. They then received the second anointing on their grandparents' behalf. "Laboring for the dead is a labor of love and productive of the most pleasant thoughts and feelings in life," wrote Brigham Jr. in his diary. For many Latter-day Saints, and presumably for Brigham Young himself, these rites salved anxieties about parents, grandparents, and other loved ones. Such worries were widespread in the mid- to late-nineteenth-century United States, as illustrated by the millions of Americans who sought contact with their dead kin through spiritualist mediums. The Mormons contented themselves with the anticipation of eternal communion with their ancestors. "It affords me great Joy and Consolation," wrote Esias Edwards after spending three days performing rites for his father, brothers, and uncles, "to think that I have had the privilege of living in this dispensation." By the end of 1877, Mormons had performed thirty thousand baptisms for the dead in the St. George temple and thirteen thousand proxy endowments for their ancestors.[74]

Young also reintroduced two rituals not performed since Nauvoo. In certain cases, church leaders taught that children needed to be sealed to their parents. No ritual was necessary if the parents had been sealed in marriage before the birth of their children. However, children born before their parents had been sealed risked eternal separation from their mothers and fathers. In the heavens, parents would have no right to such "illegitimate" children, warned George Q. Cannon. At the St. George Temple, hundreds of Latter-day Saint parents and children participated in sealings that ensured they would spend eternity together.[75]

Finally, Young revived the ritual of adoption, which had stirred so much controversy within the church during the exodus. Since reaching the Great Basin, Young had rarely spoken about the ritual of adoption. Like his communitarian vision and his identification of Adam as humanity's God, however, the "law of adoption" retained its significance in his mind. "Men will have to be sealed to Men," he had noted in 1859, explaining the doctrine's importance, "untill the Chain is united from Father Adam down to the last Saint."[76] In St. George, Young allowed the Mormons to resume that work. Church members without faithful parents could be sealed to prominent church leaders who, as heirs of the priesthood, could link them back to Adam. In particular, a number of individuals and couples who had requested adoption into Young's family now had that privilege. Unlike in Winter Quarters, though, Young made no attempt to reassemble an extended family organization based on the principle of adoption, nor did he reflect publicly on the doctrine at the St. George Temple.

Beginning on April 6, 1877 in St. George, the church held its annual conference, which doubled as a formal dedication of the temple. Young had been apprehensive since John D. Lee's execution two weeks earlier, worried that U.S. marshals might seek his arrest after Lee's insinuation of his guilt. Still, feeling healthier, he had actively helped prepare the temple for its dedication. According to Brigham Young Jr., his father even arranged seats and laid carpets. At the conference and dedication, there was no outpouring of Pentecostal blessings as had been the case in Kirtland. Unlike in Nauvoo, there was no ritual stampede, no pressure to hastily complete as much work as possible under the pressure of mobs. Still, crowds of Latter-day Saints stood outside the temple each morning during the conference, eager to celebrate their leader and his accomplishment. In St. George and in future temples, Mormons steadily performed rites they believed would save the dead and bind human beings together for an eternity of exaltation. The temple's completion provided a season of exhilaration and a sense of accomplishment, a brief glimpse of the heavenly harmony and cooperation Young had sought with such mixed success to establish within his church.[77]

On April 8, Young delivered his final discourse in the St. George Temple. After three months of ritual work and oversight, he would soon return to Salt Lake City. Instead of reflecting on the import of the temple's completion or on its sacred rites, Young used the occasion to bitterly lament the United Order's demise. He asserted that "the First Presidency and the Twelve had stood in the way of the People entering the United Order." In other words, the order's failure rested on the shoulders of the church's top leaders. In particular, he singled out Erastus Snow for condemnation, for allegedly having complained about the burden of maintaining the Washington cotton factory. In Young's mind, the temple and the United Order were interconnected efforts to build up God's kingdom in earth and in heaven. Thus, Young could not celebrate the temple's completion without contemplating the United Order's failure. In the end, recorded the doorkeeper Charles Lowell Walker, "Brother Brigham whipped and scolded the tradesmen and almost every body and every thing." Walker could not hear all of the church president's sound and fury, for a fierce wind blew dust, sand, and rain against the building. Inside, once Young had completed his harangue, he asked the choir to sing Eliza R. Snow's beloved hymn, "O my Father." Perhaps given his recent frailty, the closing verse took on an even greater meaning than usual for him: "Then, at length, when I've completed/All you sent me forth to do,/With your mutual approbation/Let me come and dwell with you."[78]

That morning, throngs of Latter-day Saints had gathered outside the temple to make sure they found a place within its walls to worship together and listen to their leaders. Young's harsh words would not have bothered them (with the possible exception of Erastus Snow). The diatribe was characteristic of Brigham Young at such moments. He was not one to revel in accomplishments, and he could not let go of unmet goals. While Young was still very much the center of Great Basin Mormonism, the relationship between Young and the Latter-day Saints had changed considerably since the mid-1850s. During the Mormon reformation, many in his audiences quite literally felt the fear of God and man. No one could dispute Brigham Young's persistence and tenacity, but as he edged toward the end of his life he became more cantankerous than fearsome. Those who

Brigham Young, ca. 1876 *(courtesy of Church History Library, The Church of Jesus Christ of Latter-day Saints)*

dissented from his economic leadership knew they could bide their time until Young no longer led the church. Meanwhile, they cherished the spiritual blessings they obtained from his discourses and from his ritual leadership. Young might sometimes have harsh words for them, but he had with fierceness and determination defended the church for the past three decades. For that, and despite all his faults, he had his people's enduring respect and admiration. Once again, church members at the St. George Temple conference affirmed him as their "Prophet, Seer, and Revelator."

AFTER returning from the St. George Temple dedication, Young had a typically active summer. He dedicated temple grounds in Manti and Logan, undertook an extensive reorganization of the lower levels of the church hierarchy, and even revived his old dream of replacing written English with a phonetic alphabet. In mid-August, he bathed in the Great Salt Lake for the first time in many years. "Father seems in good health," wrote Brigham Jr. on August 20, "and [I] never saw him more active or in better spirits."[79]

On the evening of August 23, Young suddenly fell ill, suffering from cramps, vomiting, and diarrhea. Brigham Jr. found his father in great pain the next day. "I don't know," he said when asked if he would recover. Seymour Young, the church president's nephew and physician, labeled his illness as "cholera morbus," a nonspecific diagnosis largely equivalent to the modern lay term "stomach flu." Seymour Young later wrote that his uncle's appendix burst on August 25, but diverticulitis, perforated colon cancer, and several other diseases could also have caused his symptoms.[80]

"[H]e clung to life," reported the *Salt Lake Tribune* a week later, "with a tenacity characteristic of the living Brigham Young." That tenacity and the care of four physicians could not produce a recovery. Young had often avoided deathbed scenes, but he lived his final days with wives, children, and church leaders constantly by his side and praying for his recovery. On Wednesday, August 29, after his father had been semi-comatose for thirty-six hours and had developed a high fever, John Willard Young once again requested the administration of healing rites for his father. After Young was anointed and sealed, he said "Amen" and added "that's all right." Several hours later, he stopped breathing. "It was but a gasp or two," recorded his grandson Richard, "a slight and almost imperceptible tremor—the rush of a thimble of blood to his lips—when his pulse ceased to denote the vibrations of his heart." The Lion of the Lord was dead.[81]

Epilogue

ON SEPTEMBER 1, 1877, a great crush of mourners filed through the Salt Lake City Tabernacle to see Young's body. The next day, after the tabernacle reached its capacity, two thousand individuals stood outside the building during the funeral. After the hymns, prayers, and eulogies concluded, a large procession brought Young's corpse through the Eagle Gate outside his mansions and eventually to a family cemetery just to the east of Temple Square. At the burial service, a choir sang "O, my Father," celebrating Young's return to his heavenly, divine parents.

Not hesitating to speak ill of the dead or his religion, the *Salt Lake Tribune* expressed its hope that now "the whole decaying structure [of Mormonism] will rapidly fall to pieces." Young had positioned himself as a bulwark against the tide of political anti-Mormonism and a potential flood of Gentile capital and settlers. Perhaps with Young out of the way, the dam would break, and the Mormons would at the very least abandon polygamy and theocracy, if not the entire substance of their religion. Echoing the language of white southern Democrats who had regained control of the American South, the *Tribune* predicted that "Utah will be Americanized and politically and socially redeemed."[1]

Within three decades, several of the *Tribune*'s wishes had come true. Future church leaders eventually made the compromises Young had been unwilling to accept. John Taylor, Young's immediate successor, fiercely resisted more sweeping antipolygamy legislation and even went underground

"In memoriam Brigham Young," 1877 *(courtesy of Library of Congress)*

to avoid arrest. In 1890, however, Wilford Woodruff—who had succeeded Taylor as church president—announced in a manifesto that the church would abide by antipolygamy laws. Within another fifteen years, the church stopped sanctioning any plural marriages. Although the church retained considerable influence over Utah politics, it abandoned its more overt theocratic aspirations. The church also put the brakes on the gathering of Saints to the Great Basin, leading to the growth of Mormon communities in other parts of the United States and around the world.[2]

If Joseph Smith's murder ended the first period of Mormon history, Woodruff's manifesto seemed to bring its second era to a conclusion. Utah became a state in 1896 and even elected several non-Mormon Republicans to high office. Over the course of the twentieth century, many Latter-day Saints became super-patriotic, more fully reconciled to American capitalism, and in occasional partnership with politically conservative evangelicals. Once regarded as notorious sexual deviants by most other Americans, the Latter-day Saints eventually became vocal defenders of heterosexual monogamy. Especially after the church began excommunicating persons who married plurally in the early 1900s, some Mormons formed splinter churches that retained what they saw as key articles of the faith as expressed by Joseph Smith and Brigham Young, including polygamy. Many fundamentalist Mormons also adhered to Young's identification of Adam as God, which Young's successors gradually rejected. Most of Young's ecclesiastical descendants, however, found it necessary to move away from the aspects of his vision that could not peacefully or prosperously exist within the United States.

The rapid evolution of the church after Young's death provides an ironic testimony to the strength of his leadership. George Q. Cannon later revealed that some of his ecclesiastical associates complained that Young had "ruled with so strong and stiff a hand" that they "dare[d] not exhibit their feelings to him." Furthermore, they alleged "that the funds of the Church have been used with a freedom not warranted by the authority which he held." Probably alluding to Young's identification of Adam as God, Cannon continued that "in the promulgation of doctrine he took liberties beyond those to which he was legitimately entitled."[3] That Cannon, a stalwart Young loyalist, perceived and later articulated such concerns suggests that the disgruntlement was widespread. Young's vigor and tenacity, however, had maintained what he saw as essential. Young would retreat in the face of insurmountable opposition, as he had done when confronted by Johnston's 1857 army. For the most part, though, he had held his ground.

At the same time, just as the history of the American West (or the United States more broadly) did not dramatically change course with the closing of the frontier, mainstream Mormonism very much remained Brigham Young's church beyond the abandonment of polygamy and theocracy. The church's reconciliation with the U.S. government did not wash away other significant aspects of his legacy. Even as certain Mormon practices waned, the Church of Jesus Christ of Latter-day Saints kept its unique position within the American landscape and never drifted back toward the Protestant Christianity from which it had diverged. The church's endurance as a "new religious tradition" or a new species of Christianity was hardly inevitable. Joseph Smith III's Reorganized Church of Jesus Christ of Latter Day Saints—renamed the Community of Christ in 2001—eventually came to resemble a mainline Protestant denomination in many respects. Brigham Young's ecclesiastical descendants did not follow that path.[4]

The process of colonizing the Great Basin, building a theocratic kingdom, and resisting the force of the U.S. government had fashioned a Mormon people. For Brigham Young, individuals did not become Latter-day Saints in the waters of baptism but through trials, tribulations, and "living their religion," which meant great sacrifice and perfect obedience. "I want hard times," he once insisted, "so that every person that does not wish to stay, for the sake of his religion, will leave." In their new mountain home,

Young's followers found those hard times in abundance, suffering from famine, wars and rumors of war, the difficulty of creating harmonious plural families, and a long struggle to build viable communities in a rugged environment. "This is a good place to make Saints," Young concluded. Even though Young demanded more than some of his followers could stomach, tens of thousands flocked to and abided by his leadership, attracted by his stewardship of Smith's theological and ritual legacy, his fervent belief in and preaching of the gospel, and the close connections he maintained with his people. The memory of this collective experience still shapes American Mormon identity.[5]

Mormon theology and ritual also set the Latter-day Saints apart, in large part because of the emphasis upon temple-building that characterized the beginning and end of Young's time at the helm of the church. "We shall build Temples over north and South America," Young said in 1875 while planning the construction of a temple in Manti. With the U.S. Army camped to the east of Salt Lake City in December 1857, Young expressed a hope that, in the future, hundreds of men and women would work in "thousands of Temples" to redeem the world. Young spoke with characteristic hyperbole, yet the church has now dedicated nearly one hundred and fifty temples, some in such formerly unthinkable places as Nigeria and Washington, D.C. While Sunday morning ward meetings resemble a very low-church form of Protestantism, temple rituals (the sacred covenants of the endowment ceremony, sealings, and work for the dead) sharply demarcate Mormonism from other contemporary forms of Christianity.[6]

Could Young have accomplished what he did without leading his people into the darker chapters of Mormon history, such as the excesses of the reformation, the handcart tragedy, and the Mountain Meadows Massacre? After the setbacks of the 1850s, Young learned to restrain his rhetoric and tolerate the presence of Gentiles and ex-Mormons in Utah. Such changes in tone and practice did not weaken the church, even if they foretold the end of Mormonism's political kingdom. In large part because of the trauma of Joseph Smith's death and Young's own fear of a similar end, however, he could not understand any other way to lead the church until the final decade of his life.

Young made it clear that he would not suffer anyone to stand in the way of his drive to establish and build up the Kingdom of God on earth. "Mind Your Own Business," proclaimed the masthead of John Taylor's New York City–based newspaper *The Mormon* in the mid-1850s. What the paper identified as the "Mormon Creed," it attributed to Brigham Young. "Mind your business" or "mind your own business" was Brigham Young's advice for Saint and Gentile alike. The phrase had several meanings. Young wanted his people to choose industry over idleness, to store up a surplus in good years so that they could survive the lean. "Any man in the world filled with the Spirit of [the] Lord," Young taught, "is filled with the Spirit of industry." In preparation for Christ's return, they should build up an earthly kingdom that would one day become their heavenly Zion. At its best, Young's creed was a simple call to hard work and benevolence. "'To mind your own business,'" he said, "incorporates the whole duty of man." Young described that duty as to "do all the good he can upon the earth." Mormons should spur each other on to more righteous living, eschew vices, and help neighbors in need. "Mind your own business," in this sense, was Young's golden rule. When Young adhered to it, he was at his most impressive as a leader, as when he helped poor families leave Missouri and Nauvoo, when he dispatched rescue parties to meet the stranded 1856 handcart emigrants, and when he dispensed charity and jobs to impoverished Mormons in Utah.[7]

The Mormon Creed had other connotations as well. Some Americans termed "mind your own business" the "eleventh commandment," including southerners who suggested that northerners should not criticize the institution of slavery. The Mormons used the phrase to encourage a quiet dedication to the tasks of kingdom-building coupled with obedience to their leaders. "Every man in his own place," proclaimed Willard Richards's nephew Samuel in 1856, "minding his own business—that's Mormonism." The Saints should not stick their noses into affairs that did not concern them. For Young, "mind your own business" meant that church members should not question his decisions or pry into the private matters of church councils. Nor should they divulge sacred matters, such as the endowment ceremony, sealing rituals, or ecclesiastical deliberations. In the spring of 1852, Young became upset with what he termed "whining" among church members who wanted to know whether church leaders "intended to send out a mission this season." Such decisions could have a great impact on church members' livelihoods and ability to care for their families. "I say it is none of your business," Young told a congregation. "Mind your own business." Members of the church should recognize their place in the church hierarchy, wait to receive instruction, and respect the prerogatives of their leaders.[8]

Throughout his entire adult life, Young fiercely defended his own autonomy and independence, and he sometimes described independence as a key element of the godliness to which all Latter-day Saints should aspire. The building up of the Kingdom of God on the earth, though, required Mormons to subordinate their individual desires to those of the group. Young often stressed that he wanted church members to receive revelations for themselves, but such divine promptings would confirm, not contradict or question, his doctrine and direction. The church that Young shaped still places a high value on conformity and obedience, giving it unusual cohesion but often making it an inhospitable environment for those members more inclined to question than simply conform.

Young applied the creed in a similar manner toward non-Mormons, especially toward politicians and judges. When outsiders violated Young's creed, he did his utmost to get rid of them. In the mid-nineteenth century, many other Americans would have affirmed such an impulse for local sovereignty against outside interference. Especially after the Civil War, though, Young's desire for Mormon self-determination collided with a national government intent on more fully extending its sovereignty over the American West. While he made some adjustments in his approach to disputes with Washington, Young could not fully reconcile himself to these changes. A religious minority with theocratic pretensions could not readily coexist alongside a government that still maintained a loose, unofficial Protestant establishment. Protestant America could make peace with new denominations and isolated sects. Groups with broader claims to religious authority, such as Catholics, struggled much harder to gain acceptance. The Mormons under Brigham Young posed a unique challenge. They had the real estate to back up their kingdom-building rhetoric.

To most church members, Brigham Young was the church's earthly savior following Smith's death, an indispensable protector and benefactor. In the opinion of many other Americans, he was a treasonous heretic. Many who became better acquainted with him modulated their opinions, but among Utah's non-Mormon population Young often inspired both fear and loathing, and many church members trembled before him on occasion as well. He preserved a church and created a people, but that success damaged and even destroyed some lives. Brigham Young died with few apparent regrets about his choices and decisions. In his forty-five years as a Latter-day Saint, Young dedicated himself to Joseph Smith, boldly challenged religious, political, and economic conventions, and shaped—as far as was possible, for as long as was possible—the Mormon people in his self-image.

Notes

Abbreviations

APR   Scott H. Faulring, *An American Prophet's Record: The Diaries and Journals of Joseph Smith* (Salt Lake City: Signature Books, 2nd ed., 1989)

BYJ1   Brigham Young Journal, 1832–36, Box 71, Folder 1, BYP

BYJ2   Brigham Young Journal, 1837–45, Box 71, Folder 2, BYP

BYJ3   Brigham Young Journal, 1840–44, Box 71, Folder 3, BYP

BYOJ   Brigham Young Office Journal, 1844–46, Box 71, Folder 4, BYP

BYOJA   Brigham Young Office Journal, 11 Feb. 1852–12 July 1855; 8 Nov. 1855–20 Dec. 1856, Box 72, Folder 2, BYP

BYOJB   Brigham Young Office Journal, 16 Aug. 1852–25 March 1853; 20 Dec. 1856–24 Dec. 1857, Box 72, Folder 1, BYP

BYOC   Brigham Young Office Journal, 1857–1860, CR 1234 2, CHL

BYOJD   Brigham Young Office Journal, 1858–63, Box 72, Folder 5, BYP, published in Fred C. Collier, ed., *The Office Journal of President Brigham Young, 1858–1863: Book D* (Hanna, UT: Collier's Publishing, 2006)

BYOJ57A   Jan–May 1857, Box 72, Folder 3, BYP

BYOJ57B   May–Dec. 1857, in Everett Cooley, ed., *Diary of Brigham Young, 1857* (Salt Lake City: Tanner Trust Fund, 1980)

BYP   Brigham Young Papers, CR 1234, CHL

CHL   Church History Library (Church Archives), Church of Jesus Christ of Latter-day Saints, Salt Lake City, Utah

DN   *Deseret News* [Salt Lake City: 1850–]

D&C   *Doctrine and Covenants* (available at http://lds.org/scriptures/dc-testament?lang=eng)

EMD   Dan Vogel, ed., *Early Mormon Documents,* 5 vols. (Salt Lake City: Signature, 1996–2003)

FHL   Family History Library, Church of Jesus Christ of Latter-day Saints, Salt Lake City, Utah

GCM   General Church Minutes, CR 100 318, CHL

HBLL   Special Collections, Harold B. Lee Library, Brigham Young University, Provo, Utah

HC   B. H. Roberts, ed., *History of the Church of Jesus Christ of Latter-day Saints,* 7 vols. (Salt Lake City: *Deseret News,* 1902–1932)

HCKJ   Heber C. Kimball Journal, in Stanley B. Kimball, ed., *On the Potter's Wheel: The Diaries of Heber C. Kimball* (Salt Lake City: Signature Books, 1987)

HCKWC   Heber C. Kimball Journal, kept by William Clayton, Nov. 1845–Jan. 1846, typescript at HBLL

HOJ   Church Historian's Office, Journal, CR 100 1, CHL

HOOC   Church Historian's Office, Outgoing Correspondence, CR 100 38, CHL

HSJ   Juanita Brooks, ed., *On the Mormon Frontier: The Diary of Hosea Stout, 1844–1889* (Salt Lake City: University of Utah Press, 2009 reprint of 1964 edition)

JD   *Journal of Discourses by Brigham Young, His Two Counsellors, the Twelve Apostles and others . . .* 26 vols. (Liverpool and London: various publishers, 1854–1886)

JH   Journal History of the Church, Church Historian's Office, CR 100 137, CHL

JSP J1   Dean C. Jessee, Mark Ashurst-McGee, and Richard L. Jensen, eds., *The Joseph Smith Papers, Journals, Volume 1: 1832–1839* (Salt Lake City: Church Historian's Press, 2008)

KCMB   Fred C. Collier and William S. Harwell, eds., *Kirtland Council Minute Book* (Salt Lake City: Collier's Publishing, 1996). [Kirtland High Council Minutes, MS 3432, CHL]

LJA   Leonard J. Arrington Papers, MSS 10, Special Collections, Merrill-Cazier Library, Utah State University, Logan, Utah

MH   Manuscript History, Church Historian's Office, CR 100 102, CHL

MMM   Ronald W. Walker, Richard E. Turley, Jr., and Glen M. Leonard, *Massacre at Mountain Meadows* (New York: Oxford University Press, 2008)

MU   John D. Lee, *Mormonism Unveiled, or the Life and Confessions of the Late Mormon Bishop, John D. Lee . . .* (St. Louis: Bryan, Brand, & Company, 1877)

NEC   Devery S. Anderson and Gary James Bergera, eds., *The Nauvoo Endowment Companies, 1845–1846: A Documentary History* (Salt Lake City: Signature Books, 2005)

NYT   *New York Times*

OR   *The War of the Rebellion: A Compilation of the Official Records of the Union and Confederate Armies,* 70 vols. (Washington: Government Printing Office, 1880–1901)

RSR   Richard Bushman with Jed Woodworth, *Joseph Smith: Rough Stone Rolling* (New York: Knopf, 2005)

RMS   T.B.H. Stenhouse, *The Rocky Mountain Saints . . .* (New York: D. Appleton and Company, 1873)

SLT   *Salt Lake Tribune*

SOPM   School of the Prophets Minutes, 1867–74, CR 390/6, CHL, cf., Devery S. Anderson ed., *"The Knowledge of All Truth": Minutes of the Salt Lake City School of the Prophets, 1867–1874, and 1883* (Salt Lake City: Signature Books, forthcoming)

SYGP   Susa Young Gates Papers, MSS B-95, Utah State History, Salt Lake City, Utah

TBJ   Will Bagley, ed., *The Pioneer Camp of the Saints: The 1846 and 1847 Mormon Trail Journals of Thomas Bullock* (Spokane, WA: Arthur H. Clark, 1997)

T&S   *Times & Seasons* [Nauvoo, IL: 1839–46]

UUSC   Special Collections, Marriott Library, University of Utah

USGP   John Y. Simon, ed., *Papers of Ulysses S. Grant,* 31 vols. (Carbondale: Southern Illinois University Press, 1967–)

VW   Richard S. Van Wagoner, ed., *The Complete Discourses of Brigham Young,* 5 vols. (Salt Lake City: Smith-Pettit Foundation, 2009)

WCJ   George D. Smith, ed., *An Intimate Chronicle: The Journals of William Clayton* (Salt Lake City: Signature Books, 2nd ed. 1995)

WRJ   Willard Richards Journal, MS 1490, CHL

WWJ   Scott G. Kenney, ed., *Wilford Woodruff's Journal, 1833–1898: Typescript,* 9 vols. (Midvale, UT: Signature Books, 1983–84)

ZHJ   Zina D. Huntington Journal

Preface

1. Taylor, P. A. M., "The Life of Brigham Young: A Biography Which Will Not Be Written," *Dialogue* 1 (Autumn 1966): 101–110.

Prologue

1. Sedan chair in Brigham Young Jr. Journal, 1 Jan. 1877, MS 1236, CHL. Quotations from WWJ, 1 Jan. 1877, 7:303–320; Charles L. Walker Journal, 1 Jan. 1877, in Andrew K. Larson and Katharine M. Larson, eds., *The Diary of Charles Lowell Walker* (Logan: Utah State University Press, 1980), 1:440–443.

2. Discourse of 17 April 1853, JD, 2:123.

3. Bloodstone amulets in Brigham Young account book, esp. 5 Jan. 1858 and 16 May 1868, Vault MSS 155, HBLL; witches in HOJ, 3 Feb. 1868.

4. Discourse of 18 July 1869, JD, 13:60.

5. Discourse of 28 July 1866, transcript of George D. Watt shorthand notes by LaJean Carruth, Papers of George D. Watt, CHL. Watt recorded many of Young's sermons in Pitman shorthand. For a select number of sermons, Watt then prepared a transcript, which church leaders sometimes revised for publication in the *Deseret News* or the *Journal of Discourses* or both. Carruth's transcripts of the original shorthand notes provide more immediate access to Young's sermons.

1. A New Creature

The epigraph is from Peter Cartwright, *Autobiography of Peter Cartwright, the Backwoods Preacher* (New York: Carlton & Porter, 1857), 342.

1. "baptized under the hand," BYJ1, 9 April 1832; "History of Brigham Young," DN, 10 Feb. 1858. On the latter source, see Howard Clair Searle, "Early Mormon Historiography: Writing the History of the Mormons, 1830–1858" (Ph.D. diss., UCLA, 1979), 337–357. Young's elder's license confirms that his ordination took place on the same day. See Box 170, Folder 22, BYP. I am grateful to Michael Marquardt for pointing me to this source.

2. The following sources proved invaluable in establishing a chronology of Young's ancestry, childhood, and early adulthood: Ronald K. Esplin, "The Emergence of Brigham Young and the Twelve to Mormon Leadership, 1830–1841," Ph.D. diss., Brigham Young University, 1981 (Provo, UT: Joseph Fielding Smith Institute for Latter-day Saint History and BYU Studies, 2006), ch. 2; Leonard J. Arrington, *Brigham Young: American Moses* (New York: Alfred A. Knopf, 1985), chs. 1 and 2; Rebecca Cornwall and Richard F. Palmer, "The Religious and Family Background of Brigham Young," *BYU Studies* 18 (Spring 1878): 286–310; Richard F. Palmer and Karl D. Butler, *Brigham Young: The New York Years* (Provo, UT: Charles Redd Center, 1992).

3. Fanny Young Murray to Phineas Howe Young, 1 Jan. 1845, typescript in MS 14465, CHL; "a country broken and rocky" from Edward P. Conklin, *Middlesex County and Its People: A History*, vol. 2 (New York: Lewis Historical Publishing Company, 1927), 576. On John Young's military service, see Gene A. Sessions, *Latter-day Patriots: Nine Mormon Families and Their Revolutionary War Heritage* (Salt Lake City: Deseret Book, 1975), ch. 2.

4. Quotes in Fanny Young Murray to Phineas Howe Young, 1 Jan. 1845; 1790 U.S. Census, Hopkinton, Middlesex County, Massachusetts. See Cornwall and Palmer, "The Religious and Family Background of Brigham Young," 294–295.

5. Fanny's care for Brigham in Joseph Young Journal, 10 May 1872, MS 1741, CHL.

6. Hamilton Child, *Gazetteer and Business Directory of Windham Country, VT., 1724–1884* (Syracuse, NY: Journal Office, 1884) [reprint Bowie, MD.: Heritage Books, 2001], 1:304. On this wave of migration, see Stewart H. Holbrook, *The Yankee Exodus: An Account of Migration from New England* (New York: MacMillan, 1950); Whitney R. Cross, *The Burned-Over District:*

The Social and Intellectual History of Enthusiastic Religion in Western New York, 1800–1850 (Ithaca: Cornell University Press, 1950), 4–6.

7. Discourses of 8 Aug. 1869 ("chop logs"), JD, 14:103; 7 Sept. 1856 ("sisters"), JD, 5:97.

8. Discourse of 15 Aug. 1852, transcript of George D. Watt shorthand notes by LaJean Carruth; "that dear servant" in William Barry, *A History of Framingham, Massachusetts* (Boston: James Munroe, 1847), 114; story of Ebenezer and Sybil Goddard from Fanny Young Murray to Phineas Howe Young, 1 Jan. 1845; Susannah Howe from 8 Jan. 1845 minutes of Young family meeting, Box 1, Folder 28, GCM, CHL. On the radical religiosity of the ancestors of many converts to Mormonism, see Val D. Rust, *Radical Origins: Early Mormon Converts and Their Colonial Ancestors* (Urbana: University of Illinois Press, 2004).

9. Sweet, *Religion on the American Frontier, 1783–1840,* vol. 4 (New York: Cooper Square, 1964), 57; "nothing out today" in John H. Wigger, *Taking Heaven by Storm: Methodism and the Rise of Popular Christianity in America* (Urbana: University of Illinois Press, 2001), 21. On the New England religious frontier, see Stephen A. Marini, *Radical Sects of Revolutionary New England* (Cambridge, MA: Harvard University Press, 1982). On Hamilton, see Clark Jillson, *Green Leaves from Whitingham, Vermont: A History of the Town* (Worcester, MA: n.p., 1894), 148–149, ch. 4; D. Michael Quinn, *Early Mormonism and the Magic World View,* rev. and enl. (Salt Lake City: Signature Books, 1998), 26, 46–47.

10. "cut like a sword" and naming of children in Charles Coleman Sellers, *Lorenzo Dow: The Bearer of the Word* (New York: Minton, Balch, 1928), 91, 258–259; "odd-looking" in discourse of 15 July 1860, JD, 8:120; "can and you can't" in Lorenzo Dow, *The Opinion of Dow; Or, Lorenzo's Thoughts, on Different Religious Subjects . . .* (Windham: J. Byrne, 1804), 24; "spiritual children" in Dow, *The Life, Travels, Labors, and Writings of Lorenzo Dow* (New York: Miller, Orton and Mulligan, 1856), 177. See also Nathan Hatch, *The Democratization of American Christianity* (New Haven: Yale University Press, 1989), 36–41, 130–133.

11. "holy zeal" in George Peck, *Early Methodism within the Bounds of the Old Genesee Conference from 1788 to 1818* (New York: Carlton and Porter, 1860), 322; "a singularity" in Dow, *The Life, Travels, Labors, and Writings,* 132–134 (emphasis in original). See Wigger, *Taking Heaven by Storm,* ch. 5.

12. "middling" from Wigger, *Taking Heaven by Storm,* 5; Cartwright quoted in Sweet, *Religion on the American Frontier,* 4:55; discourses of 6 Feb. 1853 ("kept within" and "not a chance"), JD, 2:94; 5 Oct. 1856 ("word and a blow"), JD, 4:112; 15 Aug. 1852 ("taught her children"), transcript of George D. Watt shorthand notes by LaJean Carruth; "Bible-drenched" from Philip L. Barlow, *Mormons and the Bible: The Place of the Latter-day Saints in American Religion* (New York: Oxford, 1991), 11. On evangelical social aspiration, see Paul Johnson, *A Shopkeeper's Millennium: Society and Revivals in Rochester, New York, 1815–1837* (New York: Hill and Wang, 1978).

13. Joseph Young Journal, 10 May 1872; Amasa Little, "Biography of Lorenzo

Dow Young," *Utah Historical Quarterly* 14 (1946), 130; "make bread" in discourse of 7 Sept. 1856, JD, 5:97.

14. "sixteen years old" in discourse of 12 Nov. 1864, transcript of George D. Watt shorthand notes by LaJean Carruth; "carpenter" in "History of Brigham Young," DN, 10 Feb. 1858, 385; "journeyman" in discourse of 7 April 1873, JD, 16:17.

15. Discourses of 23 March 1862 ("opposed"), JD, 9:248; 27 Aug. 1871 ("temperance pledge"), JD, 14:225; 7 April 1873 ("Mr. Pratt"), JD, 16:17. On late 1820s temperance demands for complete abstinence, see Robert H. Abzug, *Cosmos Crumbling: American Reform and the Religious Imagination* (New York: Oxford University Press, 1994), ch. 4.

16. Finney, *Memoirs of Rev. Charles G. Finney* (New York: A. S. Barnes, 1876), 78; Dow in discourse of 3 June 1871, JD, 14:197; "Men were rolling" from minutes of 8 Jan. 1845; "Lo here" in discourse of 6 April 1860, JD, 8:38. On "democratic biblicism," see Mark Noll, *America's God: From Jonathan Edwards to Abraham Lincoln* (New York: Oxford University Press, 2002), ch. 18. On Mormon critiques of evangelical pluralism, see Marvin S. Hill, *Quest for Refuge: The Mormon Flight from American Pluralism* (Salt Lake City: Signature Books, 1989).

17. Minutes of 23 Sept. 1849, Box 2, Folder 14, GCM; "some things" in discourse of 6 Oct. 1870, JD, 13:267. On Baptists who advocated restricting the Lord's Supper to persons baptized as believers by immersion, see James R. Mathis, *The Making of the Primitive Baptists: A Cultural and Intellectual History of the Antimission Movement, 1800–1840* (New York: Routledge, 2004), 31–33.

18. "contagion" in Bernard Bailyn, *The Ideological Origins of the American Revolution*, enl. ed. (Cambridge, MA: Harvard University Press, 1992), esp. 246–272; "plain, unassuming" in Wesley Bailey, "History of the Reformed Methodist Church," in I. Daniel Rupp, ed., *An Original History of the Religious Denominations at Present Existing in the United States* (Philadelphia: J. Y. Humphreys, 1844), 466; other quotes from *The Reformer's Discipline* (Bennington, VT: Darius Clark, 1814), 3–4, 6–7, 22–23. On the Young family's association with Reformed Methodism, see Larry C. Porter, "The Brigham Young Family: Transition between Reformed Methodism and Mormonism," in Kent P. Jackson and Andrew C. Skinner, eds., *A Witness for the Restoration: Essays in Honor of Robert J. Matthews* (Provo, UT: Brigham Young University Religious Studies Center, 2007), 249–280.

19. Bailey, "History of the Reformed Methodist Church," 466–477; *The Reformer's Discipline*, 12; "something like Pentecost" from William Pitts, *The Gospel Witness* (Catskill, NY: Junius S. Lewis and Col., 1818), 65. On John Wesley and physical manifestations of the Spirit, see Ann Taves, *Fits, Trances, and Visions: Experiencing Religion and Explaining Experience from Wesley to James* (Princeton: Princeton University Press, 1999), 50–58.

20. "from that hour" in Phineas Young to BY, 11 Aug. 1845, Box 44, Folder 6, BYP; "averse" in "History of Brigham Young," *Millennial Star,* 27 June 1863, 407; Little, "Biography of Lorenzo Dow Young," 27–31.

21. In his 1832 account of his "First Vision," Joseph Smith Jr. wrote that "a pillar of light above the brightness of the sun at noon day come down from above and rested upon me and I was filled with the spirit of god." For commonalities between Smith's narrative and accounts of Methodist conversions, see Christopher C. Jones, "The Power and Form of Godliness: Methodist Conversion Narratives and Joseph Smith's First Vision," *Journal of Mormon History* 37 (Spring 2011): 88–114.

22. "History of Brigham Young," *Millennial Star,* 23 May 1863, 327; *Ontario Republican Times* [Canandaigua, NY], 10 Sept. 1857.

23. Discourses of 3 July 1859 ("Evil One"), JD, 7:6; 20 April 1856 ("troubled"), JD, 3:320; 30 June 1867 ("Joseph once said"), JD, 12:95; 9 Oct. 1872 ("Bible Christians"), JD, 15:165; "well remember" in Phineas Young to BY, 11 Aug. 1845. On this dynamic, see Abzug, *Cosmos Crumbling,* 75.

24. McKee to BY, 4 April 1860, Box 27, Folder 17, BYP; cf. Esplin, "The Emergence of Brigham Young," 22; BY to McKee, 3 May 1860, Letterpress Copybook 5, pages 492–495, BYP. See Dan Vogel, *Religious Seekers and the Advent of Mormonism* (Salt Lake City: Signature Books, 1988), x.

25. Johnson, *A Shopkeeper's Millennium,* 37; Phineas Young quoted in "History of Brigham Young," *Millennial Star,* 23 May 1863, 327–328. See J. Sheldon Fisher, "Brigham Young as a Mendon Craftsman: A Study in Historical Archeology," *New York History* 6 (Oct. 1980): 433.

26. 17 Feb. 1829 lease, MSS 5880, HBLL; 16 March 1830 note, MS 15905, CHL; BY to John Willard Young, 7 Feb. 1866, Letterpress Copybook 8, pages 69–70, BYP. See Palmer and Butler, *The New York Years,* 27–28. On the economic transformation of the early American republic, see John Lauritz Larson, *The Market Revolution in America: Liberty, Ambition, and the Eclipse of the Common Good* (New York: Cambridge University Press, 2010), chs. 1 and 2.

27. Both Anti-Masonry and Sabbatarianism were powerful political movements in the Rochester vicinity in the late 1820s. For a brief overview, see Sean Wilentz, *The Rise of American Democracy, Jefferson to Lincoln* (New York: W.W. Norton, 2005), 271–280.

28. Discourse of 24 Aug. 1872, JD, 15:135.

29. "discern" in Lucy Mack Smith, *Biographical Sketches of Joseph Smith the Prophet and His Progenitors for Many Generations* (Liverpool: S. W. Richards, 1853), 92; "spark of Methodism" in Orasmus Turner, *History of the Pioneer Settlement of Phelps and Gorham's Purchase,* in EMD, 3:50; "somewhat partial" in MH, A-1 [1838], page 2; cf. Dean C. Jessee, *The Papers of Joseph Smith* (Salt Lake City: Deseret Book, 1989): 1:270. On Smith's early life, see RSR, chs. 1 and 2.

30. On the creation of the *Book of Mormon* and the organization of the Church of Christ, see RSR, 8–126; Terryl L. Givens, *By the Hand of Mormon: The American Scripture that Launched a New World Religion* (New York: Oxford University Press, 2002), chs. 1 and 2.

31. 2 Nephi 5:21–23; 2 Nephi 30:6.

32. See John L. Brooke, *The Refiner's Fire: The Making of Mormon Cosmology,*

1644–1844 (Cambridge: Cambridge University Press, 1994), 184–189; Givens, *By the Hand of Mormon,* 64, 67.

33. Minutes of 8 Jan. 1845; "Synopsis of the History of Heber Chase Kimball," *Millennial Star,* 23 and 30 July 1864, 472, 487.

34. For a discussion of Anglo-American prophets from the late eighteenth to early nineteenth centuries, see Susan Juster, *Doomsayers: Anglo-American Prophesy in the Age of Revolution* (Philadelphia: University of Pennsylvania Press, 2003). The ideas about Joseph Smith expressed in this paragraph bear debts to David F. Holland, *Sacred Borders: Continuing Revelation and Canonical Restraint in Early America* (New York: Oxford University Press, 2011); Richard T. Hughes and C. Leonard Allen, *Illusions of Innocence: Protestant Primitivism in America, 1630–1875* (Chicago: University of Chicago Press, 1988), ch. 6; Samuel M. Brown, *In Heaven As It Is on Earth: Joseph Smith and the Early Mormon Conquest of Death* (New York: Oxford University Press, 2012).

35. Phineas Young quoted in "History of Brigham Young," *Millennial Star,* 6 June 1863, 360–361.

36. Solomon Chamberl[a]in, *A Sketch of the Experience of Solomon Chamberlin* (Lyons, NY: 1829), printed in Larry C. Porter, "Solomon Chamberlain's Missing Pamphlet," *BYU Studies* 37 (1997–98): 113–140.

37. "Father Chamberlain" in Minutes of 8 Jan. 1845; other quotes from "History of Brigham Young," *Millennial Star,* 13 June 1863, 374–375.

38. "something in" in "History of Brigham Young," *Millennial Star,* 13 June 1863, 375.

39. "receive the laying on of hands" in "Synopsis of the History of Heber Chase Kimball," *Millennial Star,* 30 July 1864; "History of Brigham Young," DN, 10 Feb. 1858; "not baptized" in discourse of 6 April 1860, JD, 8:38; "reasoned" in minutes of 8 Jan. 1845. On the role of rational reflection in Mormon conversions, see Steven Harper, "Infallible Proofs, Both Human and Divine: The Persuasiveness of Mormonism for Early Converts," *Religion and American Culture* 10 (Winter 2000): 99–118.

40. "pondering" in "Synopsis of the History of Heber Chase Kimball," *Millennial Star,* 6 Aug. 1864.

41. "miricles" in Joseph Young Journal, 10 May 1872; other quotes in discourse of 6 April 1860, JD, 8:38.

42. "endowed with power" in D&C 38:32. See Grant Underwood, *The Millenarian World of Early Mormonism* (Urbana: University of Illinois Press, 1993), esp. 137; Stephen J. Fleming, "'Congenial to Almost Every Shade of Radicalism': The Delaware Valley and the Success of Early Mormonism," *Religion and American Culture* 17 (Summer 2007): 129–164. On the appeal of Mormonism in rural, "backwoods" portions of the northeastern United States, see Mario S. De Pillis, "The Social Sources of Mormonism," *Church History* 37 (March 1968): 50–79.

43. Tullidge, "The Mormon Commonwealth," *The Galaxy,* 15 Oct. 1866, 356. The argument here is congruent with Rust, *Radical Origins,* esp. 4–6.

44. *Liberal Advocate* [Rochester, NY], 14 April 1832 (emphasis in original); BYJ1, 9 April 1832; "humble" in "History of Brigham Young," DN, 10 Feb. 1858, 385.

45. "getting into it" in minutes of 8 Jan. 1845.
46. Discourse of 17 July 1870, JD, 13:209; 2 Cor. 5:17.

2. The Tongues of Angels

JSP J1, 16 Jan. 1836, 159. Smith spoke the words to the then-disgruntled members of the Quorum of the Twelve Apostles.

1. Leigh Schmidt, *Hearing Things: Religion, Illusion, and the American Enlightenment* (Cambridge, MA: Harvard University Press, 2000), ch. 5.
2. Stephen Stein, *The Shaker Experience in America: A History of the United Society of Believers* (New Haven: Yale University Press, 1994), 165–200; Stephen C. Taysom, *Shakers, Mormons, and Religious Worlds: Conflicting Visions, Contested Boundaries* (Bloomington: Indiana University Press, 2011), ch. 4.
3. BYJ1, 9 April 1832; "electric shock" from draft manuscript of "History of BY," Folder 4, CR 100 475, CHL; Finney, *Memoirs of Rev. Charles G. Finney* (New York: A. S. Barnes, 1876), 20; cf. Robert H. Abzug, *Cosmos Crumbling: American Reform and the Religious Imagination* (New York: Oxford University Press, 1994), 66.
4. Discourse of 2 Aug. 1857, JD 5:97.
5. HCK, Autobiography [ca. 1842], Box 1, Heber C. Kimball Papers, MS 627, CHL.
6. A. Gregory Schneider, "The Ritual of Happy Dying among Early American Methodists," *Church History* 56 (Sept. 1987): 348–363; Samuel M. Brown, *In Heaven As It Is on Earth: Joseph Smith and the Early Mormon Conquest of Death* (New York: Oxford University Press, 2012), ch. 1.
7. Joseph Young to Lewis Harvey, 16 Nov. 1880, MS 2304, CHL; "lubberly" in "A Journal of Sketch of the Life of Joel Hills Johnson," n.d., HBLL; discourse of 20 Nov. 1864, transcript of George D. Watt shorthand notes by LaJean Carruth.
8. See Richard T. Hughes and C. Leonard Allen, *Illusions of Innocence: Protestant Primitivism in America, 1630–1875* (Chicago: University of Chicago Press, 1988), chs. 5 and 6; Terryl L. Givens and Matthew J. Grow, *Parley P. Pratt: The Apostle Paul of Mormonism* (New York: Oxford University Press, 2011), 21–36.
9. Raising the dead from Nancy Towle, *Vicissitudes Illustrated, in the Experience of Nancy Towle, in Europe and America* (Portsmouth, NH: John Caldwell, 1833), 152, 57; "prophetess" in Bruce N. Westergren, ed., *From Historian to Dissident: The Book of John Whitmer* (Salt Lake City: Signature Books, 1995); 37–38. See Mark Staker, *Hearken, O Ye People: The Historical Setting for Joseph Smith's Ohio Revelations* (Salt Lake City: Kofford Books, 2009), pt. 1. On speaking in tongues in antebellum America, see Schmidt, *Hearing Things,* ch. 5.
10. "History of BY," DN, 10 Feb. 1858, 385; singing in tongues in draft manuscript of "History of Brigham Young," CR 100 475, Folder 3, CHL; "poured out" in KCMB, 22 Jan. 1833, 6. On the "Adamic" language, see Samuel

Brown, "Joseph (Smith) in Egypt: Babel, Hieroglyphs, and the Pure Language of Egypt," *Church History* 78 (March 2009): 29–65.

11. D&C 76; "directly contrary" in *Deseret News Extra,* 14 Sept. 1852, 24; "one prayer" in discourse of 8 Oct. 1866, transcript of George D. Watt shorthand notes by LaJean Carruth; "contraction of hell" from RSR, 199. See 1 Cor. 15:40–41.

12. BYJ1, Jan.–June 1833; *The Evening and the Morning Star* [Independence, MO], June 1832, 6; Philip L. Barlow, *Mormons and the Bible: The Place of the Latter-day Saints in American Religion* (New York: Oxford, 1991), 44–46.

13. "the place" in D&C 57:2; "stake of Zion" in D&C 94; "never do" in discourse of 3 Feb. 1867, JD, 11:294; "resources," Francis Asbury quoted in John Wigger, *American Saint: Francis Asbury and the Methodists* (New York: Oxford University Press, 2009), 9; *The Evening and the Morning Star* [Kirtland, OH], May 1834. On the significance of "gathering" to early Mormonism, see Grant Underwood, *The Millenarian World of Early Mormonism* (Urbana: University of Illinois Press, 1993), ch. 2; Jan Shipps, "From Peoplehood to Church Membership: Mormonism's Trajectory since World War II," *Church History* 76 (June 2007): 245–251.

14. "any man" in discourse of 3 Feb. 1867, JD, 11:295–296; "History of George Albert Smith by Himself," Box 1, Folder 2, MS 1322, CHL; "endowment of power" in D&C 94; discourse of 7 Oct. 1857, JD 5:332. See Ronald K. Esplin, "The Emergence of Brigham Young and the Twelve to Mormon Leadership, 1830–1841," Ph.D. diss., Brigham Young University, 1981 (Provo, UT: Joseph Fielding Smith Institute for Latter-day Saint History and BYU Studies, 2006), 38.

15. BYJ, 1832–36 Journal, 4 Sept. 1833; Brigham Young Hampton Autobiography and Journal, MS 2080, 67. I am grateful to Jeffrey Nichols for sharing his transcription of the latter document.

16. Wells, "Biography of Mary Ann Angell Young," *Juvenile Instructor* 26 (1 Jan. 1891): 17; "History of BY," DN, 10 Feb. 1858, 385; BY and Mary Ann Angell (hereafter MAA) marriage license, 10 Feb. 1834, FHL; Young and Angell marriage certificate, 31 March 1834, FHL. Several sources date Joseph A. Young's birth to 14 Oct. 1834, including Wells, "Biography of Mary Ann Angell Young," 18; Susa Young Gates and Mabel Sanborn, "Brigham Young Genealogy," *Utah Genealogical and Historical Magazine* 11 (April 1920): 52. See M. Scott Bradshaw, "Joseph Smith's Performance of Marriages in Ohio," *BYU Studies* 39.4 (2000): 23–69.

17. *Missouri Intelligencer and Boon's Lick Advertiser* (Columbia, MO), 10 Aug. 1833, quoted in William Mulder and A. Russell Mortensen, eds., *Among the Mormons: Historic Accounts by Contemporary Observers* (New York: Knopf, 1958), 79. See Kenneth H. Winn, *Exiles in a Land of Liberty: Mormons in America, 1830–1846* (Chapel Hill: University of North Carolina Press, 1989), ch. 5.

18. KCMB, 24 Feb. 1834, 35; D&C 103:16. On the expulsion from Jackson County and Zion's Camp, I have relied on Peter Crawley and Richard L. An-

derson, "The Political and Social Realities of Zion's Camp," *BYU Studies* 14 (Summer 1974): 406–420; RSR, 222–230, 235–250; Esplin, "Emergence," ch. 3; Warren A. Jennings, "The Army of Israel Marches into Missouri," *Missouri Historical Review* 62 (Jan. 1968): 107–135, and "The Expulsion of the Mormons from Jackson County, Missouri," *Missouri Historical Review* 64 (Oct. 1969): 41–63.

19. "Extract from the Journal of Heber C. Kimball," T&S, 15 Jan. 1845, 773; KCMB, 29 Aug. 1834, 54.

20. "commit hostilities" in *Evening and the Morning Star,* July 1834, 176; cf. RSR, 244. On Dunklin's decision, see Crawley and Anderson, "Political and Social Realities." On the non-Mormon reaction to Zion's Camp, see J. Spencer Fluhman, "Anti-Mormonism and the Making of Religion in Antebellum America" (Ph.D. diss., University of Wisconsin-Madison, 2006), 161–165. On Mormons and the "destroying angel," see Samuel M. Brown, "Escaping the Destroying Angel: Immortality and the Early Mormon Word of Wisdom," paper delivered at the 2009 Mormon Historical Association, copy in author's possession.

21. "[I]f you will go with me" and "a good gun and bayonet" from "History of BY," DN, 10 Feb. 1858, 385; WWJ, 26 April 1834, 1:8; "white Lamanite" from WWJ, May 1834, 1:10; D&C 105:19. On Zelph, see Kenneth W. Godfrey, "The Zelph Story," *BYU Studies* 29 (Spring 1989): 31–56.

22. "gave us" in minutes of 7 Jan. 1855, Box 3, Folder 1, GCM; Zion's camp reunion from DN, 19 Oct. 1865, 11.

23. KCMB, 29 Aug. 1834, 53–54, BY appointed to Kirtland High Council, 24 Sept. 1834, 62.

24. Quotes from KCMB, 14–27 Feb. 1835. For the development of the Mormon apostolic office, see Gregory A. Prince, *Power from on High: The Development of Mormon Priesthood* (Salt Lake City: Signature Books, 1995), 56–62.

25. KCMB, 1 March 1835, 95.

26. KCMB, 2 May 1835, 115; BYJ1, May–July 1835.

27. BY to MAA, 9 Aug. 1835, MS 15616, CHL; MAA to BY, 31 Aug. 1835, Luna Thatcher Young Collection, MS 6140, CHL.

28. D&C [1835], 101:4; Minutes of 4 Aug. 1835, Letter Book 1, 90–93, Joseph Smith Collection, MS 155, Box 2, Folder 1, CHL; JSP J1, 3 Nov. 1835, 83.

29. "in the habit" from HOJ, 16 Feb. 1859; "toad's hair comb" from Minutes of 12 Feb. 1849, Box 2, Folder 8, GCM; "[H]ow much fault" from minutes of 16 Nov. 1847, typescript in LJA, Box 12, Folder 3; "snob[b]ed us" from minutes of 30 Nov. 1847, typescript in LJA, Box 12, Folder 3.

30. JSP J1, 3 Oct. 1835, 68; BY to MAA, 24 March 1837, Box 1, Blair Collection, MS 120, UUSC.

31. On this period of strife, see RSR, 294–303.

32. JSP J1, 16–17 Jan. 1836, 156–160.

33. On the Kirtland Temple, see RSR, ch. 17; Brown, *In Heaven*, ch. 6.

34. Oliver Cowdery Sketchbook, 16–22 Jan. 1836, in Arrington, ed., "Oliver Cowdery's Kirtland, Ohio, 'Sketchbook,'" *BYU Studies* 12 (1972): 416, 419, 420; JSP J1, 21–22 Jan. 1836, 166–172.

35. "History of BY," DN, 10 Feb. 1858, 386; *Messenger & Advocate* [Kirtland, OH], March 1837; JSP J1, 27 March 1836, 200–211; Young and Patten in Stephen Post Journal, 28 March 1836, in John W. Welch with Erick B. Carlson, *Opening the Heavens: Accounts of Divine Manifestations, 1820–1844* (Provo, UT: Brigham Young University Press, 2005), 351.

36. D&C 88:138. On foot washing in the United States, see I. Daniel Rupp, ed., *An Original History of the Religious Denominations at Present Existing in the United States* (Philadelphia: J.Y. Humphreys, 1844), 80, 178; Stein, *The Shaker Experience in America*, 105.

37. McLellin to Orson Pratt, 29 April 1854, in Stan Larson and Samuel J. Passey, eds., *The William E. McLellin Papers, 1854–1880* (Salt Lake City: Signature Books, 2007), 436; John Corrill, *A Brief History of the Church of Christ of Latter Day Saints* (St. Louis: n.p., 1839), 23; JSP J1, 30 March and 3 April 1836, 213–216, 219–222.

38. Discourse of 6 April 1853, JD, 2:31.

39. WWJ, 8 Nov 1857, 5:120; cf. Esplin, "The Emergence of Brigham Young," 75. The reminiscence almost certainly reflects the use of endowment robes in the subsequent Nauvoo rituals.

40. BY to MAA, 3 June and 21 July 1836, Blair Collection, UUSC; Jonathan Crosby Autobiography, Folder 1, MS 8151, CHL.

41. Edward Leo Lyman, et al., eds., *No Place to Call Home: The 1807–1857 Life Writings of Carolina Barnes Crosby, Chronicler of Outlying Mormon Communities* (Logan: Utah State University Press, 2005), 43–44.

42. See Brown, *In Heaven*, 213–218; Prince, *Power from on High*, 174–182.

43. Susa Young Gates, "Notes on the Young and Howe Families," *Utah Genealogical and Historical Magazine* 11 (Oct. 1920): 181; on members of the Works family in Kirtland, see MAA to BY, 31 Aug. 1835. See the discussion of patriarchal ordination in D. Michael Quinn, *The Mormon Hierarchy: Origins of Power* (Salt Lake City: Signature Books, 1994), 47–49.

44. Joseph Young to Lewis Harvey, 16 Nov. 1880. The most detailed history of the Kirtland Safety Society is found in Staker, *Hearken, O Ye People*, pt. 4.

45. Stephen Mihm, *A Nation of Counterfeiters: Capitalists, Con Men, and the Making of the United States* (Cambridge, MA: Harvard University Press, 2007), ch. 4.

46. Richards to Hepzibah ("Hepsy") Richards, 20 Jan. 1837, MS 12765, CHL; contract between BY and Zebedee Coltrin, 8 March 1837, Blair Collection, MS 15616, CHL; 10/15 March contract between BY and Jacob and Abigail Bump, Blair Papers, MS 120, Box 3, UUSC.

47. *Cleveland Daily Gazette*, 12 Jan. 1837.

48. WWJ, 10 Jan. 1837, 1:121; "did not believe" in discourse of 11 Sept. 1853, JD, 1:74–75; "so public" in discourse of 13 Nov. 1864, JD, 10:363; "not concerning" in discourse of 29 March 1857, JD, 4:297.

49. Joseph Young to Lewis Harvey, 16 Nov. 1880; BY to MAA, 24 March 1837, Blair Papers, Box 1, UUSC.

50. WWJ, 9 April 1837 and 28 May 1837, 1:138, 147; KCMB, 29 May 1837, 184.

51. "said across the water" in Scott A. Sandage, *Born Losers: A History of Failure in America* (Cambridge, MA: Harvard University Press, 2005), 41.
52. KCMB, 3 Sept. 1837, 184–187; "History of BY," DN, 10 Feb. 1858, 386; WWJ, 6 Jan. 1837, 1:120. See RSR, ch. 18.
53. RSR, 332; "shedding of blood" from Hepzibah Richards to Willard Richards, 18 Jan. 1838, in Kenneth W. Godfrey, et al., *Women's Voices: An Untold History of the Latter-day Saints, 1830–1900* (Salt Lake City: Deseret Book, 1982), 71–72.
54. "History of BY," DN, 17 Feb. 1858, 393; KCMB, 30 Nov. 1837, 207; MAA to BY, 12 Jan. 1838, Blair Collection, Box 1, UUSC.
55. Discourse of 29 March 1857, JD, 4:297.
56. Discourse of 5 March 1860, JD, 8:15–16.

3. Acts of the Apostles

Rigdon in Reed Peck Manuscript, 1839, MSS SC 530, HBLL Special Collections.

1. JSP J1, 13–14 March and 17 April 1838, 237–238, 257–258; "whooping-cough" from Hepzibah Richards to Willard Richards, 18 Jan. 1838, in Kenneth W. Godfrey, et al., *Women's Voices: An Untold History of the Latter-day Saints, 1830–1900* (Salt Lake City: Deseret Book, 1982), 74.
2. JSP J1, 29 March, 12 and 13 April, and 11 May 1838, 245–247, 251–257, 268; *Far West Record: Minutes of the Church of Jesus Christ of Latter-day Saints, 1830–1844*, ed. Donald Q. Cannon and Lyndon W. Cook (Salt Lake City: Deseret Book, 1983), 167–168.
3. Discussion of "salt sermon" in John Corrill, *A Brief History of the Church of Christ of Latter Day Saints* (St. Louis: n.p., 1839), 30; letter against dissenters printed in *Document Containing the Orders, Correspondence, etc. in Relation to the Disturbances with the Mormons . . .* (Fayette, MO: Boon's Lick Democrat, 1841), 103–107; JSP J1, 27 July 1838, 293.
4. JSP J1, 18 May–1 June 1838, 270–274. See Stephen C. LeSueur, "Missouri's Failed Compromise: The Creation of Caldwell County for the Mormons," *Journal of Mormon History* 32 (Fall 2005), 113–144. On Adam-ondi-Ahman, see Samuel M. Brown, *In Heaven As It Is on Earth: Joseph Smith and the Early Mormon Conquest of Death* (New York: Oxford University Press, 2012), 110–114. On Diahman and De Witt, see Leland H. Gentry and Todd M. Compton, *Fire and Sword: A History of Latter-day Saints in Northern Missouri, 1836–39* (Salt Lake City: Kofford Books, 2011), ch. 6.
5. Rigdon sermon reprinted in Peter Crawley, ed., "Two Rare Missouri Documents," *BYU Studies* 14 (Summer 1974): 517–527; "cause of our troubles" in minutes of 8 Sept. 1844, Box 1, Folder 26, GCM; Smith quoted in *Elder's Journal* [Far West, MO], August 1838, 54.
6. Lucas in *Document Containing the Orders,* 35; Albert P. Rockwood Journal, 15 Oct. 1838, in "The Last Months of Mormonism in Missouri: The Albert Perry Rockwood Journal," eds. Dean C. Jessee and David J. Whittaker, *BYU*

Studies 28 (Winter 1988): 22; Marsh in *Document Containing the Orders,* 58; John Smith quoted in Bushman, RSR, 362.

7. D&C 118.

8. "History of Brigham Young," DN, 17 Feb. 1858, 393.

9. Boggs's order in *Document Containing the Orders,* 61; Joseph Young in Alexander L. Baugh, "Joseph Young's Affidavit of the Massacre at Haun's Mill," *BYU Studies* 38 (1999): 188–202; "will make lice" in *History of Caldwell and Livingston Counties, Missouri* . . . (St. Louis: National Historical Company, 1886), 149. See Gentry and Compton, *Fire and Sword,* chs. 9 and 10, esp. pp. 337–341.

10. Albert P. Rockwood Journal, 28 Oct. 1838, in Jessee and Whittaker, "Last Months," 25; "appointed captains of fifty" in *President Heber C. Kimball's Journal* . . . (Salt Lake City: Juvenile Instructor Office, 1882), 57–58; cf. Gentry and Compton, *Fire and Sword,* 353; Corrill, *Brief History,* 41; BY 1843 testimony, T&S, 15 July 1843, 261.

11. "commenced" and "as other citizens" in BY 1843 testimony, T&S, 15 July 1843, 261–262; "see you in hell" in discourse of 20 May 1866, transcript of George D. Watt shorthand notes by LaJean Carruth; *Eastern Argus,* 5 Dec. 1838 (emphasis in original). I am grateful to Jason Thompson for the latter reference.

12. Sidney Rigdon, Joseph Smith, and Hyrum Smith to HCK and BY, 16 Jan 1839, Box 2, Folder 3, Joseph Smith Collection, MS 155, CHL.

13. "History of Brigham Young," DN, 17 Feb. 1858, 394; "mantle and bonnet" from discourse of 9 April 1853, transcript of George D. Watt shorthand notes by LaJean Carruth.

14. MH, 29 Jan. 1839; Snow to Esqr. Streator, 22 Feb. 1839 (emphasis in original), in *BYU Studies* 13 (Summer 1973): 544–552; "History of Brigham Young," DN, 17 Feb. 1858, 394.

15. Newel Knight autobiography, MS 767, CHL; cf. William G. Hartley, *"They Are My Friends": A History of the Joseph Knight Family, 1825–1850* (Provo, UT: Grandin Book, 1986), 132; Emmeline B. Wells "Biography of Mary Ann Angell Young," *Juvenile Instructor,* 1 Jan. 1891, 19.

16. Sidney Rigdon, Joseph Smith, and Hyrum Smith to HCK and BY, 16 Jan 1839; 20 March 1839 epistle in Folder 71, MS 4583, CHL; cf. Dean C. Jessee, ed., *Personal Writings of Joseph Smith,* rev. ed. (Salt Lake City: Deseret Book, 2002), 429–446; Young quoted in T&S, Nov. 1839, 15. The 20 March epistle is in the handwriting of Alexander McRae and Caleb Baldwin and contains a few corrections in Smith's hand.

17. WWJ, 26 April 1839, 1:327.

18. Smith to Presendia Buell, 15 March 1839, copy in MH, 15 March 1839; cf. Jessee, *Personal Writings of Joseph Smith,* 426–428; Willard Richards, "Pocket Companion," undated entries [ca. June–July 1838], Box 2, Folder 6, pages 16 ("tongues"), 9–10 ("himself nigh"), 19–22 ("calling and election . . . pure intelligence"), MS 1490, CHL. Richards recopied various revelations and notes on Smith's teachings into this volume while in England. On these

developments, see Bushman, RSR, 386–389; Brown, *In Heaven*, chs. 6 and 9. The phrase "calling and election sure" is from 2 Peter 1:10.

19. HCK to Joseph Fielding, Willard Richards, and William Clayton, 25 July 1839, typescript in MSS 670, HBLL Special Collections; "History of Brigham Young," DN, 24 Feb. 1858, 401; WWJ, 22 July 1839, 1:347.

20. Discourse of 4 July 1854, JD, 2:19; Leonora Taylor to John Taylor, 9 Sept. 1839, in Ronald K. Esplin, "Sickness and Faith, Nauvoo Letters," *BYU Studies* 15 (Summer 1975): 2–5; BY to MAAY, undated letter, ca. 15 Sept. 1840, Box 1, Folder 6, Blair Papers, MS 120, UUSC.

21. BY to MAAY, undated letter, ca. 15 Sept. 1840; BY to MAAY, 14 Jan. 1840, printed in Ronald O. Barney, ed., "Letters of a Missionary Apostle to His Wife: Brigham Young to Mary Ann Angell Young, 1839–1841," *BYU Studies* 38.2 (1999): 166; BY to MAAY, 14 Feb.–March 1840, in Barney, "Letters," 168.

22. On John Young Sr.'s death, see James A. Little, "Biography of Lorenzo Dow Young," *Utah Historical Quarterly* 14 (1946): 59–60; M. Hamlin Cannon, "A Pension Office Note on Brigham Young's Father," *American Historical Review* 50 (Oct. 1944): 90. On Joseph Smith Sr.'s death, see Samuel Brown, "The 'Beautiful Death' in the Smith Family," *BYU Studies* 45 (2006): 121–150.

23. BYJ2, 4 and 26 Nov. 1839.

24. BYJ2, Feb. 1840; Hosanna shout in MH, 6 April 1840; "History of Brigham Young," DN, 3 March 1858, 409; WWJ, 14 April 1840, 1:435. For the outlines of the British Mission, I have relied on James B. Allen, et al., *Men with a Mission, 1837–1841: The Quorum of the Twelve Apostles in the British Isles* (Salt Lake City: Deseret Book, 1992).

25. BY to MAAY, 6 April 1840, in Barney, "Letters of a Missionary Apostle to His Wife," 173. For succinct discussions of the depression's impact on the working classes and Chartism, see Boyd Hilton, *A Mad, Bad, and Dangerous People? England, 1783–1846* (New York: Oxford University Press, 2006), 573–576, 612–621.

26. On the struggles of English churches to retain the loyalties of the working classes, see W. R. Ward, *Religion in Society in England, 1790–1850* (New York: Schocken Books, 1972), chs. 3–6.

27. George Eliot, *Adam Bede* (New York: Harper and Brothers, 1860), 19.

28. Michael R. Watts, *The Dissenters*, vol. 2: *The Expansion of Evangelical Nonconformity* (Oxford: Clarendon Press, 1995), 189, 149; Julia Stewart Werner, *The Primitive Methodist Connexion: Its Background and Early History* (Madison: University of Wisconsin Press, 1984), 25, 19.

29. Job Smith, "The United Brethren," *Improvement Era* [Salt Lake City, UT], July 1910, 819; Ward, *Religion in Society in England*, 76; Job Smith, Autobiography, MS 881, HBLL.

30. WWJ, 23 March 1840; Woodruff discourse of 23 Feb. 1873, JD, 15:343; John Wigger, *American Saint: Francis Asbury and the Methodists* (New York: Oxford University Press, 2009), 36–39.

31. Acts 8:15; BY to Joseph Smith Jr., 7 May 1840, copy in Box 2, Folder 2, MS 155, CHL; BY to George A. Smith, 4 May 1840, Box 4, Folder 5, MS 1322, CHL.

32. "tea party" in BYJ2, 17 May 1840; WWJ, 14–19 May 1840, 1:449–451; Woodruff discourse of 23 Feb. 1873, JD, 15:344. See David J. Whittaker, "'That Most Important of All Books': A Printing History of the Book of Mormon," *Mormon Historical Studies* 6 (Fall 2005): 129, n. 47.

33. Willard Richards notes of Parley Pratt sermon at a "New York conference," Box 2, Folder 6, 37–39, MS 1490, CHL; WCJ, 29 May 1840, 53; BYJ2, 11 June 1840; BY to Richards, 17 June 1840, Richards Papers, MS 1490, CHL.

34. WCJ, 12 June 1840, 55; BY to Richards, 17 June 1840; Pratt in minutes of 19 Jan. 1851, First Council of the Seventy records, CR 3 51, CHL. See Charles Hambrick-Stowe, *Charles G. Finney and the Spirit of American Evangelicalism* (Grand Rapids, MI: Eerdmans, 1996), ch. 3.

35. WRJ, 20 April 1840; BY to MAAY, 12 Nov. 1840, Box 1, Folder 6, Blair Papers, UUSC.

36. "doe not know" and "wicked malicias" in BY to MAAY, 12 June 1840, Box 1, Folder 6, Blair Papers, UUSC; "asked my Hevenly" in BY to MAAY, 6 April 1840, in Barney, "Letters of a Missionary Apostle to His Wife," 172; "carsly" in BY to MAAY, 16 Oct. 1840, MS 6140, CHL; "sleep in the grave" in BYJ3, 29 Oct. 1840.

37. BY to MAAY (and note to Joseph Young), 16 Oct. 1840; Joseph Fielding Diary, 7 July 1840, typescript at HBLL. This conclusion reflects the argument of Stephen J. Fleming, "The Religious Heritage of the British Northwest and the Rise of Mormonism," *Church History* 77 (March 2008): 73–104; Grant Underwood, *The Millenarian World of Early Mormonism* (Urbana: University of Illinois Press, 1993), ch. 8.

38. BY to MAAY, 12 June 1840; "drank of wine" in BYJ2, 16 April 1840; "shall I break" in WWJ, 7 Nov. 1841, 2:137. For a discussion of the Word of Wisdom in its cultural context, see Lester E. Bush Jr., "The Word of Wisdom in Early Nineteenth-Century Perspective," *Dialogue* 14 (Autumn 1981): 47–65.

39. "thousands and thousands" from discourse of 17 April 1853, transcript of George D. Watt shorthand notes by LaJean Carruth; "do not recollect" in discourse of 17 July 1870, JD, 13:212; "Cloggs" in BY to MAAY, 13 March 1841, in Barney, "Letters of a Missionary Apostle to His Wife," 188–189; watch in BY to GAS, 14 Oct. 1840, Box 4, Folder 5, MS 1322, CHL; "exact likeness" in WWJ, 3 Dec. 1840, 1:567; "mostly in looking" in HCK to GAS, 12 Dec. 1840, Box 4, Folder 4, MS 1322, CHL; BY to Kelsey, 12 Sept. 1851, Box 16, Folder 22, BYP.

40. BY to Willard Richards, 17 June 1840; Parley P. Pratt to Mary Ann Pratt, 6 July 1840, Box 1, Folder 1, Parley Pratt Collection, MSS 7, HBLL. This paragraph builds on an argument made in Ronald K. Esplin, "The Emergence of Brigham Young and the Twelve to Mormon Leadership, 1830–1841," Ph.D. diss., Brigham Young University, 1981 (Provo, UT: Joseph Fielding Smith Institute for Latter-day Saint History and BYU Studies, 2006), ch. 10.

41. BY and Richards to Smith, et al., 5 Sept. 1840, ed. Ronald W. Walker, *BYU*

Studies (Spring 1978): 468–469; "May the Lord" in BY to MAAY, 16 Oct. 1840; "did not wright" and "don the verry best" in BY to MAAY, 12 Nov. 1840; "not to publish" in Nauvoo Stake High Council Minutes, 27 Oct. 1839, in John S. Dinger, *The Nauvoo Stake High Council and City Council Minutes* (Salt Lake City: Signature Books, forthcoming); Smith to the Twelve, 15 Dec. 1840, Box 2, Folder 4, MSS 155, CHL. See Linda King Newell and Valeen Tippetts Avery, *Mormon Enigma: Emma Hale Smith,* 2nd ed. (Urbana: University of Illinois Press, 1994), 88.

42. On the history of American foreign missions, see William R. Hutchison, *Errand to the World: American Protestant Thought and Foreign Missions* (Chicago: University of Chicago Press, 1987).

43. Charlotte J. Erickson, "Emigration from the British Isles to the U.S.A. in 1841," *Population Studies* 43 (Nov. 1989): 348; Pratt quoted in *Millennial Star,* Feb. 1842, 154; "no one go" in WWJ, April 16 1840, 1:439; BY to MAAY, 12 Nov. 1840; emigration statistics in Leonard Arrington and Davis Bitton, *The Mormon Experience: A History of the Latter-day Saints* (Champaign: University of Illinois Press, 1992), 129; Ezra T. Benson to BY, 21 Nov. 1856, Box 38, Folder 2, BYP.

44. "as happy" in BY to MAAY, 12 June 1840; "Brotherin" in BY to MAAY, 16 Oct. 1840, in Ronald Esplin, "Inside Brigham Young," *BYU Studies* 20 (Spring 1980): 306.

4. New and Everlasting Covenant

Wasp [Nauvoo, IL], 20 Aug. 1842.

1. "History of Brigham Young," DN, 10 March 1858, 3; D&C 126; BYJ2, 18 Jan. 1842.

2. Smith in T&S, 15 Jan. 1841, 273–274 (emphasis in original); "cornerstone" in D&C 124:2; Nauvoo charter in John E. Hallwas and Roger D. Launius, eds., *Cultures in Conflict: A Documentary History of the Mormon War in Illinois* (Logan: Utah State University Press, 1995), 23. On Mormon Nauvoo, see Robert D. Flanders, *Nauvoo: Kingdom on the Mississippi* (Urbana: University of Illinois Press, 1965) and Glen M. Leonard, *Nauvoo: A Place of Peace, a People of Promise* (Salt Lake City: Deseret Book, 2002).

3. "kissing" in minutes of 3 Nov. 1844, Seventies Record, Book B, CR 3 51, CHL; Douglas in *Illinois State Journal,* 13 June 1857; William Smith in *Wasp,* 11 June 1842; cf. Michael Hicks, "Minding Business: A Note on 'The Mormon Creed,'" *BYU Studies* 26 (Fall 1986), 125.

4. "black hair" from T&S, 15 Oct. 1840, 955; "much vivacity" from Sidney Rigdon quoted in Bennett, *History of the Saints; or, an Exposé of Joe Smith and Mormonism* (Boston: Leland and Whiting, 1842), 40; "Assistant President" in T&S, 15 April 1841, 387; BY to Levi Richards and Willard Richards, 5 Dec. 1840, Box 3, Folder 16, MS 1490, CHL. On Bennett, see Andrew F. Smith, *The Saintly Scoundrel: The Life and Times of John Cook Bennett* (Urbana: University of Illinois Press, 1997).

5. "the time had come" from T&S, 1 Sept. 1841, 521; "no presidency" from KCMB, 27 Feb. 1835; "preside over all" in KCMB, 27 Feb. 1835, 86; "take the burthen" from HC, 4:400 (see minutes of 16 Aug. 1841, Box 1, Folder 7, GCM); "nothing could be" from T&S, 1 Sept. 1841, 521; "bring of your" in T&S, 15 Oct. 1841, 568; D&C 124. See the analysis in D. Michael Quinn, *The Mormon Hierarchy: Origins of Power* (Salt Lake City: Signature Books, 1994), 58–67.

6. D&C 22:1; "who have died" in D&C 137:7. For a juxtaposition of Mormon and American Protestant soteriology, see Samuel M. Brown, *In Heaven As It Is on Earth: Joseph Smith and the Early Mormon Conquest of Death* (New York: Oxford University Press, 2012).

7. BY to MAAY, 26 May 1840, in Ronald O. Barney, ed., "Letters of a Missionary Apostle to His Wife: Brigham Young to Mary Ann Angell Young, 1839–1841," *BYU Studies* 38.2 (1999): 178–180; 1 Corinthians, 15:29; Joseph Smith to the Twelve, 15 Dec. 1840, Box 2, Folder 4, MS 155, CHL. See M. Guy Bishop, "'What Has Become of Our Fathers?' Baptism for the Dead at Nauvoo," *Dialogue* 23 (Summer 1990): 85–97; Gregory A. Prince, *Power from on High: The Development of Mormon Priesthood* (Salt Lake City: Signature Books, 1995), 142–145.

8. "no more" in T&S, 15 Oct. 1841, 523; 1 Kings 7; McBride to BY, 1 April 1871, Box 34, Folder 6, BYP; "sacred pool" from Brown, *In Heaven*, 219. See Alexander L. Baugh, "'Blessed Is the First Man Baptised in This Font': Reuben McBride, First Proxy to Be Baptized for the Dead in the Nauvoo Temple," *Mormon Historical Studies* 3 (Fall 2002): 253–261; Jonathan Stapley and Kristine L. Wright, "'They Shall Be Made Whole': A History of Baptism for Health," *Journal of Mormon History* 34 (Fall 2008), 69–112.

9. There are many helpful discussions of the Nauvoo endowment, including David John Buerger, *Mysteries of Godliness: A History of Mormon Temple Worship,* 2nd ed. (Salt Lake City: Signature Books, 2002), ch. 3; Andrew F. Ehat, "Joseph Smith's Introduction of Temple Ordinances and the 1844 Mormon Succession Crisis" (M.A. thesis, Brigham Young University, 1982), ch. 2; Devery S. Anderson and Gary J. Bergera, *Joseph Smith's Quorum of the Anointed, 1842–1845* (Salt Lake City: Signature Books).

10. HCK to Parley P. Pratt, 17 June 1842, MS 897, CHL; Joseph Fielding Journal, ca. 1843, in Andrew F. Ehat, ed., "'They Might Have Known That He Was Not a Fallen Prophet': The Nauvoo Journal of Joseph Fielding," *BYU Studies* 19 (1979): 145; Young's initiation from Mervin B. Hogan, ed., *The Official Minutes of Nauvoo Lodge, U.D.* (Des Moines, IA: Research Lodge No. 2, 1974), 24–27. For different (and partly conflicting) accounts of the relationship between Mormonism and Freemasonry, see Michael W. Homer, "'Similarity of Priesthood in Masonry': The Relationship between Freemasonry and Mormonism," *Dialogue* 27 (Fall 1994): 1–113; John L. Brooke, *The Refiner's Fire: The Making of Mormon Cosmology, 1644–1844* (Cambridge: Cambridge University Press), 244–253; and Brown, *In Heaven*, ch. 7.

11. MH, 4 May 1842; L. John Nuttall Journal, 7 Feb. 1877, typescript at HBLL; cf. Buerger, *Mysteries of Godliness,* 39.

12. "my New Name" from 28 Dec. 1845, Seventies Record, Book B, CR 3 51, CHL; BY discourse of 6 April 1853, JD, 2:31. See Brown, *In Heaven,* ch. 7.
13. Kimball to Pratt, 17 June 1842.
14. "flesh and bones" from William Clayton "Private Book," 5 Jan. 1841, in Andrew F. Ehat and Lyndon W. Cook, eds., *The Words of Joseph Smith: The Contemporary Accounts of the Nauvoo Discourses of the Prophet Joseph* (Provo, UT: Religious Studies Center, Brigham Young University, 1980), 60.
15. D&C 128.
16. "dirty, nasty, filthy affair" from Cowdery to Warren A. Cowdery, 21 Jan. 1838, Oliver Cowdery Letterbook, HM 63646, Huntington Library, San Marino, CA; Beaman's disguise from Franklin Richards Journal, 22 Jan. 1869, MS 1215, CHL. See Todd Compton, *In Sacred Loneliness: The Plural Wives of Joseph Smith* (Salt Lake City: Signature Books, 1997), chs. 1 and 3; George D. Smith, *Nauvoo Polygamy* (Salt Lake City: Signature Books, 2008), 38–43, 56–65; RSR, 323–327, 437–439.
17. WWJ, 10 March 1844, 2:364; Joseph Fielding Journal, undated entry, in Ehat, "'They Might Have Known,'" 154. On the promise of priesthood power to men and women, see Kathleen Flake, *The Emotional and Priestly Logic of Plural Marriage* (Logan: Utah State University Press, 2010).
18. I am relying on the compilation in Compton, *In Sacred Loneliness,* 4–7.
19. Almera W. Johnson, 1 Aug. 1883 affidavit, Folder 1, MS 3423, CHL.
20. Benjamin F. Johnson, 4 March 1870 affidavit, Folder 5, MS 3423, CHL.
21. Emily D. Partridge Young, 19 March 1892 deposition, in H. Michael Marquardt, "Emily Dow Partridge Smith Young on the Witness Stand: Recollections of a Plural Wife," *Journal of Mormon History* 34 (Summer 2008): 134.
22. For example, see the discussion of Sylvia Porter Sessions in Compton, *In Sacred Loneliness,* 183–184.
23. Taylor discourse of 27 June 1854, in LaJean P. Carruth and Mark L. Staker, eds., "John Taylor's June 27, 1854, Account of the Martyrdom," *BYU Studies* 50.3 (2011): 43.
24. BYJ1, 19 June 1836; Stephen Stein, *The Shaker Experience in America: A History of the United Society of Believers* (New Haven: Yale University Press, 1992), 87; Orson Hyde Journal, 11 Oct. 1832, typescript at HBLL (emphasis in original). On the Harmonists, see Karl John Richard Arndt, *George Rapp's Harmony Society, 1785–1847,* 2nd ed. (Rutherford, NJ: Fairleigh Dickinson University Press, 1972). On the Oneida Community, see Lawrence Foster, *Religion and Sexuality: The Shakers, the Mormons, and the Oneida Community* (Urbana: University of Illinois Press, 1981), ch. 3. On Fourier and his American disciples, see Philip F. Gura, *American Transcendentalism* (New York: Hill and Wang, 2007), ch. 6. On the Cochranites, see Joyce Butler, "Cochranism Delineated: A Twentieth-Century Study," in Charles E. Clark, et al., eds., *Maine in the Early Republic: From Revolution to Statehood* (Hanover, NH: University Press of New England, 1988), 146–164.
25. BYJ2, 6 Jan. 1842; Mary Elizabeth Rollins Lightner, 1902 statement, Box 1, Folder 3, Vault MSS 363, HBLL. On the Royal Arch Masonic Cipher and Young's diary entry, see Tim Rathbone, "Brigham Young's Masonic Con-

nection and Nauvoo Plural Marriages," <http://masonicmoroni.com/Docu ments/bymcpap1210.htm>, accessed 6 Sept. 2011.

26. Minutes of 16 Feb. 1849, Box 2, Folder 8, GCM. See the discussion in Smith, *Nauvoo Polygamy,* 262.

27. BYJ3, 9 March and 9 April 1841; WWJ, 12 and 14 April 1841, 2:87–88; Elizabeth Pratt's conversion in *Woman's Exponent* [Salt Lake City], 1 Dec. 1890, 14; *Millennial Star,* Feb. 1842, 156. For a discussion of the Brotherton family, see Paul B. Pixton, "The *Tyrian* and Its Mormon Passengers," *Mormon Historical Studies* 5 (Spring 2004): 40–41, 45–46.

28. T&S, 15 April 1842, 763.

29. "glut" in *Missouri Reporter,* reprinted in T&S, 1 Aug. 1842, 877; Bennett's loss of church fellowship in T&S, 15 June 1842, 830. See Smith, *Saintly Scoundrel,* 105–106.

30. Brotherton's affidavit in Bennett, *History of the Saints,* 236–240.

31. *Wasp,* 27 August 1842; McIlwrick in *Affidavits and Certificates Disproving the Statements and Affidavits Contained in John C. Bennett's Letters* (Nauvoo, 1842), HBLL; William Clayton to William Hardman, 30 March 1842, in *Millennial Star,* Aug. 1842, 74–76; Joseph Fielding to Parley Pratt, Jan. 1842, in *Millennial Star,* Aug. 1842, 76–80; "conceived" in *Millennial Star,* Aug. 1842, 73.

32. *Affidavits and Certificates.* On Elizabeth Pratt's conversion and subsequent marriage to Parley Pratt, see Terryl L. Givens and Matthew J. Grow, *Parley P. Pratt: The Apostle Paul of Mormonism* (New York: Oxford University Press, 2011), 205–206.

33. Lucy D. Young 1869 affidavit, in Joseph F. Smith affidavits on celestial marriage, vol. 2, MS 3423, CHL; BY 1836–46 Account Book, MS 17984. See also Jeffery O. Johnson, "Determining and Defining 'Wife': The Brigham Young Households," *Dialogue* 20 (Fall 1987): 60.

34. Charlotte I. Godbe, *Salt Lake Daily Herald,* 29 June 1882; Brigham Young sealings to Mary Ann Angell and Miriam Works cited in Brown, *Nauvoo Sealings,* 348, 351. I am grateful to Jeffery Johnson for sharing the Godbe quotation and other sources of information on Young's early plural marriages.

35. Kathryn M. Daynes, *More Wives Than One: Transformation of the Mormon Marriage System, 1840–1910* (Urbana: University of Illinois Press, 2001), 27.

36. Minutes, 30 Nov. 1847, transcript by Edyth Romney, Box 12, Folder 3, LJA. On Graham's understanding of sexuality, see Stephen Nissenbaum, *Sex, Diet, and Debility in Jacksonian America: Sylvester Graham and Health Reform* (Westport, CT: Greenwood Press, 1980).

37. WWJ, 18 June 1842, 2:179.

38. BY to Parley Pratt, 17 July 1842, MS 14291, CHL. See Breck England, *The Life and Thought of Orson Pratt* (Salt Lake City: University of Utah Press, 1985), 77–80.

39. BY to Pratt, 17 July 1842.

40. "angel from heaven" from Levi Richards Journal, 14 May 1843, MS 1284, CHL; WCJ, 23 May 1843, 105; discourse of 8 Oct. 1866, transcript of George D. Watt shorthand notes by LaJean Carruth.

41. BYJ3, 2 Dec. 1843.

42. Helen Kimball Whitney Autobiography, 30 March 1881, MS 744 2, CHL. On Smith's marriage to Marinda Hyde, see Compton, *In Sacred Loneliness,* ch. 9.

43. On return to England, APR, 19 April 1843, 371; MAAY to BY, 16 Aug. 1843, MS 817, CHL.

44. WWJ, 27 July, 6, and 26 Aug. 1843, 2:264, 270, 279.

45. BYJ3, undated entries. On the three Nephites, A. E. Fife, "The Legend of the Three Nephites among the Mormons," *Journal of American Folklore* 53 (Jan.–March 1940): 1–49. See 3 Nephi 28.

46. "animal magnatisem" from BYJ3, 10 May 1843; phrenological chart copied in BYJ2; "History of BY," DN, 17 March 1858, 11; WWJ, 10 and 11 Aug. 1843, 2:273. On animal magnetism, Mesmerism, and spiritualism, see Ann Taves, *Fits, Trances, and Visions: Experiencing Religion and Explaining Experience from Wesley to James* (Princeton: Princeton University Press, 1999), chs. 4 and 5.

47. WWJ, 29–30 July 1843, 6 Aug. 1843, 9 Sept. 1843, 2:266, 271, 288–295, 295–296.

48. Augusta Cobb's conversion in Samuel Smith Journal, 29 June 1832, MS 4213, CHL; Orson Hyde Journal, 2–4 July 1832, MS 1386, CHL; BYJ3, 12 Oct. 1843. For the death of Brigham Y. Cobb see *Nauvoo Neighbor,* 8 Nov. 1843; Lyndon W. Cook, ed., *Nauvoo Deaths and Marriages, 1839–1845* (Orem, UT: Grandin Book, 1994), 16. Young was not in the Northeast at the time of Brigham Y. Cobb's conception. I am grateful to Connell O'Donovan for the reference to the journals of Samuel Smith and Orson Hyde.

49. "love" from Augusta Adams Cobb Young to BY, 4 Feb. 1846, in Theodore Schroeder Papers, University of Wisconsin Historical Society; "by revelation" from Minutes, 30 Nov. 1847, transcript by Edyth Romney, Box 12, Folder 3, LJA.

50. "hiest" in BYJ3, 1 Nov. 1843; Augusta A. Young, 12 July 1869 affidavit, in Joseph F. Smith affidavit collection, vol. 2, MS 3423; BY to MAAY, 17 Aug. 1843, in Ronald W. Walker and David J. Whittaker, eds., "The Historians' Corner," *BYU Studies* 32 (Summer 1992): 92.

51. Catherine Lewis, *Narrative of Some of the Proceedings of the Mormons* (Lynn, MA: n.p., 1848); *Cobb v. Cobb,* Massachusetts Supreme Judicial Court Records, Docket 447, Massachusetts State Archives; *Boston Post,* 30 Nov. 1847; Augusta Adams to BY, undated letter, Schroeder Papers.

52. "must be a king and a priest" from WWJ, 6 Aug. 1843, 2:271; BY anointing in APR, 22 Nov. 1843, 428; "highest and holiest," APR, 28 Sept. 1843, 416. See Ehat, "Joseph Smith's Introduction of Temple Ordinances," 80–89, 94–96; David John Buerger, "'The Fullness of the Priesthood': The Second Anointing in Latter-day Theology and Practice," *Dialogue* 16 (Spring 1983): 10–44; Gregory A. Prince, *Power from on High: The Development of Mormon Priesthood* (Salt Lake City: Signature Books, 1995), ch. 6.

53. "perform all the ordinances" from WWJ, 10 March 1844, 2:362.

54. Smith 7 April 1844 discourse (as recorded by Thomas Bullock) in Box 1,

Folder 20, GCM; "Jesus had a Father" in Smith discourse of 16 June 1844 in Ehat and Cook, *Words of Joseph Smith,* 378–339. See Brown, *In Heaven,* ch. 9.

55. *Memoirs of Charles G. Finney* (New York: A.S. 1876), 341; cf. RSR, 207; BY to Richards, 8 July 1844, Box 3, Folder 22, MS 1490, CHL. See Brown, *In Heaven,* ch. 9.

56. BYJ3, 15 and 24 Jan. 1844; Nauvoo population from Flanders, *Nauvoo,* 56.

57. "Theodemocracy" from T&S, 15 April 1844. See Patrick Q. Mason, "God and the People: Theodemocracy in Nineteenth-Century Mormonism," *Journal of Church and State* 53 (Summer 2011): 349–375.

58. BYJ3, 13 March 1844, WCJ, 1 Jan. 1845 and 13 April 1844, 153, 129. On the Council of Fifty, see Klaus J. Hansen, *Quest for Empire: The Political Kingdom of God and the Council of Fifty in Mormon History* (East Lansing: Michigan State University Press, 1967) and corrections by Andrew F. Ehat, "'It Seems Like Heaven Began on Earth': Joseph Smith and the Constitution of the Kingdom of God," *BYU Studies* (1980): 253–279; Quinn, *Origins of Power,* ch. 4.

59. "whole of America is Zion" from APR, 8 April 1844, 468; Young quoted in WWJ, 9 April 1844, 2:390.

60. WWJ, 9 April 1844, 2:390.

61. BY to MAAY, 12 June 1844, MS 3486, CHL.

62. Gura, *American Transcendentalism,* 148, 209ff.; WWJ, 1 July 1844, 2:414; *Boston Evening Transcript,* 2 July 1844.

63. *Nauvoo Expositor,* 7 June 1844; APR, 10 June 1844, 489; BY to Richards, 8 July 1844.

64. Vilate Kimball to Heber Kimball, 9–24 June 1844, in Ronald Esplin, ed., "Life in Nauvoo, June 1844: Vilate Kimball's Martyrdom Letters," *BYU Studies* 19 (Winter 1979): 235.

65. BY to WR, 8 July 1844; T&S, 15 July 1844, 585. On the Masonic cry of distress, see Brown, *In Heaven,* 180, 280–281.

66. WWJ, 9 and 17 July 1844, 2:419, 422; minutes of 12 Feb. 1849, Box 2, Folder 8, GCM.

67. Discourse of 27 June 1854, transcript of George D. Watt shorthand notes by LaJean Carruth.

68. WWJ, 18 July 1844, 2:428; "History of Brigham Young," DN, 24 March 1858, 17.

5. Prophets and Pretenders

1. "humbug" in T&S, 15 Feb. 1843, 105; J. Spencer Fluhman, "Anti-Mormonism and the Making of Religion in Antebellum America" (Ph.D. diss., University of Wisconsin-Madison, 2006), esp. ch. 1. See Stephen Mihm, *A Nation of Counterfeiters: Capitalists, Con Men, and the Making of the United States* (Cambridge, MA: Harvard University Press, 2007).

2. BYJ2, 8 Aug. 1844; murder accusation against Richards and Young in *New York Tribune,* 28 May 1857; Young's response in discourse of 26 July 1857,

JD, 5:77. See the discussion of Samuel Smith's death in D. Michael Quinn, *The Mormon Hierarchy: Origins of Power* (Salt Lake City: Signature Books, 1994), 152–154.

3. WRJ, 4 Aug. 1844. On the events of early August 1844, see Ronald K. Esplin, "Joseph, Brigham, and the Twelve: A Succession of Continuity," *BYU Studies* 21 (Summer 1981): 301–341; Richard S. Van Waggoner, *Sidney Rigdon: A Portrait of Religious Excess* (Salt Lake City: Signature Books, 1994), ch. 23; Quinn, *Origins of Power,* 143–173.

4. Minutes of 7 Aug. 1844, typescript in LJA, Box 12, Folder 1. See the analysis in Andrew F. Ehat, "Joseph Smith's Introduction of Temple Ordinances and the 1844 Mormon Succession Crisis" (M.A. thesis, Brigham Young University, 1982), ch. 9.

5. Minutes of 8 Aug. 1844, folders 21–25, GCM. There are two sets of minutes in the collection. The second appears to be a slightly revised version of the first, on which I have relied.

6. Cannon from *Juvenile Instructor* [Salt Lake City, UT], 29 Oct. 1870, 174–175; Quincy in William Mulder and A. Russell Mortensen, eds., *Among the Mormons: Historic Accounts by Contemporary Observers* (Lincoln: University of Nebraska Press, 1958), 133–134; Clayton to Woodruff, 7 Oct. 1844, copy of letter in author's possession. The Clayton letter appears to be the earliest reference to the subsequently common observation that Smith's mantle had fallen on Young. I am grateful to Jason Thompson for this reference.

   Compare Lynne W. Jorgensen, "The Mantle of the Prophet Passes to Brother Brigham: A Collective Spiritual Witness," *BYU Studies* 36 (1996–97): 125–204; Richard S. Van Wagoner, "The Making of a Mormon Myth: The 1844 Transfiguration of Brigham Young," *Dialogue* 28 (Winter 1995): 1–24.

7. WRJ, 12 Aug. 1844; BY to Secretary of War William Marcy, 17 Dec. 1845, Box 16, Folder 5, BYP. See the analysis in Quinn, *Origins of Power,* 174–180.

8. BYJ2, 27 Aug. 1844; HCKJ, 1 Feb. 1845, 94; discourse of 27 June 1854, transcript of George D. Watt shorthand notes by LaJean Carruth; minutes of 7 April 1850, Box 2, Folder 18, GCM. See Barbara H. Bernauer, "Still 'Side by Side'—The Final Burial of Joseph and Hyrum Smith," *John Whitmer Historical Association Journal* 11 (1991): 17–33.

9. "come out" in BYJ2, 3 Sept. 1844; Clayton to Woodruff, 7 Oct. 1844; "wonder who is here" from minutes of 8 Sept. 1844, Box 1, Folder 26, GCM; other quotes from trial in T&S, 1 Oct. 1844, 666–667.

10. WCJ, 17 Feb. 1844, 126; BY to Vilate Young, 11 Aug. 1844, MS 5102, CHL; BYJ3, 13 and 14 Sept. 1845. On Young's relations with Emma Smith, see Linda King Newell and Valeen Tippetts Avery, *Mormon Enigma: Emma Hale Smith,* 2nd ed. (Urbana: University of Illinois Press, 1994), chs. 14–17.

11. BY to Lucy Mack Smith, 2 Aug. 1845, Box 16, Folder 3, BYP. Young later blamed William Smith for generating a conflict over the carriage. See WWJ, 13 Feb. 1859, 5:287.

12. T&S, 15 Oct. 1844, 683. Contradictorily, Young later recalled that Joseph "never appointed Hyrum to be his successor and never thought of such

a thing." Young added that three months before his death, Joseph "said if I was out of the way you are the only man living on this earth that can counsel and direct the affairs of the kingdom of God on the earth." Discourse of 8 Oct. 1866, transcript of George D. Watt shorthand notes by LaJean Carruth.

13. Minutes of 8 Aug. 1844; "hints" in John Taylor Journal, 25 June 1845, in Dean Jessee, ed., "John Taylor Nauvoo Journal," *BYU Studies* 23 (Summer 1983): 61–62; "Josephs oldest son" in William Smith to Jesse Little, 20 Aug. 1845, typescript in MS 14691, CHL; cf. Ehat, "Joseph Smith's Introduction," 240–241. On William Smith, see Quinn, *Origins of Power*, 213–226; Irene M. Bates and Gary E. Smith, *Lost Legacy: The Mormon Office of Presiding Patriarch* (Urbana: University of Illinois Press, 1996), ch. 4. On early speculation surrounding lineal succession, see Esplin, "Joseph, Brigham, and the Twelve," 312–320, 333–341; Quinn, *Origins of Power*, 213–241.

14. BYOJ, 17 Aug. 1845; *Warsaw Signal*, 3 Sept. 1845; WRJ, 31 Aug. 1845.

15. BY to Orson Hyde, 16 March 1846, Box 16, Folder 6, BYP; Isaac Haight Journal, 8 March 1846, typescript at HBLL. Statistics from Roger Van Noord, *King of Beaver Island: The Life and Assassination of James Strang* (Urbana: University of Illinois Press, 1988), 48; Dean L. May, "A Demographic Portrait of the Mormons, 1830–1980," in Thomas G. Alexander and Jessie L. Embry, eds., *After 150 Years: The Latter-day Saints in Sesquicentennial Perspective* (Provo, UT: Charles Redd Center for Western Studies, 1983), 44. On Strang's appeal, see Vickie Cleverley Speek, *"God Has Made Us A Kingdom": James Strang and the Midwest Mormons* (Salt Lake City: Signature Books, 2006); Robin Scott Jensen, "Mormons Seeking Mormonism: Strangite Success and the Conceptualization of Mormon Ideology, 1844–50," in Newell G. Bringhurst and John C. Hamer, eds., *Scattering of the Saints: Schism within Mormonism* (Independence, MO: John Whitmer Books, 2007), 115–140.

16. "offered up" in HCKWC, 25 Dec. 1845; "every day" in WCJ, 7 Dec. 1845, 193. See Quinn, "Latter-day Saint Prayer Circles," *BYU Studies* 19 (Fall 1978): 79–105.

17. BYJ2, 25 Aug. 1844; BYOJ, 12 July 1845; John Taylor Journal, 26 Dec. 1844, in Jessee, "John Taylor Nauvoo Journal," 9; George Laub Journal, 31 Dec. 1844 (retrospective), MS 9638, CHL.

18. "want rest" in Seventies Record, Book B, CR 3 51, CHL; "keep my" in minutes of 12 March 1848, Box 2, Folder 2, GCM.

19. WWJ, 18 Aug. 1844, 2:443–444; "head stake" in BYOJ, 14 Oct. 1844; "inquaired" in BYJ2, 24 Jan. 1845.

20. *Warsaw Signal*, 29 June 1844; Ford to W. W. Phelps, 22 July 1844, Box 3, Folder 20, MS 1490, CHL. See Dallin S. Oaks and Marvin S. Hill, *Carthage Conspiracy: The Trial of the Accused Assassins of Joseph Smith* (Urbana: University of Illinois Press, 1975), chs. 2 and 3. On the Philadelphia Bible Riots, see Michael Feldberg, *The Philadelphia Bible Riots of 1844: A Study of Ethnic Conflict* (Westport, CT: Greenwood, 1975).

21. Sarah Scott to Abigail Hall, 22 July and 11 Aug. 1844, in George F. Partridge, ed., "The Death of a Mormon Dictator: Letters of Massachusetts Mormons,

1843–1848," *New England Quarterly* 9 (Dec. 1936): 599; BYJ2, 16 Sept. 1844 (entry out of sequence); "got up" in HCKJ, 24 Oct. 1844, 91; Lewis, *Narrative of Some of the Proceedings of the Mormons . . .* (Lynn, MA: n.p., 1848), 6; Fielding Journal, ca. Jan. 1846, in Andrew F. Ehat, ed., "'They Might Have Known That He Was Not a Fallen Prophet': The Nauvoo Journal of Joseph Fielding," *BYU Studies* 19 (1979): 159.

22. Ford to Phelps, 22 July 1844; BYJ2, 31 Aug. 1844; "appeared" in BYOJ, 28 Sept 1844. On the "wolf hunt" episode, see Oaks and Hill, *Carthage Conspiracy,* 36–38.

23. "doomed" in minutes of 30 Jan. 1845, Box 1, Folder 29, GCM; "severed" in William Clayton Journal, 26 Feb. 1845, quoted in James B. Allen, *Trials of Discipleship: The Story of William Clayton, a Mormon* (Urbana: University of Illinois Press, 1987), 174.

24. "living constitution" in Daniel Spencer Journal, 21 Feb. 1845, MS 1566, CHL; "standing chairman" in WCJ, 4 Feb. 1845, 157. See the discussion in D. Michael Quinn, *The Mormon Hierarchy: Extensions of Power* (Salt Lake City: Signature Books, 1997), 226–235.

25. WWJ, 18 Aug. 1844, 2:446; Hyde to BY, 29 Dec. 1844, Box 39, Folder 15, BYP; *Warsaw Signal,* 5 June 1844 ("Nauvoo Bogus"), 25 Dec. 1844 "spurious coin"); John Taylor Journal, 12 Jan. 1845, in Jessee, "The John Taylor Nauvoo Journal," 21–22. See the discussion in Kenneth W. Godfrey, "Crime and Punishment in Mormon Nauvoo, 1839–1846," *BYU Studies* 32 (Winter/Spring 1992): 195–227; Marshall Hamilton, "From Assassination to Expulsion: Two Years of Distrust, Hostility, and Violence," *BYU Studies* 32 (Winter/Spring 1992): 230–248.

26. "inflammation" in minutes of 11 May 1845, Box 1, Folder 33, GCM; "intend," "go and tattle," and "Marks" in minutes of 16 March 1845, Box 1, Folder 30, GCM. See Thurmon Dean Moody, "Nauvoo's Whistling and Whittling Brigade," *BYU Studies* 15 (1992): 480–490.

27. HSJ, 3 April 1845 and 9 Jan. 1846, 1:32, 103; BY to Parley P. Pratt, 26 May 1845, in Letterpress Copybook 1, pages 13–16, BYP; "Celestial law" in WCJ, 7 Dec. 1845, 194.

28. "sufficiently united" in ZHJ, 10 Nov. 1844, in Maureen Ursenbach Beecher, "'All Things Move in Order in the City': The Nauvoo Diary of Zina Diantha Huntington Jacobs," *BYU Studies* 19 (Spring 1979): 297; "Zion is here" in minutes of 6 April 1845, Box 1, Folder 31, GCM; Susan Sessions Rugh, *Our Common Country: Family Farming, Culture, and Community in the Nineteenth-Century Midwest* (Bloomington: University of Indiana Press, 2001), 45; "fruitful field" in minutes of 4 May 1845 Minutes, Box 1, Folder 33, GCM.

29. *Nauvoo Neighbor,* 16 April 1845; minutes of 24 May 1845, Box 1, Folder 34, GCM.

30. "city of Joseph," T&S, 15 April 1845, 871; "cannot be driven" from minutes of 4 May 1845, Box 1, Folder 33, GCM; "buffalo" from minutes of 4 Aug. 1845, Box 1, Folder 36, GCM; 3,000 men in WCJ, 28 Aug. 1845, 180; "Governor" from WRJ, 31 Aug. 1845; "hurry" in BYJ2, 17 Aug. 1845.

31. *Warsaw Signal,* 3 Sept. 1845; cf. Hill and Oaks, *Carthage Conspiracy,* 194; BYOJ, 12 Sept. 1845.

32. WRJ, 11 Sept. 1845; John Taylor Journal, 11 Sept. 1845, in Jessee, "John Taylor Nauvoo Journal," 88.

33. BYOJ, 14 Sept. 1845; "proposed" in WRJ, 16 Sept. 1845; *Proclamation: to Col. Levi Williams,* 16 Sept. 1845 (Nauvoo: 1845), HBLL.

34. HSJ, 19 Sept. 1845, 1:67; "fun for us" in BYOJ, 19 Sept. 1845; BY to Backenstos, 18 Sept. 1845, Box 16, Folder 4, BYP.

35. WRJ, 14 Sept. 1845; "pray the Lord" in BYOJ, 20 Sept. 1845.

36. WRJ, 26 Sept. 1845; "Hell of a Hole" from HSJ, 26 Sept. 1845, 1:73. For the late-1845 mob activity and the Saints' agreement to leave Nauvoo, see Glen M. Leonard, *Nauvoo: A Place of Peace, a People of Promise* (Salt Lake City: Deseret Book, 2002), 525–542; Oaks and Hill, *Carthage Conspiracy,* ch. 11; and John E. Hallwas and Roger D. Launius, eds., *Cultures in Conflict: A Documentary History of the Mormon War in Illinois* (Logan: Utah State University Press, 1995), pt. 6.

37. MH, 4 Oct. 1845; minutes of 9 Nov. 1845, Box 1, Folder 41, GCM.

38. Joseph Fielding Journal, 4 Jan. 1846, in Ehat, "They Might Have Known," 158.

39. WCJ, 30 Nov. 1845, 193–194; "Report of Suits Pending in the Circuit Court of the United States for the District of Illinois at its December Term 1845," in Reports of the U.S. District Attorneys, 1845–50, National Archives, microfilm copy at HBLL. See the conflicting interpretations of Nauvoo counterfeiting in John L. Brooke, *The Refiner's Fire: The Making of Mormon Cosmology, 1644–1844* (New York: Cambridge University Press, 1994), 269–270; Leonard, *Nauvoo,* 311–312, 524, 564–565, 570.

40. "Hats and Coats" in WCJ, 23 Dec. 1845, 230; Young discourse of 23 July 1871, JD, 14:219; 24 Sept. 1845 resolution, in Box 16, Folder 4, BYP.

41. HCKWC, 13 Dec. 1845; *Proclamation of the Twelve Apostles of the Church of Jesus Christ of Latter-day Saints . . .* (n.p., 1845), 1; cf. Thomas G. Alexander, "The Reconstruction of Mormon Doctrine: From Joseph Smith to Progressive Theology," *Sunstone,* July/Aug. 1980, 28. On the Nauvoo Temple endowment ceremony, see Leonard, *Nauvoo,* 258–261; David John Buerger, *Mysteries of Godliness: A History of Mormon Temple Worship,* 2nd ed. (Salt Lake City: Signature Books, 2002), ch. 4; Kathleen Flake, "'Not to Be Riten': The Mormon Temple Rite as Oral Canon," *Journal of Ritual Studies* 9 (Summer 1995): 1–21. On shifting Mormon views of Jehovah, see Boyd Kirkland, "Elohim and Jehovah in Mormon Thought," *Dialogue* 19 (Spring 1986): 77–93.

42. "becoming a God" in minutes of 20 April 1845, Box 1, Folder 31, GCM; "innumerable posterity" in minutes of 8 Jan. 1845, Box 1, Folder 28, GCM; "Power to create" in George Laub Journal, 31 Dec. 1844; "secret of the whole thing" in minutes of 4 May 1845. On the distinctly Mormon version of the "Great Chain of Being," see Brown, *In Heaven,* chs. 8 and 9.

43. BYOJ, 12 Jan. 1846; Norton Jacob Journal, 12 Dec. 1845, in Ronald Barney, ed., *The Mormon Vanguard Brigade of 1847: Norton Jacob's Record* (Logan:

Utah State University Press, 2005), 60. For an early exposé by a disillusioned Mormon, see Lewis, *Narrative.*

44. HCKWC, 26 Dec. 1845; quotations from William Clayton Minutes, 28 December 1845, in NEC, 205–207.

45. "lion of the Lord" in T&S, 1 Jan. 1844 [1845]; "brought in" and "power of animation" in Seventies Record Book B, 17 Dec. 1845, 157, CR 3 51, CHL.

46. For text of "Upper California," see William Clayton Journal, 17 April 1845, in Allen, *Trials of Discipleship,* 177–178; "Lamanites . . . will join" from Seventies Record Book B, 30 Dec. 1845, 172; "most beautiful" and "most touching" in HCKWC, 30 Dec. 1845. Shane Chism and Ardis Parshall provided me with information on the popular song, which John Taylor adapted to fit Mormon themes.

47. HCKWC, 1 and 2 Jan. 1846. See Terryl L. Givens, *People of Paradox: A History of Mormon Culture* (New York: Oxford University Press, 2007), ch. 7; R. Lawrence Moore, "Learning to Play: The Mormon Way and the Way of Other Americans," *Journal of Mormon History* 16 (1990): 89–108.

48. BYOJ, 19 January 1846 (reminiscent account of 17 January); HSJ, 20 Jan. 1846, 1:107.

49. William Clayton, notes on BY discourse of 26 Dec. 1845, in NEC, 191; HCKWC, 28 Dec. ("never get back") and 16 Dec. ("into the upper") 1845.

50. BYJ2, 10, 19, and 20 Sept. 1844.

51. Minutes of 12 March 1848, Box 2, Folder 2, GCM.

52. List of sealings in Lisle G Brown, *Nauvoo Sealings, Adoptions, and Anointings* (Salt Lake City: Smith-Pettit Foundation, 2006), 351–353. On Phebe Morton and Jemima Angell, see Myrtle Stevens Hyde and Dean Crawford Smith, "Mormon Angells," *New England Historical and Genealogical Register* 147 (July 1993): 211–233. See the discussion in Johnson, "Determining and Defining 'Wife': The Brigham Young Households," *Dialogue* 20 (Fall 1987): 57–70.

53. Clarissa Blake Homiston to BY, undated (ca. late 1844 or 1845), Box 44, Folder 12, BYP; ZHJ, 31 Dec. 1844, in Beecher, "'All Things Move in Order,'"300; Percis (Persis) Tippett to BY, 27 Dec. 1845, Box 65, Folder 1, BYP.

54. BYJ2, 10 Oct. 1844; HCKJ, 10 and 14 Oct. 1844, 90; Clarissa Young Spencer and Mabel Harmer, *Brigham Young at Home* (Salt Lake City: Deseret Book, 1940), 76. See Jill Derr, "The Lion and the Lioness: Brigham Young and Eliza R. Snow," *BYU Studies* 40 (2001): 54–101.

55. MU, 166; Grant quoted in 9 Dec. 1847 Minutes, Box 12, Folder 4, LJA; John D. Lee Journal, 20 Dec. 1845, Box 15, Folder 5, LJA. See the description of Lee and discussion of the December 1847 council in MMM, 59–62. On Lee, see Juanita Brooks, *John Doyle Lee: Zealot, Pioneer, Scapegoat,* rev. ed. (Glendale, CA: Arthur H. Clark, 1972).

56. Augusta Adams (Cobb); Jemima Angell (Stringham); Amanda Barnes (Smith); Clarissa Blake (Homiston); Mary Ann Clark (Powers); Amy Cooper (Aldrich); Lucy Decker (Seeley); Lydia Farnsworth (Mayhew); Emily Haws (Whitmarsh); Zina Huntington (Jacobs); Mary de la Montague (Woodward);

Phebe Morton (Angell); Margaret Pierce (Whitesides); Mary Elizabeth Rollins (Lightner); Hannah Tapfield (King).

57. Lyndon W. Cook, ed., *Nauvoo Deaths and Marriages, 1839–1845* (Orem, UT: Grandin Book, 1994), 82, 111. Young's diary records a 16 Jan. 1845 visit to Robert Pierce's home, and several scholars, including Jeffery Johnson, date Young's sealings to both Margaret and her sister Mary to that day. See BYJ2, 16 Jan. 1845.

58. ZHJ, 3 and 9 May, 10/11 June 1845, in Beecher, "'All Things Move in Order,'" 21, 23; Book of Proxy Sealings, 2 Feb. 1846, photocopy in author's possession. On Zina Huntington's background and marriages, see Martha Sonntag Bradley and Mary Brown Firmage Woodward, *4 Zinas: A Story of Mothers and Daughters on the Mormon Frontier* (Salt Lake City: Signature Books, 2000), esp. ch. 5; Todd Compton, *In Sacred Loneliness: The Plural Wives of Joseph Smith* (Salt Lake City: Signature Books, 1997), ch. 4.

59. Augusta Adams to BY, 20 Jan. 1846, Box 66, Folder 7, BYP; Augusta Adams to BY, 4 Feb. 1862, Theodore Albert Schroeder Papers, Wisconsin Historical Society.

60. Augusta Adams to BY, 4 Feb. 1846, Schroeder Papers.

61. "Sealings and Adoptions," 11 Jan. 1846, in NEC, 397–398.

62. Laub Journal, 5 Feb. 1846; WWJ, 16 Feb. 1847, 3:131. See Samuel M. Brown, "Early Mormon Adoption Theology and the Mechanics of Salvation," *Journal of Mormon History* 38 (Summer 2011): 3–53; Jonathan A. Stapley, "Adoptive Sealing Rituals in Mormonism," *Journal of Mormon History* 37 (Summer 2011): 54–117.

63. BYOJ, 25 Jan. 1846; Thomas Bullock Journal, 25 Jan. 1846, in Gregory R. Knight, ed., "Journal of Thomas Bullock," *BYU Studies* 31 (Winter 1991): 45; Laub Journal, 5 Feb. 1846; Stapley, "Adoptive Sealing Rituals," 67, n. 30.

64. Brown, *Nauvoo Sealings, Adoptions, and Anointings,* 350, 353; Mary M[ontague] Woodward to BY and Council, undated (ca. 1845), Box 66, Folder 26, BYP. See Lawrence Foster, *Religion and Sexuality: The Shakers, the Mormons, and the Oneida Community* (Urbana: University of Illinois Press, 1984); Kathryn M. Daynes, *More Wives Than One: Transformation of the Mormon Marriage System, 1840–1910* (Urbana: University of Illinois Press, 2001), ch. 11.

65. Ford to Backenstos, 29 Dec. 1845 in MH, 4 Jan. 1846; BYOJ, 27 Jan., 2 and 3 Feb. 1846.

66. See Brown, *In Heaven,* esp. ch. 10; Stapley, "Adoptive Sealing Ritual," 67–81.

67. Young at Lewis's residence in HCKJ, 5 July 1844, 72; Catherine Lewis to Brigham Young, 17 Nov. 1844, Box 20, Folder 7, BYP; Lewis, *Narrative.* I am grateful to Connell O'Donovan for pointing me to the Catherine Lewis letter.

68. Lucy Mack Smith's participation in the endowment in HCK Journal (kept by William Clayton), 11 Dec. 1845, in NEC, 5; "made Bogus of it" in Lucy Messerve Smith, 18 May 1892 statement, MS 7067; cf. Newell and Avery, *Mormon Enigma,* 211.

69. Joseph Heywood to BY, 2 and 16 Oct. 1846, Box 20, Folder 20, BYP. On the continued mob activity after Young's departure and the temple's fate, see Leonard, *Nauvoo*, ch. 19 and 622–631.

70. Minutes of 3 Nov. 1844, Seventies Record, Book B, CR 3 51, CHL; Lewis, *Narrative*, 18 (emphasis in original); HCKWC, 2 Jan. 1846. Although Lewis had left and denounced the church by the time of her exposé, her recollection is in accord with other accounts of Young's commentary on the American government around this time.

6. Word and Will

Snow, "Let Us Go," in Jill Mulvay Derr and Karen Lynn Davidson, eds., *Eliza R. Snow: The Complete Poetry* (Provo, UT: Brigham Young University Press, 2009), 324.

1. Young reading Frémont's narrative in HCKWC, 29 Dec. 1845; Frémont, *Narrative of the Exploring Expedition to the Rocky Mountains . . . and to Oregon and North California* (Washington: Henry Polkinhorn, 1845), esp. 260; BY to Addison Pratt, 28 Aug. 1845, Box 16, Folder 3, BYP; "know where" John D. Lee Journal, 13 Jan. 1846, typescript in Box 15, Folder 5, LJA.

2. Feb.–Aug. 1846 Account Book, John D. Lee, MS 19826, CHL.

3. BY to Orson Hyde 21, April 1846, Box 16, Folder 6, BYP; Eliza R. Snow Journal, 9/10 Aug. 1846, in Maureen Ursenbach Beecher, ed., *The Personal Writings of Eliza Roxcy Snow* (Salt Lake City: University of Utah Press, 1995), 139; WCJ, 12 May 1846, 275.

4. "tied our hands" in WRJ, 3 May 1846; "conduct" in WRJ, 9 April 1846. See also WRJ, 19 April and 21 May, 1846.

5. WRJ, 21 and 24 May, 1846; "slap of revelation" from Heber C. Kimball Journal, 24 May 1846, typescript at HBLL.

6. Journal of Patty Sessions, 26 April and 2 Sept. 1846, in Donna Toland Smart, ed., *Mormon Midwife: The 1846–1888 Diaries of Patty Bartlett Sessions* (Logan: Utah State University Press, 1997), 47, 60–61.

7. Journal of John D. Lee, 7 and 8 Feb. 1847, in Charles Kelly, ed., *Journals of John D. Lee, 1846–47 and 1859* (Salt Lake City: University of Utah Press, 1984), 67–68; "we lay hands" in WWJ, 23 Feb. 1848, 3:325.

8. WRJ, 14 March 1847. See Jan Shipps, *Mormonism: The Story of a New Religious Tradition* (Urbana: University of Illinois Press, 1985), esp. 61–63. On the Mormon sense of Israelite lineage, see Armand L. Mauss, *All Abraham's Children: Changing Mormon Conceptions of Race and Lineage* (Urbana: University of Illinois Press, 2003), ch. 2.

9. HSJ, 15 Feb. 1846, 1:123; Sessions Journal, 6 April 1846, in Smart, 41; Kimball Journal, 10 June 1846, typescript at HBLL.

10. On the Oregon resolution and the origins of the Mexican-American War, see Daniel Walker Howe, *What Hath God Wrought: The Transformation of America, 1815–1848* (New York: Oxford University Press, 2007), chs. 19 and 20; Walter Nugent, *Habits of Empire: A History of American Expansion* (New York: Knopf, 2008), ch. 6 and 7.

11. James K. Polk Diary, 31 January 1846 ("absurd") and 2 June 1846 ("concili-

ate") in Milo Milton Quaife, ed., *The Diary of James K. Polk during His Presidency,* vol. 1 (Chicago: A. C. McClurg, 1910), 205, 444; Little to Polk, 1 June 1846, copy in Box 47, Folder 10, BYP; cf. David L. Bigler and Will Bagley, *Army of Israel: Mormon Battalion Narratives* (Logan: Utah State University Press, 2000), 32–35. On the creation of the Mormon Battalion, see Bigler and Bagley, *Army of Israel,* ch. 1; Richard E. Bennett, *Mormons at the Missouri, 1846–1852: "And Should We Die,"* 2nd ed. (Norman: University of Oklahoma Press, 2004), ch. 3; W. Ray Luce, "The Mormon Battalion: A Historical Accident?" *Utah Historical Quarterly* 42 (Winter 1974): 27–38. On Kane, see Matthew J. Grow, *"Liberty to the Downtrodden": Thomas L. Kane, Romantic Reformer* (New Haven: Yale University Press, 2009).

12. Heber C. Kimball Journal, 2 Jan. 1846, typescript at HBLL; "no *hoax*" in BY to Samuel Bent, 7 July 1846, Box 16, Folder 7, BYP (emphasis in original); "straddle the fence" from BY to Orson Spencer, 20 Oct. 1846, Box 16, Folder 9, BYP; "should we locate" from BY to James K. Polk, 9 Aug. 1846, in Box 16, Folder 8, BYP. On the hostility of many church members toward Allen's offer, see John F. Yurtinus, "'Here Is One Man Who Will Not Go, Dam'um': Recruiting the Mormon Battalion in Iowa Territory," *BYU Studies* 24 (Fall 1981): 475–487.

13. TBJ, 28 July 1847, 243.

14. John D. Lee Journal, 27 Jan. 1847, in Kelly, 60; cf. Bennett, *Mormons at the Missouri,* 127–128.

15. Taggart 1886 Autobiography, typescript in MS 1185/1, CHL; cf. Bennett, *Mormons at the Missouri,* 122; "lowest scrapings" in John D. Lee Journal, 11 March 1848, in Robert Glass Cleland and Juanita Brooks, eds., *A Mormon Chronicle: The Diaries of John D. Lee, 1848–1876* (San Marino, CA: Huntington Library, 1955), 1:5.

16. "Gospel" from BY to Nauvoo Trustees, 7 July 1846, Box 16, Folder 7, BYP; Vancouver Island in WRJ, 24 July 1846. See the discussion in Bennett, *Mormons at the Missouri,* 63–67.

17. Zina Huntington to Mary Huntington, 29 Dec. 1846, MS 15664, CHL; population from HSJ, 24 Dec. 1846, 1:219.

18. "did not know" in WRJ, 12 Sept. 1846; "did not whip them hard enough" in WWJ, 12 Sept 1846, 3:80; "Law of God" in Norton Jacob Journal, 13 Sept. 1846, in Ronald Barney, ed., *The Mormon Vanguard Brigade of 1847: Norton Jacob's Record* (Logan: Utah State University Press, 2005), 81. For Young ordering the flogging, see HSJ, 4 Sept. 1846.

19. Zina Huntington quoted in Edward W. Tullidge, *Women of Mormondom* (New York: Tullidge and Crandall, 1877), 327.

20. Eliza Partridge autobiography and journal, 15 Feb. 1846, in Scott H. Partridge, ed., *Eliza Maria Partridge Journal* (Provo, UT: Grandin, 2003), 15; Emily P. Young, 1877 Autobiography, Vault MSS 5, HBLL.

21. BY to Harriet Cook Young, 25 March 1846, VMSS 64, HBLL; BY to Harriet Cook Young, 23 June 1846, MSS 576, HBLL; Harriet Cook Young to BY, 14 June 1847, Box 44, Folder 14, BYP. See Dean Jessee, "Brigham Young's Family: The Wilderness Years," *BYU Studies* 19 (Summer 1979): 474–500.

22. See Compton, *In Sacred Loneliness,* ch. 8.

23. Henry Jacobs to Zina Jacobs, 19 Aug. 1846, MS 3248, CHL. See Compton, *In Sacred Loneliness,* ch. 4.

24. BY to Mary Woodward, 13 Dec. 1846 (emphasis in original), Box 66, Folder 27, BYP.

25. James Woodward to BY (addressed as "Father"), undated, ca. early 1847; "raise children" in Mary Woodward to BY, undated, ca. February 1847; "cannot give" in Mary Woodward to BY, undated (ca. 1851 or 1852), "same privelige" in Mary Woodward to BY, Dec. 1855 (emphasis in original), all in Box 66, Folder 27, BYP.

26. Clarissa B. Homiston to BY, 12 April 1859, Box 66, Folder 10, BYP; Lyman discourse of 5 April 1866, JD 11:207.

27. Eliza R. Snow Journal, 1 Jan. 1847 ("female family"), 26 Jan. 1847 ("2d mansion"), 1 June 1847 ("glorious time"), in Beecher, 151, 153, and 176; Zina Huntington to Mary Huntington, 29 Dec. 1846; female blessings in Patty Sessions Journal, 29 May 1847, in Smart, 82. Emphasis in original.

28. Namaah Twiss to Thomas Nichols, 29 Dec. 1846, MS 156, CHL; cf. Jessee, "Brigham Young's Family: The Wilderness Years," 487; Mary Pierce death in Eliza R. Snow Journal, 16 and 17 March 1847, in Beecher, 159.

29. WRJ, 15 Jan. and 20 March 1847. On Beaman, see Compton, *In Sacred Loneliness,* ch. 3.

30. Augusta Adams Cobb to BY, 9 June 1847, Schroeder Papers; Eliza Snow Journal, 2 and 16 June 1847, in Beecher, 176, 178–179. See BY to Mary Ann Angell, 20 April 1847, MS 5278, CHL.

31. "forever" in WRJ, 9 July 1846; Miriam B. Murphy, "From Impulsive Girl to Patient Wife: Lucy Bigelow Young," *Utah Historical Quarterly* 45 (Summer 1977): 270–288; information on sealings and deathbed requests from Pre-Endowment House and Endowment House Records, CR 344 13, CHL.

32. "head & God" in WWJ, 16 Feb. 1846, 3:137. See B. Carmon Hardy, "Lords of Creation: Polygamy, the Abrahamic Household, and Mormon Patriarchy," *Journal of Mormon History* 20 (Spring 1994): 119–156.

33. "want Sisters" in Seventies Record Book B, 9 March 1845, 78, CR 3 51, CHL.

34. "dirtier than a man" in minutes of 30 Nov. 1847, Box 12, Folder 3, LJA; "won't lie" in minutes of 9 Dec. 1847, Box 12, Folder 4, LJA; "buzzing" from minutes of 12 March 1848, Box 2, Folder 2, GCM; "don't wash their dishes" in WWJ, 16 Feb. 1846.

35. See Nancy Isenberg, *Sex and Citizenship in Antebellum America* (Chapel Hill: University of North Carolina Press, 1998), ch. 6; Sarah Barringer Gordon, *The Mormon Question: Polygamy and Constitutional Conflict in Nineteenth-Century America* (Chapel Hill: University of North Carolina Press, 2002), 66–68.

36. Minutes of 9 Dec. 1847. See the discussion in MMM, 61.

37. Seventies Minute Book B, 9 March 1845; minutes of 9 April 1844, Box 1, Folder 20, GCM. See Jonathan A. Stapley and Kristine Wright, "Female Ritual Healing in Mormonism," *Journal of Mormon History* 37 (Winter 2011): 1–85.

38. WWJ, 24 July 1846, 3:62; John D. Lee Journal, 16 Feb. 1847, in Kelly, 80.

39. WRJ, 27 March 1846; WWJ, 18 Jan. 1847, 3:118; "Big Red headed chief" in HSJ, 25 May 1847, 256–257; "Brother Brigham" from John D. Lee Journal, 16 Feb. 1847, in Kelly, 82. On adoption, see Jonathan A. Stapley, "Adoptive Sealing Ritual in Mormonism," *Journal of Mormon History* 38 (Summer 2011): 75–81. On Young's Missouri River farm, see Bennett, *Mormons at the Missouri,* 163–164.

40. WWJ, 16 Feb. 1847, 3:136–137.

41. "actually . . . came back again" from WRJ, 28 Feb. 1847; account of dream in Box 75, Folder 34, BYP.

42. WRJ, 16 Feb. 1847. See Benjamin E. Park, "'Build, Therefore, Your Own World': Ralph Waldo Emerson, Joseph Smith, and American Antebellum Thought," *Journal of Mormon History* 36 (Winter 2010): 65–70.

43. Bennett, *Mormons at the Missouri,* 90, 137; *Voree Herald* [Voree, WI], March 1846, 2; cf. Bennett, *Mormons at the Missouri,* 238, n. 47.

44. "reformation" in Norton Jacob Journal, December 1846, in Barney, 90; "must stop" in WWJ, 20 Dec. 1846, 3:100–101.

45. Young to Rich, 4 Jan. 1847, Box 16, Folder 11, BYP; WRJ, 29 Dec. 1846.

46. WRJ, 11 and 14 1846; Heber C. Kimball Journal, 19 Jan. 1847, typescript in HBLL; D&C 136, essentially unchanged from early copies such as WWJ, 3:120–124; HSJ, 14 Jan. 1847, 229.

47. Mary Haskin Parker Richards Journal, 26 Jan. and 9 Feb. 1847, in Maurine Carr Ward, ed., *Winter Quarters: The 1846–1848 Life Writings of Mary Haskin Parker Richards* (Logan: Utah State University Press, 1996), 107, 109; WRJ, 15 and 22 Feb. 1847; "very short time" and "Mormon dance" in minutes of 5 Feb. 1847, Box 1, Folder 51, GCM; "all music is in heaven" in minutes of 16 Jan. 1848, Box 2, Folder 1, GCM.

48. WRJ, 14 March 1847.

49. Bennett, *We'll Find the Place,* 74–77, 83–86.

50. John D. Unruh Jr., *The Plains Across: The Overland Emigrants and the Trans-Mississippi West, 1840–60* (Urbana: University of Illinois Press, 1979), 119, ch. 6.

51. "Commander" in Norton Jacob Journal, 17 April, in Barney, 106; Albert P. Rockwood Journal, 16 April 1847, MS 1449, CHL. For "laws regulating the camp of Israel," see TBJ, 357.

52. See Unruh, *The Plains Across,* 184–186.

53. Norton Jacob Journal, 4 May ("not the time") and 28 May ("spirit" and "Negros") 1847, in Barney, 150; "wrote some" in WWJ, 28 May 1847, 3:186; "did not care" and "in vain" in WRJ, 28 May 1847, vol. 18, MS 1490, CHL.

54. "let the brethren dance" and "dirtiest thing" from WCJ, 29 May 1847, 327; other quotes from minutes of 29 May 1847, Box 1, Folder 55, GCM. See Bennett, *We'll Find the Place,* 159–167.

55. WCJ, 30 May 1847, 333–334.

56. "crowned" in Norton Jacob Journal, 7 June 1847, in Barney, 166.

57. Willard Richards and George A. Smith to Orson Pratt, 21 July 1847, in Box 3, Folder 7, MS 1490. See Bennett, *We'll Find the Place,* 191–196.

58. Young to Lyman, C. C. Rich, 3 July 1847, Box 16, Folder 13, CHL. See Will Bagley, *Scoundrel's Tale: The Samuel Brannan Papers* (Spokane, WA: Arthur H. Clark, 1999), ch. 7.

59. Joel Palmer, *Journal of Travels Over the Rocky Mountains, to the Mouth of the Columbia River, Made During the Years 1845 and 1846*, ed. Reuben Gold Thwaites (Cleveland, OH: Arthur H. Clark, 1906), 74; Hosanna shout in TBJ, 4 July 1847, 218; "insensible" in WCJ, 13 July 1847, 357; "washed" in Norton Jacob Journal, 18 July 1847, in Barney, 212; "gazed with wonder" in WWJ, 24 July 1847, 233–234; "Promised Land" (emphasis in original) in Horace K. Whitney Journal, 25 July 1847, MS 1616, CHL.

60. My analysis is congruent with Barney, *Norton Jacob Record*, 103 n. 34.

61. Levi Jackman Journal, 28 July 1847, VMSS 79, HBLL.

62. Bennett, *We'll Find the Place*, ch. 8.

63. Erastus Snow Journal, 8 Aug. 1847, Box 1, MS 1329, Church Archives.

64. Isaiah 62:12, 2:2, 35:1; "may live" in TBJ, 28 July 1847, 243–244; "standard" in WCJ, 1 March 1845, 158; cf. Ronald W. Walker, "'A Banner is Unfurled': Mormonism's Ensign Peak," *Dialogue* 26 (Winter 1993): 72.

65. TBJ, 28 July 1847, 244.

66. Norton Jacob Journal, 28 July 1847, in Barney, 229.

67. David Sehat, *The Myth of American Religious Freedom* (New York: Oxford University Press, 2011), ch. 3, esp. 68.

68. Minutes of 4 Sept. 1847, Box 1, Folder 57, GCM.

69. 16 Nov. 1847 minutes excerpted in Gary J. Bergera, *Conflict in the Quorum: Orson Pratt, Brigham Young, Joseph Smith* (Salt Lake City: Signature Books, 2002), 54–61.

70. Minutes of 27 Dec. 1847, Box 1, Folder 61, GCM. For a discussion of these issues, see Bennett, *Mormons at the Missouri*, ch. 11; D. Michael Quinn, *The Mormon Hierarchy: Origins of Power* (Salt Lake City: Signature Books, 1994), 245–250.

71. Minutes of 5 Dec. 1847, Box 1, Folder 59; cf. Bergera, *Conflict in the Quorum*, 64–81.

72. Minutes of 27 Dec. 1847, Box 1, Folder 61, GCM.

73. Minutes of 12 Feb. 1849, Box 2, Folder 8, GCM; cf. Bergera, *Conflict in the Quorum*, 82–83.

7. A New Era of Things

1. "leader" and "passed" in John Pulsipher Journal, September 1848, typescript at HBLL; Jill M. Derr and Karen L. Davidson, eds., *Eliza R. Snow: The Complete Poetry* (Provo, UT: Brigham Young University Press, 2009), 379; "happy" in minutes of 24 Sept. 1848, Box 2, Folder 7, GCM; "dark and dreary" in minutes of 18 June 1848, Box 2, Folder 5, GCM.

2. List of church leaders' weights, 11 Sept. 1850, Box 75, Folder 4, BYP; discourse of 5 Feb. 1857, in VW, 3:1224. See Ronald W. Walker, "Raining Pitchforks: Brigham Young as Preacher," *Sunstone* 8 (May–June 1983): 5–9.

3. John W. Gunnison, *The Mormons, or Latter-day Saints ...* (Philadelphia: Lip-

pincott, Grambo, 1852), 73. See Richard Bushman, "Was Joseph Smith a Gentleman? The Standard for Refinement in Utah," in Ronald Walker and Doris Dant, eds., *Nearly Everything Imaginable: The Everyday Lives of Utah's Mormon Pioneers* (Provo, UT: Brigham Young University Press, 1999), 27–43.

4. Only swearing in the pulpit in discourse of 31 July 1853, JD, 1:166; "church debts" in minutes of 22 Jan. 1848, Box 2, Folder 1, GCM; "what I please" in minutes of 23 Sept. 1849, Box 2, Folder 14, GCM; "frequently say" in minutes of 17 March 1848, Box 2, Folder 2, GCM; "not so good" in minutes of 14 May 1848, Box 2, Folder 5, GCM; "profanes" in minutes of 12 Jan. 1851, Box 2, Folder 26, GCM.

5. For information on the publication of Young's sermons, see Ronald G. Watt, *The Mormon Passage of George D. Watt: First British Convert, Scribe for Zion* (Logan: Utah State University Press, 2009), ch. 6.

6. Minutes of 12 Aug. 1849, Box 2, Folder 13, GCM; minutes of 25 May 1851, Box 2, Folder 30, GCM.

7. "only man" in John D. Lee Journal, 3 Feb. 1849, in Robert Glass Cleland and Juanita Brooks, eds., *A Mormon Chronicle: The Diaries of John D. Lee, 1848–1876* (San Marino, Calif.: Huntington Library, 1955), 1:87; other quote in minutes of 11 Feb. 1849, Box 2, Folder 8, GCM.

8. See William G. Hartley, "Mormons, Crickets, and Gulls: A New Look at an Old Story," *Utah Historical Quarterly* 38 (Summer 1970): 224–239.

9. BY to Brannan, 5 April 1849, Box 16, Folder 17, BYP. See Will Bagley, *A Scoundrel's Tale: The Samuel Brannan Papers* (Spokane, WA: Arthur H. Clark, 1999), ch. 10.

10. Minutes of 1 Oct. 1848, Box 2, Folder 7, GCM; minutes of 12 Aug. 1849, Box 2, Folder 13, GCM.

11. "follow in the wake" in minutes of 23 June 1850, Box 2, Folder 20, GCM; "foreign coins" from BY to Amasa Lyman, 2 Nov. 1849, Box 16, Folder 18, BYP; other quotes from minutes of 7 Jan. 1849, Box 2, Folder 7, GCM. On Mormon coins and Utah paper currency, see Leonard Arrington, "Coin and Currency in Early Utah," *Utah Historical Quarterly* 20 (Jan. 1952): 56–76.

12. Stephen C. Taysom, *Shakers, Mormons, and Religious Worlds: Conflicting Visions, Contested Boundaries* (Bloomington: Indiana University Press, 2011), 96–99.

13. John D. Lee Journal, 10 March 1849, in Cleland and Brooks, 1:100; BY to Amasa Lyman and Charles C. Rich, 23 Oct. 1851, Box 16, Folder 22, BYP. See Eugene E. Campbell, *Establishing Zion: The Mormon Church in the American West, 1847–1869* (Salt Lake City: Signature Books, 1988), chs. 4 and 5; Milton R. Hunter, *Brigham Young the Colonizer* (Independence, MO: Zion's Printing and Publishing, 1945).

14. Minutes of 8 Nov. 1847, Box 1, Folder 58, GCM; BY to "the Saints in Parowan and Cedar City . . . ," undated ca. Oct.–Nov. 1851, Box 176 Folder 22, BYP; John D. Lee Journal, 2 Dec. 1850, in Gustive O. Larson, ed., "Journal of the Iron County Mission, John D. Lee Clerk," in *Utah Historical Quar-*

terly 20 (April 1952): 114; BY to Franklin Richards 30 April 1851, Box 16, Folder 20, BYP.

15. See Leonard Arrington, *Great Basin Kingdom: An Economic History of the Latter-day Saints, 1830–1900* (Cambridge, MA: Harvard University Press, 1958), ch. 4; Morris A. Shirts and Kathryn H. Shirts, *A Trial Furnace: Southern Utah's Iron Mission* (Provo, UT: BYU Press, 2001).

16. "mercantile crossroads" from Brigham Madsen, *Gold Rush Sojourners in Great Salt Lake City, 1849 and 1850* (Salt Lake City: University of Utah Press, 1983), 132.

17. "freeze out" in minutes of 7 Jan. 1849, Box 2, Folder 7, GCM; "good place" and "hard times" in discourse of 17 Aug. 1856, in JD, 4:32.

18. Minutes of 14 Oct. 1849, Box 2, Folder 14, GCM; "they can trample" in minutes of 22 Oct. 1848, Box 2, Folder 7, GCM.

19. "shit upon" from minutes of 2 July 1848, Box 2, Folder 5; "boss" and "master" from 4 Feb. 1849 minutes, Box 2, Folder 8; "daddy" from 12 Feb. 1849 minutes, Box 2, Folder 8; "walk over all" from 8 Oct. 1848 minutes, Box 2, Folder 7, all in GCM; "old Boss" from HSJ, 28 April 1846, 1:157.

20. Minutes of 11 Feb. 1849, Box 2, Folder 8, GCM; "dictate" in minutes of 14 Oct. 1849, Box 2, Folder 14, GCM. On the Council of Fifty's role in the Great Basin, I have relied on D. Michael Quinn, *The Mormon Hierarchy: Extensions of Power* (Salt Lake City: Signature Books, 1997), 235–241; Andrew F. Ehat, "'It Seems Like Heaven Began on Earth': Joseph Smith and the Constitution of the Kingdom of God," *BYU Studies* 20 (Spring 1980): 21–22.

21. Minutes of 25 Feb. 1849, Box 2, Folder 8, GCM.

22. Thomas Bullock Journal, 24 Aug. 1848, MS 1385, CHL; minutes of the Salt Lake City High Council, 2 March 1849, LR 604 107, CHL; "thief and swindler" in minutes of 12 March 1849, Box 2, Folder 9, GCM.

23. John D. Lee Journal, 3 and 4 March 1849, in Cleland and Brooks, 1:98–99.

24. Quotes from minutes of 12 March 1849; Chauncey West in HSJ, 12 March 1849, 2:348.

25. John D. Lee Journal, 17 March 1849, in Cleland and Brooks, 1:102; Joseph Fielding Journal, 18 March 1849, typescript at HBLL; SLT, 4 June 1881.

26. William Smith, "A Proclamation," *Warsaw Signal,* 29 Oct. 1845; cf. Bill Shepard, "The Notorious Hodges Brothers: Solving the Mystery of Their Destruction at Nauvoo," *John Whitmer Historical Association Journal* 26 (2006): 260–286; "do her up" in minutes of 27 Dec. 1847, Box 1, Folder 61, GCM; Snow quoted in minutes of 18 March 1849, Box 2, Folder 9, GCM.

27. John D. Lee Journal, in Cleland and Brooks, 1:27.

28. John D. Lee Journal, 31 March 1849, in Cleland and Brooks, 1:104.

29. Minutes of 23 June 1850, Box 2, Folder 20, GCM.

30. Vilate Decker to Fanny Young Murray, 1848, MS 740, CHL.

31. Minutes of 9 Dec. 1847, Box 12, Folder 4, LJA.

32. Quorum of the Twelve minutes, 29 April 1849, in VW, 1:330–331; Snow poem of 7 Jan. 1846, Box 44, Folder 21, BYP; cf. Derr and Davidson, *Eliza R. Snow,* 319. On Young's homes, see Colleen Whitley, ed., *Brigham Young's*

Homes (Logan: Utah State University Press, 2002), chs. 5 and 6; Dean C. Jessee, "'A Man of God and a Good Kind Father': Brigham Young at Home," *BYU Studies* 40 (2001): 23–53.

33. ZHJ, 16 March and 10 April 1849, in Marilyn Higbee, ed., "'A Weary Traveller': The 1848–1850 Diary of Zina D. H. Young," *Journal of Mormon History* 19 (Fall 1993): 102, 104.

34. Eliza R. Snow Journal, 13 April 1849, in Maureen Ursenbach Beecher, ed., *The Personal Writings of Eliza Roxcy Snow* (Salt Lake City: University of Utah Press, 1995), 228; ZHJ, 16 April 1849, in Higbee, 105.

35. ZHJ, "very agreeable" (26 May 1849), "paneful loneliness" (19 March 1850), in Higbee, "'A Weary Traveller,'" 107–108, 118; "step sons" in Zina Huntington autobiographical sketch, n.d., CHL, transcription by Todd Compton in author's possession; Susa Young Gates notes, Box 12, Folder 3, SYGP.

36. ZHJ, "like aples" (21 July 1850) in Higbee, 119; "gave his family" and "like a God" in ZHJ, 11 June 1854, Box 1, Folder 2, MS 4780, CHL; "sniveling" from minutes of 11 June 1854, Box 2, Folder 55, GCM; "greeted me with more kindness" in ZHJ, 18 June 1854, Box 1, Folder 2, MS 4780. See Martha Sonntag Bradley and Mary Brown Firmage Woodward, *Four Zinas: A Story of Mothers and Daughters on the Mormon Frontier* (Salt Lake City: Signature Books, 2000), ch. 7; Todd Compton, *In Sacred Loneliness: The Plural Wives of Joseph Smith* (Salt Lake City: Signature, 1997), ch. 4.

37. Emily D. P. Young to BY, 30 June 1850 and 24 Feb. 1853, Box 66, Folder 18, BYP; cf. Compton, *In Sacred Loneliness*, 416–447; "distant association" from Quorum of the Twelve Minutes, 29 April 1849, in VW, 1:331.

38. Augusta Adams, last will and testament, 21 Feb. 1848; certificate of sealing in handwriting of Thomas Bullock, 14 April 1848, both in Box 66, Folder 7, BYP; Phineas Cook autobiography, n.d., MS 6288, CHL.

39. "a negro" in Adams to BY, undated (Thomas Bullock notation "about 1 September 1852"), Box 66, Folder 9, BYP; "excursion" (30 July 1850), "Queen" (16 Feb. 1851), "consort" (2 Dec. 1855), all in Schroeder Papers; Susa Young Gates notes, Box 12, Folder 2, SYGP.

40. "children" in Adams to BY, 17 Aug. 1850, Box 66, Folder 7, BYP; "in the flesh" in Adams to BY, 12 Jan. 1850, Box 66, Folder 8, BYP; "divorce" in Adams to BY, 23 Nov. 1850, in Schroeder Papers.

41. Adams to BY, n.d. (ca. 1850s) and 30 July 1850 (dress), Schroeder Papers.

42. Mary Ann Clark Powers to BY, 18 June 1851, Box 66, Folder 13, BYP. On the above divorces, see the information and analysis in Johnson, "Determining and Defining 'Wife,'" 63. On Mary Ann Clark Powers, see also John H. Keatley, *A History of Pottawatamie County, Iowa* (Chicago: O.L. Baskin, 1883), 87. In 1855, after two remarriages, Elizabeth Fairchild obtained an official certificate of divorce from Young. See Box 67, Folder 9, BYP.

43. MSS SC 68 Margaret Pierce Young Journal Fragment, HBLL.

44. Jemima Young to BY, 9 Sept. 1866, Box 44, Folder 9, BYP; Zina Huntington autobiographical sketch, n.d., CHL, transcription by Todd Compton in author's possession.

45. See the discussion in Compton, *In Sacred Loneliness*, 655, notes vi and vii.

46. John D. Lee Journal, 23 July 1848, in Robert Glass Cleland and Juanita Brooks, eds., *A Mormon Chronicle: The Diaries of John D. Lee, 1848–1876* (San Marino, CA: Huntington Library, 1955), 1:65; Beaman to Hyde, 8 April 1849, in Todd Compton, ed., "'Remember Me in My Affliction': Louisa Beaman and Eliza R. Snow Letters, 1849," *Journal of Mormon History* 25 (Fall 1999): 51–52.

47. ZHJ, 15 April and 14 May, in Higbee, 105, 107; Beaman to Hyde, 14 July 1849, in Compton, "Remember Me," 54–55; ZHJ, 27 Feb. 1850, in Higbee, 118; GAS to BY, 28 Jan. 1851, Box 42, Folder 4, BYP. See Compton, *In Sacred Loneliness*, 55, 652.

48. Ether 2:3.

49. Ezra T. Benson and George A. Smith to BY, 10 Oct. 1848, in Box 42, Folder 3, BYP. See Ronald W. Walker, "Thomas L. Kane and Utah's Quest for Self-Government, 1846–51," *Utah Historical Quarterly* 69 (Spring 2001): 100–119.

50. Dale L. Morgan, *The State of Deseret* (Logan: Utah State University Press, 1987), ch. 2. On Deseret's creation, see Peter Crawley, "The Constitution of the State of Deseret," *BYU Studies* (Fall 1989): 7–22.

51. "standard is to be raised" from Augusta Adams to Alexander and Mary Ann Badlam, 20 July [1849], Schroeder Papers; account of festivities in 24 July 1849 minutes, Box 2, Folder 13, GCM. See the account in Ronald W. Walker, "'A Banner is Unfurled': Mormonism's Ensign Peak," *Dialogue* 26 (Winter 1993): 83–86.

52. "dictated by the revelation" from minutes of 14 July 1850, Box 2, Folder 20, GCM; "puke them" from minutes of 26 Aug. 1849, Box 2, Folder 13, GCM. On the African American relationship to the Fourth of July, see Laurie Maffly-Kipp, *Setting Down the Sacred Past: African-American Race Histories* (Cambridge, MA: Harvard University Press, 2010), 41.

53. "appointing" in BY to Bernhisel, 19 July 1849, Box 16, Folder 17, BYP.

54. See Michael F. Holt, *The Political Crisis of the 1850s* (New York: W. W. Norton, 1978), chs. 2 and 3; Joel H. Silbey, *Storm Over Texas: The Annexation Controversy and the Road to Civil War* (New York: Oxford University Press, 2005), ch. 7.

55. Matthew J. Grow, *"Liberty to the Downtrodden": Thomas L. Kane, Romantic Reformer* (New Haven: Yale University Press, 2009), ch. 5.

56. *American Whig Review,* Aug. 1850, 208; Woodruff to Kane, 27 Nov. 1849, Box 16, Folder 28, Kane Papers, HBLL; BY to John M. Bernhisel, 19 July 1849. See Nathaniel R. Ricks, "A Peculiar Place for the Peculiar Institution: Slavery and Sovereignty in Early Territorial Utah" (M.A. thesis, Brigham Young University, 2007), ch. 2.

57. Bernhisel to BY, 27 March 1850, Box 60, Folder 9, BYP; WWJ, 4 Dec. 1849, 3:513.

58. Minutes of 6 July 1851, Box 2, Folder 31, GCM. See Howard Lamar, *The Far Southwest: A Territorial History, 1846–1912* (New Haven: Yale University Press, 1966), ch. 4.

59. On the clashes between the 1851 appointees and Mormon authorities, see

Norman F. Furniss, *The Mormon Conflict, 1850–1859* (New Haven: Yale University Press, 1960), ch. 2; Thomas G. Alexander, "Carpetbaggers, Reprobates, and Liars: Federal Judges and the Utah War (1857–58)," *Historian* 70 (Summer 2008): 215–222; Gene A. Sessions, *Mormon Thunder: A Documentary History of Jedediah Morgan Grant* (Urbana: University of Illinois Press, 1982), chs. 8 and 9.

60. "pettifogging" in discourse of 1 Aug. 1852, transcript of George D. Watt shorthand notes by LaJean Carruth; "drinks champagne" in minutes of 8 July 1849, Box 2, Folder 13, GCM; Kane to BY, 19 Feb. 1851, in Box 40, Folder 10, BYP; HOJ, 20 July 1851.

61. Minutes of 23 July 1851, Box 2, Folder 31, GCM, typescript by LaJean Carruth and John Turner.

62. "Power of the Priesthood" in HOJ, 23 July 1851; A. W. Babbitt to BY, 7 July 1850, Box 21, Folder 16, BYP, CHL; minutes of 24 July 1851, Box 2, Folder 31, GCM; non-Mormon appointees in attendance from DN, 19 Aug. 1851. I am grateful to Bruce Wayne Worthen for sharing his knowledge of Taylor's stance toward the Latter-day Saints.

63. On Brocchus's political ambitions, see HOJ, 17 Aug. 1851; Brigham D. Madsen, *Exploring the Great Salt Lake: The Stansbury Expedition of 1849–50* (Salt Lake City: University of Utah Press, 1989), 673; Joseph W. Coolidge to Brigham Young, 24 June 1851, Box 22, Folder 6, BYP.

64. Minutes of 8 Sept. 1851 Box 2, Folder 2, GCM, Box 2, Folder 32, typescript by LaJean Carruth and John Turner; Wells in DN, 19 Aug. 1851, 305.

65. WWJ, 8 Sept. 1851, 4: 62; minutes of 8 Sept. 1851.

66. BY to Amasa Lyman, 31 March 1852, Box 17, Folder 1, BYP; minutes of 1 Aug. 1852, Box 2, Folder 40, GCM; WWJ, 20 Feb. 1853, 4:206.

67. Bernhisel to Willard Richards, Box 4, Folder 7, MS 1490, CHL; "send another" in discourse of 4 Feb. 1852, in VW, 1:477; "bring their bread" in BY to Jedediah Grant, 31 Jan. 1852, Box 17, Folder 1, BYP; "higher law" in BY to Bernhisel, 28 Feb. 1852, copy in 1851–1862 Letter Book, Box 14, BYP.

68. Bernhisel to BY, 8 June 1852, Box 60, Folder 13, BYP; "Three Letters to the New York Herald, from J. M. Grant, of Utah," in Sessions, *Mormon Thunder,* appendices; "runaway judges" in DN, 21 Aug. 1852, 84.

69. WWJ, 4 Feb. 1851, 4:12.

70. "philosopher and show-speaker" from Jules Remy, *Journey to Great-Salt-Lake City* (London: W. Jeffs, 1861), 2:112; cf. B. Carmon Hardy, *Doing the Works of Abraham, Mormon Polygamy: Its Origins, Practice, and Demise* (Norman, OK: Arthur H. Clark, 2007), 76. For the text of Pratt's discourse, see *Deseret News Extra,* 14 Sept. 1852.

71. Discourse of 1 Aug. 1852, transcript of George D. Watt shorthand notes by LaJean Carruth.

72. Discourse of 1 Aug. 1852; BY to JMB, 14 Sept. 1852, 1851–62 Letterpress Copybook, Box 14, page 94, BYP.

73. Discourses of 8 Aug. and ("there is not a man") 29 Aug. 1852, both in Box 2, Folder 40, GCM.

74. See Hardy, *Doing the Works of Abraham,* ch. 2.

75. BY discourse of 29 Aug. 1852, transcript of George D. Watt shorthand notes by LaJean Carruth; Pratt to BY, 25 Oct. 1854, Box 41, Folder 11. See David J. Whittaker, "Bone in the Throat: Orson Pratt and the Public Announcement of Plural Marriage," *Western Historical Quarterly* 18 (July 1987): 293–314.

76. BY to JMB, 14 Sept. 1852, 1851–62 Letterpress Copybook, Box 14, page 93, BYP; JMB to BY, 8 Nov. 1852, Box 60, Folder 13, BYP; cf. Hardy, *Doing the Works of Abraham,* 80–81; Grow, *"Liberty to the Downtrodden,"* 91.

77. 20,000 from Dean L. May, "A Demographic Portrait of the Mormons, 1830–1980," in Thomas G. Alexander and Jessie L. Embry, eds., *After 150 Years: The Latter-day Saints in Sesquicentennial Perspective* (Provo, UT: Charles Redd Center for Western Studies, 1983), 48; Stegner, *The Gathering of Zion,* 6; "near nation" from Thomas O'Dea, *The Mormons* (Chicago: University of Chicago Press, 1957), 115.

78. Minutes of 8 Sept. 1850, Box 2, Folder 22, GCM; ". . . and Seer" from minutes of 9 Sept. 1851, Box 2, Folder 32, GCM; "profitable" from minutes of 7 April 1852, Box 2, Folder 37, GCM. Smaller church conferences in England and St. Louis had already affirmed Young as their "Prophet, Seer, and Revelator." See *Millennial Star,* 1 Aug. 1848, 234.

8. One Family

Minutes of 27 Dec. 1847, GCM.

1. Minutes of 12 March 1848, Box 2, Folder 2, GCM.

2. Minutes of 29 Dec. 1847, Box 1, Folder 60, GCM; minutes of 2 July 1848, Box 2, Folder 5, GCM.

3. David Rich Lewis, *Neither Wolf Nor Dog: American Indians, Environment, and Agrarian Change* (New York: Oxford University Press, 1994), chs. 2 and 3; Ned Blackhawk, *Violence Over the Land: Indians and Empires in the Early American West* (Cambridge, MA: Harvard University Press, 2006); Jared Farmer, *On Zion's Mount: Mormons, Indians, and the American Landscape* (Cambridge, MA: Harvard University Press, 2008), ch. 1.

4. John Corrigan, "Amalek and the Rhetoric of Extermination," in Chris Beneke and Christopher S. Grenda, eds., *The First Prejudice: Religious Tolerance and Intolerance in Early America* (Philadelphia: University of Pennsylvania Press, 2011), ch. 2.

5. "grafted in" from minutes of 15 April 1847, Box 1, Folder 55, GCM; "remnant" in 3 Nephi 20:16; "marshal" in D&C 87:5; "battle axe" from minutes of 8 April 1855, Box 3, Folder 2, GCM. See Ronald W. Walker, "Seeking the 'Remnant': The Native American during the Joseph Smith Period," *Journal of Mormon History* 19 (Spring 1993): 1–33. Smith's 1840 revision to the *Book of Mormon* altered 2 Nephi 30:6 to "a pure and a delightsome people"; other editions until 1981 employed the original "a white and a delightsome people."

6. "would be connected" in WWJ, 28 July 1847, 3:241; other quotes from min-

utes of 29 Dec. 1847, Box 1, Folder 60, GCM. See Nancy F. Cott, *Public Vows: A History of Marriage and the Nation* (Cambridge, MA: Harvard University Press, 2000), 26–27; Peggy Pascoe, *What Comes Naturally: Miscegenation Law and the Making of Race in America* (New York: Oxford University Press, 2009), ch. 3.

7. See Farmer, *On Zion's Mount*, ch. 1.

8. Minutes of 26 Nov. 1848, Box 2, Folder 7, GCM; Oliver B. Huntington Journal, February 1849, MSS 162, HBLL.

9. John D. Lee Journal, 10 March 1849, in Robert Glass Cleland and Juanita Brooks, eds., *A Mormon Chronicle: The Diaries of John D. Lee, 1848–1876* (San Marino, CA: Huntington Library, 1955), 1:100–101; HSJ, 8 Jan. 1850, 2:359; George Bean statement of 12 June 1854, in CR 100 397, Box 1, Folder 12; Alexander Williams and J. Willis to BY, 7 Jan. 1850, Box 22, Folder 1, BYP.

10. "wild" in BY to the "Brethren in the Utah Valley," 8 Jan. 1850, Box 16, Folder 19, BYP; "no captain" and "go and kill them" in minutes of 31 Jan. 1850, Box 2, Folder 17, GCM; "use up" in HOJ, 1 Feb. 1850; "everything I have" in Stansbury to BY, 4 Feb. 1850, Box 22, Folder 3, BYP; prayer circles HOJ, 10–14 1850; "quit the ground" and "prophesied" in minutes of 10 Feb. 1850, Box 2, Folder 17, GCM.

11. Minutes of 31 Jan. 1850; Gunnison to Martha Gunnison, 1 March 1850, in Brigham D. Madsen, *Exploring the Great Salt Lake: The Stansbury Expedition of 1849–50* (Salt Lake City: 1988), 270; Wells to BY, 13/14 Feb. 1850, and BY to Wells, 14/15 Feb. 1850, both in Box 2, Folder 1, Utah Territorial Militia Records, Series 2210, Utah State Archives; Will Bagley, *Frontiersman: Abner Blackburn's Narrative* (Salt Lake City: University of Utah Press, 1992), 170. Emphasis in originals. See Howard Christy, "Open Hand and Mailed Fist: Mormon-Indian Relations in Utah, 1847–52," *Utah Historical Quarterly* 46 (Summer 1978): esp. 223–227.

12. Minutes of 26 May 1850, Box 2, Folder 20, GCM.

13. See Lewis, *Neither Wolf Nor Dog*, ch. 3; Farmer, *On Zion's Mount*, 85–92.

14. Ronald W. Walker with Dean C. Jessee, "The Historians' Corner," *BYU Studies* 32 (1992): 125–135; Walker baptism in BY to Isaac Morley, 24 March 1850, Box 16, Folder 19, BYP. On Walker's early 1840s exploits, see Blackhawk, *Violence Over the Land*, 139–141.

15. BY to Indian Chiefs, 6 May 1850, Box 16, Folder 20, BYP; minutes of 22 May 1850, Box 74, Folder 42, BYP; record of baptism in Box 74, Folder 43, BYP. See Farmer, *On Zion's Mount*, 77–80.

16. BY to John M. Bernhisel, draft in Box 3, Folder 10, MS 1490, CHL.

17. Luke Lea, *Annual Report of the Commissioner of Indian Affairs . . .* (Washington: Office of the Commissioner of Indian Affairs, 1850), 4; cf. Lewis, *Neither Wolf Nor Dog*, 15. On the development of the mid-century reservation system, see Francis Paul Prucha, *The Great Father: The United States Government and the American Indians* (Lincoln: University of Nebraska Press, 1984), vol. 1, chs. 12–15.

18. Account of sale in BY, 11 Jan. 1852 testimony in *United States v. Pedro León et al.,* First District Judicial Court, in Box 47, Folder 36, BYP. On the Ute slave

trade, see Blackhawk, *Violence Over the Land*, 70–78, 106–112, 140–144, 240–244; Farmer, *On Zion's Mount*, 31–34; Sondra Jones, *The Trial of Don Pedro León Luján: The Attack against Indian Slavery and Mexican Traders in Utah* (Salt Lake City: University of Utah Press, 2000), chs. 2 and 3.

19. ZHJ, 16 June 1849, in Marilyn Higbee, ed., "'A Weary Traveller': The 1848–1850 Diary of Zina D. H. Young," *Journal of Mormon History* 19 (Fall 1993): 109–110.

20. BY, 11 Jan. 1852 testimony in *United States v. Pedro León*; BYOJD, 28 Sept. 1860, 146; 1860 U.S. Census, 18th Ward, Great Salt Lake City, Utah, page 214.

21. BY, 11 Jan. 1852 testimony in *United States v. Pedro León*; "buy up" in WWJ, 12 May 1851, 4:25; BY to Orson Hyde, 28 Feb. 1850, Box 16, Folder 19, BYP. See James F. Brooks, *Captives & Cousins: Slavery, Kinship, and Community in the Southwest Borderlands* (Chapel Hill: University of North Carolina Press, 2002).

22. BY to Luke Lea, 8 June 1852, Box 55, Folder 1, BYP; "whole flock" in William H. Ellison, "The Federal Indian Policy in California," *Mississippi Valley Historical Review* 9 (June 1922): 50; discourse of 8 May 1853, JD, 1:105; Sondra Jones, "Saints or Sinners? The Evolving Perceptions of Mormon-Indian Relations in Utah Historiography," *Utah Historical Quarterly* 72 (Winter 2004): 19–46.

23. The analysis here is congruent with Paul Reeve, *Making Space on the Western Frontier: Mormons, Miners, and Southern Paiutes* (Urbana: University of Illinois Press, 2006), 102.

24. BYJ1, 1 July 1835. On black New Yorkers in the early 1800s, see Phyllis F. Field, *The Politics of Race in New York: The Struggle for Black Suffrage in the Empire State* (Ithaca, NY: Cornell University Press, 2009), ch. 1.

25. Henry J. Wolfinger, "A Test of Faith: Jane Elizabeth James and the Origins of the Utah Black Community," in Clark Knowlton, ed., *Social Accommodation in Utah* (Salt Lake City: American West Center, University of Utah, 1975), 154; Kate B. Carter, ed., *Our Pioneer Heritage* (Salt Lake City: Daughters of Utah Pioneers, 1965), 8: 502. See also Newell Bringhurst, *Saints, Slaves, and Blacks: The Changing Place of Black People within Mormonism* (Westport, CT: Greenwood Press, 1981), 228.

26. Genesis 4; Genesis 9:18–27. See Thomas Virgil Peterson, *Ham and Japheth: The Mythic World of Whites in the Antebellum South* (Metuchen, NJ: Scarecrow Press, 1978); Stephen R. Haynes, *Noah's Curse: The Biblical Justification of American Slavery* (New York: Oxford University Press, 2002); Fay Botham, *Almighty God Created the Races: Christianity, Interracial Marriage, and American Law* (Chapel Hill: University of North Carolina Press, 2009), ch. 4. On black conversion leading to lighter skin, see Jon F. Sensbach, *Rebecca's Revival: Creating Black Christianity in the Atlantic World* (Cambridge, MA: Harvard University Press, 2005), 166, 197–199.

27. Moses 7:22; Abraham 1:21, 27; 2 Nephi 26:33. See Bringhurst, *Saints, Slaves, and Blacks*, chs. 1–5. For an example of Smith's application of the Curse of Ham, see *Messenger and Advocate*, April 1836, 289–291.

28. Wolfinger, "A Test of Faith," 152; V. Jacque Voegeli, *Free but Not Equal: The*

Midwest and the Negro during the Civil War (Chicago: University of Chicago Press, 1967), ch. 1.

29. Michael Burlingame, *Abraham Lincoln: A Life* (Baltimore: Johns Hopkins University Press, 2008), 364. On McCary, see Bringhurst, *Saints, Slaves, and Blacks,* 84–86; Connell O'Donovan, "Plural Marriage and African American Mormons: Race, Schism, and the Beginnings of Priesthood and Temple Denial in 1847," unpublished paper in author's possession.

30. WWJ, 26 Feb. 1847, 3:139; minutes of 26 March 1847, Box 1, Folder 52, GCM; cf. typescript in O'Donovan, "Plural Marriage and African American Mormons."

31. Minutes of 6 Sept. 1847, typescript in MS 2737, Box 101, CHL.

32. Appleby to BY, 2 June 1847, Box 21, Folder 5, BYP.

33. Minutes of 3 December 1847, Box 1, Folder 59, GCM. On Q. Walker and Enoch Lewis, see Connell O'Donovan, "The Mormon Priesthood Ban and Elder Q. Walker Lewis: 'An example for his more whiter brethren to follow,'" *John Whitmer Historical Association Journal* 26 (2006): 48–100. See Joel Williamson, *New People: Miscegenation and Mulattoes in the United States* (Baton Rouge: Louisiana State University Press, 1995), 94–97.

34. Minutes of 13 Feb. 1849, Box 2, Folder 8, GCM; "true eternal principles" in discourse of 5 Feb. 1852, Box 1, Folder 17, CR 100 317, CHL. On the origins of the church's exclusion of black men from the priesthood, see Lester E. Bush Jr., "Mormonism's Negro Doctrine: An Historical Overview," *Dialogue* 8 (Spring 1973): 11–68; Bringhurst, *Saints, Slaves, and Blacks,* chs. 5 and 7. Compare Ronald Esplin, "Brigham Young and Priesthood Denial to the Blacks: An Alternative View," *BYU Studies* 19 (Spring 1979): 394–402.

35. Bringhurst, *Saints, Slaves, and Blacks,* 224, 66–67, 219; *Acts, Resolutions, and Memorials, Passed by the First Annual, and Special Sessions, of the Legislative Assembly, Territory of Utah . . .* (Great Salt Lake City: Brigham H. Young, 1852), 91. On the political status of black Americans in the western United States at this time, see Eugene H. Berwanger, *The Frontier against Slavery: Western Anti-Negro Prejudice and the Slavery Extension Controversy* (Urbana: University of Illinois Press, 2002 [1967]), chs. 3–6.

36. William Crosby to BY, March 1851, Box 22, Folder 6, BYP, Church Archives. See William E. Parrish, "The Mississippi Saints," *Historian* 50 (August 1988): 489–506.

37. BY to Crosby, 12 March 1851, Box 22, Folder 6, BYP.

38. HOJ, 26 March 1851; William J. Flake to Church Historian, 14 February 1894, in Dennis L. Lythgoe, "Negro Slavery in Utah," *Utah Historical Quarterly* 39 (Winter 1971): 42.

39. "free soil" in BY to Bernhisel, 19 July 1849, Box 16, Folder 17, BYP; "God forbid" in WWJ, 1 June 1851, 4:31; "throat cutting" in minutes of 6 July 1851, Box 2, Folder 31, GCM.

40. DN, 10 Jan. 1852. Message read by Bullock from JH, 5 Jan. 1852.

41. Discourse of 23 Jan. 1852, George Watt report, Box 1, Folder 14, CR 100 317, CHL. Watt revised the above-quoted portion of the transcript: "In as much as we beleive in the Bible, inasmuch as I we beleive in the ordenances of God, in the Preisthood and order, ^and decrees^ of God, I we must beleive in

slavery." See George M. Frederickson, *The Black Image in the White Mind: The Debate on Afro-American Character and Destiny, 1817–1914,* rev. ed. (Middletown, CT: Wesleyan University Press, 1987), ch. 2.

42. Discourse of 5 Feb. 1852, George Watt transcript, Box 1, Folder 17, CR 100 317, CHL.

43. *Acts, Resolutions, and Memorials* (1852), 80–82. On the creation of slavery in the Utah Territory, see Nathaniel R. Ricks, "A Peculiar Place for the Peculiar Institution: Slavery and Sovereignty in Early Territorial Utah" (M.A. thesis, Brigham Young University, 2007), esp. ch. 3. In 1859, the New Mexico legislature reversed course and enacted a slave code. See Berwanger, *The Frontier against Slavery,* 119–120.

44. On the lack of national reaction to Utah slavery, see Ricks, "A Peculiar Place," ch. 4.

45. F. McKown to BY, 31 March 1849, Box 21, Folder 16, BYP; BY to Horace S. Eldredge, 12 July 1852, Box 17, Folder 3, BYP. Daniel Wells drafted the letter to Eldredge, which he explained was sent without Young's signature because of the latter's "temporary absence." Thomas Bullock's notes, however, make clear that Young "read correspondence" with Wells that evening, suggesting that the letter's message met with his approval. 12 July 1852, HOJ.

46. *Acts, Resolutions, and Memorials* (1852), 81. See David H. Fowler, *Northern Attitudes towards Interracial Marriage: Legislation and Public Opinion in the Middle Atlantic and the States of the Old Northwest, 1780–1930* (New York: Garland, 1987), 134–220; Pascoe, *What Comes Naturally,* ch. 1.

47. DN, 25 Dec. 1852; minutes of 23 March 1856, Box 3, Folder 10, GCM. See Berwanger, *The Frontier against Slavery,* esp. 93, 119.

48. Amasa Lyman to BY, 27 July 1854, Box 40, Folder 21, BYP; BY to Lyman and Charles C. Rich, 19 Aug. 1854, Box 17, Folder 14, BYP; 1860 U.S. Census, Utah, Great Salt Lake County, Union, page 262. See the helpful discussion in Ronald G. Coleman, "A History of Blacks in Utah, 1825–1910" (Ph.D. diss., University of Utah, 1980), 38–39, 57–59. I am grateful to Margaret Young for sharing the Amasa Lyman letter.

49. Various entries on James in Boxes 91–97, BYP.

50. "Have two Blacks" in WWJ, 1 June 1851, 4:31.

51. Jane E. James to Joseph F. Smith, 7 Feb. and 12 April 1890, Box 18, Folder 12, MS 1325, CHL; "decided that she might be" in minutes of 2 Jan. 1902, Box 78, Folder 7, typescript in George Albert Smith Papers, MS 36, UUSC. See Wolfinger, "Test of Faith," 148–154; Ronald G. Coleman, "'Is There No Blessing for Me?' Jane Elizabeth Manning James, A Mormon African American Woman," in Quintard Taylor and Shirley Ann Wilson Moore, eds., *African American Women Confront the West, 1600–2000* (Norman: University of Oklahoma Press, 2003), 144–162.

9. Go Ahead

Grant, letter of 8 April 1852 to the *New York Herald,* in Gene A. Sessions, *Mormon Thunder: A Documentary History of Jedediah Morgan Grant* (Urbana, IL: University of Illinois Press, 1982), 345.

1. Dean L. May, "A Demographic Portrait of the Mormons, 1830–1980," in Thomas G. Alexander and Jessie L. Embry, eds., *After 150 Years: The Latter-day Saints in Sesquicentennial Perspective* (Provo, UT: Charles Redd Center for Western Studies, 1983), 47; BY to Orson Hyde, 30 Jan. 1856 (emphasis in original), Letterpress Copybook 3, page 546, BYP.

2. Discourse of 13 June 1852, JD 1:92.

3. HOJ, 20 Dec. 1854.

4. Minutes of 16 Jan. 1848, Box 2, Folder 1, GCM.

5. William C. Staines Journal, Aug. 1855, MS 1850. On the Endowment House, see Lisle G Brown, "'Temple Pro Tempore': The Salt Lake City Endowment House," *Journal of Mormon History* (Fall 2008): 1–68; Richard E. Bennett, "'Line upon Line, Precept upon Precept,' Reflections on the 1877 Commencement of the Performance of Endowments and Sealings for the Dead," *BYU Studies* 44 (2005): 47–53. On adoption, see Jonathan A. Stapley, "Adoptive Sealing Ritual in Mormonism," *Journal of Mormon History* 38 (Summer 2011): 81–90.

6. HOJ, 27 Feb. 1853 and 14 March 1852.

7. Minutes of 9 April 1852, 9 April 1852, Box 2, Folder 37, GCM. For this and the following paragraph, I have relied heavily on David John Buerger, "The Adam-God Doctrine," *Dialogue* 15 (Spring 1982): 14–58; Blake Ostler, "The Idea of Pre-Existence in the Development of Mormon Thought," *Dialogue* 15 (Spring 1982): 59–78; Breck England, *The Life and Thought of Orson Pratt* (Salt Lake City: University of Utah Press, 1985), chs. 8 and 9; Gary J. Bergera, *Conflict in the Quorum: Orson Pratt, Brigham Young, Joseph Smith* (Salt Lake City: Signature Books, 2002), chs. 4 and 5.

8. Minutes of 4 April 1860, Box 70, Folder 16, BYP; cf. Bergera, *Conflict in the Quorum,* 181; "father of all" in D&C 27:11; "oldest man" in Willard Richards Pocket Companion, Box 2, Folder 6, MS 1490, CHL; cf. WJS, 8–9; Samuel Brown, "William Phelps's Paracletes, an Early Witness to Joseph Smith's Divine Anthropology," *International Journal of Mormon Studies* 2 (Spring 2009): 62–82.

9. Minutes of 2 Sept. 1849, Box 2, Folder 14, GCM; discourse of 8 Oct. 1854, VW, 2:845–854; "receive our resurrected bodies" in HOJ, 14 March 1852.

10. Snow poem of Jan. 1855 in Jill M. Derr and Karen L. Davidson, eds., *Eliza R. Snow: The Complete Poetry* (Provo, UT: Brigham Young University Press, 2009), 472.

11. Pratt, "The Holy Spirit," *Millennial Star,* 15 Oct. 1850, 308 (emphasis in original); cf. Ostler, "The Idea of Pre-Existence," 65; "boundless ocean" in Pratt, *The Holy Spirit* (Liverpool: L.D.S. Book and Star Depot, 1856), 53; cf. Bergera, *Conflict in the Quorum,* 129.

12. Thomas Evans Jeremy Journal, 30 Sept. 1852, MS 1249, CHL; cf. Bergera, *Conflict in the Quorum,* 126–127; BY to Orson Pratt, 29 July 1853 (emphasis in original), Box 17, Folder 9, BYP; "Adam was our God" in WWJ, 17 Sept. 1854, 4:288; "thumping lies" in minutes of 25 Nov. 1855, Box 3, Folder 8, GCM. On the dispute over Lucy Mack Smith's autobiography, see ch. 11.

13. Samuel W. Richards Journal, 11 March 1856 (emphasis in original), vol. 11,

MS 1841, CHL; cf. Bergera, *Conflict in the Quorum*, 126–127; "written revelations" in minutes of 20 April 1856, Box 3, Folder 11, GCM; "living oracles" in discourse of 30 March 1856, Box 2, Folder 15, CR 100 317, CHL. See Philip L. Barlow, *Mormons and the Bible: The Place of the Latter-day Saints in American Religion* (New York: Oxford University Press, 1991), ch. 3.

14. "Adam" in 11 March 1856, Samuel W. Richards Journal; "drowns" from discourse of 8 March 1857, JD, 4:266–267.

15. Discourse of 8 Feb. 1857, JD, 4:217.

16. BYOJD, 22/23 Feb. 1861 (emphasis in original), 212; L. John Nuttall, 7 Feb. 1877, excerpted in David John Buerger, *Mysteries of Godliness: A History of Mormon Temple Worship*, 2nd ed. (Salt Lake City: Signature Books, 2002), 112.

17. "List of President Young's Family Living in the 18th Ward," 19 March 1855, Box 170, Folder 26, BYP.

18. HOJ, 3 June 1858.

19. BY to Lydia Farnsworth, 22 Jan. 1857, Letterpress Book 3, page 304, BYP. Ironically, Young married Lydia Farnsworth fourteen years later.

20. 1850 Utah Census, Great Salt Lake County, 75.

21. Amanda Smith to BY, 9 Sept. 1850 and 16 Feb. 1852, Box 22, Folder 22, BYP; 2 April 1852 divorce certificate, Box 67, Folder 4, BYP. For Warren Smith's complaint, Orson Hyde to BY, undated (ca. 1852), typescript in MS 2736, Box 22, Folder 8. See Hulda Cornelia Thurston Smith, "O My Children and Grandchildren: An Account of the Sealing of Amanda Barnes Smith to Joseph Smith," *Nauvoo Journal* 4 (1992): 5–8.

22. Amanda Smith to BY, 19 Sept. 1852 and 10 Jan. 1856, Box 66, Folder 22, BYP; BY to A. Smith, 25 Jan. 1868, Letterpress Copybook 10, page 611, BYP; Amanda Barnes Smith Autobiographical Sketch, 1856, MS 2005, CHL; DN, 14 July 1886.

23. BY to Snow, 10 Sept. 1859, Letterpress Copybook 5, page 239, BYP; Clarissa B. Homiston to Snow, 30 Sept. 1859, Box 66, Folder 10, BYP; Lyman Homiston death in DN, 12 Oct. 1859, 256; Clarissa B. Homiston to BY, 20 April 1861, Box 66, Folder 10, BYP; Utah State History Burials Database, http://history.utah.gov/research_and_collections/cemeteries/index.html (accessed 26 Jan. 2011). On Clarissa Blake's marriages, see the research of Connell O'Donovan at <http://connellodonovan.com/essex_mormons.pdf (accessed 23 Sept. 2011).

24. BY to Joseph Young, 9 March 1846, Box 16, Folder 6, BYP; Julia Hampton to BY, 14 March 1860, Box 22, Folder 1, BYP; BY to Eldredge, 29 July 1853, Box 17, Folder 9, BYP; Brigham Hampton Young Diary, Folder 1, MS 2080, 64–65 and 70–71.

25. "Record of the mass Quorum held in Provo City," 13 March 1857, Elias Blackburn Papers, Vault MSS 785, HBLL; BY to Isaac Haight, 5 March 1857, Letterpress Copybook 3, pages 461–462, BYP.

26. BY to Ephraim Luce, 22 Dec. 1845, Box 65, Folder 1; BY to John Price, 20 Feb. 1856, Letterpress Copybook 2, page 578, BYP.

27. Mary Richardson to BY, 22 Feb. 1857, Box 65, Folder 4, BYP.

28. Minutes of 27 Jan. 1849, Box 2, Folder 8, GCM; BY to Mary Richardson, 5 March 1857, Letterpress Copybook 3, page 464, BYP.

29. Edmund Richardson to BY, 6 Sept. 1857, Box 65, Folder 4, BYP. See Annie Richardson Johnson and Elva Richardson Shumway, *Charles Edmund Richardson: Man of Destiny* (Tempe, AZ: Publication Services, 1982), ch. 1; Clare B. Christensen, *Before & After Mt. Pisgah* (Salt Lake City: 1979), 232–234, 237, 239.

30. Sarah B. G. Phelps to BY, 6 March 1849; W. W. Phelps to BY, 18 March 1849; Sarah B. G. Phelps to BY, 20 March 1849; BY to W. W. Phelps, 30 March 1849, all in Box 66, Folder 19, BYP; WWJ, 2 June 1857, 5:56. On divorce in early Utah, see Kathryn M. Daynes, *More Wives Than One: Transformation of the Mormon Marriage System, 1840–1910* (Urbana: University of Illinois Press, 2001), chs. 8 and 9; Eugene E. Campbell and Bruce L. Campbell, "Divorce among Mormon Polygamists: Extent and Explanations," *Utah Historical Quarterly* 46 (Winter 1978): 4–23.

31. HOJ, 15 and 17 Dec. 1858.

32. Discourse of 8 Oct. 1861, Box 4, Folder 24, CR 100 317, CHL.

33. BY to TLK, 30 Oct. 1854, Letterpress Copybook 1, page 723, BYP; cf. Matthew J. Grow, *"Liberty to the Downtrodden": Thomas L. Kane, Romantic Reformer* (New Haven: Yale University Press, 2009), 153.

34. Discourse of 5 July 1852, Box 1, Folder 27, CR 100 317, CHL; "democracy of Heaven" in minutes of 6 May 1854, Box 2, Folder 52, GCM; BY to JMB, 28 Feb. 1854, Letterpress Copybook 1, page 448, BYP. See Patrick Q. Mason, "God and the People: Theodemocracy in Nineteenth-Century Mormonism," *Journal of Church and State* 53 (Sumer 2011): 349–375.

35. Sylvester Mowry to Edward Bicknall, 17 Sept. 1854 and 27 April 1855, in Mulder and Mortensen, eds., *Among the Mormons,* 274, 277; BY Jr.'s involvement in HSJ, 25 Dec. 1854, 2:536; petition in 1851–62 Letterbook, Box 14, pages 225–226, BYP. See William P. MacKinnon, "Sex, Subalterns, and Steptoe: Army Behavior, Mormon Rage, and Utah War Anxieties," *Utah Historical Quarterly* 76 (Summer 2008): 227–246.

36. Minutes of 18 February 1855, Box 3, Folder 1, GCM; John F. Kinney to Caleb Cushing, 1 March 1855, in Records Relating to the Appointment of Federal Judges, Attorneys, and Marshals for the Territory and State of Utah, National Archives, microfilm copy at HBLL. See Michael W. Homer, "The Judiciary and the Common Law in Utah Territory, 1850–61," *Dialogue* 21 (Spring 1998): 97–108.

37. Steptoe to Pierce ("My dear General"), 25 April 1855, MS2/0278, Idaho State Historical Society Public Archives and Research Library; Kinney to Cushing, 1 April 1855, in Records Relating to the Appointment of Federal Judges, Attorneys, and Marshals for the Territory and State of Utah, National Archives, microfilm copy at HBLL; discourse of 16 March 1856, in JD, 3:258.

38. Discourse of 8 July 1855, Box 3, Folder 7, GCM.

39. BY to Bernhisel, 29 April 1854 (draft), Box 60, Folder 5, BYP; BY to JMB, 29 April 1854, 1851–1862 Letterbook, pages 149–150, BYP; "had eyes" in BY

to Stephen A. Douglas, 29 April 1854, Letterpress Copybook 1, page 515, BYP. I would never have noticed the crossed-out phrase without the careful research of Ardis Parshall, http://www.keepapitchinin.org/archives/brigham-invites-a-kiss/ (accessed 12 July 2010). See Fred R. Gowans, "Fort Bridger and the Mormons," *Utah Historical Quarterly* 42 (Winter 1974): 49–67.

40. Kinney to U.S. Attorney General Jeremiah Black, 20 March 1857, published in ASP, 11; BY to Bernhisel, 29 Oct. 1856, Letterpress Copybook 3, page 152, BYP.

41. HOJ, 16 April 1854. On the passage of the Kansas-Nebraska Act, see Nicole Etcheson, *Bleeding Kansas: Contested Liberty in the Civil War Era* (Lawrence: University of Kansas Press, 2004), ch. 1. See also Sean Wilentz, *The Rise of American Democracy, Jefferson to Lincoln* (New York: W. W. Norton, 2005), ch. 22.

42. JMB to BY, 13 Jan. 1854, Box 60, Folder 15, BYP; *National Era* (Washington), 2 April 1857, 54; cf. ASP 103; BY to Stephen A. Douglas, 29 April 1854, Letterpress Copybook 1, page 514, BYP. See Sarah Barringer Gordon, *The Mormon Question: Polygamy and Constitutional Conflict in Nineteenth-Century America* (Chapel Hill: University of North Carolina Press, 2002), 54–65.

43. JMB to BY, 1 Jan. 1855, Box 60, Folder 18, BYP; BY to JMB, 29 April 1852, Box 60, Folder 1, BYP.

44. "in common" 3 Nephi 26:19; D&C 42:30–35; Minutes of 18 May 1855, Box 3, Folder 6, GCM. See Leonard J. Arrington, et al., *Building the City of God: Community and Cooperation among the Mormons*, 2nd ed. (Urbana: University of Illinois Press, 1992), ch. 2.

45. Arrington, *Building the City of God,* ch. 4, app. II.

46. Ibid., ch. 4.

47. HOJ, 22 and 27 Nov. 1853. On Franklin, see Walter Isaacson, *Benjamin Franklin: An American Life* (New York: Simon and Schuster, 2003), 220–221. On the Deseret Alphabet, see Ronald G. Watt, *The Mormon Passage of George D. Watt* (Logan: Utah State University Press, 2009), ch. 7.

48. BY to Frederick Schönfield, 29 Nov. 1858, Letterpress Copybook 5, pages 3–4, BYP.

49. Wallace Stegner, *The Gathering of Zion: The Story of the Mormon Trail* (New York: McGraw-Hill, 1964), 1; $50,000 debt in minutes of 16 Sept. 1855, Box 3, Folder 7, GCM.

50. Arrington, *Great Basin Kingdom,* 162–169; Will Bagley, "'One Long Funeral March': A Revisionist's View of the Mormon Handcart Disasters," *Journal of Mormon History* (Winter 2009): 62–65.

51. Minutes of 16 Sept. 1855.

52. Young to Franklin D. Richards, 30 Sept. 1855, Letterpress Copybook 2, pages 389–392, BYP; "if the Saints" in E. H. Davis to Leonard Pickel, 9 Sept. 1843, microfilm in MS 8829, CHL; DN, 31 Oct. 1855, 268; cf. Bagley, "'One Long Funeral March,'" 61.

The standard work on the handcart companies remains Leroy R. Hafen and Ann W. Hafen, *Handcarts to Zion: The Story of a Unique Western Migration,*

1856–1860 (Glendale, CA: Arthur H. Clark, 1960). See also William G. Hart-ley, "The Place of Mormon Handcart Companies in America's Westward Mi-gration Story," *Annals of Iowa* 65 (2006): 101–123; Lyndia M. Carter, "The Mormon Handcart Companies," *Overland Journal* 13 (1995): 2–18. For ac-counts critical of Young's leadership, see Stegner, *The Gathering of Zion,* 221–259; David Roberts, *Devil's Gate: Brigham Young and the Great Mor-mon Handcart Tragedy* (New York: Simon and Schuster, 2008); Bagley, "'One Long Funeral March.'"

53. Taylor to BY, 21 Nov. 1855 and 16 April 1856, Box 43, Folder 6, BYP; BY to Taylor, 28 July 1856, Letterpress Copybook 2, page 896, BYP.

54. BY to Erastus Snow, 30 Sept. 1856, Letterpress Copybook 3, page 87, BYP.

55. Young's uncertainty about remaining trains in BY to Snow, 30 Sept. 1856.

56. Minutes of 4 Oct. 1856, Box 3, Folder 12, GCM; BY discourse of 5 Oct. 1856, in JD, 4:113.

57. BYOJA, 31 Oct. and 28 Nov. 1856. Statistics from Hafen and Hafen, *Hand-carts to Zion,* 193.

58. Kimball discourse of 2 Nov. 1856, in DN, 12 Nov. 1856, 282.

59. "clear" in discourse of 2 Nov. 1856, in Box 3, Folder 18, CR 100 317, CHL; cf. DN, 12 Nov. 1856, 284; "suffered severely" and "mortality" in BY to GQC, 7 Dec. 1856, Letterpress Copybook 3, pages 200–201, BYP; "many times" in discourse of 16 Nov. 1856, in DN, 26 Nov. 1856, 298.

60. Discourse of 2 Nov. 1856; Daniel Spencer Journal, 8 April 1857, MS 1566, CHL.

61. Discourse of 2 Nov. 1857; BY to Taylor, 30 Oct. 1856, Letterpress Copybook 3, page 134, BYP; Taylor to BY, 24 Feb. 1857, Box 43, Folder 6, BYP.

62. Discourse of 6 Oct. 1860, JD, 8:192.

63. On the Mormon reformation, compare Paul H. Peterson, "The Mormon Ref-ormation" (Ph.D. diss., Brigham Young University, 1981); Polly Aird, *Mor-mon Convert, Mormon Defector: A Scottish Immigrant in the American West, 1848–1861* (Norman, OK: Arthur H. Clark, 2009), chs. 11 and 12.

64. Joseph Fielding Journal, 1857, HBLL; Watt discourse of 14 Sept. 1856, LR 9629 11, CHL. See the analysis in Stephen C. Taysom, *Shakers, Mormons, and Religious Worlds: Conflicting Visions, Contested Boundaries* (Blooming-ton: Indiana University Press, 2011), 169–194.

65. WWJ, 2 March 1856, 4:405; cf. Ronald W. Walker, "Raining Pitchforks: Brigham Young as Preacher," *Sunstone* 8 (May–June 1983): 5–9; discourse of 14 Sept. 1856, Box 3, Folder 17, CR 100 317, CHL.

66. Franklin Richards to Orson Pratt, et al., 1 Nov. 1856, in *Millennial Star,* 14 Feb. 1857, 109.

67. "tried it" in John Moon Clements Journal, 4 Nov. 1856, in Sessions, *Mormon Thunder,* 220–221; WWJ, 8 Dec. 1856, 4:506. On Grant and the reforma-tion, see Sessions, *Mormon Thunder,* chs. 16–19.

68. BY discourse of 21 Sept. 1856, JD, 4:55–56; "astonished" in BYOJ57, 14 Jan. 1857; "go ahead" in BY to William Barton, 5 March 1857, Letterpress Copy-book 3, page 459, BYP; "Sisters" in BY to Ezra T. Benson, 26 Jan. 1857, Let-terpress Book 3, page 320, BYP.

69. Woodruff to GAS, 1 April 1857, Letterpress Copybook 1, 439, HOOC; "young wives" in WWJ, 15 Feb. 1857, 5:22.

70. BY to Uriah Butt, 17 Feb. 1857, Copybook 3, page 408, BYP. See Butt and Joseph Parramore to BY, 17 Feb. 1857, Box 64, Folder 5, BYP.

71. HCK to John S. Fulmer, 20 March 1857, Letterpress Copybook 3, page 474, BYP. Kimball explicitly described his advice as Young's counsel.

72. "three young girls" in WWJ, 14 June 1857, 5:58; "long tail" in BY to John Steele, 18 March 1857, Letterpress Copybook 3, page 488, BYP. See the analysis in Daynes, *More Wives Than One*, 165–166; Todd M. Compton, "Early Marriage in the New England and Northeastern States, and in Mormon Polygamy: What was the Norm?" in Newell G. Bringhurst and Craig L. Foster, eds., *The Persistence of Polygamy: Joseph Smith and the Origins of Mormon Polygamy* (Independence, MO: John Whitmer Books), 184–232.

73. Lowell C. Bennion and Thomas R. Carter, "Touring Polygamous Utah with Elizabeth W. Kane, Winter 1872–1873," *BYU Studies* 48 (2009): 184.

74. "transgressors" in discourse of 21 Sept. 1856, JD, 4:53; other quotes in discourse of 8 Feb. 1857, JD, 4:219–220.

75. WWJ, 21 Sept. 1856, 4:451; Haight to BY, 29 Oct. 1856, Box 24, Folder 19; Haight to BY, 25 Feb. 1857, Box 25, Folder 17, BYP; BY to Isaac Haight, 5 March 1857, Letterpress Copybook 3, pages 461–462, BYP.

76. Excommunication in Manti Ward Record, 5 Oct. 1856, LR 5253 11, CHL; Minutes of Sanpete County Court, 20 Oct. 1856, microfilm at HBLL Family History Library; Jones to BY, 8 Nov. 1856, Box 69, Folder 7, BYP; Ann Eliza Young, *Wife No. 19, or the Story of a Life in Bondage* (Hartford, CT: Dustin, Gilman, 1875), 280; MU, 285–286.

77. BY to Elizabeth Jones, 15 Nov. 1856, Letterpress Copybook 3, page 186a, BYP; WWJ, 2 June 1857, 5:54–55.

78. Concern about thieves spreading rumors in BYOJ57, 26 Jan. 1857; cf. ASP, 79, n. 22.; "tale bearers" in BY to Johnson, 3 Feb. 1853, Letterpress Copybook 3, page 352, BYP; "on the lookout" in 6 Feb. 1856 to "Bishops and Presidents, South," Letterpress Copybook 3, page 387, BYP.

79. Ardis E. Parshall, "'Pursue, Retake & Punish': The 1857 Santa Clara Ambush," *Utah Historical Quarterly* 73 (Winter 2005): 64–86.

80. BY to John R. Wooley, 2 April 1857, Letterpress Copybook 4, page 532, BYP. On the Parrish-Potter murders, see Polly Aird, "'You Nasty Apostates, Clear Out': Reasons for Disaffection in the Late 1850s," *Journal of Mormon History* 30 (Fall 2004): 173–191.

81. BY discourse of 22 June 1861, Box 4, Folder 16, CR 100 317, CHL.

82. Townsend, *The Mormon Trials at Salt Lake City* (New York: American News Company, 1871), 30; Joseph Young to BY, 26 June 1849, Box 44, Folder 2; HOJ, 11 March 1853; BYOJD, 23 March and 2 April 1860, 61–62, 66–67. On Rockwell, see Harold Schindler, *Orrin Porter Rockwell: Man of God, Son of Thunder*, 2nd ed. (Salt Lake City: University of Utah Press, 1983).

83. Discourse of 5 July 1857, in JD, 5:6. See Wilentz, *Rise of American Democracy*, 646; Mary P. Ryan, *Civic Wars: Democracy and Public Life in the American City during the Nineteenth Century* (Berkeley: University of California

Press, 1997), 139–145; Richard Maxwell Brown, *Strain of Violence: Historical Studies of American Violence and Vigilantism* (New York: Oxford University Press), ch. 5.

84. See Brown, *Strain of Violence,* ch. 4, esp. 101.

85. HSJ, 16 April 1857, 2:625; BY to GQC, 4 July 1857, Letterpress Copybook 3, page 690, BYP; discourse of 17 April 1853, JD 2:126.

86. Woodruff to George A. Smith, 1 April 1857, Letterpress Copybook 1, 440, HOOC; Peterson, "The Mormon Reformation," 76. On the development of ward-level worship, see Matthew Bowman, *The Mormon People: The Making of an American Faith* (New York: Random House, 2012), 138–141.

87. Manti Ward Record, September 1856–February 1857. Emphasis in original.

88. ZDHJ, 8 March 1857, Box 1, Folder 5, MS 4780, CHL; discourse of 21 Sept. 1856, in JD, 4:54–55.

89. Discourse of 16 Aug. 1857, Box 3, Folder 24, CR 100 317, CHL.

10. The Whirlwind

Peter O. Hansen Journal, undated entry, end vol. 1, MS 7057, CHL.

1. James Martineau Journal, 30 Dec. 1856, in Donald Godfrey and Rebecca Martineau-McCarty, *An Uncommon Pioneer: The Journals of James Henry Martineau, 1828–1918* (Provo, UT: Religious Studies Center, Brigham Young University, 2008), 58–59; "repent and forsake" in HSJ, 30 Dec. 1856, 2:613; "new Feature" in WWJ, 30 Dec. 1856, 4:524; "treason" in Woodruff to GAS, 2 Feb. 1857, Letterpress Copybook 1, 410, HOOC.

2. 6 Jan. 1857 memorial and draft, Box 54, Folder 7, BYP.

3. BY to Kane, 31 Jan. 1857, Letterpress Copybook 3, page 356, BYP. See Philip Shriver Klein, *President James Buchanan: A Biography* (University Park: Pennsylvania State University Press, 1962).

4. James Buchanan Henry, *The Messages of President Buchanan* (New York: n.p., 1888), 7.

5. JMB to BY, 17 March and 2 April 1857, Box 61, Folder 1, BYP; cf. ASP, 103–105, 106–107.

6. "Utah and Its Troubles," *New York Herald,* 20 March 1857, in ASP, 102–103; *Washington Star,* 21 March 1857. See the analysis in MacKinnon, "And the War Came: James Buchanan, the Utah Expedition, and the Decision to Intervene," *Utah Historical Quarterly* 76 (Winter 2008): 22–37.

7. Robert Tyler to James Buchanan, 27 April 1857, in David A. Williams, ed., "President Buchanan Receives a Proposal for an Anti-Mormon Crusade, 1857," *BYU Studies* 14 (Autumn 1973): 104. On the hastiness of Buchanan's decision, see Norman F. Furniss, *The Mormon Conflict, 1850–1859* (New Haven: Yale University Press, 1960), esp. 70.

8. Douglas, speech of 12 June 1857, *Illinois State Journal,* 13 June 1857; Lincoln, speech of 26 June 1857, *Illinois State Journal,* 29 June 1857; *Remarks of the Hon. Stephen A. Douglas on Kansas, Utah and the Dred Scott Decision . . .* (Chicago: Daily Times Book and Job Office, 1857), 13; cf. ASP, 136.

9. 3 May BYOJ57A; P. Jane Hafen, "'Great Spirit Listen': The American Indian in Mormon Music," *Dialogue* 18 (Winter 1985): 135. Accounts of the trip in Box 73, folder 13, BYP; BYOJ57A. See David Bigler, *Fort Limhi: The Mormon Adventure in Oregon Territory, 1855–1858* (Spokane, WA: Arthur H. Clark, 2003); William G. Hartley, "Thomas Corless and the Fort Limhi Mission," *Mormon Historical Studies* 2 (Fall 2001): 135–162.

10. Minutes of 14 June 1857, Box 3, Folder 16, GCM; BY to Kane, 29 June 1857, Letterpress Copybook 3, pages 667–670, BYP; Dame to Wells, 22 June 1857, Box 1, Folder 35, TMR; BY to A. O. Smoot and N. V. Jones, 30 June 1857, Letterpress Copybook 3, pages 650–651, BYP. On the covert shipments, see ASP, ch. 10.

11. WWJ, 22 Jan. 1857, 5:11; 1 May 1865 minutes, Box 3, Folder 44, GCM. See the account in Terryl L. Givens and Matthew J. Grow, *Parley P. Pratt: The Apostle Paul of Mormonism* (New York: Oxford University Press, 2011), ch. 14.

12. DN, 29 July 1857, 165.

13. Quotes from BYOJ57B, 24 July 1857, in Everett L. Cooley, ed., *Diary of Brigham Young, 1857* (Salt Lake City: Tanner Trust Fund, University of Utah Library, 1980), 49. Emphasis in original. Since at least 1859, writers have speculated that Young staged the messengers' arrival for dramatic effect, but the most reliable sources confirm the above narrative. See "The Utah Expedition," *Atlantic Monthly*, March 1859, 368; Cooley, *Diary*, 49–53, n. 52. For the messengers' arrival in Salt Lake City on the evening of 23 July, see HOJ, 23 July 1857.

14. Minutes of 25 Nov. 1855, Box 3, Folder 8, GCM.

15. Discourse of 26 July 1857, JD, 5:72–78.

16. Discourse of 2 Aug. 1857, in DN, 12 Aug. 1857, 180; BY to Eldredge, 8 Aug. 1857, Letterpress Copybook 3, pages 770–774, BYP; discourse of 16 Aug. 1857, Box 3, Folder 24, CR 100 317, CHL; cf. ASP, 239–243; Elias Smith Journal, 16 Aug. 1857, MS 1319, CHL; William Staines Journal, 16 Aug. 1857, MS 1580, CHL.

17. "with or without" in BY to Jacob Hamblin, 4 Aug. 1857, Letterpress Copybook 3, pages 737–738, BYP; discourse of 26 July 1857, JD, 5:76–77; discourse of 21 March 1858, in *A Series of Instructions and Remarks . . . at a Special Council, Tabernacle, March 21, 1858* (Salt Lake City: n.p., 1858), 3.

18. BY to Lewis Robison, 9 Aug. 1857, Box 18, Folder 6, BYP; Buchanan to Walker, 12 July 1857, excerpted in ASP, 179.

19. Discourse of 16 Aug. 1857; Matthew 27:7.

20. BY to Lewis Brunson ("copy sent to I. C. Haight"), 2 Aug. 1857 (emphasis in original), Letterpress Copybook 3, page 732, BYP; minutes of 8 and 9 Aug. 1857, Parowan Stake Historical Record, LR 6778 28, CHL; William Dame to DHW, 23 Aug. 1857, Box 1, Folder 38, TMR.

21. WWJ, 13 Aug. 1857, 5:76; DHW to Dame, 13 August 1857, William R. Palmer Collection, Special Collections, Gerald R. Sherratt Library, Southern Utah University, Cedar City, Utah.

22. Dimick Huntington Journal, 31 Aug. and 1 Sept. 1857, MS 1419 2, CHL.

23. Samuel Pitchforth Journal, 15 and 17 Aug. 1857, typescript at CHL; Jacob Hamblin Journal, 25 Aug. 1857, MS 1951, CHL; for Young repeating allegations see BY to James Denver, 6 Jan. 1858, Box 55, Folder 4, BYP; cf. Juanita Brooks, *The Mountain Meadows Massacre,* rev. ed. (Norman: University of Oklahoma Press, 1962), 158–159. Hamblin's statement appears in a portion of his journal written retrospectively, probably after the massacre. At a later date, Hamblin or someone else removed at least one page from his diary shortly after the above quote.

24. MMM, 125–126; Will Bagley, *Blood of the Prophets: Brigham Young and the Mountain Meadows Massacre* (Norman: University of Oklahoma Press, 2002), 214.

25. MMM, 132–134.

26. MU, 220.

27. Samuel Pitchforth Journal, 9 Sept. 1857, typescript at CHL; BY to Haight, 10 Sept. 1857, Letterpress Copybook 3, pages 827–828, BYP; HOJ, 10 Sept. 1857. Haight's letter to Young is not extant.

28. Shannon A. Novak, an anthropologist, questions Paiute participation in the slaughter. See Novak, *House of Mourning: A Biocultural History of the Mountain Meadows Massacre* (Salt Lake City: University of Utah Press, 2008), epitaph. While Mormons did most of the killing, it seems likely that some Paiutes were involved. See MMM, ch. 13; Bagley, *Blood of the Prophets,* ch. 8.

29. See Hurt to Interior Secretary Jacob Thompson, 4 Dec. 1857, in *Message of the President of the United States, Communicating . . . information in relation to the massacre at Mountain Meadows,* 36th Congress, 1st Session, Senate Exec. Doc. 42, 92–98. The published version misdates the letter to 1859, but the context is clearly 1857. See Will Bagley and David L. Bigler, *The Mormon Rebellion: America's First Civil War* (Norman: University of Oklahoma Press, 2011), 150–154.

30. Cox to BY, 6 Oct. 1857, Box 25, Folder 4, BYP; *Daily Alta California,* 17 Oct. 1857; GQC to BY, 30 Oct. 1857, Box 38, Folder 5, BYP.

31. Bagley, *Blood of the Prophets,* xviii, xvi; MMM, xiv.

32. BY to Daniel H. Wells, encrypted telegram of 14 Nov. 1874, 1873–75 telegram copybook, Box 12, BYP, decryption courtesy of Chad Foulger and Brian Reeves.

33. Young 1875 affidavit, printed in SLT, 3 Aug. 1875.

34. This conclusion is congruent with Brooks, *Mountain Meadows Massacre,* 219.

35. Lee to BY, 20 Nov. 1857, printed in Brooks, *Mountain Meadows Massacre,* 151–152; BY to James Denver, 6 Jan. 1858; *Accounts of Brigham Young,* House Exec. Doc. 29, 37th Cong., 2nd Sess., *Accounts of Brigham Young, Superintendent of Indian Affairs in Utah Territory* (Washington: Government Printing Office, 1862), 100–104. See the discussions in Bagley, *Blood of the Prophets,* ch. 10 and 253–254; Brooks, *Mountain Meadows Massacre,* 150–159.

36. MMM, 185.

37. HOJ, 19 June 1858; GAS to BY, 17 Aug. 1858, Box 42, Folder 7, BYP. See Bagley, *Blood of the Prophets*, 186–187.

38. WWJ, 26 Sept. 1857, 5:101. In his journal, Woodruff inserted this conversation "between President Young and Capt Van Vleit" some two weeks after it had taken place.

39. "not have an article" in BYOJ57B, 8 Sept. 1857, 78; "resist the orders" in BYOJB, 8 Sept. 1857; other quotes from WWJ, 13 Sept. 1857, 95–97. See Buchanan annual message of 8 Dec. 1857, *Congressional Globe*, 35th Cong., 1st sess., appendix, 5.

40. 15 Sept. 1857 proclamation, MSS 107, HBLL, printed in ASP, 284 and 286–288.

41. BY to "the Officer commanding the forces now invading Utah Territory," 29 Sept. 1857, in DN, 13 Jan. 1858, 354; BY to George D. Grant, Robert S. Burton, and Lewis Robison, 2 Oct. 1857, Box 18, Folder 7, BYP; BY to Wells, et al., 9 Oct. 1857, Box 18, Folder 8, BYP.

42. Homer Brown Journal, 24 Nov. 1857, MS 2181 1, CHL; Hickman and John Beadle, *Brigham's Destroying Angel . . .* (New York: G.A. Crofutt, 1872), 127–130, 206–211. See the analysis in David Bigler, "The Aiken Party Executions and the Utah War, 1857–58," *Western Historical Quarterly* 38 (Winter 2007): 457–476.

43. Young to Lewis Robison, 7 Sept. 1857, Letterpress Copybook 3, pages 822–824, BYP; cf. ASP, 299; Wells et al. to BY, 15 Oct. 1857, Box 47, Folder 51, BYP; cf. ASP, 300; Callister to Wells, 18 Oct. 1857, Box 3, Folder 2, Nauvoo Legion Adjutant General Letterbook, MS 1370, CHL; Wells et al. to BY, 18 Oct. 1857 (emphasis in original), Box 47, Folder 51, BYP; cf. ASP, 300.

44. *Brigham's Destroying Angel*, 124–125; *New York Tribune*, 7 Oct. 1871 (Joseph A. Young); Townsend, *Mormon Trials*, 29–33 (Wells); Jones, *Forty Years among the Indians* (Salt Lake City: Juvenile Instructor, 1890), 129–130. See the analysis and documents in ASP, 298–312.

45. BY to Wells et al., 16 Oct. 1857, Box 3, Folder 1, MS 1370; cf. Bigler and Bagley, *Mormon Rebellion*, 220; BYOJB, 16 and 17 Oct. 1857; HSJ, 18 Oct. 1857, 2:643.

46. BY to Wells et al., 17 Oct. 1857, Box 18, Folder 8, BYP; cf. ASP, 359–361; BY to Alexander, 16 Oct. 1857, Box 18, Folder 8, BYP; cf. Bigler and Bagley, *Mormon Rebellion*, 222–223.

47. "pray" in BYOJB, 15 Nov. 1857; "slaughter yard" in William A. Carter Diary, quoted in Bigler and Bagley, *Mormon Rebellion*, 228; "torment" in Wells to Lewis Robison and Robert Burton, 10 Nov. 1857, Box 47, Folder 55, BYP; "sure indication" in Wells to BY, 21 Nov. 1857, Box 47, Folder 53, BYP; cf. ASP, 453.

48. Discourse of 28 Feb. 1858, Box 2, Folder 28, CR 100 317, CHL.

49. Buchanan annual message of 8 Dec. 1857, 5. On the army's response to Mormon provocations, see Todd M. Kerstetter, *God's Country, Uncle Sam's Land: Faith and Conflict in the American West* (Urbana: University of Illinois Press, 2006), ch. 2.

50. Discourse of 15 Nov. 1857, JD 6:41; CLWJ, 21 March 1858, 26.

51. "tremendous uproar" in BY to Appleby, 6 Jan. 1858, pages 944–47l, BYP; "spicy correspondence" in BY to Bernhisel, 6 Jan. 1858, pages 953–954, BYP; memorial printed in *Deseret News Extra,* 7 Jan. 1858, copy in Box 53, Folder 7, BYP; "millions" in Charles Lowell Walker Journal, 16 Jan. 1858, in Karl A. and Katharine Miles Larson, eds., *The Diary of Charles Lowell Walker* (Logan, UT: Utah State University Press, 1980), 1:14.

52. Urological problems in ASP, 64, n. 1; "do more" in WWJ, 25 Feb. 1858, 5:169–170.

53. "connection" in 7 May 1857, Box 75, Folder 35, BYP; other dreams from HOJ, 16 April 1858, 18 May 1858, 22 Sept. 1858, and 17 Jan. 1859.

54. On the creation of the new army, see Bigler and Bagley, *Mormon Rebellion,* 269–274.

55. HOJ, 24 May 1858.

56. John D. Lee Journal, 8 Feb. 1858, in Robert Glass Cleland and Juanita Brooks, eds., *A Mormon Chronicle: The Diaries of John D. Lee, 1848–1876* (San Marino, CA: Huntington Library, 1955), 1:149. See Bigler, *Fort Limhi,* chs. 11 and 12.

57. Buchanan to Kane, 31 Dec. 1857 (three letters of the same date), Box 14, Folder 11, Kane Papers, HBLL. See the accounts in Grow, *"Liberty to the Downtrodden,"* 160–164; ASP, 503–509.

58. BY to Kane, 25 Feb. 1858, Box 14, Folder 12, Kane Papers, HBLL; WWJ, 25 Feb. 1858, 5:169.

59. See William P. MacKinnon, "Epilogue to the Utah War; Impact and Legacy," *Journal of Mormon History* 29 (Fall 2003): 244–245; Grow, *"Liberty to the Downtrodden,"* ch. 10.

60. Offer of pardon in TLK to Buchanan, ca. 15 March 1858, Box 14, Folder 13, Kane Papers, HBLL; "destitute" in BY to Kane, 9 March 1858, Box 14, Folder 13, Kane Papers, HBLL.

61. BY to Kane, 9 March 1858, draft in Box 18, Folder 10; BY to Johnston, 25 Nov. 1857, Box 18, Folder 9; Kane to Johnston, 13 March 1858 (two letters), Box 14, Folder 13, and 16 March 1858, Box 14, Folder 14, all in Kane Papers, HBLL. See Grow, *"Liberty to the Downtrodden,"* 177–179.

62. *A Series of Instructions and Remarks.* On the Move South, see Richard D. Poll, "The Move South," *BYU Studies* 29 (Fall 1989): 65–88.

63. BY inventory of goods for Move South, Box 98, Folder 2, BYP; BY to DHW, 22 April 1858, Box 73, Folder 30, BYP; minutes of 12 June 1858, Box 3, Folder 22, GCM.

64. Jesse Gove to Family, 4 April 1858, in Otis G. Hammond, ed., *The Utah Expedition: Letters of Capt. Jesse A. Gove* (Concord, NH: New Hampshire Historical Society, 1928), 145; HOJ, 13 April 1858. See the discussion in Bigler and Bagley, *Mormon Rebellion,* 300–305.

65. HOJ, 11, 13, and 14 April 1858.

66. Young to DHW, 20 May 1858, Box 73, Folder 30, BYP. Emphasis in original.

67. Cumming discourse of 25 April 1858, in Letterpress Copybook 4, pages 157–161, BYP; HSJ, 25 April 1858 (emphasis in original), 2:658; Adams in John

Taylor discourse, 25 April 1858, Letterpress Copybook 4, pages 167–168, BYP.

68. Discourse of Gilbert Clements, 25 April 1858, Letterpress Copybook 4, pages 169–179, BYP; discourse of John Taylor 25 April 1858 (emphasis in original), pages 164, 167; "enthusiastic" in BYOJC, 25 April 1858; "friend" in discourse of 25 April 1858, Letterpress Copybook 4, pages 153–156, BYP; "fine country" in HOJ, 25 April 1858.

69. HOJ, 28 April 1858.

70. Cumming to James Orr, 12 May 1858, draft in Box 14, Folder 17, TLK Papers, HBLL; Cumming to BY, Nov. 1857, typescript in MS 2736, Box 24, Folder 1, CHL. See MacKinnon, "Epilogue," 244; Grow, *"Liberty,"* 188–189.

71. HOJ, 20 May 1858. The reference to bedding down together is probably not sexual. See D. Michael Quinn, *Same-Sex Dynamics among Nineteenth-Century Americans: A Mormon Example* (Urbana: University of Illinois Press, 1996), ch. 3.

72. Henry Ballard Journal, 10 June 1858, MS 1699, CHL; cf. Bigler and Bagley, *Mormon Rebellion,* 320; regret over temple in HOJ, 17 May 1858; BYOD, 16 Feb. 1860, 39.

73. 6 April 1858 proclamation, House Exec. Doc. 2, 35th Cong., 2nd Sess., vol. 1, 69–72.

74. ASP, 135.

75. See Bagley and Bigler, *Mormon Rebellion,* ch. 13.

76. Minutes of 11 June 1858, Box 3, Folder 21, GCM; minutes of 12 June 1858, Box 3, Folder 22, GCM. Compare Powell and Mulloch to John Floyd, 26 June 1858, in *Annual Report of the Secretary of War, 1858,* 35th Cong., 2nd Sess., vol. 2, House Ex. Doc. 1, 168–172. See Bagley and Bigler, *Mormon Rebellion,* 325.

77. BY to Warren Snow, 26 June 1858, Letterpress Copybook 4, pages 271–272, BYP; HOJ, 30 June and 1 July 1858; Campbell to GAS, 24 July 1858, Box 5, Folder 15, GAS Papers, MS 1322, CHL; *Annual Report of the Secretary of War, 1858,* 6.

78. See Arrington, *Great Basin Kingdom,* 182–194.

79. BY to Van Vliet, 22 Oct. 1858, Letterpress Copybook 4, pages 491–495, BYP.

80. Discourse of 5 May 1861, Box 4, Folder 11, CR 100 317, CHL.

11. Let Him Alone

Mormoniad (Boston: A. Williams, 1858), 33; cf. William Deverell, "Thoughts from the Farther West: Mormons, California, and the Civil War," *Journal of Mormon History* 34 (Spring 2008): 8. Emphasis in original.

1. Schaff, *America: A Sketch of the Political, Social, and Religious Character* (New York: C. Scribner, 1855), 243; discourse of 7 July 1861, Box 4, Folder 20, CR 100 317, CHL.

2. BYOJD, 7 Aug. 1861, 279; Twain, *Roughing It* (Hartford, CT: American Publishing Company, 1872), chs. 13 and 15; *Puck,* 5 Sept. 1877. See Frank Luther Mott, *A History of American Magazines* (Cambridge: Harvard University Press, 1938–1968), 3:526–527.

3. Twain, *Roughing It,* app. A and B. On Twain and the Mormons, see Nicole Amare and Alan Manning, "American Prophets: Mark Twain and Joseph Smith Revisited," *Journal of Mormon History* 37 (Fall 2011): 151–172.

4. Maria Ward, *Female Life among the Mormons . . .* (New York: J. C. Derby, 1855), 141–142. On anti-Mormon and anti-Catholic literature, see David Brion Davis, "Some Themes of Counter-Subversion: An Analysis of Anti-Masonic, Anti-Catholic, and Anti-Mormon Literature," *Mississippi Valley Historical Review* 47 (Sept. 1960): 205–224.

5. John Hyde Jr., *Mormonism: Its Leaders and Designs* (New York: W.P. Fetridge, 1857), 171; Richard Burton, *City of the Saints . . .* (New York: Harper and Brothers, 1862), 240; *New York Tribune,* 20 Aug. 1859.

6. Hyde, *Mormonism,* 154; Burton, *City of the Saints,* 240.

7. Minutes of 8 Oct. 1859, Box 48, Folder 2, BYP.

8. "sucking" and "miserable" in BY to DHW, 24 Dec. 1858, Letterpress Copybook 5, page 11, BYP; "tanned" in RMS, 402.

9. "baby Judge" in discourse of 22 June 1861, Box 4, Folder 17, CR 100 317, CHL; "cognisance in" *Valley Tan,* 26 Nov. 1858. See David L. Bigler, *Forgotten Kingdom: The Mormon Theocracy in the American West, 1847–1896* (Spokane, WA: Arthur H. Clark, 1998), 130.

10. "pistols and knives" in HOJ, 1 Dec. 1858; "melancholy" in NYT, 3 Jan. 1859; "set down" in HOJ, 26 Feb. 1859. See Donald R. Moorman and Gene A. Sessions, *Camp Floyd and the Mormons: The Utah War* (Salt Lake City: University of Utah Press, 1992), 103–106; Norman F. Furniss, *The Mormon Conflict, 1850–1859* (New Haven: Yale University Press, 1960), 208–214.

11. HOJ, 4 Nov. 1858. On Cradlebaugh's 1859 judicial activities in Utah, see Will Bagley and David L. Bigler, *The Mormon Rebellion: America's First Civil War* (Norman: University of Oklahoma Press, 2011), ch. 14; Furniss, *Mormon Conflict,* 215–221; Polly Aird, *Mormon Convert, Mormon Defector: A Scottish Immigrant in the American West, 1848–1861* (Norman, OK: Arthur H. Clark, 2009), ch. 16; Moorman and Sessions, *Camp Floyd,* ch. 6.

12. Cumming to Cradlebaugh, 18 Jan. 1859, copy in Box 48, Folder 6, BYP; Johnston to Lorenzo Thomas, 10 March 1858, in Records of the War Department, Department of Utah, Letters Sent 1857–60, National Archives, microfilm at HBLL.

13. "some person" in DN, 16 March 1859, 9; Smith to BY, 7 March 1859, Box 48, Folder 23, BYP; "cut off" in Smith to BY, 16 March 1859, Box 48, Folder 25, BYP.

14. Cradlebaugh and Sinclair to Buchanan, 7 April 1859, Records Relating to the Appointment of Federal Judges, Attorneys, and Marshals for the Territory and State of Utah, National Archives, microfilm at HBLL; "combined effort" and "turn the savages" in *Valley Tan,* 29 March 1859.

15. Quotes from HOJ, 24 April 1859 (emphasis in original). See WWJ, 23 and 24 April 1859, 5:329–330.
16. Campbell to F. J. Porter, 6 July 1859, in *Message of the President of the United States, Communicating . . . in relation to the massacre at Mountain Meadows,* 36th Cong., 1st Sess., Senate Ex. Doc. 42, 15.
17. Black to Cradlebaugh and Sinclair, 17 May 1859, Records Relating to the Appointment of Federal Judges, Attorneys, and Marshals for the Territory and State of Utah, National Archives, microfilm at HBLL. This retained draft conveys a more severe and lengthy reprimand than the version that appeared in *Message of the President of the United States,* Senate Ex. Doc. 32, 36th Congress, 1st Sess., 2–4.
18. "one eyed enemy" in BY to William Hooper, 12 April 1860, Letterpress Copybook 5, page 453, BYP. Emphasis in original.
19. Black to Wilson, 17 May 1859; Forney to Wilson, 10 Aug. 1859, both in *Message of the President of the United States,* 36th Congress, 1st Sess., Senate Ex. Doc. 32, 9–10, 32, 55.
20. HOJ, 18 June 1859; Eckels to Cass, 27 Sept. 1859, copy in Box 48, Folder 41, BYP. See Thomas Alexander, *Brigham Young, the Quorum of the Twelve, and the Investigation of the Mountain Meadows Massacre* (Logan: Utah State University Press, 2007).
21. BY to Horace Eldredge, 5 May 1859, Letterpress Copybook 5, page 130, BYP. On Lee during these years, see Juanita Brooks, *John Doyle Lee: Zealot, Pioneer Builder, Scapegoat,* rev. ed. (Glendale, CA: Arthur H. Clark, 1972), 257–302.
22. WWJ, 25 May 1861, 5:577.
23. Leavitt, quoted in Juanita Brooks, *The Mountain Meadows Massacre,* rev. ed. (Norman: University of Oklahoma Press, 1962), 183, n. 16; Carleton's allegation in WWJ, 13 March 1862, 6:32; Jenson, notes on conversation with Samuel Knight (ca. 1892), in Richard E. Turley and Ronald W. Walker, eds., *Mountain Meadows Massacre: The Andrew Jenson and David H. Morris Collections* (Provo, UT: Brigham Young University Press, 2009), 266; Purple in Barbara Jones Brown, "Mountain Meadows Monuments and the 'Marvelous Flood' of 1862," paper presented at the 2011 annual meeting of the Mormon Historical Association.
24. John D. Lee Journal, 30 May 1861, in Robert Glass Cleland and Juanita Brooks, eds., *A Mormon Chronicle: The Diaries of John D. Lee, 1848–1876* (San Marino, CA: Huntington Library, 1955), 1:314.
25. Discourse of 22 May 1859, transcript of George D. Watt shorthand notes by LaJean Carruth.
26. There are a variety of references to Young's dental issues in the 1860–1862 HOJ and BYOJD. On Young's cure for the "piles," see BYOJD, 2 March 1860, 45–46. For "tic doloreaux," see 5 Dec. 1858 BYOJD, 17. Waist size from list of measurements in Box 100, Folder 13, BYP. On Young's health, see Lester Bush, "Brigham Young in Life and Death: A Medical Overview," *Journal of Mormon History* 5 (1978): 79–103.

27. Discourse of 16 June 1861, Box 4, Folder 15, CR 100 317, CHL; "more girls" in discourse of 6 Sept. 1857, JD, 5:210; discourse of 1 June 1862, Box 4, Folder 28, CR 100 317, CHL.

28. "foundation" in discourse of 22 May 1859, transcript of George D. Watt shorthand notes by LaJean Carruth; "celestialized" in discourse of 7 Oct. 1860, JD, 8:200; "every faithful" in discourse of 27 Aug. 1867, Box 5, Folder 26, CR 100 317, CHL.

29. "not going to wait" in discourse of 23 February 1862, JD, 9:284; "come here" in 1864 memorandum book, Box 100, Folder 1, BYP.

30. "order of heaven" in discourse of 6 Oct. 1859, JD, 7:267; "absolute independence" in discourse of 19 June 1859, JD, 7:192; "being a son" in discourse of 30 Nov. 1862, in Box 4, Folder 33, CR 100 317, CHL.

31. "independent" in discourse of 6 April 1862, JD, 9:274; "still break it" in discourse of 7 April 1861, JD, 9:35. See Leonard Arrington, *Great Basin Kingdom: An Economic History of the Latter-day Saints, 1830–1900* (Cambridge, MA: Harvard University Press, 1958), 215–223.

32. BY to Lyman and Rich, 13 Sept. 1860, Letterpress Copybook 6, pages 598–600, BYP. On the down-and-back system, see William G. Hartley, "Brigham Young's Overland Trail Revolution: The Creation of the 'Down-and-Back' Wagon Train System, 1860–61," *Journal of Mormon History* 28 (Spring 2002): 1–30.

33. See the conclusion in Hartley, "Overland Trails Revolution," 3.

34. GAS to T. B. H. Stenhouse, 2 Nov. 1858, Letterpress Copybook 1, 606, HOOC; flagstaff in minutes of 17 Aug. 1864, Box 3, Folder 41, GCM. See Moorman and Sessions, *Camp Floyd and the Mormons*, ch. 15; Arrington, *Great Basin Kingdom*, 196–199.

35. Discourse of 8 July 1863, JD, 10:229. Arrington, *Great Basin Kingdom*, 199–200.

36. BYOJD, 17 Jan. 1861, 195; *Report of the Grand Jury of the Second District of Utah Territory, September Term, 1859* (Carson Valley: Office of the Territorial Enterprise, 1859); "slavery" in discourse of 25 Oct. 1863, JD, 10:271; BY to Leonard Butterfield, 5 Feb. 1864, Letterpress Copybook 7, page 756, BYP. On the creation and enlargement of the Nevada and Colorado territories, see W. Paul Reeve, *Making Space on the Western Frontier: Mormons, Miners, and Southern Paiutes* (Urbana: University of Illinois Press, 2006), ch. 3; William P. MacKinnon, "'Like Splitting a Man Up His Backbone': The Territorial Dismemberment of Utah, 1850–1896," *Utah Historical Quarterly* 71 (Spring 2003): 100–124.

37. BY consecrated deed printed in Leonard J. Arrington et al., *Building the City of God: Community and Cooperation among the Mormons*, 2nd ed. (Urbana: University of Illinois Press, 1992); *New York Tribune*, 20 Aug. 1859; "abundance" in Oregon Territory, Vol. 1, p. 278 (entry on Horace S. Eldredge), R. G. Dun & Co. Collection, Baker Library Historical Collections, Harvard Business School, Boston, Mass.

38. "best material" and "thread" in BY to Hooper, 29 Nov. 1860, Letterpress Copybook 5, pages 640–641; "roan calf" in BY to Brigham Young Jr., 24

June 1863 to Letterpress Copybook 6, page 624; "goatskin" in George Q. Cannon, Nov. 1861, Letterpress Copybook 6, page 28; piano in BY to Horace Eldredge, 5 June 1863, Letterpress Copybook 6, page 603, all in BYP. Emphasis in originals. See the discussion in Richard Bushman, *The Refinement of America: Persons, Houses, Cities* (New York: Knopf, 1992), esp. 262–279.

39. "heaps" in discourse of 15 July 1860, JD, 8:125; "not to be called" in discourse of 4 March 1860, JD, 8:12; "private affairs" discourse of 8 Oct. 1860, JD, 8:202.

40. Leonard Arrington, "The Settlement of the Brigham Young Estate," *Pacific Historical Review* 21 (Feb. 1952): 7; BY account with Trustee-in-Trust, Box 103, Folder 6, BYP.

41. List of Workers, ca. 1863–64, Box 104, Folder 11, BYP; cf. Arrington, *Brigham Young: American Moses* (New York: Alfred A. Knopf, 1985), 336–337; Clawson in 1858 Memorandum Book, Box 98, Folder 7, BYP; Ronald G. Watt, *The Mormon Passage of George D. Watt: First British Convert, Scribe for Zion* (Logan: Utah State University Press, 2009), 229–230.

42. "smart man," BYOJD, 2 Feb. 1861, 204; "many wives," BYOJD, 28 July 1861. See E. B. Long, *The Saints and the Union: Utah Territory during the Civil War* (Urbana: University of Illinois Press, 1981), which led to many of the below sources.

43. BYOJD, 2 Feb. 1861, 204; BYOJD, 9 July 1861, 266.

44. Discourse of 19 Jan. 1862, JD, 9:157; "abolish slavery" in BYOJD, 5 July 1860, 112; Hinter Rowan Helper, *The Impending Crisis of the South: How to Meet It* (New York: Burdick Brothers, 1857). See David Brown, *Southern Outcast: Hinter Rowan Helper and the Impending Crisis of the South* (Baton Rouge: Louisiana State University Press, 2006), esp. chs. 6 and 7.

45. See Alvin M. Josephy Jr., *The Civil War in the American West* (New York: Knopf, 1992), ch. 1.

46. "would be glad" in BYOJD, 16 Sept. 1861, 290; "did not wish" in WWJ, 10 March 1861, 5:559; "not seceded" in DN, 18 Oct. 1861, 189; "home guard" in BY to Bernhisel, 30 Dec. 1861, Letterpress Copybook 6, page 80, BYP; "in Hell" in WWJ, 11 Dec. 1861, 5:605. See Long, *The Saints and the Union,* 65.

47. BY to Hooper, 20 Dec. 1860, Letterpress Copybook 5, page 652, BYP.

48. BY to Dwight Eveleth, 23 July 1861, Letterpress Copybook 5, page 841, BYP; Wells to Chauncey West, 12 Aug. 1861, Letterpress Copybook 5, page 857, BYP; Smith to Hyde, 9 Jan. 1861, Letterpress Copybook 1, 959, HOOC; HOJ, 14 Feb. 1862.

49. HOJ, 28 April 1861.

50. HOJ, 22 Dec. 1861; Dawson to Wells, 21 Dec. 1861, in DN, 25 Dec. 1861, 208; Dawson to Lincoln, 13 Jan. 1862, transcribed and annotated by the Lincoln Studies Center, Knox College, Galesburg, Illinois. Available at *Abraham Lincoln Papers at the Library of Congress,* Manuscript Division (Washington, D.C.: American Memory Project, [2000–01]), http://memory.loc.gov/ammem/alhtml/alhome.html (accessed 18 Jan. 2011); WWJ, 23 Dec. 1861, 5:609.

51. "threatened" in HOJ, 30 Dec. 1861; Albina Williams affidavit of 26 Dec.

1861, Box 49, Folder 5, BYP; "choice set" in BYOJD, 1 Jan. 1862, 331; "gore" in WWJ, 1 Jan. 1862, 6:4; Dawson to Lincoln, 13 Jan. 1862; RMS, 592. See Harold Schindler, *Orrin Porter Rockwell: Man of God, Son of Thunder,* 2nd ed. (Salt Lake City: University of Utah Press, 1983), 315–318; Will Bagley, "Conan Doyle Was Right: Danites, Avenging Angels, and Holy Murder in the Mormon West," in Leslie S. Klinger, ed., *A Tangled Skein: A Companion Volume to the Baker Street Irregulars' Expedition to the Country of the Saints* (New York: Baker Street Irregulars, 2008), 7–8.

52. Discourse of 6 Jan. 1862, Box 4, Folder 27, CR 100 317, CHL; WWJ, 22 Jan. 1862, 6:10–11. See Dale L. Morgan, *The State of Deseret* (Logan: Utah State University Press, 1987), ch. 4.

53. HOJ, 18 April 1862; BYOJD, 21 April 1862, 369.

54. Thomas to BY, 28 April 1862, OR, ser. 3, vol. 2, 27; James Craig to Henry Halleck, 25 Aug. 1862, OR, ser. 1, vol. 13, 596; BY to Lorenzo Thomas, 25 Aug. 1862, Box 45, Folder 25, BYP; discourse of 8 March 1863, JD, 10:107.

55. Bernhisel to BY, 28 Feb. 1862, Box 61, Folder 5, BYP; discourse of 6 July 1862, JD, 9:322; BY to Hooper, 21 Feb. 1863, Letterpress Copybook 6, pages 493–494, BYP.

56. WWJ, 19 Jan. 1863, 6:92, 93.

57. "treasonable sentiments" in U.S. Army Headquarters District of Utah, Orders, No. 1, 6 Aug. 1861, OR, ser. 1, vol. 50, pt. 2, 55; "community of traitors" in Connor to R. C. Drum, 14 Sept. 1862, OR, ser. 1, vol. 50, pt. 2, 119–120. See Long, *The Saints and the Union,* ch. 6; Bigler, *Forgotten Kingdom,* ch. 11; Brigham D. Madsen, *Glory Hunter: A Biography of Patrick Edward Connor* (Salt Lake City: University of Utah Press, 1990), ch. 5.

58. Harding to Seward, 30 Aug. 1862, Utah Territorial Papers, U.S. Department of State, Record Group 59, National Archives, microfilm copy at HBLL; cf. Long, *The Saints and the Union,* 119–120; minutes of 30 Oct. 1862 (emphasis in original), Box 3, Folder 33, GCM; "mother and her daughters" in 37th Cong., 3rd Sess., Senate Misc. Doc. 37, 6; HOJ, 11 Dec. 1862.

59. "handsome and magnetic" from Susa Young Gates notes, Box 11, Folder 9, SYGP.

60. Anonymous to BY, Feb. 1863, Box 44, Folder 23, BYP. While there are extant letters from most of Young's other household wives, there are no identified letters from Emmeline's hand for the purposes of comparison.

61. Discourse of 7 April 1861, JD, 9:3–5; M. R. Werner, *Brigham Young* (New York: Harcourt, Brace, 1925), chs. 7 and 8; "love match" from Susa Young Gates, "Recollections," Box 12, Folder 3, SYGP.

62. Stenhouse, *"Tell It All": The Story of a Life's Experience in Mormonism* (Hartford, CT: A. D. Worthington, 1874), 282; Ann Eliza Young, *Wife No. 19, or the Story of a Life in Bondage* (Hartford, CT: Dustin, Gilman, 1875), 531; *New York World,* 17 Nov. 1869; "refrained" in Box 11, Folder 9, SYGP; Mary Ann Angell to BY, 15 Jan. 1873, Philip T. Blair Papers, MS 120, Box 1, Folder 22, UUSC.

63. WWJ, 9 Feb. 1862, 6:17; "favorite" in SLT, 11 March 1894; "could not pay" in Box 12, Folder 3, SYGP.

64. Drake and Waite to Lincoln, 6 March 1863, transcribed and annotated by the Lincoln Studies Center, Knox College, Galesburg, Illinois. Available at *Abraham Lincoln Papers at the Library of Congress,* Manuscript Division (Washington, D.C.: American Memory Project, [2000–01]), http://memory.loc.gov/ammem/alhtml/alhome.html (accessed 1 Feb. 2011); Harding to Seward, 3 Feb. 1862, State Department Territorial Papers: Utah Series, Reel 2, National Archives, microfilm at HBLL. Emphasis in original.

65. Bernhisel to BY, 6 Feb. 1863, Box 61, Folder 8, BYP; BY to Fuller, 30 March 1863 and minutes of 3 March 1863 discourse, in Letterpress Copybook 6, pages 550–555, BYP; Wright to Thomas, 30 March 1863, OR ser. 1, vol. 50, pt. 2, 369–374; Drake and Waite to Lincoln, 6 March 1863.

66. Connor to Drum, 15 March 1863, OR ser. 1, vol. 50, pt. 2, 372; Halleck to Connor, 19 March 1863, OR ser. 1, vol. 50, pt. 2, 358.

67. Creighton to Young, telegram of 5 March 1863, Box 45, Folder 26, BYP; Sibley to Stager, 10 March 1863, *Abraham Lincoln Papers at the Library of Congress,* Manuscript Division (Washington, D.C.: American Memory Project, [2000–02]), http://memory.loc.gov/ammem/alhtml/alhome.html (accessed 12 June 2011); Stenhouse to BY, 7 June 1863, Box 29, Folder 13, BYP.

68. R. C. Drum to Connor, 16 July 1864, OR, ser. 1, vol. 50, pt. 2, 909–910; discourse of 23 Jan. 1865, Wilford Woodruff transcript, Box 5, Folder 1, CR 100 317, CHL. Emphasis in original. A gimlet is a small tool that bores holes with a screw point.

69. Discourse of 30 June 1861, Box 4, Folder 19, CR 100 317, CHL; WWJ, 7 April 1861, 5:563–564.

70. Discourse of 6 Sept. 1857, JD, 5:210, 212; BYOJD, 5 Oct. 1860, 152–153.

71. WWJ, 27 Jan. 1860, 5:420–430. For a discussion of the 1860 confrontation with Pratt and generous excerpts of key documents, see Gary J. Bergera, *Conflict in the Quorum: Orson Pratt, Brigham Young, Joseph Smith* (Salt Lake City: Signature Books, 2002), chs. 6–9.

72. "makes me appear" in HOJ, 4 April 1860; minutes of 4 April 1860, Box 70, Folder 16; cf. Bergera, *Conflict in the Quorum,* 183.

73. BYOJD, 5 April 1860, 69.

74. BYOJD, 1 Oct. 1860, 148; BY to Wells, 6 Nov. 1857, Box 18, Folder 9, BYP. I am grateful to William MacKinnon for bringing the latter example to my attention.

75. Morris to BY, 13 Oct. 1858, 20 April 1860, 20 Nov. 1860, Box 87, Folders 6 and 7; cf. C. LeRoy Anderson, *For Christ Will Come Tomorrow: The Saga of the Morrisites* (Logan: Utah State University Press, 1981), 33, 50, 53. See also G. M. Howard, "Men, Motives, and Misunderstandings: A New Look at the Morrisite War of 1862," *Utah Historical Quarterly* 44 (Spring 1976): 112–132.

76. Morris revelation of 23 October 1861, in *The Spirit Prevails: Containing the Revelations, Articles and Letters Written by Joseph Morris* (San Francisco: J.A. Dove, 1886), 177; RMS, 594; NYT, 21 June 1861; cf. Val Holley, "Slouching Towards Slaterville: Joseph Morris's Wide Swath in Weber County," *Utah Historical Quarterly* 76 (Summer 2008): 248.

77. 12 Aug. 1861, BYOJD, 281; 16 June 1862, WWJ, 6:56; "Weber River prophet" from HOJ, 11 June 1862.

78. BY to JMB, 26 June 1862, Letterpress Copybook 6, pages 304–308, BYP; WWJ, 18 and 29 June 1862, 6:58, 63.

79. BY discourse of 3 June 1860, JD, 8:69. On the origins of the Reorganization, see Roger D. Launius, *Joseph Smith III: Pragmatic Prophet* (Urbana: University of Illinois Press, 1988), chs. 4–6.

80. BY discourse of 7 Oct. 1863, in Box 4, Folder 40, CR 100 317, CHL. On RLDS growth in California, see Ronald E. Romig, "The RLDS Church on the Pacific Slope," *Journal of Mormon History* 25 (Spring 2009): 43–125.

81. BY to Cannon, 12 Nov. 1861 (emphasis in original), Letterpress Copybook 6, pages 26–31, BYP; WWJ, 8 May 1865, 6:223; "go to hell" in WWJ, 24 Sept. 1865, 6:249; *Millennial Star,* 4 Nov. 1865, 698; Orson Pratt to BY, 12 Nov. 1865, Box 41, Folder 6, BYP. On Lucy Mack Smith's autobiography, see Lavina Fielding Anderson, ed., *Lucy's Book: A Critical Edition of Lucy Mack Smith's Family Memoir* (Salt Lake City: Signature Books, 2001), esp. 100–132. See also the discussion in Bergera, *Conflict in the Quorum,* ch. 11; Breck England, *The Life and Thought of Orson Pratt* (Salt Lake City: University of Utah Press, 1985), 227–230.

82. Minutes of 25 Nov. 1855, Box 3, Folder 8, GCM. See the analysis in Jan Shipps, *Mormonism: The Story of a New Religious Tradition* (Urbana: University of Illinois Press, 1985), ch. 5.

83. DN, 23 Aug. 1865, 373; cf. Bergera, *Conflict in the Quorum,* 242.

84. Connor to Grenville Dodge, 28 May 1865, OR, ser. 1, vol. 48, pt. 2, 646.

85. BYOJD, 18 March 1862. See Bigler, *Forgotten Kingdom,* 247.

86. Sarah Barringer Gordon, *The Mormon Question: Polygamy and Constitutional Conflict in Nineteenth-Century America* (Chapel Hill: University of North Carolina Press, 2002), 83.

12. The Monster in the Vale

The Utah Magazine, 8 May 1869, 9.

1. John D. Lee Journal, 14/15 May 1867, in Robert Glass Cleland and Juanita Brooks, eds., *A Mormon Chronicle: The Diaries of John D. Lee, 1848–1876* (San Marino, Calif.: Huntington Library, 1955), 2:71–72; banners in Joseph F. Smith Journal, 27 Oct.–6 Nov. 1869, MS 1325, CHL; Kane to Elisha Kane, 7 Dec. 1872, in Matthew J. Grow, *"Liberty to the Downtrodden": Thomas L. Kane, Romantic Reformer* (New Haven: Yale University Press, 2009), 264.

2. Discourse of 3 Feb. 1867, VW, 4:2412; Tullidge, "The Reformation in Utah," *Harper's,* Sept. 1871, 605.

3. "The Utah Expedition," *Atlantic Monthly,* May 1859, 583.

4. Ezra Taft Benson to BY, 31 Jan. 1863, Box 38, Folder 3, BYP; BY to John F. Kinney, 3 Feb. 1864, Letterpress Copybook 6, pages 751–52, BYP. See Brigham D. Madsen, *The Shoshoni Frontier and the Bear River Massacre* (Salt Lake City: University of Utah Press, 1985), chapters nine and ten; Scott R.

Christensen, *Sagwitch: Shoshone Chieftain, Mormon Elder, 1822–1887* (Logan, Ut.: Utah State University Press, 1999), chapters two and three; Ned Blackhawk, *Violence Over the Land: Indians and Empires in the Early American West* (Cambridge, MA: Harvard University Press, 2006), 244–266.

5. Connor to R. C. Drum, 28 April 1863, OR, Series 1, Part 2, page 415.

6. In the following paragraphs, I rely on John Alton Peterson, *Utah's Black Hawk War* (Salt Lake City: University of Utah Press, 1998).

7. BY to Orson Hyde, 16 April 1865, Letterpress Copybook 7, page 560, BYP; O. Irish annual report to D. N. Cooley, 9 Sept. 1865, in *Message of the President of the United States* (Washington, DC: Government Printing Office, 1865), 314.

8. "exterminator" in Brigham D. Madsen, *Glory Hunter: A Biography of Patrick Edward Connor* (Salt Lake City: University of Utah Press, 1990), 130; Connor to Nelson Cole, 4 July 1865, in OR, Series I, Vol. 48, pt. 2, 1049; *Virginia Daily Territorial Enterprise,* 9 April 1865, in Heather Cox Richardson, *West from Appomattox: The Reconstruction of America after the Civil War* (New Haven: Yale University Press, 2007), 36; BY to R. N. Allred, 14 April 1865, Letterpress Copybook 7, page 553, BYP.

9. "Articles of Agreement and Conversation made and concluded at Spanish Fork," Documents Relating to the Negotiation of Unratified Treaties, T494, Reel 10, National Archives, microfilm at HBLL.

10. BY to Charles C. Rich, 29 June 1865, Letterpress Copybook 7, page 679, BYP.

11. "profess to be friendly" in WWJ, 16 July 1865, 6:235; "*stop fighting altogether*" in BY to Orson Hyde, et al., 1 Oct. 1865, Letterpress Copybook 7, pages 746–47, BYP. Emphasis in original. See Peterson, *Black Hawk War,* 181–208.

12. Snow to George A. Smith, 14 March 1866, Box 6, Folder 22, Smith Papers, MS 1322, CHL; BY to Snow, 25 April 1866, Letterpress Copybook 8, page 331, BYP. See Peterson, *Black Hawk War,* 229–242.

13. "treachery" in Babcock to Brig. Gen. John Rawlins, 23 June 1866, in USGP, 16:175–177. On the Circleville Massacre, see Albert Winkler, "The Circleville Massacre: A Brutal Incident in Utah's Black Hawk War," *Utah Historical Quarterly* 55 (Winter 1987): 4–21.

14. BY to Warren Snow, 25 April 1866, Letterpress Copybook 9, page 332, BYP.

15. BY to Thomas Callister, 21 June 1866, Letterpress Copybook 9, pages 5–6, BYP; cf. Peterson, *Black Hawk War,* 295–96; Callister to BY, 15 July 1866, Box 69, Folder 19, BYP.

16. BY to Orson Hyde, et al., 28 April 1866, Letterpress Copybook 8, pages 342–352, BYP.

17. Discourse of 28 July 1866, transcript of George D. Watt shorthand notes by LaJean Carruth.

18. BY to John Brown, 19 Sept. 1867, Letterpress Copybook 9, page 372, BYP. Casualty estimates from Peterson, *Black Hawk War,* 2.

19. See Edward Leo Lyman, "Chief Kanosh," *Journal of Mormon History* 35 (Winter 2009): 188–207.

20. Huntington to BY, 21 August 1856, Box 24, Folder 22, BYP; A. Milton Musser Journal, 16 Aug. 1866, MS 8410, CHL; marriage record of 8 June 1877, CR 100 424, CHL; Callister to BY, 13 June 1877, Box 46, Folder 12, BYP; Kanosh to Huntington, 13 June 1877, Box 46, Folder 13, BYP; DN, 18 Dec. 1878, 736.

21. Minutes of 29 Dec. 1847, Box 1, Folder 60, GCM.

22. *Union Vedette* [Salt Lake City, Ut.], 4 April 1866; discourse of 8 April 1866, DN, 149.

23. McCurdy to Stanton, telegram 7 April 1866, in USGP, 16:173; Grant to Sherman, telegram 9 April 1866, in USGP, 16:173; Sherman to BY, 10 April 1866, Box 49, Folder 27, BYP; BY to Sherman, 12 April 1866, Letterpress Copybook 8, page 279, BYP; Sherman to Grant, 7 May 1866, in USGP, 16:157.

24. Connor to Judge William Carter, 23 Oct. 1866, typescript by Will Bagley in author's possession; *Union Vedette,* 26 Oct. 1866; discourse of 23 Dec. 1866, JD, 11:281. See David L. Bigler, *Forgotten Kingdom: The Mormon Theocracy in the American West, 1847–1896* (Spokane, WA: Arthur H. Clark, 1998), 247–253.

25. DN, 2 Jan. 1867, 1; "Jews here" in WWJ, 9 May 1869, 6:472.

26. Discourse of 11 Dec. 1864, JD, 11:19; discourse of 10 Feb. 1867, JD, 11:326.

27. DN, 2 Jan. 1867, 1; Ronald W. Walker, *Wayward Saints: The Godbeites and Brigham Young* (Urbana: University of Illinois Press, 1998), 96–97.

28. WWJ, 16 Dec. 1867, 6:381; Joseph F. Smith Journal, 17 June 1871; SOPM, 14 and 21 May 1870 (grasshoppers), 2 Sept. 1871 (city hygiene), and 11 and 18 June 1870 (plural marriage).

29. HOJ, 22 May 1868; Stanford to Hopkins, 9 June 1868, Box 1, Folder 12, Leland Stanford Papers, SC0033a, Stanford University Special Collections and University Archives, Stanford, Calif.; BY to Franklin D. Richards, 23 May 1868, Letterpress Copybook 10, page 866, BYP.

30. See Craig Foster, "'That Canny Scotsman': John Sharp and the Union Pacific Negotiations, 1869–72," *Journal of Mormon History* 27 (Fall 2001): 197–214; Arrington, *Great Basin Kingdom,* chapter nine.

31. SOPM, 6 Aug. 1870; "mind and will" in WWJ, 7 Oct. 1870, 6:574; *Utah Reporter* [Corinne, Ut.], 15 Jan. 1870.

32. Exodus 28:36; Truman O. Angell 1854 sketch of the Salt Lake Temple east center tower, CR 679 13, Folder 10, CHL. On the creation and early years of ZCMI, see Martha Sonntag Bradley, *ZCMI: America's First Department Store* (Salt Lake City: ZCMI, 1991), 8–54; Arrington, *Great Basin Kingdom,* 298–314.

33. See William Cronon, *Nature's Metropolis: Chicago and the Great West* (New York: W.W. Norton, 1991), 361–64.

34. Oregon Territory, Vol. 1, p. 284Z (12 Aug. 1869 entry), R. G. Dun & Co. Collection, Baker Library Historical Collections, Harvard Business School.

35. "smart, active" in Oregon Territory, Vol. 1, p. 276 (1856 entry), R. G. Dun & Co. Collection.

36. Walker, *Wayward Saints* 112–120.

37. Taves, *Fits, Trances, and Vision,* chapters four and five; Ann Braude, *Radical Spirits: Spiritualism and Women's Rights in Nineteenth-Century America* (Boston: Beacon Press, 1989), esp. 4.

38. SLT, 27 Nov. 1873. See Walker, *Wayward Saints,* 112; Michael W. Homer, "Spiritualism and Mormonism: Some Thoughts on Similarities and Differences," *Dialogue* 27 (Spring 1994): 171–90.

39. Jewish cemetery in Annegret S. Ogden, ed., *Frontier Reminiscences of Eveline Brooks Auerbach* (Berkeley: Friends of the Bancroft Library, 1994), 13; "work of the Devil" in discourse of 12 Feb. 1854, Box 2, Folder 28, CR 100 317, CHL. See also discourse of 10 July 1870, JD, 14:72.

40. Brigham Young Jr. to BY, 20 Nov. 1869, Box 44, Folder 35, BYP. On Godbe's marriage to Charlotte Cobb, see Walker, *Wayward Saints,* 138.

41. *Utah Magazine,* 11 Sept. 1869, 295 (emphasis in original); *Utah Magazine,* 16 Oct. 1869, 376–378.

42. Salt Lake Stake Historical Record Book, 25 Oct. 1869, typescript published in Devery S. Anderson, ed., *"The Knowledge of All Truth": Minutes of the Salt Lake City School of the Prophets, 1867–1874, and 1883* (Salt Lake City: Signature Books, 2012), appendix. See Walker, *Wayward Saints,* chapter nine.

43. See Walker, *Wayward Saints,* chapter eleven.

44. See ibid., chapter fifteen.

45. BY to Carrington, 23 April 1870, Letterpress Copybook 12, page 101, BYP.

46. Hooper to BY, 31 Jan. 1869, Box 62, Folder 12, BYP; BY to Hooper, 13 Feb. 1866, Letterpress Copybook 8, page 106, BYP. I am grateful to Paul Reeve for sharing the first reference.

47. BY to TLK, 26 Oct. 1869, Letterpress Copybook 11, page 845, BYP.

48. See Richardson, *West from Appomattox,* esp. chapters three and four.

49. *The Mormon Question: Being a Speech of Vice-President Schuyler Colfax . . .* (Salt Lake City: Deseret News, 1870), 3–5.

50. See James B. Allen, "The Unusual Jurisdiction of County Probate Courts in the Territory of Utah," *Utah Historical Quarterly* 36 (Spring 1968): 132–142; Lawrence L. Linford, "Establishing and Maintaining Land Ownership in Utah Prior to 1869," *Utah Historical Quarterly* 42 (Spring 1974): 126–143.

51. Testimony in *Execution of the Laws in Utah,* House Report 21, 41st Cong., 2nd Sess.; draft of Cullom bill in *Congressional Globe,* House of Representatives, 41st Cong, 2nd Sess., 1367–1369. See Bigler, *Forgotten Kingdom,* 281–285; Gustav Larson, *The "Americanization" of Utah for Statehood* (San Marino, Cal.: Huntington Library, 1971), 64–72.

52. DN, 12 Jan. 1870, 574; cf. Walker, *Wayward Saints,* 215; "Vigilance Committee" in DN, 4 Jan. 1870, 2; BY to Hooper, 4 Jan. 1868, Letterpress Copybook 10, page 580, BYP; Hooper to BY, 24 April 1870, Box 62, Folder 13, BYP.

53. DN, 19 Jan. 1870, 554–556; Pratt in SOPM, 29 Jan. 1870. See Bigler, *Forgotten Kingdom,* 283–284.

54. Shaffer to Hamilton Fish, 1 and 27 ("absolute power") April 1870, State Department Territorial Papers, Utah Series, National Archives, microfilm at HBLL; Shaffer to Grant, 7 July 1870, copy in Shaffer to Hamilton Fish, 7 July 1870, State Department Territorial Papers, Utah Series.

55. Shaffer to Wells, 27 Oct. 1870, in DN, 2 Nov. 1870, 453. See the discussion in Bigler, *Forgotten Kingdom,* 286–288.

56. Cannon to George A. Smith, 29 May 1872, Box 8, Folder 4, Smith Papers. On McKean, see Thomas G. Alexander, "Federal Authority Versus Polygamic Theocracy," *Dialogue* 1 (Autumn 1966): 85–100.

57. BY to Hickman, ca. Jan. 1868, Letterpress Copybook 10, page 609, BYP; Hickman and John Beadle, *Brigham's Destroying Angel . . .* (New York: G.A. Crofutt, 1872), 190–193. See Hope A. Hilton, *"Wild Bill" Hickman and the Mormon Frontier* (Salt Lake City: Signature Books, 1988), chapter fifteen.

58. HOJ, 27 Sept. 1871. See Mark R. Grandstaff, "General Regis de Trobriand, the Mormons, and the U.S. Army at Camp Douglas, 1870–71," *Utah Historical Quarterly* 64 (Summer 1996): 204–223.

59. "[g]overnment of the United States" in *Corinne Reporter,* 13 Oct. 1871; "new judicial era" from SLT, 2 Nov. 1871; Boss Tweed comparison from SLT, 8 Nov. 1871; *Corinne Reporter,* 23 Oct. ("hoary libertine") and 30 Oct. 1871 ("the butcher of Zion" and "high priest"); "strong hope" in A. M. Musser telegram to BY, 27 Oct. 1871, Box 46, Folder 5, BYP.

60. *New York Tribune,* 5 and 14 Oct. 1871.

61. Wells to BY, telegram of 25 Oct. 1871, Box 43, Folder 17; George A. Smith Journal, 6 Nov. 1871, Smith Papers.

62. BY and GAS to DHW, telegrams of 26 Oct. 1871 ("continue" and "hired girls") and 28 Oct. 1871 ("a little stormy"), both in Box 73, Folder 34, BYP; John W. Young to TLK, 9 Nov. 1871, Thomas L. Kane Papers, Box 16, Folder 30, HBLL.

63. Clawson to BY, telegram of 11 Dec. 1871, Box 34, Folder 3, BYP.

64. See Bates to Akerman, 7 Dec. 1871, Letters Received by the Attorney General, 1871–84, Record Group 60, National Archives; Akerman to Bates, 19 Dec. 1871, Letters Sent by the Department of Justice, Instructions to U.S. Attorneys and Marshals, 1867–1904, Record Group 60, National Archives; cf. Stephen Creswell, *Mormons & Cowboys, Moonshiners & Klansmen: Federal Law Enforcement in the South & West, 1870–1893* (Tuscaloosa, Ala.: University of Alabama Press, 1991), 85; McKean to Bates, 18 December 187, Box 34, Folder 6, BYP; BY cipher telegram to Wells, 14 Dec. 1871, Box 73, Folder 34, BYP; SOPM, 16 Dec. 1871. I used an cryptogram decoder to decrypt the substitution cipher telegram: <http://www.blisstonia.com/software/Web Decrypto/index.php>. See Edwin Olson, "Robust Dictionary Attack of Short Simple Substitution Ciphers," *Cryptologia* 31 (Oct. 2007): 332–342.

65. *Corinne Reporter,* 3 Jan. 1871; Seymour B. Young Journal, 11 and 29 January 1872, Box 3, Folder 4, MS 1345, CHL.

66. GQC to BY, 15 April 1872, Box 38, Folder 15, BYP.

67. For text of the proposed measure, see SLT, 12 April 1872.

68. *New York Tribune,* 22 Nov. 1871.

69. Cannon to DHW, 16 April 1872, Box 38, Folder 15, BYP. See Ardis E. Parshall, "Codes and Ciphers in Mormon History (Part III)," www.keepapitchinin.org <accessed 16 April 2011>.

70. Joseph F. Smith Journal, 26 April 1872; Wells telegram to Cannon, 29 April

1872 and BY telegram to Cannon, 16 May 1872, both in Telegram Book 1, Box 12, BYP.

71. Hooper and GQC to BY, 22 April 1872, Box 38, Folder 15, BYP; Bernhisel to BY, 24 March 1862, Box 61, Folder 5, BYP; BY to Bernhisel, 15 April 1862, Letterpress Copybook 6, page 206, BYP; Bates to George Williams, 8 Jan. 1872, Letters Received by the Attorney General of the United States, 1871–84, Record Group 60, National Archives; collaboration in Hooper to GAS, 1 April 1872, Box 8, Folder 6, Smith Papers. See Will Bagley, *Blood of the Prophets: Brigham Young and the Mountain Meadows Massacre* (Norman: University of Oklahoma Press, 2002), 282; David L. Bigler and Will Bagley, *Innocent Blood: A Documentary History of the Mountain Meadows Massacre* (Norman, OK: Arthur H. Clark, 2008), 304, n. 6.

72. "small-pox" in Cannon to BY, 5 Feb. 1873, Box 38, Folder 17, BYP. On the Crédit Mobilier scandal, see Richardson, *West from Appomattox,* 136–39; Richard White, *Railroaded: The Transcontinentals and the Making of Modern America* (New York: W.W. Norton, 2011), 28–36, 62–66.

13. The Soul and Mainspring of the West

1. SOPM, 19 Nov. 1870.
2. "Nevada" from Brigham Young Jr. Journal, 29 March 1870, Box 2, Folder 3, MS 1236, CHL; other quotes from SOPM, 19 Nov. 1870. See Milton R. Hunter, *Brigham Young the Colonizer* (Independence, MO: Zion's Printing and Publishing, 1945), 356.
3. Brigham Young Jr. Journal, 28 March 1870.
4. Seymour B. Young Journal, 1 Dec. 1875, MS 1345, CHL.
5. BY to William Stevens, Sr., and "Directions how to use the Catheter," 19 Jan. 1876, Letterpress Copybook 14, pages 136–138, BYP. I found this letter and episode because of the careful research of Ardis Parshall, http://www.keepapitchinin.org/2009/12/01/random-reasons-why-i-like-brigham-young-three/ (accessed 1 May 2011).
6. BY to John Van Cott, 6 Jan. 1863, Letterpress Copybook 6, page 450, BYP; Provo home in BY to Hiram Clawson, 17 March 1868, Letterpress Copybook 10, page 732, BYP. See Susa Young Gates notes, Box 12, Folder 3, SYGP.
7. BY to Elias Smith, 9 Dec. 1865, Letterpress Copybook 7, page 850, BYP; Elias Smith Journal, 23 Dec. 1865, MS 1319, CHL; Andrew Cahoon to BY, 7 July 1867, Box 64, Folder 10, BYP; Ann Eliza Young, *Wife No. 19, or the Story of a Life in Bondage* (Hartford, CT: Dustin, Gilman, 1875), ch. 27; list of ladies belonging to the Deseret Dramatic Association (including "Miss E A Webb"), BY Account Book, 1856–77, Vault MSS 155, HBLL.
8. Divorce certificate of 28 Oct. 1856 in Box 67, Folder 11, BYP; Elizabeth Jones to BY, 5 June 1858, Box 66, Folder 16, BYP; discourse of 23 Jan. 1852, CR 100 317, Box 1, Folder 14; "Welsh Queen" in Rex LeRoy Christensen, "The Life and Contributions of Captain Dan Jones" (M.A. thesis, Utah State University, 1977), 54.
9. Ann Eliza Young, *Wife No. 19,* 280–286; record of deed in Brigham Young

Real Estate Book A, 153, MS 10324, CHL; BY to Charles Crabtree, 3 Jan. 1875, Letterpress Telegram Book, 1873–75, Box 12, BYP. On Forest Farm, see Todd Compton, *In Sacred Loneliness: The Plural Wives of Joseph Smith* (Salt Lake City: Signature Books, 1997), 417–418.

10. Lydia Farnsworth to BY, 20 Jan. 1857, Box 64, Folder 4, BYP; BY to Lydia Farnsworth, 22 Jan. 1857, Letterpress Copybook 3, page 304, BYP; 1870 U.S. Census, Utah Territory, Utah County, Pleasant Grove, page 4.

11. Hannah T. King to BY, 22 Nov. 1874, Box 35, Folder 8, BYP.

12. "always thought" in HOJ, 23 Dec. 1863; "receive kindly" in HOJ, 11 April 1866.

13. Mary Ann Angell's Gardo House residence in Brigham Young Jr. Journal, Box 2, Folder 7. See Sandra Dawn Brimhall and Mark D. Curtis, "The Gardo House," in Colleen Whitley, ed., *Brigham Young's Homes* (Logan: Utah State University Press, 2002), 173–175.

14. WWJ, 20 Sept. 1869, 6:494; discourse of 18 July 1869, JD, 13:61; Susa Young Gates notes, Box 1, Folder 9, SYGP. On Young and women's medical education, see Thomas W. Simpson, "Mormons Study 'Abroad': Brigham Young's Romance with American Higher Education, 1867–1877," *Church History* 76 (Dec. 2007): 788–795.

15. Jill Mulvay Derr, et al., *Women of Covenant: The Story of Relief Society* (Salt Lake City: Deseret Book, 1992), chs. 2 and 3.

16. "have given as good" in Brigham Young Jr. Journal, 21 June 1875, Box 2, Folder 6. See Jill M. Derr, "The Lion and the Lioness: Brigham Young and Eliza R. Snow," *BYU Studies* 40 (2001): 54–101; Derr, "Woman's Place in Brigham Young's World," *BYU Studies* 18 (Spring 1978): 377–395.

17. Augusta Adams to BY, 17 Dec. 1861, Theodore Albert Schroeder Papers, Wisconsin Historical Society. Emphasis in original. I am grateful to Connell O'Donovan for providing a transcription of this letter.

18. "dope fiend" in Susa Young Gates, "My Father's Wives," Box 12, Folder 3, SYGP; cf. D. Michael Quinn, *The Mormon Hierarchy: Extensions of Power* (Salt Lake City: Signature Books, 1997), 771; Brigham Young Family Store Ledger, 1874–1875, Box 123, Folder 2, BYP; BY to Emmeline Free, 8 Dec. 1874, in Letterpress Telegram Book, 1873–75.

19. 1870 U.S. Census, Utah Territory, Salt Lake City, 18th Ward, 5; "orphans" in Zina D. H. Young autobiography, in Martha Sonntag Bradley and Mary Brown Firmage Woodward, *Four Zinas: A Story of Mothers and Daughters on the Mormon Frontier* (Salt Lake City: Signature Books, 2000), 196; Brigham Young Family Store Ledger, 1870–1871, Box 122, Folder 4, BYP.

20. BY telegram to James Jack, 4 Jan. 1874, Letterpress Telegram Book, 1873–75; Brigham Young Family Store Ledger, 1874–1875, Box 123, Folder 2, BYP; Emily Dow Partridge Young Journal, esp. 16 April 1874, 2 Aug. 1874, 1 Feb. 1875, VMSS 5, HBLL.

21. Augusta Adams to BY, 11 April 1869 ("Their Father"), Blair Papers, MS 120, Box 2, Folder 12, UUSC. I am grateful to Connell O'Donovan for sharing this reference.

22. Discourse of 9 August 1874, JD, 17:160; Emily Dow Partridge Young Journal, 17 July 1877.

23. Susa Young Gates notes, Box 12, Folder 3, SYGP.

24. Townsend, *The Mormon Trials at Salt Lake City* (New York: American News Company, 1871), 46; "Richelieu" in Arthur I. Street, "The Mormon Richelieu," *Ainslee's Magazine,* Jan. 1900, 706.

25. Todd Compton, "John Willard Young, Brigham Young, and the Development of Presidential Succession in the LDS Church," *Dialogue* 35 (Winter 2002): 111–134.

26. "would rather" in WWJ, 1 Jan. 1861, 5:536. On Brigham Young Jr., see Davis Bitton, *The Ritualization of Mormon History and other Essays* (Urbana: University of Illinois Press, 1994), ch. 7.

27. BY to Mary Ann Angell, 5 Dec. 1874, Letterpress Telegram Book, 1873–75; Clara Young to BY, 4 March 1875, Box 44, Folder 25; Andrew Moffitt telegram to BY, 6 Aug. 1875, Letterpress Telegram Book, 1873–75.

28. Brigham Young Jr. Journal, 5 Sept. 1871; wept in *Millennial Star,* 4 Oct. 1875, 638.

29. SLT, 3 Jan. 1877 and 13 Jan. 1878.

30. SLT, 23 Sept. 1877.

31. BY to John W. Young (emphasis in original), 17 Dec. 1875, MS 2184, CHL; Brigham Young Jr. Journal, 14 Feb. 1876, Box 2, Folder 7. On John Willard Young, see M. Guy Bishop, "Building Railroads for the Kingdom: The Career of John W. Young, 1867–91," *Utah Historical Quarterly* 48 (Winter 1980): 66–80.

32. Brigham Young Jr. Journal, 14 March 1876, Box 2, Folder 7; Nibley, *Reminiscences of Charles W. Nibley, 1849–1931,* privately published in 1934, copy at CHL; WWJ, 8 Oct. 1876, 7:286.

33. SLT, 1 Aug. 1873. On the Ann Eliza Young case, see Wallace, *The Twenty-Seventh Wife* (New York: Simon and Schuster, 1961), chs. 7 and 8; John Gary Maxwell, *Gettysburg to Great Salt Lake: George R. Maxwell, Civil War Hero and Federal Marshal among the Mormons* (Norman, OK: Arthur H. Clark, 2010), ch. 8 and 237–241.

34. Minutes of 23 June 1875, San Pete Stake, LR 8046 29, Folder 1. See Richard Wightman Fox, *Trials of Intimacy: Love and Loss in the Beecher-Tilton Scandal* (Chicago: University of Chicago Press, 1999).

35. Ann Eliza Young to Hiram Clawson, 11 Sept. 1873, Box 66, Folder 26, BYP; SLT, 27 Nov. 1873.

36. James Burton Pond, *Eccentricities of Genius: Memories of Famous Men and Women of the Platform and Stage* (New York: G. W. Dillingham, 1900), xx–xxii; *Rocky Mountain News,* 10 Dec. 1873; "sheltered haven" in Young, *Wife No. 19, 576.*

37. Cannon to BY, 18 April 1874, Box 38, Folder 19, BYP; *National Republican* [Washington, D.C.], 3 June 1874.

38. McKean's decision in SLT, 26 Feb. 1875; Seymour B. Young Journal, 11 March 1875, Box 2, Folder 1.

39. "carpet-baggers" in SLT, 17 March 1875. On McKean's removal, see Thomas

G. Alexander, "Federal Authority Versus Polygamic Theocracy: James B. McKean and the Mormons, 1870–1875," *Dialogue* 1 (Autumn 1966): 97–99.

40. BY to Arta D. and Lorenzo D. Young, 21 Oct. 1876, Letterpress Copybook 14, pages 587–590, BYP. See Leonard Arrington, ed., "Crusade against Theocracy: The Reminiscences of Judge Jacob Smith Boreman of Utah, 1872–1877," *Huntington Library Quarterly* 24 (Nov. 1960): 33–35, 39–41.

41. On Ann Eliza's marriage to Denning, see Wallace, *The Twenty-Seventh Wife,* 395–401.

42. Hicks to BY, 4 Dec. 1868, Box 32, Folder 15, BYP; BY to George Hicks (emphasis in original), 16 Feb. 1869, Letterpress Copybook 11, pages 362–363, BYP. See the discussion in Will Bagley, *Blood of the Prophets: Brigham Young and the Mountain Meadows Massacre* (Norman: University of Oklahoma Press, 2002), 258–261.

43. Franklin D. Richards Journal, 9 Oct. 1870, Box 2, Vol. 18, Richards Papers, MS 1215, CHL. John D. Lee Journal, 21 Nov. and 19–29 Dec. 1870, in Robert Glass Cleland and Juanita Brooks, eds., *A Mormon Chronicle: The Diaries of John D. Lee, 1848–1876* (San Marino, CA: Huntington Library, 1955), 2:147, 149–151. Unlike Lee, Haight apparently regained his membership several years later.

44. John D. Lee Journal, 11 Nov. 1871 and 5 April 1874, in Cleland and Brooks, 2:174, 336; SLT, 16 April 1874.

45. Affidavit of "Philip Klingon Smith," printed in full in Juanita Brooks, *The Mountain Meadows Massacre,* 2nd ed. (Norman: University of Oklahoma Press, 1962), 238–242; Lee's arrest in MU, 297–301; BY to Daniel H. Wells, encrypted telegram of 14 Nov. 1874, Letterpress Telegram Book, 1873–75, decryption courtesy of Chad Foulger and Brian Reeves.

46. Bates telegram to James Jack, 16 July 1875, Letterpress Telegram Book, 1873–75. For Lee's July 1875 "confession," see *Salt Lake Herald,* 21 July 1875.

47. Affidavit printed in Brooks, *Mountain Meadows Massacre,* 284–286; affidavit and draft in Folder 2, MS 2674, CHL; Bates to John W. Young, 9 Aug. 1875, Box 16, Folder 3, Kane Papers, HBLL. See HOJ, 29 and 30 Sept. 1857; WWJ, 29 Sept. 1857, 5:102–103.

48. SLT, 24 and 27 July, 8 Aug. 1875; Bates to John W. Young, 9 Aug. 1875. See also NYT, 24 Aug. 1875.

49. Baskin quoted in SLT, 6 Aug. 1875; Lockley in SLT, 29 July 1875; NYT, 9 Aug. 1875.

50. Bates to John W. Young, 9 Aug. 1875.

51. DHW telegram, 16 Sept. 1876, 1875–77; Letterpress Telegram Book, 1873–1875; William Nelson and Howard to Alphonso Taft, 20 Sept. 1876, Letters Received by the Attorney General, 1871–84, Record Group 60, National Archives, microfilm at HBLL.

52. John D. Lee to Rachel Lee, 24 Sept. 1876, and John D. Lee to Emma B. Lee, 9 Dec. 1876, copies in Papers of John Doyle Lee, Huntington Library, San Marino, CA; cf. David L. Bigler and Will Bagley, *Innocent Blood: A Documentary History of the Mountain Meadows Massacre* (Norman, OK: Arthur H. Clark, 2008), 313, 315, 323.

53. SLT, 11 Oct. 1876.

54. William Bishop to John D. Lee, 23 Feb. 1877, Lee Papers, Huntington Library; "Aim at my heart" in Josiah Rogerson telegram, 23 March 1877, Box 46, Folder 15, BYP; "done nothing designedly wrong" in SLT, 24 March 1877; John D. Lee to BY, 2 May 1856, Box 69, Folder 7, BYP; "old man" in SLT, 24 March 1877. I am grateful to Chad Orton for pointing me to the first quote.

55. *New York Herald,* 24 March 1877. See Bigler and Bagley, *Innocent Blood,* 338–352.

56. *New York Herald,* 22 March 1877; MU, 223–225. On *Mormonism Unveiled,* see Richard E. Turley Jr., "Problems with Mountain Meadows Massacre Sources," *BYU Studies* 47 (2008): 147–151.

57. Howard to Charles Devens, 26 April 1877, Letters Received by the Attorney General, 1871–84, Record Group 60, National Archives, microfilm at HBLL.

58. John W. Young telegram to Calder et al., 31 March 1877, Letterpress Telegram Book, Received, 1877–1879, Box 13, BYP; draft of a telegram to Hayes in Box 46, Folder 15, BYP.

59. *New York Herald,* 6 May 1877, reprinted in DN, 12 May 1877.

60. Brigham Young Jr. Journal, 27 June 1875, Box 2, Folder 5, MS 1236, CHL.

61. Discourse of October 9, 1872, JD, 15:221.

62. Discourse of 7 April 1869, JD, 13:2; Genesis 5:24; Hebrews 11:5; Moses, 7:18.

63. Acts 4:32 (see 3 Nephi 26:19 and discourse of 23 June 1867, JD, 12:65). See Leonard J. Arrington et al., *Building the City of God: Community and Cooperation among the Mormons,* 2nd ed. (Urbana: University of Illinois Press, 1992), ch. 6.

64. Article of Agreement, St. George United Order, ca. March 1874, Box 76, Folder 15, BYP. See Arrington et al., *Building the City of God,* ch. 8.

65. James Jack to George Gibbs, 30 March 1874, Letterpress Copybook 13, page 549, BYP; "live as one family" in BY to Salt Lake City "brethren," telegram of 11 March 1874, Letterpress Telegram Book, 1873–75; "all labors" in James G. Bleak, Annals of the Southern Utah Mission, 11 Jan. 1874, Box 1, Folder 3, MS 318, CHL; JH, 31 May 1874.

66. Stegner, *Mormon Country* (New York: Duell, Sloan and Pearce, 1942), 109. See Arrington et al., *Building the City of God,* chs. 7 and 8.

67. Brigham Young Jr. Journal, 22 June 1875.

68. Discourses of 23 June 1874 and 9 Aug. 1874, in JD 18:248 and 17:157–158; cf. Arrington et al., *Building the City of God,* 148–149; WWJ, 17 Aug. 1872, 7:79.

69. SLT, 31 March 1874.

70. "being built" in MH, 10 Jan. 1875.

71. "thank thee" in Charles Lowell Walker Journal, 1 Jan. 1877, in Karl A. and Katharine Miles Larson, eds., *The Diary of Charles Lowell Walker* (Logan: Utah State University Press, 1980), 1:441; "sedan chair" from Brigham Young Jr. Journal, Box 2, Folder 5, MS 1236, BYP.

72. Young's effort at revision in WWJ, 21 March 1877, 7:340; L. John Nuttall Journal, 7 Feb. 1877, typescript at HBLL; cf. David John Buerger, *The Myster-*

ies of Godliness: A History of Mormon Temple Worship, 2nd ed. (Salt Lake City: Signature Books, 2002), 111–112.

73. WWJ, 14 and 15 March, 1877, 7:339; "rob the dead" in Susa Young Gates notes, Box 12, Folder 3, SYGP. On endowments for the dead, see Richard E. Bennett, "'Line upon Line, Precept upon Preceipt': Reflections on the 1877 Commencement of the Performance of Endowments and Sealings for the Dead," *BYU Studies* 44 (2005): 38–77.

74. Brigham Young Jr. Journal, 29 March 1877, Box 2, Folder 7; Esaias Edwards Journal, 25 March 1877, MSS 184, HBLL; statistics from Bennett, "'Line upon Line,'" 67.

75. Minutes of 23 June 1875, San Pete Stake, Folder 1, LR 8046 29, CHL.

76. WWJ, 11 Dec. 1859, 6:508.

77. Brigham Young Jr. Journal, 2 and 3 April 1877, Box 2, Folder 7, MS 1236, CHL; Charles L. Walker Journal, 4 April 1877, in Larson and Larson, 1:455.

78. Charles L. Walker Journal, 8 April 1877, in Larson and Larson, 1:457; hymn request in *Millennial Star,* 21 May 1877, 324.

79. Brigham Young Jr. Journal, 20 Aug. 1877.

80. Brigham Young Jr. Journal, 24 Aug. 1877; Seymour B. Young Journal, 24 Aug. 1877, USHS. Compare this conclusion to that of Lester Bush, "Brigham Young in Life and Death: A Medical Overview," *Journal of Mormon History* 5 (1978): 92–103. I am grateful to Drs. Samuel Brown, Elissa Turner, and Robert Kiskaddon for reviewing Young's medical history and final illness for me.

81. SLT, 30 Aug. 1877; Franklin Richards Journal, 29 Aug. 1877; Richard Young Journal, 29 Aug. 1877, MS 382, CHL.

Epilogue

1. SLT, 30 Aug. 1877.

2. See Kathleen Flake, *The Politics of American Religious Identity: The Seating of Senator Reed Smoot, Mormon Apostle* (Chapel Hill, NC: University of North Carolina Press, 2004).

3. George Q. Cannon Journal, 17 Jan. 1878, excerpted in *The Instructor* [Salt Lake City], June 1945, 259; cf. Quinn, *Extensions of Power,* 40–41.

4. "new religious tradition" from Jan Shipps, *Mormonism: The Story of a New Religious Tradition* (Urbana: University of Illinois Press, 1985), esp. pp. 148–149.

5. Discourse of 17 Aug. 1856, JD, 4:32.

6. Brigham Young Jr. Journal, 25 June 1875, MS 1236, Box 2, Folder 6, CHL; discourse of 25 Dec. 1857, VW, 3:1384.

7. Discourse of 15 May 1864, JD, 10:295.

8. Samuel W. Richards in DN, 9 July 1856, 140; discourse of 9 [misdated 8] April 1852, in DN, 12 Jan. 1854. See Michael Hicks, "Minding Business: A Note on the 'Mormon Creed,'" *BYU Studies* 26 (Fall 1986): 125–132.

Acknowledgments

Joseph Smith and Brigham Young believed that individuals could not obtain their salvation on their own. In their minds, human beings needed each other in order to obtain a full measure of celestial glory. Historians also need a great deal of help in order to achieve their earthly goals, and this project has provided me with a keen sense of that dependence. Even when a book bears a single name, scholarship is by its nature a collaborative enterprise, building on the work of men and women from the distant past and relying on the help of archivists, librarians, and colleagues.

A large number of institutions made their documents and photographs available to me, but several institutions and repositories deserve special mention. The Church History Department of the Church of Jesus Christ of Latter-day Saints enabled access to the entirety of the massive Brigham Young Papers and several other key collections, including the diary of Brigham Young Jr. and the typescripts of a vast assortment of correspondence, journals, and church minutes made by Edyth Romney. In particular, I am grateful to Marlin K. Jensen and Richard E. Turley Jr. for their courtesy and encouragement. Most Thursday nights over the past four summers, I presented Bill Slaughter with long lists of urgent archival requests. Chatting with Bill about all things Mormon was as pleasurable as obtaining the needed documents and photographs. Robin Jensen, Mark Ashurst-McGee, Chad Orton, Chad Foulger, Brian Reeves, Mark Staker, and Mike Landon all went to great lengths to answer research queries. Other employees of the Church History Department and staff at its library helped locate manuscripts, discussed points of research, and shared their expertise.

The Charles Redd Center for Western Studies at Brigham Young University (BYU) supported this project with several visiting scholarships. These grants facilitated a great deal of the research for this book and also gave me opportunities to better understand contemporary Mormonism. Brian Cannon and Jessie Embry merit special thanks. The Special Collections of BYU's Harold B. Lee Library—through David Whittaker, Russ Taylor, Tom Wells, and many others—also provided considerable assistance with archival materials and photographs. It was a pleasure to work with summer research assistants Whitney Cross, Matt Joslin, and Jason Thompson.

This project would probably not have come to pass save for the support and encouragement I received from the University of South Alabama (USA), which gave me time for research and initial funding. I am grateful to my colleagues and students at USA, many of whom have endured and appeared to enjoy stories about Brigham Young and the Latter-day Saints.

Many other archivists and librarians provided me with needed assistance: Brad Cole and several others at the Special Collections of Utah State University's Merrill-Cazier Library; Doug Misner at the Utah State Historical Society; Stan Larson and Krissy Giacoletto at the Special Collections of the University of Utah's Marriott Library; Peter J. Blodgett and Katrina Denman at the Huntington Library; Carol Nielson at the International Society of Daughters of Utah Pioneers; Aimee Morgan at the Stanford University Archives; Ronald E. Romig and Rachel Killebrew at the Community of Christ Archives; Orion Teal at the Duke University Library's David M. Rubenstein Rare Book & Manuscript Library; Babette Huber at the Victor Historical Society of Victor, NY; Becki Plunkett at the State Historical Society of Iowa; Abigail Thompson at the Baker Library of Harvard Business School; Janet Seegmiller at the Special Collections of Southern Utah University's Gerald R. Sherratt Library; and Carolyn Ruby at the Idaho State Historical Society.

I am especially grateful to the following persons, many of whom read significant portions of the manuscript: Will Bagley, Phil Barlow, Gary Bergera, Brian Cannon, LaJean Carruth, Todd Compton, Jill Derr, Jessie Embry, Spencer Fluhman, Terryl Givens, Matthew Grow, David Grua, Sondra Jones, William MacKinnon, Mel McKiven, Laurie Maffly-Kipp, Rahul Maitra, Patrick Mason, Clyde Milner, Quincy Newell, Ben Park, Paul Reeve, Brent Rogers, Gene Sessions, and Richard Turley.

Many other persons were unusually generously with their insights, expertise, and research materials, including Barbara Jones Brown, Richard Bushman, Kathy Daynes, Rick Grunder, Brent Herridge, David Howlett, Jeff Johnson, Anne Leahy, Mike Marquardt, Jeff Nichols, Connell O'Donovan, Josh Probert, D. Michael Quinn, Ardis Parshall, Peggy Pascoe, Lisa Olsen Tait, Laurel Thatcher Ulrich, Dan Vogel, Bruce Worthen, and Margaret Young.

For several years, LaJean Carruth has extended me unusual courtesy and assistance. Her transcripts of Pitman shorthand notes of Brigham Young's sermons and other valuable documents are themselves treasures, and I cannot begin to express my appreciation to her for facilitating my access to them. I admire her attention to detail and passion for historical accuracy.

Andrew Smith of South Royalton, Vermont, created the four maps included in this book. I appreciate his forbearance in light of the countless historical maps and suggestions I sent to him.

When one is in a strange land, one needs guides in order to reach one's destination. Jonathan Stapley, Sam Brown, Chris Jones, and Matt Bowman have patiently answered hundreds of questions about Mormonism and Mormon history. They are true saints and extended me scholarly credits I will never be able to repay.

Joyce Seltzer of Harvard University Press believed in this project at a very early stage. I am grateful for her encouragement and for her candor, both of which are essential for the improvement of a manuscript. Kate Brick carefully and patiently shepherded my manuscript through its production at Harvard. I also wish to thank Brian Distelberg and Lisa LaPoint for their roles in the publication and promotion of this book.

One of the pleasures of my research was the chance to learn about Brigham Young's many wives. While several achieved prominence within the church, many lived obscurely in the shadow of their husband's ecclesiastical luminance. Nearly all lived fascinating lives in their own right. Still, I was never jealous of Brigham for his large family, being quite content with an earthly kingdom that more than makes up for its lack of quantity with unmatched quality. Thus, I am grateful most of all to my wife, Elissa, and our daughter, Evelyn, for extending to me considerable patience and for providing me with even more joy.

Index